TEACHING THE LANGUAGE ARTS

Forward Thinking

in Today's Classrooms

Elizabeth Dobler
EMPORIA STATE UNIVERSITY

Denise Johnson
THE COLLEGE OF WILLIAM AND MARY

Thomas DeVere Wolsey
WALDEN UNIVERSITY

Holcomb Hathaway, Publishers
Scottsdale, Arizona

Library of Congress Cataloging-in-Publication Data

Dobler, Elizabeth.
    Teaching the language arts : forward thinking in today's classrooms / Elizabeth Dobler, Emporia State University, Denise Johnson, the College of William and Mary, Thomas DeVere Wolsey, Walden University.
      pages cm
    ISBN 978-1-934432-80-8 (ebook) — ISBN 978-1-934432-95-2 (print book)
    1. Language arts. I. Johnson, Denise, author. II. Wolsey, Thomas DeVere, author. III. Title.
      LB1576.D583 2013
      372.6—dc23

                                                                                    2013003899

DEDICATION

For Emily and Eric, who continually teach me about the ways we learn and use the language arts.

                                                                                    E.D.

For the colleagues, mentors, teachers, and preservice teachers I have had the privilege to collaborate with through the years, and to Travis and Derek, who are my inspiration.

                                                                                    D.J.

To the teachers and preservice teachers with whom we work and who teach us so much.

                                                                                    T.D.W.

We have made every effort to contact copyright holders, students, teachers, and other parties for permission to reproduce borrowed material. We regret any oversights that may have occurred and will be pleased to rectify them. In some cases we have changed names to protect the privacy of teachers, students, and their families.

    We have made every effort to provide current website addresses and links throughout this book. However, because these items change often, it is inevitable that some of the links used here will change following publication of this book. We will strive to update these in each version of the book.

Holcomb Hathaway, Publishers, Inc.
8700 E. Via de Ventura Blvd., Suite 265
Scottsdale, Arizona 85258
480-991-7881
www.hh-pub.com

10 9 8 7 6 5 4 3 2 1

Bundle ISBN: 978-1-934432-92-1
Ebook ISBN: 978-1-934432-80-8
Print ISBN: 978-1-934432-95-2

Printed in the United States of America.

Contents

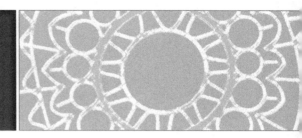

8   ASSESSING THE RECEPTIVE MODES   229

9   WRITING AS A PROCESS   245

10   WRITING TOOLS FOR ENHANCING MEANING   291

Preface

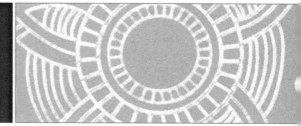

A Word About Our Title

Throughout this book, we will refer to it as *Forward Thinking,* for this reason: Though the book's complete title is *Teaching the Language Arts: Forward Thinking in Today's Classrooms,* we feel the concept of "forward thinking" best describes an important aspect of this book, in which we have incorporated new tools, technology, and pedagogy readers will use in their own classrooms. Our goal is to help them envision their future classrooms and imagine the possibilities as they combine the traditional and the new to motivate and excite their students and give them the best learning experience possible.

This Print Book

This text was conceptualized and written as a multimedia digital text. We realize, however, that having a print version may be useful in some situations and have thus made this companion print version available. Because of the rich resources available from within the digital book, we recommend that this print companion be used in conjunction with the enhanced ebook rather than as a replacement for it.

THE KERNEL

A book project begins with the kernel of an idea. For *Forward Thinking,* the kernel is the idea that the language arts are about the ways we communicate, whether face to face, on a cell phone, or electronically through a post, a tweet, a text; whether verbally or graphically; and so on. To say that the ways in which we communicate, and thus the language arts, are changing rapidly is an understatement. We wrote *Forward Thinking* with the philosophical stance that the nature of literacy is constantly evolving, and this change is driven in part by the influence of technology. The term *new literacies* is used to describe the view that adeptness with information and communications technologies is directly linked to what it means to be literate in today's global society (Coiro, Knobel, Lanskshear, & Leu, 2008).

Yet, underlying the changes in the ways we communicate, one constant remains: the value of clearly communicating our ideas to others and the need for skills to interpret the messages being shared by others. The language arts are the modes for expressing and receiving ideas. The six modes of language arts—reading, writing, listening, speaking, viewing, and visually representing—provide the organizational framework for *Forward Thinking* and, with the help of technology, bring alive the pedagogy of language arts instruction.

WHY AN ENHANCED EBOOK?

For a book about teaching the language arts, it seemed imperative to us that learners should be able to access information and create ideas using all six modes of the language arts. To best achieve this goal, we knew a multimedia digital book would be needed. An enhanced etextbook has the potential to change the ways we teach and learn because readers interact with the text in a variety of ways. Media elements enrich the traditional mode of reading: for example, learners can watch lessons being taught; they can hear the voices of children and teachers. They can quickly access relevant resources online. In addition, when digital notes are shared among students and the instructor, class members create a learning network. Community knowledge is created, and seeing ideas acknowledged and understood by others can be a powerful motivator for learning.

In these ways and others, a multimedia digital book promotes learning. Technology and the language arts themselves facilitate learning *about* the language arts.

Responsive to continuous change

The language arts, like other content areas in schools, are strongly influenced by digital literacies. Many of today's students go beyond word processing and use web publishing, microblogging, video editing, and podcasting on a daily basis. A textbook preparing future teachers must reflect and keep up with the constant evolution of digital literacies. While this is a challenge for print textbooks, an ebook allows for more frequent updating, keeping the book timely without disrupting course preparation.

Instant access to multiple resources

Many readers today are digital natives; they have grown up using digital technologies, such as cell phones and the Internet, nearly every day that they can remember. These tech-savvy readers are adept at using technology to access and understand information. A multimedia digital text gives today's students a format for learning that matches their skills and experiences. Ideas are not shared simply through text—they are enhanced with videoclips, podcasts, graphics, and links to relevant websites and resources. In this book, these learning aids can be accessed instantly, as needed by individual learners to enhance their own understanding.

Scaffolding and support for learning

Although readers may be adept at using technology when seeking information, they may be less knowledgeable about using technology in their teaching to enhance their students' learning. This book models ways in which electronic resources can be integrated with and used to augment traditional classroom materials to take full advantage of both. Access to the multimedia elements of *Forward Thinking* gives novice teachers the opportunity to read about, listen to, and view experienced teachers in action as they integrate literacy and technology in their classrooms.

Certain features of an enhanced ebook such as this one offer readers scaffolding for their learning, increasing the likelihood of comprehension and success. Because ideas can be connected and explored through links, readers of etextbooks have the advantage of being able to bolster background knowledge in areas that may need extra work. For example, if an individual is reading about the writing process and wishes to know more about what this term encompasses, an etextbook can offer not only the chapter description, but also electronic access to a definition, several websites with information in both graphic and written form, a videoclip of students using the writing process, and a teacher's podcast describing writing workshop. Information presented in such a variety of formats more fully meets diverse learning needs than when presented in only one format.

Using the features of *Forward Thinking,* readers can

- Learn by reading, listening, and viewing
- Apply and reflect learning by writing, speaking, and visually representing using "Think Like a Teacher" activities
- Access information instantly from relevant websites
- Create digital notes and highlights as reminders of important information
- Search the book for key words
- View definitions of bolded vocabulary instantly
- Navigate through chapters easily using the left-column content listing and clicking on a heading, an image, or a multimedia element
- Check learning along the way with the Points2Ponder review feature

Ease of use for instructors

We envision several ways this multimedia digital book can be used. These include, but are not limited to, the following:

- *Forward Thinking* can be used as a traditional text, with students asked to read the chapters and explore the links at home before or after a face-to-face class. The suggested speaking, writing, and visual representing activities might then be incorporated as in-class activities.
- An instructor might ask students to read/peruse the text at home and then, during a face-to-face class, the instructor can project portions of the text so that the whole group can view the resources. The suggested speaking, writing, and visual representing activities can be incorporated as in-class activities.
- *Forward Thinking* can be the focal point of content during face-to-face course meetings. When viewed on laptops (individually or shared) during the class session, the chapter and related links can serve as the class content. A workshop approach can be used in which the instructor sets the purpose and the students then read the chapter and explore the links during a class work-time. This process can also be followed for an in-class writing or speaking activity from the chapter. Finally the group can come back together to summarize and share what has been learned.
- For an online class, whether the class format utilizes Blackboard, another learning management system, or a website model, *Forward Thinking* will be an ideal text. The suggested speaking/writing/visually representing activities can be facilitated through web conference, chat room, discussion board, instant messaging, or blogging. The embedded and linked videos and podcasts provide foundational knowledge and can supplement instructor lectures for key concepts.

Whether you as an instructor already share digital resources as you teach or are new to this process, this ebook provides an exciting collection of digital resources, organized to be relevant to your course content. Our hope is that this book's content and its features will facilitate teaching and learning in your college classroom, and will help your students assume responsibility for their own learning. This, after all, will be their goal as teachers in their own classrooms.

THE MANY VOICES OF FORWARD THINKING

The multimedia digital format allows us to incorporate many voices with our own as we explore how to teach language arts effectively in modern classrooms.

Classroom voices that bring teaching to life

In creating *Forward Thinking,* one of our goals is to bring the classroom to future teachers. While writing this book, we visited classrooms, interviewed teachers and students, photographed classroom events, observed lessons, and collected student work samples, all in order to bring to life the everyday language arts activities of the classroom. Readers of *Forward Thinking* will hear the voices of practicing teachers and witness student learning by listening to podcasts and watching videos created from these classroom visits. The feature Stories from the Classroom describes real world classroom activities, allowing readers to accompany us, peek briefly into these same classrooms, and observe a great variety of language arts instruction.

Literacy leaders' voices

While new teachers can learn much from experienced teachers and their students, valuable information about teaching and learning can also be gained from leaders in the field of literacy. The feature Spotlight on a Literacy Leader shares a bit of background about various literacy leaders, including Nell Duke, Don Leu, and Dorothy Strickland. These brief descriptions include the key ideas, theories, research, or projects the leader is known for, and often we have also included opportunities to hear from and see the individuals themselves through podcasts and videos. The work of leaders such as these guides our thinking and grounds our literacy practices.

Authors' voices

We as authors want to be an active part of each reader's learning experience, and our goal has been to create a textbook that models the collaborative experiences of teaching and learning. In the feature Author's Story we begin in Chapter 1 by presenting our reasons for writing this ebook. In each subsequent Author's Story, one of us briefly describes the ways we use and teach language arts, offering real world application of the book's ideas. In another feature, Comprehension Coach podcasts, we suggest ways for readers to apply comprehension strategies while reading this enhanced ebook.

Readers' voices

While the book's digital features promote multimodal access of information, learners really begin to own new ideas when given the opportunity to think deeply and share new learning with others. The social networking features of *Forward Thinking* encourage readers to synthesize, reflect, and apply new ideas by writing about, speaking about, and visually representing new learning and by sharing this learning with others. Think Like a Teacher activities at the end of each chapter place readers into teaching situations and allow them to apply the new ideas they've learned.

To promote the sharing of ideas, instructors may create a private discussion group in which classmates are able to share their virtual notes and comments with each other. All of these tools, whether used in a face-to-face or online setting, promote the development of a personal learning network, a collection of resources a person can use to learn something new.

Forward Thinking is not intended to be a book that is opened, read, then put on a shelf. Our goal is for it to be a vibrant, connected learning tool, and we invite you and your students to become part of that learning community.

THE BOOK'S ORGANIZATIONAL FRAMEWORK

A multimodal textbook may be new to some readers, so Chapter 1 opens with a discussion of "reading" an enhanced ebook. We describe the book's digital features and also offer suggestions for applying comprehension strategies—for example, activating prior knowledge and making inferences—when reading, listening, and viewing. Chapters 2, 3, and 4 lay the groundwork for understanding the language arts, creating face-to-face and virtual classroom environments for promoting literacy development, and planning for and assessing the language arts.

Organization around the language arts modes

Chapters 5–12 present information on the theory, research, teaching, and assessment of the six modes of the language arts, with this breakdown: In Chapters 5 through 8, we focus on the *receptive language arts*—the ways learners receive or understand information. Chapters 9 through 12 focus on the *expressive language arts*—the ways learners express ideas.

Specifically, Chapters 5 and 6 address the reading process; Chapter 7 shares information about listening and viewing; and Chapter 8 focuses on assessing the receptive language arts. Chapters 9 and 10 address the writing process, spelling, grammar, and handwriting; Chapter 11 explores speaking and visually representing; and Chapter 12 shares assessments for the expressive modes.

Focus on assessment

When discussing the important topic of assessment, writers of language arts textbooks face this dilemma: whether to (a) consolidate the discussion (e.g., in one chapter), and if so whether to place that assessment chapter at the beginning or the end of the book, or (b) thread assessment information throughout the book. Arguments can be made for and against each of these options. Readers likely need basic information about literacy concepts to aid their understanding of assessment, which suggests an end-of-book placement. Yet, in the classroom, assessment should guide instruction, which argues for an earlier and/or threaded discussion.

In *Forward Thinking,* we address assessment in three ways: First, Chapter 4 provides an early overview of assessment. Second, each chapter on the language arts includes assessment information specific to that mode. Third, Chapters 8 and 12 focus on specific assessments for the receptive and expressive language arts, respectively, using a unique chapter format. These chapters emphasize the need to understand the rationale and procedure for using various informal and formal literacy assessment instruments. Each assessment description includes relevant College and Career

Readiness Standards and the Common Core State Standards, along with a suggested grade level range, and a description of the assessment and how it might be used in the classroom. The digital format of *Forward Thinking* lets readers easily click between the assessment and the instructional information in other chapters related to the assessment.

We hope that this three-pronged approach promotes a strong link between instruction and assessment.

INSTRUCTOR RESOURCES

Ancillaries

An Instructor's Manual and PowerPoint Presentation are available to instructors upon adoption of the text. The Instructor's Manual provides ideas for assignments, in class or electronic discussions, and activities based on the many multimedia and online resources. Additional ideas for how to get the most from using this book with your students are available on the book's blog: www.hhpcommunities.com/teachinglanguagearts

Digital book support

Forward Thinking is a multimedia digital book available on the Inkling platform. To find information about working with this platform, a brief overview of the support is available at either of the following two URLs:

http://support.inkling.com/forums/20719816-reading

http://support.inkling.com/forums

In addition, Holcomb Hathaway has created videos for instructors and students with specific information about navigating both the online and tablet versions of *Forward Thinking*:

For Instructors:

- Navigating the Online Version: www.hhpcommunities.com/teaching languagearts/HowToUse/PC.mp4
- Navigating the iPad Version: www.hhpcommunities.com/teaching languagearts/HowToUse/Ipad.mp4

For Students:

- Navigating the Online Version: www.hhpcommunities.com/teaching languagearts/HowToUse/StudentPC.mp4
- Navigating the iPad Version: www.hhpcommunities.com/teaching languagearts/HowToUse/StudentIpad.mp4

To set up note sharing and discussion threads with your class, email support@inkling.com with the name of this book *(Teaching the Language Arts: Forward Thinking in Today's Classrooms)* and your email address (this must be the same email address that you use for your Inkling account). Using that information, the Inkling engineering team will make your notes a color different from your students' notes. To see your notes, each student in your class will need to "Follow" you. For more information: http://support.inkling.com/entries/20295887-follow-someone-by-email-address

Please note that some websites included in the book require Flash and Quick Time player. These resources will not be available on the iPad. To view, readers should visit the sites on other devices.

It is our hope that you and your students will be motivated by *Forward Thinking* and that its unique features will yield a deeper understanding of effective ways to teach the language arts. We welcome your comments regarding the content, design, and operation of this digital book, and we welcome suggestions for its improvement. Finally, if you discover links that are not functioning, please let us know. Contact us in care of our publisher:

Holcomb Hathaway, Publishers, feedback@hh-pub.com

ACKNOWLEDGMENTS

Creating this digital book required a leap of faith for all those involved. For us as authors, this is the first digital textbook we have written, and for our publisher, in particular Colette Kelly, Executive Editor, and Gay Pauley, Production Director, this is the first textbook designed and published originally as a digital rather than print product. When we began work, none of us knew what form the finished ebook would take because the world of digital book publishing changes rapidly. It's a challenge to write a book when you're not sure what the book will look like in the end! We want to acknowledge Colette and Gay's support and their belief in this book as an interactive digital production.

We want to extend our sincere appreciation to those who reviewed the book as it was being written and developed: Kathy Brashears, Tennessee Tech University; Lisa Clayton, University of North Alabama; Laurie Henry, University of Kentucky; Kim Higdon, St. Leo University; Katherine Kinney, University of North Alabama; Lotta Larson, Kansas State University; Jessica Mangelson, Benedictine University; Micheline Manzi, University of Wisconsin Oshkosh; John E McEneaney, Reading and Language Arts, Oakland University; Aimee Morewood, West Virginia University; Ian O'Byrne, University of Connecticut; Joan Rhodes, Virginia Commonwealth University; Tammy Ryan, Jacksonville University; Elizabeth Petroelje Stolle, Grand Valley State University; and Ruth Sylvester, University of South Florida. Your honest comments and concrete suggestions were helpful as we revised the book.

We also want to thank the teachers with whom we worked directly for this project and others who shared ideas and thoughts that influenced our knowledge and our thinking; these include Sarah Lucero, Scott Ritter, Pam Albin, Ginger Lewman, Erin Fitzpatrick, Charlie Mahoney, Mark Camacho, Robin Dixon, Amee Martin, Amanda Arndt, Carla Goertzen, Gina Bennett, Lucy Burdiek, Angie Burkett, Jessica Asbury, Cherise Smith, Lori Rainey, Andrea Keller, Sara Schwerdtfeger, Theresa Livingston, Diane Kimsey, Sharon Bedolla, Ryan Wilson, Preeti Singh, Krista Hughett, Chelsea Mitchell, Cheryl Isaacson, Wendy Lucy, Kristen Schweitzer, Leslie Panaro, Julie Lipscomb, Susan Alis, and Vicki Altland. A special thanks goes to the hundreds of students (and their school districts) who shared their ideas, written and graphic work, and digital projects with us. Through these students' sharing a bit of themselves, future teachers will come to better understand the varied and amazing ways students learn to communicate.

Elizabeth Dobler
Denise Johnson
Thomas DeVere Wolsey

About the Authors

Elizabeth Dobler began her career as a classroom teacher, teaching kindergarten, first, third, and sixth grades for 13 years. She earned her Ph.D. at Kansas State University and is now a literacy professor at Emporia State University, in Emporia, Kansas; there, she teaches courses in language arts, reading, and children's literature. She also directs the Professional Development School program in Topeka Public Schools, where she supervises student interns. Dobler's research interests have focused on web literacies as well as the instructional practices of preservice and novice teachers. She is an active member of the Kansas Reading Association, the International Reading Association, and the Literacy Research Association. Her other publications include the books *Reading the Web: Strategies for Internet Inquiry* and *A Report Card on Report Cards,* and journal articles in the *Kansas Journal of Reading, Reading Research Quarterly, Journal of Adolescent and Adult Literacy,* and *Journal of Reading Education.*

Denise Johnson is a professor and director of the Literacy Leadership Program at the College of William & Mary, in Williamsburg, Virginia. She received her Ed.D. in Reading from the University of Memphis. She has worked as an elementary classroom teacher, a middle school reading specialist, and a Reading Recovery teacher; she now teaches graduate and undergraduate courses in reading and language arts methods and children's literature. Her research interests include literacy, children's literature, and the integration of technology into preservice and inservice education courses and in elementary classrooms. Johnson has written several books, including *The Joy of Children's Literature,* and has published articles in *The Reading Teacher, Journal of Adolescent and Adult Literacy,* and *Literacy Teaching and Learning.* She has been awarded the Instructional Leadership Award by the Virginia Association of Colleges of Teacher Education and was awarded the John Chorlton Manning Public Service Award by the International Reading Association.

Thomas DeVere Wolsey is a program director for the literacy master's programs at Walden University, where he teaches and supervises graduate courses related to literacy and technology. He worked in public schools for more than 20 years, teaching English, social studies, and elective classes. He earned his doctorate at the University of San Diego/San Diego State University, and he also holds a master's degree in educational administration from California State University at San Bernardino. Wolsey's articles on literacy and technology have appeared in *The Journal of Adolescent and Adult Literacy, Action in Teacher Education, The International Journal on e-Learning, The Journal of Education, The Journal of Literacy Research and Instruction,* and others. He serves on the review boards of several journals, including *The Reading Teacher* and *The Journal of Adolescent and Adult Literacy.* His recent books include *Learning to Predict and Learning from Predictions: How Thinking about What Might Happen Next Helps Students Learn, Literacy Growth for Every Child,* and *Transforming Writing Instruction in the Digital Age: Techniques for Grades 5–12.* Wolsey is interested in how literacy intersects with online and physical learning spaces, writing as a feature of learning about disciplines (e.g., mathematics, social studies), and reading in digital environments.

Access the book's Glossary, which defines the key terms boldfaced in this chapter, at www.hhpcommunities.com/teachinglanguagearts/glossary.pdf

1.1

WHY A MULTIMEDIA DIGITAL BOOK? THE STORY BEHIND THIS EBOOK

An author does not just sit down and start writing a book, especially one that makes use of new formats, such as an enhanced ebook. There is always a story behind a book, and although this is an enhanced ebook, its beginnings are not so different from a traditional print book. Knowing the story of this ebook's beginnings may give you some insight as you read, listen, and view this ebook.

First, a word about our title. Throughout this book, we will refer to it as *Forward Thinking,* for this reason: Though the book's complete title is *Teaching the Language Arts: Forward Thinking in Today's Classrooms,* we feel the concept of "forward thinking" best describes an important aspect of this book, in which we have incorporated many of the new tools, technology, and pedagogy you will use in your own classrooms. Our goal is to help you envision your future classroom and imagine the possibilities as you combine the traditional and the new to motivate and excite your students and give them the best learning experience possible.

> *"We are all part of this immense digital experiment, and we know not where it leads."*
>
> **KATHLEEN PARKER**
> nationally syndicated columnist

author's story

ELIZABETH DOBLER

The idea for this book came to me from a series of seemingly unconnected events that began with cleaning the house. After putting off housework for too long, I was forced to find something for my four-year-old son, Eric, to do while I tended to the dusting and vacuuming. I needed an activity that would not create another mess for me to clean up just as I finished cleaning the first mess, so I sat him at my computer. Eric had played a few games on the computer at his preschool, but had never been on the Internet. I brought up the Lego site, gave him a 30-second tour, and then proceeded to my work. After a few minutes, I noticed his adeptness at navigating the website, and I felt a sense of awe. Here was a boy who had little experience navigating the online world and who had limited reading skills, and yet he could make enough sense of the website to entertain himself (later, he drew the self-portrait in Exhibit 1.1). The housecleaning once again fell by the wayside as I watched with fascination. I began to wonder what things he would need to learn during his school years that would facilitate his success with reading on the Internet.

About this same time, I was working on my doctorate, which included an emphasis in reading instruction. When I was an elementary school teacher, I had been especially interested in the reading process, specifically the ways we make sense of and comprehend what we read. This interest, along with my observation of Eric, led to a doctoral study of Internet comprehension. The field of reading and technology was in its infancy, and I worked with colleagues to explore the comprehension strategies we use when reading a website, and how these are alike and different from the strategies we use when reading printed text (Coiro & Dobler, 2007; Eagleton & Dobler, 2007).

I also increased my use of technology in my personal life. I met my husband through an online dating site, where we used instant messaging to get to know each other, even though we lived only two miles apart. I observed our children constantly texting on their cell phones. By the time Eric was in middle school, he could practically text blindfolded. At the dinner table, he and our four other children talked about how cell phones, computers, and the Internet were used—or not used—in school.

For 12 years I had been teaching a language arts methods course to preservice teachers at the university. One semester I received a sabbatical to visit classrooms and study the ways teachers integrate technology into language arts instruction. The idea for this book developed from there, with the enhanced format stemming from my online background.

View my digital essay about my sabbatical (8:15) to better understand what I learned and how it influenced me to write this book. (*Access this essay in the digital version of this book.*)

Eric's Internet.

Because writing a book of this scope alone is challenging, I asked two respected colleagues, Denise Johnson and Thomas DeVere Wolsey, to serve as coauthors. We were not aware of any published ebooks like this one, so we considered this project an adventure—we felt a little like Lewis and Clark as they set off on their western expedition in the early 1800s.

author's story

DENISE JOHNSON

When Elizabeth asked me to be part of this project, I immediately thought of my own reading habits. When in bed at night or at my desk reading a book, I often reach for my tablet or computer so I can find out more about a concept in the book, an idea sparked by the book, or to learn more about resources discussed in the book. But the process of moving back and forth seems clunky, at best. The idea of creating a multimedia digital book that seamlessly integrates these resources was exciting. This ebook pulls together information and resources about teaching language arts in a way that makes sense and supports learning from a 21st-century perspective. Writing this book has been an immense learning experience for me, both exhilarating and challenging!

author's story   THOMAS DEVERE WOLSEY

When Beth asked if I would like to participate as an author of this ebook, I felt like a member of the Corps of Discovery (the name of Lewis and Clark's famous expedition) headed off to explore territory that was uncertain but very promising. We have been learners in the adventure of creating this ebook for you. It seems odd for the author of an ebook to say, but I still like the heft of a printed book, the feel of the paper, the satisfaction of actually turning a page. But I have several ebooks saved on my computer and ereader, and I have come to appreciate the qualities ebooks can add to the reading experience in certain circumstances.

One of my interests as a learner, researcher, and author is how words and images work together. While books have included illustrations since *Orbis Pictus* (Comenius, 1658), the Internet offers the reader seemingly limitless options to start with an illustration provided by the authors and explore from there. Videos and audio podcasts can bring the author's voice, literally, to the reader. In this ebook, you will also hear and see some of the seminal thinkers in the field of literacy education. Part of the adventure in writing this book derived from combining video, audio, and written words that we hope convey a sense of belonging to a community of literacy professionals. Together, we will improve the world for the students with whom we work.

We share these stories to provide background on the collection of experiences, information, and insights that have gone into creating this digital book, including not only our own experiences, but those of teachers, students, administrators, and parents. The unique format of this ebook gives you, the reader, an opportunity to learn about the language arts from a variety of sources and in a variety of ways.

1.2

HOW DO WE LEARN?

This textbook represents a new way to share information, but an old way of learning. Typically, we learn by taking in information through our senses and trying it out for ourselves. Information is gathered through the processes of reading, listening, and watching (viewing). When we have collected enough information to feel a certain level of confidence, we try out our new knowledge. Practice with using new knowledge is crucial for learning and may take the form of talking, writing, or creating something *about* or *with* what we have learned. When we incorporate all of these elements, active learning takes place.

Cone of Experience

Edgar Dale created the Cone of Experience (1969) and we have adapted this model to show the impact of learning to teach through several differ-

EXHIBIT 1.2

Cone of Experience for learning to teach.

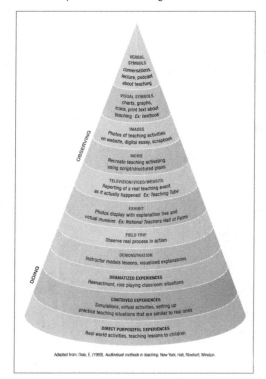

VERBAL
SYMBOLS
conversations,
lecture, podcast
about teaching

VISUAL SYMBOLS
charts, graphs,
icons, print text about
teaching Ex: textbook

IMAGES
Photos of teaching activities
on website, digital essay, scrapbook

MOVIE
Recreate teaching activating
using script/structured plans

TELEVISION/VIDEO/WEBSITE
Reporting of a real teaching event
as it actually happened Ex: Teaching Tube

EXHIBIT
Photos display with explanation live and
virtual museum Ex: National Teachers Hall of Fame

FIELD TRIP
Observe real process in action

DEMONSTRATION
Instructor models lessons, visualized explanations

DRAMATIZED EXPERIENCES
Reenactment, role playing classroom situations

CONTRIVED EXPERIENCES
Simulations, virtual activities, setting up
practice teaching situations that are similar to real ones

DIRECT PURPOSEFUL EXPERIENCES
Real world activities, teaching lessons to children

OBSERVING

DOING

Adapted from: Dale, E. (1969). *Audiovisual methods in teaching*. New York: Holt, Rinehart, Winston.

ent formats (see Exhibit 1.2). In his model, Dale identifies learning through reading or listening alone as the least effective format, while learning through seeing and hearing combined as a more effective format, although this may vary for different learners in different situations. According to his research, the bedrock of learning occurs through simulated situations and actual experiences that involve all of the senses. Traditional textbooks provide opportunities to learn at the visual symbols level (e.g., letters and words). *Forward Thinking* gives you, the reader, an opportunity to learn using the various language arts (reading, writing, speaking, listening, viewing, and visually representing) by presenting information through various modes (e.g., speaking, writing, visual images), thus creating a multimedia text and multisensory experience (Anstey & Bull, 2006).

In *Forward Thinking,* you are actively learning by using the language arts to learn about language arts. Chickering and Gamson (1987) describe active learning for college students in this way: "Learning is not a spectator sport. Students do not learn much just by sitting in class listening to teachers, memorizing repackaged assignments, and spitting out answers. They must talk about what they are learning, write about it, relate it to past experiences, apply it to their daily lives. They must make what they learn part of themselves." The goal of this ebook is to share resources that you can use to prepare yourself to be an effective teacher of the language arts. The most productive way to do this is to present information in various formats so that you can actually interact with the textbook. Through this interaction and the opportunity to solve problems with your new information, you will *learn to understand,* rather than *just learn a procedure* (Hendrickson & Schroeder, 1941). This deep learning does not come easily and requires much thought and flexing of your mental muscles.

Layers of learning information

If we learn more effectively when we are active, exactly how active must we be? With an enhanced ebook like *Forward Thinking,* must you read, watch, listen, and respond to every podcast, video, link, and activity? This decision is up to you. Consider an analogy to help with your decision. The text that you typically read in a textbook is like a hamburger. A hamburger fresh off the grill is tasty, just as reading the textbook is a good way to learn. Now take that basic hamburger and add cheese, and you have an even tastier burger. The same is true with this ebook. If you read the text *and* watch the suggested videos or listen to the recommended podcasts, you have enhanced your learning. Consider these activities to be like the cheese on the burger, an additional layer of resources for learning. Now take this cheeseburger and add two pieces of bacon; then you have a delicious burger. In the same way, if you take the basic text of this ebook, and layer it with videos or podcasts, then add an additional layer of a related speaking or writing activities, you are actively learning.

Each area of language arts that is incorporated into *Forward Thinking* provides an additional layer of learning, thus increasing the likelihood you will remember and use the information to become an effective teacher. In order to gain the most information, you should embrace the whole experience of a multimedia textbook. A teacher who gains a wide variety of information from a wide variety of resources is better prepared to take on the challenges of the language arts needs of the diverse group of multimodal learners found in the classrooms of today.

Learning from the *Forward Thinking* ebook

Exactly how does the ebook format facilitate learning? The following features of *Forward Thinking* give readers the chance to take in information in several different ways.

- **Text accompanied by images.** Chapters with written text are used to share information, which is not so different from a traditional textbook. Yet, images are interwoven among the words that can inspire connections and enhance the meaning of the text.
- **Key vocabulary defined instantly.** Words that are key to developing a strong understanding of the text can be defined by clicking on the word.
- **Links to websites.** Credible, relevant, and useful websites are easily opened in a separate window by clicking on the linked text. Close out that window to return to the text.
- **Stories from the Classroom.** Descriptions of classroom activities create a visual image of what teaching and learning are like in real classroom settings.
- **Examples of students' work.** Throughout the text you will encounter and can link to examples of real students' work, including writings, drawings, podcasts, projects, and presentations.
- **Comprehension Coach.** These author-created podcasts offer hints for improving your comprehension as you read *Forward Thinking* and, we hope, subsequent readings.
- **Spotlight on Literacy Leaders.** Various leaders in the field of literacy education are featured in many chapters. Read about their accomplishments and their influence on teaching and learning language arts.
- **Teachers' experiences in their own words.** Podcast interviews allow classroom teachers to share their experiences and insights about language arts instruction.
- **Videos/photo essays.** Graphics and audio are combined to present experiences with the language arts from the perspective of teachers and students.
- **Points2Ponder.** You will periodically come across questions about the information just covered in the chapter. Pause in your reading at this point, or return to the questions after reading the chapter. These questions serve as a review of the most important ideas of the chapter. Take a moment to formulate your own answer to the question before clicking to show the answer.
- **Links within the text.** Digital texts allow readers to link between ideas in two different chapters with only a touch or click. For example, information about literacy assessments can be viewed in two ways. A reader can use the traditional approach and read each chapter in sequence; for example, reading Chapter 8, Assessing the Receptive Modes, after reading the chapters about teaching the receptive language arts (5, 6, and 7) and reading Chapter 12, Assessing the Expressive Modes, after reading the related expressive chapters (9, 10, 11). Or, when reading any of the content chapters (5, 6, 7, and 9, 10, 11), you can explore hyperlinks connecting information about instruction directly to an assessment teachers use to evaluate a specific content or skill. Thus, connections between ideas are clear and instantaneous.
- **E-notes.** Electronic notes can be created within the text and shared with others to remind yourself of connections you made while reading.

■ **Virtual highlighting.** Highlighting can be used to help you organize and locate information when you return to the text for clarification.

When combined, these elements help present a multidimensional view of language arts. Why is this important? Being an effective language arts teacher requires you to draw from your pool of knowledge about teaching, learning, and communication. The larger we can make this pool, the more instructional tools you will have at your disposal.

1.3

WHAT *IS* TEXT IN A MULTIMEDIA DIGITAL BOOK AND AM I *REALLY* READING?

In the classroom, the word *text* usually means a book. Some might go so far as to say that it means a textbook, but certainly novels, chapter books, picture books, and informational books also come to mind when defining *text*. Although this definition is a start, it is narrow and limiting. A plethora of objects around us every day require us to develop an understanding, including signs, newspapers, websites, instructions, icons, and posters, just to name a few. In a broader sense, these are all texts. In fact, any source of information from which we make meaning is a text. *Forward Thinking* is a multimodal text (Kress, 2003), one in which meaning is created through modes such as viewing, listening, and reading. The definition of *text* that we would like to promote in this book, which is widely supported by research, includes the following criteria:

1. A text is any sign that communicates meaning (Saussure, 1966). A sign can include written words, abbreviations, symbols, icons, and gestures. Many texts, including electronic texts, rely on visual images as much as words to convey meaning (see Exhibit 1.3).
2. A text represents a *chunk of meaning* (Rowe, 1987), and can be any size and occur at many levels. A text may be a novel, a brief summary, a single word, or an icon. A text may also be an idea, a concept, a theme, or some other flexible unit of meaning (Lemke, 1985). Rather than focusing on individual words, real world texts often convey ideas through icons, diagrams, maps, timelines, and a host of other types of graphics.
3. A text is composed of elements of other texts (Orr, 2003) and is never totally a new creation. The Latin meaning for the word *text* is *woven*, as in a fabric with a woven network of threads all anchored elsewhere in other texts (Hartman, 1992). With electronic texts, graphics or images play an integral role and often ideas are connected through hyperlinks. This connectedness lets the reader easily move from one idea to the next, but also requires focused attention in order to remember the path of meaning or how one idea is connected to another.

Based on these criteria, lots of the things that we read every day are considered texts, including street signs, comic books, or illustrations. Notice that within this broad definition, images play a key role in conveying meaning. The term **visual literacy** describes the ways we construct meaning from visual images (Flood & Lapp, 1997/1998). When a person *reads* a picture, he or she incorporates many of the same processes involved in

EXHIBIT 1.3

Making meaning from a symbol.

reading a story. For example, a reader considers what he or she already knows in relation to what he or she sees in the image or illustration. A reader interprets the illustrator's intended meaning, just as when making sense of an author's words. In fact, some literacy scholars consider reading to be only one type of literacy (Gee, 1996; Street, 1993, 2003). Thus, the term **literacies** is often used to encourage educators to think beyond the printed page to include a wide variety of ways we share and receive information based on our culture, values, and experiences. With the influx of new technologies that shape how we communicate, the term **new literacies** has been coined to describe the ways we consider and use language and literacy, especially those related to technology (Lankshear & Knobel, 2002; Leu, Kinzer, Coiro, & Cammack, 2004).

Based on our understanding of the terms *text* and *literacy*, we use the term *reading* loosely when describing how you will interact with this book. Sometimes you *are* reading; sometimes you are viewing; sometimes you are listening; and sometimes you are combining two or three areas of language arts together at the same time just like your students will do when they learn new information both in school and out of school (see Exhibit 1.4). In this chapter, we use the term *reading*, but keep in mind that in a multimedia book, this term means much more than interpreting the words on a page or screen.

EXHIBIT 1.4

Creating meaning through various modes.

Understanding and remembering what we read

We previously described what it means to actively learn. Let's take this idea one step further and apply it to reading. A reader can easily become complacent by letting the words soak in and assuming they are being understood. But to gain the most you can from a textbook—especially this textbook—you must interact with the text. This means you must be constantly thinking while you are reading. As Tapscott wrote, "It's not just point and click. It's point, read, think and click" (1999, p. 63).

Understanding and remembering what we read is reading comprehension. While Chapters 5 and 6 explore effective ways to teach comprehension to students, this chapter focuses on becoming aware of and developing your own comprehension strategies (see Exhibit 1.5). To effectively teach others about comprehension in the digital age, *you* must effectively comprehend what you read. The enhanced aspects of *Forward Thinking* will put a new spin on comprehension, whether you are already skilled or want to improve how you read.

EXHIBIT 1.5

Comprehension strategies.

Before reading

Several thinking activities can occur before reading that will set you up for success in understanding and remembering what you read. Think of these as mental warm-ups or stretches, much like a runner does before a big race. Although it is tempting to skip these steps and get right to the reading, pausing first can make your reading more successful. By success, we mean understanding and remembering what you read and being able to act on this new knowledge, all of which should be your goal when reading.

Consider your purpose. Before embarking on a reading adventure consider your purpose for reading. In the case of *Forward Thinking*, your general purpose likely is to gain knowledge to be a skilled teacher of language arts, so you can develop and enrich the literate lives of your students. The broad purpose of learning more should always be in the back of your mind when reading this book. So if you ask yourself, "Do I really need to listen to that podcast, or look at that writing sample?" the answer lies in your purpose. Ask yourself, "Will doing so help me to become a skilled teacher of language arts?"

In addition to a general purpose, skilled readers also set more specific purposes. For example, when reading *Forward Thinking,* as you begin each section or chapter, identify the specific information you hope to gain, thus further considering your purpose for reading. As a specific example, in Chapter 10, Writing Tools for Enhancing Meaning, you might want to read to find out if understanding the parts of speech is necessary for an elementary teacher or if handwriting or keyboarding should be emphasized in elementary school. Once you have identified this purpose, then you will be continually seeking details to help you build an understanding of this focus while you are reading.

Preview the text or screen and make predictions. Before jumping right in and getting started, an experienced reader recognizes the importance of looking over the text, whether it be on a screen or on paper. Taking the time to preview helps the reader to determine which information is important and where to read carefully. First, glance at the chapter title. Make a prediction about the information you think will be included in the chapter based on this title. In *Forward Thinking,* you will find a list of key ideas at the beginning of each chapter. Take a close look at these (even though you might be tempted to skip them). Pause and think about what is coming up in the chapter. Then glance at the chapter headings. Again, predict the type of information that you will likely encounter. By doing this, you are giving yourself a mental "heads-up" of what to expect. As you are reading, your mind will begin to search for what you expected to find before you began. This process helps to keep you focused while reading.

Activate your prior knowledge. Before reading, consider what you know about the topic of the chapter and the format of the text. This will guide you in determining how to read the text. Call to the front of your mind what you already know about the chapter topic from your experiences as a child, adolescent, or adult learner. Recalling what you know may take only a moment or two, but it should give you several mental hooks on which to hang the new information you are about to gain. For example, before reading Chapter 3, Creating a Learning Environment in Face-to-Face and Virtual Classrooms, think about the classrooms where you were a student. Call to mind elements in these classrooms that you enjoyed or did not enjoy as a learner. Then when you are reading the chapter, mentally connect the text with your own experiences to build stronger links of understanding.

Be careful when activating prior knowledge. Sometimes we think we know about a topic already, so we do not read as carefully as we should. Even if you are already familiar with the topic, watching a video or listening to a podcast related to that topic may give you new insights. Numerous opportunities to gain information about a topic can help cement that knowledge into your brain.

During reading

To some, reading is an effortless process. To others, reading is painstaking and slow. Either way, what happens in your mind when reading can make the difference between remembering and understanding versus getting to the end of a section and not having any idea of what you just read. Consider the following comprehension strategies as ways to raise your awareness of what you do when you read and to increase your likelihood of comprehending and remembering what is read.

Make connections. *Before* reading you activated your prior knowledge. *During* reading, you should be constantly looking for details that can be connected to what you already know. Our brain seeks to connect new information to our past experiences (text-to-self), to other things we have read or seen (text-to-text), and to our general knowledge about the world around us (text-to-world). Some readers find it helpful to make these connections visible by writing them down right in the text. Making these tracks while reading gives you a record of your thinking during the reading process that goes beyond merely highlighting important ideas. Later you can return to these tracks to quickly remind yourself of what was important to you while you were reading. Use the note-taking feature in *Forward Thinking* provided for this purpose.

EXHIBIT 1.6

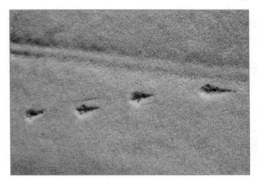

Making tracks when reading.

Ask yourself questions. Questions guide our reading regardless of the text. When reading a novel, we are constantly wondering, "What will happen next?" "Who will solve this problem?" "Will there be a happy ending?" Reading informational text like *Forward Thinking* is also driven by questions, including, "What information is worth remembering?" "How can I use this information in my teaching?" "What does that mean?" "Where will this link take me?" and "How does this image help me understand?" The answers to these questions often reveal the important information in the chapter. Asking questions when reading helps you to do the following:

- focus on what you are reading.
- bring to the front of your mind what you already know about the topic.
- check yourself to make sure you are making sense of what you read.
- clarify ideas that are unclear.

EXHIBIT 1.7

Asking questions.

While reading, notice the questions you ask yourself. If you are like most adult readers, you are probably not aware that you are even asking yourself questions. Just by noticing, however, you will likely begin asking more questions. You may even find it helpful to write down some of these questions. These questions are *not* meant to be mental roadblocks but rather a guide for what you are reading and how closely you are reading (or listening or viewing) the text. Also, when you locate the answers to your questions in the text, highlight what is important for later review. A word of caution: Before highlighting, ask yourself if the information is really important. If you are not sure, check the heading for that section, which will clue you in to what is important. Also, consider if the information helps you to meet your purpose for reading. More information on how you can remain mentally aware without disrupting your process while reading can be found later in this chapter.

Monitor comprehension. Constantly check your level of understanding while reading. Every so often, pause and mentally summarize what you have read so far. If you cannot remember what you have just read (we all experience this at some time), reread the text. Rereading takes more time, but what is the point of reading if the information does not stay with you? Instead of rereading, let's call it second draft or third draft reading. Much like a writer takes another look at what he or she has written, seeking ways to make it better, a second draft reading gives the reader the chance to gain more information. Come to the realization that when embarking on reading informational text, it might take two or three drafts of reading to really absorb the important information. Rereading does not mean you messed up the first time. It means you are looking again to find important ideas you may not have discovered the first time.

Use the links, images, podcasts, and other multimedia elements to layer your comprehension and fill in gaps when reading alone does not create a clear understanding. As with reading, comprehending multimedia elements may take a second or third draft viewing. Some may see additional viewings as extra work, while others see them as opportunities to learn at a deeper level. Remember, one purpose for reading *Forward Thinking* is to become a skilled teacher of language arts. Rereading puts you on the path toward making new information about language arts your own.

Adjust your reading rate. Experienced readers (like yourself) adjust their rate of reading much like a race car driver shifts gears to pick up speed. A slow reading rate is typically used when reading a text with new information, including unfamiliar words and concepts, especially if there are details a reader wants to remember.

Scanning is used to find specific information quickly or to preview headings and other features. **Skimming**, a very quick pace of reading, provides an overall glance to the text. Readers typically consider the length, format, and topic of the text and formulate a plan for reading when skimming. Notice during your own reading just how much information you can remember when you scan or skim versus when you read carefully. Think about adjusting your reading rate when you encounter different types of information. For example, when reading Chapter 5, Reading Fundamentals, you might scan to gauge the general information addressed in the chapter. Then, if you have a special interest in teaching young students, you might skim, looking for key words related to early reading, such as *alphabet, rhyming,* or *picture books*. If you are especially interested in teaching older students, you may scan for photographs of students reading chapter books independently or working together on group projects. After scanning and skimming, you are better prepared to read the chapter. The key idea is that at any point along the way, you, the reader, make a decision about what to read and how to read it based on your purpose.

Some experienced readers adopt a big chunk/little chunk approach by doing a first draft reading of big chunks (headings, paragraphs), and then returning to small, specific chunks to look at more closely. Consider the big chunk/little chunk strategy as one way to read *Forward Thinking*. You might find it more effective to read all of the text in a chapter or section, then return to look at the linked features, not wanting to interrupt the initial flow of reading. Or you may choose to pause in your reading to access the links immediately. There is no one right or wrong way to read an ebook. Know your reading style and use the strategies that will work best for you.

After reading

The mental work of reading is not finished once the last word has been pronounced or the last image viewed. In order for the information to really stay with you, you will likely find it helpful to take anywhere from a few seconds to a few minutes to mentally review.

EXHIBIT 1.8

Adjust your reading rate.

Summarize/synthesize. Pause and think about what you just heard, read, or viewed. What was it about? Sift through the words, the images, the audio, and interpret the main message for yourself. This process begins with **summarizing,** whereby you mentally crunch ideas into the kernel or most important point(s), often done while reading. Upon completing a text, the reader then mentally links these kernels together to form a personal understanding or summary of the text as a whole. A summary is a restatement of what is important from the text. A **synthesis** occurs when a reader pulls together the most important information, then interprets these details to create a personal understanding of the text. The mental links we create to tie together bits of information are unique for each person, reflecting our own understanding, background, culture, and values. *Forward Thinking* provides opportunities to write, speak, and visually represent your individual synthesis of ideas in "Think Like a Teacher" activities, found at the end of each chapter.

Evaluate. To *evaluate* means to judge the value or worth of something, in this case a text. Determine how well a chunk of text (paragraph, chapter, video, podcast, website, etc.) meets your purposes. Were your initial questions answered? Were the predictions you made when previewing the text accurate? When reading a website, listening to a podcast, or viewing a video, you are not only evaluating the usefulness of the information, but also its truthfulness. Do this by considering the accuracy and timeliness of the information and the credibility of the source.

Although evaluation can occur while reading, afterward we can more thoughtfully consider the information gained from the text as a whole. Does evaluation happen naturally when we read? Not necessarily. We think deeply and purposefully about a text by weighing the new information against our experiences, values, background, and beliefs. Readers must learn how to recognize bias and confirm information with other sources. Be a bit of a skeptic and do not take information at face value.

Transform. The real test of reading comprehension occurs when the reader takes new knowledge and transforms it into a product that can be shared with others, whether through a discussion, an artistic representation, a written journal entry, or some other form. Consider how your purpose for reading guided you through the reading process. Occasionally while you are reading, and always after you finish reading, ask yourself, "What will I do with this information?" In a broad sense, the information from *Forward Thinking* will be used to transform you into a knowledgeable teacher of language arts. In each chapter, you will have opportunities to demonstrate the development of that knowledge through speaking, writing, and visually representing what you have learned. Think Like a Teacher activities include responding to classroom scenarios, instructional challenges, and descriptions of individual students. These activities are designed to teach you when, where, and how to use your new knowledge.

Develop an awareness of your thought processes

Hopefully, you have noticed that each of the comprehension strategies we have described occurs in the mind. Taking in information by reading, listening, and viewing takes brain power. When you are actively involved with learning, you are *really thinking* about the information you are taking in through your eyes and ears, although at times you may be tempted

EXHIBIT 1.9

Thinking about thinking.

to switch to autopilot. If you catch yourself falling into the pattern of glossing over words and images, give your brain a mental jolt and force yourself to be aware of your thinking. This awareness is typically known as **metacognition**, but is also known as memory-monitoring or self-regulation. Basically, metacognition means being alert to the thought processes you use when reading, learning, or completing a task.

Some might think all of this *thinking about thinking* would be confusing to a reader. Actually, some of these strategies occur in a split second, and you already use many of them without realizing it. So the question becomes, if you can read and understand without consciously thinking about the process, do you need to be aware of these before, during, and after strategies? First, consider the fact that you are now preparing to teach these strategies to children. This is a great time to become more aware of the thinking you use when reading. This awareness of what *you* do when reading will help you to explain the process to your future students.

1.4

MANAGING INFORMATION

One important feature of *Forward Thinking* is that the body of information is not bound within the covers of a book. Instead, the information that can be gleaned from this enhanced ebook is in some ways limitless. Links to websites are given, but one of the helpful, yet challenging, aspects of the Internet is that one link leads to another, ad infinitum. For instance, when you visit a website about spelling instruction, you will encounter links to other books, websites, online discussions, and videos about teaching spelling. The never-ending quality of online exploration can be both a blessing and a curse.

In this section we explore how others handle the plethora of information encountered online each day, whether accessed from a smartphone, tablet, or computer. We also suggest effective habits for keeping your electronic information organized, whether it relates to teaching language arts or some other aspect of your personal or professional life. Finally, we stress the importance of creating a personal learning network (PLN) as a way to connect with others who share an interest in becoming teachers of language arts.

Establish organization routines

How will you handle the torrent of information you will encounter in both print and digital forms when reading *Forward Thinking*? The best advice is to get organized. Make organizing your digital world a priority, just as you would organize your bedroom, your desk, or your backpack. We encourage you to adopt our suggestions for electronic organization as you begin reading *Forward Thinking*. This book is full of linked resources that will lead to additional material, and you may also prepare electronic resources as you read (e.g., summaries, notes, sketches). Electronic organization allows you to sort, save, and easily return to the resources you want to explore further. Instead of saying, "That's a really good website, I should remember that for when I am teaching," our e-organization suggestions will help you create a system that will be useful in both your professional and personal life to easily locate digital information.

Develop your digital identity

Give yourself a digital identity by selecting a standard name or user ID to use each time you create an account on a website. This standard name helps people locate and connect to you through social networking or **web conferencing** sites such as Skype (www.skype.com) or Twitter (https://twitter.com). Begin by selecting a user ID. Remember, this user ID will likely follow you into your professional career, so choose carefully. Avoid user IDs such as *bellydancer92* or *partyanimal8*. Consider creating a user ID related to your name or the field of education, such as *sjohnson* or *booklover*. Next, visit a website such as Namechk (http://namechk.com) that compares your user ID to the user IDs that are available on over 72 social networking and social bookmarking websites. These sites will let you know if your user ID is not unique so you can modify it. Issues about safety and your digital identity are explored in Chapter 3, Creating a Learning Environment in Face-to-Face and Virtual Classrooms. For now, remember to share only necessary information and do not post anything online you would not want your grandmother or your future boss to see.

Create digital folders

Think of your computer as an electronic file cabinet. To keep your collection of e-documents organized, set up folders for email, word processing documents, photos, and videos. Within your email system, create folders related to coursework, colleagues, and friends/family. After reading an email, immediately sort it into the correct folder if you want to save for later review. Or set up rules within your email program to automate the sorting process for you. This system will be invaluable in the future when you are communicating with parents, colleagues, and an assortment of others through email.

When beginning a new project in Word or another program, immediately create a new folder in which to save all elements of the project. Take a look at your desktop and move each item into the proper folder whenever possible. Setting up these folders takes some time at the beginning, but it saves time later on.

Backup, backup, backup

Set up a regular schedule to back up your hard drive onto a flash drive, external hard drive, or online storage site. Put a backup time on your calendar, just like getting the dog his shots or going for a haircut. You will greatly appreciate these scheduled backups one day if your computer crashes right before a school assignment is due or a report is due to your principal. Consider using online backup systems as a way to store your documents at a secure online site rather than on your computer or on a hard drive.

Save in more than one location

Most of us know this, but it bears repeating: Save important items in more than one place, especially between your scheduled backups. Your coursework or the work of your students is valuable and should be treated as such. Word processing documents, podcasts, photos, videos can all be saved on a document sharing site such as Google Docs (http://docs.google.com) or Box (www.box.com). Photos can be saved on your hard drive and a photo sharing site such as Snapfish (www1.snapfish.com/snapfish/welcome) or

Flickr (www.flickr.com). These sharing sites also make your items available to others if you choose. Saving items to an online location, **cloud computing,** means that your data is stored virtually on remote servers.

> Visit the Common Craft site for a brief video about cloud computing (3:00, www.commoncraft.com/video/cloud-computing) to see how it can be used in both our professional and personal lives.

Use social bookmarking

Social bookmarking allows us to create a digital trail of useful and interesting resources by saving, organizing, and sharing our favorite websites. Rather than just bookmarking these websites on our computers, we can save these sites onto a bookmark sharing website, such as Delicious (http://delicious.com) or Diigo (www.diigo.com). This allows us to access the sites from any device with Internet access.

> Visit Common Craft for a brief video about Delicious (3:22, http://commoncraft.com/bookmarking-plain-english), and visit Learn It in 5 (3:59, http://learnitin5.com/Diigo), a website with technology how-to videos for teachers, to view a brief video about Diigo.

Use tagging, annotating, and subject lines

Tagging means giving a label or an electronic nametag to an online posting or a website. The tag sorts resources into groups that make them easier to locate. For example, a website with information about spelling activities might be tagged with the terms *spelling, language arts, word study, writing tools.* Then on your favorite bookmarking website, you can search for the website by using one of these terms. Annotations are brief written descriptions about a website and can be written yourself or cut and pasted directly from the website. An annotation for the Spelling City website (www.spellingcity.com) might read: "Create spelling games using words from your own spelling list." Subject lines, usually found in email and discussion boards, give the message a brief title that helps the reader to know what to expect and can be used to search for the message at a later time. When writing an email or contributing to a discussion board, think carefully about this line to be sure that it is descriptive of the note or post's content. All three of these resources take just a minute or two to complete but can be quite helpful when looking for information online.

Build your personal learning network

If we emphasize nothing else in this chapter, we hope to make the point that a textbook such as this one gives you the opportunity to learn new information in a variety of ways. However, reading this ebook is only one step in your journey as a teacher and a learner. Another step along that journey takes place when you begin to build your **personal learning network (PLN)** (also known as personal learning environment). A PLN is the collection of tools and communities that you use to direct your own learning. Not unique to language arts, PLNs can be formed by connecting with others who have similar interests in anything, such as basketball, cancer awareness, or recycling. Leu, Kinzer, Coiro, & Cammack (2004) describe the importance of building these connections: "In both the workplace and at home, the new technologies of literacy allow us to take advantage of the intellectual capital that resides in others, enabling us to collaboratively construct solutions to important problems by drawing from the expertise that lies outside ourselves" (p. 1598).

PLNs represent a shift from consuming information through a textbook toward a model of learning that develops from a matrix of resources you select and organize. To get started, watch the video Sketchy Explanations: Starting a PLN (1:51, www.you tube.com/watch?v=MqSH5TMYIz4), which presents quick and easy tips for creating your own PLN.

In order for your personal learning network about language arts instruction to evolve, you must consider and reflect upon the specific tools and resources that will lead you to a deeper engagement. **Social networking** and **media networking** tools such as Edmodo (www.edmodo.com), Plurk (www.plurk.com), Twitter (https://twitter.com), Ning (www.ning.com), and TeacherTube (http://teachertube.com) provide opportunities for creating, collaborating, and communicating among educators. Keep in mind that your PLN is unique because it reflects what *you* want to learn about, the groups *you* want to connect to, and the technology *you* feel comfortable using. As your knowledge and comfort level grow, your PLN will change and grow. Remember, it is not important whether or not you tweet or whether you use Delicious or Diigo, but it is important that you become more aware of *how* you make these choices. For example, a decision about whether to use Skype or Google Voice for web conferencing should consider the following:

- what you want to learn.
- who else uses the tool.
- where you will be when accessing the tool, whether at home, school, or public location, and whether your computer and/or connection will support the tool.
- what equipment you need (microphone, webcam, scanner, digital camera).
- how much you know about using the tool or accessing assistance (although lots of tutorials for many web tools exist online).

A PLN puts you in charge of your own learning, challenging you to reflect on the tools and resources that help you learn best. The responsibility for creating the PLN, and for learning, lies with the learner. Start with one or two PLN tools. Use these tools until you feel confident, whether that takes six days or six months, then add another tool to your network. If you follow this advice, you will increase your knowledge about teaching as you increase your adeptness with technology, and that makes for efficient learning.

1.5

APPLICATION OF NEW LEARNING

Reading the chapter, electronically highlighting important ideas, jotting down connections on electronic sticky notes, all of these facilitate learning. But remember from the previous section on comprehension that how well you understand something is gauged by what you can do or create based on this knowledge. Ericsson, Krampe, and Tesch-Roemer (1993) believe that *deliberate practice* is important to learning and requires the learner to actively monitor one's own learning. The end of each chapter in *Forward Thinking* provides activities that give you the chance to show what you know and to reflect on it. You will be asked, "What can you do after reading this chapter that you could not do before?" The goal is for you to *demonstrate* your new understanding of when, where, and why to use your new knowledge, which moves you from a novice toward an expert (Bransford, Brown, & Cocking, 1999). You will also find activities that give you a chance to write, talk with others, or create a project related to the information in the chapter. These activities are designed to help you build on your knowledge and demonstrate what you have learned so far.

1.6

CHAPTER SUMMARY

Reading an enhanced textbook may be a new experience for you, but many of the skills you have developed as an experienced reader will help you along the way. Keep in mind that the uniqueness of an ebook provides you with a variety of ways to learn new information even though you will be using many of the same thinking processes involved in reading print texts. Be conscious of the strategies you use before, during, and after reading, listening, and viewing, because these are the strategies that will help you to understand and remember. Consider the steps you currently take to manage information and the steps you might want to include in your regime to help you prepare for the unexpected. Your personal learning network (PLN) will be your first stop for seeking information about issues surrounding language arts instruction.

APPLICATION ACTIVITIES

think like a teacher

Online Reading Habits

Consider this scenario: Salena is a college student who earns pretty good grades. She attends class regularly, takes lots of notes, and sometimes reads her textbook. She might be inclined to read her textbook more, but she does not really get much out of it and frequently cannot remember much about what she reads. In fact, Salena is not really sure she was taught how to read well, because her other friends highlight lots of information when reading and complete their reading assignments quickly. Now consider what happens when Salena's instructor assigns an enhanced ebook for one of her courses.

1. Think, discuss, and write about the following issues:
   - What difficulties or challenges might Salena encounter when reading an enhanced ebook?
   - What features of a multimedia book might help a college student like Salena? How?

2. Listen to the podcast Online Reading Comprehension (12:55, www. voiceofliteracy.org/posts/26036) with Dr. Julie Coiro, Associate Professor at the University of Rhode Island and a leading researcher in the field of online comprehension. Then look back at the section in this chapter titled "Understanding and Remembering What We Read." Review the before, during, and after strategies suggested for improving comprehension.

3. Create a plan for Salena to help her be successful with reading a multimedia ebook. Give her three to five suggestions to improve her comprehension, and explain how these suggestions will boost her knowledge and confidence with online reading.

Managing Information

How do you handle the information that you encounter in our technology-filled world? Do you feel overwhelmed by all of the information available? Have you lost important information in cyberspace? This activity encourages you to explore your own experiences and to make plans to "beef up" your online organizational practices.

1. Read through the comments from journalists collected by the online magazine The Atlantic Wire (www.theatlanticwire.com/features/view/feature/Terry-Gross-What-I-Read-1058). Notice the connections you make to similar reading practices.

2. Create a descriptive list of your online reading practices or the ways you keep up with the large amounts of information encountered throughout the day from both print and electronic resources.

3. Share your list with two or three others in class and note similarities and differences.

4. Write a paragraph or two describing ways you want to improve your reading practices with print and electronic resources.

Personal Learning Network

Before establishing your PLN, consider what you want to learn about language arts.

- What have you seen or experienced yourself related to language arts that you wonder about or question?
- What do you wish you knew more about when it comes to teaching language arts?
- What do you anticipate might be challenging for you as a language arts teacher?

Reflect on these and any of your own questions. Your thoughts should lead you to forming two or three goals for what you hope to learn while studying language arts instruction in this course. These goals will then guide the development of your PLN. For this activity, complete the following:

1. Write down the two or three goals for your learning in the area of language arts. If you haven't done so already, watch the video discussed earlier in this chapter, Sketchy Explanations: Starting a PLN (www.youtube.com/watch?v=MqSH5TMYlz4) by Will Richardson.

2. Select two of the web resources mentioned in the video or in the PLN section in this chapter. Set up an account at each of your choices and explore their resources. Many of the resources include a brief tutorial to help you get started. Use this information to search for resources related to your goals.

3. Once your PLN is under way, reflect on what you have learned so far. Consider if these resources meet your learning needs or what additional resources you would like to explore.

REFERENCES

Anstey, M., & Bull, G. (2006). *Teaching and learning multiliteracies: Changing times, changing literacies.* Newark, DE: International Reading Association.

Bransford, J. D., Brown, A. L., & Cocking, R. R. (1999). *How people learn: Brain, mind, experience, school.* Washington, DC: National Academy Press.

Chickering, A. W., & Gamson, Z. F. (1987). Seven principles for good practice. *American Association of Higher Education Bulletin, 39,* 3–7. Retrieved from http://www2.honolulu.hawaii.edu/facdev/guidebk/teachtip/7princip.htm.

Coiro, J., & Dobler, E. (2007). Exploring the online comprehension strategies used by sixth grade skilled readers to search for and locate information on the Internet. *Reading Research Quarterly, 42*(2), 214–257.

Dale, E. (1969). *Audio visual methods in teaching.* New York: Holt, Rinehart, and Winston.

Eagleton, M., & Dobler, E. (2007). *Reading the Web: Teaching strategies for Internet inquiry.* New York: Guilford.

Ericsson, K. A., Krampe, R. Th., & Tesch-Roemer, C. (1993). The role of deliberate practice in the acquisition of expert performance. *Psychological Review,* 100, 363–406.

Flood, J., & Lapp, D. (1997/1998). Broadening conceptualizations of literacy: The visual and communicative arts. *The Reading Teacher, 51,* 342–344.

Gee, J. P. (1996). *Social linguistics and literacies: Ideology in discourses.* London: Falmer.

Hartman, D. (1992). Intertextuality and reading: Reconceptualizing the reader, the text, the author, and the context. *Linguistics and Education, 4,* 295–311.

Hendrickson, G., & Schroeder, W. H. (1941). Transfer of training in learning to hit a submerged target. *Journal of Educational Psychology, 32,* 205–213.

Kress, G. (2003). *Literacy in the new media age.* London: Routledge.

Lankshear, C., & Knobel, M. (2002). Do we have your attention? New literacies, digital technologies, and the education of adolescents. In D. E. Alvermann (Ed.), *Adolescents and literacies in a digital world* (pp. 19–39). New York: Peter Lang.

Lemke, J. L. (1985). Using language in the classroom knowledge: Reading lessons. *Curriculum Inquiry, 15,* 247–279.

Leu, D. J., Jr., Kinzer, C. K., Coiro, J., & Cammack, D. W. (2004). Toward a theory of new literacies emerging from the Internet and other information and communication technologies. In R. B. Ruddell & N. Unrau (Eds.), *Theoretical models and processes of reading* (5th ed., pp. 1570–1613). Newark, DE: International Reading Association. http://www.readingonline.org/newliteracies/lit_index.asp?HREF=leu/.

Orr, M. (2003). *Intertextuality: Debates & contexts.* Cambridge, UK: Polity.

Parker, K. (2010, July 9). A world of lone rangers. *Topeka Capital Journal.* Retrieved from http://findarticles.com/p/articles/mi_qn4179/is_20100709//ai_n54495831/.

Rowe, D. W. (1987). Literacy learning as an intertextual process. In J. D. Readence & R. S. Baldwin (Eds.), *Research in literacy: Merging perspectives, 36th Yearbook of the National Reading Conference* (pp. 101–112). Rochester, NY: National Reading Conference.

Saussure, F. (1966). *A course in general linguistics.* New York: McGraw Hill.

Street, B. (1993). Introduction: The new literacy studies. In B. Street (Ed.), *Cross-cultural approaches to literacy* (pp. 1–21). New York: Cambridge University Press.

Street, B. (2003). What's "new" in new literacy studies? Critical approaches to literacy in theory and practice. *Current Issues in Comparative Education, 5*(2), 77–91.

Tapscott, D. (1999). *Growing up digital: The rise of the net generation.* New York: McGraw Hill.

Access the book's Glossary, which defines the key terms boldfaced in this chapter, at www.hhpcommunities.com/teachinglanguagearts/glossary.pdf

2.1

OUR INNER DRIVE TO COMMUNICATE

Language is at the heart of all human interaction. The language arts are the modes, or ways, people communicate, by sending and receiving messages. A transaction occurs whenever we tell a joke, write a play, read a **blog**, or send a text. A message is sent and a message is received; the message is the center of the action. Humans share a need to communicate, a need to be heard, a need to be known. We strive to be recognized, and in turn, others strive for us to recognize them. Whether through words, symbols, or a combination of the two, people seek to leave their impression on others. Thus we write because we have something to say, and we speak for the same reason. Notice the pile of rocks in Exhibit 2.1. Each one has been placed on the pile by a person who has climbed to the top of Mount Royal, Colorado. The climb up this steep summit takes so much effort that those who reach the top want to leave their mark, letting the rest of the climbing world know "I was here."

Hundreds or even thousands of years ago, the ancestors of Native Americans communicated by making petroglyphs, or rock drawings (see

> *"Language is the curriculum of elementary school."*
>
> **BILL MARTIN JR.,**
> author of
> *Brown Bear, Brown Bear*

EXHIBIT 2.1

Rock pile shows "I was here."

EXHIBIT 2.2

We can only guess the meaning of a petroglyph.

Exhibit 2.2). Some petroglyph symbols are recognizable, such as animals, people, and crosses, while other symbols remain a mystery. These images were literally carved into the stone. Because their creation took an inordinate amount of time, the meaning and the location of each petroglyph was carefully planned. Anthropologists think that the petroglyphs represent an intricate cultural network among the native people. These chiseled images likely told others about travel, food, leaders, traditions, and sacred locations. These simple carvings obviously held much meaning for those who walked the land centuries ago, and we today still seek to understand them.

Young children and communication

Babies are born with a desire to communicate. Within a few minutes of birth, a newborn recognizes the voices heard while in the womb. Crying is a baby's primary way of communicating; caregivers quickly recognize the different cries of a baby who wants food, a diaper change, or has been overwhelmed by sight and sound. At an early age, this joyful bundle is already getting her message across and is alert to the coos and talk of others. Within the first couple of months, a baby communicates by making vowel sounds such as "ah-ah" or "ooh-ooh." These are a baby's way of developing the tongue and facial muscles needed to speak, as well as experimenting with sound. These initial attempts at making sounds are music to the ears of new parents, who can encourage this practice by praising the baby's efforts to communicate. Soon fingers and hand gestures are combined with grunts and coos to form an intricate system of communication as most babies developing at a normal pace find ways to get their message across.

By the time a child is a toddler, she is on the cusp of a language explosion. At 18 months, she can say 10 to 15 words learned through hearing them repeatedly. At about 20 months, a child can say 20 to 50 words and understand many more. Shortly before age two, a child will be learning 10 or more words a day. Toddlers have various means of getting their message across with a mixture of one or two word phrases and pointing. In fact, some parents teach their toddler to communicate using sign language before wants and needs can be communicated verbally. For young children, the mind is a powerhouse of receptors, taking in what is going on around their world and converting thoughts into some type of message. This process, and the increased control over saying and understanding words, is due to the brain's ability to connect three systems: visual, cognitive, and language. In other words, the toddler is able to see, understand, and name various elements in the world around him, which makes this one of the richest times for language growth. As he continues to increase in age from two, three, to four years old, he is better able to string a series of words together to form a complete thought, relying less on gesturing and more on talking. Early communication frustrations are left behind as he becomes able to share his needs and desires, although a tantrum in the cereal aisle is not out of the question.

Early childhood is also the time for experimentation with simplistic forms of writing, usually called scribbles. Those crayon marks made on the wall, annoying as they are, represent the first steps of written communication. Exhibit 2.3 provides a glimpse at the initial stage of written language development from four-year-old Eric. Consider the knowledge he is demonstrating in this simple writing sample by answering the following questions:

1. What can this child do related to written language?
2. What might a child need to know in order to do this?

Notice Eric's use of recognizable letters written in rows across the page, a mixture of capital, lowercase, forward, and backward letters. Although his writing does not make sense to us, we can see his budding awareness of the way symbols, or a collection of letters and images, convey an idea (Halliday, 1978). Eric has acquired amazing knowledge for one so young, and his writing shows he is headed toward the next phase of using letters to create words that others can recognize.

Communication, whether oral or written or for the young or old, centers around stories. To adults, the word *story* brings to mind Hansel and Gretel or a novel from *The New York Times* bestseller list. For young children, stories are simple, often involving gestures and just a few words, but these early attempts are how infants and toddlers begin to organize their experiences and make sense of the world around them. For all, stories help our brain organize thoughts and experiences and answer questions. For young children, these crucial processes promote language development.

Read the article, "Stories and Their Powerful Role in Early Language" (3 pp., www.naeyc.org/files/yc/file/200701/BTJRocknroll.pdf) published by the National Association for the Education of Young Children. Identify three benefits of stories for infants and toddlers.

EXHIBIT 2.3

The writing of a young child reveals knowledge, even if on a simplistic level.

School-aged children and communication

Children enter school with a natural desire to communicate with others, while facing a vocabulary learning task that is enormous. The vocabulary of five- to six-year-olds is between 2,500 and 5,000 words, although they may only be able to read a few words the first day of school (Beck & McKeown, 1991). By the end of elementary school, their reading vocabulary likely will increase to 25,000 words (Graves, 2004).

Most new students have successfully communicated with those around them at home and expect to continue this success at school. Our job as teachers is to nurture this desire by teaching the skills needed to send and understand messages clearly. Spelling, handwriting, and grammar are taught so what we say, write, and create has meaning to others. This process of communication is enhanced as students in the early grades develop the ability to recognize sounds within words, which leads to later reading and writing ability. Simultaneously, students are learning new words, how to use those words grammatically, and how those words may be interpreted by others. Increasingly, school-aged children develop and practice these skills through the use of technology. Cell phones in the hands of elementary students are not uncommon, and students send texts and emails to keep in touch with family and friends.

Young students greatly increase the pace of their written language development when they begin school, and the number of words they understand and use rapidly increases. Additionally, identifying, making, and combining letters to form words is the foundation of school literacy instruction. If, at the same time, an effective teacher creates a learning environment where all age-appropriate literacy activities are available, a perfect storm is created where the ingredients needed for written language work together to create a budding reader and writer.

The website Writing Development: One Child's Journey from Scribbles to Stories (7 pp., www.pbs.org/parents/education/reading-language/reading-milestones/writing-development-one-childs-journey-from-scribbles-to-stories) provides a digital display of the written language development of a young boy, Toby, as he moves from kindergarten to third grade. Click through the images of Toby's writing and read about his understanding of literacy as demonstrated in his writing. Notice the way each piece of writing becomes increasingly sophisticated, moving from scribbles to recognizable letters to words that can be pronounced by saying the letter sounds, and finally to writing that clearly communicates an idea.

points2ponder

QUICK REVIEW 1 How do stories promote communication?

(Access the answer in the digital version of this book.)

Children develop their literacy skills in a fairly identifiable sequence (although each child does so at an individual pace), similar to how babies follow a specific pattern of development when learning to walk: first they scoot across the floor, then crawl, then pull themselves up, and finally walk. A **developmental continuum** displays, in visual form, the chain of progression for learning a new skill. Developmental continuums serve as a guide, helping teachers to better understand what to expect from their students at a given time, such as the end of the quarter, the school year, or at a particular age. Many teachers use a developmental continuum as a guide, for instance, to indicate what words a typical third grader can spell, or what to expect from a fifth grader in terms of punctuation in writing.

Developmental continuums will be further explored in several chapters in *Forward Thinking,* but as an introduction, explore the Reading Continuum (www.hhp communities.com/teachinglanguagearts/IL-02-A.pdf) and the Writing Continuum (www.hhpcommunities.com/teachinglanguagearts/IL-02-B.pdf). These continuums show what students who are developing at an average pace can do during the preschool, kindergarten, the early grade years, and beyond in reading and writing development. Familiarity with typical development is vital for teachers to plan for instruction. Using the Writing Continuum, return to Toby's writing samples discussed above. For each sample, try to identify the continuum level for each piece of Toby's writing.

Teens and communication

For young adults, technology rules communication. Teen cell phone use is almost equal to that of adults. Seventy-seven percent of 12- to 17-year-olds own a cell phone, although cell phones are used by teens for texting more than for talking (Lenhart, 2012). For young people, technologies of old give way to the new. Email is being replaced with **microblogging** and **social networking.** Although a high school student's reading vocabulary will climb to 50,000 words (Graves, 2004), brief messages—the hallmark of microblogging—abound in the tweeting and texting world of adolescents. A tweet must be succinct to be broadcast on Twitter. Although some adults lament the loss of spelling skills due to instant messaging and texting, research does not support the occurrence of such a loss (Lenhart, 2008). Young adults recognize the various contexts for communicating and understand that there are differing expectations for the conventions of language (i.e., spelling, grammar, punctuation) depending on the audience receiving the message. Spelling in a text message may contain textisms, or texting shorthand (e.g., "BRB" for "be right back"), while spelling in a science fair report would be expected to be conventional and accurate. The audience influences the writer's tone, perspective, and even word choice. Research indicates teens can address and switch audiences as needed, and teens consider texting and instant messaging as communication, while writing is composition (Lenhart, 2008).

Adolescents strive to create messages that reflect their uniqueness while still fitting in with their peer group. Podcasts, texts, videos, photographs, blogs, Facebook pages, and online posters are all ways these soon-to-be adults make themselves known. Online, a global audience is only a few clicks away.

An online example from sixth grader Sissie illustrates the ways adolescents can represent their new learning. Sissie's glog or online poster (http://sissyjo261. glogster.com/human-services) displays her learning in a study of human services.

points2ponder

QUICK REVIEW 2 How is a developmental continuum a useful tool for a teacher?

(Access the answer in the digital version of this book.)

Foundational skills are still important

At no previous time in history have we been able to send and receive messages more easily, more rapidly, and in more formats. And yet, as literacy researcher Don Leu (2000) describes, the need for the foundational skills of what has traditionally been the realm of language arts continues to remain important (see Spotlight on a Literacy Leader, Don Leu).

spotlight ON A LITERACY LEADER

DONALD LEU

Donald Leu, Ph.D., has been instrumental in building a bridge between the fields of literacy and technology. He is the Director of the New Literacies Research Lab at the University of Connecticut, where educational researchers seek to understand these new skills and strategies and how best to prepare students for using them. His work as a researcher and leader in education spans over 25 years. Leu has led several research projects and written over 100 research publications and 17 books, many focusing on the new skills and strategies required to read, write, and learn online.

Listen to a podcast (10:41, http://spectrum.ieee.org/podcast/at-work/education/do-you-believe-this-headline) by Don Leu as he shares his thoughts on online reading. As you listen, consider our need for bound books, traditional libraries, and even our use of paper to record information and communicate in light of the transition to reading online. Also, think about other ways our world is changing because of the Internet and Leu's beliefs about how these changes influence literacy education.

Whatever the format, a person must make his or her message clear enough for others to understand, which requires attention to spelling, grammar, punctuation, clarity, and organization. Text messages may utilize their own unique form of spelling or shortcuts, and in this informal setting, such a style may be appropriate. However, a cover letter for a job application, whether in print or online form, must have impeccable spelling to even be considered. So our job as teachers is to prepare students for the various ways they are expected to communicate, now and beyond school. To do this, students must have strong foundational skills that let them easily move between the various formats of communication. How do we help students achieve this? By creating a variety of classroom experiences so students are communicating and practicing the very same skills they will need to use in the world outside of school. The following Stories from the Classroom share the ways teachers integrate writing into real-world experiences.

stories FROM THE CLASSROOM

Creating a science fair collaborative space

Erin Fitzpatrick teaches science to fifth through eighth graders. The students in her classes use an online collaborative space (a wiki) to collect, display, and share their science projects. The first page of this wiki includes a *Wallwisher/Padlet,* a webpage where contributors can add an electronic sticky note with a brief message.

See how Erin and language arts teacher Ginger Lewman use this page to have students introduce the science fair projects (http://tplcsciencefair2010.wikispaces.com), reflect on their work, and share their projects with the wiki visitors, including their families and others in the school community.

stories FROM THE CLASSROOM

Posting class news on the school website

Students in Ginger Lewman's language arts class are learning to report the news by creating a classroom newspaper that is posted on the school website (see Exhibit 2.4). Ginger begins news time with a mini-lesson focusing on the skills students need to communicate effectively. For example, one lesson might review the use of quotation marks and commas; another might cover the importance of students writing interesting leads and conclusions to their brief articles. Lewman chooses topics based on the needs of her students, which she has observed during previous news sessions. Consider how a school newspaper has changed with increased use of technology and what writing skills students now need to successfully communicate the news in their world.

EXHIBIT 2.4

News posted on a school website.

Our discussion about language development thus far centers on the concept of words. Although the language arts are about the message, each message is more than a matter of words. The phrase "a picture is worth a thousand words" is not far off the mark. Words hold powerful meaning, but that meaning is enhanced tenfold when coupled with an image. For example, if a person uses the term *snowpocalypse,* one might wonder if it is some type of winter sporting event. But if the term is accompanied by a picture of a warehouse roof sagging from the weight of three feet of snow, then the meaning becomes clear. Technology is pivotal in bringing together words and images. Take this book as an example. With technology, *Forward Thinking* is able to connect the written and spoken word with visual images. Both forms of communication work together to enhance meaning. Students encounter these powerful connections between words and images when they view a website, send a photo on their cell phone, or read a picture book. Creating and understanding messages is more than just talking, writing, or reading. Language holds layers of meaning, which makes communication a complex, yet fascinating, process.

2.2

WHAT DO WE MEAN BY THE TERMS *LANGUAGE* AND *LANGUAGE ARTS*?

EXHIBIT 2.5

Communicating with gestures.

In its most basic form, **language** is a systematic way of communicating ideas and feelings using gestures, symbols, sounds, and images. The term *systematic* in this definition refers to the notion that those using the language have agreed upon meaningful representations of ideas. People agree that a thumbs-up, a star on a homework paper, and the word *good* all mean a job well done (see Exhibit 2.5). This acceptance of meaning is at the heart of language and is what lets us easily create and understand messages. It also lets us create an infinite variety of messages, always with the purpose of communicating with others. To help make the meaning of our messages understandable, we have standard ways of expressing ideas through spelling, grammar, and punctuation. These are like the rules of the road that keep drivers safe; they give consistency to the meaning of our spoken and written words.

The umbrella term **language arts** describes the various ways we use language to communicate. Because communication is a two-way street, the six modes of language arts (reading, writing, speaking, listening, viewing, and visually representing) are organized into two categories: messages we receive (receptive) and messages we send (expressive). It is rather simplistic to separate these categories because often the messages we send through talking, writing, or creating images are integrally connected to the messages we receive through listening, reading, and viewing. For example, a student creating a poster advertising the school play should be thinking about the information the person reading the poster needs to know. Or, a student listening to a classmate read his writing aloud to the class is also thinking about what kind of oral feedback he can give his classmate. Communication does not exist in a vacuum, but for the purposes of this explanation, let us consider the categories and modes of language arts as separate and distinct.

As stated above, the **receptive** category involves a person taking in, or receiving, a message, which occurs when we read a book, listen to a song, view a billboard, and so forth. Our mind takes in the information using mostly our senses of sight and hearing, although the other senses can also add to this experience. For example, a person who is visually impaired uses touch to read Braille. Sight and hearing combine to receive a message when children watch a puppet show or see a concert.

COMPREHENSION *coach*

Determining important ideas: Virtual sticky notes Having trouble picking out what is important in this chapter? Does it all seem important? Listen to this podcast by Elizabeth Dobler for comprehension coaching. *(Access this podcast in the digital version of this book.)*

The **expressive** category involves a person creating, or expressing, a message, which occurs when talking to a friend, making a sign, texting a message, and so forth. We create a message because we have something to say, and each person makes dozens of decisions every day about the best way to convey our message to others. Gestures form an integral part of expressing a message. Our meaning can be enhanced with a smile, a pointed finger, or a fist pump.

The previous explanation of the language arts stems from work done by the International Reading Association and the National Council of Teachers of English (1996). Other definitions of language arts, such as those from dictionaries, typically include such elements as reading, composition, spelling, literature, English, and grammar. Certainly, each of these elements has a place in expressing and receiving messages. Without a doubt students need to know how to use quotation marks and be familiar with works of literature. However, the language arts are more than just a collection of school subjects. First and foremost, language in its many forms is about thinking and so are the language arts. The messages we create are merely a visual or auditory representation of our thinking.

Classroom teacher Ginger Lewman believes strongly in the connection between language arts and thinking, and she plans classroom activities to promote this connection because it does not always happen naturally. Listen to Lewman's podcast Writing Begins as Thinking (2:32) for the perspective of a classroom teacher in action. *(Access this podcast in the digital version of this book.)*

In Lewman's podcast, she describes her role in promoting the language arts with her students. She has been teaching for several years and can do this effectively; some novice teachers may struggle a bit with identifying their own role in promoting the language arts. The next section of this book explores ways teachers can make language arts a priority in their classroom.

points2ponder

QUICK REVIEW 3 Give an explanation of what is meant by the term *language arts*. Which modes of language arts are expressive? Which are receptive? What are the two terms used to designate categories of the language arts?

(Access answers in the digital version of this book.)

2.3

THE TEACHER'S ROLE IN PROMOTING THE LANGUAGE ARTS

Students come to school with a natural desire to communicate, so what role do you play in helping students develop the skills they need to send and receive messages? Arrange classroom activities to promote purposeful talk with each other in small groups and among the whole class. As a teacher, you will model how you communicate with others by describing experiences that occur both in and out of school and thinking aloud about the thought processes you use to create and understand messages. For example, you may share a piece of junk mail you received and talk through the thinking you used to decide whether to open and read it or throw it away. Or you may hold a class meeting to facilitate a discussion about playground rules and model how students should receive ideas shared by classmates. Also, you will provide opportunities for students to create messages in various contexts for various content (e.g., poetry, science fair projects, math instructions, historical timelines) and in various forms (e.g., podcasts, diagrams, virtual posters, word processing documents). To facilitate the language arts, encourage students to construct their own messages, as opposed to filling in the blanks of a worksheet. Active participation in purposeful and real-life language arts activities allows students to develop the practical life skills they will need to communicate throughout their lives. You can become a facilitator, guide, and learner yourself, especially when using new technologies to bring the world into the classroom (see Exhibit 2.6).

EXHIBIT 2.6

Teaching with a tablet or mobile device brings the world into the classroom.

Key components to successful language arts teaching

In today's **global society**, language arts are more important than ever. When we can communicate with one, a few, hundreds, or thousands of people with a few clicks, we must create messages clearly and quickly. Doing so requires a set of foundational skills in language arts that can be taught through a variety of techniques.

Configuring the classroom for learning

Students, like all of us, communicate in a variety of ways, such as chatting on the playground or in class, texting, phoning, or chatting online. Some people prefer the intimacy of a small group, while others like the anonymity of a large group. To meet the needs of each student, create a variety of configurations for learning activities. Through a **writing conference**, personal, one-to-one communication occurs. Use a small group setting to assist a few students who need extra help with a specific skill, such as placement of quotation marks. Whole class lessons are a useful format when all students can benefit from hearing the same information. Incorporating various configurations every day lets you tap into the natural communication preferences of students while also stretching their comfort zones in order to prepare them for the varied ways they will communicate in the future (see Exhibit 2.7).

EXHIBIT 2.7

Communication occurs face-to-face and online.

Modeling

Modeling is a crucial form of teaching (Fisher, Frey, & Lapp, 2009) that involves showing students how to do something, often while vocalizing your thought process. Modeling gives students support as they progress from watching to doing an activity with you or with each other and then trying it on their own. As students progress along a developmental continuum, they are continually adding to their foundational knowledge in order to move on to the next set of skills. Watching you, their teacher, model a process is crucial for the development of their own knowledge. Even though

EXHIBIT 2.8

Precision and clarity are keys in modeling.

EXHIBIT 2.9

A teacher models writing during a writing conference.

students come to school able to speak and listen, they will still benefit from modeling when it comes to the language arts. We cannot assume that students will learn the complexities of creating and understanding messages by merely watching and listening to those around them. Some students need a more explicit, direct method of teaching. They need to see and hear another person pose relevant questions, work through problems, and formulate comments (Roehler & Cantlon, 1997).

Modeling for language arts begins with a clear explanation of a process by an expert, which is you, the teacher (see Exhibit 2.8). The expert thinks aloud the thoughts she uses during the communication process by saying things like, "When I send an email, I try to use words that are very clear since I am not there to explain my ideas. I might choose the word *today* instead of *sometime,* so the person reading my email understands exactly what I mean." By thinking aloud, a teacher is giving a verbal demonstration of exactly what is being done, so the students develop a clear picture of what they should do. Modeling helps students see how the teacher works through the activity, what happens when she encounters roadblocks, and how she resolves these challenges (see Exhibit 2.9).

Modeling is the hallmark of good teaching. It must be explicit (i.e., crystal clear) and frequent (i.e., used daily). Don't assume that modeling is not needed if students don't have any questions. Often those who benefit the most from modeling are those who hesitate to ask questions. In fact, a student may not realize what she does not know until she sees what someone else *does* know. Also, the more experienced person may not always be the teacher. Classmates and older students can be helpful models.

Focusing on real-world skills

The language arts are experienced both in and out of school and form an integral part of any human relationship. Language arts are also the foundation for learning in the other content areas, including math, science, social studies, health, and the fine arts. Because language arts touches all aspects of our lives, practicing these skills in school should reflect the various real world ways students will use these skills, rather than just practicing for the sake of practicing. For example, spelling words and grammar patterns are learned to help create a cohesive, understandable message. Real-world language arts skills are developed by giving students lots of opportunities to use language in ways that match language use out of school and the ways language will be used in their future.

stories FROM THE CLASSROOM

Real world applications

Middle-school teacher Charlie Mahoney recognizes the real world application of language arts skills in the global studies class he teaches. Within a class period, students may create an information chart about ancient civilizations using Google Docs and visit an obscure Chinese museum by using Google Earth. He chooses language arts skills and communication tools to fit the learning situation. Listen to Charlie as he describes how blogs are used to bring together global studies and language arts (3:44) in a manner similar to the ways people encounter information and share it in the real world. Blogs are just one of many online communication tools students can use to communicate globally with a real world audience. *(Access this podcast in the digital version of this book.)*

The **21st-Century Learning Model** calls for students to effectively use real world tools, to think deeply, to communicate effectively, and to develop a sense of global awareness (North Central Regional Education Laboratory, 2003). These practices do not begin the day students graduate from high school; they begin now. These qualities, which are not limited to language arts, form a framework for successful learning in all of the content areas (see Exhibit 2.10). The emphasis is on the thinking and communication skills needed to prepare students to be successful in a global society, no matter their future career choice. For instance, teaming, collaboration, and interpersonal skills are three elements of the effective communication concept of the 21st-century learning model. Document sharing, email, and video conferences are ways that students can practice developing these skills, along with the more traditional methods typically used in school, such as cooperative learning and peer editing. Granted, some students may have limited access to technology both at home and at school, but this does not diminish the need for digital communication skills. In these cases, you must adjust your instruction to match the technology available to students; however, students and teachers can often find creative ways to access technology, whether at the local public library, through a cell phone, or using the school computers before or after school.

The term *literacy 2.0* (Knobel & Wilber, 2009) describes a way of thinking and a set of practices that value participation, collaboration, and distribution of expertise. New ways of reading, writing, listening, and viewing have emerged as a result of new technologies, which have made new forms of collaboration possible. For example, blogs and wikis enable students to be both producers and publishers of knowledge. (See Stories from the Classroom below for examples of how one teacher is using a class blog to encourage his students as writers.) An important goal of literacy instruction in today's schools is to prepare students to be "self-directed, self-motivated, lifelong learners who are network-literate in their creation and participation in [online] spaces" (Richardson, 2009). Learning how to use new digital tools effectively requires a shared expertise between the students and the teacher. Technology changes so rapidly that no one person can be expected to know everything. Students and teachers alike must learn from each other. Through this learning, we can create language arts activities that reflect the real-life skills our students need today and in their future.

EXHIBIT 2.10

The 21st-Century Learning Model.

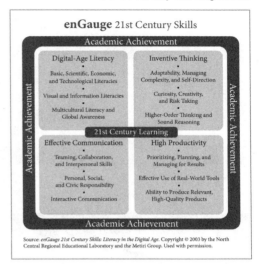

Source: *enGauge 21st Century Skills: Literacy in the Digital Age.* Copyright © 2003 by the North Central Regional Educational Laboratory and the Metiri Group. Used with permission.

stories FROM THE CLASSROOM

A class blog

Scott Ritter, a third grade teacher, created a classroom blog to which his students contribute during literacy center time (see Exhibit 2.11). He posts a topic and invites students to write a response. Topics focus on classroom activities or current events in the community or world. Scott looks for topics he thinks will spark an interest in his students, such as year-round school, summer plans, or suggestions of music for his iPod. His goal is to encourage students to respond to the topic and each other through writing.

Visit Scott's classroom blog (www.roomthreezerotwo.blogspot.com). Be sure to read the comments prepared by his students. Consider what third graders might learn from writing on a blog. Think about the motivation students might experience with blog writing and what they might feel when friends and family are able to access the blog and read their written work. Locate the entry that had the most student responses and consider why it elicited the most responses.

EXHIBIT 2.11

Contemplating what to write on the class blog.

Creating an atmosphere to promote the language arts

This book introduces the process of how students learn the language arts. Understanding the complex process of communication among students is a process itself. Reading professional materials, taking courses in language arts instruction, and forming a personal learning network go a long way toward developing a strong foundation of knowledge; however, much can also be learned from talking to, listening to, observing, and analyzing the communication of students in the classroom, on the playground, or even in the lunchroom. Creating a classroom where communication is welcomed and respected is an important first step. Such an atmosphere can be obtained by implementing the following ideas:

1. Immerse children in language.
2. Create a learning environment where language is important.
3. Model the variety of ways language is used in real-world situations.
4. Create a wide variety of opportunities for students to use language in authentic ways (see Exhibit 2.12).
5. Guide students in the ways they can take responsibility for their own language learning.
6. Accept and respect emerging attempts at new ways to use language.
7. Respect students' language differences while maintaining high expectations.
8. Give students and their caregivers accurate and useful feedback about levels of performance related to language usage.

These eight elements can serve as a guide as you create a classroom environment, design instruction, and evaluate students' progress in language development.

EXHIBIT 2.12

Salida is engrossed in her writing.

points2ponder

QUICK REVIEW 4 What do the words *explicit* and *frequent* mean when referring to the topic of modeling?

(Access the answer in the digital version of this book.)

2.4

STANDARDS

In this world of rapidly changing communication techniques, how do teachers know what to teach? What foundational skills do students need to successfully use language now and in the future? One way to answer these questions is to turn to standards. **Standards** guide our instruction by providing a list of those skills and concepts educational professionals have identified as being important for students to learn before they reach a certain grade level. Educators are expected to know the standards at the local, state, and national levels because these standards not only guide instruction, they also guide the assessment of language arts skills. Although standards from state to state may vary, teachers can turn to two places for sets of standards at the national level.

Read the answers to some of the most frequently asked questions about educational standards: www.hhpcommunities.com/teachinglanguagearts/IL-02-01.pdf

Common Core State Standards (CCSS)

First adopted in 2010, the Common Core State Standards describe the essential skills students should master for college and career readiness by laying out a "vision of what it means to be a literate person in the twenty-first century" (Common Core State Standards Initiative, 2012). Written for the K–12 level, these standards are based on the premise that preparation for college and career must begin in kindergarten and be reinforced throughout elementary, middle, and high school.

The CCSS are broken down to levels K–5 and 6–12 to help facilitate their implementation. Standards for the 6–12 level also focus on literacy skills in history/social studies, science, and technical subjects. English language arts and mathematics are the two content areas currently covered by the standards. At both the elementary and secondary levels, the English language arts standards are divided into reading, writing, speaking/listening, and language. The integration of media and technology into instruction is seen as an integral part of these standards. The CCSS guide teachers in developing lessons and creating a classroom environment that promote the development of knowledge and skills. Students, teachers, parents, and other community members have access to the curricula goals. In addition to the national standards described in this chapter, individual states have also developed their own standards, often based on the CCSS. State standards guide the development of curricula for school districts and also give structure to the state assessments.

As a teacher, your goal should be familiarity with all grade level standards for the state in which you teach. A closer scrutiny is needed for standards at your specific grade level and several grade levels preceding and following to know what students have been taught before they arrive in your classroom and what they will be taught after they leave your classroom.

To become familiar with the standards, select a grade level and go to the Common Core Standards link (www.corestandards.org/ELA-Literacy) for that grade level, or download the Common Core Standards app. Look for the key ideas taught in language arts at the selected grade level, and recall the language arts skills you learned as a student. Consider the differences and similarities.

International Reading Association Standards for Reading Professionals

The International Reading Association (IRA) is one of the leading professional organizations for educators focusing on literacy education. With over 60,000 members worldwide, the IRA represents a large number of educators at various levels. In 2010, the IRA revised the Standards for Reading Professionals, which describe what teachers are expected to know in relation to literacy instruction. These standards set the tone for teacher preparation. The document (see link below) lists the six standards for reading professionals along with specific indicators and a research-based rationale for each. The six standards are:

Standard 1: Foundation Knowledge about Literacy
Standard 2: Curriculum and Instruction
Standard 3: Assessment and Evaluation
Standard 4: Diversity
Standard 5: Literate Environment
Standard 6: Professional Learning and Leadership

These standards are an important tool for teachers, especially new teachers, because their goal is to define what teachers need to know in order to teach students the literacy skills students need to be successful now and in the future. The standards do not define how to teach, but rather describe the knowledge needed to be an effective teacher of the language arts.

Pause in your reading to look over the IRA Standards (www.reading.org/General/CurrentResearch/Standards/ProfessionalStandards2010.aspx), focusing on those standards for the pre-k through elementary teacher. Scroll down the list of elements and consider which you have already learned in your literacy coursework and which you hope to learn more about, whether in this course or other literacy courses.

Standards give structure to our teaching by guiding instructional and assessment decisions. Standards should not, however, cause us to lose sight of the heart of language arts, which lies in the interaction between people. There is a special word used by those who practice the art of yoga. The word is *namaste* and means "the spirit within me honors the spirit within you." The spirit within drives each of us to communicate, whether we learn English as a second language, stutter when speaking, or use sign language because of deafness. As teachers, we accept our students where they are at in their language development and always strive to move them forward. Our mission as teachers is to help students develop the skills and strategies needed to communicate effectively.

points2ponder

QUICK REVIEW 5 The CCSS English Language Arts (ELA) Standards are divided into four areas. What are these?
What is the purpose of the CCSS? The IRA Standards for Reading Professionals?

(Access the answers in the digital version of this book.)

2.5

CHAPTER SUMMARY

Each person is born with an innate desire to communicate. Our abilities become more sophisticated as we develop the language arts skills of reading, listening, viewing and writing, speaking, and visually representing. Teachers strive to give students opportunities to grow and develop in each of the areas through one-to-one, small group, and whole class interactions. Modeling and providing real world experiences are central to the ways teachers can facilitate language development in the classroom. Local, state, and national language arts standards give teachers a framework for planning language arts instruction and assessing student progress toward goals. Teachers must honor the language experiences their students bring to school and work to help them move forward in their literacy development.

think like a teacher

Explore the Common Core State Standards

Consider this scenario: Andrew recently graduated from a teacher education program at a Midwestern university, received his teaching license, and was hired for a third grade teaching position. Enthusiastic and excited, Andrew reviews the third grade teachers' manuals over the summer so he can be prepared to teach in the fall. A few days before school begins, he receives a phone call from the principal letting him know that because of an unexpected shift in enrollment, he will now be teaching a combined second and third grade classroom. With school beginning in just a few short days, Andrew starts to panic because he is familiar with the third grade curriculum, but not the one for second grade. He recalls learning about the Common Core State Standards at the university, so he turns to this resource to help bring him up to speed with expectations for second grade.

Now, put yourself in Andrew's shoes. Imagine his excitement, then his sense of panic. This activity is designed to encourage you to take a closer look at the standards with the purpose of identifying similarities and differences at grade levels, just as Andrew did.

At the CCSS website (www.corestandards.org/ELA-Literacy), select two consecutive grade levels between kindergarten and fifth grade (e.g., first/second, third/fourth). Closely study the standards at these two grade levels, noting how the expectations change and the key vocabulary used to describe these expectations. Create a chart displaying similarities and differences between the standards for each grade level in the areas of reading, writing, speaking/listening, and language. Then share your chart with a partner who studied a different grade level combination. Discuss the expectations on students as they move from grade to grade and the challenges faced by teachers.

Language Arts in My Everyday Life

Understanding our own personal development as a literate person is equally important to knowing the content and pedagogy of language arts instruction. Our experiences and values greatly influence how and what we teach. Never underestimate the power you have to influence the literacy behaviors of your students. Examples of ways you use the various elements of language arts in your everyday life can have a powerful influence on the literacy choices your students make each day. This activity asks you to create a project to share your own literacy preferences, experiences, and values with your (future) students. The way you share this information is up to you, but the project must meet the following criteria.

1. Use technology to create your project.
2. Include examples (artifacts) of the ways you use language arts in your everyday life.

3. Reflect on the examples you use. A reflection should be an explanation of how or why you use something.

Review and print the evaluation criteria for the Language Arts in My Everyday Life Project Rubric: www.hhpcommunities.com/teachinglanguagearts/IL-02-02.pdf.

How to Prepare Your Project

1. Gather artifacts that represent the ways you use language arts in your everyday life.
2. Consider why you chose each artifact, how it reflects what you do, and why it is important to you.
3. Visit the Presentation Zen website (www.presentationzen.com/presentationzen/2010/04/making-presentations-that-stick.html) and watch two brief videos (3:19, 2:23) about creating effective digital presentations. Watch for key ideas that will help you effectively display your language arts ideas.
4. Decide on a format for sharing your project. Try something new, for example:

    A. PowerPoint: Create a PPT display with photos of your artifacts and written reflections.
    B. Prezi (http://prezi.com): Instead of the traditional PowerPoint, give Prezi a try. It's an easy presentation tool that jazzes up PPT presentations. You can import pictures, videos, and sound. You can receive an upgraded account for free if you use your school email address.
    C. Glogster (edu.glogster.com): Create a digital poster on Glogster, similar to a digital scrapbook page. See the sample Glog (http://sissyjo261.glogster.com/human-services).
    D. Voice Threads: Spoken words and images can be combined in an online format on Voice Threads. Others can listen to a thread and add feedback of their own. Click on the *About* link at the Voice Threads website (2:20, http://voicethread.com) for a tutorial video for creating your own voice thread.
    E. iMovie (Mac) or MovieMaker (Windows): These tools are good for presenting photos and or video clips and then publishing them in a photo essay or digital story. This software is a little more challenging to use than some of the other choices.
    F. Photo Story 3 for Windows: (Refer back to the author's digital story in Chapter 1, created using Photo Story.) This free download is an easy tool for creating a photo essay that can include voice, music, and photos.

For sample projects, check out the following links. Of course, these projects only serve as inspiration. Your project will be your own.

Amy Hillman's project (9:00): http://ahillman.glogster.com/glog-1258)

Cherise Smith's project (1:29): www.youtube.com/watch?v=Obi4dVeOjuM)

Creating a Classroom Atmosphere That Promotes the Language Arts

An essential aspect of learning to teach the language arts is learning how to create an atmosphere in which communication is welcomed, respected, and expected. As a first step in this learning process, use the observation sheet (www.hhpcommunities.com/teachinglanguagearts/IL-02-03.pdf) in your next classroom visit to see how the teacher promotes the language arts. Be sure to record specific examples of the teacher's methods so that you can adapt them to your own classroom.

REFERENCES

Beck, I. L., & McKeown, M. G. (1991). Conditions of vocabulary acquisition. In R. Barr, M. L. Kamil, P. Mosenthal, & P. D. Pearson (Eds.), *Handbook of reading research* (Vol. 2, pp. 789–814). White Plains, NY: Longman.

Common Core State Standards Initiative. (2012). The Standards: English Language Arts Standards. Retrieved from http://www.corestandards.org/ELA-Literacy.

Fisher, D., Frey, N., & Lapp, D. (2009). *In a reading state of mind: Brain research, teacher modeling, and comprehension instruction.* Newark, DE: International Reading Association.

Graves, M. F. (2004). Teaching prefixes: As good as it gets? In J. F. Baumann & E. J. Kame'enui (Eds.), *Vocabulary instruction: Research to practice* (pp. 81–99). New York: Guilford Press.

Halliday, M. K. (1978). *Language as social semiotic: The social interpretation of language and meaning.* Baltimore, MD: University Park Press.

International Reading Association and the National Council of Teachers of English. (1996). *Standards for the English Language Arts.* Urbana, IL: Author.

Knobel, M., & Wilber, D. (2009). Let's talk 2.0. *Educational Leadership, 66*(6), 20–24.

Lenhart, A. (2008). Writing, technology and teens. Pew Internet and American Life Project. Retrieved from http://www.pew internet.org/Reports/2008/Writing-Technology-and-Teens.aspx.

Lenhart, A. (2012). Teens, smartphones, and texting. Pew Internet and American Life Project. Retrieved from http://www.pew internet.org/Reports/2012/Teens-and-smartphones/Summary-of-findings.aspx.

Leu, D. J. (2000). Literacy and technology: Deictic consequences for literacy education in an information age. In M. L. Kamil, P. Mosenthal, E. D. Pearson, & R. Barr (Eds.), *Handbook of reading research* (Vol. 3, pp. 743–770). Mahwah, NJ: Erlbaum.

North Central Regional Education Laboratory. (2003). *EnGAUGE 21st century skills for 21st century learners.* Available: http://pict.sdsu.edu/engauge21st.pdf

Richardson, W. (2009). Becoming network-wise. *Educational Leadership, 66*(6), 26–31.

Roehler, L. R., & Cantlon, D. J. (1997). Scaffolding: A powerful tool in social constructivist classrooms. In K. Hogan & M. Pressley (Eds.), *Scaffolding student learning: Instructional approaches and issues* (pp. 6–42). Cambridge, MA: Brookline.

Creating a Learning Environment in Face-to-Face and Virtual Classrooms

Access the book's Glossary, which defines the key terms boldfaced in this chapter, at www.hhpcommunities.com/teachinglanguagearts/glossary.pdf

3.1

THEORIES AND THEIR ROLE IN TEACHING AND LEARNING

The Big Bang theory, besides being a television show, was proposed by scientists to explain the origins of the universe. This theory is described by the National Aeronautics and Space Administration (NASA) as a general principle offered to explain an observed phenomenon, which is the origin and evolution of our universe (NASA, 2012). Proposed by George Lemaitre, a Belgian priest, in 1927, the Big Bang theory is based on Albert Einstein's early twentieth-century work. Not all scientists agree with the Big Bang theory, but many non-scientific people have heard of it. While the theory explains how the universe began, it does not help us understand literacy instruction. It does, however, provide a model for understanding the usefulness of theories.

Theories help explain where ideas come from and predict where they might lead. In terms of communication, theories help explain how and why humans create and receive messages. When it comes to learning, theories help explain how and under what conditions students learn best. This chapter looks at how learning theories guide teachers' creation of a learning environment, whether learning takes place face-to-face or virtually. So

"Not only are things changing but we have to be willing to go along with the change and prepare our students to be flexible and roll with all the changes."

CHERISE SMITH,
third grade teacher

why are theories important to *you* as a teacher? Are they merely what professors and researchers use to sound educated? Resoundingly, we say *no*! Theories deserve your attention because they support and give structure to the hundreds of decisions you will make over the course of the teaching day. A theory can explain how students use language, but it can also guide simple decisions you make on a daily basis, such as how to arrange students' desks, what materials to put in your writing center, or how long you should spend reading aloud each day. A theory can also predict what your students will need to know about communication in the future.

Although school districts and administrators provide teachers with curriculum guidelines, decisions about the minute-to-minute flow of activities in your classroom are up to you. These decisions should not be taken lightly, nor should they be made randomly. Theories give us guidance, help back up our decisions, and provide guidance in the face of uncertainty. In essence, theories "make us smarter about our practice and thereby increase the likelihood that our instructional decisions will be effective" (Baker, 2010, p. 7). Theories provide a lens through which to view the ways we learn to communicate. Don't shy away from theories; rather, embrace them as tools for understanding.

Theories lead to a philosophy of teaching

Theories should form the basis for your teaching philosophy, which you may be called upon to share with employers or the families of your students. Your philosophy is the collection of theories, beliefs, and values that you bring to your teaching and to interactions with students and their families. It is unique to you, forms the tone or style of your teaching, and influences the everyday decisions you make in the classroom. Your philosophy is the mosaic (see Exhibit 3.1) of theories that match your beliefs.

A teaching philosophy is like a mosaic with many elements that come together to form a cohesive whole.

author's story   ELIZABETH DOBLER

My Philosophy of Teaching

One component of my philosophy is that I believe in the value of choice as a motivator in learning, so I build into my instruction ways for students to make choices about format and content in assignments. I teach from the belief that we do not all learn the same way, thus we do not have to demonstrate learning the same way, as long as we demonstrate an understanding of the concept. This belief, while based on some of my own personal experiences, is rooted in Donald Graves's Conditions for Effective Writing (1994) (see Chapter 7 for further explanation), Howard Gardner's Theory of Multiple Intelligences (1983) (see Chapter 4 for further explanation), and Louise Rosenblatt's Reader Response Theory (1978) (see Chapter 6 for further explanation). These theories have helped form my beliefs, or philosophy, which then guide my actions as a teacher.

Justin's reflection.

I have learned that I need to work on my time management. Throughout all of my lessons, I have gone over time. I need to make sure to set a buzzer or have a student check the time for me so that I do not go over on my time. I have also learned through planning that it is better to plan out too much than too little. Comparing this phonics lesson and my math lesson, I planned a lot more for this lesson and it went better.

A philosophy is not written in stone; it evolves and is guided by reflection on our own teaching. (Exhibit 3.2 shows a sample reflection by soon-to-be teacher, Justin.) We know that effective teachers evaluate their teaching (Schon, 1987) by looking back on a lesson and identifying what worked and what did not work, and their role in this instruction. Next these thoughtful teachers make adjustments in their teaching based on their experiences. This reflection is the hallmark of a good teacher and, when collected over time, provides another source for defining our beliefs or philosophy. Thus, philosophy guides practice, and practice guides philosophy.

Both evolve and intertwine. (See Exhibit 3.3 and Exhibit 3.4 for a sample philosophy from Sara and Tammy, future teachers).

Foundational theories for literacy instruction

You are in the process of formulating your philosophy and beliefs based on theories you are encountering in your teacher preparation program. The beginning part of this chapter is designed to touch on four prominent theories forming the foundation for literacy instruction. Our hope is that knowledge of these and other theories will guide the creation of your own philosophy of literacy teaching. We have chosen to highlight only some from the many useful theories available in education, and our explanations only scratch the surface. We encourage you to further explore theories that strike a chord for you as a teacher and learner.

Behaviorist theory: Learning about language by breaking down a task

Language stems from the combination of individual letters and their sounds. Behaviorist theory focuses on breaking down a task, such as learning to read, into individual components and becoming proficient by progressing step-by-step from simple to complex. The teacher presents information for each step of the task and supports new learning through practice and reinforcement, often in the form of a reward. According to Skinner (1974), progress must be observable and measurable. In fact, many of Skinner's behaviorist principles can be found in computer-based learning games where students practice basic skills, are rewarded for correct answers, and move up to the next level. The principles of behaviorism are often used to teach the basic skills that serve as the foundation for higher-order thinking. For example, earning how to form letters correctly through handwriting practice leads to the legible writing required to write and publish a poem in a class book (see Exhibit 3.5).

For more information, visit the webpage Behaviorism: http://projects.coe.uga.edu/epltt/index.php?title=Behaviorism

Semiotics theory: Learning about language by understanding symbolic forms

There is more than one way to express an idea, and the semiotics perspective focuses on the role of various symbolic forms in communicating (Eco, 1976). Words, images, gestures, and objects all convey meaning. A student hoping to convince classmates to recycle might create a poster, video, podcast, news article, announcement, poem, flyer, or all of these. Michael Halliday coined the term *social semiotics,* which refers to the ways signs and symbols are created and understood by a society. Halliday (1978) described three functions of language as:

- *Ideational function:* Language represents the world around and inside us.
- *Interpersonal function:* Language facilitates social interactions.
- *Textual function:* Elements of language in a text are interconnected.

When multiple sign systems are used together, the meaning of the message broadens and deepens. "Constructing meaning from multiple perspectives, using multiple media sources, provides a richer understanding of complex information, especially if one lacks prior knowledge about a topic" (Kinzer

Sara's philosophy of teaching.

My Daily Teaching To-Do List

- **Create a safe learning environment**
  School should be a place for students to feel protected and free of harm. It is my job to create this atmosphere every day for every student.

- **Show love and acceptance**
  Students deserve to feel loved and accepted. Sadly, this does not happen for every child. I must take the time to show kindness, talk to my students, and find a way to make each one feel welcome.

- **Provide effective and meaningful instruction**
  Each classroom has a diverse group of students; the teaching should reflect this. For each student to succeed, I must find the way each student learns best.

- **Use positive reinforcement**
  I must take the time to praise my students regularly and focus on all of the great attitudes, good behaviors, and hard work found every day in my classroom. I need to keep a positive attitude and reinforce in the same way.

- **Work closely with students' parents**
  I need to get parents involved so that they can see what is taught in the schools, what is needed in the schools, and what is lacking in the schools. This will allow the parents to act as a voice in the community to help better the schools.

- **Never stop learning**
  Teaching strategies are always changing. I must stay current in educational trends, so that as education changes, I am renewed in my own experience.

Tammy's philosophy of teaching.

I believe that all students need:

- Encouragement
- Support
- High expectations
- A positive learning environment
- Responsibility
- Fun

My role as a teacher is to:

- **Encourage all my students, no matter what their learning ability is or might be.**
  As a teacher it is important to constantly encourage students, and show them that I, the teacher, believe in them. It can mean the difference between a student succeeding or failing.

- **Support each and every one of my students.**
  It is important for me as the teacher to remember that each child has his/her own unique perspective brought from home. With this in mind, I show every student support and love, regardless of background, ethnicity, or gender.

- **Hold each student to a set of high expectations.**
  I, the teacher, will hold every student to a set of high expectations, no matter what their level of learning. EACH AND EVERY STUDENT CAN ACHIEVE TASKS ASKED BY THE TEACHER.

- **Create a positive learning environment.**
  It is my role as the teacher to create a learning environment that is safe for every student. Respecting each other will be the center of everything the students do in my classroom.

- **Give students responsibility within the classroom.**
  All students will have responsibilities within the classroom, as well as responsibilities to me, the teacher, as well as their classmates.

- **Make sure that students have fun while they are learning.**
  School is a serious matter, but students will be able to have fun while in my classroom.

I leave you with one last thought that my mother has told me for years: "Never judge other people. You never know what they have been through, or what challenges they face every day."

Practice as a key element of the behaviorist theory.

& Leu, 1997, p. 130). The teacher's role in semiotic theory is to teach students to express their message in various ways and to make wise choices about which system is effective in which situation. Each sign system expresses an idea in a unique way, and students need guidance in choosing the most effective way to express their ideas (Labbo, 1996).

For more information about semiotics, view the video *Semiotics: The Study of Signs* (3:28): www.youtube.com/watch?v=rEgxTKUP_WI

Sociocultural theory: Learning about language through interacting with others

Learning about language occurs through our interactions with other people. Each one of us is crafted from an *identity kit* based on our values, beliefs, and ways of thinking, all of which stem from our culture or family, community, religion, race, ethnicity, gender, and socioeconomic status. When we interact with others, these factors influence what we say and do. In essence, learning does not occur in isolation, but is nestled within our own personal collection of experiences. "It is difficult if not meaningless to isolate various aspects of mental processes for separate analysis" (Wertsch, 1991, p. 14); thus, sociocultural theory may be considered contrary to behaviorism.

Students' learning is dependent on all the ways ideas are communicated, through the teacher, classmates, instructional tools, classroom, school environment, and the social interactions among students, teachers, parents, and the community. As described by Vygotsky (1978), "human learning presupposes a specific social nature and process by which children grow into the intellectual life of those around them" (p. 88). Classroom arrangement, management techniques, instruction, and assessments all must take into account the unique sociocultural background each student brings to class.

Read more about sociocultural theory in the article "Guided Participation": www.education.com/reference/article/guided-participation/#C

Constructivist theory: Learning by doing

We learn to write by writing; we learn to speak by speaking. Language is learned by actively using language, and this concept lies at the heart of the constructivist perspective. Words like *discovery, hands-on, active learning,* and *collaboration* are all used to describe constructivism. Piaget (1972) believed that learning is the interaction between experiences and ideas. Our **schema,** or way of organizing knowledge, is like a mental file cabinet in which we store these experiences and ideas, with drawers for concepts, and file folders holding more specific information. When we learn something new, our mental file cabinet accepts this new information and stores it in an existing file folder (**assimilation**) or adjusts the file system to make room for this new bit of information (**accommodation**). This process of making meaning, or constructing knowledge, is unique to each person and can be developed through interactions with others who already know the information, whether they are peers or more experienced adults (Vygotsky, 1978). The role of the teacher is to create an environment and plan activities where students can gain experiences and ideas about language and thus expand their mental file folders. In a constructivist classroom, the teacher facilitates rather than lectures; coaches and observes rather than prescribes and measures. The teacher also helps students understand the patterns of thinking used when learning to communicate. **Metacognition** is a person's own awareness of his or her thinking when completing a task or process (Flavell, 1976), and when used in the context of learning it could refer to an awareness of the thought processes used to understand a newspaper article or to figure out an unfamiliar word when reading. Constructivism is about brain power, problem solving, and creating meaning.

For more information, visit the webpage Piaget's Constructivism to find written text and video clip explanations (4:00): http://projects.coe.uga.edu/epltt/index.php?title=Piaget%27s_Constructivism

Connecting teaching theories to teaching philosophies

Now that you are familiar with four key learning theories, let's see if you can apply them. Revisit the two sample philosophies in Exhibits 3.3 and 3.4. As you reread Sara's and Tammy's philosophy statements, look for hints of the theories each used to guide her philosophy. Did you notice Sara's use of positive reinforcement, a key element of the behaviorist theory? Maybe you observed Tammy's view of the teacher's role as one who supports each student, taking into account family, cultural, and economic differences among students, which matches sociocultural theory. Can you identify any other connections to the theories described in this chapter or other familiar learning theories?

Impact on teaching the language arts

These four key theories—behaviorism, semiotics, socioculturalism, and constructivism—form the building blocks for learning about the language arts. Certainly, there are other worthy theories that help explain many aspects of language arts instruction, but we chose to focus on these four theories because of their wide acceptance in the learning community. What do these theories mean for teaching the language arts? Theoretical decisions form the basis for effective teaching. Exhibit 3.6 shares classroom activities matching each learning theory explored in this chapter. Typically, teachers incorporate aspects of various theories into their classroom activities, although one theory may be predominant. Theories overlap somewhat, because researchers build on the work of those who came before them.

COMPREHENSION *coach*

Did you know that looking over the text before reading can set you up for success when reading? Hard to believe? *(Access this podcast in the digital version of this book.)*

points2ponder

QUICK REVIEW 1 The four theories presented in this section are the foundation for the remainder of this book. How well do you remember this information? Can you

EXHIBIT 3.6

Classroom activities based on learning theories.

Based on the **behaviorist perspective**, in a classroom I would expect to see:
- Flash cards for practicing words
- Workbooks for practicing skills
- Teacher leading the activities and doing most of the talking
- Reward system for good behavior
- A computerized reading program where children advance to the next level once a skill is mastered

Based on the **sociocultural perspective**, in a classroom I would expect to see:
- Group discussions about literature
- Student writing that reflects their family and culture
- Children's and young adult literature representing diversity
- Collaboration on group projects through discussion, video conferencing, online chatting
- Individual conferences between teacher and students

Based on the **semiotic perspective**, in a classroom I would expect to see:
- Lots of visual images (posters, photographs, charts, drawings, paintings, and picture books)
- Equipment for creating and interpreting content of various sign systems (microphone, digital camera, mp3 player, computer, tablet, writing center, art supplies, classroom library)
- Alphabet charts
- Labels for common objects around the classroom
- Picture clues for students learning English or less-skilled readers

Based on the **constructivist perspective**, in a classroom I would expect to see:
- Desks arranged in groups to facilitate collaboration
- Journals used for reflecting on learning
- Access to the Internet for several, if not all, students at the same time
- Materials for hands-on activities (real objects, letter tiles, writing materials, art supplies, science materials, math manipulatives)
- Students working in learning teams

name the four theories, explain each in a sentence, and name an educational theorist associated with the theories?

(Access answers in the digital version of this book.)

3.2

STANDARDS AS GUIDES FOR CREATING A LEARNING ENVIRONMENT

Apart from theories and philosophies guiding our creation of a learning environment, knowledgeable teachers also turn to professional standards. As discussed in Chapter 2, standards are a collection of best practices based on research that addresses the expectations set by a certain group. The International Reading Association (2010) has created the Standards for Reading Professionals (www.reading.org/General/CurrentResearch/Standards/ProfessionalStandards2010.aspx), which speak directly to the creation of a learning environment to promote the language arts. These standards are based on the following key ideas:

- An effective literate environment offers both visible and *invisible* support (e.g., psychological, social, emotional) to learners as they expand their literacies.
- The goal of the literate environment is to create a flexible border between the world outside the classroom and the world within (i.e., making the curriculum permeable to the social context). Learners require a literate environment that affords them the opportunity to engage in meaningful ways by providing time, accessibility, tools, choice, and support.
- Student learning is positively impacted by positive teacher dispositions, such as high expectations, a carefully crafted physical environment, and a safe, low-risk social environment.
- To meet the needs of learners, a co-constructed literate environment must continually change as interests and focal points for learning shift over time.

These major assumptions, based on research, provide a rationale for creating an effective learning environment. The IRA standards call for teachers to "create an environment that fosters and supports students' traditional print, digital, and online reading and writing achievement" (p. 13). As a teacher, you will make decisions regarding which elements to implement in your classroom, based on your teaching philosophy and knowledge of best practices. We have chosen to focus on the physical, social, and online environments when considering the best ways to promote language arts learning. Each of these realms requires a unique set of tools, although skilled teachers often find ways to integrate all three realms into instruction.

3.3

DESIGNING THE PHYSICAL ENVIRONMENT

Creating a physical environment that promotes learning involves planning, organization, and creativity. Haphazard decisions about where to place the classroom library or what to display on a bulletin board do not take advantage of the powerful influences the physical environment can have on learning. Even a seemingly simple decision, such as where to place the class pet, should be made in a thoughtful way, based on a teacher's philosophy. For example, consider that Bernard, a pet lizard, is a popular attraction. He is also a potential source of interaction between students and should be located in a spot where students can easily discuss interesting observations. Sociocultural theory, which emphasizes learning through interaction, would guide a teacher to place the lizard in an open area where students can easily congregate and interact. Elements of the four learning theories presented previously in this chapter can serve as a beacon or guide when making these decisions that strongly influence teaching and learning in the classroom.

An organized learning space can do the following:

- motivate students
- enhance learning
- reduce behavior problems

The Reggio Emilia approach (New, 1993) to early childhood education compares the influence of an effective physical environment to the influence of an extra teacher in the classroom. The positive influence of a teacher's informed decisions about the classroom environment can influence children's learning. This section of Chapter 3 focuses on two aspects of the physical environment: visual displays and room arrangement. Both contribute to creating organized learning space and reflect a teacher's philosophy of teaching.

Visual displays

Classroom walls tell the story of learning within a classroom, so teachers are encouraged to make purposeful decisions about what is displayed and where it is displayed. Create a plan for visual displays, considering the space available on walls, bulletin boards, doors, file cabinets, and other upright surfaces. Displays should reflect organization of ideas along with proper English and spelling. Visual displays are key tools for promoting the symbolic forms of language, as expressed in the semiotics theory. Students need to see various forms of letters, words, and images to gain new knowledge and build their vocabulary. For example, in a bilingual English-Spanish classroom, a teacher incorporates elements of semiotic theory when including labels for classroom objects written in both English and Spanish (see Exhibit 3.7) or creating an autumn nature center with labeled objects, children's books, and photographs.

When selecting what to display in the classroom, keep the message simple and clear (see Exhibit 3.8). Closely monitor the messages that classroom walls give to students as well as families and other visitors. Visual displays can include a wide variety of materials, including the following:

- alphabet/number cards
- seasonal displays
- routines
- word walls
- motivational posters
- behavior expectations
- daily schedule
- upcoming events

- calendar
- safety reminders
- students' names/birthdates
- student work
- math or science concepts
- record keeping charts
- information about books/authors

Teachers sometimes organize the classroom around various content areas, creating displays for science near the science equipment and posters promoting writing, along with pencils and paper, near the writing center.

Classroom labels.

Keep the message simple.

These displays often focus on classroom routines, serving as a reminder of the schedule and familiar procedures designed to make learning consistent and help the classroom run smoothly. For example, a poster might remind students of the sources of information for figuring out how to spell an unknown word or the color coding system used to identify easy, medium, and challenging books in the classroom library.

Interactive visual displays provide opportunities for students to practice new learning by adding to or manipulating an element of the display. Having students work together to add a new word to an interactive spelling bulletin board demonstrates a teacher's enactment of sociocultural theory. **Anchor charts** are commonly used to display important information students should remember, such as ideas for writing or proofreading or editing marks. The most helpful anchor charts use borders, headings, and color to organize ideas (see Exhibit 3.9). Include pictures along with words as cues for English language learners. Anchor charts may also be used to break a task into steps using arrows and numbers, such as a chart demonstrating how to make the capital letter B. This type of chart reflects the behaviorist theory. Anchor charts should focus on the crucial information and should be changed as students learn new concepts.

Whatever the display, the message should focus on sharing information, teaching a concept, or motivating students to learn. Avoid clutter by periodically asking a colleague for feedback or taking a photograph of the displays and judging them with a critical eye, all the while being conscious of students' learning needs.

Room arrangement

The various possibilities for classroom arrangement are limited only by your imagination, the furniture, and the shape of your classroom. So where do you begin? What do you consider when sizing up the classroom on the first teacher workday, before the students arrive? Begin with a clear philosophy reflecting your beliefs about teaching and learning, and use this knowledge to effectively configure space to promote these beliefs and facilitate learning (see Exhibit 3.10). Keep in mind "classroom space impacts everything: instruction, behavior and our children's and teachers' sense of well-being" (Diller, 2008, p. 11). The following section shares some key concepts to consider when making arrangement decisions that support your learning goals.

Don't look for a magic bullet

There is no one correct way to arrange a classroom. Every configuration has advantages and disadvantages. Your job is to weigh each of these against your beliefs and what you know about effective instruction and to make the best professional decision possible. Give careful consideration to arrangements that facilitate classroom management. Fred Jones, co-author of the teaching resource, *Tools for Teaching* (2007) says, "Either you work the crowd or the crowd works you" (p. 30). Classroom arrangement decisions you make impact the ways students interact with each other and with you. Make decisions that promote the types of interactions that enhance learning rather than detract from learning. For example, desks organized in columns and rows may promote the behaviorist theory by encouraging individual practice of skills. At the same time, desks organized in groups of two or three facilitates collaboration, a hallmark of the constructivist theory. At any time, each arrangement may be the best choice to promote the teacher's

EXHIBIT 3.9

Anchor chart.

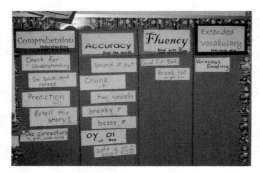

EXHIBIT 3.10

Room arrangement.

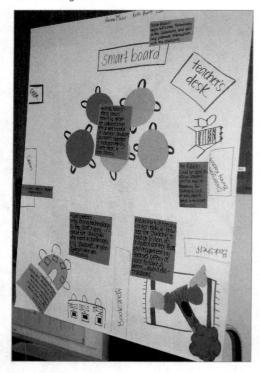

goals and philosophy. Flexibility is a key in determining the best arrangement for the class, the room, and the activities.

Be flexible

A classroom arrangement should change as needed. A teacher's recognition of learning needs, the addition of new students, and the acquisition of new equipment can and should cause a change in classroom arrangement.

On the Classroom Architect site (http://classroom.4teachers.org), teachers can develop an electronic classroom floor plan including rugs, bookshelves, desks, and so on by choosing an object and dragging it to the grid or by drawing objects not found in the collection. This tool promotes the flexible arrangement plans. Use this website as a place to design, revise, and save a plan for your future classroom. (This site requires Flash. An alternative for the iPad is the Classroom Layout app.)

Know that limitations abound

Your classroom arrangement plan will be limited by physical barriers such as the size and shape of the room, the location and number of electrical outlets, or the quantity, type, and size of furniture. Assess these limitations before you begin arranging and consider whether they can be addressed (e.g., through the use of surge protectors with longer cords). These limitations will require you to be creative in designing learning spaces. One primary goal should be to allow broad walkways to facilitate movement.

Design around a purpose

Benjamin Franklin said, "A place for everything, everything in its place." This adage is especially true in a classroom. Consider the purpose of each object, visual display, and piece of furniture and weigh this against what you know about best practices for literacy instruction. For example, a computer can be a useful tool for practicing letter sounds with a phonics game (aligning with behaviorist theory), but it also can be a tool for displaying a class poem on the school website (aligning with sociocultural theory) and for videoconferencing with a guest speaker (aligning with constructivist theory). Place computers where they can serve multiple purposes. Also create spaces that can serve a single specific purpose, such as providing a quiet reading spot in a reading center. Maneuver a rainbow-shaped table into the corner of the room so that the students can move in close to the teacher and face away from the visual and auditory distractions of the classroom.

Be aware of student needs

Consider the learning needs of individual students in the class by viewing the room through their eyes. Sit down in various students' desks and see the classroom from their vantage point. Make adjustments to anything in the physical environment that is a distraction, from a child's point of view. Think about light, temperature, noise, visual displays, and proximity to you and other students. Give special consideration to those students with hearing or vision impairments or other special learning needs. Designate a central spot to display picture cues and real objects for communicating ideas to English language learners.

Get students involved

When students play a role in creating their learning environment, they feel ownership in the classroom and feel like a vital part of the learning community. Some teachers begin the school year with blank walls and rely on students' help to create an arrangement that reflects both the teacher's and students' learning priorities. In this way, a teacher is aligning the learning environment with sociocultural theory by encouraging interactions that will help craft the identity of the class as a group.

Plan for necessary classroom spaces

Although there is much to consider when planning for room arrangement, Debbie Diller, in her book *Spaces and Places,* suggests five must-have elements in classroom arrangement:

1. Whole group area. Typically, whole group activities for younger students are held on a rug on the floor, whether in the center or to the side of the room. The rug is important for setting off the learning area and providing comfort to students and teacher. Teachers tend to forgo having a whole group area with older students, which may or may not be the best decision. A whole group area brings students and the teacher closer together. It provides a change of scenery and removes the distractions from elsewhere in the room. In whole group areas, the teacher may read aloud, record students' ideas on chart paper, whiteboard, or an interactive whiteboard, or call on students to share written or oral projects. (See Exhibit 3.11 for a whole group area in a kindergarten classroom and Exhibit 3.12 for a whole group area in a fourth grade classroom.)

2. Small group area. A small group area provides a designated space for small group instruction or one-on-one conferences between the teacher and students (see Chapter 4 for more information about forming learning groups). Arrange the area so you have a clear view of the students both in the group and those working at their seats. Usually, the area will feature a rainbow- or kidney-shaped table that can seat six or so students along with the teacher. Have a wall or board for displaying charts and posters at hand, along with a portable whiteboard or other tool on which to write or draw. Shelves nearby provide easy access to materials during a

EXHIBIT 3.11

Whole group area in a kindergarten classroom.

EXHIBIT 3.12

Whole group area in a fourth grade classroom.

EXHIBIT 3.13

EXHIBIT 3.13

Small group area in a kindergarten classroom.

EXHIBIT 3.14

Small group area in a fourth grade classroom.

reading or writing lesson. (See Exhibit 3.13 for a small group area in a kindergarten classroom and Exhibit 3.14 for a small group area in a fourth grade classroom.)

3. Classroom library. Bookshelves and tubs for books are a must when planning a classroom library. To make the classroom library inviting, you can add a lamp, rug, plants, and comfortable pillows and chairs. If short on space, the classroom library can double as a whole group learning area. Books might be organized into plastic tubs or baskets with labels for authors, genres, or level of difficulty. (See Exhibit 3.15 for a classroom library in a kindergarten classroom and Exhibit 3.16 for a classroom library area in a fourth grade classroom.)

4. Literacy centers or work stations. When a teacher is working with a small group, the other students are often expected to work on literacy activities at different stations or centers. These areas are usually designed for students to work individually or in groups of two or three and typically focus on activities such as reading, writing, spelling, vocabulary, listening, phonics, and handwriting. A computer work station where students can independently use computers to practice skills or create projects may also be part of the design.

EXHIBIT 3.15

Classroom library in a kindergarten classroom.

EXHIBIT 3.16

Classroom library in a fourth grade classroom.

EXHIBIT 3.17

Literacy work station in a kindergarten classroom.

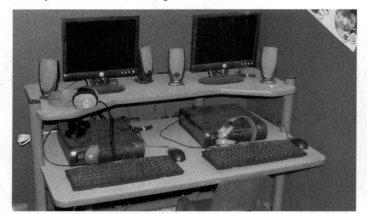

EXHIBIT 3.18

Literacy work station in a fourth grade classroom.

(See Exhibit 3.17 for a literacy work station in a kindergarten classroom and Exhibit 3.18 for a literacy work station in a fourth grade classroom.)

Listen to Amee Martin describe in this podcast (2:41) how she created a classroom library and reading center in her third grade classroom. Amee has pulled together what she knows about small group and whole class workspaces to create a classroom arrangement that meets the needs of her students. (Access this podcast in the digital version of this book.)

5. Desks/tables. Students' individual workspaces may be grouped together to save space or promote collaboration while at the same time providing for easy access for the teacher and other students. Students have their own space for independently practicing language arts, math, science, and social studies, although supplies may be kept in a basket in the middle of a table or group of desks. (See Exhibit 3.19 for a desk arrangement in a kindergarten classroom and Exhibit 3.20 for a desk arrangement in a fourth grade classroom.)

EXHIBIT 3.19

Desk arrangement in a kindergarten classroom.

EXHIBIT 3.20

Desk arrangement in a fourth grade classroom.

In addition to these considerations, you are encouraged to add a personal touch to the classroom. This could be anything from displaying your stuffed frog collection (see Exhibit 3.21) to sharing works by your favorite children's author. Some teachers display motivational posters to inspire students (see Exhibit 3.22).

It's impossible to know the configuration of your future classroom, but you can begin to formulate your personal philosophy, which will guide your future decisions. Exhibit 3.23 explores how personal beliefs and theoretical perspectives might influence decisions about classroom arrangements. Consider which statements apply to you and the ways you might translate those beliefs into the learning environment of your classroom.

EXHIBIT 3.21

A teacher's frog collection.

BOOK REVIEW

Spaces and Places: Designing Classrooms for Literacy
BY DEBBIE DILLER

The book *Spaces and Places: Designing Classrooms for Literacy* is full of color photographs of classroom areas that promote literacy instruction. Diller focuses on the essentials, other options you might like, and each element's role in instruction. This is a *must have* book for teachers. A spiral binding, thick pages, and color photographs make this book a durable and vibrant instructional resource. Readers are provided with hundreds of specific ideas for designing the physical aspects of the classroom, all with an eye toward meeting the varying needs of students. Put this practical resource high on your list of books to buy.

Locate a copy: www.worldcat.org/title/
spaces-places-designing-classrooms-for-literacy/oclc/213765735

points2ponder

QUICK REVIEW 2 What is the value of a visual display beyond decorating the classroom?

(Access answers in the digital version of this book.)

EXHIBIT 3.22

Motivational poster.

EXHIBIT 3.23

Links between beliefs and classroom arrangement.

A TEACHER'S BELIEFS	A TEACHER'S ACTIONS	PREDOMINANT THEORETICAL PERSPECTIVE
I believe students learn best when the classroom is quiet and under control . . .	. . . thus I will arrange the desks in rows with all students facing forward.	Behaviorism
I believe students learn to read and write by being surrounded by print . . .	. . . thus I will make space for students to view posters, labels, charts, and signs on the walls of the classroom.	Semiotics
I believe students learn when they explain their thinking to others . . .	. . . thus I will arrange the desks in groups of 2 or 3.	Socioculturalism
I believe students learn best through individualized practice . . .	. . . thus I will keep a class chart of practice times and accomplishments.	Behaviorism
I believe the classroom should be a place to honor the culture of all students . . .	. . . thus I will have a bulletin board where a different student each week displays photos and a written description about his or her life outside of school.	Socioculturalism
I believe English language learners should have many opportunities to use English . .	. . . thus I will have literacy centers where students can interact with others while focusing on developing language arts skills.	Socioculturalism
I believe students learn best through social interaction . . .	. . . thus I will create a technology center where students have access to a web camera and can use video conferencing with students in other schools, communities, and countries.	Socioculturalism
I believe students construct ideas for their writing based on experiences . . .	. . . thus I will have a class pet and keep a journal recording interesting observations and ideas for stories about the pet.	Constructivism

3.4

DESIGNING THE SOCIAL ENVIRONMENT

A learning environment is made up of more than desks and posters; it also includes the atmosphere and spirit of the classroom. Charlotte Danielson, a leader in the field of professional development for educators, encourages teachers to ask themselves, "If you were to walk into a classroom, what might you see or hear there (from the students as well as the teacher) that would cause you to think that you were in the presence of an expert?" (n.d.). The teacher has the opportunity to set the tone for the classroom. How does he or she do this? By communicating what is important in that classroom. Return to your philosophy of teaching; this is your set of values for teaching and learning. Built into that set of values are your core beliefs about the conditions that must be in place for effective learning.

Themes for creating a social environment

The tone, or classroom climate, can be discerned within the first few minutes a visitor spends in the classroom. Skilled teachers shape this tone through their words, actions, tone of voice, and attitude. According to Danielson (2007), five common themes teachers can use as a guide for creating a social environment conducive to the learning of all students are:

Equity

Fairness is important to learners of all ages. Children, especially, seek to be reassured about their importance in the classroom. The key word in a definition of equity is *all*. A teacher encourages all students to feel valued by showing respect and establishing rapport with them. By giving feedback to all students, a teacher gives everyone an equal chance to grow as learners. By inviting all students to participate in a discussion about a work of literature, a teacher gives the message that all opinions are valued. Public schools must serve all students equally well, even if this has not always been the case in the past. You must be particularly sensitive to the inclusion of English language learners, students living in poverty, and gender differences and provide additional support for students belonging to groups with a history of being underserved.

Cultural sensitivity

You must be keenly aware of the cultural backgrounds of your students. Use this awareness to initiate learning about the families' culture, traditions, and religious backgrounds so that the classroom environment is one where students feel like these differences are embraced. Honor the students' culture by learning about the traditions and sharing this knowledge with the class as a whole. Age-appropriate literature can be a helpful tool for this (see Exhibit 3.24). Give special care to communicating with families from various cultural backgrounds. Learn about subtle communication cues used in those cultures so communication is smooth with those students and their families.

High expectations

Full disclosure is the key to setting high expectations in the classroom. Students often rise to meet our expectations, but only if these expectations are clearly spelled out to them. High achievement takes place when students know what is expected and how to meet those expectations. Just as students can strive to meet high expectations, they can also match our expectations if we set these too low. When rigorous instructional standards require hard work and perseverance, you need to communicate your confidence in the student's ability to learn. Planting the seed of confidence can lead to the bloom of a child learning new concepts.

EXHIBIT 3.24

Age-appropriate literature about cultural traditions.

Bringing in the New Year by Grace Lin (2008). New York: Alfred A. Knopf. Younger readers.

Day of the Dead by Tony Johnston & Jeanette Winter (1997). San Diego: Harcourt. Middle readers.

Children Just Like Me by Barnabas Kindersley & Anabel Kindersley (1995). New York: Dorling Kindersley. Middle readers.

I Am African American by Ruth Turk (1997). New York: PowerKids Press. Younger readers.

Fourth grade teacher Carla Goertzen believes in sharing her expectations with students and caregivers from the first day of school. View a digital version of the class handbook (http://goertzensguidebook.wikispaces.com/4th+Grade+Handbook) Carla has prepared, which clearly spells out her expectations.

Developmental appropriateness

Be familiar with the patterns of development students tend to follow, despite the individual differences common in all classrooms (see Chapters 5 and 7 for stages of reading and writing). Students will engage in new concepts in various ways, depending on their level of understanding. Knowing this, you can stretch students to think beyond their personal level of development during instruction and discussion through strategic questions and problem-solving activities. The constructivist approach guides teachers to encourage students to construct meaning at whatever level of their understanding.

Accommodating individual needs

Learning is basically an individual act, even though it may occur within a group setting. You must design a classroom environment that supports students' learning at various levels, being especially sensitive to students with special needs, whether those be intellectual, emotional, or physical. A skilled teacher designs activities and sets up learning opportunities that challenge students to learn at various levels. A desk in a secluded part of the classroom can be used to minimize distractions. A quiet classroom with the lights dimmed can provide a calming effect following a noisy interactive activity. You set the tone in the classroom by showing an awareness of and accommodating students' needs. Other students will watch and follow in your footsteps.

points2ponder

QUICK REVIEW 3 What two adjustments could a teacher make in the classroom to accommodate a student with limited vision or a hearing impairment?

(Access answers in the digital version of this book.)

The teacher's role

The IRA Standards for Reading Professionals call for teachers to "design a social environment that is low risk and includes choice, motivation, and scaffolded support to optimize students' opportunities for learning to read and write" (2010, p. 28). This aspect of creating an environment for learning is a bit more challenging than determining a classroom floor plan. Designing the social environment means creating a climate where each student feels welcome, safe, and respected. The most influential factor in creating this climate is your attitude and actions. A teacher's words, tone of voice, and gestures all work together to convey an attitude of respect for students and families and the idea that all are working together toward a common goal. When students and their families see this value in their teacher, they gain a sense of what is important in that particular classroom. A teacher can also convey the importance of students collaborating and treating each other with respect through the following ways:

- Share literature that promotes positive social interactions (see Exhibit 3.25 for a list of age-appropriate books).
- Create problem-solving activities in which students must work together.
- Remind students of each individual's uniqueness and the value of this uniqueness for generating ideas and solving problems.
- Display signs and posters promoting collaboration and respect.

EXHIBIT 3.25

Age-appropriate literature for promoting positive social interactions.

How to Be a Friend: A Guide to Making Friends and Keeping Them by Laurene Krasny Brown (1998). Illustrated by Marc Brown. Boston: Little, Brown. Younger readers.

Whoever You Are by Mem Fox (1997). New York: Harcourt. Younger readers.

I'm Like You, You're Like Me: A Child's Book about Understanding and Celebrating Each Other by Cindy Gainer (1998). Minneapolis, MN: Free Spirit Publishing. Younger readers.

I Like Being Me: Poems for Children about Feeling Special, Appreciating Others, and Getting Along by Judy Lalli and Douglas Mason-Fry (2007). Minneapolis, MN: Free Spirit Publishing. Younger/middle readers.

The Recess Queen by Alexis O'Neill (2002). Illustrated by Laura Huliska-Beith. New York: Scholastic. Younger/middle readers.

- Set boundaries about noise level and politeness that emphasize the rights of all to learn.
- Use the language of collaboration: "Let's do this together." "This helps our class." "Friends help friends."
- Reinforce the notion that all ideas are respected.
- Create a supportive environment where those who are less skilled at written or oral language are encouraged to collaborate in their own ways.
- Cultivate an attitude of *learning together* for the teacher, the students, and the family.

The role of group work

When working together, students develop valuable skills used not only in school, but also in the community and the world of work. Through collaboration and by respectfully defending their own ideas and challenging the ideas of others, students create deeper and more meaningful connections (Johnson, Johnson, & Smith, 1998; Slavin, 1995) and begin to understand alternative points of view (Cunningham, 1992). The 21st century learning model shared in Chapter 2 illustrates the need for the development of skills important for students' abilities to work with others now and in their future. Educators often use the terms *collaboration* and *cooperative learning* to describe group work in the classroom. Although sometimes used as synonyms, these terms actually represent two types of group work. See Exhibit 3.26 for an explanation of these differences. Collaboration reflects the constructivist perspective because students are working together to construct a new interpretation of an idea, such as when a group of students designs a recycling program for the school. Cooperative learning aligns more with the sociocultural perspective because students learn through language, sometimes from more experienced peers, by completing a specific task together. Think, Pair, Share, a cooperative learning activity, can be used when students read the book *Snow* by Cynthia Rylant. Students think about their favorite indoor activities when it snows (or rains if the local weather doesn't include snow) and share them with a partner.

Merely putting students into groups to work together does not guarantee positive results. You must give clear expectations, model appropriate behavior, and recognize students' attempts at working together. Teachers should also be sensitive to students' cultural and family backgrounds; working in a group may not be valued at home as much as in the classroom (Kozar, 2010). Individual differences may inhibit some students from working together. A skilled teacher recognizes these differences and adjusts expectations as needed. A group may need more guidance from the teacher or more time to complete a task.

EXHIBIT 3.26

Cooperative learning vs. collaboration.

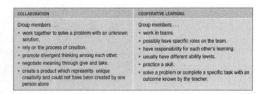

COLLABORATION	COOPERATIVE LEARNING
Group members . . .	Group members . . .
• work together to solve a problem with an unknown solution.	• work in teams.
• rely on the process of creation.	• possibly have specific roles on the team.
• promote divergent thinking among each other.	• have responsibility for each other's learning.
• negotiate meaning through give and take.	• usually have different ability levels.
• create a product which represents unique creativity and could not have been created by one person alone	• practice a skill.
	• solve a problem or complete a specific task with an outcome known by the teacher.

🔊 Listen as third grade teacher Amee Martin describes in this podcast (5:17) how she begins building a learning community on the first day of school. *(Access this podcast in the digital version of this book.)*

points2ponder

QUICK REVIEW 4 How can teachers and students reading literature together help create a positive social environment in the classroom?

(Access answers in the digital version of this book.)

3.5

DESIGNING THE ONLINE LEARNING ENVIRONMENT

The previous section focused on the decisions a teacher makes to create a positive and productive learning environment in a traditional classroom, where decisions about shoulder partners, desk clusters, and literacy centers are the norm. Now let's explore decisions a teacher makes when designing an online learning environment that meets the learning needs of students.

points2ponder

QUICK REVIEW 5 In an upcoming section you will read about the digital etiquette, or netiquette. What does this term mean? Name two ways you think a person might show their digital etiquette. When you get to the section Digital etiquette (p. 63), see if your ideas match what is shared in this book.

(Access answers in the digital version of this book.)

Creating a rationale for an online learning environment

The decision to use technology when teaching is not one to be made lightly. Up until about the early 2000s, technology in schools was mostly used for input and output, such as students using word processing to print a story or poem, creating a slide show in PowerPoint, or practicing math facts or reading skills using computer software. In 2004, the term *Web 2.0* was coined to describe new applications that created a virtual space promoting collaboration, information sharing, and creation of user content. Since then online **social networking** practices such as blogging, tweeting, and texting have proliferated. You may decide to use online learning tools in a face-to-face classroom, which would be considered **blended learning** or *hybrid education* (see Exhibit 3.27). Or a teacher may design a unit or even an entire course to be conducted online. Some teachers may teach for a virtual school, where interactions with students occur through a web camera, email, and a cell phone. Whether in a brick-and-mortar school, on a blog, or in a virtual chat room, your instructional decisions and learning environment hinge on your philosophy and sound knowledge of effective instructional practices (see Exhibit 3.28).

Arne Duncan, U.S. Secretary of Education during the Obama administration, underscored the important role technology plays in education: "In the 21st century, students must be fully engaged. This requires the use of technology tools and resources, involvement with interesting and relevant projects, and learning environments—including online environments—that are supportive and safe. . . . In the 21st century, educators must be given and be prepared to use technology tools; they must be collaborators in learning—constantly seeking knowledge and acquiring new skills along with their students" (Duncan, 2010).

The impact of digital literacies begins with our youngest learners. Although they may not use a cell phone or instant message, they are aware of their siblings, parents, and caregivers who use these technologies. Being raised in a digital culture impacts students at all ages as they watch and learn from others. Blanchard and Moore (2010), researchers in the field of literacy for young children, predict that exposure to all this technology will cause shifts in

EXHIBIT 3.27

Learning in a blended educational setting.

EXHIBIT 3.28

Creating online learning experiences.

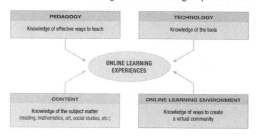

their developmental milestones. They suggest that children's attention spans will adapt as they become increasingly surrounded by digital media. Visual and/or auditory processes will be refined more rapidly, and children will be adept at learning new information through these flexible pathways.

points2ponder

QUICK REVIEW 6 What is blended learning?

(Access answers in the digital version of this book.)

Technology and College and Career Readiness (CCR) Standards

Students' experiences with the various modes of the language arts create a strong foundation of communication skills. In order for these experiences to include the digital literacy skills students need, technology must be integrated into school and across content areas. The Common Core State Standards provide educators with anchor standards, or the skills that all students must demonstrate by the end of their K–12 school experience, also known as College and Career Readiness (CCR) Standards. Several CCR anchor standards address the skills of gathering, assessing, and applying information from print and digital sources (National Governors Association, 2010). The standards state that by the end of high school students should be able to:

- Use technology, including the Internet, to produce and publish writing and to interact and collaborate with others.
- Gather relevant information from multiple print and digital sources, assess the credibility and accuracy of each source, and integrate the information while avoiding plagiarism.
- Prepare for and participate effectively in a range of conversations and collaborations with diverse partners, building on others' ideas and expressing their own clearly and persuasively.
- Integrate and evaluate information presented in diverse media and formats, including visually, quantitatively, and orally.
- Make strategic use of digital media and visual displays of data to express information and enhance understanding of presentations.

Consider the CCR English Language Arts Anchor Standards (www.core-standards.org/ELA-Literacy) the goal for your teaching and for your students. A closer look at the Common Core State Standards will show the specific grade level standards leading up to the CCR anchor standards. Although it may be years before your students are ready for college or a career, the foundation for their eventual success is being laid each day in your classroom. Incorporating online learning activities into face-to-face or virtual learning settings moves students toward the goal of being successful, literate members of society.

Online learning tools

Online learning tools have arisen from an underlying goal of creating connections between people. An online learning activity may utilize a private chat room for discussing a children's novel or a Skype session with a class in New Orleans to share Mardi Gras traditions. In order to facilitate these types of connections using online tools, a teacher must draw upon a clearly articulated philosophy of teaching, set the learning objective and purpose for using the online tool, and then choose the appropriate technology tool in order to accomplish the learning goals. Sounds simple enough? Moving through this planning process successfully requires you to be familiar with online tools. The best way to do this is to use the tools yourself. For example, design an events page on Facebook for your family reunion before working with students to design a page for the school carnival. Your own experiences using online tools will be invaluable for teaching your students how to use them. The following discussion focuses on the supporting theories and the knowledge of best practices teachers use when selecting and using online tools, whether in the physical classroom or a virtual environment.

Deciding whether to use online learning tools

A crucial question instructors and teachers at all levels consider when making decisions about using online learning tools for teaching is whether our students can learn something more easily, more interestingly, or more distinctively with these tools than without. This question is the key for us, because, frankly, teaching with technology is fraught with challenges, such as unreliable Internet access, broken links, uncooperative computers, and privacy risks. You must be committed to incorporating technology into your teaching in order to prevent or solve these problems. Even still, you might wonder, why bother? Isn't having a literature discussion group meet face-to-face just as effective as having one meet through Skype? Isn't writing in a journal just as good as writing on a blog? Certainly, each learning tool chosen by a teacher has advantages and disadvantages. Every day teachers weigh these factors to determine which tools best meet the goal and the learning needs of the students. Sometimes these decisions include online technology and sometimes they do not. Remember, technology should help your students learn in new and different ways; technology should not merely be used for technology's sake. Focus on choosing the most effective tool for the situation and needs of students.

author's story   ELIZABETH DOBLER

Collaboration, Technology, and Work

My husband is a civil engineer. He has been trained to design roads, bridges, and water systems and uses various computer applications and software to complete these tasks. He does not design these projects alone, but rather in collaboration with colleagues in different offices, buildings, cities, states, and even countries. To do this, he must not only be able to communicate effectively, but he must also be able to use technology such as video conferencing, instant messaging, and texting, because his profession and his employer expect it. To be successful, engineers and other professionals must know how to do their job, but also be able to work with others. A focus on collaboration in both face-to-face and online teamwork prepares our students to effectively share their ideas and work with others.

Selecting online learning tools

Another challenge teachers face when it comes to choosing online tools is the decision about which tool to use in which situation. Just as when selecting tools in the traditional classroom environment, selecting tools for the online environment requires an awareness of the special needs of students, but high expectations for all learners are still a must. In an online setting, sensitivity to cultural and learning differences should continue to remain in the front of your mind. In addition to these considerations, some online tools provide unique learning opportunities and can even the playing field for students with special learning needs. English language learners can gain information from videos and podcasts along with printed text. More advanced students can find additional ways to learn about new concepts that go beyond the traditional materials found in the classroom. For students with vision or hearing impairments, access to technology for learning helps them fully participate in learning activities through the use of enlarged screens, voice readers, or software that turns speech into typed text.

Before making a decision about online learning tools, first identify a learning objective. Second, ask yourself, "Which online tool will help create the conditions under which students will learn this objective successfully?" For instance, if the objective is to prepare a piece of writing for publication, and a teacher wants students to receive private feedback on a piece of writing from a peer or himself, then email, instant message, or a document sharing site would be the best choice. If a teacher wants students to receive public feedback on a piece of writing, possibly a reaction to the writer's ideas rather than the editing details, then a blog would be a better choice because readers can post comments for all to see. In essence, when making a decision about which online tool to use, the goal for learning drives the tool selection. Online tools do not replace effective teachers, and they are not a substitute for the sound pedagogical practices that guide a teacher's daily instructional decisions.

Listen to the podcast from teacher Ginger Lewman (5:50) about the decision-making process she uses for selecting online communication tools to use with her students. *(Access this podcast in the digital version of this book.)*

Five key priorities impact each teacher's decision about which online tools best match his or her classroom learning goals:(1) enhancing communication, (2) engaging students, (3) promoting collaboration, (4) creating content and opportunities for feedback, and (5) accessing information.

The Compendium of Online Tools (www.hhpcommunities.com/teaching languagearts/IL-03-01.pdf) describes various online learning tools. This is not an exhaustive list; other useful tools exist and new ones are continually being created, but this list is a place to begin. Make it a personal goal to learn more about one or more of the tools you may be unfamiliar with. If you are familiar with the tools, consider how the tools can be used in an educational setting.

Enhancing communication. As with other important decisions, learning through communication in a virtual space should be grounded in best practices and learning theories. For example, a key element of constructivist theory is the use of a group's collective knowledge to solve a problem. Virtual chatting during a project work time through instant messaging or a private chat room, also known as back channeling, both provide a way for the teacher and students to communicate instantly. The teacher's role is to guide the discussion, model appropriate comments, and provide feedback, while the students discuss new ideas, ask questions and summarize information. Read the upcoming Stories from the Classroom about the ways middle school teacher Charlie Mahoney and third grade teacher Scott Ritter use instant messaging and back channeling to spark discussion, manage behaviors, model thinking, and pace learning activities.

stories FROM THE CLASSROOM

Instant messaging

Charlie Mahoney sets the students on a task to locate information about the aftermath of an earthquake in Haiti. He asks that while students are conducting online research that they instant message interesting information they come across to their groups, which Charlie has organized prior to this activity (see Exhibit 3.29). Because Charlie is a member of each instant message group, he monitors the understanding and key ideas the students are sharing during this project. He also monitors their work time and sends an instant message to students who need a reminder to return to the task at hand when their attention wanes. Charlie knows that during their reading about Haiti, students may come across unfamiliar vocabulary words. He anticipates their learning needs and sends an instant message to the students with an explanation of a key word or a tip for using a context clue to determine a word's meaning. Through instant messaging, Charlie also periodically gives reminders of the class time remaining for this project. Charlie uses instant messaging in a face-to-face classroom as a tool to facilitate learning in an online environment. Instant messaging is not the only way students learn in this lesson, but it does give Charlie the opportunity to reach students who might otherwise not respond. It also presents a learning environment that is both motivating and collaborative.

EXHIBIT 3.29

Instant messaging with fifth and sixth graders.

stories FROM THE CLASSROOM

EXHIBIT 3.30

Third grader using back channeling to participate in class discussion.

Back channeling

Third grade teacher Scott Ritter uses the website Today's Meet to create a free private chat room so his class can carry on a virtual discussion during project work time in his face-to-face classroom (see Exhibit 3.30). By having students communicate in this way during work time, Scott can attend to the individual needs of students face-to-face while those who have general questions can pose them to the group and a classmate can answer, all without causing a disruption to others. For one activity the students use the Internet to identify the five highest mountain peaks in the world. As Scott sets up the **virtual meeting room** for the entire class, he encourages students who have questions during the activity to post them in the meeting room for all to see. Then he responds in the meeting room so all can see, or he invites other students to respond, which facilitates students learning from each other. The students are encouraged to follow the conversation during their Internet search, which requires them to multitask between looking for information and following the virtual class discussion. Scott knows that this will be a challenge for some of his students, but he finds that even students lacking strong reading skills are highly motivated to participate in the discussion. Two English language learners in the class have developed stronger skills in written communication than oral, so the meeting room is a place for them to more fully participate in a class discussion. Another student has a speech impediment and rarely contributes orally during class discussions because she is self-conscious. For her, back channeling provides the

chance to be a full participant without the usual hesitancies that occur when she speaks in front of the entire group. Between posting comments, Scott moves around the room, noticing which students need more individualized support. He might respond to students in person or through his comments in the chat room, which may help clarify ideas for all students reading the discussion.

Engaging students. A cutting-edge virtual activity that is likely to engage students are 3-D learning environments and the integration of video gaming principles into educational settings (see Chapter 9 for more information about video gaming in education). In Sloodle, an online tool that uses 3-D elements to encourage collaborative and interactive learning, each student creates an avatar, a character that represents him- or herself. The student designs the character, choosing physical features, then the character participates in class activities as the student. In one example, created in Second Life and displayed on the Sloodle website, English teacher Mike McKay has created a virtual room, a den complete with fireplace, oak bookshelves, and comfortable chairs, where five students meet to discuss a reading assignment (see Exhibit 3.31). As a student shares reactions to the reading assignment, Mr. McKay records feedback and grades assignments, which are made available on the Moodle website and inworld via the SLOODLE module. Throughout the discussion, the students and teacher view this virtual room, see each other's avatars, and communicate with each other via voice chat. The teacher has crafted a virtual world with the Second Life building tools that promotes student interaction, a key factor of engagement in learning. Virtual learning environments provide opportunities to present information and organize activities in a way that is novel and motivating for many students (and teachers).

A virtual learning classroom shared on Sloodle.

Take a few minutes to explore Sloodle. Log-in is now required (https://www.sloodle.org/), but once logged in you may watch the tutorial video (Part 1: 4:25; Part 2: 6:46; Part 3: 3:54). After viewing, consider the pros and cons of using Sloodle to introduce a new unit or to review information at the end of a unit. Then decide for yourself whether you are interested in further exploring the topic of learning in a virtual setting.

Encouraging students to learn from and work with others. Online tools let students make connections across space and time, both in the classroom and beyond its walls. Students can be full participants in our global society through email pen pals, video conferencing with experts from around the world, and online chats with a small group from around the globe or in their own classroom. The foundation behind the development of many online learning tools stems from a value of sharing, a prominent theme of the constructivist theory. If, as Piaget believed, learning is the interaction between experiences and ideas, then the collaborative nature of online tools promotes these valuable interactions. Wikis and document sharing websites provide opportunities for two or more people to collaborate on the same document, giving the chance for writing, revising, and editing to be a truly collaborative endeavor. Collaborative games, such as *Words with Friends,* played on a smartphone or a tablet encourage virtual friends to build on each other's vocabulary knowledge. Social bookmarking websites, such as Diigo, let students and teachers collect, store, and share websites relating to a specific topic, such as outer space or the children's/young adult author Lois Lowry. An online discussion board, like the one in Edmodo, lets students extend a face-to-face discussion beyond the class session or beyond the classroom walls. Learn how Jan Wells, a fourth grade teacher in Kansas, and Paula Naugle, a fourth grade teacher in Louisiana, encourage collaboration between their classes using Skype, Edmodo, and Google Docs in the upcoming Stories from the Classroom.

stories FROM THE CLASSROOM

Video conferencing

Jan Wells and Paula Naugle, both fourth grade teachers, follow similar social studies curricular standards, although they teach in Kansas and Louisiana. One of the standards calls for students to study the United States Constitution. Paula arranges for a guest speaker to share information about the Constitution and invites Jan's class to join the presentation via Skype. During the presentation, Paula and Jan each select four students to summarize ideas from the speaker on a discussion board in Edmodo, available to both classes. After the presentation, individual students from both classes are able to ask the speaker questions or to share a personal connection with the groups. The next day, the classes jointly prepare a list of frequently asked questions (FAQs) and answers about the Constitution using Google Docs. The finalized list will be published to the class website. Although the activity promotes learning about the Constitution, students gain many other important skills through collaboration and the use of technology.

Learning from and working with others are skills that benefit students long after they leave our classrooms. Purposeful use of online learning tools arms students with the skills they need to meet head-on the changes occurring both in school and in the world of work. The use of such tools is purposeful when it is linked directly to learning objectives and best practices. For example, a wiki may have two main uses in the classroom. One is to serve as a place to store and display information, where several people can add elements, but the elements basically remain static. Another more dynamic use of a wiki is for a group to collaborate on a project that may include written text, images, web links, and video/audio files. Group members can add, delete, and edit, and the wiki stores a record of all changes. Grounded in both the sociocultural and constructivist theories, a wiki used in this collaborative way can become a collection of the group's insights and knowledge.

Fifth grade teacher Diane Kimsey and her students created a wiki to collect their learning about the Revolutionary War. This collaborative effort served not only as a culmination of their unit but also promoted a feeling of pride and a sense of accomplishment among the class as a whole. After viewing the Revolutionary War wiki (http://meadows-ss-project.wikispaces.com) mentally list three ways students might have collaborated in its creation.

Creating content and opportunities for feedback. Online tools and the accompanying attitude of sharing provide users with various formats for creating messages along with access to an audience. Content creation tools such as Glogster, Voice Thread, and Vimeo give users the opportunity to create content, receive feedback, and give feedback to others. With the popularity of mobile devices and apps, such as GoKnow, students can create documents, sketches, video, and audio files using a smartphone and then upload or email the work directly to a computer so projects can be shared with others. Because content creation tools utilize images, sound, video, and text, the semiotic theory provides an underpinning for their use in the classroom. In the presence of an audience, teachers, and hopefully their students, will place a high priority on grammar, spelling, and punctuation, recognizing the importance of getting their message across to others professionally. In the upcoming Stories from the Classroom, Erin Fitzpatrick addresses the need for an awareness of audience when using the microblogging tool Twitter to report the school news.

stories FROM THE CLASSROOM

Microblogging

Erin Fitzpatrick works with intermediate students to publicize classroom events and news in a microblogging format (see Exhibit 3.32). Although students do write traditional news articles about school happenings and post these on the school website, they also compose tweets, or microblog entries, to share through the school Twitter account. Anyone who has signed up to follow the school on Twitter will receive the announcements of school news on their Twitter feed. Erin encourages students to consider three things when writing a tweet: what is happening, who is reading the tweet, and how can it be summarized in only a few words. Each tweet can be only 140 characters, so when a student's message is too long, the textbox forces the student to edit until the character limit is met. Erin helps students identify the key point of their message, parsing away unnecessary words while retaining meaning, which is not a simple task for some writers.

Erin requires standard English conventions be used by students, although some microbloggers develop a form of shorthand that uses **emoticons** and **textisms** to condense messages into fewer characters. Because these messages represent the school to the outside world, Erin does not feel these shortcuts are appropriate. Erin continually reminds students their audience could be anyone who chooses to follow the school on Twitter, but more specifically it will be their families, their principal, and their fellow classmates. Such a wide audience motivates even the most reluctant writers to make sure their work represents their best skills.

EXHIBIT 3.32

School news on Twitter.

Today we had a Global Nomads Conference. We were talking with other people around the world discussing Haiti.
10:00 AM Mar 24th via web

Our 6/7/8 Graders helped some college students with presentation tools, while the Fifth and Sixth were in a Video Conference with Haiti.
9:53 AM Mar 24th via web

Today in Global Studies we have been showing off our Ancient China Artifacts for our Ancient China Museum.
12:45 PM Mar 23rd via web

Today in science, we learned about the human anatomy.
10:12 AM Mar 23rd via web

This quarter we are starting a new way of doing things in news. We are going to be broad casting the articles that we will be writing.
9:53 AM Mar 23rd via web

We are about to skype with the high school to discuss "The Art of Learning".
7:10 AM Mar 23rd via web

A blog is another tool for creating content and receiving feedback. Typically, bloggers share their own thoughts and opinions, often purposefully enticing controversy to promote discussion. When used in the classroom, teachers and students should develop a set of expectations for blog posts that ensure everyone feels they can respond safely and without being judged.

To begin thinking about the blogging expectations you and your students might set for your classroom, view this list of blogging do's and don'ts: www.hhpcommunities.com/teachinglanguagearts/IL-03-02.pdf

Simple to create, a blog can also be used as an alternative to a website for those who consider themselves less than savvy with technology. Teachers who use blogs should be aware that not all students and families have access to computers on a regular basis. A blog can be seen as an extension of the classroom, but teachers should still make efforts to communicate with parents in ways that do not require a computer.

Kindergarten teacher Laura Patrick has created the blog Kinderkids (http://lpatrick29.edublogs.org), in which she shares information for her students and their parents. She also invites students and parents to post comments of their own, thereby extending the dialogue of learning beyond the classroom.

Providing instant access to information. Smartphones and other mobile devices, such as tablets, make information portable. Information now lies in the palm of our hands, to be consumed or created at our will. Instant access to information can impact the ways we teach and what we learn. For example, a behaviorist view of learning might promote the memorization of the 50 states and their capitals. A constructivist view would support using the Internet for finding a specific state capital and then incorporating that information into a digital learning project. Whatever your philosophy, it is impossible to ignore the impact of our ability to find information quickly via mobile devices. Access to so much information provides teachers with the opportunity to model efficient ways to use the Internet to answer both specific and big idea questions (see upcoming Stories from the Classroom). Issues of Internet safety surface as teachers look for ways to direct students to appropriate and useful information on websites. Social bookmarking tools, such as Diigo (text-based, www.diigo.com), Pinterest (picture-based, www.pinterest.com), and Symbaloo (icon-based, www.symbaloo.com), can be used to create a collection of teacher-approved websites students can use for their Internet research.

stories FROM THE CLASSROOM

Smartphones to access information

In her combination first and second grade classroom in Boulder City, Nevada, Pam Albin uses her smartphone to help students access information. During a science lesson on animals of Africa, the students discussed how weather conditions in Africa affected the animals. One student asked what the temperature actually was in Africa, and Pam used her smartphone to check the current weather conditions in Monrovia, a city in Liberia, in West Africa. She then used this information to begin a graph on a piece of poster paper. Each day, Pam and the students added the updated weather conditions to the graph. Each day they compared the weather conditions in Liberia to those in Nevada and discussed the reasons why the conditions might be similar or different. Pam modeled for her students how to instantly access information and how it can facilitate learning (see Exhibit 3.33).

EXHIBIT 3.33

Checking the weather conditions in Africa using a smartphone.

Instant access to information does not always come from the Internet; sometimes it comes from each other. Texting gives students the opportunity to communicate with others quickly. Seventy-five percent of 12- to 17-year-olds have a cell phone, and 88 percent of adolescent cell phone owners send text messages. An earlier study showed just over half of all adolescents texting on a daily basis (Lenhart, 2010), and that percentage is surely higher now. Data for children under 12 are not available, although anecdotal evidence

Cell phones in school.

from elementary school teachers indicates students as young as seven or eight are bringing cell phones to school more frequently than ever before. When asked about the use of mobile devices in the classroom, teacher Carol Dolman says, "The more we discover what we can do with them, the more valuable they are. If you can harness what students are interested in, you have massive amounts of potential. And if you can get that into the classroom, you're set" (Rapp, 2009). How can teachers channel the energy and enthusiasm for texting into an educational purpose? See Exhibit 3.34. In districts that allow it, some teachers are working to do just that (see this Stories from the Classroom) in ways that keep students engaged in learning while at the same time addressing safety and ethical issues.

stories FROM THE CLASSROOM

Using cell phones to promote spelling

Middle school teacher Tony Ramirez knows that most of the students in his language arts class have a cell phone hidden in a pocket or backpack. Occasionally, he catches a glimpse of these devices, which are expected to be put away during class. One day he surprises the students by asking them to take out their phones for an activity. He asks them to text three people who are not in school and ask them to spell a difficult word. Within seconds, the challenging spelling words begin to arrive on the screens. Friends and family share words like *broccoli* and *vacuum,* and Tony makes a list of the various spellings on an interactive whiteboard. He then has them put away their phones and continues the lesson, discussing difficult spots in tricky words. In this activity, cell phones captured students' attention and motivated them to discuss spelling.

Issues with the online learning environment

Previously in this chapter, we described the use of tools like Skype, Blogger, or Wikispaces in promoting learning, but let's look more specifically at how these tools should and should not be used with students. We will explore the value and limitations of using virtual learning tools in the classroom and instructional resources available for topics such as netiquette and online ethics. Researchers at Harvard University have studied the *good play* of technology, in other words, "online conduct that is both meaningful and engaging to the participant and responsible to others in the community and society in which it is carried out" (James et al., 2008, p. 2). Such uses of technology pose definite benefits to students. Through the Internet, young people can feel empowered by contributing their expertise to knowledge communities and building connections to those near and far. This empowerment helps to establish their identity, gives them confidence, and builds their knowledge of the world both on- and offline. When a first grader shows her parents where her teddy bear poem is published on the class website, she gains confidence as a writer. When a third grader visits the blog of his favorite author, Seymour Simon (www.seymoursimon.com/index.php/blog) and reads about Simon's own antics as a child, he feels a connection to that author. When a fifth grader speaks to a student in India through the Digital Nomads program, he broadens his understanding of the world.

Throughout this chapter, we have shared the ways online tools can be used to promote collaboration and communication. Now let's focus on the cautions and responsibilities that come with using such tools, because issues of safety are every teacher's responsibility.

Digital etiquette

As in any public community, rules of politeness and respect ensure that everyone can coexist, and these rules are known as etiquette. These rules include listening quietly when someone else is talking and saying "hello" and "good-bye" when speaking on the telephone. Although not necessarily written down, rules of etiquette are seen as common courtesy. An online learning environment is a virtual public learning community, and a collection of commonly accepted rules on ways people should communicate online is known as *netiquette* or network etiquette. Both etiquette and netiquette give structure to communication and remind us to consider the needs of readers, listeners, and viewers. Online, people, including students, may forget that a real person exists beyond their representation on the screen. Many individuals send emails, text messages, or tweets they later regret because they did not consider the other person's feelings and interpretations before hitting the send button.

As a public community, Internet users are expected to act in a way that makes the digital world a safe and pleasant experience for all. Sharing this digital space is a positive experience when people speak politely; are considerate of others when using computers, Internet access, and cell phones in public; and give credit to the work of others in the course of their research. Kathy Furgang, in her book *Netiquette: A Student's Guide to Digital Etiquette* (2011), suggests the following guidelines for students working on a school project:

- Keep all emails professional by using proper English and punctuation.
- Be aware of the needs of others when using public Internet access: limit your time on public computers and focus only on necessary work; do not "borrow" Internet access from unknown wi-fi sources, otherwise known as piggybacking.
- Give credit to others' work by citing your sources for written words, videos, and audio files, including podcasts and songs found on the Internet. Provide the date accessed and the URL, and seek permission to use copyrighted material. (More specific information about Internet copyright policies can be found in Chapter 10.)

The key to netiquette is having a constant awareness of others, both virtual and face-to-face, along with an understanding of how our words and actions portray ourselves. We as teachers, parents, and community members must help young people understand that digital communication, including texts, photos, emails, and instant messages, can be shared with anyone else. We may trust the person to whom we are sending the message, but no one knows what the future holds or where that message may end up. This can be a difficult concept for young people to grasp, and teaching netiquette must begin when students first encounter technology. Since the language arts are about sending and receiving messages, these lessons fall into the realm of language arts instruction, but they can be taught by all teachers. Personal netiquette suggestions include:

- Share limited information online. Encourage students to only share a first name or pseudonym and no other personal information.
- Post only photos that show you behaving responsibly.
- Keep online messages (including texting) positive and polite. Cyberbullying involves insults, put-downs, along with threats and harassment. Before hitting the send button, pause and reconsider your words.

- Put away your cell phone when in a face-to-face conversation, a classroom, or a public performance. Texting and talking on a cell phone while someone else is talking is impolite.

Although it would appear that there are no boundaries in cyberspace, this is absolutely not true. Students need the guidance of adults in understanding and setting these boundaries for themselves. Politeness may simply involve wearing headphones when listening on a public computer or moving to another room during a cell phone conversation. As in any communication with others, our words and actions reveal much about us, including our own levels of caring and self-restraint. The eighteenth-century German poet Johann Wolfgang von Goethe wrote, "A man's manners are a mirror in which he shows his portrait." He could not have imagined how accurately his words would be applied to the digital age some 200 years later.

Digital footprints

Our **digital footprint** is the record of our online activities and reveals much about us to those who seek such information. This footprint is constantly growing and changing as we join new groups, share information about ourselves, and conduct more business online. Some elements of the trail have been purposefully put there by us, such as a Facebook page or a travel blog of our trip to the Grand Canyon. Other elements are added through our membership in organizations, participation in events, payment of taxes, or even receipt of a traffic ticket. This digital footprint is a reflection of our choices, actions, beliefs, and values. If you are unsure about your own digital footprint, take a minute and check out the inset for "Protecting Your Digital Identity."

Protecting your digital identity

Google yourself. Type your first and last name in the search box and see what you come up with. Then go back and add your middle name and see what is different. First, determine which entries are truly about you and not someone with the same name. Note how much information is available to anyone who Googles you, say a future employer, a scholarship application committee, or even the family of your students. Ask yourself if this is the image you want to portray. If not, consider the possibility of adding online elements to enhance what people know about you, like keeping a blog to document your hobby of dog training or joining Shelfari (www.shelfari.com), a social network for those who like to read. Locate online elements that you are less than proud of, such as unflattering photographs or tweets about activities that portray you in a less than positive light. Remove as many of these as you can. For example, you can contact the blog host and ask for a comment to be deleted. Remove those questionable photographs from your Facebook page or other site. Although we may not have complete control over our digital footprint, we can shape our digital destiny with awareness and diligence.

When crafting your digital footprint, the goal is to reveal enough information without revealing too much, an important concept for teachers and students alike. Utilizing various online features lets others find us more easily and facilitates connections and the sharing of information, all of which can be both good and bad. An online presence enhances our ability to make personal connections, such as inviting a long-lost schoolmate to the class reunion, sharing information with someone else who gets cluster headaches like you do, or finding your true love (as in the case of one of this textbook's authors). However, an online presence puts us at risk for exploitation by those who are less than scrupulous. Being aware of the benefits and risks of having your own online presence is an important first step toward conveying this valuable information to your students.

spotlight ON A LITERACY LEADER

WILL RICHARDSON

Will Richardson is on a mission to share the value of bringing online learning tools into classrooms with educators, students, and parents. Being a public school teacher for 22 years, a parent, a speaker, and an author have shaped his thinking about the need for educators to fully utilize the benefits the Internet has to offer. Web 2.0 tools provide boundless opportunities for classroom education, if they are undertaken with thought, planning, and skill. Richardson questions the status quo and challenges others to do the same on his blog, Read. Write. Connect. Learn. (http://willrichardson.com), on Twitter (@Willrich45), and through video clips and published books. Consider adding Will Richardson's Twitterfeed or blog to your personal learning network.

View Will Richardson on the video Personal Learning Networks (3:42, www.youtube.com/watch?v=mghGV37TeK8) as he talks about the shift among teachers and students to reach out from their classrooms to build online connections and find new information from trusted sources. Chapter 2 introduced the idea of creating your own personal learning network. Consider what you have done in the past week or two to use or add to your personal learning network and use online tools to learn new ideas for school and for your personal life.

Because of security concerns, some might like to avoid the Internet altogether, though this is not advised. Even though you may not want to share information about yourself, in many instances you cannot prevent it when your name is part of the public record or when it is distributed by others. Pew Research reports that, even while Internet users are becoming more aware of their digital footprints, surprisingly few of them try to limit access to their information (Madden, Fox, Smith, & Vitak, 2007). As the saying goes, "the best defense is a good offense," which means you should craft your digital footprint to reflect the qualities you want others to see. This may also mean limiting access to your profile on Facebook or making your blog private instead of public. In creating a Twitter account, users encounter the following statement in the terms of agreement: "What you say on Twitter may be viewed all around the world instantly. You are what you Tweet!" (Twitter, 2010). Some employers have come to expect to find you on the Internet. Having such a presence can not only reveal a level of professionalism, but it can also demonstrate your technical knowledge, as well as an awareness of the role social networking plays both in and outside the field of education.

To learn more about your digital footprint, view the video Digital Dossier (4:24, www.youtube.com/watch?v=79IYZVYIVLA). Then share this video with a friend or family member. Next, talk together about the emotions each of you felt watching this video clip.

Students should not be left to develop their own digital footprint for various reasons. Students must be 13 years old to create a social media account on many sites such as Facebook, Twitter, Shelfari, and Blogger. The creation of an account is considered a legally binding agreement that goes into effect when the user checks the "I agree" box. Younger children typically do not have the maturity or experience to understand the responsibilities and issues that such an agreement entails. Teachers should help students understand this and not encourage them to disregard these guidelines. Some sites, such as Edmodo (www.edmodo.com) are designed to give students of all ages access through a teacher's account, so no private information is required of the students. Explore these sites carefully and be familiar with your school district's policies for classroom Internet use before using an online tool for an instructional project. Teachers can and should use online tools with students to prepare them for the time when they are able to create their own account.

Students, and even some adults, fail to understand the long-term implication of inappropriate posts on the Internet. They need guidance in understanding that online posts may follow a person long into their future, so careful decisions are a must. Such an important lesson can be taught using a scaffolded environment. This means teaching students how to use social media through the modeling and guidance of an adult. One way to scaffold, or provide some structure, is for the teacher to create a social media account, such as a blog, which belongs to the class. Before posting any written work, the class and teacher develop a list of netiquette expectations, which is also shared with families. Early on, all posts must be approved by the teacher. As trust and experience develops, the teacher can share the user ID and password for the blog so that students can post their own work. Classmates and families are charged with policing the class blog to ensure appropriateness and report netiquette violations to the teacher. Through this guided activity, students learn the art of crafting digital messages that reflect a positive image.

points2ponder

QUICK REVIEW 7 What is your digital footprint? What are two things a person can do to craft their digital footprint?

(Access answers in the digital version of this book.)

Public is the new private: Online safety

Even with all of the opportunities for collaboration, learning, and creating, an online learning environment can be fraught with hidden and not-so-hidden dangers for students. Educators must actively seek ways to protect the very students they are teaching while at the same time teaching students how to protect themselves. This protection begins with teaching students about their digital footprint. Help them become aware of the information already available about themselves and the need to make careful choices about future online sharing. Careless over-sharing can have a long-term effect on young people of all ages. Weber (2006) asserts that "public is the new private. Young people often realize that their blogs and homepages are public and accessible, but they trust that only their peers are interested enough to view them." Silverstone (2007) calls for a proper distance where online users preserve individual privacy while at the same time creating an air of openness to community. Privacy is the overarching theme in these lessons, with an emphasis on carefully managing the disclosure of information. Some may say these are issues best left to middle and high school teachers. Because of children's privacy issues, little reliable data exist regarding the number of elementary school children sharing personal information on the Internet. However, since issues of privacy and safety are so crucial, one could make the argument that waiting until students are able to use the social networking tools on their own is too late to begin this instruction. Online safety typically falls into the categories of safety and judgment, both of which require much guidance from more experienced adults.

Safety focuses on keeping private any information that reveals more about a person than others need to know. Adults must help young people find a balance between the dangers of not guarding their identity and the powerful learning opportunities of collaboration within a virtual environment. Young people tend to believe that the Internet is anonymous. Although they may have a vague notion of Internet predators, they often think they will be able to easily recognize an online predator and nothing bad will happen as a result. These are false impressions that can expose students to safety risks. The Children's Internet Protection Act (www.fcc.gov/guides/childrens-internet-protection-act) and other federal, state, and local laws address many of these safety risks, but implementation of these laws often falls to parents and other adults who monitor Internet use by young people. Educators must communicate with parents exactly how the Internet will be used in class and for what purpose.

points2ponder

QUICK REVIEW 8 Why would a teacher want to allow public access to information he/she posts on the Internet?

(Access answers in the digital version of this book.)

stories FROM THE CLASSROOM

Internet safety

The teachers at Turning Point Learning Center, a charter middle school, created an Internet use policy to clarify to students, families, and educators the ways the Internet will be used at their school. The policy includes a rationale for using the Internet as a learning tool, a detailed description of how students will be using the Internet, and how this use will be monitored. Also spelled out are the Internet use expectations for students, teachers, and families. Sharing this information at the beginning of the school year opens the dialogue for Internet safety issues because monitoring students' use is a partnership between home and school. Both students and caregivers sign the form to show their commitment to Internet safety. Read an excerpt from the Turning Point Learning Center Internet Use Policy: www.hhpcommunities.com/teachinglanguagearts/IL-03-03.pdf.

Another important step is to teach students to never talk to people online they do not know in person and to guard their identity by not revealing their full name or place of residence during online communication. Screen names should include only a first name or be a pseudonym so that only selected friends and family know the student's true identity.

The website I Keep Safe (http://ikeepsafe.org) has additional information about Internet safety issues. Visit this website, click on the "For Parents" link, and decide which resource you would recommend families view first as a starting point for learning about digital reputation, the myth of anonymity, and cyberbullying.

Some online issues are not necessarily safety concerns, but instead portray a person in an unfavorable light and reflect poor judgment. The seemingly anonymous nature of the Internet contributes to this problem. People tend to put thoughts into words that they would otherwise not say directly to a person, as may be the case with cyberbullying. **Flaming** refers to hostile or insulting comments people make back and forth to each other and demonstrates the importance of using good judgment and thinking carefully before sending a message. Often, others can see these comments, whether it's an email message gone **viral** or a comment on someone's Facebook page. As described previously, teachers can play a key influential role in helping students develop good judgment by modeling their own words and actions online. Talk with students about what it means to be a good digital citizen, or **digicitizen,** meaning being polite, ethical, and safe when communicating online. Scaffolding provides a safety net for students to learn the valuable lessons of collaboration and awareness of a global society without putting them at risk.

Listen to this podcast with Ginger Lewman on digital citizenry (3:43). How does she define being a digital citizen? How does she help students learn that they are not anonymous and need to communicate responsibly online? *(Access this podcast in the digital version of this book.)*

Where to begin with online learning environments?

Teachers who use technology themselves put more emphasis on twenty-first century skills in their own teaching, including collaboration, critical thinking, problem solving, and self-direction (Grunwald & Associates, 2010). To receive the full educational benefits from using technology for promoting learning, follow these practices:

- Be as fearless as your students. Make a commitment to learning new technologies and applications.
- Seek out or create opportunities to collaborate with and learn from your peers when it comes to new technologies.
- Evaluate continuing education opportunities and consider options that integrate technology and twenty-first century skills development into the curriculum.
- Communicate with parents about classroom expectations for students using social networking technologies.

For some, integrating technology into your teaching will be seamless because you have already integrated technology into many aspects of your life. But having a Twitter account and using Twitter to learn about teaching the language arts may be two very different things. Others may have embraced technology in their personal lives on a limited basis, sticking with tried and true email and texting for close family and friends. No matter where you fall on the technology spectrum, keep in mind the need for flexibility and openness to change. Don Leu, in his work on new literacies, describes the challenges of dealing with the continuous and rapid change of technology (2000). This continuous change sends out a ripple, which impacts the ways we communicate with others. As with a ripple in a pond, this change goes on and on. Change is the one thing we can count on, so let's prepare our students for this continuous change in the ways we communicate with each other.

3.6

CHAPTER SUMMARY

This chapter focuses on ways for students to collaborate and communicate in any type of learning environment. To promote these skills, you must first articulate your personal beliefs about teaching by developing your own philosophy. This philosophy, based on experiences and knowledge of learning theories, guides your decisions about the learning environment. You design an environment or choose tools to promote learning, whether face-to-face or virtual, that reflects best practices identified by standards and a personal philosophy based on learning theories and experiences, with an emphasis on the ways students can collaborate and communicate. In Chapter 4 we will look at the nuts and bolts of teaching by exploring the alignment between what we teach (objectives) and how we teach (instruction).

APPLICATION ACTIVITIES
think like a teacher

Designing a Classroom

Consider this scenario: You are a student teacher in a third grade classroom. Your mentor teacher, Ms. Omni, has been teaching third grade in the same classroom for 17 years. This year she wants to try something new; she wants you to design the classroom because she expects you to have fresh and innovative ideas. Ms. Omni is willing to let you try just about anything with the room arrangement, as long as you can justify your choices with professional knowledge. She thinks it's important you know the following about the 25 students who will soon arrive in the classroom:

- one student is legally blind
- four students are identified as gifted
- five students are English language learners
- two students have issues with anxiety and/or aggression

Your task is to design a classroom that gives careful consideration to the special needs of these students along with the learning needs of the group as a whole. Draw upon the knowledge you gained from Chapter 3 about learning theories, visual displays, and room arrangement. The following are must-haves in your classroom: A whole group area, small group area, classroom library, literacy work stations, and desks/tables. With other classroom design elements, you have free rein. Because this is a simulation, and we have not listed specific equipment or furniture, the sky is the limit with the other details of your classroom design. You choose the tool for creating your design, whether it's a piece of graph paper, chart paper, poster, or a design created with an online tool like Google SketchUp (http://sketchup.

google.com), Classroom Architect (http://classroom.4teachers.org/), or the Classroom Layout app for the iPad. Along with your design, create a written rationale for your decisions. Make specific references to the learning theories discussed in Chapter 3 (behaviorism, socioculturalism, semiotics, and constructivism) and other key elements about classroom design described in the chapter.

Comparing Social Bookmarking Sites

So many online tools, and so little time! This activity gives you the opportunity to collaboratively evaluate which of two social bookmarking sites will work best for you. The two sites we suggest are Diigo and Delicious, although you can substitute another for this activity if you choose. In Chapter 3, we discussed what a social bookmarking site is and how it might be used in the classroom. As a first step, review this information and watch the video about bookmarking on Common Craft (www.commoncraft.com/video/social-bookmarking). Then do the following:

- Increase your general knowledge about social bookmarking in general, and Diigo (http://en.wikipedia.org/wiki/Diigo) and Delicious (http://en.wikipedia.org/wiki/Delicious_%28website%29) more specifically, by reading about each on Wikipedia (http://en.wikipedia.org/wiki/Social_bookmarking). Take notes to help you remember similarities, differences, and interesting information so you can compare and contrast the two sites before making your decision.
- Next, learn about Diigo and Delicious by visiting their websites. Watch their tutorial videos, explore the site, and take notes about the specific features. Read the website blog where users describe their experiences with the site. Look for satisfied and unsatisfied users and note their reasons.
- Synthesize your findings to create a display that compares and contrasts the two social bookmarking sites. This display can be created on paper, a poster, or a computer to be shared with others. Consider what you found to be the most interesting information you found, and decide on a format that best facilitates sharing this information.
- Once you've created your display, practice orally presenting your information, which will be the next step of this project.
- After viewing the oral presentations and displays, decide whether you will use Diigo or Delicious as a teacher. Weigh the pros and cons of each, then write down your choice and give a written explanation for making it. Support your opinion with specific examples about the site.

Writing Your Philosophy of Teaching

Where do you begin writing your philosophy of teaching? For some, writing this philosophy will come easily; the words will just flow. For others, this activity will be quite challenging, and that challenge begins with deciding what elements make up your philosophy. If you already have your ideas formulated, this sequence may not be necessary. If not, then consider this sequence a scaffold to set you on the path.

- **Brainstorm.** A philosophy is based on your experiences, so begin by bringing these experiences to the front of your mind. Grab a piece of paper or bring up a blank word document on your computer and make a two-column chart. Label one column "positive experiences" and the other "negative experiences," then list specific learning experiences you enjoyed or did not enjoy during your school career. Keep it brief. For example, list "group projects" rather than the story of how you were always paired with a student who did not pull her weight and who you felt took advantage of your hard work. Also, consider all levels of schooling including elementary, middle, high school, and college. Aim for five to ten items in each column.

- **Identify professional knowledge.** Just below your two-column chart, list a few learning theories to which you have made a personal connection. Include the theory and four to six examples of how that theory would impact decisions in the classroom. For a model, refer back to Exhibit 3.6. The four theories described in this chapter (behaviorism, semiotics, socioculturalism, and constructivism) are merely a starting point. You may also include other theories you have learned during your teacher education program.

- **Consider a motivational saying or phrase.** Although not required, some teachers will include a motivational saying or phrase that inspires them or represents their beliefs about teaching and learning.

- **Add your values.** Consider aspects of your future classroom that fall into the categories of "must haves" and "might be nice." A "must have" might be a strong emphasis on writing. A "might be nice" could be having class meetings once a week to sort out social issues or plan class activities.

- **From this collection of ideas, your philosophy will emerge.** Remember, there are no wrong answers when it comes to your teaching philosophy. You simply must be able to articulate your philosophy in an organized and clear manner. Do not write what you think others will want to read, but write what represents you as a knowledgeable professional. Choose a format for the philosophy. This can be a descriptive paragraph, a bulleted list, or some other style. Give careful attention to editing. Get a friend or classmate to read over your work, give suggestions, and point out misspellings. Let the person who will read your philosophy (future employer, scholarship application committee, teaching abroad coordinator) know that you have given careful attention to grammar, punctuation, and spelling so that your work displays your professional knowledge and skills.

REFERENCES

Baker, E. A. (2010). *The new literacies: Multiple perspectives on research and practice.* New York: Guilford.

Blanchard, J., & Moore, T. (2010). The digital world of young children: Impact on emergent literacy. Pearson Foundation http://www.pearsonfoundation.org/downloads/EmergentLiteracy-WhitePaper.pdf.

Cunningham, D. J. (1992). Beyond educational psychology: Steps toward an educational semiotic. *Educational Psychology Review, 4*(2) 165–194.

Danielson, C. (n.d.). The framework for teaching. http://www2.parkridge.k12.nj.us/PDFs%20technology/Framework_for_Teaching_C_Danielson.pdf

Danielson, C. (2007). *Enhancing professional practice: A framework for teaching,* 2nd ed. Alexandria, VA: Association for Supervision and Curriculum Development.

Diller, D. (2008). *Spaces and places: Designing classrooms for literacy.* York, ME: Stenhouse.

Duncan, A. (2010). Using technology to transform schools. http://www.ed.gov/news/speeches/using-technology-transform-schools%E2%80%94remarks-secretary-arne-duncan-association-american-

Eco, U. (1976). *A theory of semiotics.* Bloomington: Indiana University Press.

Flavell, J. H. (1976). Metacognitive aspects of problem solving. In L. B. Resnick (Ed.), *The nature of intelligence* (pp. 231–236). Hillsdale, NJ: Erlbaum.

Furgang, K. (2011). *Netiquette: A student's guide to digital etiquette.* New York: Rosen.

Gardner, H. (1983). *Frames of mind: The theory of multiple intelligences.* New York: Basic Books.

Graves, D. (1994). *A fresh look at writing.* Portsmouth, NH: Heinemann.

Grunwald & Associates. (2010). Education, technology, and 21st century skills: Dispelling five myths. Walden University. http://www.waldenu.edu/Documents/Degree-Programs/Report_Summary_-_Dispelling_Five_Myths.pdf

Halliday, M. K. (1978). *Language as social semiotic: The social interpretation of language and meaning.* Baltimore, MD: University Park Press.

International Reading Association (IRA). (2010). *Standards for reading professionals—revised 2010.* Retrieved from http://www.reading.org/General/CurrentResearch/Standards/ProfessionalStandards.aspx.

James, C., Kavis, K., Flores, A., Francis, J. M., Pettingill, L., Rundle, M., & Gardner, H. (2008). *Young people, ethics, and the new digital media: A synthesis from The Good Play Project.* Harvard Graduate School of Education. http://www.pz.harvard.edu/eBookstore/PDFs/Goodwork54.pdf

Johnson, D. W., Johnson, R. T., & Smith, K. A. (1998). *Active learning: Cooperation in the college classroom,* 2nd ed. Edina, MN: Interaction Book.

Jones, F. H., Jones, P., Lynn, J., & Jones, F. (2007). *Tools for teaching: Discipline, instruction, & motivation.* Santa Cruz, CA: Fredric H. Jones.

Kinzer, C., & Leu, D. J. (1997). The challenge of change: Exploring literacy and learning in electronic environments. *Language Arts, 74*(2), 126–136.

Kozar, D. (2010). Towards better group work: Seeing the difference between cooperation and collaboration. *English Teaching Forum* (2), 16–23. http://exchanges.state.gov/englishteaching/forum/archives/docs/files-folder111111/48_2-etf-towards-better-group-work-seeing-the-difference-between-cooperation-and-collaboration.pdf

Labbo, L. D. (1996). A semiotic analysis of young children's symbol making in a classroom computer center. *Reading Research Quarterly, 31*(4), 356–383.

Lenhart, A. (2010). *Teens and mobile phones.* Pew Internet and American Life Project. http://pewinternet.org/Reports/2010/Teens-and-Mobile-Phones.aspx

Leu, D. J. (2000). Literacy and technology: Deictic consequences for literacy education in an information age. In M. Kamil, P. B. Mosenthal, P. D. Pearson, & R. Barr (Eds.), *Handbook of reading research,* Vol. 3 (pp. 743–770). Mahwah, NJ: Erlbaum.

Madden, M., Fox, S., Smith, A., & Vitak, J. (2007). *Digital footprints: Online identity management and search in the age of transparency.* Pew Internet and American Life Project. http://www.pewinternet.org/pdfs/PIP_Digital_Footprints.pdf

National Aeronautics and Space Administration (NASA). (2012). http://www.nasa.gov/

National Governors Association Center for Best Practices & Council of Chief State School Officers. (2010). Common Core State Standards. Washington, DC: Author. http://www.corestandards.org/the-standards/english-language-arts-standards

New, R. (1993). Reggio Emilia: Some lessons for U.S. educators. http://www.ericdigests.org/1993/reggio.htm

Piaget, J. (1972). *To understand is to invent.* New York: Viking.

Rapp, D. (2009). Lift the cell phone ban. http://www2.scholastic.com/browse/article.jsp?id=3751073

Rosenblatt, L. (1978). *The reader, the text, the poem: The transactional theory of the literary work.* Carbondale, IL: Southern Illinois Press; rev. ed., 1994.

Schon, D. A. (1987). *Educating the reflective practitioner: Toward a new design for teaching and learning in the professions.* San Francisco: Jossey-Bass.

Silverstone, R. (2007). *Media and morality: On the rise of the mediapolis.* Cambridge, UK: Polity Press.

Skinner, B. F. (1974). *About behaviorism.* New York: Random House.

Slavin, R. E. (1995). *Cooperative learning* (2nd ed.). Boston: Allyn and Bacon.

Twitter. (2010). Terms of service. https://twitter.com/tos

Vygotsky, L. (1978). *Mind in society: The development of higher psychological processes.* Cambridge, MA: Harvard University Press.

Weber, S. (2006, 12 December). Sandra Weber thinks that "public" is young people's new "private." MacArthur Spotlight blog. http://spotlight.macfound.org/main/entry/sandra_weber_public_young_people_private/

Wertsch, J. (1991). *Voices of the mind: A sociocultural approach to mediated action.* Cambridge, MA: Harvard University Press.

CHILDREN'S LITERATURE CITED

Rylant, C. (2008). *Snow.* New York: Houghton/Harcourt.

Planning and Assessment in the Language Arts

Access the book's Glossary, which defines the key terms boldfaced in this chapter, at www.hhpcommunities.com/teachinglanguagearts/glossary.pdf

KEY IDEAS

- Lesson planning is an integrated act of thinking about overarching goals that are often reflected as standards.

- While there are many formats for lesson plans, most share key attributes.

- Lesson plans require interactive adjustments as the lesson unfolds.

- Assessment helps inform the instruction, thus making it part of an assessment and instruction cycle.

4.1

THE ROLE OF PLANNING IN TEACHING

Teaching may seem at first to be simply a presentation of material that constitutes a lesson; however, this definition is too simplistic. Teaching involves understanding curricular goals set forth in standards, pacing guides, and teachers' editions of textbooks. Teaching means knowing your students and how to help them meet those curricular goals. It means knowing how your students are progressing and making the necessary adjustments to help them meet learning goals without losing them in the process. Just as important, teaching involves understanding the concerns of parents, faculty colleagues, administrators, legislators, and other policy makers. This may sound like an impossible balancing act, but meeting these demands in a way that results in student learning and meeting instructional goals is at the heart of what it means to be a teacher. The foundation for success in teaching is planning. While teachers want to work with their students, sufficient planning is the starting point for success. As the quote at the beginning of this chapter suggests, failing to plan ends with failure. For teachers, this is critically important because when they are not successful, neither are their students.

"He who fails to plan is planning to fail."

attributed to
WINSTON CHURCHILL

A word about curriculum

Curriculum is a term often heard in staff rooms, colleges of education, legislative halls, and school district offices. Most teachers know what curriculum is, but defining it is not as easy as it sounds. Wiles and Bondi (1984) defined **curriculum** in two parts. First, curriculum is a plan for learning that is based on a vision or philosophy that embeds values about society's purpose and beliefs regarding education. Second, curriculum is a structure that translates the vision into learning experiences for students. Generally, curriculum is a way to think about broad swaths of learning experiences that encompass a given period of time (e.g., a unit, a semester, a year), a content or disciplinary area (e.g., language arts, mathematics, science). These learning experiences are often expressed as **pacing guides,** which indicate the resources and activities to introduce at different points in time.

Open and review the two pacing guides listed below, noting the similarities and differences between them. These two pacing guides will be featured in one of the "Think Like a Teacher" activities at the end of this chapter.

Second Grade Pacing Guide Language Arts for Camden County School District (10 pp.): www.camden.k12.nc.us/info/pace/gps/2english.pdf

Bullitt County Public Schools Suggested Pacing Guide for English/Language Arts (9 pp.): www.bullittschools.org/wp/wp-content/uploads/2011/06/BCPS-Fifth-Grade-ELA-Pacing-Guide-FINAL.pdf

Curriculum may also include a plan for the learning experience and discipline elements that occur across grade levels or between and among different courses. Curriculum development is often a collaborative effort between teachers, administrators, members of the community, and sometimes students.

4.2

MANAGING TIME IN THE CLASSROOM

Important aspects of implementing a curriculum include planning how much time lessons and units will take. Several structures help teachers and students manage the time allocated to achieving learning objectives and standards.

Unit plans

A **unit** is a collection of lessons on a similar topic that help students meet curricular standards. Often, unit plans are interdisciplinary in nature. For example, a unit on dinosaurs may have opportunities for students to work on math standards as they calculate relative size and weight of various dinosaurs. Students may practice the reading strategy of finding the main idea by reading nonfiction texts about dinosaurs. Geography may be included by having students identify the locations of dinosaur skeletons on maps of Utah, Montana, or China. Science may be integrated as students learn about the geologic time scale. Units might also focus on a specific theme or genre within one disciplinary area. For example, a unit in a language arts class might focus on poetry, including a study of the poet Shel Silverstein, reading Silverstein's poems, and writing humorous poems.

Weekly outlines

Later in this chapter, we discuss how content and processes are part of lesson planning; however, two primary considerations of any lesson are time and available resources. Neither time nor resources can be a reason for not teaching what students need; rather, how you make use of time and acquire necessary resources are variables in any lesson. By looking at the lessons on a week-by-week basis, you can decide how to organize time and plan to have resources on hand. Exhibit 4.1 shows a **weekly outline** for a series of lessons in science that allots a specific amount of time for the activities to result in student learning. It is also a portion of a much larger unit that will encompass lessons for several weeks. Exhibit 4.2 is a weekly plan for an elementary classroom that includes lessons for math, social studies, literacy, and group work to reinforce prior learning.

EXHIBIT 4.1

Weekly outline for a series of science lessons.

A	B	C	D
	DAY 1	DAY 2 & 3	DAY 4
	Activity #2	Activity #6	Activity #5
Title of Lesson	Introduction to Genetics	Mendelian Genetics	Genetic Traits
Objectives	Students will understand that DNA is the genetic material of living organisms. They will also learn the importance of genes and genetic inheritance.	Students will understand Mendelian Genetics and genetic inheritance.	Students will understand that inheri[...] traits can be determined by one or [...] genes.
California Content Standards: *7th Grade Life Science*	2 (C-E) *(see attachment)*	2 (B-E); 7 (C, E) *(see attachment)*	2 (B-E) *(see attachment)*
California Content Standards: *7th Grade English Language Arts*	Reading: 1.0, 1.2, 1.3, 2.0, 2.1, 2.2 *(see attachment)*	Reading: 1.0, 1.2, 1.3 Writing: 1.0, 1.1, 1.2, 1.3, 1.4, 1.6, 1.7 *(see attachment)*	Reading: 1.0, 1.2, 1.3, 2.0, 2.1, 2.[...] *(see attachment)*
Materials and Resources	*Double Helix: A Personal Account of the Discovery of the Structure of DNA* by James Watson; *Rosalind Franklin: The Dark Lady of DNA* by Brenda Maddox; *Linus Pauling: Advancing Science, Advocating Peace* by Naomi Pasachoff; *The Sky's the Limit: Stories of Discovery by Women and Girls* by Catherine Thimmesh.	Recessive/Dominant activity worksheet; Punnett Square activity worksheet; Lab Notebook	*Genes and DNA* by Richard Walker; Supplies for Breeding Critter Activity; Styrofoam ball, toothpicks, pipe cleaners, thumbtacks, etc.
Anticipatory Set (Motivation)	Warm-up questions; ▲Class discussion of responses to questions.	Warm-up activity: Day 1: Show and discuss photos of animals to demonstrate the following ☼vocabulary words: purebred, hybrid, dominant, and recessive. Day 2: ▲Review previous day's Phenotyping Classmates Activity; Discuss homework assignment.	Warm-up questions; ▲Class discus[...] of responses to questions.
Instructional Input	History and science of DNA; ☼Introduction to vocabulary.	Day 1: Intoduction to Gregor Mendel and experiments with pea plants; Day 2: ▲Re-cap previous day's instruction on Gregor Mendel. Introduction to Punnett squares.	☼Introduction to vocabulary words[...] Lesson on important players in gene[...] inheritance; ☼Introduction to *Genes and DNA* book.
Guided Practice/ Activity	☼▲Research Activity: Usage of external books as a source of information.	Day 1: ☼▲Phenotyping Classmates Activity; Day 2: ☼▲Punnett Square Activity	☼▲Breeding Critter Activity; Us[...] activity to demonstrate how to stru[...] writing prompt assignment fro[...] previous day.
Independent Practice/Closure	Summary of day's lesson and activities; ▲HW: Journal Question	HW: Day 1: ☼▲Compare their phenotypes with their parents'; Day 2: ☼▲Writing Prompt, due at the end of the Unit	Summary of day's lesson and activiti[...] ▲HW: Journal Question

EXHIBIT 4.2

Weekly plan for an elementary classroom for several subjects.

TIME	15-Apr	18-Apr	19-Apr	20-Apr	21-Apr	22-Apr
8:20	Pick up students from gym and take to class. Have students put backpacks away, get ready for the day, take attendance and lunch account.					
8:35-9:20	PE/Music Take students to PE/Music and pick them up at 9:20.					
9:20-9:30	Students will use the restroom and get drinks at the bathrooms downstairs.					
Math 9:30-11:00	Lesson 9.10	Review for Test	Test over unit 9	Lesson 10.1	Lesson 10.2	Lesson 10.3
Social Studies 11:00-11:50	Lesson 3	Tax collecting activity Finish lesson 3 Skits	Junior Achievement Lesson 4	Junior Achievement Lesson 4	Junior Achievement Lesson 5	Junior Achievement Lesson 5
Lunch 11:50-12:20	Take students to lunch in the cafeteria. Stand in line with them to make sure all have checked off on the list. Pick students up from recess outdoors across from the cafeteria at 12:20					
12:20-12:30	Students will use the restroom and get drinks at the bathrooms downstairs.					
12:30-12:40	Students will read silently at their desks.					
Reading 12:40-1:25	Spelling test	Introduce story vocabulary words and activity	Listen to Name This American on tape	Grammar verbs spelling activity	Activity students read play	Spelling test/ new spelling list
Stations 1:25-2:30	Table: introduce books, context clues/vocabulary	Descriptive language	Main idea/ supporting details	Sequence	Cause/Effect	Compare and contrast
	Computer: Vijay	States and capitals	Harcourt reading	Harcourt reading	Spelling City	Math
	Seat: Annie	Vocabulary in red notebook	Workbook pages	Current events	Social studies worksheet	Writing activity
Recess 2:30-2:45	Take students and pick up from recess by outside doors across from the cafeteria.					
Miscellaneous 2:45-3:15	Buddies	States and Capitals Quiz	Library	Counselor	Read Aloud	Buddies
Class Meeting 3:15-3:30	Students will fill out agendas and have them signed. Students will pack up bags to leave and engage in a class discussion about daily events.					

Daily schedule

A **daily schedule** focuses on the activities planned for all the time in the school day. Exhibit 4.3 shows how a weekly plan is broken down into a daily schedule to help the teacher manage time. Some teachers organize their lessons in file folders, which include the daily schedule as well as handouts, worksheets, and other resources that will be used each day (see Exhibit 4.4). Sharing the daily schedule with students (see Exhibit 4.5) is also a good way to help students plan the day and eliminate unpredictability that can detract from learning. Students who must constantly guess what happens next are less likely to focus on what really matters.

Lessons

Individual **lessons** are the operational details of learning experiences in the classroom and represent how teachers interpret and implement the curriculum on a daily basis. Teachers often include a time estimate for each component of a lesson. Some instructional activities go much more quickly than planned or may take longer than estimated. Also, teachers need to consider the constraints that are a regular part of the school day (e.g., recess, lunch break, art class). Planning the amount of time for each element of the lesson is a good way to ensure that lessons are completed in a way that allows students to move forward without getting bogged down or sidetracked in their learning. Flexibility is a key at all stages of planning, but especially for the individual components of the lesson. A check for understanding, or an informal assessment of learning along the way, may reveal the need to devote more or less time to a specific activity.

Lesson planning

Consider: What do you predict students will do given the learning conditions in the classroom, the processes the students know and can be taught, the content they are to learn, and your teaching approach?

EXHIBIT 4.3

Breaking down a weekly plan into a daily schedule.

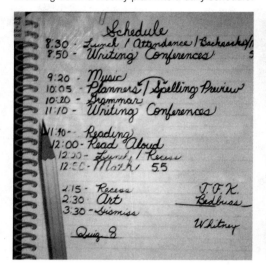

EXHIBIT 4.4

Organizing lessons using file folders.

EXHIBIT 4.5

Sharing the daily schedule with students.

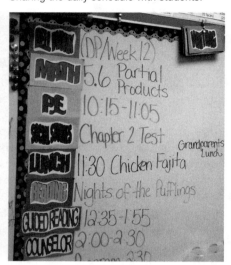

Lesson planning is one of the most basic activities of teaching, but it is also one of the most complicated. Planning for instruction occurs with your philosophy in mind and a keen sense of the learning needs of each student in your classroom. In addition, lesson planning requires attention to standards and development of objectives that will result in student achievement. Even more complicated is predicting how your students will respond to instructional tasks and when to let students gradually assume responsibility for their own learning.

On the surface, lesson planning might appear to be as simple as turning the page in the teacher's edition of the textbook. But even if the textbook and the curriculum are well-designed, the teacher must know the content, the instructional goals, resources, instructional techniques, and ways to assess student learning (Danielson, 1996), all in relation to the particular needs of the students in her given classroom. Only the teacher knows how those students might respond to instructional activities and their capacity to work with the resources provided. It is the teacher who adjusts the learning events, adapts the tasks, chooses the resources, and determines the learning environment that makes learning through literacy possible.

In planning a lesson, teachers make decisions about content, expected student behaviors, and their own behaviors that promote learning (Hunter, 1982). Corollaries to these factors are the conditions of learning, which include classroom climate and the processes of learning; that is, if the climate of the classroom is not conducive to learning, or the teacher has not considered the cognitive development of the students, no lesson plan will succeed.

Lesson plans

A lesson plan book or tool, whether electronic or paper, is typically where teachers record their plans for the day, the week, or the school year; it is more like the note cards for a speech rather than a word-for-word script. In preparing speech note cards, all the work that goes into planning the speech is not plainly visible. Similarly, the hard work of lesson planning is not always apparent in the written notes of a lesson plan book. The deep thinking and decision making behind the creation of a lesson plan cannot fit into the two-inch box found on a lesson plan page. Novice teachers are often expected to write detailed lesson plans. This expectation usually begins in a teacher education program and may extend into the early years of teaching. Professors, principals, and mentor teachers may expect detailed lesson plans, but as a novice teacher gains more experience, lesson plans typically encompass less information as more details are stored mentally. In whatever form your written plans appear, there are key elements for you to consider, which are explored in this chapter.

Fortunately or unfortunately, there seem to be as many types of lesson plans as there are school districts and professors who teach lesson planning. For example, compare the lesson plan template from the ReadWriteThink.org (www.readwrite think.org/files/resources/lesson_images/lesson181/lessonplan.pdf) site and a plan from the Teacher Planet site: http://www.lessonplans4teachers.com/guidelines.php

Granted, these lesson plan templates look somewhat different. One is a plan for a reading lesson, the other could be used with any content area. One gives a five-day overview, while the other is a plan for a single lesson. One lists the elements of a reading lesson, while the other lists the method for conveying the information to students. Despite these differences, a general pattern emerges. Lesson plans record our thinking and document our approaches to learning. Plans help us manage time and resources within the lesson and across a unit, or collection of lessons. Lesson plans incorporate a means of addressing student learning needs through a variety of scaffolding approaches. These approaches help move students from what they know at the outset of the lesson to creating new knowledge, transforming existing knowledge, or transferring knowledge from one domain of learning to another.

Planning is, in many ways, a predictive activity. At the beginning of this section, we asked what you predict students will do given the learning conditions in the classroom, the processes the students know and can be taught, the content they are to learn, and your teaching approach. As you plan lessons, consider how students might respond based on the knowledge they already have as well as the knowledge of processes and content that the lesson is designed to convey. At the end of this chapter, you will find "Think Like a Teacher" activities that further help you understand lesson planning.

points2ponder

QUICK REVIEW 1 How are lessons aligned with time designations that are part of the school day (a class period, recess, lunch break, etc.)?
(Access the answer in the digital version of this book.)

4.3

LESSON PLAN ELEMENTS

As we explained earlier, there are many different lesson plan formats; however, common elements do exist among them. This section explores these

Lesson plan template. (Print a copy of this template: www.hhpcommunities.com/teachinglanguagearts/ IL-04-01.pdf)

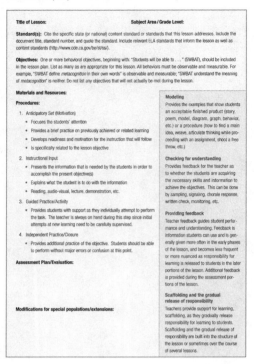

A fourth grader using an organizational structure for writing.

elements as shown in the lesson plan in Exhibit 4.6. You will likely notice that this lesson plan is not substantially different from the lesson plan templates you encountered previously in this chapter.

In some ways, we have simplified the lesson format in Exhibit 4.6; for example, no component asks for a description of the lesson. On the other hand, teachers have room to explain why they included specific learning tasks or chose to eliminate some aspects of the lesson. Some aspects of lesson planning are sequential, and those will be examined in this section. However, other instructional elements, such as modeling and checking for understanding, are integrated into various phases of the lesson and appear on the side column of the lesson plan. Modeling and guided practice are not considered separate steps, but can occur throughout a lesson and will be further discussed in upcoming sections of this chapter.

Here is a list of some of the lesson planning apps that are available: www.hhp communities.com/teachinglanguagearts/IL-04-02.pdf

Standards

Standards are the big ideas that guide curriculum design and lesson development. Professions are often defined by the standards they embrace. We expect certain standards of care from our doctors, and we insist on standards of accuracy from our accountants. Teaching is no different, and the standards we use can help us design our curriculum, our lessons, and our interactions with students.

Wiggins and McTighe (2005) suggest what they call a "backward" design for approaching learning experiences and instruction. In their backward design approach, Wiggins and McTighe have teachers ask themselves "why?" for every learning task in their classrooms. Why do students need to read this book? Why should students complete this worksheet? Why should students talk in small groups about their performance on a collaborative task? Each "why" should lead back to the standards or goals that lead to student achievement. For example, in grade four, the Common Core State Standards for English Language Arts in writing (Common Core State Standards Initiative, 2012) call for students to "introduce a topic or text clearly, state an opinion, and create an organizational structure in which related ideas are grouped to support the writer's purpose." Specific lessons are the learning opportunities teachers create for students to meet the goal of clearly communicating ideas through writing. Within a lesson, smaller steps are taken to move along the path of achieving the standard, and these steps are the lesson-specific objectives. Exhibit 4.8 shows graphically how standards inform unit planning, the development of objectives with attention to literacy tasks embedded in any lesson, and the actual lesson activities. In the video, you will learn more about how the Common Core State Standards contribute to lesson planning and development as well as how the standards were developed.

Learn more about the development of the Common Core State Standards by viewing the video Common Core State Standards: Principles of Development (8:00): http://teachertube.com/viewVideo.php?video_id=253458&title=Common_Core_State_ Standards__Principles_of_Development.

Keep in mind, standards are broad statements. In the previous paragraph, a standard called for students to introduce a topic, state an opinion, create an organizational structure, and so on. A single fourth-grade lesson would likely not result in students achieving this standard; however, if a teacher divided the standard into smaller parts, and clearly, sequentially, and consistently built lessons that led toward this standard, it could be done. Each step along the way needs its own signpost, and those signposts are called objectives.

Objectives

Every effective lesson format includes a provision for determining what students know or should be able to do at the end of the lesson. This may take the form of outcomes or objectives, and the more recent versions of lessons include a place to link the lesson to the standards selected by the school district or the state. Sometimes the general term *goal* is used when referring to an objective. Regardless of the terminology used, **objectives** are statements that are observable and measurable so that both the teacher and the students will know if they have been successful. Thus, an objective for a single lesson related to the standard above could be: *Students will be able to identify opinions and differentiate facts in an article selected from the student newspaper.* A subsequent objective for a lesson on the following day might be: *Students will be able to write an opinion in the form of a letter to the editor suitable for publishing in the student newspaper, organized according to the newspaper's guidelines for letters to the editor.* In this way, the teacher designs the building blocks of the lesson through clear objectives, which lead to the overall standard(s).

Serdyukov and Ryan (2008) suggest that objectives indicate what students will be able to do under specific conditions and at a specific level of acceptable attainment. The means by which students demonstrate what they know is important as well; however, keep in mind the idea of backward design discussed in the previous section (Wiggins & McTighe, 2005). For instance, it is of little practical use to write an objective such as this one: *Students will be able to complete a worksheet on the topic of opinion pieces in the newspaper.* "Why?" you start to ask, before realizing you already know the answer. Completing a worksheet does not necessarily indicate that learning has occurred, because completion of a worksheet does not equal mastery or even understanding of the objective of writing a letter to the editor.

Although worksheets are plentiful, keep backward design in mind. We are only interested in worksheets, or any other activities, insofar that they lead students to understand something they did not before the lesson began. The content on the worksheet is far more important than the fact that the learning task is a worksheet. The above worksheet lesson plan objective does not indicate what learning, relevant to the standards, will take place. We have not indicated the conditions under which students will perform the task, and there is no level of acceptable attainment specified. Well-written objectives keep students and teachers on the road toward understanding and mastery of standards chosen by colleagues, district administrators, and state education agencies. Stating actions in objectives is important, and we explore this next.

Verbs are useful for stating actions in objectives for lessons. Remember that an objective is a statement indicating what students will know (a verb) or be able to do (another verb). Fortunately, educators have a tool for choosing verbs. In 1956 Benjamin Bloom headed a group of educational psychologists who developed a classification of levels of intellectual behavior important in learning. During the 1990s a new group of cognitive

EXHIBIT 4.8

Relationship of standards, objectives, learning tasks, and lessons.

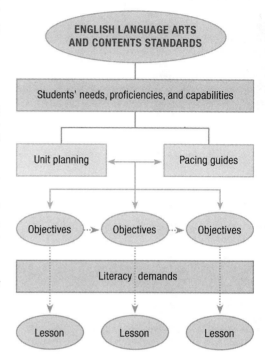

psychologists, led by Lorin Anderson (a former student of Bloom), updated the taxonomy to reflect relevance to twenty-first-century work. The latest version of the Bloom's Taxonomy (Anderson & Krathwohl, 2001) is built around verbs as a way to build instructional objectives (e.g., remember, understand, apply, analyze, evaluate, create). These are the actions of learning, and these actions should guide our instruction.

View Bloom's Taxonomy (ww2.odu.edu/educ/roverbau/Bloom/blooms_taxonomy.htm) to compare the latest version to the previous version. Particularly consider the changes in verbs from the old version to the new. Ponder why the authors recommended such changes. Why is it important to compare the two? You will sometimes encounter lesson objectives written with the older taxonomy in mind. As you write your own lessons, keep the new version at the forefront of your thinking. Think of a lesson you recently observed or taught; then use a verb from the revised version of Bloom's Taxonomy to create a reasonable objective for the lesson. With the right verb, as part of a well-written objective, learning stays on target.

Educator Kathy Schrock offers a reimagining of Bloom's taxonomy (www.schrockguide.net/bloomin-apps) and uses it to link to what she refers to as "Bloomin' Apps": applications that support Bloom's revised taxonomy.

If all the learning experiences in a lesson are properly aligned to the objective and to the standard for learning, assessments should demonstrate how well students achieved a lesson-specific objective. Assessments are not always about tests, however. Assessments, an upcoming topic in this chapter, are about how teachers and students know what they have learned and to what degree.

Materials and resources

Another key element of lesson plans is a section for listing resources. Sometimes, all you need for a lesson is the textbook, paper, and a pencil. At other times, a lesson may require children's literature, science equipment, or access to the portable computer lab. Now and then, a lesson will require materials from a retail store that you keep at home or maintain in a storage area of the school. One teacher arranged for her butcher to save a cow's bone and saw it in half so students could see the marrow. Without this teacher's prior planning, the students would not have experienced and handled a real bone, noting its structure in ways a photograph or simulation could not reveal. Putting even the most obvious of resources on the lesson plan list is important because there is little worse than planning an activity to publish students' writing and finding that the classroom is out of paper or planning to video a field trip and finding the camera's battery has not been charged. Planning for resources means making sure that the resources you need are gathered and available at the time you need them.

Procedures

Anticipatory set: Getting started with instruction

In the lesson format provided in Exhibit 4.6, a step for linking to prior knowledge is included. The **anticipatory set** is the step that links what students already know to what they will be learning (Hunter, 1982). An anticipatory set can also focus students on the upcoming lesson, inspire motivation to learn, and give a preview of what is to come. An anticipatory set activity might consist of reading a picture book, showing photographs, passing around real objects, listening to a guest speaker, or even taking a field trip. This is a small, but mighty, step in the lesson sequence, so give careful thought to plan an effective beginning.

COMPREHENSION *coach*

Did you know that activating your prior knowledge can set you up as a reader for successful comprehension? Listen to this podcast from Dr. Wolsey for ways to bring to the front of your mind what you already know and thus better remember, and comprehend, what you are reading. *(Access this podcast in the digital version of this book.)*

Similar strategies, such as sponge, bell-ringer, or do-now activities, often serve a similar purpose as the anticipatory set, but these two types of activities are not synonymous. A sponge, bell-ringer, or do-now is typically used to make use of every moment of learning time from the very start of class, often by reviewing past learning, whereas an anticipatory set is directly linked to a lesson and its objectives. This is no small difference. Sponge activities keep students engaged and occupied from the beginning of a learning period, a task that may or may not be linked to a lesson objective to follow.

Suppose, for example, that you have selected the following Common Core State Standard for your first-grade lesson: Students will be able to identify the main topic of a passage (CCSS Initiative, 2012). Then you write a related objective: Students will be able to identify the main topic of the predictable text *Have You Seen My Cat?* (Carle, 1987). In this case, a sponge activity at the beginning of the language arts period might be a review of sight words, such as *cat* and *boy*. These terms, although not related to the objective of identifying the main topic, are a review of content that would be useful in the learning required to meet the current objective; without word recognition and vocabulary proficiency, identifying a main topic would be fruitless. An anticipatory set for this lesson, however, might ask students to recall the lesson last week in which they learned to retell a simple narrative in a different genre.

Other possible anticipatory set activities include the following:

- A video clip that piques students' interest in the topic
- A problem that seems difficult to solve
- A lead-in to a story or narrative that sets the tone or purpose for a later reading task
- A discovery experience that leaves students wondering why a particular event occurred

Instructional input

Input is simply the information students have available to them and that they must apply or with which they must engage. This could be a reading selection, a video, a teacher's lecture, or information provided by peers. How information is organized and presented during a lesson is critically important

(Hunter, 1982). Gick and Holyoak (1983) demonstrated that even graduate students struggled to apply familiar strategic knowledge in an unfamiliar domain. In their experiments, participants who were presented with a scenario and a solution in one domain (in this case, a military scenario) did not easily note the attributes of the scenario in a new domain (a medical scenario), even though the strategy was the same for both problems. Teachers encounter this phenomenon daily. Students who appear to understand a concept on Tuesday struggle with the same idea presented under slightly different conditions on Thursday. This is a problem of transfer; that is, how lessons connect with each other and, more important, how lessons connect with concepts that extend to the world at large. Part of the solution lies in the organization of the material to be presented. Concepts should be presented in multiple ways; only through many encounters with a concept in many different ways will students be able to apply new learning in new situations (CAST, 2011). Lessons that apply this principle tend to help students connect ideas and transfer them to new learning situations inside and outside school.

Input is the key information students need to meet the objective or to accomplish the goal or purpose of the lesson. This information could be shared by reading a book, watching a video, listening to a teacher's lecture, or participating in a peer discussion. How this key information is organized and presented during a lesson is critically important (Hunter, 1982). Concepts should be presented in multiple ways; only through many encounters with a concept in many different ways will students be able to apply new learning in new situations (CAST, 2011). Gick and Holyoak (1983) demonstrated that even graduate students struggled to apply familiar strategic knowledge in an unfamiliar domain. In their experiments, participants who were presented with a scenario and a solution in one domain (in this case, a military scenario) did not easily note the attributes of the scenario in a new domain (a medical scenario), even though the strategy was the same for both problems. Teachers encounter this phenomenon daily. Students who appear to understand a concept on Tuesday struggle with the same idea presented under slightly different conditions on Thursday. This is a problem of transfer, that is, how lessons connect with each other and, more important, how lessons connect with concepts that extend to the world at large. Part of the solution lies in the organization of the material to be presented. Lessons that present content in multiple ways help students connect ideas and transfer them to new learning situations inside and outside school.

What a teacher does or says is the explicit instruction part of the lesson. **Explicit instruction** is the clear and purposeful presentation of the information about how and what students are to learn and why they are to learn it under certain conditions. The teacher plays a significant role in what students learn, although that role varies depending on the age or maturity of the students, the difficulty of the lesson objective, and novelty of the learning. Direct or explicit instruction may include whole class or small group instruction, and it may also include one-on-one instruction. Durkin (1990) characterized instruction as "what someone or something does or says that has the potential to teach one or more individuals what they do not know, do not understand, or cannot do" (p. 472). She goes on to explain that direct instruction can be planned or unplanned; it can be part of a whole class lesson or a small-group instructional plan. It may also be something the teacher does in the moment when an unanticipated learning situation arises. Examples of formats for direct instruction include the following:

1. You present information to the whole class using a digital whiteboard or other data projector.

2. You work with a small group of students to accelerate their understanding based on their readiness to move ahead of the class.

3. You notice that two students are struggling with a difficult concept as they work individually or in small groups. You stop to provide unplanned direct instruction to help them move toward achievement of the lesson objective and standard.

Teacher presentation, sometimes in lecture format, is an important part of learning, and it does have a place in instruction (Bransford, Brown, & Cocking, 2000). Freire (1970/1993) cautions teachers against what he calls a "banking approach" to education. The banking approach is where the teacher has all the knowledge and fills the students with what she knows. Although teacher presentation has a place in learning, banking knowledge can easily become a major teaching method to the exclusion of what students can do to promote their own learning. As opposed to the banking approach, some instructors have learned to *flip* their classrooms. In a **flipped classroom,** the instructor remains an important and insightful source of information, but much of the content is delivered in a way that enables students to work independently, such as via the Internet (e.g., a YouTube video or podcast). Students then access this information at home, in the library, or on their smartphones before they come to class. As a result, class time is freed up for active engagement with peers and the teacher. Imagine a thoughtful presentation that a teacher prepares to assist students with determining how and when context cues can assist with meaning-making during reading. If the teacher captures that presentation using video, audio, or other presentation software and uploads it to the Internet, students who are trying to put context cues to work in their own thinking can return to the presentation at any time.

At other times, students engage with readings, view videos, or listen to peers' presentations that serve as instructional input and with which they work in the practice phases of the lesson. In some cases, students seek out their own resources in this phase with guidance from the teacher. To be clear, students should consider the teacher as an important source of information, but they need to look beyond the teacher as the main or only source of ideas, knowledge, and wisdom, as well. Thus, direct instruction should be more than just teacher presentation.

The Knewton site (www.knewton.com/flipped-classroom) offers more information about the growing use of flipped classrooms.

Guided practice and collaborative work

Students must have many opportunities to practice application of ideas in order for them to understand difficult or challenging concepts or principles. When students are confronted with a challenging concept or task, they need to work with someone who can guide or facilitate their learning in **guided practice.** Often, that someone is a teacher. If learning were simply a matter of students reading and following directions, teaching would be much less complex. However, when tasks are challenging, as they should be most of the time, students need to work with ideas while an expert guides them. That expert can be a teacher. At the same time, working with others who are also trying to understand that difficult concept can result in effective learning. Sometimes teachers provide guidance as students work alone, and sometimes teachers provide guidance as students work together in synergistic and collaborative groups.

Earlier, we described explicit instruction, which includes what you say or do to assist students in how, what, and why they are learning something. Kolb states that "learning is the process whereby knowledge is created through the transformation of learning" (1984, p. 38). Zull (2002) took Kolb's ideas about learning as a cycle and added one more dimension: Learning is grounded in concrete experience. From concrete experiences, attentive learners are able to reflect on what they know and how they come to know it. Zull hypothesized a transformation at this point where **reflection** and experience combine to produce learning that is more abstract and applicable to many other contexts. As the learner gains momentum and greater understanding, learning progresses from abstract thinking to a stage of active experimentation wherein the ideas are challenged and contexts manipulated for greater understanding. Active experimentation, naturally, leads the learner right back to new concrete experiences, and the cycle starts once more.

Kolb and Zull argue well for a great theory, but how does it apply to teaching literacy? What does transformation have to do with the practice phases of the lessons in a classroom every day? These are good questions, ones that demonstrate many of the ideas both Kolb and Zull explain through their theory of learning. An example will prove helpful. Read the following classroom story to see how learning theory should inform lesson planning. Nowhere is this more important than in the practice phases.

stories FROM THE CLASSROOM

Active learning

Anna is a kindergarten student in Ms. Mitchell's classroom, and it is the first months of the new school year. Kindergarten is a big adventure, and Anna is excited about learning how to really read. She already knows that spoken words can be segmented into individual sounds, and she knows that those sounds are related to letters she sees on billboards, television, and in the books her parents read to her every day. She is quite bright, but being just five years old she cannot put these understandings into words. But the concepts are workable in her mind as she starts to apply the principles of phonemic awareness and the alphabetic principle during class. Soon Anna will apply phonics learning to the words she sees and will read these words herself. This learning will not happen magically for Anna. She needs a good teacher who can make explicit the seemingly hidden process of reading, and fortunately, Anna has Ms. Mitchell.

Ms. Mitchell knows that presenting Anna and her classmates with a definition of phonics—the relationship of the written letters to the sounds of the spoken language (Harris & Hodges, 1995)—is not the most effective way to teach this important skill. If Ms. Mitchell just tells Anna that phonics means recognizing the correspondence between letters and sounds, Anna will not learn how to read. Instead, Ms. Mitchell builds on what Anna already knows. Since Anna can clap out the sounds of words and tell Ms. Mitchell that the word *mom* starts and ends with the *mmm* sound, the teacher knows that Anna is on the right track. Over several lessons, Ms. Mitchell, Anna, and the other students talk about sounds, associate those sounds with letters written on letter cards, move the cards to form new words, combine words Anna will come to know as families, such as the *at* family and the *am* family, and so forth. To be sure, Ms. Mitchell will present these during instructional input by reading a story that includes words from these families and providing directions for what students will be doing during the practice phases.

Review Ms. Mitchell's lesson plan on the short /a/ sound: www.hhp communities.com/teachinglanguagearts/IL-04-03.pdf

Ms. Mitchell employs several useful approaches in her lesson. Each activity is carefully aligned to the objectives, which in turn are aligned to the Common Core State Standards. By using a lesson template as the foundation for her thinking, she builds in the idea of moving students from working with new ideas to practice with teacher guidance, then to independence with the task. Each phase of the lesson includes opportunities for the teacher to check for understanding and adjust instruction if necessary. Students also have models that inform them about how processes help them understand the idea initially, but they can return to these models during the practice phases. For Anna, the abstract concept of associating letters with sounds, combining the letters and sounds, and associating those with words is grounded in the concrete representations of those words as she encounters them in the story, the associations with words she already knows, and the opportunity to practice. Essential to the idea of practice is that simply repeating a task over and over is insufficient. Indeed, practice that is imprecise can lead to learning that actually impedes progress. As others have said (Hunter, 1982; Jones, 2007) practice without appropriate guidance may only make poor learning permanent.

Independent practice and closure

Later in this chapter, we explore how students can move from reliance on the teacher and peers for understanding to increasingly independent mastery of concepts and responsibility for learning. Practice with concepts and processes is integral to successful learning. In the scenario involving Ms. Mitchell's phonics lesson, students wrote sentences using new vocabulary terms for the word wall during independent practice.

Hunter (1982) proposed that some practice is "massed"; in other words, several opportunities for practice occur closely together in time. **Massed practice** depends on multiple iterations of learning, rather than replication of the same task over and over. For example, students learning to associate the short /a/ sound might read several books that emphasize this sound and work with them in writing and discussion tasks. Massed practice is helpful when a concept is new because new learning does not easily stay with the learner until it is experienced in several ways.

Distributed practice emphasizes what students have learned and over time associates it with other concepts. To understand how to decode words with the short /a/ sound, students work with this sound across several lessons and compare it to other short vowel sounds and perhaps long vowel sounds, as well. Massed and distributed learning, when successfully engineered by an expert teacher, can result in a gradual release of responsibility, a concept we explore later in this chapter, that turns over to students the control for what they know and when to apply that learning in various contexts.

Closure may be a separate phase of the lesson or embedded in the independent practice. In either case, students are given the chance to synthesize their learning during the lesson. Ms. Mitchell provided closure to her lesson by having students share the sentences they wrote during independent practice. A good rule of thumb for closure activities is that they permit students to be able to answer the questions their parents often ask, such as, "What did you learn today?" and "Why is that important?"

Assessment plan/evaluation

Few concepts in education are as all-encompassing as assessment. When it comes to literacy learning and learning content through literacy, assessment is a cornerstone of what we do as teachers. Later in this chapter we describe various types of assessments. For now, keep in mind the twofold role assessment plays in planning and instruction. Before the lesson, assessment lets the teacher know what students already know, reveals gaps, and determines what students are ready to learn. After a lesson, assessment lets you and the students know what has been learned.

As a feature of lesson planning, assessment is directly related to the objective. Simply put, how will you know that students have met the objective and are on track to achieve literacy and content standards? Assessment informs every step of the lesson, but is especially connected to the lesson objective and guides a teacher toward determining if students have met the objective and are on track to achieve literacy and content standards. Assessment is information about student learning that helps us know where to begin the lesson; there is little point in repeating what students already know or asking them to learn what is well beyond their capacity. Assessment tells us whether students are successfully grappling with the challenging topics and concepts that lead to long-term learning as they encounter new information during the instructional input phase and work with that information during the guided and independent practice phase. Assessment is the information you use to provide feedback to students so they can adjust their performance, and it is the information that tells you they have achieved the outcomes you set for them. Sometimes this valuable information comes from an informal assessment, such as observing or listening to students during a lesson and comparing what you notice to an objective. At other times a rubric, quiz, or test can be a useful tool for revealing what students know. There are likely as many ways to gather assessment information as there are ways to teach a concept. In the example lesson, you saw how Ms. Mitchell observed Anna to determine if she and her classmates were making progress toward the lesson objective and were able to put their learning into practice when they read words that included the short /a/ sound. Ms. Mitchell recorded her observations using anecdotal notes, and at the end of the lesson gave word list and nonsense word tests.

Lesson plan modifications for special populations

Classrooms are composed of students with diverse learning needs. Sometimes, those needs are specific to the student, such as the student who has a visual impairment and needs Braille texts or enlarged texts. At other times, those needs are addressed by providing multiple access points, such as the student who needs to hear a story read aloud or look up unfamiliar words in an online dictionary. The particular needs of English language learners are sometimes considered as *just good teaching* that works with any learner. In every classroom, however, the students' learning needs must be identified and instruction must be specific to these needs. The instructional practices used last year may not be the best methods for students in the class this year. The upcoming sections on literacy approaches and differentiation share more information and examples about the specific ways you can adjust instruction to meet the literacy learning needs of all students. Including these specific adjustments in a lesson plan is crucial. Their inclusion reflects the conscious consideration given to each student's learning needs before the lesson occurs. During the lesson, many competing forces vie for your attention. If these adjustments are written down in a lesson plan, they are more likely to be integrated into the flow of the lesson. Additional modifications will likely come to mind while teaching, but those included in a lesson plan are an important starting point. Notice that Ms. Mitchell included in her lesson plan specific modifications for Anna, for example, placing her in a guided group for phonemic awareness help, as well as modifications for high-achieving students.

points2ponder

QUICK REVIEW 2 How do effective teachers align daily lessons with standards and long-term goals as found in curriculum plans and pacing guides?
Why are verbs a useful foundation for thinking about lesson planning?

(Access the answers in the digital version of this book.)

4.4

INSTRUCTIONAL METHODS IN LESSONS

Modeling, checking for understanding, providing feedback, and gradually releasing responsibility are critical components of any lesson plan; these elements should not be treated as afterthoughts, but integrated into the various phases of the lesson. Just as the individual activities students complete are important, so are the models of products, processes, and behaviors that help students move toward increasingly sophisticated performances and understandings. The same is true of checking for understanding. Effective teaching means consistently checking to see how well students are making progress toward lesson objectives and agreed-upon standards. Notice that we did not say to periodically check for student understanding. Models that are useful to students and checking for understanding are not separate steps in the lesson planning process. Rather, they are integral to all other aspects of the teaching and learning processes. With that in mind, this section discusses the various instructional methods used in lessons.

Modeling

When it comes to new learning, context is everything. Modeling provides the learner with context, or a visual and auditory explanation of how new learning fits into the context of what is already known. A great example of modeling is a chef on a television cooking show. The chef demonstrates slicing, dicing, and sautéing, while providing the viewer with a clear example of how to cook up the dish at home. His or her explanations, demonstrations, and advice give even the most reluctant cook the confidence to give it a try.

Of course, modeling how to whip up a soufflé does not compare to teaching a child to read, or does it? In both cases, modeling is about showing and telling. Modeling a process, such as revising and editing a piece of writing, and providing a model of a learning product, such as a journal entry, are important ways to demonstrate what we want students to know and be able to do. When students encounter substantively new learning, modeling provides the context that facilitates linking new learning to what students already know. Effective modeling shows learners how a complex task can be broken down into parts and how complex ideas fit with other ideas as a whole. Thinking aloud, a key component of modeling, is especially useful when teaching an in-the-head process, such as reading, listening, or viewing, which is typically difficult to demonstrate.

We have all experienced a situation where we were asked to do something new without being given a model, whether it was solving a math equation, writing a haiku, or making a soufflé. Without a model, students will likely feel some instructional disequilibrium (Fisher, Frey, & Lapp, 2009). We may have no prior experience on which to draw and ask ourselves, "How do I do this?" Research tells us that when we learn something new, neurons in our brain are linked together to form a pathway. The more we experience or practice this new idea, the stronger the pathway becomes. Ironically, the brains of our ancestors were not originally wired for learning language. These pathways developed over thousands of years as humans began communicating by mimicking each other's actions, then mimicking their spoken utterances and eventually words, then writing these words down for later use. Modeling is a foundation for teaching, because that is how our brains are wired to learn (Fisher, Frey, & Lapp, 2009, p. 13):

- Watch me as I do this.
- Let's do it together.
- Let's talk about it or write about it.

In this sense, modeling may be the single most important step of instruction, and thus deserving of strong consideration in the lesson planning process. Good modeling does not happen on its own. Good modeling techniques do not just pop into a new teacher's mind in the midst of the lesson. Effective modeling entails

- planning specific examples,
- crafting what will be said during a think-aloud, and
- thinking through how best to show and tell this information to students.

To help develop a clear understanding of what is entailed by modeling, view this lesson for English language learners (7:00, http://youtu.be/I3aTwIwwU40) that shows a teacher integrating key instructional elements in her second-grade class. Notice how the teacher models by pointing to the key words the students should learn, using a sentence frame students should use, as she also models the behaviors she expects of the students as they prepare for the collaborative activity.

author's story   THOMAS DEVERE WOLSEY

As a seventh-grade teacher, I wanted my students to work with a stack of cards bound together with rubber bands and paper clips. What students were to do with the office supplies was a process. Without instruction, seventh graders could quickly turn the rubber bands and paper clips into something other than a way to keep stacks of cards bound together. Before the activity began, I showed the students how to put the rubber band inside the envelope that contained the cards. The paper clips were to be counted and then placed in the envelope as well. The instruction took only a minute, and as the students were told what to do with the rubber bands and paper clips, I modeled each step putting the rubber band in an envelope, counting the paper clips, and then placing them inside the envelope as well. The modeling step was simple; however, with an explicit model of the process, students knew exactly what to do. Even better, they did not use the rubber bands or paper clips in any other inventive manner, because they had a model to follow.

A more complex process that can be modeled involves revising, a process embedded as part of a larger writing process and one that students often struggle with (e.g., Emig, 1971). In Mrs. Shea's second grade class, for example, students found it difficult to revise their work to make their message clear to their readers (Lapp, Shea, & Wolsey, 2011). Because the idea of an audience (see Chapter 7 for more on this concept) is abstract and somewhat complex, Mrs. Shea first constructed a blog post of her own, then she asked her students to respond to it by telling their classmates what they learned from reading it. She also read through her blog post explaining her thinking about each element (e.g., Baumann, Jones, & Seifert-Kessell, 1993; Wilhelm, 1999, 2001). However, Mrs. Shea wanted her students also to be critical readers who could suggest or *push* her to think about what might be confusing or to identify details about which readers would like to learn more. By creating a blog post and inviting students to respond, she modeled the behaviors, products, and processes she wanted her students to emulate in their responses to each other's written work and in revising their work based on their peers' responses.

Checking for understanding

Modeling helps students understand important details and put them in the context of other learning. At the same time, you assess students to ensure that learning is taking place and to adjust instruction as needed. Assessment is a multifaceted concept that will be addressed in more detail in Section 4.7; however, informal checks for understanding are informal mini-assessments that occur throughout each lesson and guide your decisions on-the-fly or in the midst of the lesson. One of the most common misused checks for understanding is when teachers stop and ask students, "Are there any questions?" Far more is involved in **checking for understanding** than a one-stop pass asking if everyone's "got it." Almost everyone knows that questions develop over time. Good questions often evolve when content and processes are applied in real time; moreover, because students are novices with the content knowledge and processes, they do not always know what questions to ask if information is not clear to them. Students may actively be working on a learning task, but it is dangerous to mistake effort and hard work, or nods and smiles, for understanding. Read the Stories from the Classroom to learn how a fifth-grade teacher's careful observations determined if a student understood the lesson objective.

stories FROM THE CLASSROOM

Checking for understanding

Mr. Atkinson, a fifth-grade teacher, works with his students on making inferences from their reading using quotes to support their conclusions (Common Core State Standards Initiative, 2012). The students are to use quotes from the story and explicitly link those to the conclusions they draw about the story. While most students appear to work intently, Mr. Atkinson notices that Aamir is dutifully copying quotes from the story his small group has read, but the quotes he chooses seem random and unrelated to any conclusion he may have drawn from the text. An observer might think Aamir is learning because he is working diligently. Mr. Atkinson, however, is a careful observer, and as he walks around the room, he asks students to explain why they chose certain quotes to support their conclusions. In his brief discussion with Aamir, he quickly discerns the problem and provides some feedback so Aamir will know how to create a connection between the quotes and the inferences he makes as a reader. Mr. Atkinson is checking for understanding based on the standard and lesson objective that will help Aamir improve his performance.

EXHIBIT 4.9

Checking for understanding.

USING ORAL LANGUAGE	When students talk (and we add, students should be talking!), teachers should listen. As they listen, teachers can note features of what Michaels, O'Conner, and Hall (2010) call accountable talk, which features clarification and explanation, justifications of proposals and challenges, recognition and challenge to misconceptions, and calls for evidence of claims and arguments. Students may also interpret and "revoice" others' statements. In small groups and partner work, students can retell key points. Each provides an opportunity for teachers to check for understanding of key ideas aligned with standards.
USING QUESTIONS	Questions are a time-honored method of checking for understanding and comprehension. Later in Chapter 9, we explore how questions are effectively used and how they may be misused in the classroom.
USING WRITING	Not all work written by students is a finished product, and much of what students write can help the teacher know the degree to which students are making progress toward achievement of standards. Short writing tasks, such as exit slips and journal entries, can effectively inform instruction and learning, for example.
USING PROJECTS AND PERFORMANCES	Projects and performances require students to engage in learning, often as a result of integrating many concepts as the project develops. In addition to final assessments of the project or performance, teachers may enhance learning by conferring with students about critical understandings as the project moves forward, and they may use rubrics as a basis for reflection at benchmarks along the way.
USING TESTS	Tests are an important means of checking for understanding. If the items are correctly constructed, and the results are used for "increasingly precise instruction for individual students" (p. 119), tests can be a very useful method of checking for understanding.
USING COMMON ASSESSMENTS AND CONSENSUS SCORING	Common assessments are frequently based on an agreed upon process of implementing a curriculum, determining the pace of instruction (e.g., pacing guides), and then evaluating student progress on a common assessment, frequently called a benchmark assessment. As with tests, above, such assessments can assist teachers and students with guideposts along the path toward achievement of standards.

Adapted from Fisher, D. & Frey, N. (2007). *Checking for understanding: Formative assessment techniques for your classroom.* Alexandria, VA: Association for Supervision and Curriculum Development.

Checking for understanding is closely aligned with feedback, and it is an ongoing part of every lesson. A first step in checking for understanding is to have a concept of what students do or do not know. The next step is for you to use that understanding to help move students forward. Without this process, students can work their hearts out and still miss the mark or appear to understand without really understanding. Checking for understanding involves you looking for evidence of how well students are meeting the lesson objective at key points in the lesson. Much like the signal from the air traffic control tower to an airplane, checking for understanding is the signal to you that students are ready to move on to the next step of learning. When planning is clearly aligned to instructional objectives and standards for learning, and you know what students are able to do, then the likelihood of successful learning increases.

In 2007, Fisher and Frey developed a framework for approaches to checking students' understanding. This framework is grounded in the idea that teachers who know what they expect students to learn and can key those expectations to specific objectives and standards are more apt to precisely target their teaching to the learning needs of each student. We have summarized and adapted the approaches to checking for understanding from Fisher and Frey's work in Exhibit 4.9. You can check for understanding in a myriad of ways, depending on the types of information about student learning you hope to gather.

This presentation (5:00) demonstrates how teacher Krista Hughett uses back channeling in the classroom as a tool to check for understanding and to give all students a voice (This resource requires Flash.) *(Access this video in the digital version of this book.)*

Providing feedback

Closely aligned with checking for understanding is providing feedback. **Feedback** gives learners information about how well they are progressing and what needs more attention. Feedback should be specific, targeted to the learner and the learning situation. Praise, one type of feedback, can be helpful if precise, but if it is too general it feels good but provides no useful information (e.g., "good job" or "this is terrific"). Exhibit 4.10 provides a *typology*, an organized list of features, of feedback characteristics based on the work of Hattie and Timperley (2007) and Wolsey (2008). Notice there are three key questions: "How am I doing?" "Where am I going?" and "Where to next?" Put another way, students should understand how they are progressing on the task at hand, how that task leads them to achieve the learning objectives, and how the task connects to new learning or how they can extend that learning.

What you say and do to scaffold student learning is critical to assisting students in understanding the attributes of the learning problems they encounter. An effective way to provide feedback is to adopt a strategy called praise, prompt, leave (Jones, 2007). With the instructional objective in mind, move from student to student or group to group, offering a word of specific praise linked to the objective and avoiding generic praise that offers no useful feedback. Then, prompt the student or group to correct errors and suggest an alternate route, or another way to move forward with the task.

stories FROM THE CLASSROOM

Giving useful feedback

As you will recall from the previous story, Mr. Atkinson is working with his students to help them make appropriate inferences for comprehending texts. He has asked students to find quotes from the text to support their inferences. As Mr. Atkinson moves around the room, he has noticed that Aamir does not understand how to use quotes to support the inferences he is making. Mr. Atkinson stops by Aamir's desk and praises him for accurately copying quotes from the source text (praise). He then prompts Aamir by asking what the main idea of the passage is and how it relates to the quote Aamir has copied (prompt). Aamir's face lights up as he realizes that he has missed an important point of the activity, which he now knows how to fix, and Mr. Atkinson moves on to the next student (leave).

To read more about specific ways to provide feedback to students, read the article "How Do Teachers Provide Feedback?" (http://suite101.com/article/how-do-teachers-provide-feedack-a201608). Giving focused, helpful feedback is an art, which even experienced teachers continue to cultivate through professional reading and practice. The Praise, Prompt, Leave model is introduced in this article, but other feedback ideas are also explained. Find at least one additional feedback strategy you would like to incorporate into your own teaching.

Scaffolding and gradual release of responsibility

An effective plan for teaching a lesson takes into account the background or prior knowledge students bring with them to the lesson. These experiences can help students with new and challenging learning. Near the beginning of the twentieth century, the Russian psychologist Lev Vygotsky (1978) theorized what he called a "zone of proximal development." The term is

Feedback typology.

PURPOSES (Hattie & Timperley, 2007)	TYPES	QUALITIES	FORMS
Feed back (How am I going?) Feed up (Where am I going?) Feed forward (Where to next?)	**Affirmations (simple)** *Example:* "Nicely done placing the comma between two main clauses." **Affirmations (complex)** *Example:* "While we read our last novel, you seemed to struggle with in-text connections, but in our discussion of the reading today, you clearly noticed how the main character foreshadowed the tragic accident later in the book." **Clarifications** *Example:* "Right here [pointing to key word in a text] is an example of a verb being used as a noun like the one you noticed earlier." **Observations** *Example:* "I noticed that you are writing this paragraph in third person." [Note: involves no value judgment, just the observation to highlight what it is the student is doing.] **Corrections: content** *Example:* "I think I see what you are saying, but if we go back to the science book and read the section on motion, we may find some different information about the Coriolis effect." **Corrections: mechanics, usage, spelling** *Example:* "Take a look at this word here [points to word]. The letters sound right, but the spelling of 'spaghetti' is a different than we might normally expect because of the silent h." **Questions** *Example:* "Your short story is shaping up nicely. How might you use dialog to tell your readers more about what this character is thinking right now?" **Exploratory** *Example:* "When I read the script for your science project podcast, I started thinking about how geysers erupt. Do you think this example might help your listeners understand thermal energy? Maybe you can think of other examples too." **Personal** *Example:* "Your descriptive podcast about thermal energy brought back vivid memories of the time I visited Yellowstone National Park and watched the Old Faithful geyser erupt."	Identified positive aspects of the work Explains rather than labels Perceptive Corrective Compassionate Useful Timely Linked to specific criteria Expands, clarifies, elaborates	Written during Written after Oral during Oral after Teacher Peers Other parties Link to feed forward . . .

© Thomas DeVere Wolsey, 2012. Sources: Hattie, J. & Timperley, H. (2007). The power of feedback. *Review of Educational Research*, 77(1), 81-112, 2007. DOI: 10.3102/003465430298487. Wolsey, T. D. (2008). Efficacy of instructor feedback in an online graduate program. *International Journal on eLearning*, 7(2), 311-329.

fancy, but it represents a familiar idea to us in this century: Learners can do some tasks on their own, but other tasks are frustrating. Between these two points are tasks that learners can do if they have assistance. Usually, assistance comes from teachers or capable peers. An American professor took this idea and came up with a metaphor for the helping interaction; Bruner's (1978) term for what teachers and capable others do to help learners succeed is called *scaffolding*.

author's story   ELIZABETH DOBLER

When my daughter was five years old, I took her to swimming lessons one summer at the city pool. She enjoyed the water in a baby pool, but was a bit apprehensive at the shallow end of the big pool. At her first lesson, Emily clung to the edge until her teacher pried Emily's fingers off, held her hands, and gingerly trolled her around the shallow end of the pool. This went on for a few days, until the teacher wanted Emily to try a back float. Emily hesitated, but the teacher gently insisted, then laid Emily out on her back, placing her hands under her back for support. A few lessons later, the teacher laid Emily on her back, and this time pulled Emily around the pool, holding on to her hands. By the end of the swimming lesson session, Emily could float on her back independently. This perceptive teacher knew that when her scaffolding created enough of a sense of confidence in her student it was time to lessen it and move her closer toward independence.

Many teaching methods, tools, and instructional routines (Wolsey & Fisher, 2009) can help the scaffolding process; however, scaffolds should not be confused with the actual tools or techniques. **Scaffolding** is what a teacher does for students who need support to learn, just as Emily needed support to learn to back float. Scaffolding tools can facilitate this support, but they are not a substitute for quality instruction from a teacher. Here are some examples of tools, instructional routines, and instructional concepts that can be included in literacy lessons and result in scaffolding:

- Graphic organizers
- Questions asked by peers or the teacher that help break down the concept to cognitively manageable bits
- Anchor projects or models of finished products that meet or do not meet the expectations
- Modeling behaviors and processes through thinking aloud
- Incremental steps
- Collaborative activities in which students may ask each other for assistance or learn from the knowledge each brings to the group.

If a graphic organizer helps a specific student or group of students to learn, that is scaffolding. However, if the student or group could learn without the graphic organizer, it is no longer considered scaffolding; indeed, such a tool when it is not necessary could hinder the thinking process. A tool, instructional routine, or technique is only a scaffold if it works to promote learning (Cazden, 2001).

The relationship between learning and teaching is nuanced and specific to the needs of the students, the demands of the curriculum, the resources available, and many other factors (e.g., an unscheduled announcement on the loud speaker that interrupts reading time). Responsibility for learning is shared between teacher and students, both as individuals and as a group of learners working together. A popular and useful way to think about new and challenging learning is the I Do, We Do, You Do approach. This approach is grounded in the idea that teachers cannot and should not bear the sole responsibility for student learning; the responsibility for learning must be transferred to students in a way that recognizes how learning occurs. Students who always rely on the teacher will not become independent learners. Instruction that helps students become proficient and independent over time follows a model of **gradual release of responsibility** (Fielding & Pearson, 1994; Pearson & Gallagher, 1983).

In this approach you explicitly teach a key concept: the "I Do" phase (see Exhibit 4.11). Then, you work with students so they can manipulate and apply their learning in the "We Do" phase (see Exhibit 4.12). Finally, learners are expected to manipulate and apply their learning on their own in the "You Do" phase (see Exhibit 4.13). To take the idea of the gradual release of responsibility a step further, a collaborative or cooperative phase can be added so that students work together without the teacher to create a shared understanding (Fisher & Frey, 2008; Frey & Fisher, 2009). Right away, a correspondence of the gradual release of responsibility and the lesson elements emerges (see Exhibit 4.14) where some key features of the lesson plan are compared with other useful planning models.

Explore this PowerPoint presentation (www.fisherandfrey.com/wp-content/uploads/2009/03/walkthroughs-grr-elementary-blog.ppt) to learn more about gradual release of responsibility from Nancy Frey. Slides 12 through 17 will help you visualize how gradual release of responsibility looks in graphic form.

EXHIBIT 4.11

I do: Teacher models.

EXHIBIT 4.12

We do: Teacher and student together.

points2ponder

QUICK REVIEW 3 Modeling behaviors, processes, and products is an important part of a lesson, but it is not a separate step. Why?

What is the relationship between checking for understanding and feedback?

How does scaffolding help students achieve lesson objectives and standards for learning?

(Access the answers in the digital version of this book.)

EXHIBIT 4.13

You do: Student does the task independently.

EXHIBIT 4.14

Comparing lesson planning elements with the gradual release of responsibility.

LESSON ELEMENTS	GRADUAL RELEASE OF RESPONSIBILITY
Anticipatory set	
Instructional input or explicit instruction	I do *(Responsibility for the lesson focus mainly rests with the teacher.)*
Guided practice and collaborative practice	We do *(Responsibility for learning is shared between teacher and students.)* You do it together *(Students collaborate to gain greater understanding.)*
Independent practice	You do it alone *(Students can assume nearly all of the responsibility for understanding and applying the concepts and content.)*
Closure	
Assessment and evaluation	

4.5

INSTRUCTIONAL APPROACHES TO INTEGRATING LITERACY TASKS IN YOUR LESSONS

A lesson plan represents your knowledge about standards, content, and effective ways to encourage students to advance in their learning. A language arts lesson plan is essentially a snapshot of the literacy learning that will occur in a single lesson on a certain day; it represents an approach to teaching. Students have lots of opportunity to read, write, speak, or listen in class; however, a more formal approach to teaching language arts will guide your planning. This section presents three approaches that guide the structure of language arts learning tasks as they fit within the context of the lesson in order to help students make sense of seemingly difficult learning challenges.

Before, during, and after approach

Many textbooks used in teacher preparation programs suggest a three-prong approach (before, during, and after) to teaching literacy as a key means of knowing and learning (Betts, 1946; Ryder & Graves, 2003; Tompkins, 2003), with some variations on that theme. Betts called this approach the directed reading activity. It is important to note that the before-during-after approach was first conceptualized as a way to approach reading tasks; however, it works well with other literacy learning tasks as well.

When students are asked to read challenging or instructional texts, lesson planning should account for what students need to know before reading; that is, what students do to prepare for reading challenging materials. This may be known as preparation for reading, prereading, or simply before reading. Make provisions for guiding students during reading by breaking down long texts into manageable chunks and helping to establish a purpose for reading. Finally, learning experiences should take into account the necessity of thinking about and working with ideas after reading is finished. This approach is popularly characterized as before-during-after reading; however, it is worth considering that each phase can support learning in different ways.

Prereading, for example, is a good time to engage students by helping them set a purpose for reading and making connections between the knowledge they already have and the learning that will result. This often serves the purpose of helping students become fluent readers by addressing new or partially familiar vocabulary prior to the reading. *Prereading* activities may also expose gaps in students' knowledge that can be addressed prior to the activity, thus improving the likelihood that students will learn from the reading. *During,* or guided, reading activities provide opportunities for students to practice cognitive strategies or to learn material relevant to the objective and standard. As students read, they continually see new purposes for their reading and narrow their focus based on the new information acquired. After students read, they should have the chance to revisit key skills and strategies (Afflerbach, Pearson, & Paris, 2008) and following up to extend or reinforce content, literacy learning, and understandings that result from the reading.

While there are different ways to stretch or compact the method of thinking about what students should learn before, during, and after they read, one way to think about it is to compare the lesson elements with the directed reading activity (Betts, 1946). Notice the similarities between the steps of the directed reading activity (i.e., before, during, after reading) and the lesson plan elements described previously in this chapter (see Exhibit 4.15). Pre-reading is akin to the anticipatory set and instructional input. During reading activities may be similar to the guided or collaborative section of a lesson plan. The pattern of introducing a concept and laying groundwork, providing instruction and guiding learning, then following up is prevalent in many models of learning. Although some elements match up for a single lesson, at times reading tasks are stretched over several lessons. A vocabulary activity, for example, may be the focus of an entire lesson, and it may be interspersed into all phases of the lesson. At other times, a review of vocabulary may only be part of the before reading step or the anticipatory set. Subtle nuances of how an approach, such as before, during, and after, integrates into daily language arts lessons develop with your increased level of knowledge and experiences.

EXHIBIT 4.15

Comparing lesson planning elements and the directed reading activity.

LESSON ELEMENTS	DIRECTED READING ACTIVITY
Anticipatory set	Prereading
Instructional input or Explicit instruction	Prereading
Guided practice and Collaborative practice	• Guided or during reading (especially if focused on learning new reading skills)
Independent practice	• Guided or during reading • Follow-up, extension, or after reading learning experiences.
Closure	Follow-up and extension (e.g., discussion and reflection).
Assessment and evaluation	

Whole-part-whole approach

Some argue that teaching students to look at the parts of language without providing context in ways that are recognizable and familiar is not as effective as activities that surround those skills in the context of language students will recognize (e.g., Smith, 2003). In other words, it does students little good to learn that the letter /b/ makes the sound "buh" if students cannot associate that learning with words they know: boy, bounce, big, bed, etc. Even better for young readers is if those words are found in the context of sentences, and even better yet is if those words are also found in stories that students know or to which they are introduced. Fortunately, there is no need to debate whether we can teach skills, such as phonics, and meaningful literature at the same time. Both support each other. Strickland (1998) argues for an approach that she calls *whole-part-whole,* which emphasizes context for learning many literacy skills. In this approach, Strickland proposes three conditions of a grounded framework for reading instruction: "Teaching is:

1. Whole: is grounded in fundamental understandings about whole texts such as stories, informational books, and poems;
2. Part: allows for in-depth focus on specific skills; and
3. Whole: includes planned practice within the context of meaningful reading and writing." (p. 7)

A skilled teacher begins with a meaningful text, embeds instruction of the skills students need, and returns to the text for additional practice and skill development. By now, you can probably see a pattern; this approach fits nicely into the lesson design we explored earlier. The point is that teaching skills outside of a meaningful context is not likely to result in effective learning.

4.6

DIFFERENTIATION

Differentiation is a term teachers hear and use frequently. The idea seems simple. Students should be taught according to their abilities, talents, strengths, and learning challenges. Educators try to avoid the term *weakness* when discussing students' capabilities. However, making differentiation work in a classroom with 25 or more students is a challenge, or it may seem so at first.

To promote your thinking about differentiation, let's begin with a short anticipation guide (Duffelmeyer, Baum, & Merkley, 1987). Use this book's notetaking feature to indicate whether you agree or disagree with each statement.

1. Differentiation means that the teacher develops a lesson plan for each student to address the needs of each.
2. Differentiation recognizes that students have different strengths, talents, learning challenges, and learning styles.
3. Differentiation is not really that different from planning a good lesson; it's just good teaching.
4. Differentiation means that learning tasks should cater to student learning strengths.
5. Differentiation tasks should be aligned with students' ability levels.
6. Groups based on needs are not very effective.

Now, as you read, make note of anything that confirms or refutes your view about each statement.

Let's begin by stating what differentiated instruction is not. It is not individualized learning where every student moves through material at a different pace. Differentiation is a way to think about how a teacher can meet students' learning needs in the classroom. This means thinking about how students will be grouped and the effects of that grouping on learning. It means thinking about the strengths students bring with them and their needs as compared to the objectives and standards of the lesson. Differentiation, in short, means

- noting important similarities in students' learning attributes,
- designing tasks that help all students meet the learning objectives,
- grouping students in flexible ways depending on specific learning objectives.

Differentiating a lesson can take many forms. However, a general framework for differentiation is based on identifying students' learning needs via thoughtful assessment. Instruction is then directed toward achievement of curricular goals, typically found in standards and iterated in the objectives for lessons. Differentiation also means considering how processes, products, content, or the learning environment might address students' identified needs (e.g., Tomlinson, 2001a, 2001b). For you, this means knowing the curriculum, the students, and the skills required for the content. The matrix in Exhibit 4.16 shows how curricular goals and learning needs intersect. For a given element of the lesson, you find the intersection of learning needs and curricular demands that addresses both. A fifth-grade teacher working at a school serving students at a military base could very well have students who come from many regions of the United States. For a unit on creation myths, the content might be differentiated based on student interest in a myth from a region near where they were born or last lived. Remember that differentiation is always about how you work with variation and diversity in the classroom. Thus, at any one intersection, multiple tasks are designed to address those needs and curricular goals. For more information about using this matrix, visit the LiteracyBeat site: http://literacybeat.com/2012/06/18/differentiation-tech.

EXHIBIT 4.16

Differentiation matrix.

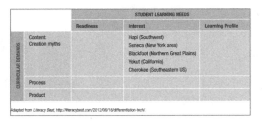

Adapted from *Literacy Beat*, http://literacybeat.com/2012/06/18/differentiation-tech/

Differentiating by student learning attributes

A popular means of differentiating tasks is based on learning profile. *Learning profile* and *learning style* are not interchangeable terms, and there are at least 12 different models describing various learning styles (e.g., Tendy & Geiser, 1998–1999). A **learning profile** can include a number of factors about the ways a person prefers to learn, including orientation to group work (i.e., some students prefer to work alone while others prefer to work with groups), cognitive and learning styles, learning environment preferences, and intelligence preferences (Tomlinson, 2001b). Conversely, a learning style framework might focus on perceptual modalities: visual, aural, tactile, and so on.

Differentiation can also incorporate intelligence theories, such as Gardner's theory of multiple intelligences. In the article "Frequently Asked Questions—Multiple Intelligences and Related Educational Topics" (http://howardgardner01.files.wordpress.com/2012/06/faq_september2012.pdf), Howard Gardner describes the important differences between learning style and intelligences. Simply put, a **learning style** is the customary way a person approaches a learning task or learning materials, while an **intelligence** is a person's potential for learning about certain content.

spotlight ON A LITERACY LEADER

HOWARD GARDNER

Howard Gardner is the John H. and Elisabeth A. Hobbs Professor in Cognition and Education at the Harvard Graduate School of Education. He is well known for his work in the area of multiple intelligences, a theory he developed from his background in cognition and education. Gardner was inspired by Jean Piaget's quest to understand the deepest levels of human thought. In 2005 and 2008, he was named as one of the world's top 100 most influential public intellectuals.

View Big Thinkers: Howard Gardner on Multiple Intelligences (7:55, www. edutopia.org/multiple-intelligences-howard-gardner-video) to hear Gardner talk about the theory of multiple intelligences and what it means for teachers and for students.

Differentiation according to learning needs or learning styles is not as complicated as it first sounds. Though there is some disagreement about learning styles and how they affect learning, they can be an effective way to provide helpful choices to students. Some students learn best by knowing the goals they are to master. Some learn best by working with others. Some learn through the journey of discovery, and still others learn through self-expression (e.g., painting or writing about a concept). Exhibit 4.17 provides an example of a task based on learning style (Silver, Strong, & Perini, 2000). The overall task is for students to compare the geology of the area where they live and share it with a class in another part of the country or even the world using email or a threaded discussion.

Differentiating by task

For some tasks, differentiation based on the learning styles framework will help all learners achieve science and literacy objectives. However, sometimes students need learning tasks that are based on their challenges. This may be thought of as their readiness for the learning that is to occur. In the task card, below (Exhibit 4.18), several tasks are tiered according to the students' capacities to read and understand a topic.

Read the following Stories from the Classroom to see how first-grade teacher Jessica Asbury uses tablet computers to manage grouping and differentiated activities geared toward meeting the needs of her students. In this example, Ms. Asbury differentiates her curriculum to guide all students to success by determining their readiness level and providing tasks that challenge them at that level.

EXHIBIT 4.17

Twenty-first-century pen pals tasks.

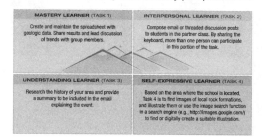

MASTERY LEARNER (TASK 1)	INTERPERSONAL LEARNER (TASK 2)
Create and maintain the spreadsheet with geologic data. Share results and lead discussion of trends with group members.	Compose email or threaded discussion posts to students in the partner class. By sharing the keyboard, more than one person can participate in this portion of the task.
UNDERSTANDING LEARNER (TASK 3)	SELF-EXPRESSIVE LEARNER (TASK 4)
Research the history of your area and provide a summary to be included in the email explaining the event.	Based on the area where the school is located, Task 4 is to find images of local rock formations, and illustrate them or use the image search function in a search engine (e.g., http://images.google.com/) to find or digitally create a suitable illustration.

EXHIBIT 4.18

Sample task card.

Objective: Students will read to understand and explain the phenomenon of global warming.

Directions: Read the information about global warming on the EPA climate change page (http://www.epa.gov/climatechange/kids/basics/index.html). If you want to learn more, read the three linked webpages you find at the bottom of that page.

Next, choose one task from the list below.

If you understand this objective and want a challenge	Read *The down-to-Earth guide to global warming* by David, L. and Gordon, C. (New York: Scholastic, 2007).
	Explain what global warming is in one paragraph based on what you read on the EPA webpage and in the book.
If you need more practice with this objective	Read Murphy, G. (2008). *A kid's guide to global warming.* Sydney: Weldon Owen Pty. Ltd.
	Compare this nonfiction book with EPA webpage information. Use a Venn diagram to compare the two sources of information.
If you aren't sure you understand this objective	Read the EPA climate change page about the impacts of global warming.
	Use a story board or paper folded into six boxes to illustrate some of those impacts. Why did you choose these? Then, read *Global warming: The threat of Earth's changing climate* by L. Pringle (New York: SeaStar Books, 2001). Explain what you learned in the book that you did not find on the webpage.

EXHIBIT 4.19

Students practice skills from their differentiated folder in pairs.

EXHIBIT 4.20

Spelling practice is designed for each student's level.

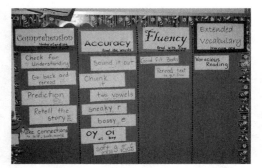

stories FROM THE CLASSROOM

Using tablets to differentiate instruction

Jessica uses tablets to promote differentiation during literacy center time. While she meets with a guided reading group, students are working at various literacy centers that include writing, reading to self or a partner, completing morning work, and using the tablet with a partner to practice a certain set of skills each day. To prepare for the tablet use, Jessica creates three folders in the tablet, titled red, blue, and green. Each folder contains educational apps chosen by Jessica to meet the different levels of learning needs for students in the corresponding groups. As students rotate through the literacy centers, pairs of students have a turn with the three tablets (see Exhibit 4.19). Periodically, Jessica reviews new educational apps and makes adjustments to the leveled folders based on the interests and learning needs of her students.

In addition to the three guided reading groups, the first graders are also organized into five leveled groups for spelling instruction and practice. On Wednesdays, the tablets are used for spelling practice during literacy centers. Students practice their own spelling lists using various apps to spell words with Morse code, sign language, electronic glitter letters, a digital whiteboard, and a dozen other ways that each student can choose based on individual interests (see Exhibit 4.20).

For tablet use at center time, Jessica encourages higher-level students to challenge themselves by working with apps that require knowledge beyond the grade level expectations. At the same time, students who still need to meet grade-level standards can develop their skills by using apps for this level of practice. Jessica explains her instructional decisions regarding the tablet: "In every classroom you are going to have a wide range of abilities. So if you don't allow for these levels within center time, it's not as productive. My students know their color group and know where they are supposed to work."

Differentiating by grouping

Managing the logistics of groups and lessons, while keeping all students moving forward, requires organization. You can conceptualize classroom management of groups in several ways (Lapp, Fisher, & Wolsey, 2009). One way to visualize how students might move from whole class, collaborative groups, and needs-based groups is depicted in Exhibit 4.21. However, this approach can vary depending on the needs of the students, their interests, and the demands of the curriculum. One critical consideration is to avoid grouping students in such a manner that they begin to think of themselves as underperforming or below grade level. Labeling students, however inadvertently, can work against them as they work toward challenging learning objectives and standards. Differentiated tasks should be challenging without being overwhelming; thus, different tasks will be available for various groups of students. Tasks for learners at every level must be substantive, respecting all students' right to learn. A student who is asked to simply color a picture of a plant, for example, while other students draw and label a plant's parts, may not be learning much about the plant. In that case, the activity is not differentiated and it is not respectful because little or no learning results.

In this video (9:13, http://youtu.be/IkRLikNR-UY), Dr. Wolsey describes the critical aspects of differentiation and provides three examples of differentiation that account for students' learning needs and curricular goals. Note how technology is used to enhance the differentiated tasks.

Finally, refer to the anticipation guide at the beginning of this section. What new ideas about differentiation do you now have? Which ideas are confirmed? Which ideas would you like to continue to explore?

4.7

ASSESSMENT

All elements of instructional design—anticipating different learning needs, designing effective learning tasks, creating an appropriate lesson plan—hinge on one key piece of information. What do the students know? Creating an accurate picture of a student's learning looks more like a mosaic than a still life. Because learning about language is an active process, assessment of language skills must be multifaceted. The assessment process provides both the teacher and students with information about what the students know and can do, which can then help determine what students need to learn next, based on expectations and standards. In this way, assessment guides instruction. Keep in mind, *assessment* and *evaluation* are not the same, although these terms are often used interchangeably. **Assessment** is gathering evidence of what students know and can do (e.g., collecting a written retelling, giving a spelling test) and using the evidence to inform instruction. **Evaluation** is making a judgment about the progress students are making based on this evidence (e.g., determining a developmental level, assigning a grade or score).

Determining what a student knows and is able to do and using this information to guide instruction requires you to make professional judgments and recommendations along the way. You can do this skillfully when you have a solid knowledge base about how students learn the language arts. This knowledge base does not appear overnight or merely after reading a chapter or two in a multimedia textbook. This knowledge base grows through your experiences with students and professional reading and discussions, along with a focus on implementing standards. This section of Chapter 4 builds your professional knowledge about key ways to assess and evaluate students' progress in the language arts by taking a multifaceted approach to looking at students' learning. Keep in mind, assessment is an ongoing process, from the first day of school to the last. As we assess our students, we also assess ourselves. We discover what, how, and when to teach specific things (Bridges, 1996). Some assessment occurs before we teach and some after; some assessment is formal with identified levels of criteria, and some is informal, relying on your keen sense of observation. Self-evaluation is also a crucial piece of the puzzle, so students can recognize what they know, develop a sense of their own learning growth, and use this knowledge and guidance from you and caregivers to set goals for future learning.

A model for assessment

The development of language arts skills is a complex process, which, as described in Chapter 3, is influenced by a person's culture, family, beliefs, and experiences. A single score placed on an assignment or test does not let you adequately evaluate progress, give specific feedback, and plan what to teach. Read the story about the author's daughter, who received a single score on a piece of writing.

EXHIBIT 4.21

A model for working with the whole class, heterogeneous groups, and needs-based groups.

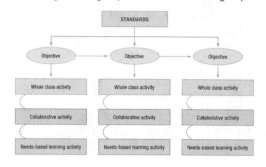

EXHIBIT 4.22

How valuable is this feedback?

Emily's Edition

Volume 1   February 7, 2001

The Plane wreck
By: Emily E. Schmar

We are hear at home and this is what hapend. We were going to see my aunt Angie in New Jersy. Our plane crashed on a mountain that was not even on the map. I was very suprised. Well of corse we have no food since it blue up with the plane. Well we were in luck there was fruits, and berries.

Well, we have been there for a week. We've ben sending signals and finaly some one came. It was not for us and we were out of food. Luckaly when the plane whent by, it dropped food just in case, butten more days later a plane came by. Then we were out of food and thirsty. Then a rescue party came and saved us. It brought us back. That is what I am telling you now. By the way, I am still hungry.

I for got to introduce my family. This is my mom, Beth and my dad, Tom and my brother, Eric. O ya I for got me Emily. I told you all I could. From now on you nead to talk to the rescu crew. Thank you.

26/30   87%
B-
nice story
check spelling and
make your details stronger

author's story   ELIZABETH DOBLER

My daughter Emily received this writing assignment back from her teacher with corrections and feedback written in green (see Exhibit 4.22). How helpful is this feedback? What does 26 out of 30 mean when it comes to writing? Twenty-six what out of 30 what? And what about the 87%? How can feedback on something as complex as writing be reduced to a single score? What exactly does B minus quality writing look like? The comments are only marginally more specific. "Nice story" is an attempt at a positive comment, but what about it is "nice"? Advice about spelling would be more helpful if given before the paper was graded. "Make your details stronger" is helpful, but suggesting specific details would be even better. If I have all of these questions and concerns, how did nine-year-old Emily feel? Confused? Disappointed? When I asked her how she felt about the feedback she said, "I don't care. . . . I don't like writing anyway." But maybe she would like writing more if she received feedback that recognized her strengths and weaknesses rather than vague comments that do not speak directly to her as a writer.

In order to create an accurate picture of what your students are able to do, you assess by gathering information all along the learning path and at the point where the path meets the learning goal. **Formative assessment** is at the heart of effective teaching because it provides information you can use to make adjustments along the learning path. A wide range of activities can be categorized as a formative assessment, including an entry in a science journal, a discussion of literature, or a handwriting worksheet. A **summative assessment** occurs at the end of a unit or at a specific point in time (e.g., week, quarter, grade level), and summarizes what the student has learned up to that point. A summative assessment could be a standardized test, a portfolio, or a final project.

The most useful assessments, whether formative or summative, are the ones that provide information you can use to adapt your teaching to meet the students' needs. A model for assessment provides evidence of the breadth and depth of student learning that supports your instructional decisions. To create this multidimensional view of the learner, you will collect learning evidence by monitoring, observing, and analyzing (Bridges, 1996).

Monitoring

Just as a baker monitors the loaf of bread in the oven, a teacher continually monitors student progress. These checks are often informal, evidence-gathering ventures. You may create an assessment tool for recording the evidence of learning, adapt one found in a teaching resource, or find one on the Internet. These formative assessments check progress along the way and may include a checklist, an inventory, or a project log.

Checklist. A checklist (Rowlands, 2007) is a tool for systematically monitoring students' progress by marking off what each student knows and is able to do in relation to grade level expectations. Students can also use checklists to monitor their own progress. Checklists can provide "an ongoing chronicle of the student's acquisition of fundamental skills" (Campbell-Hill, 2001, p. 161). A checklist must identify the essential elements of learning, but not include too many details as to be overwhelming. Second grade teacher Sarah Lucero describes her use of a checklist in this way: "I use checklists with a variety of structures but mostly for self-check during revising and peer-edit during the editing process. I'll use checklists for specific traits that I am currently working on. I always try to make sure the checklist is kid-friendly." Use professional judgment to determine if an existing checklist fits the learning needs of your students and make adjustments as needed. Checklists are also helpful in keeping track of day-to-day progress on specific projects or as a quick check of progress during writing time. Exhibit 4.23 offers an example of a writing skills checklist. A checklist can often be used as a precursor to a rubric, an assessment tool described in an upcoming section.

Inventories, profiles, and surveys. An interest inventory, a reading/writing profile, and an attitude survey are similar questionnaire tools for collecting information about the affective aspects of learning, or the attitudes, emotions, and preferences of learners. You can create or find existing tools in either paper or electronic form that will help you gauge your students' interests and attitudes about language arts both in and out of school. If you create your own, consider what you want to know about your students' language arts habits and attitudes and how their feelings and experiences may help or hinder learning. Although an inventory, profile, or survey helps you get to know your students, they may find it interesting to review their comments later on to see how their views have changed over time. Exhibit 4.24 displays an interest inventory from a third grader. An online version of the same inventory could be created through online survey tools such as Survey Monkey (www.surveymonkey.com).

Project log. A project log, such as a writing log or a reading log, is an individual record of what students are currently working on. Keeping track of this information holds students accountable and provides you with a written record of literacy center or writing time activities. A digital listening log, such as the one used in Exhibit 4.25, shows the digital books Ana listened to at the listening center. Her record could become part of a portfolio showing what she has accomplished over the last marking period.

EXHIBIT 4.23

A writing skills checklist.

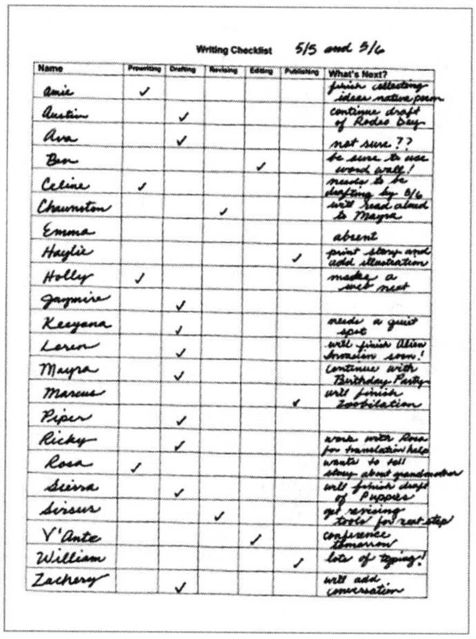

Writing Checklist 5/5 and 5/6

Name	Prewriting	Drafting	Revising	Editing	Publishing	What's Next?
Amie	✓					finish collecting ideas native poem
Austin		✓				continue draft of Rodeo Day
Ava		✓				not sure??
Ben				✓		be sure to use word wall!
Celine	✓					needs to be drafting by 5/6
Chaunston			✓			will read aloud to Mayra
Emma						absent
Haylie					✓	print story and add illustration
Holly	✓					make a web next
Jaymira		✓				
Keeyana		✓				needs a quiet spot
Loren		✓				will finish Alien Invasion soon!
Mayra		✓				continue with Birthday Party
Marcus					✓	will finish Zoobilation
Piper		✓				
Ricky		✓				work with Rosa for translation help
Rosa	✓					wants to tell story about grandmother
Sierra		✓				will finish draft of Puppies
Sirius			✓			get revising tools for next step
Y'Ante				✓		conference tomorrow
William					✓	lots of typing!
Zachery		✓				will add conversation

EXHIBIT 4.24

Interest inventory.

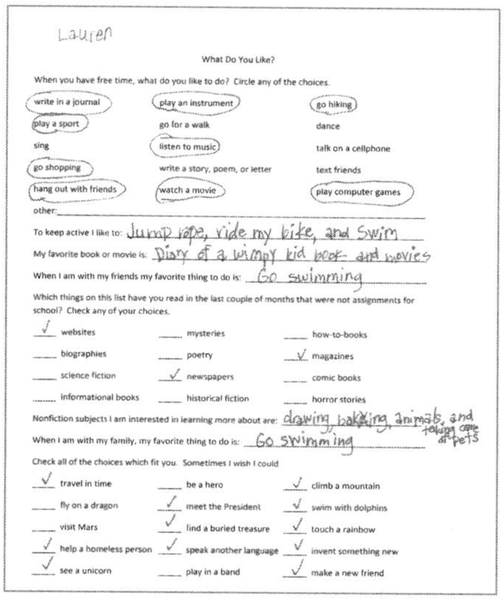

Lauren

What Do You Like?

When you have free time, what do you like to do? Circle any of the choices.

(write in a journal) (play an instrument) (go hiking)
(play a sport) go for a walk dance
sing (listen to music) talk on a cellphone
(go shopping) write a story, poem, or letter text friends
(hang out with friends) (watch a movie) (play computer games)

other: ______

To keep active I like to: Jump rope, ride my bike, and Swim

My favorite book or movie is: Diary of a wimpy kid book and movies

When I am with my friends my favorite thing to do is: Go swimming

Which things on this list have you read in the last couple of months that were not assignments for school? Check any of your choices.

✓ websites ___ mysteries ___ how-to-books
___ biographies ___ poetry ✓ magazines
___ science fiction ✓ newspapers ___ comic books
___ informational books ___ historical fiction ___ horror stories

Nonfiction subjects I am interested in learning more about are: drawing, bakking, animals, and taking care of pets

When I am with my family, my favorite thing to do is: Go swimming

Check all of the choices which fit you. Sometimes I wish I could

✓ travel in time ___ be a hero ✓ climb a mountain
___ fly on a dragon ✓ meet the President ✓ swim with dolphins
___ visit Mars ✓ find a buried treasure ✓ touch a rainbow
✓ help a homeless person ✓ speak another language ✓ invent something new
✓ see a unicorn ___ play in a band ✓ make a new friend

(Print a blank Interest Inventory: www.hhpcommunities.com/teachinglanguagearts/IL-04-04.pdf)

EXHIBIT 4.25

Digital listening log.

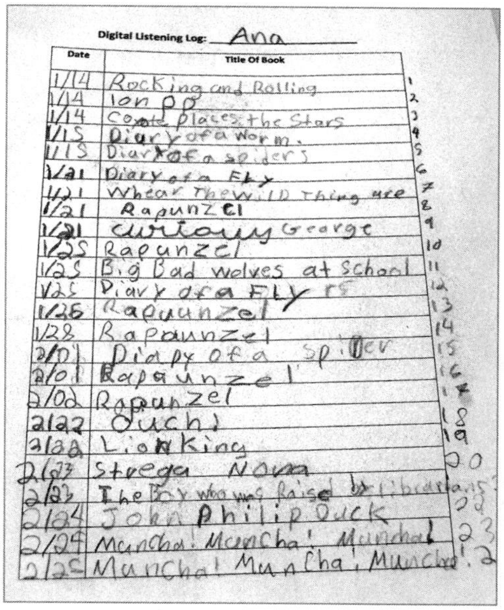

Digital Listening Log: Ana

Date	Title Of Book	
1/14	Rocking and Rolling	1
1/14	lon po	2
1/14	Coyote places the Stars	3
1/15	Diary of a Worm.	4
1/15	Diary of a spiders	5
1/21	Diary of a Fly	6
1/21	Whear The wild Thing are	7
1/21	Rapunzel	8
1/21	curious George	9
1/25	Rapunzel	10
1/25	Big Bad wolves at School	11
1/25	Diary of a Fly	12
1/26	Rapuunzel	13
1/28	Rapaunzel	14
2/01	Diapy of a spider	15
2/01	Rapaunzel	16
2/02	Rapunzel	17
2/22	Ouch!	18
2/22	Lion King	19
2/23	Strega Nona	20
2/23	The Boy who was Raised by librarians	21
2/24	John Philip Duck	22
2/24	Muncha! Muncha! Muncha!	23
2/25	Muncha! Muncha! Muncha!	24

Anecdotal records.

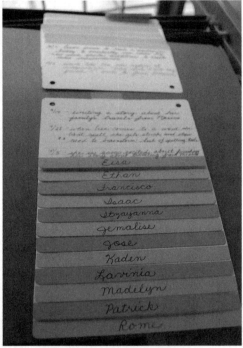

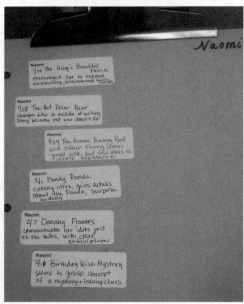

Observing

A student leaves clues about what she knows and can do. The role of the teacher is to recognize, interpret, and use these clues to help guide instruction. Noticing clues begins with a keen eye. The term *kidwatching* (Goodman, 1985) was coined to describe the combination of a teacher's constant and focused observation of students and knowledge of developmental levels and learning styles. Recorded observations serve as evidence of learning and can be used to help make decisions about modifying and adapting teaching to meet the individual needs of students. In addition, organized and effective records of your observations provide a tool for tracking growth and setting goals, while also giving colleagues and families specific examples of student progress.

Anecdotal records. Anecdotal records, or brief written notes based on classroom observations of students, allow you to capture the moment and describe various aspects of student learning and behavior as they are occurring. When collected over time, you can look for patterns within the notes and use this information to guide instruction. Early on, when developing a system for collecting and organizing anecdotal notes, decide

- the purpose of the notes
- the specific learning you expect to observe
- who else besides you might see the notes
- how the notes will be recorded and stored.

The three R's of anecdotal notes are *remember, record, reflect,* which focus on consistently recording brief notes about observations and reflecting on their connection to instruction. Write down with what you notice, noting especially the details that fill you with awe or worry. Look for signs of progress both large and small, such as the consistent use of paragraphs or the correct spelling of a tricky word. Your observations should be guided by grade level expectations for your state or local standards and your own objective for the day's lesson. Anecdotal notes are not only about looking for what is missing in your students' learning, but also the many skills they have learned. Anecdotal notes are often recorded on sticky notes, file cards, mailing labels, or with a tablet or digital voice recorder (see Exhibit 4.26). "Anecdotal records readjust the teacher's vision of who and where the student is and sharpens teachers' insights into how each student travels along his or her own path to learning" (Matthew, 1992, p. 169).

Developmental continuum. As was discussed in Chapter 2, a **developmental continuum** presents the stages of learning in a visual form. A continuum is unique from the other assessment tools because it displays previous and future levels of learning, so those working with the student know what to expect next. Some teachers use highlighters of various colors to indicate a student's progress on the writing continuum from one marking period to the next. A continuum shows clear benchmarks for growth, which help a teacher know what students of a certain age can be expected to do. In addition, a continuum can serve as an observation guide, pinpointing specific literacy behaviors or actions a teacher should watch for during learning. In order to use a continuum to show progress in literacy, we as teachers must become very familiar with the stages of development and the descriptors for each stage. However, please note that continua such as those linked below tend to describe typical of progress; great care should be taken in applying these to individual students.

View the Reading Continuum: www.hhpcommunities.com/teachinglanguage arts/IL-02-A.pdf

View the Writing Continuum: www.hhpcommunities.com/teachinglanguagearts/IL-02-B.pdf

View the Stages of Spelling Development: www.hhpcommunities.com/teaching languagearts/IL-10-01.pdf

---

Samples of a student's work, anecdotal notes, and completed checklists serve as the evidence of a student's abilities. As you collect a wide variety of evidence throughout the marking period, you begin to identify each student's stage of development, based on what you have seen the student do. For example, if the continuum says a student labels pictures with words, then samples of the student's writing should support this statement. Once enough evidence is gathered, and typically at a certain point in the school year, you will mark a developmental stage on the continuum for each student. Then the document is usually shared with others, such as the reading specialist, caregivers, and also the student. When communicating with families, use the continuum to move the discussion beyond grades to a model of growth. A continuum is about focusing on the positive by noticing what a student can do right and what we should watch for next.

Analyzing

Analyzing may be the most challenging of the three elements of a teacher's assessment tasks, although all are equally important. Monitoring is checking for learning; observing is watching for learning. Analyzing is determining the essential features of learning. Synonyms for *analyze* include *examine* and *investigate*. This means you are looking closely at what students are doing to demonstrate their learning and how well they are doing it. Whether using student work in a portfolio or data from a test, a teacher pulls together assessment information to draw conclusions about a student's progress.

Portfolios. Assessing a complex skill, such as any one of the modes of language arts, requires a collection of various sources of evidence to demonstrate a student's proficiency. A **portfolio,** whether paper or electronic, can be used as a tool for collecting and saving assessment data and samples of students' work that represent their learning. A portfolio may simply be a manila or pocket folder or it may be electronically created on a document sharing site or a private school district website. The organization and use of a portfolio reflect a teacher's or school's purpose. In order to show growth, a portfolio could be a collection of student work to share at a fall and spring parent/teacher conference. A portfolio could be aligned with standards and contain work samples that demonstrate a student's proficiency with certain grade level expectations. For example, a collected spelling test could show mastery of grade level spelling words, and a writing sample could be included to support this same expectation. Individual items collected in the portfolio may have already been assessed, or the portfolio as a whole, when created as a final project, may be a single item for assessment. Portfolio formats, uses, and sources of evaluation information are as varied as the teachers who design them. Live Binder is a useful tool for creating an online portfolio because it allows students to upload files, scanned documents, and weblinks to create an online space for storing evidence of their learning. Some educators even use Live Binder to create an electronic teaching portfolio to use for job interviews.

To learn more, wiew the video at the Live Binder homepage (1:33): www.live binders.com (click on the graphic image at right to access the video).

Standardized assessment. A **standardized test** is an assessment that is administered and scored in a uniform way in order to give consistent and reliable data. The results from a standardized assessment are used to show how a student performs compared to other students who took the assessment (**norm referenced**) or compared to a set criteria or standard (**criterion referenced**). Standardized assessments can be developed at the local, state, or national level and may be used not only to document individual student progress but also to show the proficiency of a group of students (e.g., all fourth graders at a school, in a district, or a state). In addition, standardized assessment data may be used to determine the success of teachers and administrators. Standardized tests typically have multiple-choice questions and bubbles that the test taker blackens. When applied to standardized tests, the term *high stakes* means important decisions are made based on the test results, such as a student passing to the next grade or graduating. Not all standardized test data are used this way, but standardized tests do receive much attention from teachers, administrators, and the public. Some standardized assessments entail students demonstrating their learning verbally rather than on a computer or with paper and pencil. A performance standardized assessment is typically given individually; one example is the DIBELS (Dynamic Indicators of Basic Early Literacy Skills), which assesses phonological awareness, phonics, accuracy, fluency, comprehension, vocabulary, and oral language.

More information about DIBELS: https://dibels.uoregon.edu. Although you may feel pressure for students to do well on standardized assessments, such as DIBELS, keep in mind these tools are just one kind of many used to determine student progress.

Rubric. At the basic level, a **rubric** presents levels of quality, which compare expectations to a finished product or performance. For example, the creators of Ben and Jerry's ice cream have identified their expected level of quality characteristics for their blueberry cheesecake ice cream, which includes the elements of smoothness, flavor, and the proper amount of cheesecake chunks. In the classroom, a rubric for learning assessment lists the characteristics you expect to see, providing levels of quality, ranging from beginning to developing or proficient. A useful rubric for assessing students' learning includes criteria that are significant, clear, and constructive. These criteria are crucial, because a rubric, besides being an assessment tool, can also serve as an instructional tool, providing you with direction for what to teach next in order to help a student reach the expected level of quality.

A teacher may choose between two types of rubrics, holistic and analytic. A holistic rubric looks at learning as a whole. For example, a holistic rubric considers a piece of writing to be the sum of its parts. In other words, the teacher looks at the piece of writing as a whole and determines how closely the writing matches expectations.

Third-grade teacher Jennifer Gold has created a holistic retelling rubric (www. mrsgoldsclass.com/Word%20Files/Retelling%20Rubric.doc) that lists four levels of quality: capable, developing, beginning, and novice. Each level provides a score to be assigned to the retelling of a story. Holistic assessment provides a quick and relatively simple way to determine the quality, while also providing general feedback to the learner.

Analytic assessment involves analyzing individual traits to determine if a set of expectations or criteria are being met, usually spelled out in an analytic rubric. An analytic rubric provides more detailed information about the individual elements of learning than a holistic rubric. The Six +1 Trait writing model (discussed in Chapter 12) uses an analytic rubric or scoring guide to break down writing into various elements with a score given to each element. Analyzing the components of writing gives you the opportunity to provide specific feedback about strengths and areas for growth.

One key to using rubrics successfully is giving students access to the criteria we expect them to meet before we assess their work. Jenny Fitzgerald, a kindergarten teacher, posts a writing rubric in her classroom near the writing center (see Exhibit 4.27). This simple tool lets young writers know the progression their writing should follow as they become more skilled and encourages them to compare their own writing to these expectations on a regular basis. Third grade teacher Scott Ritter shares a project rubric with the students on the day he introduces the animal project assignment (see Exhibit 4.28). From the beginning, the students know Mr. Ritter's expectations for the project and they know the end point.

Listen to the two segments of this interview to hear how third grade teacher Scott Ritter uses feedback and rubrics to increase student achievement. In particular, note how Mr. Ritter's students provide feedback to each other in addition to the feedback from the teacher.

Segment 1 Feedback (5:00), Segment 2 Rubrics (3:54) *(Access these podcasts in the digital version of this book.)*

Whenever possible, assessment should be a partnership between you and the student, and you should clearly communicate evaluation criteria to students before embarking on the learning journey. Few things are more frustrating for a learner than trying to meet learning criteria without knowing what these criteria actually include. You have probably had the experience of writing a paper or creating a project while wondering exactly what the teacher expects. When both teachers and students know what is expected (Stiggins, 2005), each can move forward with an eye on the target. Each can become integrally involved in the circle of assessment, where clear criteria leads to learning (see Exhibit 4.29).

Choosing the assessment tool to use

As described earlier, a variety of assessment tools exist to determine what students know and can do when it comes to language arts. You will use your professional knowledge to choose the most appropriate and useful assessment to meet the purpose, whether it is anecdotal notes, a develop-

EXHIBIT 4.27

Kindergarten writing rubric.

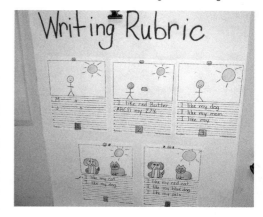

EXHIBIT 4.28

Third grade project rubric.

	ANIMAL EXPERT	ANIMAL FRIEND	KEEP LEARNING
Clearness	Proper grammar, spelling, and vocabulary are used throughout the presentation. The four topics are clearly stated. The meaning was clear.	Proper grammar, spelling, and vocabulary are used in most of the presentation. Three topics are clearly stated.	Grammar, vocabulary and spelling are not acceptable. Fewer than three topics are presented in a clear manner.
Facts	Facts are stated. Supporting evidence from the research is provided.	Facts are stated.	No or few facts are stated.
Information	Presentation informs others about the animal.	Presentation tries to inform others about the animal.	Presentation does not try to inform others about the animal.

EXHIBIT 4.29

Teachers and students as partners in the circle of assessment.

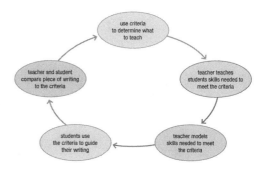

EXHIBIT 4.30

Which assessment tools should I use?

ASSESSMENT TOOL	USE
Interest Inventory	Determines the interests of children and guides selection of reading materials and writing topics
Literacy Profile	Determines interests, attitudes, and experiences with various aspects of literacy
Attitude Survey	Determines attitudes toward various aspects of literacy
Anecdotal Notes	Systematically records your observations of what students know and can do during classroom literacy experiences
Developmental Continuum	Shows the developmental stages students transition through in language arts
Checklist	Keeps track of skills mastered or completed by each student
Rubric	Show levels of quality and clarifies expectations for performance tasks (i.e., reading aloud, writing a poem, creating a multi-media project)

mental continuum, or a rubric, or another tool (see Exhibit 4.30). This notion of meeting a purpose is important. In no way would you be expected to use all of the assessment tools described in this chapter every day for every student. If this were the case, teachers would spend all their time assessing and little time teaching. To determine which assessment tool to use in a given situation, ask yourself, "What do I want to know about the students, and which is the most effective way to gain this information?"

These broad explanations about assessments are only a starting point in understanding the various types of assessments and how they can be used to guide instruction. Chapters 5, 6, and 7 provide information about teaching the receptive modes of language arts (reading, listening, viewing), and Chapters 9, 10, and 11 present information about the expressive modes (writing, speaking, visually representing). Each chapter also mentions and links to relevant assessments (which are gathered in the following two chapters: Chapter 8, Assessing the Receptive Modes, and Chapter 12, Assessing the Expressive Modes). For a more sequential reading of *Forward Thinking*, you may decide to wait and study the assessment descriptions and examples in the assessment chapters rather than linking to them as you read the content chapters.

points2ponder

QUICK REVIEW 4 Why is it important to provide students with criteria from a rubric before assessing their work?

(Access the answer in the digital version of this book.)

4.8

REFLECTING ON YOUR TEACHING

Reflecting on your teaching means becoming aware of yourself and noticing the nuances of your growth and development (Sheerer & Glatthorn, 2004). It helps you to:

- find focus
- make sense through the written word and digital media
- search for meaning
- share insights
- change behavior

Think of reflection as a means of navigating the space between what is learned in your everyday professional practice and the possibilities of what that practice might look like tomorrow under more complex conditions. Reflection is situational and asks you to utilize all your cognitive resources. In describing Schön's model of professional reflection, Romer (2003) suggests that teaching practice is legitimate in its own right, not just as a product of enacting theory. Teachers deal with limited resources, many models and paradigms that sometimes conflict with each other, numerous stakeholders, and contending interests. Reflection helps you bring unity and coherence to these complex systems. "The learning process may then be described as a circular structure involving the elements of framing, experiment, situational backtalk, evaluation, and reframing. This process may, of course, go on infinitely" (Romer, 2003, p. 86).

An important avenue of reflection is engagement with other professionals. Fortunately, there are many ways to engage with other professionals, including through the organizations discussed below.

The Association for Supervision and Curriculum Development offers a forum for professional engagement and reflection: http://ascdedge.ascd.org.

A first step toward professional development is joining the professional associations in your state and region, as well as connecting through professional learning communities (often abbreviated as PLC) at your school and in your district. These professional growth opportunities will provide resources and renewal throughout your entire career. Visit the IRA website for a list of local and state IRA associations: www.reading.org/General/LocalAssociations.aspx.

4.9

CHAPTER SUMMARY

Lesson planning is one of the most basic aspects of teaching, but just because it is basic does not mean we can assume it is simple. Rather, many elements, some of which do not remain constant throughout a lesson, must be brought together to promote student learning and achievement. Experienced teachers do much planning in their heads, although many continue to create lesson plans in some type of format (e.g., list, outline, graphic organizer) well into their teaching years. For novice teachers, creating a complete and thorough lesson plan is imperative. This plan serves as evidence of the myriad of considerations given to the lesson prior to teaching. Teaching requires juggling many balls: presentation, time, behavior management, checking for understanding, language and learning needs—not to mention the occasional fire drill, assembly, or bloody nose. Preparing the predictable—a full and detailed lesson plan—lets you focus on the what is unpredictable in the lesson.

Literacy learning is a particularly complex domain (e.g., Spiro, 2004), and it does not lend itself easily to fixed notions of how best to proceed. Teachers must be knowledgeable about pedagogy, language arts, and their students' learning needs in order to help them become proficient, lifelong readers. Effective teachers also recognize the critical role assessment plays in all aspects of planning and instruction. The circular connection between these three elements leads to the idea of lesson planning as a continuous process.

APPLICATION ACTIVITIES

think like a teacher

Comparing Lesson Plans

Many different lesson planning guides exist, which may be a bit confusing at first. Remember, one size does not fit every circumstance when it comes to planning and teaching. There is no perfect lesson plan format. Professors and administrators may expect a certain format, so future and practicing teachers must be familiar with a variety of formats. Many lesson planning resources are available through a collection of weblinks available at Delicious.com; visit the lesson plan format links there. Use the links at this site and the Lesson Plan Format Comparison Chart to compare several lesson plans in order to better understand their possibilities. Even though the names of different components change depending on the authors' perspectives, several main ideas emerge.

On the Delicious link stack, visit the lesson plan format links: https://delicious. com/#tdwolsey/Lesson%20Planning%20and%20Assessment

Access and print the Lesson Plan Format Comparison Chart: www.hhp communities.com/teachinglanguagearts/IL-04-05.pdf

Question the Lesson Plan

Online lesson plan sites have plans all written up and seemingly ready to go. These are useful resources; however, the lessons you find online may not meet your curricular needs or feature all the elements of lesson plans that will help your students achieve learning goals that are appropriate for them.

Visit this site, https://delicious.com/#tdwolsey/Lesson%20Planning% 20and%20Assessment, and choose three lesson plans for the grade level you teach or plan to teach from the sites linked there. Next, choose your state or content standards (www.educationworld.com/standards) or the Common Core State Standards (www.corestandards.org).

Ask yourself:

- What are the **objectives** for the lesson? Are they appropriate for your students? How are they aligned with the standards for your state or school district? Do the lessons include opportunities for differentiating student learning experiences? If so, how, and if not, what adjustments could be made? Are those differentiated learning tasks appropriate for the students with whom you work?
- Do the lessons include **models** to help students with new or complex learning? If not, what models would you incorporate?
- How would this lesson fit with other lessons designed to help students achieve their learning goals?

Comparing Pacing Guides

A pacing guide maps out what is to be taught at a certain grade level and when it is to be taught. For this activity, read over the two pacing guides listed below, one for second grade, and one for fifth grade. Use the four-box Pacing Guide Comparison Contrast handout (www.hhpcommunities.com/ teachinglanguagearts/IL-04-06.pdf) to compare and contrast them. The purpose of this activity is to give you a chance to dig deeper into the functions of a pacing guide and how you might use one effectively as a teacher. After completing the handout individually, meet with a small group of other students to discuss the similarities and differences between the pacing guides. Then, as a group, identify three key features you feel are the most important or helpful and share these with the whole group. Use this collaborative list to construct a broad explanation of how a pacing guide may be used in the classroom to guide instruction.

REFERENCES

Afflerbach, P., Pearson, D., & Paris, S. G. (2008). Clarifying the differences between reading skills and reading strategies. *Reading Teacher, 61*(5), 364–373. DOI: 10.1598/RT.61.5.1.

Anderson, L. W., & Krathwohl, D. R. (Eds.). (2001). *A taxonomy for learning, teaching, and assessing: A revision of Bloom's taxonomy of educational objectives.* New York: Longman.

Baumann, J. F., Jones, L. A., & Seifert-Kessell, N. (1993). Using think alouds to enhance children's comprehension monitoring. *Reading Teacher, 47*(3), 184–193.

Betts, E. A. (1946). *Foundations of reading instruction with emphasis on differentiated guidance.* New York: American Book Company.

Bransford, J. D., Brown. A. L., & Cocking, R. R. (Eds.). (2000). *How people learn: Brain, mind, experience, and school.* Washington, DC: National Academy Press. Retrieved from http://www.nap.edu/catalog.php?record_id=9853.

Bridges, L. (1996). Assessment (Strategies for teaching and learning professional library). Portland, ME: Stenhouse.

Bruner, J. (1978). The role of dialogue in language acquisition. In A. Sinclair, R. J. Jarvelle, & W. J. M. Levelt (Eds.), *The child's concept of language* (pp. 241–256). New York: Springer-Verlag.

Campbell-Hill, B. (2001). *Developmental continuums.* Norwood, MA: Christopher Gordon.

CAST (2011). *Universal design for learning guidelines version 2.0.* Wakefield, MA: Author. Retrieved from http://www.udlcenter.org/aboutudl/udlguidelines/principle1

Cazden, C. B. (2001). *Classroom discourse: The language of teaching and learning* (2nd ed.). Portsmouth, NH: Heinemann.

Cennamo, K., Ross, J., & Ertmer, P. (2009). *Technology integration for meaningful classroom use.* Mason, OH: Cengage Learning.

Common Core State Standards Initiative (2012). Common core state standards for English language arts & literacy in history/social studies, science, and technical subjects. Council of Chief State School Officers and the National Governors Association. Retrieved from http://www.corestandards.org/assets/CCSSI_ELA%20Standards.pdf.

Danielson, C. (1996). *Enhancing professional practice: A framework for teaching.* Alexandria, VA: Association for Supervision and Curriculum Development.

Duffelmeyer, F. A., Baum, D. D., & Merkley, D. J. (1987). Maximizing reader-text confrontation with an extended anticipation guide. *Journal of Reading, 31,* 146–150.

Durkin, D. (1990). Dolores Durkin speaks on instruction. *Reading Teacher, 43,* 7, 472–726.

Emig, J. (1971). *The composing processes of twelfth graders.* Urbana, IL: National Council of Teachers of English.

Fielding, L., & Pearson, P. D. (1994). Reading comprehension: What works. *Educational Leadership, 51*(5), 62–68.

Fisher, D., & Frey, N. (2007). *Checking for understanding: Formative assessment techniques for your classroom.* Alexandria, VA: Association for Supervision and Curriculum Development.

Fisher, D., & Frey, N. (2008). *Better learning through structured teaching: A framework for the gradual release of responsibility.* Alexandria, VA: Association for Supervision and Curriculum Development.

Fisher, D., Frey, N., & Lapp, D. (2009). In a reading state of mind: Brain research, teacher modeling, and comprehension instruction. Newark, DE: International Reading Association.

Freire, P. (1970/1993). *Pedagogy of the oppressed: 30th anniversary edition.* New York: Continuum.

Frey, N., & Fisher, D. (2009). The release of learning. *Principal Leadership, 9*(6), 18–22.

Gick, M. L., & Holyoak, K. J. (1983). Schema induction and analogical transfer. *Cognitive Psychology, 15,* 1–38.

Goodman, Y. (1985). Kid watching: Observing children in the classroom. In A. Jaggar and M. T. Smith-Burke (Eds.), *Observing the language learner.* Newark, DE: International Reading Association, and Urbana, IL: National Council of Teachers of English.

Harris, T. L., & Hodges, R. E. (1995). *The literacy dictionary.* Newark, DE: International Reading Association.

Hattie, J., & Timperley, H. (2007). The power of feedback. *Review of Educational Research, 77*(1), 81–112, 2007. DOI: 10.3102/003465430298487.

Hunter, M. (1982). *Mastery teaching.* Thousand Oaks, CA: Corwin Press.

Jones, F. (2007). *Tools for teaching* (2nd ed.). Santa Cruz, CA: Fredric H. Jones.

Kolb, D. A. (1984). *Experiential learning.* Englewood Cliffs, NJ: Prentice Hall.

Lapp, D., Fisher, D., & Wolsey, T. D. (2009). *Literacy growth for every child: Differentiated small-group instruction K–6.* New York: Guilford.

Lapp, D., Shea, A., & Wolsey, T. D. (2011). Blogging and audience awareness. *Journal of Education, 191*(1), 33–44.

Matthew, C. (1992). An alternative portfolio: Gathering one child's literacies. In D. Graves & B. Sunstein (Eds.), *Portfolio portraits* (pp. 158–170). Portsmouth, NH: Heinemann.

National University (2010). *Student teaching handbook.* Retrieved from http://www.nu.edu/assets/resources/departmentResources/Student%20Teacher%20Handbook%202010%20Final.pdf.

Pearson, P. D., & Gallagher, M. C. (1983). The instruction of reading comprehension. *Contemporary Educational Psychology, 8,* 317–344.

Romer, T. A. (2003). Learning process and professional content in the theory of Donald Schön. *Reflective Practice, 4*(1), 85–93.

Rowlands, K. D. (2007). Check it out! Using checklists to support student learning. *English Journal, 96*(6), 61–66.

Ryder, R. J., & Graves, M. (2003). *Reading and learning in the content areas* (3rd ed.). New York: John Wiley & Sons.

Serdyukov, P., & Ryan, M. (2008). *Writing effective lesson plans: The 5-star approach.* Boston, MA: Pearson.

Sheerer, M., & Glatthorn, A. A. (2004). *The teacher's portfolio: Fostering and documenting professional development.* Lancaster, PA: Proactive Publications.

Silver, H. F., Strong, R. W., & Perini, M. J. (2000). *So each may learn: Integrating learning styles and multiple intelligences.* Alexandria, VA: Association for Supervision and Curriculum Development.

Smith, F. (2003). *Unspeakable acts, unnatural practices: Flaws and fallacies in "scientific" reading instruction.* Portsmouth, NH: Heinemann.

Spiro, R. (2004). Principled pluralism for adaptive flexibility in teaching and learning to read. In R. B. Ruddell & N. Unrau (Eds.), *Theoretical models and processes of reading* (5th ed., pp. 654–659). Newark, DE: International Reading Association.

Stiggins, R. J. (2005). *Student-involved assessment for learning* (4th ed.). Upper Saddle River, NJ: Pearson.

Strickland, D. (1998). What's basic in beginning reading? Finding common ground. *Educational Leadership, 55*(6), 6–10. Retrieved from http://www.ascd.org/publications/educational-leadership/mar98/vol55/num06/What's-Basic-in-Beginning-Reading%C2%A2-Finding-Common-Ground.aspx.

Tendy, S. M., & Geiser, W. F. (1998–1999). The search for style: It all depends on where you look. *National Forum of Teacher Education Journal, 9*(1), 3–15.

Tomlinson, C. A. (2001a). Differentiation of instruction in the elementary grades, *ERIC Digest*. Retrieved from http://www.ericdigests.org/2001-2/elementary.html.

Tomlinson, C. A. (2001b). *How to differentiate instruction in mixed-ability classrooms* (2nd ed.). Alexandria, VA: Association Supervision and Curriculum Development.

Tompkins. G. (2003). *Literacy for the twenty-first century (3rd ed.). Upper Saddle River, NJ: Merrill Prentice Hall.*

Vygotsky, L. S. (1978). The mind in society: The development of higher psychological processes. Cambridge, MA: Harvard University Press.

Walden University. (2006). ERL lesson plan template. Retrieved from http://inside.waldenu.edu/c/Student_Faculty/Student Faculty_2462.htm.

Wiggins, G., & McTighe, J. (2005). *Understanding by design* (Expanded 2nd ed.). Alexandria, VA: Association for Supervision and Curriculum Development.

Wiles, J., & Bondi, J. C. (1984). *Curriculum development: A guide to practice.* Columbus, OH: Charles E. Merrill.

Wilhelm, J. D. (1999). Think-alouds boost reading comprehension. *Instructor, 111*(4), 26–28.

Wilhelm, J. D. (2001). *Improving comprehension with think-aloud strategies: Modeling what good readers do.* New York: Scholastic Professional Books.

Wolsey, T. D. (2008). Efficacy of instructor feedback in an online graduate program. *International Journal on eLearning, 7*(2), 311–329.

Wolsey, T. D., & Fisher, D. (2009). *Learning to predict and predicting to learn.* Upper Saddle River, NJ: Merrill Prentice Hall.

Wormeli, R. (2007). *Differentiation: From planning to practice, 6–12.* Portland, ME: Stenhouse.

Zull, J. E. (2002). *The art of changing the brain: Enriching teaching by exploring the biology of learning.* Sterling, VA: Stylus Publishing.

CHILDREN'S LITERATURE CITED

Carle, E. (1987). *Have you seen my cat?* New York, NY: Aladdin Paperbacks.

David, L., & Gordon, C. (2007). *The down-to-Earth guide to global warming.* New York: Scholastic, Inc.

Murphy, G. (2008). *A kid's guide to global warming.* Sydney: Weldon Owen Pty. Ltd.

Pringle, L. (2001). *Global warming: The threat of Earth's changing climate.* New York: Seastar books.

Read Naturally, Inc. (2006). *A rat.* [Read Naturally Phonics Series, Level .8]. St. Paul, MN: Author.

Reading Fundamentals

Access the book's Glossary, which defines the key terms boldfaced in this chapter, at www.hhpcommunities.com/teachinglanguagearts/glossary.pdf

KEY IDEAS

- A teacher's skill and knowledge is the most powerful variable in determining whether or not a student learns to read, especially a student in poverty.

- The reading process is the simultaneous extraction and construction of meaning through interaction with written language.

- Balanced literacy is an instructional approach that includes the research-based components of comprehension, composition, literature, and language.

- Differentiating instruction through grouping allows teachers to meet the diversity of students' instructional needs.

- Phonological instruction should be explicit, systematic, and match students' developmental levels.

- The instructional context in which reading is taught is critical to meaningful and engaging instruction.

- Effective routines for managing classroom instruction are critical and must be meaningful and productive.

5.1

INFLUENCES ON LITERACY ACQUISITION

What are your early memories of learning to read? Maybe a family member or a teacher read to you. Or, maybe you remember reading a book that left a lasting impression, such as E. B. White's *Charlotte's Web* or J. K. Rowling's Harry Potter series. You may also have memories of which you are not so fond, such as being placed in the lowest reading group or being asked to read aloud when you did not feel confident doing so. Our early experiences with reading can leave an indelible impression that lasts a lifetime. Teachers have a powerful influence on their students, and their instructional practices must encourage students to take ownership of literacy for lifelong success.

Students continue to learn to read throughout their years of education, and family members and teachers play an important role in the development of the students' increasingly complex levels of literacy learning. However, for some students, teachers are their best hope for achieving literacy. Duane Alexander, Director of the National Institute of Child Health and Human Development (NICHD), testifying before the House Senate Budget Committee, stated that "Reading skills are essential to function in our society.

"Meeting the instructional needs of all students is essential. Frustration as a teacher comes into play when you're not able to challenge students or able to reach students. The ability to meet the needs of students on multiple levels is what makes a teacher successful."

RACHEL GRANATA,
first grade teacher

111

Yet many children, particularly children born in poverty, never learn to read. This inability to read has profound and long term implications for the children in terms of their health, their participation in civic life, and their ability to function in an increasingly complex world" (NICHD, 2002). The teacher's skill and knowledge is the most powerful variable in determining whether or not a young child learns to read, including socioeconomic status (Nye, Konstantopoulos, & Hedges, 2004). Therefore, your role as a teacher of reading has the potential to be life-changing.

According to a position statement by the IRA (2000), a research-based description of the distinguishing qualities of excellent classroom reading teachers includes those who:

- Understand reading and writing development and believe all students can learn to read and write.
- Continually assess students' individual progress and relate reading instruction to students' previous experiences.
- Know a variety of ways to teach reading, when to use each method, and how to combine the methods into an effective instructional program.
- Offer a variety of materials and texts for students to read.
- Use flexible grouping strategies to tailor instruction to individual students.
- Are good reading coaches; that is, they provide help strategically (see Exhibit 5.1).

In addition, excellent reading teachers have strong content and pedagogical knowledge, manage classrooms so that there is a high rate of engagement, use strong motivational strategies that encourage independent learning, have high expectations for students' achievement, and help students who are having difficulty (IRA, 2000, p. 1).

From this list of distinguishing qualities of knowledge and practice, it is easy to see why excellent reading teachers make a difference in students' reading achievement and motivation to read (see Exhibit 5.2). With the exception of knowledge of the reading process, many of these characteristics are discussed in other chapters of this book because they are critically important to highly effective teaching of the language arts and will be reinforced in this chapter in relationship to teaching reading.

EXHIBIT 5.1

Jessica Asbury reading with Austin.

EXHIBIT 5.2

Maria and Jacob reading.

5.2

PHASES OF READING DEVELOPMENT

Literacy acquisition is a developmental process that takes place from birth through adulthood. Researchers have described this process as a sequence of developmental phases (Chall, 1983; O'Donnell & Wood, 2004). Though researchers have used different terms to delineate the phases, most have similar descriptions. All students move through these phases while growing and developing as readers, but not all students progress at the same rate. For example, some children enter kindergarten with emergent literacy skills, such as knowledge of the letters of the alphabet or how to write their name, while others will not. The developmental sequence of learning is influenced by one's ability, sociocultural background, environment, attitude, and motivation. The Reading Continuum (www.hhpcommunities.com/teachinglanguagearts/IL-02-A.pdf) displays the phases of reading development a typically developing student moves through during the school-age years. A knowledgeable teacher watches for literacy behaviors that match these benchmarks as evidence of a student's progress. Understanding the development nature of literacy acquisition gives you the perspective that learning is a reflection of what the student understands at the moment and what he or she can do with assistance.

stories FROM THE CLASSROOM

Early reading

Ginny, a kindergarten teacher, spent the first several weeks of school observing her students as they interacted with a variety of books. She placed the picture books in a book box between two students and asked them to look at the books together. As they interacted, she observed many of her students opening the books from the bottom and leafing through the pages from left to right. Most students also looked at the pictures and not the text. In the following weeks, Ginny used big books (large books that all students could see) to model the correct way to open a book and which way to turn the pages. She also pointed to the words as she read, modeling the correct direction to read the words. As she read, she invited the students to join her during the parts that were familiar. Ginny's modeling, within the context of meaningful reading in which the students were also participating, allowed the students to begin acquiring these important concepts about print.

 The developmental phases outlined in the Reading Continuum can be used as benchmarks to assess where students are in their development and what they need to learn with assistance. The video Thalia Learns the Details (26:48, www.learner.org/libraries/readingk2/thalia/index.html) provides an example of this developmental process of literacy acquisition. The video follows the progress of kindergartner Thalia over the year as she engages in a variety of reading and writing activities that develop her awareness of letters, sounds, and words. Her English-language teacher, Jim St. Clair, uses poems, songs, predictable books, reports on classroom activities, and student journals to build on her emergent literacy skills and to promote a love of reading and writing.

5.3

THE READING PROCESS

Think of the last book you read. Why did you read it? To be transported vicariously into another place and time? To be entertained or to gain knowledge? Or, did a friend or teacher ask you to read it? We read for lots of different reasons, and these reasons play a role in the reading process. As you read a book, you utilize many thought processes to understand what you read. This section focuses on the deep thinking the reading process entails.

author's story   DENISE JOHNSON

Recently my husband, who is a history buff, asked me to read an article in *Newsweek* on the Iraq War. I was motivated to read the article because he asked me, but my background knowledge and vocabulary concerning the war were not adequate to fully understand the article. Though I could read all of the words, I didn't understand some concepts and events, which made reading the article difficult and less than engaging, and I didn't gain as much information from it as my husband did. Later in the day, however, I picked up a new book by one of my favorite authors. Because I was familiar with the genre and writing style of fantasy, I slipped easily into the author's world, became totally absorbed in the story, and lost track of time. My comprehension varied greatly between these two reading events due to the difference in my prior knowledge, the texts, and the activity itself.

What is the reading process?

In the *Newsweek* scenario above, as the reader extracted information from the nonfiction text, she was simultaneously trying to access and connect to the appropriate background, vocabulary, and concept knowledge to construct meaning; however, her comprehension was limited due to insufficient knowledge in these areas. As defined by the RAND Reading Study Group (2002), comprehension "is the process of simultaneously extracting and constructing meaning through interaction and involvement with written language" (p. 12). Extracting and constructing meaning from text is a complex cognitive socio-psycholinguistic activity that involves the simultaneous execution of the processes of attention, memory, language, and motivation (Snow, Burns, & Griffin, 1998).

Because this process is so complex, the RRSG created a heuristic, or mental model, of the process, which can assist educators with making instructional decisions based on their understanding of the process. In the heuristic, the three elements of reading comprehension—the *reader,* the *text,* and the *activity* of reading—are depicted within a Venn diagram that shows the unique exchange between the elements and the larger sociocultural context that shapes and is shaped by the reader (see Exhibit 5.3).

The heuristic in Exhibit 5.3 is based on the assumption that the reader is reading linear text, typical of most traditional written communication, such as books or articles. The implications for reading nonlinear text, which includes online information, have not been taken into consideration in the heuristic. The RAND Reading Study Group (2002) acknowledges that "electronic text presents particular challenges to comprehension (e.g., challenges stemming from the nonlinear nature of hypertext), but it also offers the potential to support comprehension by providing links to definitions of unknown words or to other supplementary material" (p. xv). Some researchers have argued that conventional understandings of these four elements (including context) are not always sufficient in electronic and networked information environments (e.g., Coiro, 2003; Coiro & Dobler, 2007; Kymes, 2005; Leu, Kinzer, Coiro, & Cammack, 2004).

For example, Coiro & Dobler (2007) found that successful online reading experiences appeared to simultaneously require both similar and more complex applications of prior knowledge sources. Readers were required to draw upon their prior knowledge of the topic and their knowledge of printed informational text structures, as they would for traditional text. However, they were also required to use their prior knowledge of informational website structures and online search engines, which are only required in online reading environments.

Coiro, Knobel, Lankshear, and Leu (2008) state that "literacy is no longer a static construct; it has now come to mean a rapid and continuous process of change in the ways in which we read, write, view, listen, compose, and communicate information" (p. 5). In other words, the skills required to

A heuristic for thinking about reading comprehension.

READER (will vary among and within individuals):

- cognitive capabilities such as attention, memory, critical analytic ability, inferring, visualization
- motivation or purpose for reading and interest in the content
- prior knowledge of vocabulary, topics, language, and comprehension strategies
- experiences

TEXT: The structures of any text have a large impact on comprehension. The reader constructs meaning from the text that is based on:

- the exact wording of the text
- the ideas within the text
- the way in which information is processed for meaning

ACTIVITY: The reading activity involves:

- one or more purposes or tasks, which can change as the reader encounters information that raises new questions or changes the original purpose for reading
- decoding the text, higher-level linguistic and semantic processing, and self-monitoring for comprehension
- outcomes of performing the activity, which can include an increase in knowledge, a solution to some real-world problem, and/or engagement with the text

SOCIOCULTURAL CONTEXT

This refers to the varying sociocultural environments in which children live and learn to read. Learning and literacy are acquired through social interactions, but they also represent how a specific cultural group or discourse community interprets the world and transmits information. There are a range of sociocultural differences in communicative practices that are often correlated with group differences such as income, race, ethnicity, native language, or neighborhood.

Adapted from: RAND Study Group (2002). *Reading for understanding: Toward an R&D program in reading comprehension.* Arlington, VA: RAND Corporation.

communicate proficiently with technology require traditional as well as new reading, writing, and communicating skills. These **new literacies** have been defined as the "skills, strategies, and dispositions necessary to successfully use and adapt to the rapidly changing information and communication technologies and contexts that continuously emerge in our world and influence all areas of our personal and professional lives" (Leu et al., 2004, p. 1572). Effective teachers understand the importance of being able to read and understand visual and print-based information in order to fully participate in our quickly changing technology-based society (see Exhibit 5.4).

spotlight ON LITERACY LEADERS

JULIE COIRO, SARA KAJDER

Over the past few decades, we have seen a great flow of technological tools to assist literacy learning from computers to cell phones to MP3 players. Today, digital technology enables readers and writers to integrate text, image, sound, animation, and voice in new ways. The challenge for teachers is to integrate these constantly evolving digital technologies into meaningful and motivating instruction. In the podcast, linked below, Julie Coiro from the University of Rhode Island and Sara Kajder from Virginia Tech University share their thoughts about available digital tools and how they might transform classrooms and literacy learning. Coiro and Kajder are researchers in the field of literacy and technology whose work has contributed significantly to our current understanding of online reading and the integration of technology into literacy instruction. As you listen to these researchers, consider how they suggest that teachers help their students care about their digital footprints. Also consider how they suggest that teachers select the technology for their students to learn (28:00, http://media. ncte.org/library/audio/c0a4452e-ff84-4bc0-bca9-bf4b41813eec.mp3).

Language cueing systems

Students come to school equipped with a powerful source of information with which to begin their journey to literacy—full knowledge of their native language. Since birth, children have been acquiring an understanding of the phonology, words, grammar, and socially influenced meanings of the language they speak. Knowledge of this complex system of language serves as a source of clues or a set of **cueing systems** (see Exhibit 5.5) in a student's acquisition of literacy.

The **phonological system** is the sound system of a language. The English language has 44 **phonemes** or units of sound (see Exhibit 5.6). Regional differences may affect the way some phonemes are pronounced. These sounds are put together into words that have meaning to speakers of English. Children come to school with an implicit understanding of these sounds and words but will need assistance in learning how these sounds are represented in writing by the 26 **graphemes** or letters of the alphabet. Teachers often assist students by promoting **phonemic awareness,** the ability to orally manipulate phonemes in words, and **phonics,** the phoneme-grapheme correspondences and rules.

The **syntactic system** is the structure or grammar of a language that governs how words are combined into phrases and sentences that make sense. Syntax in this sense does not refer to the correctness of grammar; rather, it refers to our understanding of the order of nouns, verbs, adjectives, and other words in a sentence. For example, if someone says, "The dog again barked,"

EXHIBIT 5.4

Darius reading on a computer.

EXHIBIT 5.5

Language cueing systems.

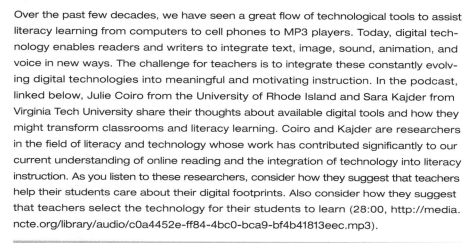

EXHIBIT 5.6

Phoneme chart.

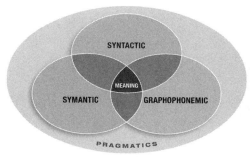

a child is likely to know that the statement is not syntactically correct, or recognize that it does not sound right because the order of the words is unusual. Children come to school already understanding these rules to a large extent, though they will continue to develop an understanding of more complex sentence structures over time. Syntax is a powerful source of information when reading. When a student comes to an unknown word in a sentence, she can substitute a word that sounds right or fits structurally. For example, if the text is, "the boy is flying" and the student reads it as "the boy as flying," the fact that the incorrect reading does not sound right could prompt her to go back and reread. This helps the student monitor her reading. Books written for emergent readers often mimic the natural syntax with which children are familiar and then later introduce literary language.

The **semantic system** is the meaning system of a language. Meaning comes from understanding words and word parts, or **morphemes,** which are the smallest meaningful unit of language (e.g., the word *buyers* consists of three morphemes: *buy, er, s*). Words have multiple meanings that can only be derived within the context of the sentence, or no meaning, as in the case of idioms unless you are familiar with these expressions. Meaning also comes from the text taken as a whole.

The **pragmatic system** is the social use of language in a culture. Our language changes according to immediate social situations and audiences. For example, our discourse at a school faculty meeting might be different than at a football game. Additionally, **dialect,** also referred to as registers, changes according to social class, ethnic group, or geographic locations. The formal dialect of school is called **Standard English,** whereas other forms, such as those spoken in Appalachia or African American English, are nonstandard and differ in the phonology, syntax, and semantics from Standard English. Nonstandard forms of English are not inferior to Standard English; rather they reflect a particular community of people. Recognize the value of educating students about language diversity in ways that honor all students' linguistic and cultural backgrounds while also teaching the rules, norms, and conventions of Standard English that students need to succeed in school and life (Charity-Hudley & Mallinson, 2011). Teachers also need to emphasize the importance of adapting language to the audience and the social context.

Visible versus invisible sources of knowledge in reading

These four cueing systems represent a vast amount of *in the head* or invisible sources of knowledge that students bring to the task of reading. Some students who have been read to at home may have also acquired additional knowledge about how texts work, such as different types of texts or genres, text structures, and literary elements. Visible sources of information such as symbols and signs, print conventions, and text tools also provide valuable information when reading.

When learning to read, a child must draw upon both invisible and visible sources of information simultaneously. For example, while the child recognizes the letters in the words she is reading (visible information), she must simultaneously associate these letters with their sounds and put the sounds together into meaningful words (invisible information). While reading words, the child must simultaneously think about the content and her personal knowledge of these words. In the early phases of literacy development, this process will be slow and deliberate. As the reader becomes more proficient, however, he will use this complex system of strategic actions in a highly orchestrated and efficient way, which allows for fluency and comprehension.

Each student's use of visible and invisible information in the reading process is unique. Knowing what information a student does or does not use while reading can provide teachers with valuable data to be used for guiding instruction. Teachers can analyze an individual student's use of the cueing systems through a coding system called **running records**. Running records, developed by Marie Clay (1993), capture students' text processing strategies through oral reading and can be used throughout the year to inform instructional decisions. The teacher uses a blank sheet of paper and the coding system in Exhibit 5.7 to record the student's reading of a text. The running record can be analyzed for accuracy to determine the kinds of information the student is using to process the text. Even very good readers make errors when reading. The difference is when the errors, or **miscues,** lead to lack of comprehension of the text. Exhibit 5.8 shows an analysis of errors using the cueing systems.

From an analysis of oral reading patterns and responses to comprehension questions, you can get a picture of how a student figures out unknown words in context, how she constructs meaning, and her approximate reading level. With running records of text reading, you can record and analyze reading behaviors and monitor progress over time. Keep in mind, reading is not only about accuracy but also about how well students are learning to recognize and solve the reading problems they encounter. Based on this ongoing assessment information gathered over time, you can determine oral reading or comprehension areas where students need more instruction and practice.

Chapter 8 offers additional discussion of running records and miscue analysis.

The video Teaching for Transfer: Strategic Activity (8:00, http://fdf.reading recovery.org/index.php/teaching-for-transfer) demonstrates how effective teachers provide many opportunities for students to successfully read and write texts. These opportunities allow the students to strengthen neural pathways in order to pick up information, work on that information, make decisions, and evaluate their responses. The video also shows examples of teachers working with students individually and in small groups, making instructional decisions based on what they know about each student's reading process. As you watch, consider how the teachers help students build strategic processing systems. After viewing, select a key point from the video. Using chart paper, an individual whiteboard, or a mobile device, draw your interpretation of this key point. Then share your drawing and explanation with classmates.

Fluency and comprehension

author's story   DENISE JOHNSON

I often listen to audiobooks in the car, especially during my hour-long drive to work. Sometimes when I pull into the parking lot at work, I don't remember getting there because I was so engrossed in the story. Driving the same route every day for years, I have developed a routine that has become automatic and largely unconscious. If something changes during my drive, such as the need to stop suddenly, my routine is interrupted and I adjust my driving to meet the demands of the situation. When this happens, I might need to replay part of my audiobook because I missed key details during the interruption. The reading process can also be performed unconsciously. The simultaneous use of the cueing systems and integration of visible and invisible information during the reading process, when developed over time, become automatic, or fluent.

EXHIBIT 5.7

Coding reading behaviors.

BEHAVIOR	CODE	COUNTED AS ERROR
Accurate reading	✓ / text word	NA
Substitution	incorrect word / text word	Yes
Self-correction	incorrect word | SC / text word	No
Repetition	← R / text word (s)	No
Repetition with self-correction	incorrect word | R | SC / text word	No
Omission	___ / text word	Yes
Insertion	inserted word / ___	Yes
Long pause	# / text word	No
Told	text word | T	Yes

(Print a blank version of Coding Reading Behaviors at www. hhpcommunities.com/teachinglanguagearts/IL-05-01.pdf as a quick review sheet when coding a running record.)

EXHIBIT 5.8

Analysis of oral reading miscues.

Semantically acceptable: The word makes sense in the context of the text.

In the following example, the student's substitution is not semantically acceptable since *ailment* alters the meaning of the sentence. If the student had substituted *homework* instead, it would be a semantically acceptable error.

Student: *ailment*
Text: The assignment did not seem interesting to the girl.

Syntactically acceptable: The word fits grammatically in the sentence.

In the following example, the substituted word *didn't* for *did not* is syntactically acceptable since it fits grammatically in the sentence.

Student: *didn't*
Text: The assignment did not seem interesting to the girl.

Graphically similar: The word is visually or phonetically similar to the accurate word.

In the following example, the substituted word "ailment" is visually similar, so the student is using some visual information, but the substitution doesn't make sense.

Student: *ailment*
Text: The assignment did not seem interesting to the girl.

A person reading aloud with fluency captures listeners' attention. Oral reading flows smoothly as the reader's voice rises and falls with a natural rhythm. Fountas and Pinnell (2006) say that **fluency** entails

- Accessing visible and invisible information rapidly and integrating it smoothly.
- Reconstructing written signs into language in a largely unconscious process.
- Performing all operations rapidly and smoothly.
- Reading with ease so that the greatest amount of attention is freed to think about the text.
- Reading phrase units or groups of words with the voice in a way that shows recognition of the deeper meanings of the text. (p. 31)

Notice that this description does not include speed or fast reading. The speed or rate of reading reflects a reader's purpose for reading. Students often give a slow, careful reading of a textbook when studying for a test and a quick reading of the ball game scores at ESPN.com. Fluent readers adjust their rate of reading according to purpose and context. This does not mean that reading with momentum or pace should be ignored. Excessively slow or fast reading can be an indication of a dysfluent reader. The accuracy with which we read is critical to understanding a text. The ability to read words automatically and quickly with little effort means readers have more mental attention available for comprehension. **Prosody,** or the ability to read with expression, is also important. Prosody includes the pausing, phrasing, stress, and intonation appropriate for the text being read. Fluent readers do not use a monotone reading voice; they interpret the intention of the author and read strategically with appropriate inflection, tone, and pace to make the text sound like spoken words.

To determine a student's **reading rate,** time her reading and divide the number of words in the passage by the time it took to read it. A study by Pinnell et al. (1995) found that 64 percent of fourth grade students read at 124 words per minute or slower; however, students who read at 130 words per minute or higher had the highest average proficiency scores on the NAEP Integrated Reading Performance Oral Reading Fluency Scale (see Exhibit 5.9). The scale can be used as a general guideline for determining students' reading fluency.

Fluency, accuracy, and prosody can be influenced by:

- what is being read
- familiarity with concepts and/or genre
- accessibility of language structures
- vocabulary, the number of known words
- the number of unknown words that are easy to figure out.

All of these aspects contribute to text difficulty, which in turn affects fluency. Thus, the more resources a reader brings to the text, the quicker, more accurate, and more expressive the reading becomes. All of these elements of fluency work together to help the reader build a strong foundation for comprehension. You assess a student's fluency by listening to oral reading and comparing what is seen and heard to a set of expectations, usually presented as a rubric. (Chapter 8 offers more information about fluency assessment.)

EXHIBIT 5.9

NAEP's Integrated Reading Performance Record Oral Reading Fluency Scale.

LEVEL 4	Reads primarily in large, meaningful phrase groups. Although some regressions, repetitions, and deviations from text may be present, these do not appear to detract from the overall structure of the story. Preservation of the author's syntax is consistent. Some or most of the story is read with expressive interpretation.
LEVEL 3	Reads primarily in three- or four-word phrase groups. Some smaller groupings may be present. However, the majority of phrasing seems appropriate and preserves the syntax of the author. Little or no expressive interpretation is present.
LEVEL 2	Reads primarily in two-word phrases with some three- or four-word groupings. Some word-by-word reading may be present. Word groupings may seem awkward and unrelated to larger context of sentences or passage.
LEVEL 1	Reads primarily word by word. Occasional two-word or three-word phrases may occur, but these are infrequent and/or they do not preserve meaningful syntax.

From *Listening to Children Read Aloud* by U.S. Department of Education, National Center for Education Statistics, 1995, Washington, DC.

Assessing the reading process

Determining how well a student can read is fraught with complexities because the reading process itself is complex. Much of what occurs when we read takes place in our mind, and monitoring, observing, and analyzing the elements of assessment described in Chapter 4 require a trained eye and the knowledge to dig beneath a reader's pronunciation. A running record and fluency rubric, both discussed previously, provide useful glimpses at students' decoding skills and reading fluency. Both of these, although important, represent only a portion of the reading process. Standardized multiple choice reading tests, widely used for reading assessments, also provide data about one aspect of the reading process—comprehension. Getting at the heart of the reading process in a single assessment is challenging at best. Portfolios pose one effective way of capturing the multidimensional essence of reading, because you can collect different types of evidence to represent what a student can do. An electronic portfolio, first introduced in Chapter 4, could contain a series of oral reading podcasts and beginning- and end-of-the-year fluency rubrics that show a student's progress over the course of the school year, along with copies of running records and periodic retellings that show growth in comprehension. Such a wide variety of items gives a richer picture of a student's progress with learning to read. Another reading assessment, the informal reading inventory (IRI), collects evidence representing the many facets of the reading process. The basic element of an IRI is similar to a running record in that the student reads orally while the teacher codes words that are different from what appears on the paper or screen. However, an IRI has additional components not found with a running record, including comprehension questions, a word list, and in some cases a fluency rubric. When it comes to providing a teacher with the breadth and depth needed to assess student reading progress, an IRI is the most comprehensive tool. (Chapter 8 offers additional information about one kind of informal reading inventory, the *Qualitative Reading Inventory,* and the pros and cons of using an IRI for reading assessment.) Keep in mind that when given the opportunity to choose a reading assessment, you should look for one that generates the information that will be the most helpful when planning for instruction, establishing small groups, and determining what students know and can do.

In the next sections of this chapter, you will learn the various instructional contexts and teaching strategies you can employ to assist students in developing their understanding of written language. Teachers can assist students in using invisible and visible sources of information to develop the skills and strategies necessary to develop a proficient processing system that leads to fluency and comprehension.

points2ponder

QUICK REVIEW 1

A. Why is a teacher's understanding of the reading process important?
B. What are the new literacies and how have they affected the teaching of reading?
C. List several sources of invisible and visible information used when reading.
D. Why is reading fluency important?

(Access the answers in the digital version of this book.)

5.4

A BALANCED, COMPREHENSIVE APPROACH TO LITERACY INSTRUCTION

A balanced approach to literacy instruction is grounded in the belief that ownership of literacy is central to students' lifelong success (Pearson, Raphael, Benson, & Madda, 2007), and this ownership of literacy motivates students to continue reading even when reading becomes challenging. Au (2011) writes, "the first task a teacher faces . . . is to make sure that students are engaged in meaningful literacy activities, so they realize that literacy can serve real purposes in their own lives" (p. 130). In order for literacy to be meaningful and for engagement ultimately to develop into a sense of ownership, the literacy curriculum must be designed to reflect the diverse needs of students who come from different cultural and linguistic backgrounds.

What is balanced literacy?

Balanced literacy is an instructional approach that allows teachers to provide all of the important ingredients that go into creating thoughtful, avid readers, and writers (Cunningham & Allington, 2011). Characteristics of a balanced literacy classroom for students and teachers are as follows:

- Students engaged in authentic, meaningful reading and writing:
    - across the day and the curriculum,
    - in the content areas,
    - that emphasizes higher level thinking.
- Teachers who:
    - explicitly teach reading and writing skills through modeling, coaching, and demonstration.
    - use a variety of formats to provide instruction, including whole class, small group, individual instruction, and collaborative groups, changing the format depending on what will best achieve their goals.
    - use a wide variety of materials.
    - have well-managed classrooms with high levels of engagement in which the activities are relevant and important to the students.

The characteristics of a balanced literacy approach are exemplified in an instructional program that includes the research-based components of comprehension, composition, literary analysis, and language conventions (see Exhibit 5.10). Three of these components are described in this chapter and Chapter 6, while composition is discussed in Chapters 9 and 10. As teachers we must provide comprehensive and balanced literacy instruction because too much time spent on one component typically results in too little time spent on another. Although the scope and sequence of the literacy curriculum is often determined by the school district, teachers still have a great deal of leeway in deciding how to use materials, what kinds of instructional formats to use, and how to create an engaging environment.

Implementing the components of balanced literacy instruction requires teachers to possess a deep knowledge of individual students, the reading process, and the curriculum. Using both formal assessment and informal assessments such as developmental checklists and running records previously discussed in this chapter, we are able to **differentiate instruction** to

EXHIBIT 5.10

Components of a balanced literacy curriculum.

COMPREHENSION	COMPOSITION	LITERATURE/LITERARY ANALYSIS	LANGUAGE
Background Knowledge: Prediction	**Writing Process:** Planning (Prewriting)	**Literary Elements:** Theme	Sound Symbol
Text Processing: Summarizing Sequencing Identifying importance	Drafting Revising Editing Publishing	Plot Character Setting	Grammar Syntax Interaction
Monitoring: Clarifying Planning	**Writing as a Tool** **Writing from Sources** **Writing on Demand**	**Response to Literature:** Personal Creative Critical	
		Text Structures: Description Problem/solution Chronological/sequencing Comparison/contrast Cause/effect	
		Text Features*: Glossary Headings/subheadings Table of contents Boldface vocabulary Photo captions Bibliography Author's notes Graphics Index Questions	
		*May include other features in addition to those listed.	

Adapted from Pearson, P., Raphael, T., Benson, V., & Madda, C. (2007). Balance in comprehensive literacy instruction: Then and now. In L. Gambrell, L. Morrow, & M. Pressley (Eds.), *Best practices in literacy instruction* (3rd ed., pp. 31–54). New York: Guilford.

meet the diverse needs of our diverse students (also see the discussion of differentiating instruction in Chapter 4). Using information gained through ongoing assessment allows teachers to be flexible and tailor their teaching to provide meaningful engagement with reading for all learners. "Balanced literacy instruction should give students of diverse backgrounds the best of both worlds: motivation to use literacy in everyday life, for the purposes they set for themselves, and proficiency in the literacy skills and strategies necessary to accomplish these purposes" (Au, 2011, p. 130).

As teachers, we must know when to provide more explicit support, or **scaffolding,** through modeling and demonstration and when to gradually decrease scaffolding and allow students to take over the responsibility through guided and independent practice until they are able to use a skill or strategy independently. As Pearson, Raphael, Benson, and Madda (2007) note, "Achieving balance is a complex process that requires flexibility and artful orchestration of literacy's various contextual and conceptual aspects" (p. 33). Exhibit 5.11 depicts how the instructional contexts of **reading aloud, shared reading, guided reading,** and **independent reading** allow for varying levels of teacher scaffolding and student participation and lead to a gradual assumption of responsibility by students. These instructional contexts, used to teach the components also listed in Exhibit 5.11, will be described in more detail later in this chapter.

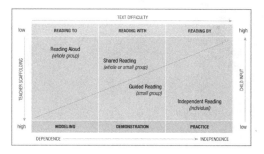

EXHIBIT 5.11

Levels of instructional scaffolding and context.

Grouping for effective instruction

As previously mentioned, children come to school with varying developmental levels of literacy acquisition. Grouping is an organizational response to meeting the diversity of students' instructional needs. Differentiating instruction through grouping is a common trait of highly effective schools. (See also Differentiation by Grouping in Chapter 4.)

Research has shown **small group instruction** to be a critical component of effective reading instruction (Allington & Johnston, 2002; Gibson & Hasbrouck, 2008; Taylor, Pearson, Clark, & Walpole, 2000). Teachers make decisions for small group instruction using assessment data and an understanding of the unique needs of each student in the classroom. Data-informed teaching uses materials that match text difficulty to student reading levels. Good teachers lead skills-focused lessons that include student engagement and guided practice with constructive feedback from themselves or a student peer. Within a balanced literacy classroom, groups are formed and reformed for different purposes.

Ability grouping, in which students are organized into low, middle, and high reading groups according to skill levels that are often determined by standardized tests (Schumm, Moody, & Vaughn, 2000), is a prevalent practice (Chorzempa & Graham, 2006). In contrast to the flexible groups described above, groups designated by ability tend to remain static throughout the year with students in all groups reading the same material and receiving the same instruction, but at a different pace. Ability grouping has many negative effects for diverse learners, including:

- Students from minority groups are more likely to be assigned to low ability groups.
- Students who did not have preschool experience are more likely to be assigned to low ability groups.
- Students in low ability groups may receive lower quality instruction, spending more time doing **round-robin reading** (in which each student

EXHIBIT 5.12

Grouping for instruction.

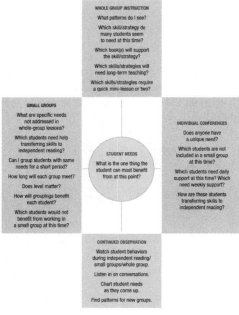

Source: Sibberson, F., & Szymusiak, K. (2003). *Still learning to read: Teaching students in grades 3-6*. Portsmouth, NH: Stenhouse.

EXHIBIT 5.13

A visual word wall.

reads a short passage, continuing where the last student left off) and workbook assignments than students in high ability groups.

- Students in low ability groups are more likely to exhibit inattentive behaviors than students in high ability groups.
- Students in low ability groups have lowered academic expectations and suffer damage to self-esteem and social relationships.
- Teachers typically interrupt low readers more often during oral reading when they miscue.

Quality instruction reflects a balance between various group combinations, including whole group, small group, and individual instruction. You must use professional judgment, including knowledge of the content and research, all couched within your teaching philosophy to provide a rationale for various grouping decisions. When small groups are the most appropriate choice, a teacher creates the groups based on formal and informal assessment information, grouping together students with similar learning needs, based on the data. As these learning needs change from one lesson to another or one unit to another, the groups also change. Exhibit 5.12 provides questions you can ask yourself when making decisions about grouping for effective instruction. At some schools teachers of each grade level form a team and meet weekly, biweekly, or monthly to discuss assessment data with each other and an instructional coach or literacy specialist. These meetings provide teachers with support for the process of organizing small group instruction.

Text matters

A critical factor in a balanced literacy classroom is creating a **print-rich environment** with a variety of literacy materials to support instruction. A print-rich environment is one in which students see their own writing and drawing and other printed materials all around them through class-created books and charts, poems, student-created stories on bulletin boards, environmental print, word walls (see Exhibit 5.13), magazines, and the classroom library, just to name a few. In such an environment, students come to recognize the value of many different types of writing. The texts available to students for reading aloud, small group instruction, and independent reading are also important and should include authentic texts from a range of genres in order to develop skilled readers (Duke & Pearson, 2002).

An **authentic text** is "real-world" writing that occurs naturally in the lives of readers; for example, newspaper and magazine articles, books, and online articles. Authentic texts include **trade books,** which are written for the public and available at bookstores or libraries. Trade books come in a variety of formats (including picture books, easy readers, chapter books, informational books), and many genres (including fantasy, realistic fiction, historical fiction, poetry, and nonfiction). Providing access to a range of quality authentic texts for whole group lessons, small group reading instruction, and independent reading helps to satisfy each student's interests and abilities. Authentic texts help students understand different text structures. And importantly, when reading authentic texts students are more likely to encounter topics, cultures, and people of various abilities and talents that they might not otherwise meet. A synthesis of research by Shanahan et al. (2010) indicates that

> [E]arly exposure to different types of text builds the capacity to understand the large variety of reading material that students will encounter as

they move from grade to grade. Not only should teachers introduce students to a variety of texts, but teachers should also ensure that a selected text (1) is rich in depth of ideas and information, (2) has a level of difficulty commensurate with the students' word-reading and comprehension skills, and (3) supports the purpose of the lesson. (p. 30)

Commercial materials such as **basal series,** which are prevalent in classrooms across the United States, are specially constructed materials that contain a series of graded stories, poems, and nonfiction. Some basal series include stories available as trade books that may have been edited in order to be included in the basal series. For example, picture books included in a basal series may not include illustrations that are in the original, and chapter books may include only an excerpt rather than the whole story. Other basal series consist of texts that have been specially written with limited vocabulary that is introduced in a controlled manner, which gradually increases in difficulty across the grade levels. One of the biggest drawbacks of commercial reading programs is the number of brief stories for students to read. Research has found that these core reading programs provide an average of 15 minutes of reading volume per day. The National Center on Education and the Economy (2001) asserts that "Too often students are not given the opportunity to read full-length books because of curricular restraints, a lack of resources, or a lack of access to books. The missed opportunity results in a tremendous loss of potential literacy skills that can only be developed when students become habitual readers" (p. 20). Teachers often rely on a combination of texts to meet students' reading needs. Exhibit 5.14 shares six different types of texts and suggests ways to use them. Later in this chapter, you'll find more information about reading aloud; mini-lessons; and shared, guided, and independent reading.

Cunningham and Allington's (2011) synthesis of research on effective instruction found that exemplary teachers use a wide range of materials for reading instruction. If teachers are to meet the diverse needs and interests of their students, then it makes sense that they would need a range of materials for instruction and independent reading. If your school or district has adopted a basal series, you can still bring lots of trade books into the classroom from the school or local library and provide access to texts via a computer, tablet, or ereader. Audiobooks, whether purchased or teacher created, are also valuable resources that can be included in a listening center or made available for independent reading time. Teachers can also supplement social studies, science, and math textbooks with fiction and nonfiction trade books that can serve as a magnifying glass to enhance the students' interaction with a subject and provide motivation, enthusiasm, and insight into just about any aspect of the curriculum (see Exhibit 5.15).

Selecting texts for instruction

Matching text to readers is an important component in providing instruction within a student's zone of proximal development. The book needs to be easy enough for the student to read yet present enough challenges to provide opportunities for learning with the support of the teacher—in other words, just right. A *just right* book is considered an **instructional level** text whereas an **independent level** text is easy reading and a **frustration level** text is too difficult.

Research has shown that students demonstrated improved time on task while reading texts at their instructional level, compared to tasks at the frustration and independent levels (to read more about determining these

EXHIBIT 5.14

Books found in the classroom.

TEXT TYPE	DEFINITION	WHEN TO USE
Trade Book	A book designed for the general public and available through an ordinary bookseller.	Reading Aloud Mini-lessons Independent Reading
Big Book and Enlarged Text	An enlarged version of a trade book, with illustrations and very large print, usually used to learn about concepts of print and early reading strategies.	Shared Reading Mini-lessons
Decodable Text	Story written with limited vocabulary introduced in a controlled manner that gradually increases in difficulty.	Guided Reading
Leveled Text	Book that has been organized along a continuum of difficulty based on a combination of text characteristics. Includes trade books and books written with specific characteristics in mind.	Guided Reading
Basal/Anthology	A grade-leveled series of textbooks produced by an educational publisher that can include decodable text or excerpts of trade books. A teacher's manual provides guidance as to how to teach and extend each lesson.	Guided Reading
Electronic Text	CD/DVD storybooks, ebooks, online encyclopedias and dictionaries, blogs, and other websites.	Reading Aloud Mini-lessons Shared Reading Independent Reading

EXHIBIT 5.15

Books can enhance science, social studies, or math learning.

reading levels for students, refer to the section Informal Reading Inventory in Chapter 8). Comprehension was highest at the independent level and lowest at the frustration level (Treptow, Burns, & McComas, 2007; Gickling & Armstrong, 1978). Furthermore, Allington (2009) states that "the single-most critical factor in designing instruction that will determine the success of the effort is matching struggling readers with texts they can actually read with a high level of accuracy, fluency, and comprehension" (p. 144). In other words, text difficulty is critical to reading success.

Text difficulty is determined by many factors. Texts make demands on readers in terms of how they are written, illustrated, and designed. Take into consideration the following *qualitative* text characteristics:

- Genre
- Text structure
- Content
- Themes and ideas
- Language and literary features
- Vocabulary
- Words
- Illustrations
- Book and print features

Readers must learn to navigate each of these characteristics proficiently in order to fully understand the text. Quantitative text characteristics also play a role in text difficulty, including the number of sentences, words, and syllables in the words. Reader characteristics, such as prior knowledge, motivation, and purpose for reading, also affect how difficult the text will be to read.

Teachers must understand how text characteristics place demands on young readers. For example, a student may be able to read the words in a book, but she may not understand the content or concepts presented. Therefore, even though the student can read the book, the lack of background knowledge about content or concepts can make it too difficult. The teacher may need to make another text selection or provide enough background knowledge for the student to be successful. In other words, the texts that teachers select should be just right for students. The texts should be interesting and offer an appropriate level of challenge by being not too easy and not too difficult.

View the video Selecting Texts That Are Just Right (7:45, http://fdf.reading recovery.org/index.php/selecting-texts) to see a teacher selecting a *just right* text. As you watch, consider what suggestions and criteria these teachers offer for selecting such a text.

Texts should be within each student's control and encourage successful problem solving. Effective teachers carefully selecting an appropriate text, then think about the best way to help students orient themselves to it. Introductions will vary according to the text itself and the knowledge the students bring to it. The ultimate goal is for students to learn how to take responsibility for orienting themselves to new texts as they enjoy becoming successful independent readers.

Many text leveling systems created by literacy experts, book publishers, and other companies take some or all of the qualitative and quantitative text characteristics into consideration. When using a specific system, be aware of the characteristics used to determine the text difficulty. Systems such as Fountas and Pinnell's Guided Reading Levels and the Developmental Reading Assessment use qualitative characteristics, such as those listed above, to determine text difficulty. Other systems use only quantitative characteristics, plugging the number of sentences or sentence length and number of words or syllables into a readability formula that calculates text difficulty. Examples of these quantitative systems are the Lexile Reading Framework and the Flesch-Kincaid, the latter being available on most computers. These leveling systems are convenient and can help you match readers to text, but you must always take into consideration the reader's personal characteristics, too. Assess the suitability of the reading material as well as the capacity of the students to read materials in the classroom. One of the difficulties students face when given a reading task is that the reading demands more of them than their current proficiencies permit (Allington, 2002). This is not to say that students should not read challenging materials. Students who are consistently given texts that are far too simple do not make progress, because the material fails to challenge them appropriately.

Additional tools for estimating readability are available at Readability Tools: http://delicious.com/tdwolsey/readability

The Common Core State Standards (Common Core State Standard Initiative, 2012) incorporate the idea of complex texts that are appropriate for the grade level, devoting an entire standard to text complexity. Standard 10: Range, Quality, and Complexity, defines a grade-by-grade staircase of text complexity that increases from second grade to the college- and career-readiness levels. This reading standard places equal emphasis on the sophistication of what students read and the skill with which they read. The standard states that "the use of qualitative and quantitative measures to assess text complexity is balanced in the Standards' model by the expectation that educators will employ professional judgment to match texts to particular students and tasks" (Common Core State Standard Initiative, 2012, Appendix A, p. 7).

To find out more about this standard, read Appendix A of the Common Core State Standards (43 pp.): www.corestandards.org/assets/Appendix_A.pdf

Word matters

Earlier in this chapter, we explained language as a set of phonological, syntactic, semantic, and pragmatic cueing systems working together in a way that allows people to think, communicate, and construct knowledge. In this section, we discuss the phonological system in more detail.

Students come to school with an understanding of oral language and its meaning in communicating at home and in their communities. However, basic to the ability to learn to read is an understanding of the **alphabetic principle** or the idea that the speech sounds (phonemes) in words are represented by letters (graphemes). Phonemic awareness is the understanding that spoken words are made up of a sequence of individual phonemes, and phonics is the relationship of phonemes to graphemes. While some students come to school with an understanding of both areas, research supports the need for many students to receive explicit, systematic **phonological instruction** (instruction in the sound system of a language) that matches students' developmental levels (National Reading Panel, 2000).

Phonemic awareness

Phonemic awareness is the ability to orally segment or take words apart and to orally blend the sounds back together again (Cunningham & Allington, 2011). It is an important factor in learning to read. Students who have difficulty hearing and manipulating the sounds of spoken words will find it challenging to relate these sounds to the letters in written words. In addition, students come to school speaking different dialects, which may impact their ability to discern the sounds of some phonemes; however, language patterns and dialects will not be a deterrent in learning to read (McIntyre, Hulan, & Layne, 2011).

A student who is phonemically aware is able to manipulate the word *dog* in the following ways:

- **Isolate phonemes:** /d/ is the beginning sound in *dog* or /g/ is the ending sound in *dog*.
- **Blend phonemes:** /d/-/o/-/g/ makes the word *dog*.
- **Segment phonemes:** the word *dog* has the following sounds, /d/-/o/-/g/.
- **Substitute phonemes:** if you change the /d/ for /h/ you have the word *hog*.

Students can more easily manipulate larger units of language than smaller units, so finding a rhyming word for *dog* is easier than segmenting *dog* into its individual sounds (Adams, 1990). Therefore, a progression of introducing students to a rhyming poem, for example, could lead to finding rhyming words in the poem, then looking at the syllables of the rhyming words, and then segmenting the syllables into phonemes (see Exhibit 5.16).

Meaningful, authentic activities with language, such as engaging students in poetry, nursery rhymes, songs, riddles, jump rope rhymes, wordplay and tongue twisters, and reading books that emphasize alliterative sounds such as Dr. Seuss' *There's a Wocket in My Pocket,* provide a fun way to develop phonemic awareness that actively involves students in exploring and manipulating the sounds in language. Word games and activities for teaching phonemic awareness, as well as phonics, provide students with hands-on opportunities to manipulate letters and sounds. Read about activities for teaching phonemic awareness and phonics: www.hhp communities.com/teachinglanguagearts/IL-05-02.pdf.

You can assess phonemic awareness as a way to determine if students understand how to segment a spoken word into sounds. This foundational knowledge is key to later success with blending sounds, recognizing letter–sound correspondence, and eventually **decoding** (translating printed words into sounds) and **encoding** (spelling, writing). Assessment information about phonemic awareness serves as an important guide for planning the instruction that meets the needs of students. The Yopp Singer Test of Phoneme Segmentation and elements of the Dynamic Indicators of Basic Early Literacy Skills (DIBELS) (https://dibels.uoregon.edu/) are both assessments of phonemic awareness, typically administered in kindergarten. More detailed information is presented on those assessments in the linked chapters.

EXHIBIT 5.16

Poetry for phonemic awareness.

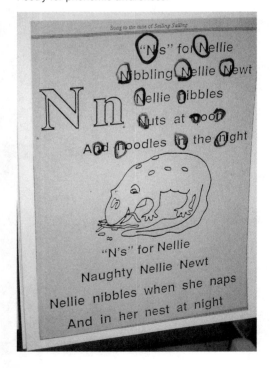

Phonics

Phonics is the process of relating sounds to letters and letter clusters. Some languages such as Russian, Spanish, and Italian are close to being completely phonemic in that they have a one-to-one correspondence between spoken sounds and letter representations; however, English does not have a one-to-one correspondence. English has 44 sounds represented by only 26 letters. These sounds have been classified as consonants and vowels (see Exhibit 5.6). Some words in the English language have a simple one-to-one phoneme/grapheme match, such as *dog*; however, other words, such as *duck*, are more complex because more than one letter represents a sound. Readers must learn to go beyond the sound/symbol match to understand the more complex ways that sounds are represented by letters and letter clusters, which in turn influence the recognition of word patterns and word structure.

In the past, experts thought that phonics rules or generalizations could help students understand the complexity of reading in the English language. For example, you may remember the rule, *when two vowels go walking, the first one does the talking*, which was intended to help readers remember that the first vowel in a word with two vowels side-by-side is pronounced and the second vowel is silent. However, most of these rules do not apply most of the time (*shoe*, *biscuit*, and *guest*, for example, are exceptions to the two-vowel rule). Nonetheless, here are a few important phonic concepts for you to know:

- **Diagraphs:** A diagraph is a letter combination that represents a single sound. The most common consonant diagraphs are *ch*, *sh*, *th*, and *wh*. Examples of vowel diagraphs are *ai*, *ay*, *ea*, *ee*, *ei*, *ey*, *ie*, *oa*, *oo*, and *ow*.
- **Diphthongs:** A diphthong is when two vowels represent a glide from one vowel to the other. Two consistent diphthongs are *oi* and *oy*.
- **Consonant blends:** A consonant blend is when two or three individual consonant sounds are blended together such as *spr*, *gr*, and *bl*.
- **Schwa:** A vowel that is pronounced as "uh" as in *other* or *about* is called a schwa and represented by an e upside down, _.
- **R-controlled vowels:** When one or more vowels are followed by an *r*, the vowel is pronounced differently and is called an r-controlled vowel as in *car* and *heart*.

Young readers typically progress from learning common consonants (e.g., *b*, *d*, *m*, *t*) in kindergarten to less common consonants (e.g., *c*, *g*) and short vowels to consonant blends, diagraphs, long vowel sounds, and vowel diagraphs to vowel diphthongs and r-controlled vowels by the end of third grade. Beginning readers should move quickly from analyzing words letter-by-letter to recognizing the way words and syllables follow patterns that recur throughout the English language. These patterns are:

- **Consonant-vowel-consonant pattern (CVC, *dog*):** When a one-syllable word has only one vowel and the vowel comes between two consonants, it is usually short (an exception is *told*).
- **Consonant-vowel-consonant-silent *e* pattern (CVCe, *give*):** When there are two vowels in a one-syllable word and one of them is an *e* at the end of the word, the first vowel is long and the final *e* is silent (three exceptions are *have*, *come*, and *love*).
- **Phonograms:** Spelling patterns that represent the sounds of **rimes** (parts of words or syllables within words that begin with a vowel). Words connected by rimes (e.g., words ending in the letters –*at*) are called **word families.** When an **onset** (the first part of the word or syllable) is

added to the rime –*at*, then many words can be generated, including *rat, cat, hat, mat, sat, fat, bat,* and *pat.*

- **Affixes:** Prefixes and/or suffixes added to a root word that change the function or meaning of the word; for example, the prefix *re-* added to the word *appear* makes the new word *reappear.* The suffix *-ed* added makes the word *reappeared,* which changes its function from present to past tense.

The process of recognizing patterns and word parts starts out slowly and then becomes rapid and largely unconscious, allowing the reader to focus on comprehension. Before phonics skills become automatic, an assessment such as the Names Test may aid you in determining the types of phonics sounds and patterns students know and those that still need support and practice. (Chapter 8 offers more specific information about the Names Test.)

Software, online activities, and mobile device apps can also be used to support phonemic awareness and phonics instruction with young students. A synthesis of research by the Northeast and the Islands Regional Technology in Education Consortium (NEIRTEC, 2004) found positive results: "These studies support the idea that computers are able to combine text-to-speech capabilities with visual material to create a unique resource to support and enhance traditional methods of phonics instruction" (p. 9). These digital tools can provide an opportunity for independent practice of literacy skills, but should be used in moderation and in concert with teacher instruction and independent reading.

The websites listed below provide activities and games intended to reinforce phonological awareness and early literacy skills for young students. Visit these sites to become familiar with their functions before sending students to them. First, select a game or an activity. Then, think about the skills a student will need to navigate the program and whether it will appropriately engage the student in learning or reinforcing the literacy skill.

Professor Garfield (www.professorgarfield.org)

Starfall (www.starfall.com)

PBS kids (http://pbskids.org/games)

Scholastic kids (choose "Kids" link) (www.scholastic.com)

Sesame Street (www.sesamestreet.org)

RIF's Reading Planet (www.rif.org/kids/readingplanet)

spotlight ON A LITERACY LEADER

DOROTHY STRICKLAND

Dorothy S. Strickland, Ph.D., is the Samuel DeWitt Proctor Professor of Education, Emerita at Rutgers University. A former classroom teacher, reading consultant, and learning disabilities specialist, she is a past president of both the IRA and the IRA Reading Hall of Fame. Her publications include *Literacy Leadership in Early Childhood* (2007) and *Teaching Phonics Today* (1998).

Listen to Dr. Strickland in her podcast Rethinking Phonics for the 21st Century (11:00): www.jackstreet.com/jackStreet/WIRA.Strickland.cfm

Keep in mind that the phonological system is just one of the four language systems; in a balanced, comprehensive classroom, instruction in phonological awareness and phonics is only one component of meaningful beginning reading instruction. In order to grow in literacy skills, students need meaningful interactions with language and print in authentic contexts that are guided and supported by the teacher. How do you create these authentic contexts? Ground your daily instructional decisions in research and your philosophy about effective teaching and learning. Exhibit 5.17 presents guiding principles for teaching phonemic awareness and phonics. These principles can contribute to your rationale for making instructional decisions about phonemic awareness and phonics instruction.

EXHIBIT 5.17

Guiding principles for teaching phonemic awareness and phonics.

- Students should spend most of their school language arts time reading and writing.
- Language play—exposure to books, songs, poetry, and chants—makes learning phonemic awareness and phonics fun.
- Instruction should first assess what students already know.
- Lessons must be systematically, not haphazardly, delivered.
- Phonemic awareness can be taught and learned at the same time or before phonics instruction.
- The daily instruction should build on the skills of yesterday's lesson.
- Instruction should often be conducted in small groups that match students' needs.
- Decodable text might be one tool for some students at some times in their reading practice, but little research suggests it is essential or even positive for students. Use a variety of types of texts for reading practice.
- Look for what students use but confuse (Bear et al., 2004). This means that sometimes students use a word pattern correctly and other times they don't. This is a signal that they are ready to learn that skill.
- Use words students can read and have them analyze them.
- Avoid rules, or at least avoid insisting that they learn the rules. If they do learn them, great. But it isn't necessary.
- Return to meaningful texts.

From McIntyre, E., Hulan, N., & Layne, V. (2011). *Reading instruction for diverse classrooms*, p. 82. New York: Guilford. Used with permission.

BOOK REVIEW

When Readers Struggle:
Teaching That Works

BY GAY SU PINNELL AND IRENE FOUNTAS

This book is an excellent resource on struggling readers written by two widely respected literacy experts and leaders in the field of reading. It's filled with numerous examples and descriptions of teaching ideas for helping students in kindergarten through grade three who are having difficulty in reading and writing. *When Readers Struggle* focuses on small group and individual interactions during reading and writing, how to observe readers closely to make the best possible teaching decisions for them, and how to support struggling readers in whole-class settings. Abundant examples of running records, appropriately leveled texts, teaching opportunities, and learning activities are included throughout.

Locate a copy: www.worldcat.org/title/when-readers-struggle-teaching-that-works/ oclc/259253974

points2ponder

QUICK REVIEW 2 What are some of the negative effects of ability grouping for diverse learners?

What are some meaningful authentic ways to engage students in learning phonemic awareness?

(Access the answers in the digital version of this book.)

5.5

INSTRUCTIONAL CONTEXTS FOR LITERACY INSTRUCTION

The instructional context in which reading is taught is critical. In the next section, the contexts of reading aloud, shared reading, guided reading, and independent reading are discussed. These contexts will provide you with opportunities to assess individual students' progress and ways to support and guide their instructional needs.

Reading aloud to students

Reading aloud is one of the most powerful ways experienced readers can pass on the reading tradition to others. This phenomenon is not new, but the simplicity of the concept often causes its impact to be overlooked. *Becoming a Nation of Readers,* a report from the Commission on Reading, states that "the single most important activity for building the knowledge required for eventual success in reading is reading aloud to children. . . . There is no substitute for a teacher who reads children good stories. . . . It is a practice that should continue throughout the grades" (Anderson, Hiebert, Scott, & Wilkinson, 1984, p. 51). Research shows that reading aloud to students results in increased motivation and engagement, vocabulary development, listening comprehension, and language and literary development (Dickinson & Smith, 1994; Holdaway, 1979; Sulzby, 1985). A recent meta-analysis of research on the effects of storybook read-aloud interventions for students at risk for reading difficulties found significant, positive effects on students' language, phonological awareness, print concepts, comprehension, and vocabulary outcomes (Swanson et al., 2011).

The beauty of reading aloud is that the reader can be a caregiver, relative, friend, or teacher. Why does reading aloud to students have such a strong effect on learning? According to Daniels and Zemelman (2004):

> Reading aloud evokes the time-honored human experience of listening to stories, telling family and cultural histories, trading "war stories," hearing lessons from elders—around a fire, at the dinner table, in family gatherings, at business conferences, wherever people meet in groups. It helps students grasp the big ideas, fascinations, and questions that make our subjects meaningful to us as thoughtful adults. Good teachers have learned that reading strong writing aloud draws in students who would otherwise resist engaging in school topics. (p. 110)

A variety of texts can serve as read-alouds, including newspaper and magazine articles, short stories, chapter books, and digital texts; however, picture books may be one of the best resources. Picture books are short, serve a variety of purposes for instruction, and promote visual literacy. "Picture books provide a unique opportunity to assist children in learning how to sort, recognize and understand the many forms of visual information because they are able to return to the visual images to explore, reflect, and critique those images" (Johnson, 2012, p. 98). Visual literacy, described further in Chapters 7 and 11, is increasingly important as visual images play a dominate role in online, television, and print media in our society.

Students benefit from hearing and seeing a model of expressive, fluent reading. All of the sites below provide an online read-aloud experience in which a student can listen as a book is read aloud. Some of the sites provide the option for the student to read the book independently or have it read aloud. Additionally, some of the sites highlight individual words or phrases as the text is read. As with any online resource, carefully review the books on these sites beforehand to be sure they are developmentally appropriate for your students.

Consider using the following online read-aloud sites with your students. To enhance the list's usefulness, annotate it with the read-aloud features available at the site.

Storyline Online (www.storylineonline.net)

TumbleBook Library (http://kids.nypl.org/reading/Childrensebooks.cfm)

Between the Lions (http://pbskids.org/lions/stories/)

Kids' Corner (http://wiredforbooks.org/kids.htm)

BookHive.com's Zinger Tales (www.bookhive.org)

Clifford the Big Red Dog Stories (http://pbskids.org/clifford/index-brd-flash.html) (Requires Flash)

Speakaboos (www.speakaboos.com/stories)

PBS Kids (http://pbskids.org)

Barnes and Noble Storytime (www.barnesandnoble.com/storytime)

Bookpop (www.bookpop.com)

Scholastic's Nonfiction Listen and Read (http://teacher.scholastic.com/comm club/index.htm)

Before reading aloud

For the read-aloud to be a meaningful event that supports literacy development, you must make many decisions (Morrow & Brittain, 2003). Though texts for reading aloud can and should be selected just for fun, read-alouds should also be based on your ongoing assessment of students' needs. For example, books may be selected that lend themselves to teaching certain comprehension strategies. Harvey and Goudvis (2007) point out that "realistic fiction and memoirs often spur connections and questions in readers. Poetry is likely to stimulate visualizing and inferential thinking. We frequently choose nonfiction pieces to teach determining importance and synthesizing information when we read" (p. 53). Additional guidelines for selecting texts to read aloud include choosing texts that

EXHIBIT 5.18

Second grade teacher Wendy Lucy reading aloud.

- are developmentally appropriate and sustain readers emotionally and intellectually.
- evoke a range of aesthetic responses and connect to students' lives.
- reflect high literary quality and include believable characters, engaging plots or topics, memorable language, and universal themes in fiction and engaging accurate and reliable nonfiction.
- facilitate relevant curricular connections.

After the text has been selected, practice reading it aloud so you are able to effectively communicate the mood and meaning of the story and characters through vocal variation and pace, body position, expression, and eye contact. When reading aloud to students, hold the book up so everyone can see the pictures.

During reading aloud

While reading, you can model engagement and use of reading strategies by sharing your thoughts through think-alouds. Thinking aloud can make the invisible processes of reading visible. Thinking aloud is when you model your thinking by voicing all the things you notice, see, feel, or question while processing the text. "Think-alouds allow all students to hear how others sleuth out and make sense of all these text clues so that they can recognize and adopt these strategies as their own" (Wilhelm, 2001, p. 19). For example, figuring out unknown words in context or making inferences between what the author states and what the reader knows are complex processes that take place while reading text.

EXHIBIT 5.19

A record of thinking while reading.

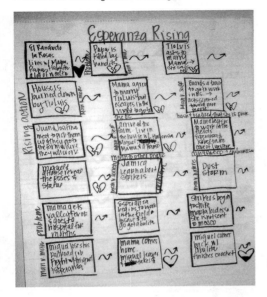

Wilhelm (2001) suggests that think-alouds be used to model:

- General processes of reading, such as predicting, monitoring, and summarizing
- Task-specific processes like understanding symbolism, irony, or bar graphs
- Text-specific processes like understanding the structure of an argument and evaluating its effectiveness (p. 28)

See Stories from the Classroom with Wendy Melzer in Chapter 6 (Section 6.4) for an example of a think-aloud on comprehension strategies.

You may record think-alouds on chart paper, overheads, or as a podcast. Providing a record of your strategies allows students to make connections to other texts later (see Exhibit 5.19). Once students have observed the think-aloud process with a particular strategy numerous times, let them practice it on their own. Students can use sticky notes to record their thinking to share with you in conferences or with a peer.

COMPREHENSION *coach*

Having trouble inferring? Listen to this podcast by Denise Johnson for comprehension coaching. *(Access this podcast in the digital version of this book.)*

After reading aloud

Provide opportunities for students to discuss the read-aloud with you and with each other. One effective strategy for engaging students in discussion with each other is turn and talk. First, present students with a question about the characters' actions or the outcome of events, or ask them to predict what would happen next if the story continued. Then, ask students to take turns sharing their thoughts about the question or prediction with someone sitting close by. The discussion should be focused and brief. Finally, bring the students back together and ask if anyone would like to share their thoughts with the class. Turn and talk gives everyone a chance to participate in the discussion.

Another activity that engages students in reflecting on the text after reading is sketch to stretch. Students draw a quick sketch to illustrate their thinking and understanding of key ideas of the text. Students can use their illustrations as a springboard for discussions with each other and the teacher.

🔊 Listen to this podcast by reading specialist Wendy Lucy, a former second grade teacher, as she talks about the importance of reading aloud (Part A, 4:15) and using anchor charts (Part B, 3:39) for scaffolding instruction. *(Access this podcast in the digital version of this book.)*

Shared reading

Shared reading is an interactive experience in which students join in the reading of a text while being supported by the teacher. The shared reading approach is intended to provide all students with the benefits that come from the experience of reading with a family member that many children experience before entering school. The process involves big books or enlarged text so students can see the words and illustrations. Whereas reading aloud exposes students to books that might be above their reading level, shared reading involves text they can read with the teacher's support. Big books and other enlarged texts cross all topics and content subjects. For example, shared reading of nonfiction texts can serve as a way to learn about science, social studies, or math as well as a way to learn to read a variety of informational text structures with the teacher's support (see Exhibit 5.20). Shared reading and the use of big books is an appropriate instructional strategy for both beginning and older readers. However, consider the learning needs of your students when selecting appropriate text. Exhibit 5.21 provides suggested guidelines for making these developmentally appropriate instructional decisions.

Before shared reading

Numerous studies have found shared reading to be an effective instructional strategy (Eldredge, Reutzel, & Hollingsworth, 1996; Maynard, Pullen, & Coyne, 2010; Pollard-Durodola et al., 2011); however, as with reading aloud, many decisions must be made beforehand for the experience to be meaningful for students.

The effectiveness of shared reading depends on selecting an appropriate text and modeling strategies based on your knowledge of students' reading strengths and needs and your ability to provide flexible scaffolding during students' reading. The enlarged text allows you to visibly scaffold students' understanding of conventions of print and reading strategies such as:

- Conventions, such as title, table of contents, author, illustrator, front/back of book.
- Early concepts about print, alphabetical knowledge, and phonemic awareness.
- Rereading for fluency and to monitor comprehension.
- Learning new information and searching for additional information.
- Author's craft.
- Text structure.
- How to figure out unknown words.
- Literary elements.
- Comprehension strategies.
- Enjoyment of reading.

Shared reading lessons can also be created and shared on an interactive whiteboard, which projects the text onto a large screen so all students can easily see it, as described in Exhibit 5.22.

During shared reading

Once you have selected a text, engage the students by reading it aloud with expression and fluency. For younger students,

- invite them to join in the reading during repetitive refrains.
- use a pointer to point to each word or phrase to focus students' attention on the words or group of words.

EXHIBIT 5.20

Fourth grade teacher Lori Rainey uses a big book for shared reading.

EXHIBIT 5.21

Guidelines for selecting texts for shared reading.

FOR BEGINNING READERS	FOR OLDER READERS
• quality literature	• quality literature
• highly engaging, informative, and meaningful	• highly engaging, informative, and meaningful
• connects to students' interests, needs, culture, and curriculum	• connects to students' interests, needs, culture, and curriculum
• print is large enough to read up to 15 ft. away	• print is large enough to read up to 15 ft. away
• words are well spaced, and font is familiar (the typeset *a* and *g* are known by students)	• is close to the reading level of most of the students
• predictable text with repeated patterns, refrains, pictures, and rhymes	• contains elements that support fluent reading
• contains easily understood concepts	• contains elements that lend themselves to demonstration and deeper understanding, such as a table of contents, index, maps, diagrams, charts, a glossary, and illustrations with captions found in informational books
• familiar vocabulary—the number of unknown words should be enough to read with support from the teacher and not overwhelming	• lends itself to comprehension, higher-level thinking, and critical reading
• print is consistently placed on the same part of the page rather than moving around from page to page	• connects to other texts
• connects to other texts	
• lends itself to comprehension and student response	

From Johnson, D. (2012). *The joy of children's literature.* New York: Wadsworth.

EXHIBIT 5.22

Creating a shared reading lesson with the interactive whiteboard.

1. **Select a text.** Short poems, nursery rhymes, and songs make good shared reading. The text can be entered in the word processing software and illustrated with clip art. You can also project texts from online resources such as *A Rhyme A Week* at http://curry.virginia.edu/go/wil/rimes_and_rhymes.htm.

2. **Identify skills and strategies to teach.** You may choose to focus on phonemic awareness, phonics, strategies such as using context clues, or even punctuation or grammar.

3. **Read a poem or other text selection together with the students.** Pointing to each word as you read will help younger readers learn concepts about print such as directionality and one-to-one word matching. Maintain students' interest during repeated readings by reading the text in groups or adding motions or sounds.

4. **Teach skills or strategies using the text.** For example:
   - Use colored rectangles to cover words and have students use context clues to predict the word.
   - Use highlighter tape to focus students' attention on high frequency works and onset or rimes.
   - Let students manipulate and sequence the lines of the text.
   - Let students manipulate word parts to create words from the text and similar words.
   - Focus students' attention on elements within the text (such as contractions) as a way to introduce a follow-up lesson.

5. **Extend students' learning through writing activities.** These might include such activities as writing a variation of the text, which can be published in book format or as a PowerPoint, Prezi, or Soundslides presentation. Students' new versions of a text can then be used for further shared reading.

Adapted from Gill, S., & Islam, C. (2011). Shared reading goes high-tech. *The Reading Teacher,* 65(3), 224–227. Reprinted with permission of The International Reading Association, via Copyright Clearance Center.

■ engage students in predicting what might happen next in the story.

As indicated in Exhibit 5.22, lessons using an interactive whiteboard allow students and teachers to interact with the text by circling, underlining, or highlighting words and phrases.

During the first reading of the text, model appropriate reading behavior for the students, allowing young readers to hear proper phrasing and to see how you, the teacher, interact with the text.

After shared reading

A critical factor in shared book reading is the interactive talk that takes place between you and the students (DeTemple, 2001; Dickinson, 2001a, 2001b; Wasik & Bond, 2001). After the first reading, engage students in a discussion of the text with you and with each other. The turn-and-talk peer discussion technique described in the read-aloud section above also works well in the shared reading context. Engage students in thinking about the text by providing them with the opportunity to talk about their favorite part of the text, why they think certain events happened or characters acted in specific ways, or if they would like to be the main character. Then invite the students to read along as you go through the text again.

Subsequent shared readings

Young students enjoy rereading familiar stories, poems, songs, rhymes, and other texts. Familiarity with the text also provides many opportunities for you to engage students in learning many skills and strategies. Additional activities can include:

■ Using highlighter tape, frames, or color overlays to point out specific features of text such as rhyming words or high frequency words.
■ Using word frames (or students can use their fingers as a frame) to locate letters or words in the texts.
■ Using sticky notes to cover words that can then serve as a **cloze technique** in which some letters or words are hidden and students must use their knowledge of words and context clues to figure them out. (Chapter 8 will describe more about ways the cloze technique can be used as a reading assessment.)
■ Retelling the story through dramatic play or storyboarding.

Rereading a particular text can take place many times over one or more weeks and can focus on one or more of these skills and strategies as students become more familiar with the text.

This online shared reading learning module (http://eworkshop.on.ca/edu/core.cfm?p=main&modColour=1&modID=21&m=111&L=1), developed for elementary teachers by the Ontario Ministry of Education, provides an in-depth look at how teachers of students at various developmental levels plan shared reading lessons, select texts and skills/strategies, and engage their students in multiple readings of the text. The module provides videos of teachers in action, activity sheets, lesson plans, and more. Additionally, the module provides an opportunity for you to apply your own knowledge of shared reading in the *Let Me Try* section.

Guided reading

Students develop the skills and strategies of good reading at different rates, therefore it is important for all of them to receive instruction that builds on their particular strengths and needs. Research has shown that small group instruction, similar to that used in guided reading, is a critical component of effective instruction. In their foundational book *Guided Reading: Good First Teaching for All Children,* Fountas and Pinnell (1996) provide the following definition of guided reading:

> Guided reading is a context in which a teacher supports each reader's development of effective strategies for processing novel texts at increasingly challenging levels of difficulty. The teacher works with a small group of children who use similar reading processes and are able to read similar levels of text with support. The teacher introduces a text to this small group, works briefly with individuals in the group as they read it, may select one or two teaching points to present to the group following the reading, and may ask the children to take part in an extension of their reading. (p. 2)

Guided reading follows the gradual release of responsibility model, as described in Chapter 4. You select an appropriate text based on students' strengths and needs and prepare an introduction to the text based on the support students will need to read the text easily. You then turn over responsibility to the students to silently read the text individually. A variety of texts can be used for guided reading (see Exhibit 5.23); however, it is important for the text difficulty to be within the students' **zone of proximal development,** as discussed in Chapter 2.

Your ongoing assessment will inform you of the skills and strategies that need to be taught during guided reading to meet each student's needs. Based on this information, you will select an appropriate text that will be supportive but provide a few manageable challenges. Then you will prepare an introduction to the story that will help students build or access background knowledge and/or vocabulary they will need in order to make predictions and use strategies to ensure comprehension.

Before the reading

Before students start reading, briefly introduce the story, keeping in mind the meaning, language, and visual information in the text, and the students' knowledge, experience, and skills, but leave some unanswered questions. During the introduction, engage students in a conversation about the text by raising questions, making predictions, and/or noticing information when previewing the text.

During the reading

Students read the whole text or a unified part of the text (softly or silently) by themselves. As the students read, the teacher observes and monitors their reading behaviors and provides support as necessary. For example, when a student stops to analyze a word the teacher may offer a strategy to assist the process, or when the student reads a word incorrectly that affects comprehension the teacher may suggest a strategy that prompts the student to go back and reread for meaning. If the book is a good match for the reader, the challenges are solvable using reading strategies already familiar to him. If necessary, provide assistance through questions that prompt the students to use effective word-solving strategies.

EXHIBIT 5.23

Texts for guided reading.

- Leveled stories within basal readers
- Sets of trade books
- Sets of leveled books
- *Weekly Reader, Scholastic News,* or other nonfiction magazines
- Articles from Internet sites
- Poetry
- Nonfiction texts including content area texts

After the reading

After reading, engage the students in a discussion about the story and offer a teaching point based on your observations of students' needs. For example, if several students needed assistance with a strategy for word solving, you may quickly model the strategy for the whole group. You may assign a follow-up activity to reinforce or extend the students' knowledge through such activities as drama, writing, art, or more reading. You may also have students reread the story to a partner or independently for fluency and to practice strategy use. Notes made during the reading may be used to guide follow-up discussion and direct future teaching decisions.

It is critical for every minute of the brief 15 to 20 minutes of a guided reading group to be spent engaged with those students and not be interrupted by other students in the class. Instruction during a guided reading group is pinpointed to the needs of those students and may be one of the most powerful instructional times of the school day. Section 5.6 of this chapter describes the use of literacy centers to provide meaningful literacy learning opportunities for the other students in the classroom during guided reading time.

Many instructional decisions must be made in order for guided reading to be effective, run smoothly, and meet students' learning needs. Listen to classroom teacher Amanda Arndt as she discusses (2:33) how she incorporates guided reading into her first grade classroom. In what ways does she use the strategy to differentiate instruction? (Access this podcast in the digital version of this book.)

Independent reading

Research clearly shows that there is a powerful relationship between volume of reading and reading achievement. In their summary of research on independent reading, Morgan, Mraz, Padak, and Rasinski (2009) noted that students' independent reading was associated with growth in word recognition, vocabulary, fluency, language syntax, comprehension, and motivation for reading. This research review provides insights into the benefits of independent reading and why teachers must provide time for students to read every day. Ample time for independent reading allows students the opportunity to orchestrate the skills, strategies, and knowledge that are important to skillful reading. Fielding and Pearson (1994) define ample time for reading as "more time to read than the combined total allocated for *learning* about reading and *talking or writing* about what has been read" (p. 63).

Some schools set aside a specific time each day for self-selected reading, sometimes called SSR (sustained silent reading) or DEAR time (drop everything and read). These schools value the importance of providing students with time to read every day and believe this commitment can make a difference in reading achievement. In fact, Rasinski and Padak (2011) point out the cumulative benefit of daily reading over the course of a school year: 25 minutes of independent reading per day $\times$ 4 days per week $\times$ 36 school weeks $\times$ 300 students = 1,080,000 minutes! "Reading a million minutes over a school year is a significant accomplishment that can change students for a lifetime" (Rasinski & Padak, 2011, p. 555).

For students to realize the benefits, independent reading time must be intentional, well thought through, and informed by assessment and student observation, just as reading aloud, shared reading, and guided reading are. Allington (2002) found that in the classrooms of more effective teachers, independent reading was characterized by how effectively the time was allocated. Given one hour for reading instruction, the teachers spent five to ten minutes preparing students to read, 40 to 45 minutes conferencing individually with students while the others read independently, and five to ten minutes engaging students in follow-up activities related to their reading. This format follows the reading workshop organizational structure that will be described further in the next section of this chapter.

Independent reading can also include online reading. Many free online books and other texts meet students' reading preferences and provide choice (see the chart summarizing some of the many online resources for independent reading (www.hhpcommunities.com/teachinglanguagearts/IL-05-03.pdf). Free books as apps or ebooks are also available for mobile devices. Keep in mind that many digital book sources do not screen books for content or quality. Established publishing companies that convert print books to a digital format or create ebooks specifically for digital devices typically put these materials through a rigorous publication process. Other digital books are self-published by novice writers who have little or no publication experience. Teachers, caregivers, and students must become gatekeepers and filter out ebooks with spelling and punctuation errors or inappropriate language or content.

BOOK REVIEW

Balancing Reading & Language Learning: A Resource for Teaching English Language Learners, K–5

BY MARY CAPPELLINI

Cappellini begins this book with a story about her husband Cézar's arrival in the United States from Argentina. He did not speak English and "felt like his tongue was cut off," she states. "How many of the students in our classrooms feel the way Cézar felt? How many of our students feel frustrated at people's expectations of them?" It is clear from the beginning that Mary is passionate about working with English language learners. She begins with a discussion about creating an environment of inclusion and ways to motivate and engage students in meaningful learning opportunities based on interests and curiosity. Mary introduces the stages of English language proficiency and discusses how they compare to the stages of reading development and how to use them to assess and plan for individual students. She shares a collection of in-depth lessons and mini-lessons based on students' language proficiency and reading strategy needs; she incorporates ongoing assessment and teacher reflection, and emphasizes choosing the right books to match students' reading and language levels. Additionally, the book provides extensive resources, including observation sheets; planning sheets; literature response sheets; focus sheets for shared and guided reading; lists of books for read-alouds, shared reading, and thematic units; and lists of recommended guided reading series appropriate for English language learners. This book supports an effective balanced reading program, while at the same time valuing the native culture and first-language skills of the English language learner.

Locate a copy: www.worldcat.org/title/balancing-reading-language-learning-a-resource-for-teaching-english-language-learners-k-5/oclc/60373703

points2ponder

QUICK REVIEW 3 What are some conventions of print and reading strategies that can be taught during shared reading?

(Access the answer in the digital version of this book.)

5.6

ORGANIZING THE CLASSROOM FOR READING INSTRUCTION

In a balanced literacy classroom, the teacher and students are engaged in whole group, small group, and independent literacy activities. When students are not working directly with you, they must be able to manage their own learning; yet, it is not productive for students to be filling in worksheets or coloring pages. Students must be engaged in instructional activities that "rival the power of instruction that takes place with the teacher" (Ford & Opitz, 2002, p. 710). This begs the question, *While the teacher is working with small groups, what are the other students doing?* The following sections are some instructional routines teachers use for managing their classrooms for small group instruction.

EXHIBIT 5.24

Centers chart.

Literacy centers

Literacy centers, also called literacy corners or workstations, are "small areas within the classroom where students work alone or together to explore literacy activities independently while the teacher provides small-group guided reading instruction" (Ford & Opitz, 2002, p. 711). Deciding what instructional activities to include in centers will depend on your ongoing assessment of students as readers and writers. Possibilities include: listening, writing, reading, ABC, poetry, buddy reading, word study, reader's theater, big books, and computer centers (see Exhibit 5.24).

The literacy activities in centers must be at a level in which students can participate independently yet advance their literacy by practicing skills previously taught by the teacher. This may seem impossible without creating a plethora of activities to meet the diverse needs of the class. However, you can create centers with tiered activities. For example, one center could focus on phonological skills and include picture, letter, and word cards. Students at this center would be required to sort the cards according to their current level of phonological understanding. By including the three types of cards, many sorts are possible that will meet most students' instructional needs. (See also, in Chapter 4, the discussion of differentiation and Jessica's classroom story, about using tablets to create tiered activities during literacy center time.)

The activities in centers should be familiar. For example, students should know how to conduct sorts with picture, letter, and word cards before participating in the center. Another center might be a big book center in which the big book you have read to the class many times is available. Students will be familiar with it and able to read it independently or with a partner.

Make centers part of the daily routine and ensure that students are able to work independently, so there are no interruptions while you conduct small group instruction. You will need to engage students in mini-lessons that explain how to complete each center, along with directions on what to do if the unexpected occurs. Role playing opportunities give students the chance to solve problems ahead of time.

Create a system for assigning students to centers each day and rotating them through each one throughout the week. Place a chart or work board in a central location so students can easily find where they are supposed to be. In the system shown in Exhibit 5.25, the teacher places in the pockets the names of the students who are to go to each center for the day. The names rotate to a different pocket each day until all students have participated in each center by the end of the week. Often, the schedule for assigning students to centers revolves around guided reading groups, which can serve as one of the centers. The groups rotate every 30 minutes or when they are finished.

Include an accountability system in which students either show the work they have completed or indicate they have completed the tasks in the center. For example, students may have a composition book they take to centers each day in which they write down the sort they completed in the word study center or the new ending they created to the story in the big book center. Or, each student can have a center card on which he marks the centers he has completed for the day.

🔊 In this podcast, second grade teacher Susan Alais shares ways literacy centers can support literacy development (8:03). *(Access this podcast in the digital version of this book.*

EXHIBIT 5.25

A system for assigning students to centers.

Activities in literacy centers should be as engaging, authentic, print-rich, purposeful, and meaningful as all other literacy instruction in a balanced literacy classroom. By using assessment, careful planning, tiered activities that build on what students know, routines, and accountability, literacy centers can be as powerful as teacher instruction.

Reading workshop

Reading workshop is an organizational framework in which students are actively engaged in reading, responding, discussing, and sharing books with the teacher and peers. You conduct a mini-lesson based on students' strengths, needs, and curricular goals, and then confer with individual students during independent reading time. Exhibit 5.26 is a sample breakdown of a one-hour reading workshop. A brief discussion of these components follows.

Mini-lessons

A **mini-lesson** provides brief, powerful, explicit instruction that clearly demonstrates a principle or process to students. In determining the focus of a mini-lesson, draw upon students' needs as determined from reading conferences, observations, and curricular goals. Mini-lessons fall into three categories:

1. **Procedures and organization:** Early in the school year, the management of a reading workshop is most important for successful independent reading. These mini-lessons might focus on respecting the learning of others, how to buddy read, or how to select a *just right book.*

2. **Reading strategies and skills:** Based on assessment information, these mini-lessons are designed to assist students with becoming aware of

EXHIBIT 5.26

Schedule for a one-hour reading workshop.

READING WORKSHOP	
5–15 minutes	Mini-lesson
30–45 minutes	Individual reading Conferring Written response
5–10 minutes	Group share

information in a text and learning how to understand and use that information to become a better reader. Mini-lessons might focus on problem-solving unknown words, comprehension strategies, characteristics of texts, such as the organization of narrative and expository texts, and reading with fluency.

3. **Literary analysis:** Based on assessment information, these mini-lessons are designed to assist students with becoming familiar with techniques and devices authors use to create quality literature. Mini-lessons might focus on elements of fiction or nonfiction texts, such as characterization, setting, plot, making connections to the text and between texts, understanding the author's perspective, critically analyzing texts for accuracy or bias, or evaluating a website.

Mini-lessons on a specific principle or process may last a week or longer, depending on your ongoing observation of students' internalization of the principle or process. Calkins (2001) suggests that teachers design mini-lessons with the following question in mind, "How will I teach this content in ways that make a lasting impact?" (p. 84). Another good question to ask is, "What will students be able to do after this mini-lesson that they could not do before?" Designing mini-lessons with these questions in mind keeps students' needs in the forefront of your planning.

Independent reading and individual conferences

While students are reading independently (see Exhibit 5.27), work one-on-one with some students every day in reading conferences to monitor their reading and provide specific feedback. By working with students individually, you not only provide individualized feedback, but you also gain an understanding of how individual students are applying the skills and strategies previously taught, thus informing future instruction. During reading conferences, your role is to:

- Have authentic conversations with the student about the texts she is reading.
- Assist the student with understanding aspects of the routines of independent reading (e.g., self-selecting *just right* books, reading for a sustained period of time).
- Teach the student effective reading skills and strategies.
- Observe the student's oral reading to ensure fluency and phrasing.
- Discuss the student's journal responses.

While conferencing with students, you can use a conference sheet for making notes about each student's reading progress (see Exhibit 5.28).

Writing in response to reading

Writing *is* reflection, so responding to reading through writing can be a great way for students to reflect on their reading; however, students must understand that there are many ways to respond to texts. One way to scaffold students' understanding of how to respond to reading is through the use of sticky notes to record your thinking while modeling for students. As you read aloud and talk about your own use of reading strategies by thinking aloud, stop to write down your connections, questions, or predictions on sticky notes and place them on the appropriate pages in the book. Afterward, go back and read the notes as a way of reflecting on your

EXHIBIT 5.27

Ariel and Josh engaged in reading.

EXHIBIT 5.28

Independent reading conference form.

Independent Reading Conference

Name: Deionta Jones   Date: 10/25

1. Ask the student to bring the book he or she is currently reading independently to the conference.

Title of Book: Horrible Harry's Secret by Suzy Kline   Genre: realistic fiction

2. Then ask:
- Why did you choose this book?
"I like the Horrible Harry books. I've read a lot of them."

- Is this book ☐ hard ☐ easy ☑ just right for you?
- What is this book about so far?
Harry meets Song Lee and really, really likes her.

- Start reading the book out loud from where you stopped. (Take notes as the student reads silently or orally.)
Reads the book fluently with expression, make no errors, and laughs at certain parts that are funny.

- What do you remember about what you just read?
Harry doesn't know how to tell Song Lee he likes her so he tells his best friend Doug about it. But, he's driving Doug crazy.

- What do you think are your strengths as a reader and what do you need to work on?
Strengths: "I know all of the words. I can figure out words I don't know."

Goals: "To read different kinds of books. I've read almost all of the Horrible Harry books."

(Print a blank form: www.hhpcommunities.com/teaching languagearts/IL-05-04.pdf) thinking about the book. Were your questions answered? Were your predictions correct? What thoughts or ideas would you like to talk about with a partner? Point out to students that your connections, questions, and predictions might be different from theirs and that each student will respond differently based on his or her experiences.

Sticky notes can be removed and placed in a student's reading response journal and used as a scaffold for writing a response to the book in the journal. Using a composition notebook or folder as a reading response journal, students can record the date, title, and genre of all the books they read on a page attached to the inside front cover (see Exhibit 5.29). During reading workshop mini-lessons, model how to write responses to reading and provide many examples of journal entries over several weeks so students understand what is expected. Some teachers develop criteria that students use as guidelines (see Exhibit 5.30). Sticky notes and written responses are also very important for literature discussion groups. As students read, sticky notes remind them of what they want to talk about with their peers.

Blogs provide unique opportunities for reading response. Due to their interactive nature, blogs allow students to create content in ways not possible in a traditional paper-and-pencil environment. Students can read and respond to each other's posts. This shift in audience from the teacher to the class or the world fundamentally changes the motivation for and engagement with written response for students (Thompson, 2009) and is a major reason for involving students in blogging. Moreover, rather than simply using the blog as a context to post a response that could be written on paper, blogs make it possible for students to link to and connect ideas. For example, when students respond to a book or poem, the response could include links to the author's blog, to book reviewers' blogs, other students' blogs, or other online resources. To do this, students must engage in close reading and reflection, think critically within and across sources of information, and form a clear and concise message for a real audience.

To learn more about blogging with students, read the *Education Week* article "The Courage to Blog with Students": www.edweek.org/tm/articles/2011/04/27/tln_ratzel_courage.html

Reading response journals and blogs gives you and your students a quick way of seeing the breadth and depth of genre reading. A reading response journal provides the student with many ways to think about reading and provides you the teacher with information for assessing students' literary understanding.

Group sharing

After independent reading time, it is important to bring the students together for a brief period to share what and how they are reading and to evaluate how the group is working together. During this time, invite individuals to share what they are reading with the whole class or ask students to discuss their books with each other in groups of twos or threes. Book sharing creates an environment in which students learn from each other, which is a strong influence and motivator (see Exhibit 5.31). When students give and take book recommendations, they reinforce strategy use, enhance literary understandings, make connections to previous learning, and broaden their perspectives.

EXHIBIT 5.29

Reading response journal log, for inside the journal's front page or cover.

#	TITLE	AUTHOR	GENRE	DATE FINISHED	EASY JUST RIGHT HARD
1	The Penderwicks	Jeanne Birdsall	RF	10/18	JR
2	Young Fredle	Cynthia Voigt	F	11/2	E
3	Amelia Lost	Candace Fleming	NF	11/9	H

EXHIBIT 5.30

Response log criteria.

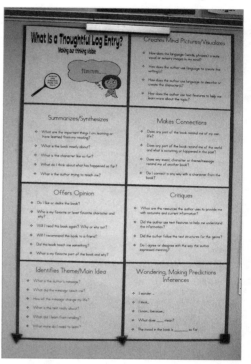

EXHIBIT 5.31

Students sharing during reading workshop.

stories FROM THE CLASSROOM

Active readers

First grade teacher Hildi Perez expects "every child in the classroom to read, at their full potential, by the end of first grade." Watch this video of Hildi Perez's first grade class (26:48, www.learner.org/libraries/readingk2/perez/index.html) to see how she guides students to become active readers and writers who problem-solve when they have difficulty and who articulate their problem-solving strategies. Observe how she uses ongoing formal and informal assessments to address a wide range of student needs with whole group, small group, and individual instruction. Also, notice how Ms. Perez carefully chooses appropriate literature for each student and balances independent work with explicit instruction throughout the literacy block.

Classroom library

A classroom library can support the development of literacy by providing students with immediate access to varied and authentic texts. Students will be motivated to read if they are allowed to self-select books from a collection that reflects a range of interests, preferences, and genres, and gives them access to a great variety of fiction and nonfiction books and curricular resources (Edmunds & Bauserman, 2006; Pachtman & Wilson, 2006). A well-stocked and well-designed library can benefit students in a variety of ways, by

- supporting literacy instruction
- helping students learn about books
- providing a central location for classroom resources
- providing opportunities for independent reading and curricular extensions, and
- serving as a place for students to talk and interact with books (Reutzel & Fawson, 2002).

For the classroom library to play an integral role in students' literacy motivation and development, give careful consideration to its purpose and function. Classroom library organization can assist students with book choices. Use this Classroom Library Checklist (www.hhpcommunities.com/teaching languagearts/IL-05-05.pdf) when planning and creating a classroom library.

Exhibit 5.32 shows ways to categorize books in the library; you can indicate categories with labels or signs. Your goal should be to have approximately 20 books per student in the classroom library, which for a class of 28, would be 560 books. This collection should include various types of narratives, informational texts, persuasive texts, and poetry at varying levels of difficulty.

Book baskets can be an effective and flexible way to organize books. They can be easily labeled and moved around for browsing. Baskets provide a way to display books to maximize students' exposure to new authors, genres, and topics (see Exhibit 5.33).

Plan to administer an attitude/interest inventory to students at the beginning of the year to learn more about their reading preferences. For a description of two interest inventories available for use in the classroom, see the Chapter 8 discussions of the Reading Interest Inventory and the Elementary Reading Attitude Survey.

EXHIBIT 5.32

Examples of ways to categorize books.

Curriculum topics	Authors' names
Genres and subgenres such as mysteries, sports, graphic novels, and memoirs	Favorite series books
Magazines and comics	Teacher recommendations
Students' recommendations	Favorite characters
Award-winning books	Books written by students in the class
Books with memorable language	Funny books

EXHIBIT 5.33

Book tubs.

Many organizations are dedicated to providing teachers and students with information about quality literature that makes the task of finding appropriate books easier. The following are just a few such resources:

- The American Library Association's (ALA) Newbery and Caldecott Award winners along with other book awards and notable book lists (www.ala.org/awards grants/awards).

- Notable book lists by content area organizations such as the National Council of Teachers of Social Studies (www.socialstudies.org/notable) and the National Science Teachers Association (www.nsta.org/publications/ostb).

- The IRA's Children's, Young Adult, and Teacher's Choice awards are also great sources for book recommendations because the books are chosen by children, young adults, and teachers themselves. These book awards are voted on annually and the winners are listed in *The Reading Teacher* and available online (www.reading.org/Resources/Booklists.aspx).

Creating and maintaining a classroom library can be a time-consuming, but valuable, endeavor. One way to manage this project is to enlist the help of students and caregivers. The video Getting Kids Involved in Planning the Library (7:30, www.readingrockets.org/article/29298/#video) shares how two teachers involve their students in the planning and management of the classroom library. While viewing the video, identify three specific steps you could utilize for creating a classroom library in your future classroom.

Wendy Melzer's classroom library.

stories FROM THE CLASSROOM

Making children's literature meaningful

Wendy Melzer, a second grade teacher, immerses her students in rich and meaningful read-alouds every day. She teaches her students about the important role illustration plays in reading and understanding picture books. She surrounds them with the best in illustrated picture books (see Exhibit 5.34). She engages them in activities that help them learn how elements of illustration, such as line, color, shape and different media, affect their understanding of the story. Slowly, Wendy's second graders become picture book experts as they study authors and illustrators. Wendy also tells her students about the prestigious Caldecott Award bestowed by the ALA each year for the best illustrated story. One day, student Gillian expresses to Wendy's class her belief that *Night in the Country*, written by Cynthia Rylant and illustrated by Mary Szilagyi, should have won the Caldecott, and the class agrees. So, Gillian creates a new award that the class can bestow on any book they think deserves an award but has somehow been overlooked by the ALA: the Melzercott! In Exhibit 5.35, see Gillian holding *Night in the Country* with the new Melzercott attached!

Gillian and the Melzercott award winner.

points**2**ponder

QUICK REVIEW 4 What are the three categories of mini-lessons taught during reading workshop, and how can you decide on the instructional focus of the mini-lesson?

(Access the answer in the digital version of this book.)

5.7

CHAPTER SUMMARY

Reading is a complex process in which the simultaneous extraction and construction of meaning takes place between the reader, the text, and the activity of reading, and is unique to each individual. A teacher's skill and knowledge in how to best promote the reading process for each student in his or her classroom is the most powerful variable in determining whether or not a young student learns to read.

Though students come to school with a rich knowledge of oral language, in order to learn to read, they need support in how to apply that knowledge to the written system of communication. Learning the alphabet, developing phonemic awareness, learning how to recognize words through phonics and sight vocabulary, fluency, and reading comprehension are key components of literacy that students acquire as they move through the stages of reading development.

To engage students, literacy activities must be meaningful and serve real purposes in the students' lives. A balanced literacy approach places a student's ownership of literacy at the center of instruction by using formal and informal assessment to determine his or her needs and to differentiate instruction. A gradual release of responsibility model is used to provide explicit instruction through modeling, demonstration, and guided and independent practice. Appropriate grouping and text selection are also critical to meeting individual students' instructional needs.

The instructional context in which reading is taught is critical to meaningful and engaging instruction. In this chapter, reading aloud, shared reading, guided reading, and independent reading were presented as instructional contexts that provide opportunities for students to learn to read and for teachers to use ongoing assessment to support and guide instruction. The use of instructional routines such as centers and reading workshop are effective for managing classroom instruction and providing meaningful and productive instruction for all students.

APPLICATION ACTIVITIES

think like a teacher

Jigsaw

Before coming to class view the video Thalia Learns the Details (26:00, www.learner.org/libraries/readingk2/thalia/summary.html), which follows the progress of Thalia, a kindergartner and emergent reader, over the year as she engages in a variety of reading and writing. Before and after viewing the video, read the questions under the *Analyzing the Video* and the *Looking Closer* section and mentally formulate responses to the questions. During class, divide into teams formed by class members each drawing a number corresponding to one of the questions. First, individually spend ten minutes or so composing a written response to the selected question. Then meet in a small group with others responding to the same question. Discuss. Then meet with a group consisting of one person for each of the six questions. Share your responses and discuss. Return to your starting point and record five key ideas from your discussions that were not included in your original response. The developmental phases outlined in the

Reading Continuum (www.hhpcommunities.com/teachinglanguagearts/IL-02-A.pdf) can be used as benchmarks to assess where students currently are in their development and what they need to learn with assistance. Thus, you and your group should use the continuum to assess where Thalia currently is in her development. Finally, your group should meet with all other groups to discuss your assessments.

Selecting a Text

View the video Selecting Texts That Are Just Right (7:00, http://fdf.reading recovery.org/index.php/selecting-texts), which discusses the importance of selecting an appropriate text. The ultimate goal is for students to learn how to take over the responsibility for orienting themselves to new texts as they enjoy becoming successful and independent readers. Before viewing the video, read the questions below; then after viewing, respond:

- What are the important factors for selecting books for instructional reading?
- What are the important elements of a book introduction?

Before the next class period, find a children's picture book and bring it to class. When selecting your book, consider which elements of the book would make it just right for your pretend class, a first grade at an urban school, fourteen boys and seven girls, four English language learners, and 90 percent from low socioeconomic backgrounds. Be ready to identify five elements that help to make your book just right for this class.

Phonemic Awareness/Phonics Activity

Choose one of the Activities for Teaching Phonemic Awareness and Phonics (www.hhpcommunities.com/teachinglanguagearts/IL-05-02.pdf). Use the online resource provided below for each activity to find more information about how to develop and teach the activity. Prepare the activity and present it to your classmates.

Sorting, online resource: ReadWriteThink (www.readwritethink.org/classroom-resources/lesson-plans/word-sorts-beginning-struggling-795.html). This site provides a framework for introducing short-vowel word sorts to beginning and struggling readers using authentic literature.

Elkonin Boxes, online resource: Reading Rockets (www.readingrockets.org/strategies/elkonin_boxes). This site provides step-by-step instructions on how to use Elkonin boxes with young readers.

Building/Making and Manipulating Words, online resource: ReadWriteThink (www.readwritethink.org/classroom-resources/lesson-plans/word-wizards-students-making-150.html). This site provides a lesson for guiding students through a making words activity. Students then use the online Word Wizard interactive to apply these strategies independently.

Writing Words, online resource: Reading Online. The article "Making and Writing Words" (www.readingonline.org/articles/words/rasinski.html), written by Timothy Rasinski, provides a rationale, sample activities, and how-to plan for making words and writing words activities.

Working with Words in Continuous Print, online resource: Scholastic's Read and Listen (http://teacher.scholastic.com/commclub). This site provides access to 54 nonfiction read-along books. The text can be read independently by the student, or the student can listen while the text is read aloud. The text is highlighted as it is read, and students can look and listen for words they know in the text.

Letter/Word Games, online resource: PBS Kids (http://pbskids.org/games). This site provides interactive games that allow students to work with letters and words.

Setting Up the Classroom Library

Organizing the Classroom Library (www.readingrockets.org/article/29298) is a collection of information on the Reading Rockets website on how to set up a classroom library. Read the information on this site up to the video at the bottom of the page. What information did you find helpful? Why? Now, watch the video *Getting Kids Involved in Planning the Library* (7:30). *(Access this video in the digital version of this book.)* Why should teachers involve their students in creating and managing the classroom library? Work in groups of three to four to create a two-column chart of pros and cons of involving students in creating the classroom library. Share with the class.

REFERENCES

Adams, M. (1990). *Beginning to read: Thinking and learning about print.* Urbana-Champaign, IL: University of Illinois.

Allington, R. (2002). What I've learned about effective reading instruction from a decade of studying exemplary elementary classroom teachers. *Phi Delta Kappan, 83,* 740–747.

Allington, R. (2009). *What really matters in response to intervention?* New York: Addison Wesley Longman.

Allington, R., & Johnston, P. (2002). *Reading to learn: Lessons from exemplary fourth-grade classrooms.* New York: Guilford.

Anderson, R., Hiebert, E., Scott, J., & Wilkinson, I. (1984). *Becoming a nation of readers.* Champaign-Urbana, IL: Center for the Study of Reading.

Au, K. (2011). *Literacy achievement and diversity.* New York: Teachers College Press.

Bear, D. R., Invernizzi, M., Templeton, S., & Johnston, F. (2004). Words their way: Word study for phonics, vocabulary, and spelling instruction (3rd ed.). Upper Saddle River, NJ: Pearson Prentice Hall.

Calkins, L. (2001). *The art of teaching reading.* Portsmouth, NH: Heinemann.

Chall, J. (1983). *Stages of reading development.* New York: McGraw-Hill.

Charity-Hudley, A., & Mallinson, C. (2011). *Understanding English language variation in U.S. schools.* New York: Teachers College Press.

Chorzempa, B. F., & Graham, S. (2006). Primary-grade teachers' use of within-class ability grouping in reading. *Journal of Educational Psychology, 98,* 529–541.

Clay, M. (1993). *An observation survey of early literacy achievement.* Portsmouth, NH: Heinemann.

Coiro, J. (2003). Reading comprehension on the Internet: Expanding our understanding of reading comprehension to encompass new literacies. *The Reading Teacher, 56,* 458–464.

Coiro, J., & Dobler, E. (2007). Exploring the online reading comprehension strategies used by sixth-grade skilled readers to search for and locate information on the Internet. *Reading Research Quarterly, 42*(2), 214–257.

Coiro, J., Knobel, M., Lankshear, C., & Leu, D. (Eds.). (2008). *Handbook of research on new literacies.* New York: Lawrence Erlbaum.

Common Core State Standards Initiative. (2012). Common core state standards for English language arts & literacy in history/social studies, science, and technical subjects. Council of Chief State School Officers and the National Governors Association. Retrieved from http://www.corestandards.org/assets/CCSSI_ELA%20Standards.pdf.

Cunningham, P., & Allington, R. (2011). *Classrooms that work* (5th ed.). New York: Pearson.

Daniels, H., & Zemelman, S. (2004). *Subjects matter: Every teacher's guide to content-area reading.* Portsmouth, NH: Heinemann.

DeTemple, J. (2001). Parents and children reading books together. In D. K. Dickinson & P. O. Tabors (Eds.), *Beginning literacy with language* (pp. 31–51). Baltimore, MD: Paul H. Brookes.

Dickinson, D., & Smith, M. (1994). Long-term effects of preschool teachers' book readings on low-income children's vocabulary and story comprehension. *Reading Research Quarterly, 29,* 105–122.

Duke, N., & Pearson, P. (2002). Effective practices for developing reading comprehension. In A. Farstrup & S. Samuels (Eds.), *What research has to say about reading instruction* (3rd ed.). Newark, NJ: International Reading Association.

Edmunds, K., & Bauserman, K. (2006). What teachers can learn about reading motivation through conversations with children. *The Reading Teacher, 59*(5), 414–424.

Eldredge, J., Reutzel, D., & Hollingsworth, P. (1996). Comparing the effectiveness of two oral reading practices: Round-robin reading and the shared book experience. *Journal of Literacy Research, 28*(2), 201–225.

Fielding, L., & Pearson, P. (1994). Reading comprehension: What works. *Educational Leadership, 51*(5), 62–68.

Ford, M., & Opitz, M. (2002). Using centers to engage children during guided reading time: Intensifying learning experiences away from the teacher. *The Reading Teacher, 55*(8), 710–717.

Fountas, I., & Pinnell, G. (1996). *Guided reading: Good first teaching for all children.* Portsmouth, NH: Heinemann.

Fountas, I., & Pinnell, G. (2006). *Teaching for comprehending and fluency.* Portsmouth, NH: Heinemann.

Gibson, V., & Hasbrouck, J. (2008). *Differentiated instruction: Grouping for success.* New York: McGraw-Hill.

Gickling, E., & Armstrong, D. (1978). Levels of instructional difficulty as related to on-task behavior, task completion, and comprehension. *Journal of Learning Disabilities, 11,* 559–566.

Gill, S., & Islam, C. (2011). Shared reading goes high-tech. *The Reading Teacher, 65*(3), 224–227.

Harvey, S., & Goudvis, A. (2007). *Strategies that work* (2nd ed.). Portland, ME: Stenhouse.

Holdaway, D. (1979). *The foundations of literacy.* Sydney, Australia: Ashton Scholastic.

International Reading Association. (2000). *Excellent reading teachers: A position statement of the International Reading Association.* http://www.reading.org/Libraries/Position_Statements_and_Resolutions/ps1041_excellent.sflb.ashx

Johnson, D. (2012). *The joy of children's literature.* New York: Wadsworth.

Kymes, A. (2005). Teaching online comprehension strategies using think-alouds. *Journal of Adolescent & Adult Literacy, 48,* 492–500.

Leu, D., Kinzer, C., Coiro, J., & Cammack, D. (2004). Toward a theory of new literacies emerging from the Internet and other information and communication technologies. In R. B. Ruddell & N. Unrau (Eds.), *Theoretical models and processes of reading* (5th ed., pp. 1570–1613). Newark, DE: International Reading Association.

Maynard, K., Pullen, P., & Coyne, M. (2010). Teaching vocabulary to first-grade students through repeated shared storybook reading: A comparison of rich and basic instruction to incidental exposure. *Literacy Research and Instruction, 49*(3), 209–242.

McIntyre, E., Hulan, N., & Layne, V. (2011). *Reading instruction for diverse classrooms.* New York: Guilford.

Morgan, D. N., Mraz, M., Padak, N., & Rasinski, T. (2009). *Independent reading: Practical strategies for grades K–3.* New York: Guilford.

Morrow, L., & Brittain, R. (2003). The nature of storybook reading in elementary school: Current practices. In A. van Kleeck, S. Stahl, & E. Bauer (Eds.), *On reading books to children: Parents and teachers* (pp. 140–158). Mahwah, NJ: Erlbaum.

National Center on Education and the Economy and the University of Pittsburgh. (2001). *Performance standards: Elementary.* Pittsburgh, PA: Author.

National Institute of Child Health and Development. (2002). *Director's Opening Statement on the FY 2003 President's Budget Request for the House Subcommittee on Labor-HHS-Education Appropriations.* http://www.nichd.nih.gov/about/overview/approp/testimony/dir_FY2003.cfm

National Reading Panel. (2000). Teaching children to read: An evidence-based assessment of the scientific research literature on reading and its implications for reading instruction. Washington, DC: National Institute of Child Health and Human Development, National Institutes of Health.

Northeast and the Islands Regional Technology in Education Consortium. (2004). *Technology and teaching children to read.* http://www.neirtec.org/reading_report/rdgreport.pdf

Nye, B., Konstantopoulos, S., & Hedges, L. (2004). How large are teacher effects? *Educational Evaluation and Policy Analysis, 26*(3), 237–257.

O'Donnell, M., & Wood, M. (2004). *Becoming a reader* (3rd ed.). New York: Pearson.

Pachtman, A. B., & Wilson, K. A. (2006). What do the kids think? *The Reading Teacher, 59:*680–684. doi:10.1598/RT.59.7.6

Pearson, P., Raphael, T., Benson, V., & Madda, C. (2007). Balance in comprehensive literacy instruction: Then and now. In L. Gambrell, L. Morrow, & M. Pressley (Eds.), *Best practices in literacy instruction* (3rd ed., pp. 31–54). New York: Guilford.

Pinnell, G., & Fountas, I. (2009). *When readers struggle.* Portsmouth, NJ: Heinemann.

Pinnell, G., Pikulski, J., Wixson, K., Campbell, J., Gough, P., & Beatty, A. (1995). *Listening to children read aloud: Data from NAEP's Integrated Reading Performance Record (IRPR) at grade 4.* Report NO. 23-FR-04. Prepared by Educational Testing Service under contract with the National Center for Education Statistics.

Pollard-Durodola, D., Gonzalez, J., Simmons, D., Kwok, O., Taylor, A., Davis, M., Kim, M., & Simmons, L. (2011). The effects of an intensive shared book-reading intervention for preschool children at risk for vocabulary delay. *Exceptional Children, 77*(2), 161–183.

RAND Study Group (2002). *Reading for understanding: Toward an R&D program in reading comprehension.* Arlington, VA: RAND Corporation. http://www.rand.org/pubs/monograph_reports/2005/MR1465.pdf

Rasinski, T., & Padak, N. (2011). Who wants to be a (reading) millionaire? *The Reading Teacher, 64*(7), 553–555.

Reutzel, R., & Fawson, P. (2002). *Your classroom library: New ways to give it more teaching power.* New York: Scholastic.

Schumm, J. S., Moody, S. W., & Vaughn, S. (2000). Grouping for reading instruction: Does one size fit all? *Journal of Learning Disabilities, 33,* 477–488.

Shanahan, T., Callison, K., Carrire, C., Duke, N., Pearson, P. D., Schatschneider, C., & Torgesen, J. (2010). *Improving reading comprehension in kindergarten through 3rd grade.* What Works Clearinghouse, Institute of Education Sciences (IES) Practice Guide.

Sibberson, F., & Szymusiak, K. (2003). *Still learning to read: Teaching students in grades 3–6.* Portland, ME: Stenhouse.

Snow, C., Burns, M., & Griffin, P. (Eds.). (1998). *Preventing reading difficulties in young children.* Washington, DC: National Academy Press.

Strickland, D. S. (1998). *Teaching phonics today: A primer for educators.* Newark, DE: International Reading Association.

Strickland, D. S., & Riley-Ayers, S. (2007). *Literacy Leadership in Early Childhood: The essential guide.* New York: Teachers College Press.

Sulzby, E. (1985). Children's emergent reading of favorite story-books: A developmental study. *Reading Research Quarterly, 20*(4), 458–481.

Swanson, E., Vaughn, S., Wanzek, J., Petscher, Y., Heckert, J., Cavanaugh, C., Kraft, G., & Tackett, K. (2011). A synthesis of read-aloud interventions on early reading outcomes among preschool through third graders at risk for reading difficulties. *Journal of Learning Disabilities, 44*(3), 258–275.

Taylor, B., Pearson, P., Clark, K., & Walpole, S. (2000). Effective schools and accomplished teachers: Lessons about primary grade reading instruction in low-income schools. *Elementary School Journal, 101*(2), 121–166.

Thompson, C. (2009). Clive Thompson on the new literacy. *Wired Magazine, 17*(9). http://www.wired.com/techbiz/people/magazine/17-09/st_thompson

Treptow, M., Burns, M., & McComas, J. (2007). Reading at the frustration, instructional, and independent levels: The effects on students' reading comprehension and time on task. *School Psychology Review, 36*(1), 159–166.

Wasik, B., & Bond, M. (2001). Beyond the pages of a book: Interactive book reading and language development in preschool classrooms. *Journal of Educational Psychology, 93*, 243–250.

Wilhelm, J. (2001). *Improving comprehension with think-aloud strategies.* New York: Scholastic.

Reading to Enhance Meaning

Access the book's Glossary, which defines the key terms boldfaced in this chapter, at www.hhpcommunities.com/teachinglanguagearts/glossary.pdf

MOTIVATION FOR READING

Motivation to read can be defined as the likelihood of engaging in reading or choosing to read (Gambrell, 2009; 2011). Motivation to read plays a critical role in reading development. Students who are motivated to read want to spend more time reading, read widely for a variety of purposes, and create situations that extend opportunities for literacy. In the recent Program for International Student Assessment (PISA, 2009), which tests the skills and knowledge of 15-year-old students in 70 participating countries, students who enjoyed reading the most performed significantly better than students who enjoyed reading the least. Clearly, instruction that provides students with decoding and comprehension skills and strategies is not sufficient for creating lifelong readers. Malloy and Gambrell (2010) state that "the most basic goal of any comprehension program is the development of highly motivated readers who can read, and who choose to read for pleasure and information. . . . [I]t is clear that if our students are not motivated to read, they will never reach their full literacy potential" (p. 163).

"Though my students differ in the range of abilities and skills they bring with them, they all want to read and enjoy learning."

JULIE LIPSCOMB,
fourth grade teacher

EXHIBIT 6.1

Serena reading.

Research has found that as students proceed through school, motivation to read steadily declines. Pressley (2006) notes that children in kindergarten and first grade "believe they can do anything. If you ask them whether they are going to learn to read, they are certain of it" (p. 373). By fifth or sixth grade, however, students are much less confident, much more aware of their failures than their successes, and less enthusiastic about reading. In the PISA report cited above, 37 percent of the 15-year-old students reported that they do not read for enjoyment at all. Motivation is so important that the International Reading Association's Literacy Research Panel (*Reading Today,* 2012) has identified motivation and engagement as a critical issue facing literacy today, stating that "student motivation currently appears devastatingly low" (p. 9).

Teachers can do much to motivate their students to read. Ruddell's (2004) research found that influential teachers positively affect students' attitudes toward reading by tapping their internal motivation as they encourage students to engage with the text. Ruddell (2004) states that "influential teachers are highly effective in taking an instructional stance that uses internal reader motivations and incorporates students' prior knowledge, experiences, and beliefs in the meaning-negotiation and construction process" (p. 993). As students' motivation to read increases, they want to spend more time reading. The more time they spend reading, the more engaged they will become (see Exhibit 6.1). Engaged reading is when a reader reads frequently for interest, enjoyment, and learning (Baker, Dreher, & Guthrie, 2000).

author's story   ELIZABETH DOBLER

When I was a third grade teacher, my student Justin appeared to be a struggling or reluctant reader. During class reading time, Justin fidgeted, daydreamed, talked, and did just about anything he could think of besides reading. I assumed Justin did not like to read, possibly because he found it difficult. When his mother came to school for a parent–teacher conference, we discussed Justin's reluctance to read. She encouraged reading at home, but still felt that Justin was not as engaged as he could be. I gave her a few book suggestions, and she told me she would take Justin to the public library over the weekend. First thing Monday morning, Justin came into the classroom and excitedly showed me the book he had borrowed from the library. I was shocked to see Justin's enthusiasm over a book and stunned to see that the book was *Treasure Island* by Robert Lewis Stevenson. Justin gave me a clear synopsis of what he had read so far, thus confirming he could indeed understand this challenging classic. He taught me an important lesson about the power of motivation and choice. Justin chose his own book and was motivated to read a book above the level I would have selected for him. Just like the saying, "don't judge a book by its cover," teachers should not jump to conclusions about what students can and want to read. Get to know your students, their tastes, interests, and abilities; then make book recommendations based on this valuable information.

The following seven research-based rules of reading engagement indicate that students are more motivated to read under the following conditions:

- The reading tasks and activities are relevant to their lives.
- Readers have access to a wide range of reading materials.
- Readers have ample opportunities to engage in sustained reading.

- Readers have opportunities to make choices about what they read and how they engage in and complete literacy tasks.
- Readers have opportunities to socially interact with others about the text they are reading.
- Readers have opportunities to be successful with challenging texts.
- Classroom incentives reflect the value and importance of reading (Gambrell, 2011).

Many of the guidelines for engagement, which are integral to balanced literacy instruction, were discussed in Chapter 5; however, one important point bears repeating. Access to books that students enjoy reading plays a critical role in motivation. "No other features of classroom instruction [are] as powerful in improving both reading comprehension and motivation" (Allington, 2009, p. 144).

Listen to this podcast (22:00) by distinguished educators and researchers Linda Gambrell, Barbara Marinak, and Jacquelynn Malloy to learn more on the important topic of motivation (www.reading.org/general/publications/podcasts.aspx).

To motivate students and provide access to books students will enjoy and want to read, discover your students' attitudes about reading and the types of books they like. Jill Cole, a second grade teacher, conducted a classroom study of her students' motivations to read by conducting interviews and observations and reading students' journals. She found that "the students were motivated by very different books, activities and other classroom components. They had their own beliefs, purposes, and reactions. In short, each one had a unique 'literacy personality'" (Cole, 2003, p. 326).

Like Jill, you can use a variety of methods to discover your students' literacy personalities. In addition to interviews, observations, and reading response journals and writing samples, you can also use attitude/interest inventories. An example of an informal reading interest inventory and the more formal Elementary Reading Attitude Survey, also known as the Garfield test, are further described in Chapter 8.

Reading authentic texts

Reading authentic texts is one way to motivate students. One type of authentic text is **real world texts** (e.g., menus, brochures, newsletters, cereal boxes, directions for operating electronic devices, medicine bottle labels, train schedules, bills, maps) that people read in the real world every day. Students learn the importance of these types of text and even how to read some of them before they come to school. For example, while riding in the car, a child might see the red octagon on the street corner and immediately recognize it as a stop sign. Similarly, a child might watch his father reading the directions in a recipe he is making for dinner. She may not be able to read the directions, but she understands that they are important to making dinner. Students of all ages and reading abilities read and experience real world text every day. Even children at the pre-k level who are not yet reading per se display knowledge about how to use books for reading. The Concepts of Print assessment is an observation tool for teachers to learn what young children know about books and reading. See Chapter 8 for more detailed information about this assessment and how it can be used by teachers of young children.

Teacher Sarah Lucero sharing good books.

Ask students to bring meaningful real world texts to class. Using such texts provides them with real life purposes for reading, which is motivating, meaningful, and responds to their individual needs. You can demonstrate that they use the same strategies for reading these texts as they do books or other materials. This can help students make the important connection between in school and out of school reading.

Trade books, introduced in Chapter 5, are also authentic texts. These books are written for the public and available at bookstores, libraries, or online and include a range of formats such as picture books, easy readers, chapter books, informational books, magazines, and newspapers, and a range of genres, which include fantasy, realistic fiction, historical fiction, poetry, and nonfiction. Research shows that authentic, high-quality literature promotes reading engagement.

The chart Genres of Children's and Young Adult Literature (www.hhp communities.com/teachinglanguagearts/IL-06-01.pdf) describes genres and gives examples of books for each.

Make sure that the texts available in the classroom meet the diverse needs and interests of all students in the classroom, including those from various socioeconomic backgrounds, religions, genders, and exceptionalities and struggling/reluctant readers, which may include boys. (Exhibit 6.3 shows a chart offering students advice about how to choose a book.) According to a PISA report (2011), "Girls and socio-economically advantaged students read more for enjoyment than boys and disadvantaged students, and there is evidence that the gap in reading patterns widened between 2000 and 2009" (p. 1). Including diverse forms of quality literature, including multicultural literature, helps teachers close this reading gap.

Inclusion of **multicultural literature** is critical for presenting readers with models of diverse characters, settings, and life situations that can help them connect their lives and the text. When students can relate to a text or find a piece of themselves in a story, they are more likely to read. Multicultural literature in the classroom library is beneficial in additional ways because it includes:

- Quality literature that meets the criteria of literary artistic merit.
- Information and knowledge about the historical and continuing contributions of the people of diverse cultures who live in the United States.
- Information that exposes young people to the world through diverse viewpoints other than the mainstream.
- Fostering an awareness, appreciation, and understanding of people who are different from and similar to themselves.
- Critical inquiry into issues of equal representation of how people of diverse cultures are depicted in all books (Johnson, 2012, p. 323).

Quality multicultural literature can play an important role in providing vicarious experiences in relating to and understanding others, whether they are like ourselves or very different.

For more information on finding quality multicultural literature, see Celebrating Cultural Diversity Through Children's Literature (www.multiculturalchildrenslit.com).

Additionally, a classroom library should include books that may not be deemed *high-quality* by adults but are popular with students; such books include the *Big Nate* series by Lincoln Peirce, *The Heroes of Olympus* series by Rick Riordan, *The Dork Diaries* series by Rachel Russell, and *The Diary of a Wimpy Kid* series by Jeff Kinney. Nonfiction series titles such as the *Amazing Science* books in the Eyewitness Junior series and the *Scientist in the Field* series are distinguished by spectacular photographs and concise text. All these popular books may appeal to struggling/reluctant readers and boys. Reading real texts for real purposes, such as to learn more about sharks or to be entertained by funny graphic novels, will increase the likelihood that students will transfer the use of strategies to their independent reading.

Children's book author Jon Scieszka *(The Stinky Cheese Man, The True Story of the Three Little Pigs)* created the website Guys Read (www.guysread.com) with the goal of encouraging boys to become self-motivated, lifelong readers. The site includes book recommendations.

Choice in reading materials

When real world readers choose a text, they are reading to learn and to enjoy themselves. They accomplish these tasks by selecting a text that fulfills their needs. Selecting what to read is a major part of becoming a reader (Ollman, 1993). Self-selecting literature is so essential to the reading process that without its inclusion in a reading program, reading development will not occur (Darigan, Tunnel, & Jacobs, 2002). For students to engage with a text, they must feel that they have control over which materials they read.

EXHIBIT 6.3

"How to pick a book" chart.

Many adults believe that young people should read only what adults consider quality literature; yet, an adult's interests often differ from a child's (Chatton, 2004; Worthy, Moorman, & Turner, 1999). When given the option, students will make positive selections based on their individual interests and abilities. Research suggests that students can and do make choices that increase their awareness and extend their literacy skills (Fresch, 1995; Schlager, 1978; Worthy, 1996). However, research has also shown that some students need assistance with selecting a just-right book for independent reading (Donovan, Smolkin, & Loxmax, 2000; Flowerday, Schraw, & Stevens, 2004). You can use several methods to help students learn to choose books, including posting a chart with guidelines such as the one shown in Exhibit 6.3.

Another specific strategy is what Ohlhausen and Jepson (1992) call the Goldilocks strategy. This strategy teaches students to find books that are not too hard or not too easy, but just right. You model how to choose a just-right book through mini-lessons that show students how to identify books that are too hard, too easy, or just right. When introducing the Goldilocks strategy, explain ways to identify these categories:

- *Too hard:* A book the student would like to read but for which she does yet not have the strategies for figuring out unfamiliar words and/or unfamiliar concepts.

- *Just right:* A book the student is interested in and for which he has the strategies to figure out most unfamiliar words and/or unfamiliar concepts.

- *Too easy:* Books the student likes to read for fun; books she has read before.

Five finger test chart.

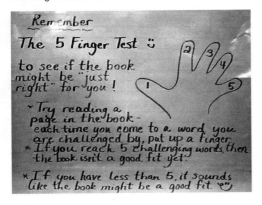

CLICKS strategy for book selection.

Students evaluate potential books to assess these factors:	
C	Connections to anyone or anything
L	Length of page or book
I	Interest in topic
C	Count five unknown words
K	Know about topic, author, illustrator
S	Sense and understanding

From Giordano, L. (2011). Making sure our reading CLICKS. *The Reading Teacher, 64*(8), 612–619. Used with permission via Copyright Clearance Center.

The five-finger method (see Exhibit 6.4) is another strategy students can use to choose appropriate books. Instruct students to open the book to any page and begin reading. As they read, tell the student to put up one finger for each word with which she is not familiar. If the student finishes the page and is holding up all five fingers, she will know that the book is too difficult. If she is holding up no fingers, the book choice is too easy. If two or three fingers are held up, the selection is probably a just-right book. The five-finger method is a fairly simple way to help students choose appropriate books.

Finally, the CLICKS strategy, developed by second grade teacher Linda Giordano (2011), provides an acronym students can use to help them to identify a just-right book (see Exhibit 6.5). Giordano explains that she finds CLICKS to be "a more concrete, effective way to get students to take ownership for book selection than the Goldilocks method and the Five-Finger rule" (p. 613).

Giordano taught her students the six strategies of the CLICKS acronym, one each day, modeling and demonstrating each component at the beginning of the year. She then revisited steps throughout the year as needed. Giordano noticed that as the year progressed, the quality of the students' explanations of their book choices became richer:

> Early on they might say, "This book looks funny" or "That dog is cute." Responses given later in the year were more specific: "I've read Henry and Mudge books before, but not this one," "I've checked, and I can read the pages without mistakes," or "I noticed that's the same author who wrote *Brave Irene*. " (p. 619)

As important as knowing how to find a just-right book is knowing when to abandon a book that may be too difficult or boring and knowing when to persist with a book that is interesting but challenging. Give your students strategies for knowing when to abandon a book after giving it a fair chance. Teach them ways to work through difficult text using highlighters, sticky notes, two-column charts, and other strategies. Modeling your own reading habits and talking through your decision-making process is one of the most effective ways to teach students how they can make informed decisions about their own reading.

stories FROM THE CLASSROOM

Choosing your own reading material

Third grade teacher Leslie Panaro recognizes the influence choosing your own reading material can have on a reader's motivation. She knows this to be true for herself as an adult and, out of respect for her students, she seeks to give them the same opportunities to decide what to read.

To learn more about the ways Panaro integrates self-selection of reading materials into her class routines, watch The Power and Purpose of Self-Selected Reading (5:29). *(Access this podcast in the digital version of this book.)* During the podcast, Panaro mentions a bar code scanning system that she uses to keep track of which books her students are reading. One such system is Intelliscanner: www.intelliscanner.com/index-classroom.html.

Ebooks, tablets, and ereaders in the classroom

"Some weeks I completely forgot about TV. I went two weeks with only watching one show, or no shows at all. I was just reading every day." This quote from Eliana Garcia, age 11, is in response to getting an ereader as a Hanukkah gift. Her comment was followed by her mother's response, "There's something I'm not sure is entirely replaceable about having a stack of inviting books, just waiting for your kids to grab. But I'm an avid believer that you need to find what excites your child about reading. So I'm all for it" (Bosman, 2011). Eliana and her mother's responses are typical of those heard around the world about reading ebooks on ereaders or tablets, which often include an initial hesitation followed by excitement and increased motivation to read.

Because ebooks often include interactive tools that allow the reader to search for key words, look up unfamiliar words, change the font size, and hear the book read aloud through a text-to-speech feature, they are well-suited for young readers. Ebooks can embed video, audio, and hyperlinks, and these features support readers' background knowledge and comprehension. Additionally, some devices or ebooks allow the reader to engage in reading response by highlighting or underlining text; adding comments by inserting notes, attaching files, or recording comments; and changing the page format, text size, and screen layout. Many of these interactive features can assist teachers with differentiating reading instruction and provide students with individual support (Larson, 2010). However, the interactivity of the format in which the book is delivered does not outweigh the importance of quality and how it aligns with the personal preferences of the reader (Jones & Brown, 2011).

Larson (2009) believes that "integrating e-books into an otherwise traditional literacy program is an effective move toward new literacies instruction" (p. 256). See Exhibit 6.7 for suggested steps for acquiring and using ebooks, tablets, and **ereaders** in the classroom.

EXHIBIT 6.6

Students reading on a tablet.

EXHIBIT 6.7

Steps for acquiring and using ebooks, tablets, and ereaders in the classroom.

- Communicate closely with school administrators and technology staff to develop common literacy and technology goals.
- Discuss funding options for acquiring ebooks, tablets, or e-readers (e.g., grants, PTA/PTO support, or fund-raisers).
- Decide how to effectively use the devices during whole-class instruction, literature circles, and individual reading experiences. Consider having students share devices on which multiple book titles have been downloaded.
- Model for the class how to operate and care for the devices. Be sure to discuss what to do if it stops working or if something unexpected happens. Also, demonstrate how to effectively use the many tools and features of the ebook or device such as making notes, highlighting words and passages, turning on the text-to-speech, changing the font size, and using the dictionary. Follow-up lessons can provide information to students on how to share digital notes or favorite text passages with their classmates.
- Create a rotation schedule during independent reading time that allows each student access to the device.
- Establish class expectations for note taking and markings in the ebooks, particularly if multiple students share a device. Decide if students have the right to access one another's books and if they can read one another's notes. Also, consider if multiple students may add notes in the same book—possibly responding to one another's notes and comments.
- Observe students' reading behaviors when they access and use ebook tools and features. Analyze students' notes and highlighted passages for strategy use; during individual conferences, use this assessment information to move students toward a broader repertoire of response options. Also, encourage students to share how the ebooks or devices support their individual reading processes.

Adapted from Larson, L. (2010). Digital Readers: The next chapter in e-book reading and response. *Reading Teacher, 64*(1), 15–22.

BOOK REVIEW

The Book Whisperer: Awakening the Inner Reader in Every Child

BY DONALYN MILLER

I am a member of a literacy study group that meets monthly and consists of district level reading/language arts coordinators from across the state. During our first meeting, we each shared a book that has impacted our learning about reading/language arts. The first recommendation was *The Book Whisperer*. The person who recommended it said that "this book reminded me of why I'm an educator and helped me to refocus on what's important in our English classrooms." Subsequently, several other members of the group read the book and completely agreed. It is about how joyous reading should be for our students and ways to help our students achieve that joy.

In the introduction, Miller writes that she is "not a reading researcher. I am not a reading policy expert. I do not have a Ph.D. What I am is a reading teacher, just like many of you." Miller is a sixth grade language arts and social studies teacher in Keller, Texas, and in the tradition of "whisperers" (i.e., those who seem to have preternatural knowledge of a specific topic), she has never met a kid she could not convert into a reader. In Miller's classroom, students read an average of 40 to 50 books a year, with no drills or worksheets. Her love of books and teaching is both infectious and inspiring. The book includes "The Nerdy Book Club," a dynamite list of recommended "kid lit" that Miller compiled with two other educators. Also visit The Nerdy Book Club website (http://nerdybookclub.wordpress.com).

Locate a copy of The Book Whisperer: www.worldcat.org/title/book-whisperer-awakening-the-inner-reader-in-every-child/oclc/251208607

points2ponder

QUICK REVIEW 1 Why is it so important for students to be motivated to read? Why is providing students with choice in the materials they read important?

(Access the answers in the digital version of this book.)

VOCABULARY OVERVIEW

Vocabulary, or knowledge of words, is made up of both general terms used in everyday language and academic terms used in specialized subjects such as math and science. Everyone's vocabulary knowledge is unique, based on their background knowledge, experiences with books, and parents' vocabulary level. Students from high socioeconomic status (SES) homes typically have a vocabulary greater than those from low SES homes (Beck, McKeown, & Kucan, 2002). Additionally, students from high SES homes continue to grow their vocabularies at a faster pace. Estimates indicate that the average child from a high SES home entering kindergarten has a vocabulary of approximate 3,500 words, and the average high school graduate from a high SES has a reading vocabulary of between 40,000 and 50,000 words. Thus, students from high SES homes learn somewhere around 3,000 words per school year, while students from low SES homes learn at a much slower rate. Research confirms that students who reach fourth grade with limited vocabularies are very likely to struggle to understand grade-level texts (Chall & Jacobs, 2003; RAND Reading Study Group [RRSG], 2002).

Numerous studies have documented that vocabulary knowledge is highly predictive of reading comprehension. Logically, this makes sense; the more words a reader knows, the better she will be able to understand what she reads. Specifically, in a review of 100 years of research on vocabulary, Graves and Watts-Taffe (2002) found that:

- Vocabulary knowledge is one of the best indicators of verbal ability.
- Vocabulary difficulty strongly influences the readability of text.
- Teaching the vocabulary of a selection can improve students' comprehension of that selection.
- Growing up in poverty can seriously restrict the vocabulary students learn before beginning school and make attaining an adequate vocabulary a challenging task.
- Disadvantaged students are likely to have substantially smaller vocabularies than their more advantaged classmates.
- Lack of vocabulary can be a critical factor underlying the school failure of disadvantaged students. (p. 141)

The task of learning vocabulary is all-encompassing. Since vocabulary applies to all content areas, vocabulary instruction and modeling occur throughout the entire school day, which makes all educators vocabulary teachers, including the music, art, and physical education teachers. It takes a concerted effort to help all students learn vocabulary, especially those with limited English skills. For young people of poverty and English language learners, it is especially critical to have many and varied experiences with words in order to build vocabulary.

Levels of word knowledge

In *The Mighty Miss Malone,* written by Christopher Paul Curtis (2012), the main character, 12-year-old Deza, hears the word *epiphany* used by a doctor to describe an event that happened to her brother. Deza, unfamiliar with the word, goes home and looks it up in the dictionary: "*Sudden intuitive perception of or insight into the reality or essential meaning of something, usually initiated by some simple, commonplace occurrence or experience.*" Despite this, Deza still does not understand the meaning of the word. She says, "That's the only bad thing about dictionaries. You start by looking up one word and end up having to look up seven others to understand the first one." At dinner, Deza asks her parents about the meaning of *epiphany.* Her father replies, "Think of a light going on. An epiphany is being surrounded by darkness and bumping around. Something happens or is said that causes a light to be switched on and everything becomes clear. It's when you suddenly understand something. The moment you *really* get it." Deza's father defines the word epiphany beautifully, through use of images and emotions. Teachers hope students have an epiphany about new words on a daily basis. The goal is for students to hear an unfamiliar word and to make a connection to their background knowledge as a way to understand it. The goal is not to have students hear a word and instantly think of a definition. This would be impractical and disconnected from the ways people come to understand words and the world around us.

However, definitional approaches to vocabulary instruction, such as weekly vocabulary tests that require students to memorize definitions of words, predominate in classrooms regardless of research that shows that students' ability to define words has no effect on reading comprehension (Cunningham & Allington, 2011, p. 95).

Good vocabulary instruction involves far more than looking up words in a dictionary and using them in a sentence, as is made evident in *The Mighty Miss Malone.* Deza loves telling stories with the help of her beloved dictionary and thesaurus and thinks that since she wants to be a teacher, her writing should display a large vocabulary. However, she often does not really understand the words she chooses, so her writing is sometimes overly verbose, stilted, or even nonsensical. According to Beck, McKeown, and Kucan (2002), knowledge of a word follows a continuum:

- No knowledge: the word is completely unknown.
- Incidental knowledge: the word may have been seen before, but is unknown.
- Partial knowledge: one definition of the word is known or it can be used in one context.
- Full knowledge: multiple meanings of the word are known and can be used appropriately in multiple contexts.

Using this continuum, Deza is at the partial knowledge point with the word *epiphany.* She knows two definitions of the word (one from her father and one from the dictionary) and has heard the word used in one context. Yet, there are at least two other definitions of the word *epiphany* (e.g., a Christian festival observed in January and the manifestation of a deity). For Deza to fully understand or have ownership of the word *epiphany,* she must be able to understand its meaning when listening and reading and to use it to express her thoughts when writing and talking. To develop this level of understanding, she will need to be actively involved in multiple opportunities to use and think about the word's meanings and in creating an understanding of the word in multiple contexts. This is especially true for academic words, which are particularly challenging for English language learners. Looking up words in the dictionary and memorizing definitions are of little value to a student with limited English proficiency (Nagy & Townsend, 2012). Students need repeated exposures and authentic opportunities to use the word in order to develop full word knowledge. Only through using new words in a variety of contexts will an English language learner, or even a native English speaker, begin to own these words and use them with ease. The levels of word knowledge can be used to create an informal assessment of students' vocabulary. The Vocabulary Knowledge Scale (discussed in Chapter 8) is a self-knowledge rating scale on which students indicate their vocabulary knowledge about words selected by the teacher. The simple act of asking about word knowledge for certain words makes readers more aware of the words as they are reading, and encourages vocabulary development. In addition, results from the scale provide teachers with an informal assessment of the class's word knowledge as a whole and can be used to guide vocabulary instruction within a lesson or a specific text.

points2ponder

QUICK REVIEW 2 List the stages in the continuum of word knowledge. How can teachers help students move along the continuum?

(Access the answers in the digital version of this book.)

6.3

MULTIFACETED VOCABULARY INSTRUCTION

Multiple exposures to vocabulary in multiple contexts require multifaceted vocabulary instruction. Graves and Watts-Taffe (2002) outline a four-component program that promotes vocabulary learning: (1) wide reading; (2) teaching individual words; (3) teaching word learning strategies; and (4) fostering word consciousness.

Wide reading

Jared and Wyatt reading.

One of the best ways of building students' vocabulary is through reading a wide variety of materials from a wide variety of genres. "Increasing the volume of students' reading is the single most important thing a teacher can do to promote large-scale vocabulary growth" (Nagy, 1988, p. 32). Reading materials selected for wide reading should be of high quality, utilizing words students know along with less familiar words.

In a balanced literacy classroom, students are immersed in a word-rich environment. Words are displayed around the room and students are given opportunities to learn vocabulary through wide reading across the day. Teachers read aloud to students, teachers and students read shared texts together, students read independently (see Exhibit 6.8), and teachers and students read during guided or content area instruction.

When reading authentic texts independently, students encounter rich vocabulary in context. Good literature can take young people to places that classroom experiences cannot, such as a visit to Narnia in *The Lion, the Witch and the Wardrobe*, a trip to Nazi-occupied Denmark during the Holocaust in *Number the Stars,* or a microscopic view of arachnids in *Amazing Spiders.* These vicarious experiences provide a powerful way to learn word meanings. While reading, have students write new words they discover in a vocabulary notebook (see Exhibit 6.9). Encourage students to include three for four new words a week from a variety of genres. You may wish to have students include the same information as for the words placed on the word wall. The purpose of a vocabulary notebook is to promote students' independent vocabulary knowledge and to provide multiple contexts in which the student becomes familiar with the word.

Another way to bring attention to words is for students to find them in the books or materials they are reading independently. For example, if your class is studying homophones (words that sound the same but are spelled differently and have different meanings), have students find homophones in their reading then write them on sticky notes and place them on a chart or draw a picture of the homophones and place them on a bulletin board (see Exhibit 6.10).

Students can also learn vocabulary from reading and listening to books online. For example, the PBS Kids website (http://pbskids.org/lions/stories) offers several interactive stories that are read aloud. Students can listen to the story and follow along with the highlighted words. Audiobooks are also a good way for students to hear books that use rich vocabulary; a person can listen and understand a text at a higher level than a text that he or she can read. The American Library Association bestows the Odyssey Award (www.ala.org/alsc/awardsgrants/bookmedia/odysseyaward/odyssey past) annually to the best audiobooks for children and young adults. The list of award winners and honors can be found at the Odyssey Award Winners website.

Teaching individual words

Research indicates that students do acquire new vocabulary through explicit vocabulary instruction (RRSG, 2002). Classroom lessons and activities can focus on specific words during reading, writing, and content area instruction. But the element of teaching individual words is just one of the four parts of a multifaceted vocabulary approach. Students need to grow their vocabulary at such a fast rate that it would not be possible to directly teach all of the words they need to know. Many words must be learned through daily experiences, conversations, and reading (as we discussed above), along with direct teaching. Traditionally vocabulary was taught by having students look up words in the dictionary and copying the definition. This is not teaching; it is merely copying. Teaching vocabulary entails giving an explanation and guiding practice, and this process begins with selecting appropriate words to teach.

Selecting words to teach

Determining which words to teach is important because you only have time to teach a limited number, so every word must count. To guide teachers with selecting words, Beck, McKeown, and Kucan (2002) determined three levels or tiers of words:

- **Tier 1 words:** Frequently occurring, everyday words.
- **Tier 2 words:** Words frequently used in written texts that have high utility.
- **Tier 3 words:** Words that are technical or specific to particular contexts and content areas.

EXHIBIT 6.9

Example of a vocabulary notebook.

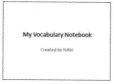

EXHIBIT 6.10

Homophone bulletin board created with student contributions.

Given this criteria, the word *epiphany* would be a tier 2 word. It is not an everyday word, but it also isn't technical or content specific. Beck and colleagues believe that words in tier 2 are most worth highlighting and teaching to elementary students, because those are the words students are most likely to incorporate into their reading, writing, listening, and speaking vocabularies. Yet, without direct instruction in school these words may never be learned. Applying this criteria can be helpful as you select words to teach across learning contexts.

To get you started identifying tier 2 words, let's use the picture book *Grandfather's Journey* (1993) by Allen Say. This book is about the author's grandfather traveling from Japan to the United States at the turn of the twentieth century. From the following words found in the book, choose five that you think would be appropriate tier 2 words to teach: European, steamship, astonished, New World, riverboat, sculptured, amazed, bewildered, marveled, Sierra Mountains, surrounded, exchanged, warblers, silvereyes, longing, homesick. Record your selections before comparing them to those selected by one of *Forward Thinking*'s authors.

See the words author Denise Johnson selected as tier 2 words for instruction: www.hhpcommunities.com/teachinglanguagearts/IL-06-02.pdf

Instructional contexts for teaching individual words

Reading aloud. Students can learn individual word meanings from reading aloud experiences in which the teacher scaffolds learning by asking questions, adding information, or prompting students to describe their thinking before, during, and after listening to a book. When reading aloud, teachers can pause to define specific words that students might not know, model how to use strategies to figure out an unknown word, or think aloud about how the author's word choice affects the reader's understanding.

Word walls. Drawing students' attention to words while reading aloud is one of the best ways for students to learn words. Selected words can be placed on a word wall for students to refer to during independent reading and writing. The word can include:

- the original sentence in which the word was found,
- synonyms or other words associated with the new word,
- a new sentence created by the class using the word.

For example, if you are reading *The Mighty Miss Malone* aloud and want to include *scheme,* the word on the wall might look as shown in Exhibit 6.11. Provide students with the definition, characteristics, and relevant examples of these words to help them activate prior knowledge, make connections to existing schema, and organize knowledge into categories.

EXHIBIT 6.11

Word wall example for use in independent reading and writing.

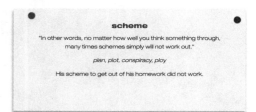

scheme

"In other words, no matter how well you think something through, many times schemes simply will not work out."

plan, plot, conspiracy, ploy

His scheme to get out of his homework did not work.

stories FROM THE CLASSROOM

Utilizing a word wall

Third grade teacher Vicki Altland began using a "Powerful Words!" wall in conjunction with reading aloud in her classroom several years ago (see Exhibit 6.12). Her students really enjoyed helping her select the words for the word wall, but the proof of its effectiveness is in her students' use of the word wall in their writing. One picture book Vicki read aloud to her students was *Stellaluna* by Janell Cannon, which is about a baby bat that falls into a bird's nest and is raised like a bird until she is reunited with her mother. The story begins, "In a warm and sultry forest far, far away, there once lived a mother fruit bat and her new baby." The students chose the word *sultry* as the *powerful word*. Later, the students took the state-mandated writing test. Afterward, one of the students informed Vicki that she had used a *powerful word* on the test. The writing prompt was to write about a day at the beach and the student wrote, "One hot sultry day at the beach." When students are able to use words flexibly and in multiple contexts, they truly own those words.

EXHIBIT 6.12

A "Powerful Words" wall.

Guided reading. Guided reading provides a beneficial context for you to build students' knowledge of individual words. The texts have been selected specifically for each group of students so that the challenges and supports within the text are just right. During the book introduction, you conduct a **picture walk** of the book, leading students through the pages as a way to preview the story and making sure they hear and attend to any challenging features. During this introduction, you can incorporate a discussion of any words or phrases that might be new or used in a new way in which students may be unfamiliar.

For example, in one guided reading book, a mother and her young son Ben are going to the store. When they reach the front door, Ben's mother says, "We are here. In you go!" This is an unusual phrasing. Most often, a mother would say something similar to "We are here. Please go in." To prepare students for this unusual phrasing, you may use the phrase in your introduction so students can hear how it sounds. If you want to raise the level of scaffolding, you could also ask the students to find the phrase on the page. This same process can be followed for unknown words.

Content area reading. General vocabulary and word identification strategies are usually the focus of vocabulary instruction in the primary grades. As students progress into content area reading that is more difficult, they encounter a greater number of abstract words used as labels for concepts; such words can best be understood through repeated exposure in a variety of meaningful contexts. For example, the word *photosynthesis* represents the entire concept of how plants turn light into energy. The definition is abstract, and without other experiences with photosynthesis, the student may have difficulty learning the concept. To develop students' understanding of photosynthesis, you may show them a diagram of the process and engage them in a science experiment in which one or more plants receives light and others do not. Without light, the plant cannot make the energy it needs to live. Effective vocabulary development activities should focus on the authentic ways people learn word meanings through use in a variety of contexts. Some vocabulary programs focus only on memorizing definitions, breaking words into syllables, looking for prefixes and suffixes or other word chunks, and using pronunciation keys. These strategies have limited value, and they must be coupled with strategies for understanding the complex meanings of many subject-specific unfamiliar words.

Specialized vocabulary learning requires direct instruction to promote understanding and the eventual development of independent strategies for figuring out unknown words. Simply telling students a definition is insufficient. The ultimate goal should be preparing students to determine

Activities for direct instruction of vocabulary.

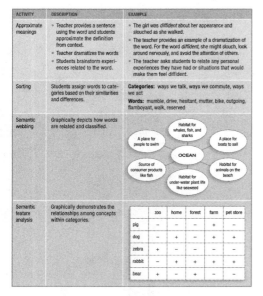

WordSift and related screens for material from a chapter on cells from a fifth grade science textbook.

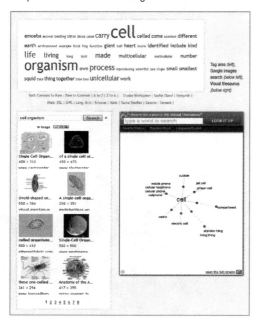

word meaning on their own. You can directly scaffold students' vocabulary development by using graphic organizers such as word webs and concept maps to help them make connections to existing words or concepts. Exhibit 6.13 provides examples of vocabulary building activities to assist students as they learn general and academic vocabulary.

Online resources are also helpful, especially visual dictionaries and thesauri. WordSift was created by experts at Stanford University to help teachers manage vocabulary and academic language in their text materials, which may be helpful in supporting English language learners.

Type or cut and paste any text into the WordSift program and it will create a *tag cloud* of these words with the most important words appearing larger than others (see Exhibit 6.14). The program also includes a visual word thesaurus and Google search that displays images and videos of the most important words from the text. Also, clicking on any word in the tag cloud displays instances of sentences in which that word is used in the text. Visit WordSift and watch a video tour (5:00): www.wordsift.com/site/videotour/newFeat

A review of research by Blachowicz, Fisher, Ogle, and Watts-Taffe (2006) found that electronic texts "can be both motivating and effective for word learning when they provide or couple their presentations with facilitation that calls on the students to actively engage with the words" (p. 533). In other words, when using an online resource such as WordSift, you should involve students in a discussion of the visual and graphical results and support students as they integrate that information with the text they are reading. Ereaders and tablets have built-in dictionaries and/or access to online dictionaries. Together, this and note-taking features make understanding unfamiliar words in a digital text an instant and active process.

stories FROM THE CLASSROOM

Vocabulary instruction

Teaching about word meaning is an important job, one that fourth grade teacher Julie Lipscomb takes very seriously. She seeks various ways to impress upon students the importance of learning vocabulary and provides a variety of instructional activities to capture students' attention and keep them engaged with learning about words.

Listen to Julie's Vocabulary Instruction podcast as she discusses the many ways she teaches vocabulary in her classroom (5:49). *(Access this podcast in the digital version of this book.)*

Teaching word learning strategies

Research supports the practice of teaching students strategies such as context clues and morphology (analyzing word structure) for inferring the meaning of unknown words (Nagy & Townsend, 2012). As mentioned earlier, even when students use context clues, vocabulary may remain inaccessible due to the students' lack of prior knowledge or lack of context clues in the passage. In such cases, morphology is a useful tool.

Teach students to use context clues

One of the most useful strategies for figuring out unknown words is through **context clues** (Graves & Watts-Taffe, 2002). Good readers tend to use context clues instinctively while less strategic readers tend to isolate unknown words from relevant context. With general vocabulary, students might not know a word, but prior knowledge and experiences play an important part in the student's ability to use context clues for comprehension. For example, a student might not know the word *consumed* in the sentence, "The young woman was consumed with curiosity about the movie after watching the movie trailer." Yet, drawing on prior knowledge of movie trailers and how they show the most exciting aspects of an upcoming movie and usually end in a thrilling cliffhanger, the student may be able to approximate the meaning of the word. In addition, an author might provide the definition, a synonym, an antonym, or an example to support the meaning of an unfamiliar word.

Baumann, Ware, and Edwards (2007) recommend discussing with students the value of context clues, displaying explicit examples, then together creating a chart of guidelines for using context clues. A chart might include the following:

> *Context clues:* Ideas or hints about the meaning of a word contained in the surrounding words and sentences.
>
> - Look for context clues both before and after a hard word. Sometimes they are close to a word, but other times they may be several sentences away.
> - Some context clues will be strong or really obvious, but others will be weak. Sometimes context even might be confusing or misleading.
> - Use the Vocabulary Rule: (1) use context, (2) look for word-part clues, (3) use context again to check meaning.

During reading aloud, model how to use context clues to figure out unknown words. Then create anchor charts (see Exhibit 6.15) to help students remember these strategies during guided reading and when reading independently.

Teach students to analyze word parts

Morphology, the study of the structure of words or the breaking down of words (for example, identifying prefixes, root words, and suffixes), is a strategy used effectively by average and above average word learners. (Exhibit 6.16 shows a chart for teaching suffixes.) A study by Kieffer and Lesaux (2007) found that fourth grade and fifth grade native speakers and English language learners in an urban setting with a greater understanding of morphology became more successful at learning academic vocabulary and comprehending text. Kieffer and Lesaux recommend four principles for teaching morphology to improve students' vocabulary and reading comprehension:

Principle 1. *Teach morphology in the context of rich, explicit vocabulary instruction.* Morphology should be just one component of a comprehensive vocabulary program. There are many effective strategies for figuring out unknown words, and no single strategy works for everyone or every word. Morphology should be considered another tool in the arsenal of strategies a student has for learning vocabulary.

Principle 2. *Teach students to use morphology strategically.* When a student comes across an unfamiliar word, one strategy he might try is to look for parts of the word that he knows. Some teachers call this strategy **chunking,**

EXHIBIT 6.15

Chart for figuring out unfamiliar words.

EXHIBIT 6.16

Chart for teaching suffixes.

where students look for familiar parts or chunks of the word (such as *auto* in *autobiography*). If the student recognizes a word part, he can use that knowledge to hypothesize a meaning for the word and then check to see if his hypothesized meaning makes sense in the context of the text. Plan to model this process explicitly several times with various words, and then give students time to practice. In this way, you will gradually release responsibility to the students.

Principle 3. Teach the underlying morphological knowledge needed in two ways, both explicitly and in context. In order to use morphology effectively, students must know three types of language knowledge:

1. *Knowledge of prefixes, and suffixes:* Help students learn high-frequency prefixes and suffixes by providing a cumulative word wall with these prefixes and suffixes grouped by meaning and by allowing students to add new examples of word parts from their own reading.

2. *Knowledge of how words get transformed:* Students must understand the changes in sound and spelling that are often required in order to extract roots from derived words (e.g., strategy [noun], strategic [adjective], strategize [verb], and strategically [adverb]). Create a word chart that displays these various forms of key words selected from the texts students are reading (Kieffer & Lesaux, 2007, p. 141).

3. *Knowledge of roots:* To understand new words by extracting roots from derived words, students must know the meaning of the roots. You can teach some of the most common Latin and Greek roots, which should not be presented as a list to be memorized but taught in meaningful context, such as when comprehending particular text (p. 141).

Most common prefixes and suffixes in alphabetical order: www.hhpcommunities. com/teachinglanguagearts/IL-06-03.pdf

Common Latin and Greek roots: www.hhpcommunities.com/teachinglanguage arts/IL-06-04.pdf

Principle 4. *For students with developed knowledge of Spanish, teach morphology in relation to **cognate** instruction.* Teaching **cognates** (words with similar spelling and meaning in two languages: banana, cereal, gas) can be a powerful way for English language learners to use their first language to improve their English reading comprehension (Kieffer & Lesaux, 2007). Divide your word wall to include a section for cognates and encourage students to find them along with common prefixes and suffixes that are also cognates; for example, anti-, bi-, -ble, -itis.

For help in creating a word wall with cognates, a list of cognates can be found at Spanish-English Cognates (5 pp.): www.colorincolorado.org/pdfs/articles/cognates.pdf

All of the activities for teaching morphemes discussed in this section can also be taught during the contexts described earlier in this chapter. For example, when reading aloud, model using your knowledge of morphemes to figure out an unknown word and adding words to the word wall.

Fostering word consciousness

When students are engaged in learning vocabulary in the numerous ways described in this section, words become something they are keenly aware of all the time. Words surround them on the walls; they discuss and analyze words during lessons throughout the day; they keep words in notebooks; and they put words on sticky notes and bulletin boards. This consistent attention to words and their meanings creates awareness and interest in words that Graves and Watts-Taffe call *word consciousness*. Word consciousness involves both cognitive and affective awareness of words. Graves and Watts-Taffe (2008) emphasize that

> [T]his awareness involves an appreciation of the power of words, and understanding of why certain words are used instead of others, knowledge about the differences between spoken and written language, and a sense of the words that could be used in place of those selected by a writer or speaker. (p. 186)

Word consciousness is about finding joy in words; marveling at a familiar word used in an unfamiliar way or at discovering a new word, as this Author's Story describes.

author's story   ELIZABETH DOBLER

Reading the children's book *Frindle* by Andrew Clements to my third grade students heightened my interest in words. In the book, Nick creates the word *frindle* for *pen*, mostly as a prank, but the word takes off and begins to have a life of its own. My enthusiasm for *Frindle* caused me to purchase a small magnetic whiteboard to display on our refrigerator at home. We take turns adding a word of the day. The word might be one that piques a person's interest, like *catawampus,* or one that is difficult to spell, like *broccoli.* Someone may add an illustration to the word or take a suggested word and morph it into another word. *Wink* became *Twinkie,* which became *pinkie.* Thinking about and sharing words has become a game that has brought our family much laughter and lively discussions and raised our awareness about words.

In addition to the activities already discussed in the chapter that promote word consciousness, the following approaches are recommended.

Modeling, recognizing, and encouraging adept word usage

One effective way to build word consciousness is through your attitudes and interest in words as displayed in your classroom. When reading aloud, pause and point out a word that interests you. Discuss why the author's use of a specific word makes a difference in a reader's understanding of the story. For example, you might compare the following sentence from *The Mighty Miss Malone* to an adapted one beneath it:

There, along with the spilled cereal, was an **army of teeny-weeny, wiggling-squiggling, wormy-looking** bugs and beetles trying to hide under the flakes of oatmeal.

There, along with the spilled cereal, was a **bunch of moving** bugs and beetles trying to hide under the flakes of oatmeal.

Discuss with students the different words being used and why the author, Christopher Paul Curtis, may have chosen words like *teeny-weeny* and *wiggling-squiggling* to convey adeptly a sense of what the main character, Deza, was feeling.

Promoting word play

In addition to conveying meaning, students need to be aware that "words and phrases can simultaneously feel good on the tongue, sound good to the ear, and incite a riot of laughter in the belly" (Graves & Watts-Taffe, 2008, pp. 147–148). Homophones, homographs, idioms, clichés, and puns provide word play opportunities for students to investigate language. Children's books can be a great resource, such as *How Much Can a Bare Bear Bear?: What Are Homonyms and Homophones?* by Brian Cleary, *In a Pickle: And Other Funny Idioms,* and *It Figures! Fun Figures of Speech* by Marvin Terban.

Consistently engaging in activities that promote word consciousness will result in students who are motivated to learn words, who have a deep and lasting interest in words, and who develop powerful vocabularies.

For additional resources and information on vocabulary instruction, visit the vocabulary page on the Reading Rockets website (www.readingrockets.org/atoz/vocabulary), which offers information on the relationship between vocabulary and comprehension coupled with practical ways parents can introduce new words to their children through videos, articles, and webcasts.

6.4

READING COMPREHENSION OVERVIEW

The purpose of reading is comprehension. **Reading comprehension,** as defined in Chapter 5, "is the process of simultaneously extracting and constructing meaning through interaction and involvement with written language" (RRSG, 2002, p. 12). In essence, comprehension is about making meaning of what is read. The three elements of reading comprehension—the *reader,* the *text,* and the *activity*—intersect to determine the extent of comprehension. Variables dealing with the importance of text and the reader's purposes or motivation for reading have been discussed thus far.

In 1978, Delores Durkin published a research study of reading comprehension instruction revealing that less than 1 percent of the time spent during reading at school was devoted to comprehension instruction. The vast majority of classroom time was spent assessing comprehension through recitation, that is, the teacher asking questions about what students had been assigned to read. This finding resulted in great attention to research on comprehension instruction that continues today. In 2002, the RAND Reading Study Group's extensive review of research on comprehension found that typical classrooms across the primary and upper elementary grades still do not devote adequate time and attention to comprehension instruction; however, the group did find the following:

- Effective comprehension instruction provides students with a collection of strategies for fostering comprehension.
- Explicit teaching of comprehension strategies can have an impact on learning, especially for low-achieving students.
- Connecting comprehension strategy instruction to content area learning, such as health or history, fosters comprehension.
- A student's knowledge of text structures, an important factor in fostering comprehension, can be enhanced by reading a wide variety of genres.

■ Choices, challenges, and collaboration, when built into learning, increase students' comprehension of text and motivation to read.

spotlight ON A LITERACY LEADER

NELL K. DUKE

Nell K. Duke is a professor of teacher education and educational psychology and co-director of the Literacy Achievement Research Center (LARC) at Michigan State University. Her areas of expertise include development of informational literacies in young children, comprehension development and instruction in early schooling, and issues of equity in literacy education. In the video *Building Comprehension*, Duke defines comprehension and reviews the multiple strategies proficient readers use.

Watch Building Comprehension (28:25, www.learner.org/workshops/teach reading35/session3/index.html) to learn how to use explicit instruction that promotes active, thoughtful learning.

6.5

GUIDELINES FOR READING COMPREHENSION INSTRUCTION

A combination of reading lots of authentic texts for real purposes along with explicit instruction and modeling of comprehension strategies will provide students with the proficiency and motivation for deep comprehension. Guidelines for teaching comprehension are presented in the sections that follow.

Provide explicit instruction in comprehension strategies

Explicit strategy instruction has repeatedly been shown to have positive effects on comprehension, especially for students who struggle with comprehension (Fielding & Pearson, 1994; RRSG, 2002). Comprehension strategies were first introduced in Chapter 1 to guide your reading of this book. Exhibit 6.17 lists the strategies researchers have found to be most effective in aiding comprehension. Researchers identified these strategies by studying what skilled readers do to make sense of text and looking for ways to scaffold these strategies for less-skilled readers. Selecting which strategies to teach should be based on your assessment from running records, guided reading, literature discussions, and individual conferences.

When providing instruction on comprehension strategies, tell your students that readers do not use any single comprehension strategy in isolation of others. Skilled readers actually use multiple strategies simultaneously. For example, when a person starts to read a new book she will make predictions based on the cover, title, pictures, and information on the inside flap or back of the book. Based on this information, the reader may make connections to her background knowledge and understanding of the structure of the story, and then formulate questions about the plot or events. Learning to execute the use of multiple strategies such as making predictions, using background knowledge and text structure, and asking questions, are all important comprehension strategies that will assist the reader in comprehending the text.

EXHIBIT 6.17

Comprehension strategies.

COMPREHENSION STRATEGY	DEFINITION
Prediction/activating prior knowledge	Engaging students in making predictions about a story has been shown to increase interest and memory for stories, especially when the students' predictions are explicitly compared to text ideas during reading. Activating prior knowledge helps students make connections between existing knowledge and the new information they will be learning.
Determining importance	This occurs when readers distinguish main ideas from details in narrative or acquire knowledge in nonfiction.
Making inferences	The reader uses the information from the author and combines it with his or her own knowledge to "read between the lines" and reach a deeper understanding of the text.
Visual representations of text	The use of various visual tools such as semantic maps and webs has been shown to improve students' ability to organize what they are learning when teachers involve students in constructing the visual displays.
Synthesizing	Synthesizing requires students to sift through large amounts of information, differentiate important from unimportant ideas, and then synthesize those ideas into a new text that contains the essential components of the original text. Synthesizing is a difficult task for many students and requires much instruction and practice.
Answering and generating questions	Much research supports the need for teachers to ask students higher level—inferential and evaluative—questions that require them to connect information in the text to their own knowledge base to improve their comprehension. Additionally, students must learn to ask questions themselves as they are reading.

EXHIBIT 6.18

Ways to teach comprehension strategies.

STRATEGY	INSTRUCTIONAL PROCEDURES
Activating background knowledge	• Students complete an anticipation guide. (Teacher creates a list of true/false statements about the text the students will read.) • Students participate in a brainstorming activity. • Students develop a K-W-L chart. (Teacher creates a chart that asks students what they *know*, what they *want to know* about a topic, and then after instruction what they have *learned*.)
Predicting	• Students make and share predictions during read-alouds. • Students write a double-entry journal with predictions in one column and summaries in the other. • Students make predictions during guided reading lessons.
Determining importance	• Students create graphic organizers. • Students make posters highlighting the big ideas.
Visualizing	• Students create portraits of characters, in which they illustrate aspects of a book's character at important times during the story. • Students draw pictures of episodes from a book they're reading. • Students role-play episodes from a book they're reading.
Summarizing	• Students write a summary using interactive writing (see Chapter 9). • Students create visual summaries on charts using words, diagrams, and pictures.
Questioning	• Students brainstorm a list of questions during read-alouds. • Students ask questions during discussions. • Students analyze the type of questions they pose (literal, inferential, evaluative).

You may introduce a strategy in isolation, but once students practice it, you should encourage them to integrate it into their repertoire (Dorn & Soffas, 2005; Duke & Pearson, 2002).

As discussed in Chapters 4 and 5, using the gradual release of responsibility model provides modeling, demonstrations, and guided practice of comprehension strategies. You will teach mini-lessons on comprehension strategies based on your students' needs. These lessons will serve as an anchor for scaffolding student learning. Exhibit 6.18 lists ways to teach comprehension strategies.

stories FROM THE CLASSROOM

Comprehension strategies

Kristen Schweitzer, a K–5 reading specialist, understands the challenge of teaching students to comprehend text. She has seen firsthand the struggles some students face with understanding what they read. In the upcoming podcast, Kristen describes the explicit reading comprehension strategies she uses with struggling readers in grades three to five. As a teacher who continually works with struggling readers, Kristen worries about her students' progress and takes pride in their accomplishments.

🔊 Notice the strategies that Kristen uses as you listen to the Comprehension Strategies podcast (4:34). (*Access this podcast in the digital version of this book.*)

Because we cannot actually see how a person comprehends, making mental processes clear to students is challenging. In math, addition can be taught by taking two groups of pennies and combining them. Demonstrating comprehension is not so simple. Modeling and thinking aloud while reading are crucial for exposing the types of thought processes we want students to understand and use. Explicit instruction of comprehension strategies can help readers understand and remember what they read.

📹 To view an example of a think-aloud lesson (2:55, www.eworkshop.on.ca/edu/core.cfm?p=modView.cfm&L=1&modID=37&c=3&navID=modView), click on the third video in the window with the description "The teacher uses a think-aloud strategy on a large sample text to demonstrate how to ask analysis questions."

COMPREHENSION *coach*

Are you uncertain about how to use the questions you formulate while reading to help you understand? Listen to this podcast by Denise Johnson for comprehension coaching. (*Access this podcast in the digital version of this book.*)

Engage in literary analysis

Literary analysis is the ability of the reader to examine a work of literature for personal response, interpretation, judgment, or critical evaluation. As with any analysis, literary analysis is a process that requires the reader to break the subject down into its component parts. In the elementary grades, the ability to analyze literature begins with understanding reader response and text structure.

Understanding reader response

Reader response stresses the importance of the reader's role in interpreting texts. This theory holds that the individual *creates* his or her own meaning through a *transaction* with the text since all readers bring their own emotions, concerns, life experiences, and knowledge to their reading. Many scholars believe that Louise Rosenblatt's influential book *Literature As Exploration*, originally published in 1938, marked the beginning of reader-response theory.

spotlight ON A LITERACY LEADER

LOUISE ROSENBLATT

Louise Rosenblatt was an American professor and author of Literature as Exploration (www.worldcat.org/title/literature-as-exploration/oclc/32969110), who influenced the fields of education and literary studies. She believed that "the reading of any work of literature is, of necessity, an individual and unique occurrence involving the mind and emotions of some particular reader and a particular text at a particular time under particular circumstances" (Rosenblatt, 2004, p. 1363).

View the video Reader Response (58:00, www.learner.org/workshops/hslit/session1) to learn more about this theory and to see reader response in action. Students in this high school classroom are reading and responding to multicultural poetry by authors Pat Mora and James Welch. Experts on reader response comment on the classroom vignettes. Authors Pat Mora and James Welch also visit the class and discuss their works and the students' response to their work.

Understanding text structure

Text structure refers to the ways that authors organize information in text. Knowledge of how genres are structured allows students to anticipate what to expect and to make inferences based on those expectations, thus making reading easier.

Narrative text structures. Fiction or narrative texts are organized around characters, setting, events, and resolution. Young children internalize story structure from hearing books read aloud and from reading stories themselves. Teachers can also explicitly teach narrative structure, or how stories work, through grammar or story maps, such as the one in Exhibit 6.19. The grammar or elements of a story include the title, author, setting, main characters, conflict and resolution, events, and conclusion. The **story map** provides students with a framework for understanding the sequential structure these elements follow in narrative text.

Once completed, a story map can then be used as a scaffold for **retelling.** The ability to retell a story reveals whether a student can identify the key story elements and is a good indicator of comprehension. Teachers should always model how to give a retelling first before asking students to retell a story. While modeling a retelling, refer to the story map and remind students of the key story elements (see Exhibit 6.20 for a sample story elements chart). When students read a different story, have them retell it individually or in small groups while referring to an anchor chart with the story elements. If students are unable to recall certain elements, provide prompts such as: Who was in the story? Where did it take place? What

EXHIBIT 6.19

Fiction story map.

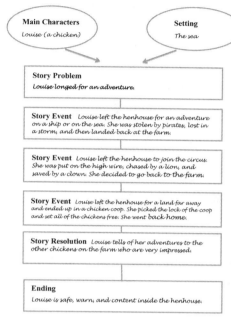

(Print a blank story map: www.hhpcommunities.com/teachinglanguagearts/IL-06-05.pdf)

EXHIBIT 6.20

Story elements chart.

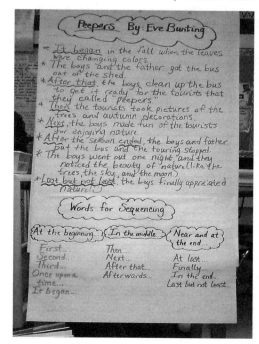

EXHIBIT 6.21

Text structures in informational texts.

TEXT PATTERN	DEFINITION	KEY WORDS	MAPS/WEBS
Description	Provides descriptive details about characteristics, actions, or events	Descriptive adjectives and words like on, over, beyond, within	
Problem/ Solution	Sets up a problem and proposes its solutions	Propose, conclude, a solution, the reason for, the problem or question	
Chronological/ Sequencing	Gives information in order of occurrence	First, second, before, after, finally, then, next, earlier	
Comparison/ Contrast	Looks at two or more items to establish similarities/ differences	While, yet, but, rather, most same, either, as well as, like and unlike, as opposed to	
Cause/Effect	Gives a reason or explanation for happening	Because, since, if/then, due to, as a result, for this reason, on account of, consequently	

Sources: Adapted from Hoyt, Mooney, & Parkes, B. (2003); Fountas & Pinell (2001); compiled by Teresa Thentault, Free tips and tools, www.literacyspecialists.com.

EXHIBIT 6.22

Nonfiction charts showing text features.

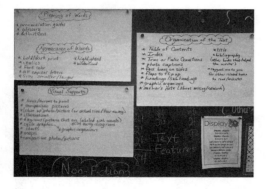

was the problem in the story? How was the problem solved? As students conduct more retellings, they will begin to internalize these story elements.

Nonfiction text structures and features. Nonfiction texts are organized quite differently from fiction texts. Nonfiction texts use five major organizational structures: description, problem/solution, chronological/sequencing, comparison/contrast, and cause/effect. (See Exhibit 6.21 for definitions of these terms.) The organization of nonfiction text can often be identified through key words that signal the structure (e.g., the word *first* signals a sequence). You can teach these structures and key words to students during read-alouds and through maps to guide students' comprehension of nonfiction. In addition to various nonfiction text structures, a reader can find features of the text that facilitate organization and comprehension. **Text features** may include boldfaced words, arrows, or captions. See Exhibit 6.22 for additional text features.

Anchor charts, introduced in Chapter 3, can also be an effective scaffold for students' learning about text structures during instruction. **Anchor charts,** which are created by the teacher and students, highlight specific guidelines or behaviors for performing a particular literacy strategy, or they can serve as a concrete representation of students' thinking. The anchor charts should be posted in a prominent place in the room and serve as a temporary scaffold for students' learning over time. The charts shown in Exhibit 6.22 are anchor charts on nonfiction text features created during read alouds.

stories FROM THE CLASSROOM

A comprehension mini-lesson

Wendy Melzer is a second grade teacher who uses picture book read-alouds as a springboard for thinking aloud and making mental reading strategies visible. The following scene is from a mini-lesson Wendy is teaching on cause and effect relationships.

> **Wendy:** *Today we are going to read the story* Scarecrow *by Cynthia Rylant. You are already familiar with Cynthia Rylant because we have read so many books written by her. Who can tell me some of the stories we've read by Cynthia Rylant?*

Several students respond with titles such as *The Relatives Came, Night in the Country, The Old Woman Who Named Things,* and *The Great Gracie Chase.*

> **Wendy:** *Today, as we read this new book by Cynthia Rylant, we are going to think about how cause and effect is used in this story.*

Wendy writes the definition of cause and effect on a chart and reminds students of some key words that might indicate a cause and effect relationship.

> **Wendy:** *Before we start, let's brainstorm what we know about scarecrows.*

Students respond with various information, indicating that most understand that the purpose of scarecrows is to scare away birds.

> **Wendy:** *As I read today, I will pause to think out loud about the story, like I always do, and I want you also to be thinking about the story as you are listening.*

Wendy begins reading. The first few pages of the story provide a brief explanation of what makes a scarecrow: a borrowed hat, suit, hands, and eyes. But, then the text moves to the character of the scarecrow.

Wendy reads the text: *"It takes a certain peace, hanging around a garden all day. It takes a love of silence and air. A liking for long, slow thoughts. A friendliness toward birds."*

Wendy stops reading: *Hmmmm. I'm thinking that this scarecrow isn't like the scarecrows we described before we started reading, because the text says that this scarecrow is friendly toward birds. I am wondering how a scarecrow can do his job of scaring birds if he is friendly toward them. I'm going to keep reading so I can find out.*

Wendy reads the next page: *"Yes, birds, crows, grackles, starlings, jays. Ask them how they feel about a scarecrow, and they'll say, 'Lovely.' They ignore the pie-pan hands and the button eyes and see instead the scarecrow's best gift: his gentleness."*

Wendy stops reading: *So, on this page I found out that this scarecrow doesn't scare birds at all! I am thinking that because he is friendly or gentle, so then the birds ignore all of the things that are supposed to make him scary and instead they think he is lovely.*

Several students raise their hand and indicate that they know Wendy just shared the cause and effect relationship in the book. Wendy asks the students to turn to their neighbor sitting next to them and tell each other the key words she used.

After finishing the book, Wendy asks the class for their response. Then she revisits the lesson: What was the cause and effect relationship in the book? Together, the class reformulates the statement and Wendy writes it on the chart (see Exhibit 6.23). Wendy then links the importance of understanding cause and effect relationships to the students' reading by stating: "When you are reading, understanding the causes and effects of events in the story helps you to think carefully about the consequences of characters' actions and about how different actions might have different effects." She asks if anyone has any questions and then dismisses the students to their independent reading.

EXHIBIT 6.23

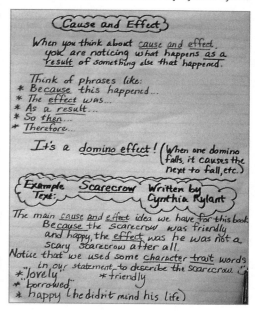

Anchor chart for *Scarecrow* by Cynthia Rylant.

Engage students in active processing

Active processing is when the reader actively builds meaning while reading in ways that promote attending to important ideas and establishing connections between these ideas (McKeown, Beck, & Blake, 2009). One way to promote active reading is to alternate reading with discussion while students are reading texts (Exhibit 6.24 includes questions used during reading of *The Firekeeper's Son*). Research by McKeown, Beck, and Blake (2009), found the value of this practice to be threefold:

EXHIBIT 6.24

Questioning before, during, and after reading.

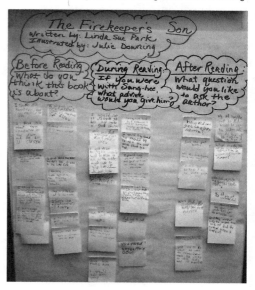

- It gives students with poor decoding skills access to the text by sharing models of the comprehension process.
- It gives students access to the thinking of others, promoting the collaborative development of an understanding of the text.
- It gives the teacher an opportunity to support meaning-building of students.

The teacher also gains the following threefold benefit from this format:

- The opportunity to observe confusion as it occurs.
- Understanding of the individual uniqueness and complexity of the comprehension process.
- Information to guide decisions on how to intervene to support students.

The questioning approach employed to activate the comprehension processing during reading is important. Fast-paced, low-level, question-and-answer routines limit students' opportunities to talk, formulate their own questions, and express extended ideas about complex issues. Effective questioning builds in think time immediately following the question. Skilled teachers resist the temptation to call on the first hand raised and encourage those with the answer to wait for others to finish thinking.

Questioning the Author (QtA) (Beck & McKeown, 1998) is a technique in which the teacher supports students' interactions with the text by intervening at selected points and asking guiding queries related to the author's purpose, methods, and so forth, with the goal of improving students' understanding of the text. Here are examples of questions found to be useful in addressing nonfiction text:

Initiating Questions

- What do you think the author is trying to say here?
- What is the author's message?
- Why do you think is the author telling us that?

Follow-Up Questions

- In your opinion, what does the author mean here?
- Does the author explain this clearly?
- Do you have ideas about how the author could have said things more clearly?
- What would you say instead?

Through this exchange, you lead the students to a deeper understanding of the implied message in the text. QtA provides students with a set of useful thinking strategies for all genres but can be especially helpful with textbook reading since the discussion can help students understand that textbooks do not always provide the depth of information necessary to fully understand the concept. Allington (2006) writes, "QtA is a powerful strategy for helping struggling readers not only better understand the texts they read, but also understand that some texts are just hard to understand for any number of reasons. This 'blame the author' feature—she just didn't write it very clearly—can be empowering for struggling readers" (p. 135).

When planning a QtA lesson, keep in mind three goals (Allington, 2006, p. 74):

1. Identify the major understandings students should construct and anticipate potential problems in the text.
2. Segment the text to focus on information needed to build understandings.
3. Develop queries that promote the building of those understandings.

QtA also provides a scaffold for students' independent book discussions.

stories FROM THE CLASSROOM

Deep thinking about text

Let's join Julie Lipscomb, a fourth grade teacher, as she uses QtA with a chapter on slavery in Virginia from the class's social studies textbook. The opening page of the chapter, titled "The Issue of Slavery," begins with the following journal entry:

November 1824

We arrived at Montpelier, the home of James Madison, late yesterday. It is a beautiful home in beautiful country. I am grateful that our visit here will last four days. Traveling with the Marquis de Lafayette on this tour of the United States has tired me. Today we looked around the large property. Lafayette is most interested in visiting Mr. Madison's workers—slaves. He cannot understand how a country so in love with freedom can allow slavery. I have overheard Lafayette say to his old friend, "All men without exception have a right to liberty." (Scott Foresman, 2004, p. 268)

The text does not indicate who wrote the journal entry, nor does it have any connection to the next section of the chapter. In her QtA, Julie reads the entry aloud and then asks, "What is the author trying to say in this journal entry?"

Jamie: That slavery is wrong.

Julie: What gives Jamie that idea?

John: Because it says Lafayette doesn't understand why there's slavery when we love freedom.

Julie: I think you are both right—Lafayette thinks slavery is wrong because all people have the right to freedom. Why do you think the author is telling us what Lafayette thinks about slavery in Virginia?

Amy: Maybe because Lafayette is an important person.

Hannah: Yeah, I remember we learned about him when we studied the Revolution. He's from France and helped us win.

Julie: [restating Amy's comment] So, the author is telling us Lafayette's thoughts because he is someone whose opinion America values. But why do you think the author is giving us Lafayette's thoughts at the very beginning of the chapter?

Justin: So we know that even though we had slavery in Virginia, important people like Lafayette, who helped us get our freedom, didn't think it was right.

This QtA lesson gave students a deeper understanding of the implied message in the text and may have also helped them understand that a textbook should be a starting point rather than an end point when it comes to seeking information.

The **question–answer relationship (QAR) strategy** (Raphael, 1984) is another questioning approach useful in comprehension processing. QAR is a framework for comprehension instruction that helps students understand the difference between four basic types of questions and where they can find the information to answer them.

- **Right there questions:** The answer can be found "right there" in the text. Often the same words used in the question are the same words found in the text.
- **Think and search questions:** The answer is in the text but must be gathered from various parts of the text and put together to make meaning.
- **Author and you questions:** The answer is based on information provided in the text, but the student is required to relate it to his own experience.
- **On my own questions:** The answer is not in the text. The reader must use her prior knowledge and experiences to answer the question.

Teaching QAR should start with assisting students to understand that information can either be found *in the book* or *in the reader's head*. You can model this concept by reading a text aloud, asking questions, and then explaining where students should look to find the answers. Once students understand the two sources of information, expand each to include the four types of questions. Model the process and have students practice using several texts, gradually releasing responsibility to students.

QAR instruction can be adjusted for use across grade levels and content areas. Students can use this process to identify the types of questions asked on worksheets, in content area textbooks, and on tests in order to then determine the sources of information needed to answer the questions. Through QAR instruction, students learn to recognize the different types of questions on different tasks and tests.

Raphael and Au (2005) argue that QAR can provide a framework for comprehension instruction with the potential of closing the literacy achievement gap because it provides teachers with a shared language for improving questioning practices, brings coherence to literacy practices within and across grade levels, and provides a responsible approach to preparing students for high-stakes tests.

Teach using instructional routines

Several research-based instructional routines that reflect the gradual release of responsibility model are effective for comprehension instruction (Duke & Pearson, 2002). Instructional routines, when applied to reading comprehension, help students understand text by developing a collection of reading strategies students can use on any text, which is especially important when reading independently (Duke & Pearson, 2002).

Reciprocal teaching (Palincsar & Brown, 1984) is a highly effective instructional routine for encouraging students to think about and share their comprehension strategies (Hattie, 2009). It promotes the use of predicting, questioning, clarifying, and summarizing to improve students' comprehension. A teacher models by explaining and applying the strategies in his own reading, then has students monitor their reading comprehension in the same way. Reciprocal teaching capitalizes on the social nature of learning by providing opportunities for students to reflect on their strategy use and share these reflections with others. The flexible nature of reciprocal teaching makes it useful in the whole class and small group settings.

Reciprocal teaching takes the form of a dialogue between you and your students around sections of text. The dialogue is structured by the use of four strategies: question generating, summarizing, clarifying, and predicting. In the beginning of reciprocal teaching, you provide extensive modeling of comprehension strategies. As you release responsibility, you and your students take turns assuming the role of teacher in leading this dialogue (Duke & Pearson, 2002).

A typical reciprocal teaching session includes:

- A review of the previous lesson and making predictions about the new text.
- Students reading a chunk of the text (i.e., paragraph, page, chapter) silently to themselves.
- Assigning a student to act as teacher, modeling strategies by:
  a. asking questions about the text chunk
  b. summarizing the text chunk

c. clarifying questions from the group

d. predicting what might be in the next text chunk

You will serve as a guide throughout the process and remind students of why these strategies are important and how they will be helpful in their reading. As time goes on, students assume increasing control over strategy use, eventually using the strategies with little or no support. According to Oczkus (2010), "Reciprocal teaching is a flexible tool that you use to strengthen and differentiate the comprehension instruction in any core reading program or curriculum model" (p. 243). Oczkus recommends that reciprocal teaching complement the core reading program and maintains that students who participate in at least two weekly reciprocal teaching lessons improve their comprehension.

Visit the webpage Classroom Strategies: Reciprocal Teaching (www.readingrockets.org/strategies/reciprocal_teaching) for more information, resources, and video clips of reciprocal teaching in action. View the two videos "Reciprocal teaching in action" and "Students take charge" (6:00, 2:15).

BOOK REVIEW

Reciprocal Teaching at Work: Powerful Strategies and Lessons for Improving Reading Comprehension (2nd ed.)

BY LORI OCZKUS

Oczkus asks the reader of *Reciprocal Teaching at Work* to "think of reciprocal teaching as a reading vitamin that ensures reading success and strengthens overall comprehension instruction" (p. 4). The book focuses on four evidence-based and classroom-tested strategies that good readers use to comprehend text—predicting, questioning, clarifying, and summarizing—within whole class, guided reading, and literature circles. This new edition includes 35 lessons and a plethora of materials, such as reproducible pages for assessment, comprehension posters, a lesson planning menu, and more. Additionally, there is a free online professional development guide and online classroom video clips.

Locate a copy: www.worldcat.org/title/reciprocal-teaching-at-work-strategies-for-improving-reading-comprehension/oclc/52720643

Encourage independent discussion

Literature discussion groups, such as book clubs and literature circles, provide a time for students to come together in small groups to discuss their reading and allows them to engage in conversations about books that are directed by their own questions, thoughts, and perspectives. Based on 30 years of teaching experience, Ardith Cole (2003) writes that "literature conversations provide a platform for deep, rich comprehension of text. By developing these classroom structures for talk, teachers can help students collaborate, substantiate their ideas, and negotiate" (p. xiv). Conversations about reading during read-alouds, shared reading, guided reading, and to some extent, independent reading, are typically teacher directed. Though students will initially need teacher support (discussed below), book clubs should eventually become student directed and response driven (see Exhibit 6.25).

EXHIBIT 6.25

Students participating in a literature discussion group.

The selection of literature for discussion groups should be based on your knowledge of quality literature and students' interests, cultural background, reading strengths and needs, independent reading levels, and cross-curricular goals. The use of interesting and relevant texts increases student motivation and enhances discussions. Possible books for literature circles can be grouped into text sets, or books that are connected in some way. Ways to create text sets include:

- Student interests or suggested books
- Author/illustrator study
- Genre study
- Math, science, or social studies connections
- Thematic study such as friendship, appreciating differences, or taking responsibility
- Books with multiple character perspectives
- Books with global perspectives
- Fiction/nonfiction pairs on the same topic

After selecting the books, conduct a brief book talk on each and then allow students to choose the book they want to read. You could use a sign-up sheet to have students indicate up to three different books they are interested in reading. Then, you match students to books based on interest and reading level. Explain to students that not everyone will get to read their first choice every time.

Literature discussion groups are heterogeneous, with no more than five or six members, and based on books the students have chosen to read, though students who read different books on the same topic could also form a literature discussion group. Students who have read each of the books could form a group to talk about the different perspectives and issues discussed across the books. Although students' reading abilities may differ, they still should be able to engage in high level discussion about topics of interest.

Although students participate in many conversations both in and out of school, these conversations are not often about books. Thus, some students have little understanding of what it is like to engage in a meaningful conversation about their reading. You may need to conduct mini-lessons on ways to discuss a book. Modeling and dramatization are effective ways to share expectations for these conversations. Based on mini-lessons and observations of book clubs in action, you can involve students in creating a list of *rules of engagement,* in which they create a list of the behaviors that would make for an effective book club. Additions and changes can be made as they learn from their ongoing participation.

Once students have decided on their selections and the groups are formed, each group meets with the teacher (see Exhibit 6.26). Despite the earlier brief book talk, they still need to build background knowledge, set a purpose for reading, and decide how much to read before the first group discussion. When you meet with the students, work with them to create a chart documenting their prior knowledge, questions, and predictions that can be revisited during the first discussion group (Exhibit 6.27 includes examples of such "before" questions). Sometimes students get excited about reading a book and assign an unrealistic number of pages to read before the first group meeting. You can model how to judge an appropriate number of pages based on the number of days before the group meets and where a good stopping point might be.

Over the next week students read the assigned pages during independent reading time. Responding to their reading should be something they have

EXHIBIT 6.26

Teacher working with a small group.

EXHIBIT 6.27

Questioning before, during, and after reading using sticky notes.

already learned during mini-lessons. (Exhibit 6.28 shows an example mini-lesson on noticing characters while reading.) By now your students should be used to jotting down their thoughts on sticky notes and writing in response journals (see Exhibit 6.29). During a book club discussion, however, students are reading with a new mind-set by considering questions, thoughts, predictions, and critiques to be shared with discussion group members, which can open up a whole new way of thinking. The notes are critical to meaningful, thought-provoking discussion. Once the group has finished discussing the book, it is disbanded and new groups are formed for subsequent book clubs.

The following is an overview of considerations for teacher/student roles in book clubs:

Teacher's role:

- Select texts to be read
- Provide mini-lessons and model ways to have productive conversations
- Build students' prior knowledge
- Scaffold students' engagement in conversations about the text
- Slowly remove support and allow student to take responsibility

Students' role:

- Read assigned pages
- Take notes about thoughts, questions, ideas to discuss with book club members
- Come to the book club prepared and ready to participate
- Discuss ideas from sticky notes

The opportunity to self-select books across genres, read and write about the books they select, and share their thoughts in book discussions with others is a powerful motivator for students.

The next section provides literature extension activities that, when carefully selected, can extend or broaden students' thinking about the books they read.

Provide extension activities

A purposeful extension project can provide readers with additional ways to revisit their reading and extend or broaden their thinking about concepts, themes, or characters. However, extension projects should not be contrived, complicated, or busy work that takes time away from instruction or independent reading. Harvey and Goudvis (2007) state that

> For too many years, kids in classrooms all over the United States have been asked to do a laundry list of activities when they finish reading books. You know the ones, dioramas, shadow boxes, word jumbles, word searches, and so on. Reading response is more than these. (p. 52)

The following activities, on the other hand, can extend students' understanding of texts:

- Storytelling
- Readers theater and drama
- Making books based on creative writing or research
- Choral reading
- Author/illustrator study

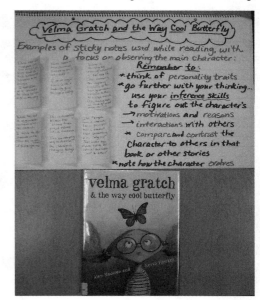

EXHIBIT 6.28

A mini-lesson on noticing characters when reading.

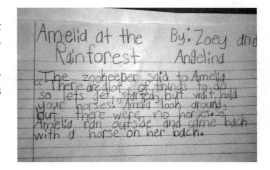

EXHIBIT 6.29

Writing in a response journal.

- Creating digital stories and publishing writing/projects on the Internet
- Online literature discussion

points2ponder

QUICK REVIEW 3 What is active processing during reading? What are two strategies for engaging students in active comprehension processing? Why is it important for students to have the opportunity to discuss the texts they are reading? What are some extension activities you can use to extend students' understanding of texts?

(Access the answers in the digital version of this book.)

6.6

ONLINE READING COMPREHENSION

Now that we have studied the foundations of learning and teaching reading comprehension, let's explore how these key ideas and other new ideas can be applied to the comprehension of online texts. The RAND Reading Study Group (2002) acknowledged that "electronic text presents particular challenges to comprehension (e.g., challenges stemming from the nonlinear nature of hypertext), but it also offers the potential to support comprehension by providing links to definitions of unknown words or to other supplementary material" (p. xv). Online reading research has built upon what we already know about the reading process. Applying this knowledge to digital texts, classroom contexts, activities, and readers online helps us to better understand what is involved in online reading.

One way to determine online comprehension is to look at whether the attributes employed by the reader to read informational print text are the same, different, or more multifaceted for reading on the Internet. Coiro and Dobler (2007) examined the reading process of 13 skilled sixth graders who were asked to locate, critically evaluate for relevancy, and synthesize information from the Internet. They found that successful Internet reading experiences appeared to require simultaneously both similar and more complex applications of the very same strategies used for reading traditional books. As when reading print, online readers activate prior knowledge, make inferences, check their comprehension along the way, and are influenced by their own motivation and confidence as readers. One of the additional complexities is *forward inferential reasoning.* When selecting hyperlinks, readers are required to anticipate the possible direction the text could take before continuing on with their internal meaning construction. Another important factor related to forward inferential reading is self-regulated reading. Coiro and Dobler explain that skilled Internet readers must be able to regulate their movement between

- newer online search and evaluation processes that typically occur very rapidly across hundreds of short Internet texts, and
- less spontaneous, more traditional self-regulation strategies within longer text passages that require more time and effort.

Coiro and Dobler (2007) point out that "an increased need to make forward inferences about *text* appeared to compound an already complex process of making bridging inferences about *content* in a manner that may prompt additional complexities to the process of reading online" (p. 242). Exhibit 6.30 provides information on these online reading strategies.

When you are aware of the supports and challenges of online reading, you can teach students to use supports effectively and to employ the strategies necessary to overcome the challenges. For example, prior knowledge of the genre or structure of digital text is critical to successful online reading comprehension. Digital texts are distinguished from other genres by the interactive or linked structure that allows readers to move through the text in a nonlinear fashion. Such terms as *navigation, search,* and *scroll* describe the online reading process. Students must understand the concepts and structures of how digital environments work before they attempt to make meaning from them.

Though many students come to school with experiences using **digital media,** they do not necessarily know how to fully access, comprehend, and use these media as learning tools. For many of our students, the Internet may typically be used to connect with their friends or watch funny cat videos rather than to gain useful information from reputable sources. Because using the Internet is highly motivating for students and presents a wealth of information within a click or two, teachers have a responsibility to prepare students to be effective online readers. The term *readers* is used loosely here, because when it comes to the Internet, information may also be gained by listening to podcasts and viewing video clips. You can capitalize on students' motivation for online reading and extend their understanding, motivation, and engagement in authentic ways. At the same time, you can extend opportunities to acquire the skills and strategies needed to live and work in the rapidly changing technological world.

With the increased use of online resources comes the need for instructional strategies that make the Internet both effective and efficient. For success now and in the future, students need to learn how to locate, understand, and use information from digital contexts (Leu, Kinzer, Coiro, & Cammack, 2004). For years, finding information in traditional venues like the library has proven challenging for learners, but locating and comprehending information on the Internet may be even more challenging. At minimum, students need to be able to identify their question, determine which online resources will answer their question, evaluate the information they find, read (and view and listen to) and synthesize information from multiple sources, and perhaps even transform all those pieces of information into something original. This is a highly complex process, one that many learners of all ages find difficult. The next two sections provide a model and a context for teaching these important strategies.

Internet inquiry: The QUEST model

The **QUEST model** of Internet inquiry was developed by Eagleton and Dobler (2007) to specifically address the importance and uniqueness of Internet reading as a means of acquiring information to answer a question or solve a problem. **Internet inquiry** is the term used to describe the process of generating a question and using the Internet to locate an answer. A question may be as simple as, *What is the weather forecast for today?* Or as complex as, *What is the difference between a landfill and a dump?* The acronym QUEST illustrates the recursive nature of Internet inquiry by linking the processes of Questioning, Understanding resources, Evaluating, Synthesizing, and Transforming information. Internet inquiry becomes an iterative process, not a one-time event (see Exhibit 6.31). QUEST engages and supports students as they tackle the complexities of reading on the web. It also serves

EXHIBIT 6.30

Online reading strategies.

Reading comprehension strategies	Similarities between the comprehension processes of printed informational text and Internet text	Additional complexities associated with the comprehension processes of Internet text
Prior knowledge sources	Skilled readers draw upon their a. prior knowledge of the topic b. prior knowledge of printed informational text structures	Skilled readers also draw upon their a. prior knowledge of informational website structures b. prior knowledge of web-based search engines
Inferential reasoning strategies	Inferential reasoning strategies are informed by a reader's conventional use of a. literal matching skills b. structural cues c. context clues	Inferential reasoning strategies are also characterized by a. a high incidence of forward inferential reasoning b. multilayered reading processes across three-dimensional Internet spaces
Self-regulated reading	Self-regulated reading processes a. independent fix-up strategies for comprehension monitoring and repair b. connected components of a larger strategic reading process	Self-regulated reading processes also occur as a. cognitive reading strategies intertwined with physical reading actions (such as clicking on links or navigating through a website) b. rapid information-seeking cycles within extremely short text passages

Adapted from Coiro, J., & Dobler, E. (2007). Exploring the online reading comprehension strategies used by sixth-grade skilled readers to search for and locate information on the Internet. *Reading Research Quarterly, 42*(2), 214–257.

EXHIBIT 6.31

The QUEST model of Internet inquiry.

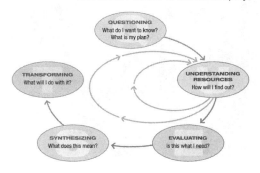

EXHIBIT 6.32

A fifth grade student's view of the Internet search process.

> List every step a person needs to do when searching for information on the Internet.
> 1. Get on the computer
> 2. Choose a website like Google, Yahoo!, or any others you can think of
> 3. Type the website and press go
> 4. Make sure it is where you can search the web
> 5. Type in what you're looking up
> 6. Press go
> 7. Choose the one you think is the best

EXHIBIT 6.33

Processes in the QUEST model.

PROCESS	WHY IS IT IMPORTANT?	WHEN IS IT USED?
Q	Questioning is used to activate prior knowledge, enabling the student to figure out what information he wants to know and create a plan for finding it.	Before the search to formulate key words, during the search to monitor results, and after the search to guide decision making about search results.
U	Understanding how to utilize digital resources and strategies and how to efficiently and effectively locate information on the Internet is critical to successful Internet inquiry.	Before the search to identify resources, manage computers, utilize the Internet, chose search tools, and select key words.
E	Evaluating websites to determine the usefulness and truthfulness of information found on the Internet is important for gathering valid information.	When analyzing key word search results to determine usefulness of websites included in the results and when reading a selected website from the search results to determine truthfulness.
S	Synthesizing strategies help students integrate ideas within and across websites including text, graphics, and multimedia.	Once search results have been gathered, students must form a mental thread between the collection of facts and ideas that are important to create a personal interpretation or understanding.
T	Transforming the newfound knowledge into a format that can be shared with others is useful in the real world.	After students have synthesized search results, they transform the information into knowledge using the strategies of note-making, organizing information, citing sources, creating a product, and presenting a final product to others.

EXHIBIT 6.34

Scott Ritter and Nadar during Internet workshop.

as an ideal metaphor for the active *quest* for information that characterizes our daily lives, whether at home, in school, or in the workplace.

Eagleton and Dobler suggest that before teaching the QUEST model, you should assess students' web search strategies. The most effective way to do this is to observe students and determine which steps they take to find information on the Internet, including: (1) turning on the computer; (2) logging on to the school network; (3) launching a browser; (4) going to a search engine; (5) entering key words; (6) choosing a website; (7) scanning for information; and (8) finding relevant information. If a student does not find relevant information on the first website, observe and record her recovery strategies for (1) choosing a new website; (2) choosing a new search engine; or (3) choosing new key words. If you do not have enough time to assess each student individually, you can ask students as a group to write down the steps they would use to search for information on the Internet. Knowledge of students' Internet search strategies will inform your instructional decisions as you teach the QUEST model (see Exhibit 6.32).

Giving students choices in selecting topics for Internet inquiry is just as important as giving students choices in book selection. Motivation and engagement will be much higher when students have the opportunity to learn about a topic that is of interest to them. Exhibit 6.33 further explores the processes in the QUEST model.

Your role during Internet inquiry is to scaffold all aspects of the process until learners are able to self-reflect and self-regulate. Eagleton and Dobler state that "as teachers, we can reinforce these strategies by conducting our own inquiry projects alongside our students while providing appropriate modeling, scaffolding, practice, and feedback" (p. 95).

Internet workshop

Internet workshop is an instructional framework developed by Don Leu (2002) that is much like reading/writing workshop. It is designed to scaffold the Internet reading process for students and to promote learning how to learn, as opposed to just finding the right answer. "It is not just that we want students to know how to read and write; we want them to know how to continuously learn new skills and strategies required by the new technologies of literacy that will regularly emerge" (Leu, 2002, p. 467). Internet workshop generally includes the following procedures:

1. Locate a site on the Internet with content related to a classroom unit of instruction and set a bookmark for the location. This ensures the site is appropriate for the age and readability of the students and limits random surfing.

2. Design an activity, inviting students to use the site as they accomplish content, critical literacy, or strategic knowledge goals in your curriculum (as students progress, you may also invite them to develop independent inquiry projects). (Exhibit 6.34 shows teacher Scott Ritter working with his student, Nadar, on such a project.) This step introduces students to the site and develops important background knowledge and navigation strategies for effective Internet use. The activity should be open-ended so students have some inquiry options about the information they will share at the end of the workshop.

3. Complete the research project. Assigning students to a schedule will assure they have enough time during the week to complete the activity.

4. Have students share their work, questions, and new insights at the end of the week during a workshop session. You may also use this time to prepare students for the next workshop experience, which may extend opportunities to explore questions or interests raised from the previous workshop activity.

This framework can be used to explore many topics through simulations, *WebQuests,* and inquiry/Internet projects. In addition to content, students learn important critical literacy skills and strategies, such as how to conduct an effective search on the Internet; how to determine if information on the Internet is valid, reliable, and current; how to use the Internet to extend learning beyond traditional forms of information; and how the Internet facilitates communication with others around the world to broaden our perspectives and understanding.

Watch the video New Literacies of the Internet (28:25, www.learner.org/work shops/teachreading35/session5/index.html) to find out more about how the Internet has changed traditional views of literacy instruction, what reading strategies are necessary to comprehend text on the Internet, and what challenges teachers face in providing instruction in the new literacies in grades three through five.

points2ponder

QUICK REVIEW 4 What are some similarities between print and online reading? What are some differences? What is Internet inquiry, and what are the processes of the QUEST model?

(Access the answers in the digital version of this book.)

6.7

CHAPTER SUMMARY

In this chapter, we discussed several key factors that affect comprehension. A student's motivation to read plays a critical role in reading development. Motivation and engagement in reading can be promoted by providing students with authentic, interesting, high-quality literature and the opportunity to select books of their own choice.

A deficit in students' vocabulary knowledge can be detrimental to their learning to read; yet explicit vocabulary instruction can make a difference. Effective vocabulary instruction actively involves students in multiple opportunities to use and think about word meanings in multiple contexts.

Explicit instruction in research-based comprehension strategies can be effective in providing students with a repertoire of strategies that promote comprehension monitoring. The use of instructional routines such as Questioning the Author, reciprocal teaching, and book clubs are also effective ways to differentiate instruction and actively engage students in comprehension instruction.

Reading online offers supports and challenges to comprehension. Teachers can effectively introduce strategies such as the QUEST model that involves students in Internet inquiry in order to overcome these challenges and use the supports effectively.

think like a teacher

Before, During, and After

In the video Building Comprehension (28:00, www.learner.org/workshops/teachreading35/session3/index.html), Nell Duke discusses comprehension and reviews the multiple strategies proficient readers use. View this video to learn how you can advance students' comprehension before, during, and after reading. Before viewing the video, make a three-column chart, labeled *Before, During,* and *After.* While viewing the video, pause in three spots and add notes about reading strategies mentioned during the three phases of reading. After the video, discuss with a partner the ideas you recorded and fill in any gaps you noticed during your discussion. Then independently write a paragraph of 100 words or fewer summarizing the video.

Creating Read-Alouds

Every student deserves an award-winning read-aloud! This means that you must effectively use tone, inflection, voice variation, and pacing; make intentional connections; and think aloud to model comprehension strategies. For this activity, select a picture book to read aloud that is appropriate for modeling a specific comprehension strategy. Read through the book several times to find the appropriate tone, inflection, voice variation, and pacing that will make the book come alive. Also, think about how you will model the use of a comprehension strategy during the read-aloud. When you have sufficient practice, record the read-aloud as a podcast and share it with your classmates.

Evaluating "New Literacies"

Watch the video New Literacies of the Internet (www.learner.org/workshops/teachreading35/session5/index.html), in which literacy expert Donald Leu addresses the reading and writing strategies required for using the Internet and how these new literacies are changing the way we teach. Through commentary by Dr. Leu and classroom vignettes, you will learn how to integrate technology into your literacy curriculum and enhance literacy learning in your classroom. Some educators wonder if the term *new literacies* continues to be appropriate, because many of the technologies, and the accompanying literacies needed to utilize the technologies, are no longer new. Email, texting, and other forms of electronic communication have been integrated into our daily lives for years. After viewing the video, discuss as a class the merit of continuing to use the term *new literacies* or just consider using the term *literacies* to encompass all forms of communicating ideas. After the discussion, write an explanation of your opinion, giving at least three supporting reasons for your stance.

Vocabulary Jigsaw

Chapter 6 has provided an introduction to vocabulary instruction, but there is still much to learn. This jigsaw activity will give you an opportunity to become an expert about one aspect of vocabulary instruction and to teach what you have learned to others. Organize into groups of four students. Each group member selects a vocabulary video to view on the Reading Rockets Vocabulary page (www.readingrockets.org/atoz/vocabulary). Examples of video topics are Semantic Gradients, List-Group-Label, Concept Sort, and Building Strong Vocabulary.

While viewing, record important information on a viewing guide such as the one described in Chapter 7. Then meet together as a group and have members share new and interesting information gained from their videos. Work together to develop three summary statements that reflect your overall learning about vocabulary instruction from this activity.

REFERENCES

Allington, R. (2006). *What really matters for struggling readers: Designing research-based programs* (2nd ed.). New York: Allyn & Bacon.

Allington, R. L. (2009). *What really matters in response to intervention.* New York: Addison Wesley Longman.

Baker, L., Dreher, M., & Guthrie, J. (2000). Why teachers should promote reading engagement. In L. Baker, M. Dreher, & J. Guthrie (Eds.), *Engaging young readers* (pp. 1–16). New York: Guilford.

Baumann, J., Ware, D., & Edwards, E. (2007). "Bumping into spicy, tasty words that catch your tongue": A formative experiment on vocabulary instruction. *Reading Teacher, 61*(2), 108–122.

Beck, I., & McKeown, M. (1998). *Improving comprehension with Questioning the Author: A fresh and expanded view of a powerful approach.* New York: Scholastic.

Beck, I. L., McKeown, M. G., & Kucan, L. (2002). *Bringing words to life.* New York: Guilford.

Blachowicz, C., Fisher, D., Ogle, D., & Watts-Taffe, S. (2006). Vocabulary: Questions from the classroom. *Reading Research Quarterly, 45*(4), 524–539.

Bosman, J. (2011, February 4). E-readers catch younger eyes and go in backpacks. *New York Times Online.* www.nytimes.com/2011/02/05/books/05ebooks.html.

Chall, J. S., & Jacobs, V. A. (2003). Poor children's fourth-grade slump. *American Educator, 27*(1), 14–15, 44.

Chatton, B. (2004). Critiquing the critics: Adult values, children's responses, postmodern picture books, and Arlene Sardine. *Journal of Children's Literature, 30*(1), 31–37.

Coiro, J., & Dobler, E. (2007). Exploring the online reading comprehension strategies used by sixth-grade skilled readers to search for and locate information on the Internet. *Reading Research Quarterly, 42*(2), 214–257.

Cole, A. (2003). *Knee to knee, eye to eye: Circling in on comprehension.* Portsmouth, NH: Heinemann.

Cole, J. (2003). What motivates students to read? Four literacy personalities. *Reading Teacher, 56*(4), 326–336.

Cunningham, P., & Allington, R. (2011). *Classrooms that work* (5th ed.). New York: Pearson.

Darigan, D., Tunnel, M., & Jacobs, J. (2002). *Children's literature: Engaging teachers and children in good books.* Upper Saddle River, NJ: Merrill/Prentice Hall.

Donovan, C., Smolkin, L., & Loxmax, R. (2000). Beyond the independent-level text. *Reading Psychology, 21,* 309–333.

Dorn, L., & Soffas, C. (2005). *Teaching for deep comprehension.* Portland, ME: Stenhouse.

Duke, N., & Pearson, P. D. (2002). Effective practices for developing reading comprehension. In A. Farstrup & S. J. Samuels (Eds.), *What research has to say about reading instruction* (3rd ed.). Newark, NJ: International Reading Association.

Durkin, D. (1978–1979). What classroom observations reveal about reading comprehension instruction. *Reading Research Quarterly, 14,* 481–533.

Eagleton, M., & Dobler, E. (2007). *Reading the web: Strategies for Internet inquiry.* New York: Guilford.

Fielding, L., & Pearson, P. (1994). Reading comprehension: What works. *Educational Leadership, 51*(5), 62–68.

Flowerday, T., Schraw, G., & Stevens, J. (2004). The role of choice and interest in reader engagement. *Journal of Experimental Education, 72*(2), 93–114.

Fountas, I., & Pinnell, G. (2001). Guiding readers and writers, grades 3-6. Portsmouth, NH: Heinemann.

Fresch, M. (1995). Self-selection of early literacy learners. *Reading Teacher, 49*(3), 220–227.

Gambrell, L. B. (2009). Creating opportunities to read more so that students read better. In E. H. Hiebert (Ed.), *Read more, read better* (pp. 251–266). New York: Guilford.

Gambrell, L. (2011). Seven rules of engagement. *Reading Teacher, 66*(3), 172–178.

Giordano, L. (2011). Making sure our reading CLICKS. *Reading Teacher, 64*(8), 612–619.

Graves, M. F., & Watts-Taffe, S. M. (2002). The place of word consciousness in a research-based vocabulary program. In S. J. Samuels & A. E. Farstrup (Eds.), *What research has to say about reading instruction* (3rd ed., pp. 140–165). Newark, DE: International Reading Association.

Graves, M. F., & Watts-Taffe, S. M. (2008). For the love of words: Fostering word consciousness in young readers. *Reading Teacher, 62*(3), 185–193.

Harvey, S., & Goudvis, A. (2007). *Strategies that work: Teaching comprehension for understanding and engagement* (2nd ed.). Portland, ME: Stenhouse.

Hattie, J. (2009). *Visible learning.* New York: Routledge.

Hoyt, L., Mooney, M., & Parkes, B. (2003). *Exploring informational texts: From theory to practice.* Portsmouth, NH: Heinemann.

International Reading Association Literacy Research Panel. (2011/2012). IRA launches major initiative. *Reading Today, 29*(3), 6–9.

Johnson, D. (2012). *The joy of children's literature* (2nd ed.). New York: Wadsworth.

Jones, T., & Brown, C. (2011). Reading engagement: A comparison between ebooks and traditional print book in an elementary classroom. *International Journal of Instruction, 4*(2), 5–22.

Kieffer, M., & Lesaux, N. (2007). Breaking down words to build meaning: Morphology, vocabulary, and reading comprehension in the urban classroom. *Reading Teacher, 61*(2), 134–144.

Larson, L. (2009). E-reading and e-responding: New tools for the next generation of readers. *Journal of Adolescent & Adult Literacy, 53*(3), 255–258.

Larson, L. (2010). Digital readers: The next chapter in e-book reading and response. *Reading Teacher, 64*(1), 15–22.

Leu, D. (2002). Internet workshop: Making time for literacy. *Reading Teacher, 55*(5), 466–472.

Leu, D., Kinzer, C., Coiro, J., & Cammack, D. (2004). Toward a theory of new literacies emerging from the Internet and other information and communication technologies. In R. B. Ruddell & N. Unrau (Eds.), *Theoretical models and processes of reading* (5th ed., pp. 1570–1613). Newark, DE: International Reading Association.

Malloy, J., & Gambrell, L. (2010). New insights on motivation in the literacy classroom. In J. Malloy and B. Marinak (Eds.), *Essential readings on motivation* (pp. 163–178). Newark, NJ: International Reading Association.

McKeown, M., Beck, I., & Blake, R. (2009). Rethinking reading comprehension instruction: A comparison of instruction for strategies and content approaches. *Reading Research Quarterly, 44*(3), 218–253.

Nagy, W. (1988). *Teaching vocabulary to improve reading comprehension.* Urbana, IL: NCTE.

Nagy, W., & Townsend, D. (2012). Words as tools: Learning academic vocabulary as language acquisition. *Reading Research Quarterly, 47*(1), 91–108.

Oczkus, L. (2010). *Reciprocal teaching at work K–12.* Newark, DE: International Reading Association.

Ohlhausen, M., & Jepson, M. (1992). Lessons from Goldilocks: "Somebody's been choosing my books, but I can make my own choices now!" *New Advocate, 5,* 31–46.

Ollman, H. (1993). Choosing literature wisely: Students speak out. *Journal of Reading, 36*(8), 648–653.

Palincsar, A., & Brown, A. (1984). Reciprocal teaching of comprehension-fostering and comprehension-monitoring activities. *Cognition and Instruction, 1*(2), 117–175.

PISA. (2009). *PISA 2009 results.* http://www.oecd.org/pisa/pisaproducts/pisa2009/pisa2009keyfindings.htm.

PISA. (2011). *PISA in focus.* http://www.pisa.oecd.org/dataoecd/34/50/48624701.pdf.

Pressley, M. (2006). *Reading instruction that works: The case for balanced teaching.* New York: Guilford.

RAND Reading Study Group (RRSG). (2002). *Reading for understanding: Toward an R&D program in reading comprehension.* Arlington, VA: RAND Corporation. http://www.rand.org/pubs/monograph_reports/2005/MR1465.pdf.

Raphael, T. (1984). Teaching learners about sources of information for answering comprehension questions. *Journal of Reading, 27,* 303–311.

Raphael, T., & Au, K. (2005). QAR: Enhancing comprehension and test taking across grades and content areas. *Reading Teacher, 59*(3), 206–221.

Rosenblatt, L. (1938; 5 ed., 1995). *Literature as exploration.* New York: Modern Language Association of America.

Rosenblatt, L. (2004). The transactional theory of reading and writing. In R. B. Ruddell & N. J. Unrau (Eds.), *Theoretical models and processes of reading* (pp. 1363–1398). Newark, DE: International Reading Association.

Ruddell, R. (2004). Researching the influential literacy teacher: Characteristics, beliefs, strategies, and new research directions. In R. Ruddell & N. Unrau (Eds.), *Theoretical models and processes of reading* (5th ed., pp. 979–997). Newark, DE: International Reading Association.

Schlager, N. (1978). Predicting children's choices in literature: A developmental approach. *Children's Literature in Education, 9*(3), 136–142.

Scott Foresman. (2004). *Social studies: Virginia.* New York, Pearson Scott Foresman.

Worthy, J. (1996). Removing barriers to voluntary reading for reluctant readers: The role of school and classroom libraries. *Language Arts, 73*(7), 483–492.

Worthy, J., Moorman, M., & Turner, M. (1999). What Johnny likes to read is hard to find in school. *Reading Research Quarterly, 34*(1), 12–27.

CHILDREN'S LITERATURE CITED

Cleary, B. (2005). *How much can a bare bear bear?: What are homonyms and homophones.* Minneapolis, MN: Millbrook Press. http://www.worldcat.org/title/how-much-can-a-bare-bear-bear-what-are-homonyms-and-homophones/oclc/57432165.

Clements, A. (1996). *Frindle.* New York: Simon & Schuster. http://www.worldcat.org/title/frindle/oclc/33900128&referer=brief_results.

Curtis, C. (2012). *The mighty Miss Malone.* New York: Random House. http://www.worldcat.org/title/mighty-miss-malone/oclc/714724485.

Kinney, J. (2007). *Diary of a wimpy kid* (series). New York: Amulet Books. http://www.worldcat.org/title/diary-of-a-wimpy-kid-greg-heffleys-journal/oclc/74029165.

Montgomery, S. (2001). *The snake scientist* (*Scientist in the Field* series). New York: Houghton Mifflin. http://www.worldcat.org/title/snake-scientist/oclc/38593546.

Parsons, A. (1990). *Amazing spiders* (*Eyewitness Junior* series). New York: Knopf.

Peirce, L. (2010). *Big Nate* (series). New York: HarperCollins. http://www.worldcat.org/title/big-nate/oclc/505423938.

Riordan, R. (2010). *The lost heroes* (*Heroes of Olympus* series). New York: Hyperion. http://www.worldcat.org/title/lost-hero/oclc/526057827.

Russell, R. (2009). *The Dork diaries* (series). New York: Aladdin.

Say, A. (1993). *Grandfather's journey.* New York: Houghton Mifflin. http://www.worldcat.org/title/grandfathers-journey/oclc/27810899.

Terban, M. (1983). *In a pickle: And other funny idioms.* New York: Houghton Mifflin. http://www.worldcat.org/title/in-a-pickle-and-other-funny-idioms/oclc/8805442.

Terban, M. (1993). *It figures! Fun figures of speech.* New York: Houghton Mifflin. http://www.worldcat.org/title/it-figures-fun-figures-of-speech/oclc/26976906.

Listening and Viewing

Access the book's Glossary, which defines the key terms boldfaced in this chapter, at www.hhpcommunities.com/teachinglanguagearts/glossary.pdf

KEY IDEAS

- Listening is a process that can be taught.

- The process of listening is similar to the process of reading.

- A focus on the purpose for listening can help us become better listeners.

- Children's literature can be a useful tool in developing listening skills.

- Viewing is about making meaning from images.

- Viewing, reading, and listening share similar processes.

- Elements of images attract the viewer's attention and influence meaning.

7.1

LISTENING AND VIEWING AS RECEPTIVE MODES

Receptive skills are about receiving a message: making meaning from what we see, what we hear, and what we read. Our receptive skills give us access to information, which facilitates an understanding and leads to making informed decisions; however, receiving a message through the language arts modes of listening, viewing, and reading does not occur in a vacuum. The sociocultural theory (Vygotsky, 1978) posits that everything we hear, view, and read is interpreted through our unique ears and eyes. Every message is received within a context, and as we interpret the message, it passes through a set of filters created by our values, beliefs, and attitudes, which are shaped by our experiences, family, and culture. In addition, when we give meaning to a spoken message, or an image, or a collection of words, a connection forms between the messenger and the receiver based on this shared information. Linked together through this connection, this shared experience can form the basis for conversations and even lasting relationships. For instance, those who have read the book or seen the movie *The Hunger Games* share a common reading or viewing experience; if they

"A good listener listens with a questioning mind."

D. B. STROTHER (1987, p. 628)

"Seeing comes before words. The child looks and recognizes before it can speak."

JOHN BERGER, *Ways of Seeing*

EXHIBIT 7.1

Using the receptive modes shows very little action.

EXHIBIT 7.2

Comprehension strategies for reading, listening, and viewing.

	READING	LISTENING	VIEWING
ACTIVATE PRIOR KNOWLEDGE *Bring to the front of your mind what you know about the topic.*	Consider what you know before reading a travel brochure about Hawaii.	Consider what you know about the topic, person, situation before listening to the story of a friend's trip to Hawaii.	Consider what you know about Hawaii before watching a video about Hawaiian volcanoes.
MAKE PREDICTIONS *Make a reasonable guess about what information will be presented.*	Predict what the book will be about based on the title and cover and consider if it will help you write your report on the desert of the Southwest.	As your friend begins a conversation about living in Arizona, predict to yourself what it will be about based on what you already know.	Before watching a video about life in the desert, predict what it will be about and how carefully you will need to watch to participate in the class discussion.
MONITOR COMPREHENSION *Check yourself to make sure you are understanding.*	Pause to mentally summarize what you just read and decide to reread if necessary.	Pause to check if you are following the conversation and it's making sense. Listen more closely or ask the speaker to repeat if necessary.	Pause in your viewing to check if what you are watching makes sense. Replay if necessary.
ASK QUESTIONS *Ask yourself questions along the way as a guide and a check for understanding.*	Ask yourself guiding questions to keep your reading on track (e.g. Is this what I predicted would happen? What is going to happen next?)	Ask yourself questions to guide your listening. (e.g. Is this what I thought she would tell me? Why is she taking so long to explain this part?)	Ask yourself guiding questions to keep your viewing on track (e.g. Why did Lassie bypass the old well? Will she be able to run all the way to the mill stream?)
MAKE INFERENCES *Fill in the gaps or read between the lines to create an understanding that makes sense.*	Use what you know about a topic of the text and what the author provides in the text to fill in the gaps.	Use what you know about the speaker's topic and clues the speaker gives through gestures and facial expressions to fill in the gaps.	Use what you know about the topic and the information provided in the visual media to fill in the gaps.

want, they could join a community of others—virtually or face-to-face—to explore this connection.

Although listening and viewing together with reading are the receptive modes of language arts, receptive does not mean passive, even though one can easily make this assumption. When we watch someone who is using the expressive modes of language arts (e.g., writing, speaking, visually representing), we see action. We see fingers typing, lips moving, or hands gesturing. At first glance, when watching someone using the receptive modes, such as students listening to a story, we see very little action (see Exhibit 7.1). One might see a slight flicker of the eyes, or a look of concentration, but mostly we see a person thinking, which does not *look* very active. Do not be fooled by this apparent passiveness. Most of the action of the listener and viewer, as well as the reader, occurs in the mind.

Let's consider the thought processes used to make sense of ideas we take in through these receptive modes. Exhibit 7.2 looks at the ways readers comprehend text, as described in Chapters 5 and 6, and applies these same mental processes to listening and viewing, pointing out the many similarities among the three modes. To understand a message, the processes of listening, viewing, and reading involve the integration of a variety of skills including predicting, determining important ideas, drawing conclusions, and summarizing. All three processes are defined by their purposes and require similar skills—an understanding of words and images. For example, if a person does not know the meaning of the words, making sense of a message, whether listening or reading, can be quite challenging. Luckily, each mode provides scaffolds, or special cues, to help a person understand the message. As discussed in Chapter 6, a reader finds context clues, embedded definitions, illustrations, and a glossary to aid in understanding. In a similar way, a listener can rely on clues about vocabulary from a speaker's facial expressions, gestures, and voice inflection. When viewing a video or play, a person has the scenery or setting, background music, and the characters' words and actions to help explain unfamiliar ideas. Although the modes of reading, listening, and viewing have similar mental processes, each mode takes on unique characteristics, and the purpose of this chapter is to take a closer look at the modes of listening and viewing in light of what you have learned about reading in Chapters 5 and 6.

Although reading and writing seem to receive the most attention in school, the other areas of language arts are equal in importance when it comes to communicating. One reason for this disparity may be the assumption that if students can hear, they must be able to listen, and if they can see, they must be able to view. Anyone who has spent time with a group of young people can attest that just because they can hear, it does not guarantee they are listening. In the same vein, students may see something, but this does not necessarily lead to the higher-level thinking that occurs when making meaning through viewing.

If any doubt still remains about the need to teach listening and viewing skills in school, think about the listening and viewing skills used in everyday situations. View the commercial for fruits and vegetables, Color of Life (1:00, www.youtube.com/watch?v=D2LvrhqAPWU).

Consider the high-level thinking skills needed to understand the message of the *Color of Life* video. The viewer must interpret the message about eating fruits and vegetables, evaluate the reasons for eating these foods, identify evidence for these reasons, and decide if this evidence is compelling enough to change one's behavior. These decisions, typically made in a matter of a few seconds, may impact our quality of life to varying degrees.

As adults, we can all recall a time when we did not employ these evaluative techniques when listening to or viewing a persuasive message, and we made a decision or a purchase that we later regretted. The term *critical media literacy* is used to describe the skills individuals need to ask relevant questions about information and construct knowledge of the world, including forming social, economic, and political views (Alvermann, Hagood, & Moon, 1999; Hobbs, 2011). Listening and viewing entail thinking critically about what we hear and see. Our students can develop these skills through our explicit instruction, modeling, and guided practice.

Although some local and state curriculums, and even some published programs, address aspects of listening and viewing, consistent attention to these topics in the elementary classroom is often overshadowed by the more traditional emphasis on reading, and to a lesser extent, writing. This focus may be shifting, with increased attention being given to listening and viewing in state and national educational standards, including the Common Core State Standards (CCSS) as discussed in the next section.

points2ponder

QUICK REVIEW 1 Why might the receptive modes of listening and viewing receive less attention in school than the receptive mode of reading?

(Access the answer in the digital version of this book.)

7.2

LISTENING AND VIEWING AND STANDARDS

Educators are being called upon to teach listening and viewing skills based on expectations developed by various professional organizations. Listening is addressed specifically within the CCSS through the strand of Speaking and Listening in the English Language Arts Standards. Although listening skills develop progressively, the creation of a strong foundation for developing these skills at school can begin in kindergarten. By fifth grade, students are expected to engage in collaborative discussions, build on others' ideas, and contribute ideas of their own, all of which hinge on a foundation of strong listening skills. In addition, fifth graders are expected to summarize texts read aloud or information presented in diverse media and formats, which could include listening to a CD or a podcast (CCSS Initiative, 2012).

Although not specifically listed as a standard, viewing also is a skill of importance in the CCSS. College and Career Readiness Anchor Standards in writing call for students to "gather relevant information from multiple print and digital sources, assess the credibility and accuracy of each source, and integrate the information while avoiding plagiarism." Gathering information from a multimedia source requires the ability to determine its truthfulness and usefulness. In the Speaking and Listening Standards for fifth graders, students are expected to view and summarize information from diverse media, which may include a video or a website. In addition, within the CCSS, fifth-grade students should be able to summarize the points a speaker makes, whether live, recorded, or shared through interactive video such as Skype, and to explain how each claim the speaker makes is supported by reasons and evidence.

Read the CCSS standards for fifth grade that address listening (www.core standards.org/ELA-Literacy/SL/5). Make a mental list of the ways you, as a college student, have utilized these listening standards during the past 48 hours. Your list will likely be varied, but will represent the important role listening plays in your life.

The International Society for Technology Education (ISTE) also has a set of standards that defines learning in the digital age (ISTE, 2007). Although listening and viewing are not mentioned directly in these standards, several elements require proficiency in these important language arts modes. Students are expected to:

- interact, collaborate, and publish with peers, experts, or others employing a variety of digital environments and media.
- develop cultural understanding and global awareness by engaging with learners of other cultures.
- locate, organize, analyze, evaluate, synthesize, and ethically use information from a variety of sources and media.

Standards provide guideposts to teachers by identifying expectations for students' learning. For the areas of listening and viewing, teachers may not have experienced focused instruction in their own learning, which makes explicit standards all the more important.

7.3

LISTENING OVERVIEW

Listening is at the heart of communication and affects every aspect of our lives (see Exhibit 7.3). Listening is the first language skill most babies develop, even while they are still in the womb (Linebarger, 2001). During the school years, students acquire 80 percent of what they know through listening (Hunsaker, 1990). In interactions with friends and family, listening is the key to understanding others and helps one develop and strengthen relationships. Being aware of and monitoring sounds in our environment through listening is necessary for our own safety and knowledge. In the world of work, listening is identified as one of the top ten skills necessary for good performance (Galvin, 1997). The importance of effective listening is evident everywhere we turn, yet, adults listen with just 25 percent efficiency (Hunsaker, 1990). A successful listener must learn how to effectively use the lag time between listening and speaking to focus on the message. What other skills does a listener need and how can these skills be taught in the classroom? The next section of Chapter 7 focuses on the process of listening and ways to enhance students' abilities to understand what they hear.

author's story   ELIZABETH DOBLER

Listening and the Symphony

My husband and I attend our community symphony concerts several times a year. We spend the evening listening to talented musicians bring to life the work of composers past and present. The dramatic conductor in his full-length tuxedo leads the orchestra, and the audience enthusiastically applauds each performance. All the while, I sit in the audience feeling lost. I enjoy the music, but I simply do not understand the symphony.

EXHIBIT 7.3

The importance of listening.

I have trouble understanding the brief descriptions the conductor shares between musical selections. I peruse the concert program, looking for pieces of information that will help me make sense of what I am hearing, but instead encounter unfamiliar words (e.g., staccato, legato) or familiar words used in unfamiliar ways, (e.g., movement). Although I appreciate the music, I do not comprehend it. I steal a quick glance at those sitting nearby to see if they have guessed my secret. I clap and smile at the seemingly correct times to hide my lack of understanding. Part of my difficulty lies in the fact I have virtually no background experiences with the symphony. Music was not a part of the curriculum in my elementary school, and my small high school had only a dozen students in the marching band—not nearly enough musicians for an orchestra. I did not learn how to read music or appreciate any famous composers. My lack of prior knowledge has kept me from understanding what I hear at the concert and from developing a full listening appreciation for the symphony.

Listening is a process

Listening, both in the classroom and in everyday life, is a process not just a task. It is not an end unto itself, but provides the conduit for learning, negotiating, and developing short- and long-term relationships. According to the International Listening Association, "listening is the process of receiving, constructing meaning from, and responding to spoken and/or nonverbal messages" (Emmert, 1996). Sara Lundsteen, a listening researcher, describes listening as "the process by which spoken language is converted to meaning in the mind" (1971, p. 9). These definitions focus on listening as both receptive and constructive. Listening is an active process in which the listener is involved with the message and builds meaning from what is heard. The listening process has three elements: (1) receiving the message through spoken words and visual cues, (2) comprehending the message, and (3) interpreting the message through your own sociocultural filters; all of these appear to happen simultaneously (Opitz & Zbaracki, 2004; Wolvin & Coakley, 1996). All three elements of the process can be influenced by factors such as age, gender, habits, and cognitive abilities, as well as the listener's motivation and purpose for listening, along with the topic and social relationship to the speaker, and physical and neurological influences, such as a hearing impairment or attention disorder.

Each message received by the listener is analyzed from the perspectives of three language cueing systems, previously described in Chapter 5 in reference to the reading process (Pearson & Fielding, 1982; Williams, 1995). At the phonological level, the listener distinguishes significant phonemes and connects these together to perceive a word. The listener also picks up on **intonation** (rise and fall of speech) patterns, variations in **stress** (emphasis or loudness), and **juncture** (when a word begins and ends). At the syntactic level, the listener (and the reader) uses the arrangement of words and endings to create meaning. At the semantic level, the listener gains meaning from the way words relate to each other, and the way ideas are connected to create organized thoughts. All three cueing systems must be in place for a listener to comprehend a message in the same way as when reading a text.

When teaching the listening process to students, begin by setting a purpose for listening and focusing on the behaviors and thought processes that occur before, during, and after a listening event. See Exhibit 7.4 for specific examples of these thought processes. Your goal is to guide students to see listening as a process, not as a task. As students become more aware of the process underlying listening, they will likely become more effective listeners.

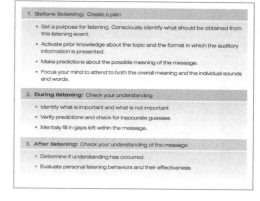

EXHIBIT 7.4

Thinking before, during, and after a listening event.

1. **Before listening:** Create a plan
   - Set a purpose for listening. Consciously identify what should be obtained from this listening event.
   - Activate prior knowledge about the topic and the format in which the auditory information is presented.
   - Make predictions about the possible meaning of the message.
   - Focus your mind to attend to both the overall meaning and the individual sounds and words.

2. **During listening:** Check your understanding
   - Identify what is important and what is not important
   - Verify predictions and check for inaccurate guesses
   - Mentally fill in gaps left within the message

3. **After listening:** Check your understanding of the message
   - Determine if understanding has occurred.
   - Evaluate personal listening behaviors and their effectiveness

This impact of increasing one's awareness about listening is especially powerful for English language learners, who rely on listening to learn a new language (Nunan, 2002). One way for all students to develop this awareness is for you to provide opportunities to develop listening strategies through a variety of authentic listening activities, while also explaining how and why students should use these strategies. Keep in mind that students who use listening strategies effectively in one situation may not use them as effectively in another. For example, a student who listens attentively to a story being read aloud in class may not be so attentive while listening to a band concert during a school assembly. Teach specific listening behaviors for specific listening situations to all students, and give students background knowledge, which can help them understand what they are listening to. Also, provide caregivers with information about how you are teaching the listening process in the classroom, so concepts can also be reinforced at home. Whether in or out of the classroom, teaching the listening process means focusing on the appropriate listening behaviors and effort required in order for students to make meaning from what they hear.

Listening as the forgotten language art

In the field of educational research, a historic lack of attention to listening skills is noted through the use of words like *ignored* and *neglected* (Landry, 1969; McPherson, 2008; Pearson & Fielding, 1982; Strother, 1987). During the 1950s and 1960s, research blossomed in the field of listening; however, this interest waned as researchers began to focus on reading in the 1970s and 1980s and placed additional emphasis on the writing process in the 1980s. In the 1990s, reading—phonics, specifically—dominated public interest, which influenced the amount of funds available for research in other educational areas. Listening fell by the wayside, even though many educational, business, and social communities agreed on the important role effective listening plays in communication. Ironically, "listening is one of the primary methods by which children acquire the beliefs, norms, and knowledge bases of their society" (McDevitt, 1990, p. 571), yet young people, like their adult counterparts, seem to have a limited view of listening. They seem unaware of the importance of being an engaged listener or even what this term might mean. Could this lack of awareness on the part of youngsters be connected to the limited knowledge about listening held by many adult listeners?

Many educators, and many outside of the field of education, hold the common belief that listening and hearing are synonymous, when actually these two skills are quite different. "We hear with our ears, but we listen with our minds" (Garman & Carman, 1992, p. 5). Hearing is the ability to discriminate among the sounds. Listening is paying attention to meaning of a sound or spoken message conveyed through verbal and nonverbal signals. Listening occurs when comprehension occurs, which involves the listener focusing on answering the question, "What does the speaker mean?" Since many people believe listening is a natural ability, little has been done to support the teaching of listening skills in schools or to address the topic of listening in the educational research community (Beall, Gill-Rossier, Tate, & Matten, 2008). The average K–12 student is expected to listen for as much as 65 to 80 percent of the school day, with little if any instruction for how to do so (Gilbert, 2005; Strother, 1987). Expecting students to listen is quite different from teaching them how to listen. Teaching specific skills brings listening to the conscious level.

Why should listening be taught?

A rationale for including listening as a pillar in language arts instruction brings to light the key reasons for teaching listening.

Listening stimulates language learning

Initial language learning, whether for a native or a second language learner, comes through listening (Lundsteen, 1979, 1990; Nunan, 2002; Rubin, 2000) and begins with the ability to hear and distinguish sounds. Learners then start to understand that specific sounds are joined together to form a word, and these words then become the foundation for their spoken and written language. This process of learning language develops with practice, and experiences, both of which are enhanced through listening.

Listening maximizes learning

Students who are better listeners are also better learners (Lundsteen, 1979; Pinnell & Jaggar, 2003; Strother, 1987). Skilled listeners are able to attend to the message amidst distractions, while applying their prior knowledge in order to make mental connections between new and known information. This process sounds similar to the process that makes for successful learning. In fact, students who comprehend well through listening also tend to comprehend through reading (Lundsteen, 1990). Strong listening skills have also been linked to early reading ability and to long-term academic success (Dickinson, McCabe, & Sprague, 2003). Quite possibly, the experiences with listening that begin in the womb lay the foundation for learning throughout life.

Listening enhances reading, writing, and speaking abilities

A growing collection of research brings to light the supportive role listening plays in developing other modes of language arts. Instruction in listening has been shown to improve phonological awareness (Morris & Leavey, 2006), reading comprehension (Badian, 1999), spelling skills, and writing (Berninger, 2000). Instruction in listening for the main idea can help improve the skill of reading for the main idea because both involve similar thought processes (Stitch, Beck, Hauke, Kleiman, & James, 1974). Students can understand more complex text when listening than when reading (for example, when listening to their teacher read a story to the class; see Exhibit 7.5), and this gap between listening and reading comprehension provides an opportunity for teachers to teach more difficult comprehension skills through listening. Young students do not have to wait until they can read all of a book's words independently before being taught how to think deeply about the text. Those students with attention difficulties or a hearing impairment may benefit from listening to information more than once or even listening to and reading the information simultaneously (Meyer & Rose, 2005). The use of audio recordings and text-to-speech software provides access to content in a more flexible or efficient mode for all learners because the information can be accessed at their own pace.

EXHIBIT 7.5

Teaching listening through reading aloud.

Effective listening skills do not always develop naturally

Although effective listening does not necessarily develop naturally, it can be taught. Adults seem to listen effectively only about one-fourth of the time, so listening skills do not necessarily increase with age and experience. In fact, as we age, our sense of hearing diminishes, which makes listening even more of a challenge. One possible explanation for adults' ineffective listening skills could be a lack of instruction. Teachers are not exempt from this gap in knowledge and must find ways to develop their own listening skills in order to effectively teach them to students.

There is a strong agreement among researchers that listening can be taught (Devine, 1978). In early research on listening (Hollow, 1955), a group of fifth graders was given systematic instruction in listening comprehension. Pre- and post-tests measured students' abilities to summarize, draw inferences, recall facts in sequence, and remember facts accurately. The difference between the control and experimental groups on the post-test was statistically significant and supported the conclusion that listening skills improve with direct instruction.

Listening is a life-skill

The consequences of poor listening skills have far reaching effects on everything from learning to finances, health, and relationships. Listening is the way we establish trust with a friend, determine the expectations of our boss, and give affirmation to an elderly relative. By teaching listening skills in school, we are developing skills our students will need for success long after leaving the classroom (see Exhibit 7.6).

Resources for teaching listening

Given that listening should be taught, where can teachers who have little or no training in this area find the resources to do so? The International Listening Association provides resources for teachers and other professionals seeking to teach effective listening skills. In addition, standards now exist to guide listening instruction. Listening has been included as a strand in the CCSS (www.corestandards.org/ELA-Literacy) (CCSS Initiative, 2012), and will likely be included in many state and local standards to align with the CCSS.

With the support of research, standards, and professionals, listening should absolutely be taught in school. The question is, how? Because listening is such an integral part of our daily lives, listening instruction should mimic the ways students will need to use their listening skills every day. Teach listening in the context of authentic classroom learning situations, through class discussions, partner writing conferences, and at literacy centers. Weave listening instruction and practice into the very fabric of the classroom, starting first with the daily learning routines.

points2ponder

QUICK REVIEW 2 Why is listening sometimes referred to as the forgotten or neglected language art?

(Access the answer in the digital version of this book.)

EXHIBIT 7.6

Listening is the integration of a variety of skills.

7.4

LISTENING ROUTINES

Auditory, rather than visual or kinesthetic learners, prefer to take in new information by listening (as in Exhibit 7.7) rather than by seeing or doing.

Students who struggle with learning in auditory ways are in particular need of listening routines in the classroom. Routines provide the structure of the classroom, letting all students know what to expect. When it comes to listening routines, such as flicking the lights off and on quickly to signal quiet time, students begin to expect the customary procedures and usually adjust their words and actions accordingly. The International Reading Association Standards for Reading Professionals call for teachers to use routines to support reading and writing instruction and to establish and maintain positive social environments (see Chapter 3 for more about creating a learning environment).

Students taking in new information by listening rather than seeing or doing.

Effective teachers strive to meet the varied learning preferences of students each school day because doing so improves the likelihood of successful learning. Students bring a variety of listening and learning styles to the classroom, based on past experiences and learning preferences. The term **listening style** refers to a listener's attitudes and beliefs about preferred ways to gain information through listening. Some listeners focus on the people delivering the message, some on the time the message is taking, some on the actions associated with the message, or some on the content of the message (Bodie & Villaume, 2007). Following are some suggested guidelines for listening routines, which can be adjusted to the listening and learning needs of students.

Set the purpose

Young people are no different than adults; both need to understand why they are listening in order to be engaged listeners. When listeners of all ages know up front what to listen for, energy and attention can be devoted toward this goal. When you say, "I am going to tell you three important things about how to solve a mystery," students' ears perk up. The teacher has set the purpose for listening and then must check afterward to see if students can identify the three things. Purposes for listening include the following:

- To gain information
- To detect bias
- To appreciate
- To give empathy

Help students experience listening for different purposes by integrating authentic listening activities into a variety of subject areas. Students can then begin to see the importance of listening as a life skill.

Give clear expectations

Encourage students to get ready to listen by setting clear listening expectations. Phrases such as *listen carefully, listen up,* and *here comes something important* are verbal cues for engaged listening. Sounds such as a bell, a clapping rhythm, or a clicking sound also serve a similar purpose. Since your goal is to create an atmosphere of listening, signals, whether verbal or non-verbal, let students know it is time to stop the previous activity and get ready to listen. You can also promote engaged listening by eliminating background noises and other distractions during a focused listening time, arranging seats appropriately, and stating a purpose for listening. Let students know what will happen after listening and avoid repeating yourself and other students' responses to encourage careful listening the first time. Doing so reinforces listening and sets your expectations, even though it can be difficult at first. Students must be taught your expectations for being an engaged listener.

Keep it brief and provide follow-up

Because students are expected to listen for a good part of the school day, often with little instruction in how to do so, some may not only find it difficult, but they may also not have developed listening as a favorite mode of learning. Keep listening experiences focused and brief in order to build listening stamina (Exhibit 7.8 shows a teacher giving focused instruction). Students with attention disorders and English language learners will especially benefit from brief listening activities, because much concentrated attention is required on their part. Hold students accountable for listening by following up shortly after the experience to assess their listening knowledge. Effective listening assessment gives students the opportunity to show what they learned, frequently by completing a meaningful task that requires listening. Determine, through observation, if students can achieve the stated listening purpose; then decide who needs additional help.

Model, model, model

If we want students to become better listeners, we need to be better listeners ourselves. "Listening is not only the heart of human interaction, but also the heart of teaching and learning" (Lundsteen, 1990, p. 213). In the absence of school-based listening instruction, students often learn listening skills by modeling their parents, teachers, and peers. Your listening behaviors provide an important model for demonstrating what engaged listening looks like. When listening to students, whether one-on-one, in a small group, or in a whole class discussion, maintain eye contact, nod your head, and keep distractions to a minimum whenever possible. After modeling these behaviors, pause and ask students if they noticed your positive listening behaviors. If you catch yourself using less than optimal listening behaviors, point this out. Say, "I am sorry I wasn't listening very well. I am finding the noise in the corner of the room to be quite distracting. Would you please say it again?" Sharing a think-aloud statement such as this helps students to become more aware of engaged listening behaviors. See Exhibit 7.9 for positive and negative listening behaviors.

By establishing listening routines in the classroom, you are letting students know that attentive listening is a priority. Explicit instruction and modeling of listening skills and opportunities to practice these new skills help students develop the ability and the confidence to handle communication situations in and out of the classroom. For English language learners, strong listening skills provide the foundation for learning a new language.

EXHIBIT 7.8

Keep listening experiences focused and brief.

EXHIBIT 7.9

Listening behaviors, positive and negative.

Behaviors that say *I am listening*

- Looking at the speaker
- Smiling
- Nodding
- Leaving arms uncrossed
- Keeping hands still
- Being quiet

Behaviors that say *I am not listening*

- Looking around
- Whispering, talking
- Making noises
- Moving around
- Touching objects or other people
- Texting while listening

points2ponder

QUICK REVIEW 3 What are two possible listening routines a teacher might use in the classroom?

(Access the answer in the digital version of this book.)

Listen Hear! 25 Effective Listening
Comprehension Strategies
BY MICHAEL F. OPITZ AND MATTHEW D. ZBARACKI

One of *Listen Hear!*'s authors begins with a personal story about his work on the book. When he told his wife that he would be writing a book about listening, she began laughing. He was not sure whether to be surprised or hurt by her response. Neither author of *Listen Hear!* considers himself an expert on listening, but both effectively shared what they have learned as experienced educators. The book provides a broad background for the reasons why listening is important while also lamenting the lack of listening instruction in schools. To help rectify this situation, the authors have designed 25 listening activities for teaching five types of listening: discriminative, precise, strategic, critical, and appreciative. The activities are interactive and most utilize children's literature as tools. The last chapter of *Listen Hear!* shares examples of informal listening assessment tools that can easily be adapted for various grade levels and activities. I took away the key idea that adults are often ineffective listeners because we have not been taught strong listening skills. The information and activities in this book are a good beginning for stimulating change for adults and the students they teach.

Locate a copy: www.worldcat.org/title/listen-hear-25-effective-listening-comprehension-strategies/oclc/55131365

7.5

LISTENING SKILLS FOR VARIOUS PURPOSES

Whether we are listening for enjoyment, to gain knowledge, or simply to be a good friend, our purposes for listening can influence various aspects of receiving a message. Identifying and understanding this purpose can focus our attention on the skills needed to become an effective listener. Listening skills can be categorized according to various purposes (Wolvin & Coakley, 1993, 1996), and instruction and experiences with each type of listening give students opportunities to reinforce, improve, or change their listening behaviors. Wolvin and Coakley believe listening skills can be developed when the listener identifies the purpose for listening and applies the associated skills through repeated practice and reinforcement until they become natural listening habits. This model of listening consists of five basic listening purposes: (1) discriminative, (2) comprehensive, (3) critical, (4) therapeutic, and (5) appreciative (see Exhibit 7.10). The next sections offer descriptions of each purpose for listening along with its associated skills and suggestions for instructional resources or activities.

Five purposes for listening.

Discriminative listening

Discriminative listening involves distinguishing one sound from another, one word from another, or one message from another. These sounds are sometimes accompanied by visual cues, and the listener's interpretation serves as the foundation for the other four listening purposes. **Auditory discrimination** involves distinguishing among verbal and environmental sounds and is closely linked to the development of oral and reading vocabularies. Auditory discrimination skills for verbal sounds for elementary students often include recognizing sounds among words, consonants, vowels, syllables, and rhyming words and attending to changes in the speaker's voice. Important environmental sounds may include distinguishing differences in tone and pitch of common sounds such as the fire drill buzzer and the recess bell. Being aware of and accurately interpreting nonverbal cues given off by the speaker, such as body posture, eye contact, head movement, and facial expression can help the listener better focus on the message.

Students develop discriminative listening skills by identifying rhyming words, reading and writing poetry, segmenting a word into sounds during phonemic awareness activities, creating words through onomatopoeia and alliteration, and listening to literature read from various dialects. Following are additional activities for developing discriminating listening.

Guess again. Encourage students to focus on the meanings of individual words by playing Guess Again. Display a group of real objects with similarities and differences or use the students in the class. Determine one object or person in the group, but keep this identity a secret. Then orally give clues, progressively making them more specific, and have students guess the identity. For example:

- I am thinking of a student who has brown hair.
- I am thinking of a student who also has short hair.
- I am thinking of a student who also has curly hair.

This activity develops discriminative listening skills by having students focus on the clue word, while also remembering previous clues.

Draw it. This listening activity focuses students' attention on the meaning of what is heard during a description of a place. Key words will include prepositions (e.g., on, above, below, near) and words describing spatial relations, two concepts especially important to English language learners. First, describe the place sentence by sentence. Then ask students to draw the scene as though they are viewing it from above based on your description. After completing the drawings, ask students to share and discuss their drawing with a partner.

> *Example description:* My dream tree house looks like a fun place. On each side of the tree are two tall roller coasters for getting into the tree house. Under the tree branches is a waterslide that goes down into a swimming pool. There are also stairs coming down from the tree house. Next to the stairs is an animal pen for my cat and dog. On the right side of the tree is a bungee cord for jumping, swinging, and bouncing. This tree fits my life! It is designed for any situation. The tree house has different rooms above the trunk. Near the windows are signs about the tree house rules. I want to live here as soon as I can drive.

See Exhibit 7.11 for an example student drawing of the dream tree house. This activity can be modified for varying levels of students by adapting the length, details, and words used in the description. An extension activity could be to have a student give an oral description to a partner while the partner draws the picture. Then the partners check the drawing for accuracy.

Comprehensive listening

Comprehensive listening, also known as precise listening (Opitz & Zbaracki, 2004), involves listening to understand the message. Through

EXHIBIT 7.11

Example student drawing based on the dream tree house description.

comprehensive listening, the listener gains knowledge. A listening event is successful if the message received by the listener is as identical as possible to the speaker's intent. Comprehensive listening is strongly influenced by the listener's ability to remember the message and recall it for future use; for example, the student in Exhibit 7.12 is listening for that purpose. Listeners should understand why the speaker is giving the message and the main ideas and important details, which they relate to their own knowledge. Listeners should be able to recall the main idea and details of the message and use this information to make inferences about the meaning of the message.

Comprehensive listening plays a critical role in elementary schools because much information is shared through oral directions, direct instruction, class discussions, and instructional media. Lessons on following directions, common in published listening programs, also focus on the comprehensive purpose for listening. Instruction in this area can help students improve their memory for oral information. Because comprehensive listening is about listening for information, using visuals can provide listeners with an additional source of information if listening skills are not strong enough alone. English language learners, and other students, too, can benefit from the use of real objects, photographs, and symbols to accompany an oral presentation, class announcements, or instructions. Also, visual cues by the teacher, such as two fingers in the air, may help students recall the oral directions for preparing to take a spelling test or some other routine activity.

In addition, a graphic organizer may be a useful tool for helping students to recall information heard during a guest speaker's presentation or when watching a video. Exhibit 7.13 displays a completed listening framework for visually organizing information gathered during a listening event. Students used the framework while listening to the podcast The Buzz-z-z on West Nile Virus (www2c.cdc.gov/podcasts/player.asp?f=8622433). As shown in Exhibit 7.13, a listening framework can be used to give a purpose for listening and to encourage the listener to give conscious attention to both the words being said and the nonverbal cues of the speaker.

Comprehensive listening plays an important role for students both in and out of school. The listener's ability to concentrate, motivation to gain knowledge from listening, and the depth of prior knowledge can influence his or her success in all types of communication. Following are activities for developing comprehensive listening.

Change it up. Changing classroom instructions from day to day makes students aware of the importance of listening carefully. Adding variety or novelty to instructions helps to keep everyone on their toes. At some point during the day, announce a special instruction and offer a small reward for those who follow the instructions correctly. Examples include:

- Return your signed field trip permission form by tomorrow, and you will get to choose your seat on the bus. Others will have their seat chosen for them.

- Come in from recess silently, and I will add a marble to our jar, which gets us closer to earning a spelling game day.

Listening centers. All students, especially English language learners, must develop listening stamina—the concentration span needed to listen to long stretches of spoken language. Listening practice activities should include

EXHIBIT 7.12

A listener must remember and recall the message for future use.

EXHIBIT 7.13

Listening framework.

(Print a blank copy of the listening framework: www.hhpcommunities.com/teachinglanguagearts/IL-07-01.pdf)

Listening centers.

clear language and a limited number of unfamiliar vocabulary words. A listening center provides an opportunity for students to listen to age-appropriate books, both fiction and nonfiction, as fluent reading is modeled and information is presented through stories and descriptions. A listening center should include a comfortable area for students to sit, listening materials, and equipment (e.g., CD player, MP3 player, tablet, laptop, desktop computer, headphones, earbuds). Exhibit 7.14 shows examples of listening centers.

View this Listening Center glog (http://bdobler.edu.glogster.com/promote-listening-7529). Click on the link for the audio file to listen to a description and view the images to see the various possibilities for creating listening centers.

Audiobooks can be found in schools and public libraries, and free online or electronic versions may also be available. The website Gizmo (www.tech-supportalert.com/free-audio-books-children), which reviews and rates free online resources, has published the list "Free Audio Books for Children." The list shares websites that legally offer free age-appropriate audiobooks. Another site, Storynory (http://storynory.com), publishes a free audiobook for young readers each week, featuring original stories, classics, and fairy tales read by professional actors. Visit these websites and listen to an excerpt of a free audiobook and consider whether you prefer reading it yourself or listening to the electronic version.

Students could create a graphic organizer, such as a story map, either while listening or after listening. Utilizing a map or outline for a listening activity holds students accountable for their listening, which is especially important if students are working independently or with a partner at a listening center.

Therapeutic listening

Therapeutic listening occurs when we lend an ear to a troubled friend or relative, or listen for the purpose of strengthening a social connection. People of all ages need someone to listen to their fears, hopes, and problems. Although young people should not take the weight of the world upon their shoulders, they can become empathetic listeners to their friends, who may have problems as simple as an unfair kickball game or as emotional as the loss of a parent. Learning therapeutic listening skills at a young age will be valuable in personal relationships throughout life.

The therapeutic listener uses a wide collection of listening skills, drawing from both discriminative and comprehensive listening skills along with skills that encourage the sharing of personal or sensitive information. Therapeutic listening is enhanced by

- focusing attention on the speaker by removing distractions.
- maintaining eye contact and receptive body language (for example, leaning toward the speaker).
- choosing a setting where the speaker feels comfortable and free to express himself.
- listening with empathy by feeling and thinking with the speaker.
- responding in a way that gives the speaker the opportunity to talk through troubles.

These may seem like high-level skills for students, especially when most of us know adults who have not yet mastered them; however, these skills can be introduced on a simplistic level for young children.

In the elementary classroom, therapeutic listening skills can be developed through class meetings and discussions. A school counselor may also be available to model behavior that develops therapeutic listening skills. In addition, you help create a climate where students feel comfortable sharing as well as provide adequate support when listening to their concerns. The topic of bullying receives much attention in the classroom, and therapeutic listening is at the center of possible solutions to this important problem. Students who are bullied may feel no one has listened or will listen to their pleas for help. The modeling of therapeutic listening skills by a teacher, counselor, or administrator can begin to open the channels of communication among students and families (Cowie, 2011). The following are activities for developing therapeutic listening.

Class meetings. Hold a class meeting or similar activity on a regular basis. The activity should have a name and established routines, rather than occurring sporadically or in an unstructured way, so that students know what to expect and can prepare for this type of listening. Prepare for the meeting by seating everyone so they can see each other, whether in chairs or on a carpeted area. Begin by summarizing what was discussed at the previous meeting and clarifying the focus for this present meeting. Review the listening and speaking guidelines, which were developed by the group before the first meeting. Share these expectations visually and orally. Utilize an object to be held by a person when speaking (e.g., a hat, a stick, a ball) as the sign for all others to be listening. Throughout the meeting, remind students as needed of the expected listening and speaking behaviors. Conclude the meeting by summing up what was discussed and giving positive recognition for appropriate listening behaviors.

Writing workshop. Sharing time during writing workshop (discussed further in Chapter 9) can be an opportunity to promote therapeutic listening in the classroom. Some students may choose to include personal information in their writing projects and then present their writing during sharing time. Students in the audience should use appropriate listening behaviors during sharing time, especially when a student reveals personal feelings or experiences. For example, a student may write about the recent death of a grandparent, and this writing may be the place where the student feels comfortable releasing pent-up emotions of sadness and loneliness. Audience members need specific instruction about how to respond when a student reveals these feelings to the group. Anticipate that this situation will occur at some point and prepare students in advance by clearly stating listening behaviors (as were shown in Exhibit 7.9), modeling these behaviors for students, and providing guided practice through role-playing situations. The goal is for the listeners to present an attitude of acceptance and understanding, but do not expect this goal to be met without modeling, guidance, and practice.

Critical listening

Critical listening is for the purpose of making a judgment regarding a message, or being persuaded to some degree by a message. Skilled critical listeners scrutinize speech, looking for faulty logic, insufficient evidence, or overt opinions and distinguishing them from the facts. They judge a message objectively and are not biased by their feelings. School-aged children are not too young to begin learning how to listen critically and to recognize a persuasive rather than a factual message by asking the following questions:

1. Who created the message?
2. What creative techniques are effectively used in the message or the media used to convey it?
3. What values are embedded in the message?
4. Why is the message being sent?

As they become productive members of our society, these same young people will be called upon to make judgments about messages from the media, politicians, sales personnel, religious leaders, medical experts, and many others. Similar thought processes are utilized for both critical listening and critical thinking, including analysis, inference, and evaluation. Critical listening and critical thinking help the listener understand another person's point of view, which may help broaden his or her own point of view. This acrostic poem communicates the idea of critical listening in a simple, yet effective format (O'Keefe, 1999, p. 21):

Listen without
Interrupting
Stay attentive
To hidden messages
Evaluate after
Noting all the facts, and
Send feedback.

Critical listening activities in school may include listening to election speeches for class or school officers, listening to persuasive arguments during a class debate, or listening to a book talk and deciding whether or not to read the book. Following are additional activities for developing critical listening.

Smokey the Bear's message. Smokey the Bear has a long tradition of sharing a persuasive message of fire safety. Have students listen to the podcast "Smokey the Bear Campfire Building and Safety" from the Minnesota Department of Natural Resources. Following the presentation, have students work in teams of three or four to create a list of the persuasive messages from the podcast. Discuss the value of these messages and ways students can pass the messages on to others. Create posters based on Smokey's messages to be displayed around the school to convince other students to be safe with fire.

🔊 Before engaging in this activity with students listen to the podcast "Smokey the Bear Campfire Building and Safety" and make a list of the persuasive messages (7:00, http://files.dnr.state.mn.us/news/podcasts/campfire.mp3).

What is your opinion? Critical listening is necessary for making informed decisions. The topic of school uniforms is both timely and of interest to students. Introduce this topic and listen to the podcast "Should All Students

Wear School Uniforms?" Have students identify the pros and cons of wearing school uniforms and record these elements on a two-column chart using the interactive whiteboard or projector. While recording on the chart, discuss each item. After completing the chart, ask each student to decide where he stands on the issue and write a paragraph stating his belief and why. Share these with the entire class or in small groups.

🔊 To prepare for engaging in this activity with students, listen to the podcast Should All Students Wear School Uniforms? Use a two-column chart to record the pros and cons (3:54, www.podfeed.net/episode/Should+all+students+wear+school+uniforms/2787288).

Appreciative listening

Appreciative listening is for the purpose of gaining enjoyment through receiving creative works of others. This type of listening is perhaps the most personal, based on each person's unique and individual preferences. The listener comprehends and interprets spoken, nonverbal, or musical language based on his experiences, background, motivation, and interest. The appreciative listener attends to the eloquence in the language and music. The listener of oral presentations appreciates the ease and conciseness, vividness, and liveliness of the language. An appreciation of music involves responses that are sensual, emotional, and intellectual. Training in music appreciation can help a listener effectively combine these perspectives and lead to further enjoyment. For the untrained symphony listener previously described, this type of training would lead to a deeper understanding and appreciation. Appreciative listening skills can be developed in elementary students through audience involvement with reader's theater, a poetry recital, audiobooks, or storytelling. Informal productions in the classroom and professional productions are both valuable listening activities (see Exhibit 7.15). Following are additional activities for developing creative listening.

A music teacher guides students during an appreciative listening activity.

🔊 Listen to Listening Enhances the Composing Process (2:09) as music teacher Mark Camancho describes an appreciative listening activity and the similarities between music and story composition. (*Access this podcast in the digital version of this book.*)

Poetry podcasts. Students will enjoy listening to podcasts of poetry performed by other students. Have them listen to an example, such as A Poetic Podcast, The Dragon Who Ate Our School (1:00, www.radioanywhere.co.uk/displayStory.php?story=2252) from the Bishops Waltham Junior School in Hampshire, England. After listening to the poem, discuss the ways these students used sound effects, rhythm, and fluctuation in their voices to create an interesting interpretation of the poem.

Joking around. People of all ages enjoy laughter, and jokes can be a source of humor for young and old alike. Begin this two-part activity by sharing the video Classic Sesame Street—Bert's Pigeon Jokes (3:00, www.youtube.com/watch?v=RK9nRJXAUzg). Discuss jokes, humor, and the importance of listening carefully to understand the humor. Then ask students to go home and find a joke to bring back to school. Require that the joke be appropriate for school and one that most students will understand. Have students write the joke and submit it to you the next day. Then review the jokes and invite students to share theirs with the class. The next step is to ask students to illustrate their joke and hang the joke and its illustration on a class bulletin board or include them both on the class website.

The purpose for listening hinges upon very personal decisions made each time the listener participates in a listening event. Most listeners are not aware of the split-second decisions the mind makes about why or how to listen in a certain way, yet these decisions set the listener on the path to listen to gain information, to be a friend, or to simply enjoy the sounds. Although categories of listening have been explained as separate and distinct, in reality our purposes for listening may overlap in various listening situations. A listener must be flexible and adapt to the expectations called for in each unique situation.

Age-appropriate literature as a tool for teaching listening for a specific purpose

Literature can be a useful tool for integrating listening skills into the curriculum. Teachers can capitalize on read-aloud or shared reading time to provide instruction in developing listening skills based on one of the five purposes for listening. A teacher can identify a purpose for listening and match this purpose to age-appropriate literature, and the teaching of skills can then be integrated into the read aloud activity.

See Matching Age-Appropriate Literature to Listening Purpose: www.hhp communities.com/teachinglanguagearts/IL-07-02.pdf

---

Keep these guidelines in mind when using literature to teach listening skills:

- Choose literature that best fits the purpose for listening (e.g., discriminative, comprehensive, therapeutic, critical, or appreciative).
- During an introduction of the literature, help the students identify the purpose for listening (e.g., therapeutic). Define a set of skills to be practiced during the listening activity (e.g., practice in thinking and feeling with another person). A teacher might say, "While you are listening to this story about Anna and her birthday, think about how Anna feels before her birthday and after she receives her surprise birthday present."
- Throughout the read-aloud activity, pause and help the students refocus on their purpose for listening. Do occasional quick checks for understanding of the listening skills being used by asking students to share orally or in writing their interpretation of the listening event.
- After reading, reiterate the purpose for listening and check to see if this purpose was met. Review the skills used, and discuss how using these skills helped the student listen more effectively.

Help students realize that listening purposes often overlap within a single piece of literature. One might listen for information but also appreciate the flow and beauty of the language. The use of age-appropriate literature as the material for enhancing listening skills gives you an abundant source of possibilities.

points2ponder

QUICK REVIEW 4 Name and explain the five purposes for listening, and for each one describe a brief example of a classroom activity.

(Access the answer in the digital version of this book.)

7.6

ASSESSING LISTENING

As described previously in this chapter, listening stems from a purpose. We receive a message and then take an action based on that message. The action may be simply giving a friend a hug, or it may be quietly and swiftly moving out of the building during a fire drill. The summative assessment of listening occurs when we take this action. Did what we hear guide us to take the appropriate action? However, teachers are also interested in the formative assessments along the way that provide information about students' uses of appropriate listening behaviors, which will increase the likelihood of listeners ultimately taking that appropriate action. Chapter 8 will discuss the Purposeful Listening Rubric (www.hhpcommunities.com/teaching languagearts/IL-08-04.pdf) and the Elementary Discussion Rubric, listening assessment tools you can use in a formal listening situation, such as listening to a guest speaker, and in a less formal situation, like listening during a class discussion. Giving these rubrics to students ahead of time will provide guidance in the types of expected listening behaviors for the situation.

Our ultimate goal as teachers is to help students be effective evaluators of their own listening skills. The Listening Checklist, discussed in Chapter 8, can also be used to help students monitor their own listening skills. The guide is intended for students in grades three through six, but descriptions of listening behaviors can be adapted for younger students. To help students learn to identify the listening skills they need in varying situations, provide students with a copy of the listening guide or display a list of the skills on a poster in the classroom. These skills can be modeled, developed, and practiced with you and your students working together. Also encourage students to use listening tools in situations outside of the classroom, such as when disagreeing during a kickball game, listening to music on an MP3 player, or having a serious discussion with a parent. Each situation requires a variety of listening skills, which students can be taught to identify and use effectively.

You should also assess your own listening skills. As discussed in Chapter 8, the Listening Classroom Checklist and the Listening Self-Assessment are both informal listening assessments that we teachers can use on ourselves, to ensure we are modeling effective listening behaviors and demonstrating to students the value of listening to all members of the classroom community.

In summary, our goal in discussing listening is to make a strong case for the need to teach listening skills in the classroom and to present various ways to do so. Using the CCSS as a guide, you can emphasize the important role listening plays in our daily lives while integrating authentic listening activities into the school day. Effective instruction in listening begins with recognizing your own listening habits and attitudes and modeling the most useful skills for your students. The teaching of listening can have a lasting impact on the ways students learn and their abilities to communicate both now and in their futures.

VIEWING OVERVIEW

author's story   ELIZABETH DOBLER

Viewing the Grand Canyon

On a recent vacation, the Dobler family traveled to see the Grand Canyon. For the children, it was their first glimpse of this vast and breathtaking view, created by the flow of the Colorado River and the uplifting of the Colorado plateau (see Exhibit 7.16). For hundreds of years people have made the trek on foot, horseback, train, plane, car, or bus to view this landform of unparalleled beauty created by the massive power of nature. A viewing device strategically placed along the rim trail gives visitors a panoramic view of the canyon. At dawn or dusk, many visitors wearing jackets and carrying blankets walk quickly to various spots to catch the sunrise or sunset across the horizon of the canyon. During the daylight, everywhere one turns along the canyon rim is a view of majestic beauty. A visit to the Grand Canyon is unquestionably about viewing, or taking in the grandeur of the canyon.

EXHIBIT 7.16

Elizabeth Dobler and her daughter view the Grand Canyon.

Viewing is the act of feasting your eyes upon new visual information. This information comes from the world around us, such as in nature, from people, and through text. The modern definition of text, as explained in Chapter 1, has expanded beyond written texts to include **multimodal texts** (e.g., street signs, maps, yard signs, billboards, websites, television programs, picture symbols, and photographs) that present ideas on more than one mode (e.g., verbal, textual, visual). Understanding these real world texts is necessary, and at times crucial, for our health, safety, and personal well-being. According to Steve Moline, the author of *I See What You Mean,* "We are all bilingual. Our second language, which we do not speak, but which we read and write every day, is visual" (2012, p. 9). **Visual literacy,** the ability to understand or to make meaning from what is seen, focuses on knowing how visual texts work and effective ways to draw conclusions from these texts.

As an introduction to visual literacy, view the video Visual Literacy Across the Curriculum (3:46, www.youtube.com/watch?v=XQNbAtK3c3g).

Teachers recognize and research supports the idea that teaching with words and images yields better outcomes than teaching with words alone (Jin & Boling, 2010). This powerful connection between words and images might lead one to wonder, what distinguishes viewing from reading? We can read a picture just as we read a book; both involve making meaning, one from an image and one from the written word. Actually, viewing and reading can happen simultaneously when print and images appear together. The key difference between viewing and reading lies not in the process of receiving the message, but in the source of the message. Images reveal meaning through color, perspective, line, medium, texture, shape and form, and tone. These elements are easily recognizable in such media as television, art, drama, and movies, as well as in graphic texts like charts, maps, graphs, and websites. Written texts reveal meaning through a collection of letters, and a sequence of words, sentences, paragraphs, and pages.

Because viewing entails receiving a message, its partner mode, visually representing, is the process of creating a message through images. The skills needed to view an image are the subject of this chapter, while the skills needed to visually represent an idea are described in Chapter 10. The design of *Forward Thinking* is to organize chapters around the receptive and expressive ways we use the language arts; however, this distinction may seem a bit unnatural at times. Viewing and visually representing do go hand-in-hand, but for purposes of our discussion, we have separated these chapters, and likewise for listening and speaking.

The process of viewing: Taking it in

EXHIBIT 7.17

Eyes provide the gateway for viewing.

The eyes provide a gateway for visual information to travel along the superhighway of neurons to the brain (see Exhibit 7.17). We can process what we see twice as fast as what we hear, and visual information can be processed infinitely faster than textual information. Website creators recognize a seven- to thirteen-second window of opportunity to capture the attention of the Internet viewer, and they focus on ways to make their websites "stickier," or more enticing to engage a viewer for longer than just a few seconds. Yet one should not assume that this speed of processing means visual texts are simple to understand or serve merely as a substitute for the written word. Images are not extraneous, but can be a highly complex way to convey an idea, requiring the viewer to make mental connections and read between the lines.

The powerful impact of images extends into various aspects of thought processes. Images link to human emotions by triggering memories, which may lead to sadness, longing, or even joy. Teachers recognize the role of images in activating prior knowledge, providing examples of new concepts, or defining words (Clark & Lyons, 2011). Images bring concepts to life and capture our interest as our eyes search for meaning and connections. Both Freud and Piaget drew similar conclusions about students' ability to understand concrete images more easily than abstract words. To put it simply, images help people to understand and remember new information.

When words and images come together through a multimodal text, the path of the message is enhanced. Together, words and images provide a context that may not be present in words or images alone, and with experience, readers learn to nimbly move between images and written words. "It is through this combination of words and images that we elevate our thinking to the highest level of understanding" (Burmark, 2002, p. 8). Infographics are an example of a multimodal text that captures the salient features of both words and images. An **infographic,** a term created by combining the words *information* and *graphic,* integrates a variety of ideas, facts, and data into a visual representation.

On the surface, viewing appears to involve watching, skimming, scanning, and browsing; however, closer scrutiny reveals a depth of thinking and mental challenge. The process of viewing actually involves finding, selecting, comprehending, and evaluating information and entertainment messages (Hobbs, 2006). Gaining meaning from images, with or without accompanying written text, requires high levels of thinking, often occurring within a mere instant. The viewer may not even be aware of this process and the sociocultural forces that influence viewing (Burmark, 2002; Hobbs, 2005). Our past experiences, personal preferences, and values all impact the conclusions we draw from what we see. Thus one person's interpretation of an image may be quite different from another's.

Viewing signals.

VIEWING SIGNALS
Pointing out information:
icon, arrow, color
Grabbing attention:
color, font, music, image
Expressing emotion:
photograph, music, color
Forming connections:
arrow, asterisk, line
Sorting information:
column, color, heading
Grouping ideas:
color, column
Separating ideas:
numbers, bullets, color

In a split second of viewing, a person creates a mental progression for looking at an image. Different from reading the written word, where our eyes move from left to right and top to bottom, the sequence of attention to elements in an image varies greatly from person to person. A graphic image may be read from bottom to top, right to left, in a circular direction or even a zigzag path. Our eyes may be drawn to a specific element because of color (a red star), line (an arrow), or location (center of the page), and what we notice first depends on our level of attention, past experiences with viewing, and the urgency of the message. Signals within the text or visual element (see Exhibit 7.18) can help guide the viewer toward more important information or motivate the viewer to give careful attention to a specific element. A graphic can quickly give information, if the viewer knows what to look for. A book cover, movie trailer, or the key on a map all serve as a preview of more to come.

In spite of all of the clues available to the viewer, the process used for viewing is similar to that used for listening and hinges on a person's purpose. Viewing is typically used to gain information or to provide entertainment. In both cases, the viewer must choose the entrance point into the text, or a place to begin viewing. An informational text, such as a website, may display several initial viewing options, including a banner across the top of the page or a list of links down the side of the page. An informational picture book full of colorful images may present a table of contents, an index, headings, or pictures with captions, all of which could be used as starting points. However, a viewer may be tempted to head down a path unrelated to his purpose by flipping through the book or clicking on an ad link.

What are QR codes?

Probably you have noticed the QR codes found on cereal boxes, in newspapers, and on posters, among other places. These Quick Response (QR) codes, when scanned by a QR reader (e.g., a smartphone or other mobile device) lead the user to a specific website. QR codes can also be used in education to direct students to preselected websites applicable to an instructional activity. Students are thus able to bypass the distractions and inappropriate websites encountered in a typical Internet search.

View Steven Anderson's Live Binder (www.livebinders.com/play/play/ 51894), which has useful resources for ways to use QR codes in the classroom. After reading some of the ideas, jot down two ways you could incorporate QR codes into your own teaching.

The viewer is constantly making decisions.

In addition to choosing the sequence of viewing, viewers (such as the young students shown in Exhibit 7.19) also make constant decisions about how much to view, which also is strongly influenced by a person's purpose for viewing (Moline, 2012). When the purpose is to gain information, a viewer typically begins with a question, for example, "What is the weather for today?" The weather forecast could be obtained by watching television, viewing a website or mobile device, or looking at the newspaper. The search continues until the viewer has gathered enough information to satisfy her curiosity; thus, the amount of viewing will likely vary from person to person.

Because the process of viewing is unique to each person's purpose and viewing entails so many different multimedia formats, creating a precise, step-by-step description for the viewing process is difficult. Just like reading and listening, viewing is a multilayered, highly synchronized mental activity. At the same time, the viewing process does utilize several elements that are common to many viewers and many multimedia elements (see Exhibit 7.20 for questions to guide the viewing process). Consider the similarities and differences between the viewing process for graphics in light of what you also know about the reading and listening process.

Social semiotics: A theory in support of visual literacy

Each sign we create represents the world around and inside us and at the same time initiates a social interaction between the creator and the reader. The video *Color of Life,* previously mentioned in this chapter, seeks to persuade people about the benefits of fruits and vegetables. Beautiful red apples and bright green broccoli are enjoyed by happy people. Snappy music adds to the upbeat mood of the video. Through images and sound, the creator hopes to convince the viewer of the great taste and nutritional qualities of fresh fruits and vegetables. Would our interpretation of this video change if we learned the producers are advocating any of the following?

- Vegetarianism
- Sustainable farming
- Diabetes awareness
- Cancer prevention

The perspective of the person or group creating an image may influence a viewer's interpretation or understanding of the message. The theory of social semiotics helps explain this idea of multiple meanings and interpretations. **Semiotics,** the study of signs and symbols, was first introduced in Chapter 3. Social semiotics refers to ways various signs and symbols are created and understood by a society (Halliday, 1978). It encourages a viewer to ask himself, "What is the message behind the message?" In order to be literate in everyday tasks, in school and in the future world of work, students need to understand that words and images convey ideas, while simultaneously containing underlying messages. Visual literacy is a life skill that extends into and beyond the classroom and requires the explicit teaching of viewing skills.

Multimodal texts provide students with opportunities to understand ideas through the use of more than one type of symbol. Each mode of communicating, whether spoken, written, or visual, can be used to express the same idea, but each mode will be received in a different way, which is social semiotics at work. The *Color of Life* video communicates ideas through images and sound. The book *Eating the Alphabet: Fruits and Vegetables from A to Z* by Lois Ehlert communicates a similar message about the value of fruits and vegetables, but through images and written words. Both of these examples represent similar ideas in different ways. Both are also multimodal texts, meaning that ideas are interpreted and presented in varied ways to the viewer. Students' learning increases more with multimodal texts than with single-mode texts (e.g., written handout, flash cards), according to a meta-analysis of several research studies (Lemke, 2008). A picture book or textbook may be considered a multimodal text when the illustrations do not merely support the text, but add their own distinct information, so the reader can see the connectedness between the language and the visuals (Kress & van Leeuwen, 2006).

EXHIBIT 7.20

Questions to guide the viewing process.

What is it you want to know?
Ask yourself questions to determine your purpose for viewing the graphic visual information (e.g., to gain information, to be entertained, to relive past experiences, to understand a topic).

What is the format?
Activate your prior knowledge by considering other visual information you have seen using this format.

What will this visual information mainly be about?
Preview the visual information. Give a quick glance at the information as a whole. Take in key aspects to gain an overall impression.

What is the purpose or main idea of the visual information?
Predict what message the visual information seeks to convey. Formulate this message in a sentence or two.

Where did the visual information come from?
Consider the source of the visual information and its credibility. Also contemplate the content and how this might have impacted the creation of the visual information.

What are the components of the visual information?
Identify the important information of the visual information by focusing on the headings, labels, captions.

What do symbols, colors, or patterns of information mean?
Infer or draw conclusions about meaning based on the information available.

What is the main idea of this visual information?
Synthesize the information you have gathered into a format you can use. Put your interpretation into your own words. Check if this synthesis matches your earlier predictions.

What information might you have missed?
Monitor your comprehension and determine if you need to view the visual information as a whole again.

Adapted from Weaver, M. (1999). *Visual literacy: How to read and use information in graphic form.* New York: Learning Express.

What is this image?

Abigail is enthralled, but with what?

The message behind the message: A need for thinking critically

Images, like spoken and written words, are not neutral. Any idea one person presents to another is the first person's own interpretation. Most adults have developed a set of skills for identifying the message behind the message based on many years of practice. Most young people do not have this same set of skills, yet they are called upon to make decisions every day, such as which cereal to eat, which cell phone has the most features, or who to vote for in the school's mock election. These future adults are being and will be called upon to locate, understand, and use information from multimodal texts.

Critically viewing an image, not to be confused with being critical of an image, involves thinking deeply about what has been included in the image and what may have been left out, and the ramifications of both (Riddle, 2009). For example, view the image in Exhibit 7.21. What does this image appear to be? Although the image provides clues (e.g., wooden, dowel-like) the exact nature of the object is unclear. Knowledge of where this photo was taken (context) what the wooden objects are being used for (purpose), and why a person might have taken this photo (rationale) might be helpful in making a determination of meaning. Keep in mind, an image is merely a snapshot in time or a slice of reality. A viewer must make interpretations. View the image in Exhibit 7.22. Abigail is enthralled with watching something in the classroom. The viewer of this photo can only see Abigail. One might wonder, what has enthralled her? Are the other students equally engaged? How long did Abigail give her undivided attention? Is Abigail learning? Some images seem to raise more questions than they answer. This is the critical nature of viewing.

Don Leu describes the importance of teaching students to be healthy skeptics (1997), especially when viewing websites. Critical consumers are those who ask questions, who do not take information at face value, who wonder about credibility and timeliness, and who compare and contrast information from various sources. In today's world, where vast amounts of information are only a click away, people need to quickly and accurately analyze messages for their meaning by interpreting the influences of popular culture and social and political forces (Hobbs, 2006). You bear the responsibility to help students learn how to apply critical thinking skills to multimedia messages both in and out of school in order to be productive members of society. In other words, "living in an image rich world . . . does not mean students naturally possess sophisticated visual literacy skills, just as continually listening to an iPod does not teach a person to critically analyze or create music" (Felton, 2008, p. 60).

spotlight ON A LITERACY LEADER

SHELLEY HONG XU

Shelley Hong Xu, professor of teacher education at California State University at Long Beach, has focused her research and professional writing on two key areas. One area focuses on developing a better understanding of English language learners as she explores students' in-school and out-of-school literacy practices. The other area focuses on the literacy practices of children and adolescents, emphasizing the reading and viewing of pop culture texts, such as comic strips, graphic novels, television shows, trading cards, and rap music. Xu's interests have merged, leading her to focus on helping teachers reach English language learners more effectively using a variety of motivating print and electronic materials and activities through publications such as *Teaching English language learners: Literacy strategies & resources for K–6* (Guilford, 2010) and *Trading cards to comic strips: Popular culture texts and literacy learning in grades K–8* (Xu & Perkins, 2005).

Locate a copy: www.worldcat.org/title/trading-cards-to-comic-strips-popular-culture-texts-and-literacy-learning-in-grades-k-8/oclc/60589032&referer=brief_results

Viewing and expectations for teachers

The CCSS and the ISTE standards describe what *students* are expected to learn. The National Board for Professional Teaching Standards (NBPTS) describe what *teachers* are expected to teach. In the area of literacy, expert teachers are expected to be skilled viewers who are "able to analyze and interpret a wide variety of visual texts" (NBPTS, 2002, p. 63) in order to describe this process to their students. These effective teachers model critical thinking about what they see. They ask questions and verbalize their thinking process used to understand the message behind the image. They help students understand the link between words and illustrations during a shared reading of a picture book or discuss the key elements on a map during a social studies lesson. These teachers also make an effort to share similar viewing experiences as their students by watching some of the same movies and visiting some of the same websites as their students. Then teachers use these shared viewing experiences as examples during lessons, thus teaching the viewing skills needed both in and out of school.

Teachers who emphasize viewing skills do the following:

- Guide students through comparisons of different texts that present the same idea. A Venn diagram may be used to compare and contrast the video version of *Where the Wild Things Are* with the print version.
- Provide opportunities to view and analyze many different types of visuals, including photos, illustrations, brochures, maps, charts, and works of art as a standard part of the curriculum.
- Point out bias and propaganda in images, advertisements, and videos, beginning at an early age.
- Include assessment, which guides decisions about further instruction. Accomplished teachers "engage in ongoing assessment of students' viewing skills and provide written and oral feedback to students aimed specifically at a student's level of development and degree of skill" (NBPTS, 2002, p. 77).

A teacher's knowledge about viewing and modeling of these skills is crucial to the success of students.

stories FROM THE CLASSROOM

Start the day with viewing

Third-grade teacher Scott Ritter strives to get each morning off to a good start by promoting a positive learning atmosphere and developing his students' viewing skills at the same time. To begin the day, Scott shares a brief PowerPoint presentation he calls Rise and Shine! The slides display written information and visual images focusing on important school news, such as the lunch menu for the week, the day's line leader, and upcoming events and reminders. Scott recognizes the value of presenting information in written form enhanced by images as a way to support those students with limited English skills. He also believes all students are more likely to remember a concept if it can be connected to a picture. Scott spends about seven minutes each morning before school preparing the slide show, and then utilizes about seven minutes presenting the slide show to the students by reading the slides and briefly elaborating as needed. Occasionally, Scott will invite a student to lead the slide show, thus providing the opportunity to develop speaking skills also.

View Scott's Rise and Shine presentation (3:00) to see how this simple activity helps Scott and his students integrate important language arts skills into the busy school day. *(Access this presentation in the digital version of this book.)*

points2ponder

QUICK REVIEW 5 What is meant by the term *visual literacy*?

(Access the answer in the digital version of this book.)

7.8

VISUAL DESIGN

What is it about the way a photograph, website, map, or other graphic text looks that influences the viewing process? A graphic makes sense if one knows what to look for, which makes instruction in viewing skills crucial for preparing students to make sense of what they see. Because visual texts rely on images to carry the meaning, effective visual texts are simple and clear. These texts tend to summarize and highlight key ideas rather than provide extensive explanations, leaving many opportunities for the viewer to fill in the gaps. Keep in mind, an image symbolizes an idea, but is not the real idea itself. Hobbs describes images as a "representation of reality which helps us make sense of our past, present, and future" (2005, p. 9).

Understanding how elements of visual design help create a visual text prepares the viewer to understand the underlying message or to consider a new perspective. Read more about the elements of visual design: www.hhpcommunities.com/teaching languagearts/IL-07-03.pdf.

The term **visual grammar** describes the conventional rules that exist for creating visual images (Kress & van Leeuwen, 2006). For instance, an English cartoon or comic is read from left to right, top to bottom, each panel in sequential order. Manga, a Japanese comic or cartoon, is read from right to left. Both follow the grammar, or rules of the culture, for creating a visual text. Knowing how to interpret and follow these conventions is essential for making meaning. If one tried to read a manga from left to right, the story would not make sense.

One way to emphasize the impact of visual design for students is to focus on the effects of color, which can evoke mood or emotion in a viewer (see Exhibit 7.23). For instance, the color red can represent urgency or importance. Encourage students to look both inside and outside the classroom for examples of the color red being used for this purpose. Knowledge about colors helps the viewer to become more aware of the ways color influences the viewing process and a person's understanding of the message.

Multimedia texts are powerful tools for conveying ideas because of the variety of paths for carrying the same message. Viewers should be aware of the plethora of elements that combine to create and share a message. We have a responsibility to teach our students how to recognize these elements and their influence on what we see. "Children need to be taught how to read, understand and critically evaluate the range of media which they are regularly exposed to or they will not be able to participate effectively in society on either a personal or professional level" (Stafford, 2011, p. 2).

stories FROM THE CLASSROOM

Communication through images

Andrea Keller teaches K–2 students with autism in Irvine, Texas. The students in Andrea's class communicate through pictures, gestures, and limited or no words. Although their speaking abilities may be limited, the students are adept at listening and viewing. Picture symbols, used with communication boards, are available as tools for promoting communication both by Andrea and the students. She creates social stories, or a picture story for communicating what is occurring in the classroom (see Exhibit 7.24). The students in Andrea's class need structure and routine to feel comfortable. When changes are going to occur, Andrea uses pictures and oral explanations to communicate these changes to the students.

🔊 Listen to Andrea as she shares the important role pictures play in communicating with her students (3:46). Consider how this sharing helps Andrea's students to prepare for changes, reduce anxiety, and hopefully head off behavior difficulties before they happen. (*Access this podcast in the digital version of this book.*)

Adjusting viewing across multiple formats: Viewers must be nimble

The process of viewing, similar to the process of reading, calls on the viewer to think about what he knows, extract new ideas while viewing, interpret these ideas, and synthesize these ideas, or make them his own. The skilled viewer must activate this process across various types of multimedia texts (e.g., websites, posters, movies, scrapbooks, billboards). A comic book presents ideas in print, but a similar version of the story may be adapted into a movie, television show, or a website. Texts may be remade into different forms (e.g., a book into a film, a film into a website, a comic into a television show). Although the viewing process is similar across all multimedia formats, the information needed to make sense of the message is unique to each format. In other words, viewers must be nimble, determining their purpose and quickly calling up what they know about visual design elements, text organization, and the topic of the text each time a new multimedia text is encountered. The following sections explore the unique features of various media in order to highlight what viewers should consider before, during, and after the viewing process, along with instructional resources for how to teach with the media.

EXHIBIT 7.23

Color's influence on mood and tone.

COLOR	MEANING
Purple	intelligence, wealth
Blue	restful and calming, truth, dignity
Green	growth, fertility, money
Yellow	happiness, cheerful, attention-getting, especially when combined with red
Orange	warmth, strength of personality
Red	warmth, urgency, passion, power, attention-getting
Black and White	historical, solemn events

EXHIBIT 7.24

A social story.

A symbol expresses an idea without words.

Images

An **image** is a visual representation of an idea, an action, or a story, and may be a photograph, a symbol, or an icon (Stafford, 2011). Because images are used to convey ideas, the viewer's job is to identify and interpret the ideas to construct an individual interpretation of the image (Collins & Blot, 2003) (refer back to Exhibit 7.20 for the process of viewing an image). **Icons** and **symbols** are images that communicate ideas across cultures, thus making the verbal visual (see Exhibit 7.25). The use of light, shadow, distance, and color all contribute to the quality of the image. Some images strive for simplicity or a focus on a single object through a close-up view or framing. Images can be powerful teaching tools because they capture our attention and can communicate ideas with English language learners who may not speak or understand the predominant language of the classroom.

Teaching students to use a systematic approach when viewing complex images can help them learn to identify and interpret ideas in images. Print the guidelines Steps for Viewing an Image (www.hhpcommunities.com/teachinglanguagearts/IL-07-04.pdf), which students can follow.

The National Archives site (www.archives.gov/education/research) provides teachers with primary source images that you can share with students and incorporate into lessons. The site presents an Image of the Day, which may include original drawings (such as a drawing of the ship USS *Constitution*), documents, and letters (such a letter from Elvis to President Nixon).

The following are additional activities for teaching students how to view images (in this case, photographs).

Zoom in. A first glance at a photograph gives the viewer a general impression, but zooming in on the details can reveal additional layers of meaning. You can integrate history and viewing for older elementary students by zooming in on historical photographs. Navigate to the website Picturing the Century: One Hundred Years of Photographs (www.archives.gov/exhibits/picturing_the_century/galleries/galleries.html) from the National Archives. Choose an era in U. S. history, possibly one connected to a unit of study in social studies or the setting of a work of literature being read in the classroom. Explain the three-step viewing process of glance, zoom in, and make inferences for viewing photographs. Model this process with one or two photographs in the chosen collection. Think aloud about what you notice at a glance. Then use your pretend binoculars to zoom in and describe the details you notice. Next, share the inferences you make from these details (e.g., coats and hats would indicate winter, bare feet in winter might indicate poverty). Then invite students to share their ideas from each of the three steps of the viewing process for this activity. Discuss these ideas at each step, pointing out the way each viewer calls to mind his prior knowledge in making inferences.

Photo analysis worksheet. For independent practice, choose a set of photos from the Picturing the Century (www.archives.gov/exhibits/picturing_the_century/galleries/galleries.html) website that are new to the students. Working in pairs, have students use the Photo Analysis Worksheet (www.archives.gov/education/lessons/worksheets/photo_analysis_worksheet.pdf) as a guide to record their observations as they follow the three-step viewing process. The combination of the photographs and the details that emerge from the structured viewing conversations will provide a wealth of vocabulary for English language learners and other students who may have few prior experiences with historical time periods.

Illustrations

Illustrations are renderings in the form of drawings, paintings, or other art forms that are created for portraying or explaining text. They convey messages without words and can serve as a catalyst for the development of words (Gambrell & Sokolski, 1983). Whether naming the ocean, describing its color or sound, or sharing an experience of finding shells along the beach, illustrations can stimulate students' oral language development. A close study of an illustration considers color, shapes, lines, and shading, and gives the viewer insight into the illustrator's style (refer back to Exhibit 7.20 for the process of viewing an illustration). The illustrator's combination of these artistic elements creates her unique style and is the foundation of the illustration's message. Examining the illustrator's style may give a viewer insight into the message the illustrator seeks to convey (Williams, 2007). You can guide students to construct a personal and creative interpretation of an illustration through modeling. Think aloud and ask yourself questions about what the details of the artistic elements might mean, and how they might be connected. Point out to students the uniqueness of each person's perspective. You may also wish to teach students to follow the Steps for Viewing an Illustration (www.hhpcommunities.com/teachinglanguagearts/IL-07-05.pdf).

Illustrations in high-quality, modern picture books present ideas by enhancing or replacing written words (Kress, 2003), and can truly be works of art. Outstanding illustrations are recognized annually by the Caldecott Medal, "awarded to the artist of the most distinguished American Picture Book for Children published in the United States during the preceding year" (Association for Library Service to Children, 2012).

Visit the Caldecott website (www.ala.org/alsc/awardsgrants/bookmedia/caldecottmedal/caldecottmedal) and read the descriptions about the Caldecott Award books for the current year. Look for past winning titles that are familiar to you. Notice the use of artistic elements in the descriptions of these award winners.

The following are additional activities for teaching students how to view illustrations.

Take a closer look. Gather a collection of 10 to 15 wordless or almost wordless picture books with detailed illustrations (see Exhibit 7.26 for sample titles). Organize the students into pairs and have them take a picture walk through the book, quickly glancing at the illustrations. Have them discuss the gist of the story with their partners. Then have the students reread the picture book, taking a close, careful look at each illustration. Have the partners take turns with each page, identifying at least one detail they did not notice the first time. Emphasize the importance of a slow, careful viewing of the illustrations, as students may want to hurry through the text, assuming they noticed all the details on the first read. After rereading, the partners should discuss

EXHIBIT 7.26

Examples of wordless picture books for Take a Closer Look activity.

- Books by Emily Arnold McCully, including

  First Snow

  Picnic

  School

- *A Ball for Daisy* by Chris Raschka

- *Flotsam* by David Wiesner

- *Korgi* by Christian Slade

- *A Boy, A Dog, and A Frog* by Mercer Maye

- *Time Flies* by Eric Rohmann

the story again, adding depth to their descriptions. Next, ask one pair of partners to join another and to give a retelling of their story, displaying only the cover of the picture book. To conclude the activity, emphasize to students the importance of taking a closer look at the illustrations when reading other books, explaining the power illustrations have in telling the story.

Comics, cartoons, and graphic texts

Reading and viewing merge in the form of graphic texts, which include comics, cartoons, graphic picture books, and graphic novels. In a picture book, illustrations enhance the text. In a graphic book, illustrations are the text, and the use of written words is limited to single words, phrases, or brief sentences. Panels or boxes are used to denote a scene or an event; speech bubbles indicate spoken words, whispers, or thoughts.

Learn more terms for graphic elements in cartoons, comics, and graphic texts: www.hhpcommunities.com/teachinglanguagearts/IL-07-06.pdf

Graphic novels refer to a comic-book-style text bound in a durable book format, rather than the magazine format of a typical comic book. Graphic texts encompass various genres, including fiction, fantasy, mystery, biography, informational, and adventure. Because graphic texts contain limited words and many illustrations, many adults consider these to be simplistic texts, containing little substance for interpretation and having little, if any, educational value. However, a closer look at graphic texts reveals that deeper thought is often needed to understand what on the surface appears to be light reading. Recognition of their substance has brought these texts to the forefront of popular literature for readers of all ages, and because of their reliance on graphics and limited use of words, graphic texts are a useful source for teaching students about visual literacy.

Access a list of graphic books: www.hhpcommunities.com/teachinglanguage arts/IL-07-07.pdf

BOOK REVIEW

Understanding Comics: The Invisible Art
BY SCOTT MCCLOUD

When my son saw me reading this book, he looked closely at the title and asked, "How hard can it be to understand comics?" I had to admit, I started off thinking the same thing, but author Scott McCloud takes readers into a behind-the-scenes view of comics with unanticipated depth. Written in comic-book style, *Understanding Comics* gives a historic background of comics, describes their artistic elements, and explains influences of Japanese comics. The graphic style may lead readers to underestimate the content of this book, which is a critical examination of what is considered by some to be a fun, frivolous phenomenon. I was particularly fascinated by the chapter "Blood in the Gutter," which explains the process of reading a comic and the way our mind fills in the gaps, or brings closure, between the panels on a page. This description reminded me of the comprehension strategy of inferencing, in which the reader brings together what is known from the text and from his own experiences to read between the lines. Through this, and several other vivid explanations in the book, I came to realize the depth of thinking required to understand comics. I shared my new respect for these seemingly simple visual texts with my son, and possibly inspired him to look at comics in a new way, too.

Locate a copy: www.worldcat.org/title/understanding-comics-the-invisible-art/oclc/30351626

Making sense of graphic texts requires the ability to mentally follow two parallel tracks, drawing clues from the limited number of words and the small illustrations in order to fill in the gaps left by what is not written or drawn. This double reading, or multitasking, demands that the reader build connections between the layers of words and images (Heath & Bhagat, 2005). Each panel illustration represents a related moment in the story, and between each panel lies the *gutter,* or empty space. Using details from the story, the viewer must use her imagination to fill in this empty space. Doing so requires the viewer to read between the lines or make a series of inferences to mentally connect the panels into a cohesive story. In addition, in order to follow the sequence of dialogue, actions, and emotions, the viewer must tap into his own mental store of experiences or activate his prior knowledge, drawing from what he knows about other comics and his own life experiences. The viewing process for graphic texts, like the texts themselves, is not simplistic and requires active viewing because the format (e.g., placement of bubbles or layout of panels) may be unpredictable from one page to the next (Weiner, 2002).

View a sample of the graphic novel *Sailor Twain or The Mermaid in the Hudson* by Mark Siegel (http://sailortwain.com/blog/2010/01/15/sailortwain-001). Click through the pages and notice the variation of layout and word placement with each new page you encounter. Think how knowledge of riverboat life and the time period would be helpful in understanding this story. Consider the challenges this graphic text might pose for struggling readers, but also the motivation it may provide to reluctant readers.

Print the Guidelines for Viewing a Graphic Text (www.hhpcommunities.com/teachinglanguagearts/IL-07-08.pdf) and use them to help view *Sailor Twain.* Consider how this form helped you and could help your students in understanding the complexities of a graphic text.

Recognition of the literary value of comics and other graphic texts is growing, and the motivational influence of these texts has long been noticed by teachers and librarians. Graphic texts are powerful tools for bringing unmotivated readers into the reading circle. Their seemingly easy format often hooks even the most reluctant reader. The strong connection between illustrations and written words makes these texts a useful choice for English language learners, who can use the picture clues to aid with developing new vocabulary.

Following are additional activities for teaching students how to view graphic novels/comics.

Reading between the gutters. With limited space and words, a comic relies heavily on the illustrations to tell the story. The combination of the comic panels, prior life experiences, and knowledge of the comics genre blend together to help the viewer fill in the gaps created by the gutters. To practice inferencing, first, locate various comics to use for the lesson. The newspaper, comic books, comic collections, and online resources such as 155 Places for Free Comic Books and Graphic Novels Online (www.tech supportalert.com/free-books-comics) are all possible sources. Select a sample comic and model your interpretation of the comic, thinking aloud about the process used to make the mental leap from one panel to the next. Point out the kinds of prior experiences you used to help formulate your inferences. Possible sentence stems include:

- "I know _____, so that is why I think _____ is happening."
- "I am guessing _____ is happening because _____ happened previously."
- "I wonder why _____ happened. I think it is because of _____."
- The _____ and the _____ in this panel are clues to tell me that _____ is about to happen."

Next, give pairs of students a comic strip copied onto a piece of paper. As the pairs read the comic, ask them to pause between each panel and write a gutter statement in the margin, drawing an arrow to indicate where the statement fits in the panel sequence. Encourage students to use one of the above sentence stems during the think-aloud. Then have two pairs join together to form a group of four and share their comics and inferences with each other.

Moving images: Film and television

Film and television take learning beyond the textbook into a place where sound and images merge to tell a story or to share information. The action and drama of film and television inspires a natural curiosity among viewers and breaks down barriers to learning by presenting ideas in a visual way. The term *film,* which once referred to the reel-to-reel film played on a projector, is now used to describe a full-length movie viewed in a theater, on a computer or television, or on a mobile device.

The compelling nature of film rests in its ability to foster intense emotional responses (Cantor, 1991) and mimic human interactions (Baines, 2005) through the vivid portrayal of people's lives and experiences. What we see in a movie or video clip is not only entertaining or informative, but it also can change our thinking or influence our beliefs. The movie *Schindler's List* (1993), for example, has shaped the attitudes of many toward the treatment of Jews in Nazi Germany and has likely been a catalyst for the creation of books, discussions, and museum exhibits focusing on the Holocaust.

Television gives viewers the opportunity to practice processing information and thus may produce a spiral effect by relying on previous viewing experiences to enhance a learner's capability to acquire new information (Neuman, 2005). Yet, what young people learn from television shows and how skillfully they do so depends on the viewing tools taught in the environment where the viewing occurs, whether at home or school. Because viewing is such an integral part of the way people gain information, teachers have a responsibility to prepare students to be effective viewers. "Television has the potential to extend learning and literacy well beyond the classroom walls. It requires, however, the guidance and supervision of parents and the skills and vision of educators building linkages between home and school learning" (Neuman, 2005, p. 20). Since television is more immediate than film and offers shorter segments, it can be a useful teaching tool that benefits adults and young people. The History Channel, the Discovery Channel, and Food Network are examples of television networks that focus on educating people of various ages. Short films are also available on the Internet in the form of web series. Like traditional television series, these online counterparts are divided into short episodes, usually around ten minutes each.

Explicit instruction in the viewing process entails teaching students to be critical viewers, by "learning to analyze and question what is on the screen, how it is constructed and what may have been left out" (Thoman, 1999, p. 133). The proper use of film or television in the classroom must be directly linked to the learning outcomes or curricular standards that match the lesson, rather than as a time filler or reward for good behavior. This expectation is set by the Copyright and Fair Use Law for the United States.

For specific information about copyright issues related to the use of video and television in the classroom see the Copyright and Fair Use Guidelines for Teachers (www6.district125.k12.il.us/staffdev/copyright_chart.pdf). Consider how this expectation for video use may be different from the experiences you had as a student in school. Identify two or three changes in our culture that might account for these differences.

Following are additional activities for teaching students how to view film and television.

Video viewing guide. Students of all ages are usually thrilled when a teacher shows a video in class because they often see it as a time to kick back and take a break from *real* learning. Although videos can be a fun and interesting way to learn, you can also make the occasion as productive and structured as possible by giving students a viewing guide. First explain the viewing guide, then model it, and then have the class practice it together. While modeling, think aloud when activating prior knowledge or when synthesizing information from a segment of a video. Pause before, during, and after viewing to give students time to formulate their thoughts and record these on the guide. After viewing, discuss the key points students identified on the guide and point out and appreciate varied interpretations. Once students have experience with the guided viewing procedure, have them complete the guide independently and use it as an informal assessment of their viewing skills. (Print a blank video viewing guide: www.hhpcommunities. com/teachinglanguagearts/IL-07-09.pdf.)

Fantastic fantasy. As a class, brainstorm a list of fantasy elements: talking animals or objects, magic, magicians, dragons and monsters, people with supernatural powers, medieval settings. Show a brief film clip (five to seven minutes or so) that contains several of these elements. Clips could be from *The Lion, the Witch, and the Wardrobe; Beauty and the Beast;* or *Harry Pot-*

ter. Have students record what they see for each category generated by the list, then discuss these elements as a class. Encourage students to form connections between elements and even between films. Through this discussion, lead students toward a stronger understanding of fantasy as a genre.

Extensions: This activity can also be done with comic books and other genres. Follow the same process of brainstorming, searching, and describing. Other genres and film clips might include the following:

Fantasy: *The Lord of the Rings; Tale of Despereaux; The Chronicles of Narnia*

Action/Adventure: *Up; The Spiderwick Chronicles; Toy Story; Jumanji; Hugo*

Comedy: *Monsters, Inc.; Scooby-Doo*

Science Fiction: *Wall-E; Fantastic Four; Star Wars Episode 1: The Phantom Menace.*

Graphic displays: Charts, graphs, maps

Graphic displays of information streamline data into an easily interpreted visual format. The use of color, lines, arrows, headings, and labels promotes clarity. Look for these elements, which provide clues to important information, during an initial viewing. Each form of graphic display presents information in a unique way, requiring the viewer to apply a slightly different set of viewing skills.

Graphic Display Formats (www.hhpcommunities.com/teachinglanguagearts/ IL-07-10.pdf) lists various formats for graphic displays and specific qualities of each, and provides links to online examples.

A process for viewing such varied texts necessitates flexibility and an eye for key words and phrases, in the form of labels or headings, that guide the viewer to the most important information. A whole-to-part process of viewing suggests the viewer first scan the graphic display to gain the big picture, then return for a closer look at the details (return to Exhibit 7.20 for the process of viewing a graphic display).

An infographic, introduced previously in this chapter, presents complex information quickly and clearly by incorporating several formats of graphic displays into one. Essentially, an infographic is a collection of graphic displays around a specific topic, requiring a viewer to apply what he knows about various forms of graphic displays to interpret the data. For example, the infographic Technology Use by 11/12 Year Old Boys is part of a teacher's blog entry titled Infographics at School (http://edtechtoolbox.blogspot.com/2011/05/infographics-at-school.html). It was created by students and Greg Swanson, a visual arts teacher in Australia.

Identify the various graphic elements used within this infographic. You may have noticed the use of pie graphs, a bar graph, icons, headings, and color to organize and display information. Use Steps for Viewing a Graphic Visual Display (www.hhpcommunities.com/teachinglanguagearts/IL-07-11.pdf) for help in reading and interpreting this graphic.

The Infographic of Infographics: How Infographics Are Made: http://thenextweb. com/dd/2011/04/06/the-infographic-of-infographics-how-infographics-are-made. An infographic displays many bits of information in an organized and visual way. View the infographic at this URL to learn how they use color, style, font, and other key elements to convey information. Then search the Internet for an infographic about a topic of interest to you. Go to your favorite image browser (e.g., Google Images). In the search box type in *infographic* + your topic of interest. For example, we tried *infographic* + *ice cream* and *infographic* + *shoes* and found lots of interesting and informative results. On the infographic you locate, notice the stylistic elements that are used to draw your attention to information or to connect or separate ideas. Think about the information students will need in order to interpret an infographic and the ways an infographic could be used by students, such as a resource for a research paper or a model for creating an infographic using class-collected data.

Following are additional activities for teaching students how to view graphic displays.

Geocaching. Described as a high-tech treasure hunt, this is an outdoor activity where students use a global positioning system (GPS) device to locate objects. Geocaching is a popular activity worldwide, with caches—boxes of trinkets—hidden in out-of-the-way places. Geocaching provides opportunities for viewers to use digital map graphic display skills to participate in a hunt for real objects left by previous geocachers. According to the website Geocaching, there are over 1 million active geocaches and 5 million geocachers worldwide. Users can try out a geocache created by others or design one of their own.

For more information or to find a geocache near you, visit the Geocaching website (www.geocaching.com).

In a school environment, traveling from site to site may not be possible, but simple geocaching activities can be designed for the school grounds. The video Lost and Found (3:04, http://blog.geocaching.com/207/08/geocaching-class-geo-caching-coms-lost-found-video) explains how a library media specialist in Texas creates geocaches for elementary school students to follow. Each cache contains a science question or an activity to complete, integrating science, mathematics, and language arts.

Simple geocaching/Educaching activities are available for younger and intermediate students. Visit the Educaching website (http://educaching. com/) for samples of hands-on, real world practice with manipulating angles and types of triangles, while also utilizing the mapping coordinates from a GPS. The Educaching Teacher's Manual (http://educaching.com/educaching_manual.html) includes links to sample activities.

Websites

A website utilizes a plethora of ways to present information (e.g., words, images, illustrations, video, sound, graphics, icons). With so many ways

Example of a bread crumb trail showing a viewer's path through a website.

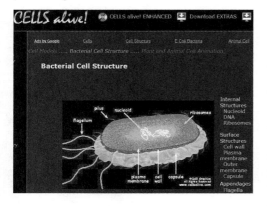

Viewing a website.

VIEWING A WEBSITE

1. **Set your purpose:** Ask yourself, "What is my guiding question? What is the information I hope to locate and understand from this website?"

2. **Activate your prior knowledge:** Consider what you know about the topic. Call to mind knowledge about websites, hyperlinks, scrolling, icons, and other elements of web literacy.

3. **Preview:** Scan the website to determine the topic and layout. Determine the credibility of the website host and the currency of the information.

4. **Closer look:** Take a longer, more focused look at the website. Read the headings, subheadings, captions, labels, and icons. Notice the connections between the words and the images.

5. **Focus your thinking:** Look for specific information related to your guiding question. Explore links within the website to seek further information. Reread to clarify.

6. **Synthesize:** Put your interpretation of the website into your own words. Use this information to answer your initial question.

to access information literally at our fingertips, the relationship between people and knowledge shifts. The individual becomes the center of knowledge (Kress, 2003) when she decides what it is she wants to know and uses the Internet to find this information. Each click on a webpage represents a thoughtful, albeit often quick, choice of what to read next as each individual literally constructs a personalized path through the text. "We see the act of deciding which path to follow on the Internet as very tightly woven within a complex process of reading and meaning making. . . . It is not simply about how quickly students can move through this online world, but more about how they decide which information is most accurate, relevant, appropriate, and useful for their purposes" (Leu, Leu, & Coiro, 2004, p. 37).

The experience of being an active meaning maker and constructing one's own path through Internet texts provides the viewer with a unique set of challenges. First, keep in mind that websites are designed to inform, persuade, and entertain, but may not be designed to meet the viewing needs of children (Kafai & Bates, 1997). The sheer volume and types of information encountered by the viewer can lead to cognitive overload, giving the brain too much information to handle at once. Scanning a website for relevancy before becoming engrossed in a careful viewing can keep a reader from getting bogged down with unnecessary information. Moreover, the constant clicks and movement through the website can leave the viewer feeling lost. A *bread crumb trail,* or a display of most recently visited links within the website, can be a helpful reminder of one's path. Exhibit 7.27 provides an example of a bread crumb trail created by a viewer when visiting the CELLS alive! website. Arriving at the CELLS alive! website, first the viewer clicks on the link for cell models on the left-hand column. A bread crumb trail then appears horizontally near the top of the page showing a logical path. The user can then click on the next link in the path for bacterial cell structure. Then, to complete the path she can click on the next link for plant and animal cell animation. Thus, the viewer sees the trail that got her to that point on the website and can easily backtrack if necessary.

Young Internet users may not know about viewing strategies such as scanning or using the bread crumb trail, even though they may have already logged many hours on the Internet. You must explain, model, and guide students through these viewing processes. "Not teaching students to be savvy Internet users leaves them to navigate the information superhighway without a map, a tank of gas, and a spare in the trunk" (Kajder, 2003, p. 49). See Exhibit 7.28 for the process of viewing a website.

Print the guidelines for Viewing a Website (www.hhpcommunities.com/teaching languagearts/IL-07-12.pdf) and use them to examine the International Reading Association (www.reading.org) website. Consider how the guide helps you and could help your students in understanding the complexities of viewing a website.

Teaching students how to view a website does not require you to start from scratch. The skills needed to make meaning from a website are built upon the skills students are already developing for comprehending print text (Coiro, 2011). Activating prior knowledge, identifying important ideas, and asking questions are all important strategies in viewing a website as well as text. However, researchers are beginning to understand that the process of Internet comprehension is both similar *and* more complex than the process of informational print text comprehension (Afflerbach & Cho, 2008; Coiro

& Dobler, 2007; Hartman, Morsink, & Zheng, 2010; see also Chapter 6). The process for viewing a website includes locating, evaluating, synthesizing, and then remembering and communicating the information. In addition, viewers must be aware of hidden—and not so hidden—social, economic, and political biases that make critical evaluation skills an integral part of understanding a website's message.

Following are additional activities for teaching students how to view websites.

WWWDOT framework. This framework (Zhang & Duke, 2011) provides an instructional approach for teaching students the critical evaluation skills needed to effectively view a website (see Exhibit 7.29). The process is divided into a series of six questions a web viewer asks in order to determine if a website is credible and useful for answering a given question. Through a gradual release of responsibility, you can first explain, model, then guide students to answer these questions about your teacher-chosen websites. Making decisions about the quality of a website takes lots of practice. At first, students may be accepting of all information on the Internet. Remember the concept of the *healthy skeptic* mentioned previously in this chapter? The WWWDOT activity is a real world application of this critical thinking.

Reader friendliness checklist. This checklist (see Exhibit 7.30) allows viewers to evaluate a website by determining if the layout or organization of the site is considerate of viewers' needs. The checklist guides viewers to consider elements such as a welcome message, the use of blank space, and the amount of clutter, all of which can help or hinder a viewer. Examples of sites that are appropriate for young people include How Stuff Works (www.howstuffworks.com), Dogo News (www.dogonews.com), National Geographic for Kids (http://kids.nationalgeographic.com/kids), and Sports Illustrated for Kids (www.sikids.com).

points2ponder

QUICK REVIEW 6 What is meant by the term *multimodal text*? Why is it important for viewers to be nimble when viewing such a text?

How does an infographic promote viewing skills?

(Access the answers in the digital version of this book.)

EXHIBIT 7.29

WWWDOT framework.

Zhang, S., & Duke, N. K. (2011). The impact of instruction on the WWWDOT framework on students' disposition and ability to evaluate websites as sources of information. *Elementary School Journal, 112*(1), 132–154. Reprinted with permission from University of Chicago Press.

EXHIBIT 7.30

Reader friendliness checklist.

Eagleton, M. & Dobler, E. (2007). *Reading the web: Strategies for Internet inquiry.* New York: Guilford. Reprinted with permission.

(Print a blank copy: www.hhpcommunities.com/teachinglanguagearts/IL-07-13.pdf)

7.9

WHAT ABOUT VIDEO GAMES AS A TOOL FOR TEACHING VIEWING?

James Paul Gee, professor of literacy studies at Arizona State University, is a proponent of video games and education: "When we think of games, we think of fun. When we think of learning we think of work. Games show us this is wrong. They trigger deep learning that is itself part and parcel of fun" (2007, p. 43).

The topic of video games as viable teaching tools may be met with bewilderment, doubt, and even disdain. Non-gamers often consider video games a waste of time and money, as well as the cause for stunted social skills. These skeptics are hard-pressed to explain the popularity of the gaming phenomenon. In the United States, 153 million people consider themselves active

EXHIBIT 7.31

Learning preferences of digital natives.

LEARNING PREFERENCES OF DIGITAL NATIVES

- Having instant access to information
- Receiving a reward for successfully accomplishing a task
- Taking personal responsibility within a collaborative setting, whether in person or virtually
- Gaining information from a variety of sources in a nonlinear order (e.g., prefer images before text)
- Having access to a networked support system for seeking ideas and sharing experiences
- Playing games rather than doing serious work

gamers, playing for 13 or more hours a week. This number skyrockets to 484 million worldwide and includes people of all professions and ages. The gaming industry is worth $15 billion. In her book *Reality Is Broken: Why Games Make Us Better and How They Can Change the World,* author Jane McGonigal describes the mass exodus from reality brought about by the popularity of video games, and believes the impact to society can no longer be ignored. Video games provide gamers with a chance to feel the heart-expanding thrill of success, the devastation of loss, and the opportunity to control their destiny, all within the confines of a virtual world. Could it be possible that what gamers learn from these experiences prepares them for other aspects of their lives? How might these lessons impact the teaching of the language arts and especially viewing?

Some educators believe the impact of technology in general has brought about a climate ripe for the emergence of alternatives to traditional teaching and learning. The term *digital native* (Prensky, 2001) describes learners who have grown up only knowing the affordances of technology. These students cannot remember a world without the Internet, cell phones, and fast computers. Instant access to information is the norm, and learning occurs best in the midst of several tasks, which may include listening to music, texting, and playing video games. Their brains have been wired for multitasking and receiving information in nonlinear ways and multimedia modes (Prensky, 2001). Exhibit 7.31 displays the learning preferences of digital natives. When one notices the connections between these preferences and video gaming, it becomes clear video games are not just for fun.

According to Prensky (2001), "Today's students think and process information fundamentally differently from their predecessors" (p. 1). As natives of the technology world, these students speak the language of Internet reading, video gaming, and digital communication. *Digital immigrants,* on the other hand, have adapted from their native world of snail mail and paper trails to the new world of email and the paperless society. These immigrants often still speak of printing off an email or developing prints of photographs. Many of us actually fall along a continuum between the native and the immigrant, depending on the technology and our purpose for using it. Digital immigrants often do not understand the digital natives' need for constant electronic tethering to friends and information. They see texting, tweeting, and video gaming as a waste of time.

Video games are presented in this section on viewing because viewing skills are at the center of gaming. Game information, threats, journeys, action, and the rewards of video gaming are experienced largely through the images of the game. A player must notice visual details within a barrage of sensory information, simultaneously watching, moving, and communicating with other players. A player is constantly taking in information from the screen and making decisions that impact his or her success within the game.

What can educators learn from video gaming that will help us reach and stimulate learning among digital natives? Teacher Mike Acedo writes on the blog Te@ch Thought about gamifying his classroom. His thought-provoking descriptions may inspire you to explore the idea of interjecting video game elements into the curriculum. Read his blog entry entitled How to Gamify Your Classroom (www.teachthought.com/teaching/how-to-gamify-your-classroom).

This discussion is not meant to imply that video games should become a standard part of the curriculum or should replace high-quality human instruction. Rather, consider the possibility that the positive aspects of video games could be applied to the curriculum in order to facilitate and promote learning engagement. James Paul Gee, who was quoted earlier and is a leader in the field of video games and education, believes many principles of good learning are built into video games (2007). After all, video game creators must entice people to play long, complex, and challenging games.

Read a summary of the good principles of learning built into good video games: www.hhpcommunities.com/teachinglanguagearts/IL-07-14.pdf

If learning looked more like video games, it would be fast-paced rather than slow-paced, parallel rather than linear, and require multitasking rather than following step-by-step processes. Learners would merge several modes of language arts into a learning game, such as reading game hints, chatting online with players, or speaking and listening to others in an alliance. Learning would be stimulating, challenging, engaging, and fun at the same time. Learners would experience what video players know—that "the best moments usually occur when a person's body or mind is stretched to its limits in a voluntary effort to accomplish something difficult and worthwhile" (Csikszentmihalyi, 1990, p. 3).

Video games combine the best of both worlds, fun and learning. Watch the interview Big Thinkers, An Interview with James Paul Gee (11:50, www.edutopia.org/james-gee-classroom-simulations) to hear more of his thoughts about the educational power of video games. Consider your own experiences with video games and your openness to the idea of incorporating video gaming principles into your teaching.

7.10

ASSESSING VIEWING

Viewing, whether a person is playing a video game or looking at a photograph, involves the process of receiving information. When it comes to assessment, we as teachers want to know, does the student understand what is being viewed? This can be a tricky question to answer as many viewing experiences involve multimedia, by mixing music, images, text, and speaking. In the viewing mode, an individual is hit with lots of information at the same time. Making sense of this information entails a process of understanding, and assessing that process is quite challenging. The Video Viewing Guide (www.hhpcommunities.com/teachinglanguagearts/IL-07-09.pdf) included earlier in the chapter can be used as an informal assessment tool that emphasizes checking students' understanding along the way, by pausing the viewing process to give students an opportunity to briefly summarize their understanding. Using an assessment tool such as this checklist, and giving it to students prior to viewing, sends a clear message that viewing is an important and useful skill and that activities such as watching a video in class are important learning activities, not merely a time for popcorn and relaxing.

7.11

CHAPTER SUMMARY

Listening is an integral part of our everyday life. Effective listeners can benefit from stronger relationships with friends and family, make more informed decisions, and take pleasure in enjoying the sounds of the environment. In the past, teaching listening skills has been left to chance or ignored, based on the assumption these skills were learned before coming to school. We now know that listening skills can be improved when taught in school and listening comprehension is closely linked to reading comprehension. Teaching students to identify their purpose for listening will help them identify skills needed in varying listening situations. A listening curriculum should center around opportunities to practice listening for different purposes and can be easily implemented when reading aloud age-appropriate literature. Through the sharing of information and an increased value of listening skills, we can establish listening as an important area of language arts.

Viewing is a complex process, which gives credence to the statement "there is more than meets the eye." Hidden values and facts lie beneath the surface of visual information, and it is each viewer's job to sift through background knowledge, cultural influences, and personal biases to make meaning when viewing. For our students, the ability to work through this process (see Exhibit 7.32) can be enhanced by quality instruction from a teacher who is aware of her own processes for viewing.

Listening and viewing, although considered separately in this chapter, often work in tandem. Their simultaneous activation gives a person more than one opportunity to make meaning. Understanding the behind-the-scenes decisions that go into creating podcast, a video clip, or a show-and-tell is a bit like peeking behind a stage curtain. This background knowledge gives the listener and viewer extra information that can enhance meaning and result in more effective communication.

EXHIBIT 7.32

Thinking deeply while viewing an image.

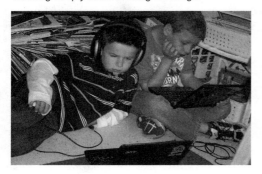

APPLICATION ACTIVITIES

APPLICATION ACTIVITIES

think like a teacher

Digital Native or Digital Immigrant?

Are you a digital native or a digital immigrant? Toward which perspective will your teaching lean? Read Marc Prensky's article "Digital Natives, Digital Immigrants" (6 pp., http://www.marcprensky.com/writing/Prensky%20-%20Digital%20Natives,%20Digital%20Immigrants%20-%20Part1.pdf). Decide where you fit on the digital spectrum, both as a learner and as a future teacher. Then complete one of these statements:

I am a digital native because I . . .

I am a digital immigrant because I . . .

Where Are We Headed?

Watch the video Big Thinkers, an Interview with James Paul Gee (www.edutopia.org/james-gee-video) and read the blog entry How to Gamify Your Classroom (www.teachthought.com/teaching/how-to-gamify-your-classroom)

about gamifying your classroom. Search online for other resources about gaming and education. Discuss the possibilities for a future in education that incorporates some of the positive aspects of video games. Brainstorm a list of pros and cons for incorporating characteristics of video games into the classroom.

What's In an Adaptation?

First, work in teams to choose and locate two sources of the same story, or material, in different formats in order to compare them. Suggestions include the following:

> **Picture book and movie:** *Where the Wild Things Are* by Maurice Sendak; *The Snowman* by Raymond Briggs; *How the Grinch Stole Christmas* by Dr. Seuss; and *Horton Hears a Who* by Dr. Seuss
>
> **Picture book and website:** *The Man in the Moon* by William Joyce, http://theguardiansofchildhoodbooks.com/mim.php
>
> **Comic book and movie or website:** *Tin Tin* by Georges Remi, http://www.tintin.com

Next, in your group discuss responses to the following prompts:

1. Your opinion about the quality of the original.
2. Your opinion about the quality of the adaptation.

Discuss elements such as illustrations, graphics, tone, and appeal of the story. Next, decide on your favorite version of the story and explain why. Then conduct a class poll of your favorite version and create a graph of the results. Finally, consider the following points about adaptations:

- Adaptation taps into the highly personal way we experience texts.
- We are already adapting when we create our own visualizations and interpretations.
- An adaptation is one person's mental processes made real.
- If your adaptation agrees with the creator, then your visualizations and interpretations are validated.
- Because it is one person's experience with a text, an adaptation is neither right nor wrong, although it may bear little resemblance to your adaptation.
- Teachers must help students move away from the idea that adaptations are only good if they follow the text directly.

REFERENCES

Afflerbach, P., & Cho, B. Y. (2008). Identifying and describing constructively responsive comprehension strategies in new and traditional forms of reading. In S. Israel & G. Duffy (Eds.), *Handbook of reading comprehension research* (pp. 69–90). Mahwah, NJ: Erlbaum.

Alvermann, D. E., Hagood, M. C., & Moon, J. S. (1999). *Popular culture in the classroom: Teaching and researching critical media literacy.* New York: Routledge.

Association for Library Service to Children. (2011). *The Randolph Caldecott Medal.* http://www.ala.org/alsc/awardsgrants/bookmedia/caldecottmedal/aboutcaldecott/aboutcaldecott

Badian, N. A. (1999). Reading disability defined as a discrepancy between listening and reading comprehension. *Journal of Learning Disabilities, 32,* 138–148.

Baines, L. (2005). Film, video, and books: Some considerations for learning and teaching. In J. Flood, S. B. Heath, & D. Lapp (Eds.), *Handbook of research on teaching literacy through the communicative and visual arts* (pp. 545–557). Mahwah, NJ: Lawrence Erlbaum.

Beall, M. L., Gill-Rossier, J., Tate, J., & Matten, A. (2008). State of the context: Listening in education. *International Journal of Listening, 22*(2), 123–132.

Berninger, V. W. (2000). Development of language by hand and its connections with language by ear, mouth, and eye. *Topics in Language Disorders, 20*(4), 65–84.

Burmark, L. (2002). *Visual literacy: Learn to see, see to learn.* Alexandria, VA: Association of Supervision and Curriculum Development.

Cantor, J. (1991). Fright responses to mass media productions. In J. Bryant & D. Zillman (Eds.), *Responding to the screen: Reception and reaction processes* (pp. 169–197). Hillsdale, NJ: Lawrence Erlbaum.

CCSS Initiative. (2012). *Common core state standards for English language arts & literacy in history/social studies, science, and technical subjects.* http://corestandards.org/assets/CCSSI_ELA%20Standards.pdf

Clark, R. C., & Lyons, C. (2011). *Graphics for learning: Proven guidelines for planning, designing, and evaluating visuals in training materials.* San Francisco: Pfeiffer.

Coiro, J. (2011). Predicting reading comprehension on the Internet: Contributions of offline reading skills, online reading skills, and prior knowledge. *Journal of Literacy Research, 43*(4), 352–392.

Coiro, J., & Dobler, E. (2007). Exploring comprehension strategies used by sixth-grade skilled readers as they search for and locate information on the Internet. *Reading Research Quarterly, 42*(2), 214–257.

Collins, J., & Blot, R. K. (2003). *Literacy and literacies: Texts, power, and identity.* New York: Cambridge University Press.

Cowie, H. (2011). Peer supporters as an interaction to counteract school bullying: Listening to the children. *Children & Society, 25*(4), 287–292.

Csikszentmihalyi, M. (1990). *Flow: The psychology of optimal experience.* New York: Harper & Row.

Devine, T. G. (1978). Listening: What do we know after fifty years of research and theorizing? *Journal of Reading, 21,* 296–304.

Dickinson, D., McCabe, A., & Sprague, K. (2003). Teacher rating of oral language and literacy (TROLL): Individualizing early literacy instruction with standards-based rating tool. *Reading Teacher, 56,* 554–564.

Eagleton, M., & Dobler, E. (2007). *Reading the web: Strategies for Internet inquiry.* New York: Guilford.

Emmert, P. (1996). President's perspective. *International Listening Association: Listening Post,* Spring (56), 2–3.

Felton, P. (2008). Resource review. *Change, 40*(6), 60–63.

Galvin, K. (1997). *Listening by doing.* Lincolnwood, IL: National Textbook Company.

Gambrell, L., & Sokolski, C. (1983). Picture potency: Use Caldecott Award books to develop children's language. *Reading Teacher, 36*(9), 868–871.

Garman, C. G., & Carman, J. F. (1992). *Teaching young children effective listening skills.* York, PA: William Gladden Foundation.

Gee, J. P. (2007). *Good video games + good learning.* New York: Peter Lang.

Gilbert, M. B. (2005). An examination of listening effectiveness of educators: Performance and preference. *Professional Educator, 17*(1/2), 1–16.

Halliday, M. K. (1978). *Language as social semiotic: The social interpretation of language and meaning.* Baltimore, MD: University Park Press.

Hartman, D. K., Morsink, P. M., & Zheng, J. (2007). From print to pixels: The evolution of cognitive conceptions of reading comprehension. In E. A. Baker (Ed.), *The new literacies: Multiple perspectives on research and practice* (pp. 131–164). New York: Guilford.

Heath, S. B., & Bhagat, V. (2005). Reading comics, the invisible art. In J. Flood, S. B. Heath, & D. Lapp (Eds.), *Handbook of research on teaching literacy through the communicative and visual arts* (pp. 586–591). Mahwah, NJ: Lawrence Erlbaum.

Hobbs, R. (2005). Literacy for the information age. In J. Flood, S. B. Heath, & D. Lapp (Eds.), *Handbook of research on teaching literacy through the communicative and visual arts* (pp. 7–14). Mahwah, NJ: Lawrence Erlbaum.

Hobbs, R. (2006). Multiple visions of multimedia literacy: Emerging areas of synthesis. In M. C. McKenna, L. D. Labbo, R. D. Kieffer, & D. Reinking (Eds.), *International handbook of literacy & technology,* Vol. 2 (pp. 15–28). Mahwah, NJ: Lawrence Erlbaum.

Hobbs, R. (2011). *Digital and media literacy: Connecting culture and classroom.* New York: Corwin Press.

Hollow, M. K., Sr. (1955). An experimental study of listening at intermediate grade level. Unpublished doctoral dissertation, Fordham University.

Hunsaker, R. A. (1990). *Understanding and developing skills of oral communication.* Englewood, CO: Morton.

ISTE. (2007). *Standards for global learning in the digital age.* Available: http://www.iste.org/standards/nets-for-students.aspx

Jin, S. H., & Boling, E. (2010). Instructional designer's intentions and learners' perceptions of the instructional functions of visuals in an e-learning context. *Journal of Visual Literacy, 29*(2), 143–166.

Kafai, Y., & Bates, M. J. (1997). Internet Web-searching instruction in the elementary classroom: Building a foundation for information literacy. *School Library Media Quarterly, 25*(2), 73–111.

Kajder, S. B. (2003). *The tech-savvy English classroom.* Portland, ME: Stenhouse.

Kress, G. R. (2003). *Literacy in the new media age.* New York: Routledge.

Kress, G. R., & van Leeuwen, T. (2006). *Reading images: The grammar of visual design.* New York: Routledge.

Landry, D. L. (1969). The neglect of listening. *Elementary English, 46,* 599–605.

Lemke, C. (2008). Multimodal learning through media: What the research says. Available: http://www.cisco.com/web/strategy/docs/education/Multimodal-Learning-Through-Media.pdf

Leu, D. (1997). Caity's question: Literacy as deixis on the Internet. *Reading Teacher, 51*(1), 62–67.

Leu, D. J., Jr., Leu, D. D., & Coiro, J. (2004). *Teaching with the Internet: New literacies for new times* (4th ed.). Norwood, MA: Christopher-Gordon.

Linebarger, D. L. (2001). Beginning literacy with language: Young children learning at home and school. *Topics in Early Childhood Special Education, 21,* 188–192.

Lundsteen, S. (1971). *Listening: Its impact on reading and other language arts.* Urbana, IL: National Council of Teachers of English.

Lundsteen, S. (1990). Learning to listen and learning to read. In S. Hynds & D. L. Rubin (Eds.), *Perspectives of talk and learning* (pp. 213–226). Urbana, IL: National Council of Teachers of English.

McDevitt, T. (1990). Encouraging young children's listening. *Academic Therapy* 25(5), 569–577.

McGonical, J. (2011). *Reality is broken: Why games make us better and how they can change the world.* New York: Penguin.

McPherson, K. (2008). Listening carefully. *Teacher Librarian, 35*(4), 73–75.

Meyer, A., & Rose, D. H. (2005). The future is in the margins: The role of technology and disability in educational reform. In D. H. Rose, A. Meyer, & C. Hitchcock (Eds.), *The universally designed classroom: Accessible curriculum and digital technologies.* Cambridge, MA: Harvard Education Press.

Moline, S. (2012). *I see what you mean: Visual literacy.* Portland, ME: Stenhouse.

Morris, T., & Leavey, G. (2006). Promoting phonological awareness in nursery-aged children through a Sure Start Early Listening programme. *International Journal of Early Years Education, 14*(2), 155–168.

NBPTS. (2002). *Early and middle childhood literacy: Reading-language arts standards.* Available: http://www.nbpts.org/userfiles/File/emc_lrla_standards.pdf

Neuman, S. B. (2005). Television as a learning environment: A theory of synergy. In J. Flood, S. B. Heath, & D. Lapp (Eds.), *Handbook of research on teaching literacy through the communicative and visual arts* (pp. 15–22). Mahwah, NJ: Lawrence Erlbaum.

Nunan, D. (2002). Listening in language learning. In J. C. Richards & W. A. Renandya (Eds.), *Methodology in language teaching: An anthology of current practice.* New York: Cambridge University Press.

O'Keefe, V. (1999). *Developing critical thinking: The speaking/listening connection.* Portsmouth, NH: Heinemann.

Opitz, M. F., & Zbaracki, M. D. (2004). *Listen hear!: 25 effective listening comprehension strategies.* Portsmouth, NH: Heinemann.

Pearson, P. D., & Fielding, L. (1982). Research update: Listening comprehension. *Language Arts, 59,* 617–629.

Pinnell, G., & Jaggar, A. (2003). Oral language: Speaking and listening in elementary classrooms. In J. Flood, D. Lapp, J. Squire, & J. Jensen (Eds.), *Handbook of research on teaching the English language arts* (2nd ed., pp. 881–914). Mahwah, NJ: Lawrence Erlbaum.

Prensky, M. (2001). Digital natives, digital immigrants. Available: http://www.marcprensky.com/writing/prensky%20-%20digital%20natives,%20digital%20immigrants%20-%20part1.pdf

Riddle, J. (2009). *Engaging the eye generation: Visual literacy strategies for the K–5 classroom.* Portland, ME: Stenhouse.

Rubin, D. (2000). *Teaching elementary language arts* (6th ed.). New York: Allyn & Bacon.

Stafford, T. (2011). *Teaching visual literacy in the primary classroom.* New York: Routledge.

Sticht, L. J., Beck, R. N., Hauke, G., Kleiman, M., & James, J. H. (1974). *Auditing and reading: A developmental model.* Alexandria, VA: Human Resources Research Organization.

Strother, D. B. (1987). Practical applications of research on listening. *Phi Delta Kappan, 68,* 625–628.

Thoman, E. (1999). Media literacy education can address the problem of media violence. In B. Leone (Ed.), *Media violence: Opposing viewpoints* (pp. 131–136). San

Villaume, W. A., & Bodie, G. D. (2007). Discovering the listener within us: The impact of traitlike personality variables and communicator styles on preferences for listening style. *The International Journal of Listening, 21*(2), 102–123.

Vygotsky, L. (1978). *Mind in society: The development of higher psychological processes.* Cambridge, MA: Harvard University Press.

Weaver, M. (1999). *Visual literacy: How to read and use information in graphic form.* New York: Learning Express.

Weiner, S. (2002). Beyond superheroes: Comics get serious. *Library Journal, 127*(2), 55–59.

Williams, R. (1995). *Beginning the balanced reading program.* Bothell, WA: Wright Group.

Williams, T. L. (2007). "Reading" the painting: Exploring visual literacy in the primary grades. *Reading Teacher, 60*(7), 626–642.

Wolvin, A., & Coakley, C. G. (1993). *Perspectives on listening.* Norwood, NJ: Ablex.

Wolvin, A., & Coakley, C. G. (1996). *Listening.* Chicago, IL: Brown & Benchmark.

Xu, S. H. (2010). *Teaching English language learners: Literacy strategies & resources for K–6.* New York: Guilford Press.

Xu, S. H., & Perkins, R. S. (2005). *Trading cards to comic strips: Popular culture texts and literacy learning in grades K–8.* Newark, DE: International Reading Association.

Zhang, S., & Duke, N. K. (2011). The impact of instruction on the WWWDOT framework on students' disposition and ability to evaluate websites as sources of information. *Elementary School Journal, 112*(1), 132–154.

CHILDREN'S LITERATURE CITED

Briggs, R. (1978). *The snowman.* New York: Random House.

Ehlert, L. (1994). *Eating the alphabet: Fruits and vegetables from A to Z.* New York: Harcourt Brace.

Joyce, W. (2011). *The man in the moon.* New York: Atheneum.

Lewis, C. S. (1994). *The lion, the witch, and the wardrobe.* New York: HarperCollins.

Numeroff, L. (1998). *If you give a pig a pancake.* New York: HarperCollins.

Rowling, J. K. (1998). *Harry Potter and the sorcerer's stone.* New York: AA Levine.

Selznick, B. (2007). *The invention of Hugo Cabret.* New York: Scholastic.

Sendak, M. (1963). *Where the wild things are.* New York: Harper & Row.

Seuss, Dr. (1954). *Horton hears a Who.* New York: Random House.

Seuss, Dr. (1957). *How the Grinch stole Christmas.* New York: Random House.

Assessing the Receptive Modes

Access the book's Glossary, which defines the key terms boldfaced in this chapter, at www.hhpcommunities.com/teachinglanguagearts/glossary.pdf

KEY IDEAS

- Assessment of the receptive modes requires a teacher to dig deeply because these processes occur within the head.

- A single assessment of one aspect of reading gives limited information about the reader as a whole.

- Various individual reading assessments can become a valuable part of a literacy portfolio.

8.1

OVERVIEW OF RECEPTIVE MODES ASSESSMENT: MINING FOR GOLD

A teacher must be a jack-of-all-trades when it comes to assessment. Chapter 4 describes a teacher's assessment tools: rubrics, checklists, portfolios, and tests. Later, Chapter 12 will describe assessment of the *expressive modes* by explaining how teachers are like bakers, meteorologists, and mechanics, using these and other tools to assess what students know and can do. In this chapter, you will learn about assessing the *receptive modes,* and how teachers are like miners, digging for understanding, or elusive nuggets of gold. Assessing the receptive language arts involves collecting evidence of students' mental processes involved in reading, listening, and viewing. Unlike learning in the expressive modes, which often leads to a finished product, such as a blog entry or a show-and-tell presentation, the receptive modes mostly occur in a person's mind. To assess how well a student is receiving a message through reading, listening, or viewing, you must collect evidence of what he or she understands. Although students may create something that represents this understanding, such as a fluent oral reading of a text, a retelling of a story, or completing a task after listening or viewing, you must act as a miner,

"Teaching reminds us that not everyone knows the same things we do."

—ANONYMOUS

229

It can be challenging to assess success in the receptive language arts (reading, listening, and viewing).

sifting through the students' words and actions by monitoring, observing, and analyzing, to extract the gold nugget—their understanding.

This chapter introduces a variety of assessments geared toward the receptive modes. The remainder of the chapter follows a consistent format; for each assessment, we provide the following information:

- The purpose of the assessment, identified by listing the types of language arts skills that are assessed.
- A suggested grade level. Note that this is only a suggestion—many of the assessments are informal and can easily be adapted for younger or older students. The more formal assessments can also be used for various age levels, although the standardized norms only apply to the grade levels listed.
- The information in columns focuses on identifying the connections between the skills to be taught and the assessment. *Left column:* Identifies the matching College and Career Readiness Standard. (Remember from Chapter 2 that these standards identify what students are able to do upon completion of high school, just prior to entering college or a career.) *Right column:* Identifies possible corresponding Common Core State Standards for the English Language Arts for an example grade level.
- A full description of the assessment, often including links to an example or a website with additional information about the assessment.

The goal is to share a range of assessments that can be used to gather data about what students know and can do in relation to the receptive language arts. Although the list of assessments is extensive, it is by no means exhaustive. Many other useful assessments exist, and with the knowledge gained from this chapter, you will be prepared to understand and determine the usefulness of these and other language arts assessments.

Recall the global description of assessment in Chapter 4, purposefully placed in the same chapter as information about instruction and planning. All of these components (planning, instruction, and assessment) work together to create a successful cycle of teaching and learning. As teachers we begin with standards, such as the CCSS or state or local standards, which guide *what* we teach. We make professional decisions about *how* to teach by implementing instructional best practices, such as the gradual release of responsibility model. Assessments provide evidence of what students have learned in relation to the standards. Let's take a closer look at assessments specific to reading, listening, and viewing by looking at the ways a teacher monitors, observes, and analyzes to determine student progress.

8.2

MONITORING

Monitoring involves a quick check on a student's progress by collecting evidence through assessment tools such as a reading log or an interest inventory. You can sift through this evidence, searching for information about what the student knows and can do. Monitoring, like panning for gold, examines what is near the surface—evidence that is fairly easy to get to—such as a reader's preferences. Panning is one of the simplest ways of extracting gold and requires only a sieved pan for catching water and sifting out the nuggets. This is a relatively small amount of equipment and effort compared to other forms of mining and represents a teacher's informal and quick monitoring of progress.

Data gathered from monitoring present early evidence of a student's progress and may lead to a teacher's deeper evaluation through observation and analysis. Tools for monitoring shared in this chapter include a reading interest inventory, an elementary reading attitude survey, the Vocabulary Knowledge Scale, a listening classroom checklist for teachers, a listening self-assessment checklist for teachers, and a listening checklist for students.

Reading interest inventory

Assesses: Interests and motivation to read

Suggested grade level: First grade and above

College and Career Readiness Standards	Common Core State Standard, grade example: Grade 2
Reading: Literature	Reading: Literature
Range of Reading and Level of Text Complexity	*Range of Reading and Level of Text Complexity*
R.10 Read and comprehend complex literary and informational texts independently and proficiently.	**RL 2.10** By the end of the year, read and comprehend literature, including stories and poetry, in the grades 2–3 text complexity band proficiently, with scaffolding as needed at the high end of the range.

Description: Knowing your students' interests and reading preferences lets you guide them toward books they will find interesting, thus creating more motivated readers. Motivated readers will read more widely and deeply, as described in the CCSS. To guide readers successfully, you must get to know them beyond how they present themselves during the school day. The best way to do this is to ask them what they enjoy, and an interest inventory provides an informal assessment tool for this task. Chapter 4 first introduced the idea of the interest inventory and presented an example. An additional example is presented in Exhibit 8.2. These inventories are meant to serve only as samples. You may easily adapt an interest inventory to fit the information you seek by designing questions appropriate for your students. A student's completed interest inventory can be stored in a portfolio, representing a glimpse of the student as a reader.

Print a blank inventory: http://www.hhpcommunities.com/teachinglanguage arts/IL-08-01.pdf

Elementary reading attitude inventory

Assesses: Attitudes about reading and motivation to read

Suggested grade level: First grade and above

College and Career Readiness Standards	Common Core State Standard, grade example: Grade 2
Reading: Literature	Reading: Literature
Range of Reading and Level of Text Complexity	*Range of Reading and Level of Text Complexity*
R.10 Read and comprehend complex literary and informational texts independently and proficiently.	**RL 2.10** By the end of the year, read and comprehend literature, including stories and poetry, in the grades 2–3 text complexity band proficiently, with scaffolding as needed at the high end of the range.

EXHIBIT 8.2

Reading interest inventory.

Description: Attitude equals motivation when it comes to learning, especially reading. A motivated reader is more likely to enjoy reading and to feel successful at it. Feeling successful will likely lead to more reading and stronger reading skills, thus strengthening the circle of learning. One sample elementary reading attitude uses cartoon faces depicting various emotions as response choices for questions about reading attitudes. The range of feelings extends from very happy to very unhappy. First- and second-grade teachers can read the survey aloud to the entire class while students respond on individual handouts. Older students can complete the survey independently. This standardized tool provides national norms so you can see how your students compare to others of the same age who took the inventory and determine a percentile. In addition to the questionnaire's score, you may also add a narrative description. This assessment data could be helpful when selecting literature, planning independent reading activities, and conferencing with students during an independent reading time.

To read more about the research supporting use of the Elementary Reading Attitude Inventory and to find a printable copy of the inventory, visit the Professor Garfield page (www.professorgarfield.org/parents_teachers/printables/reading.html) and click on "The Reading Survey."

Vocabulary Knowledge Scale

Assesses: Word meaning knowledge

Suggested grade level: Second grade and above

College and Career Readiness Standards	Common Core State Standard, grade example: Grade 4
Reading: Literature	**Reading: Literature**
Craft and Structure	*Craft and Structure*
R.4 Interpret words and phrases as they are used in a text, including determining technical, connotative, and figurative meanings, and analyze how specific word choices shape meaning or tone.	**RL.4.4** Determine the meaning of words and phrases as they are used in a text, including those that allude to significant characters found in mythology (e.g., Herculean).
Language: Vocabulary Acquisition and Use	*Language: Vocabulary Acquisition and Use*
L.6 Acquire and use accurately a range of general academic and domain-specific words and phrases sufficient for reading, writing, speaking, and listening at the college and career readiness level; demonstrate independence in gathering vocabulary knowledge when encountering an unknown term important to comprehension or expression.	**L.4.4** Determine or clarify the meaning of unknown and multiple-meaning words and phrases based on grade 4 reading and content, choosing flexibly from a range of strategies.

EXHIBIT 8.3

A sample Vocabulary Knowledge Scale.

(Print a blank copy of this scale: www.hhpcommunities.com/teachinglanguagearts/IL-08-02.pdf)

Description: Because vocabulary develops over the course of a lifetime, a single assessment may provide you with limited information about a student's vocabulary development, although it may reflect knowledge of specific words from a certain unit of study, if designed to do so. Because word knowledge is individual, one of the most useful assessments of vocabulary entails a combination of self-reporting and demonstrating word knowledge. The Vocabulary Knowledge Scale (as discussed in Chapter 6) provides a starting point for developing an informal vocabulary assessment that focuses on identifying the students' individual vocabulary knowledge for a specific set of words (Dale, 1965; Wesche & Paribakht, 1996) (see Exhibit 8.3). Many different forms of the Vocabulary Knowledge Scale exist because this assessment is designed to be used with a teacher-selected word list, as part of authentic vocabulary activities in the classroom. Thus, this informal assessment does not lend itself to making comparisons at the classroom, school, or national level, but instead works best in showing growth among individual students when designed as a pre- and post-test, as presented in Exhibit 8.4.

To administer the assessment, use the following procedure:

- Select a set of between five and fifteen vocabulary words, depending on the age of the students.
- Provide the students with the Vocabulary Knowledge Scale chart.
- Pronounce the words for the students two to three times slowly and clearly. Give no indication of meaning while pronouncing the words.
- Ask students to mark their knowledge level. If they mark a three, four, or five, ask them to also complete the sentence, filling in the missing portion for each word.
- When students have completed the chart, collect and study their responses.

You could end the assessment at this point and use the information to guide vocabulary instruction. If you choose, you could give the same assessment as a post-test, following an instruction lesson or unit, to determine if students have increased their vocabulary knowledge. Exhibit 8.4 shows a pre-/post-test chart used to display and compare individual data. Share this information with students so they can monitor their own vocabulary growth. Keep in mind, the Vocabulary Knowledge Scale is a self-reporting instrument. Impress upon students the need to respond honestly about their vocabulary knowledge. Honest responses will be more likely if students know the assessment will not be graded. Also, model your own uncertainty about word meanings to let students know it is okay to not know what words mean, and to use this as a learning opportunity.

Listening classroom checklist for teachers and listening self-assessment checklist for teachers

Assesses: A teacher's listening skills
Intended use for teacher self-assessment

College and Career Readiness Standards

Speaking and Listening: Comprehension and Collaboration

Common Core State Standard, grade example: N/A

SL.1 Prepare for and participate effectively in a range of conversations and collaborations with diverse partners, building on others' ideas and expressing their own clearly and persuasively.

SL.2 Integrate and evaluate information presented in diverse media and formats, including visually, quantitatively, and orally.

SL.3 Evaluate a speaker's point of view, reasoning, and use of evidence and rhetoric.

Description: The checklists in Exhibits 8.5 and 8.6 assist you with monitoring the classroom listening environment and your own listening behaviors, in order to create a classroom that promotes the listening standards for students discussed below. Periodically assess yourself to make sure you are modeling the types of listening behavior you expect from your students. These informal tools can serve as a helpful reminder.

EXHIBIT 8.4

Vocabulary Knowledge Scale pre-/post-test data.

Pretest – Purple
Posttest – Green
Teacher: Dahalia   Date: January 24 / February 2
Vocabulary from: *A Wrinkle in Time*, Chapter 1

	subdued	moderation	assorted	agility	exclusive
Markham	2 / 4	1 / 3	4 / 5	3 / 4	4 / 5
Eva	1 / 3	2 / 4	5 / 5	3 / 4	3 / 4
Sam	1 / 2	3 / 3	2 / 5	2 / 3	2 / 3
Derek	3 / 5	3 / 4	4 / 5	3 / 4	3 / 4
Leesha	4 / 5	5 / 5	5 / 5	5 / 5	4 / 5
Penelope	2 / 4	2 / 4	5 / 5	2 / 5	3 / 5
Mario	1 / 2	1 / 3	3 / 4	1 / 2	1 / 1

EXHIBIT 8.5

Listening classroom checklist for teachers.

Listening Classroom Checklist for Teachers

Teacher's name: _____ Date: _____ Grade: _____

_____ The desks/tables are arranged so all students can see the primary teaching area.

_____ The desks/tables are arranged so students can look at one another when speaking.

_____ Detached speakers are used for broadcasting from the computer.

_____ A listening center with headphones or earbuds gives students a quiet place to listen to books, songs, or podcasts.

_____ Student computers have working headphones, and students understand the procedures for use.

_____ Classroom routines are established that signal to students specific times for listening (e.g., clapping sequence, bell, verbal phrases).

_____ Visuals remind students of the importance of listening behaviors (e.g., posters, symbols).

_____ I model expected listening behaviors and point these out to students on a regular basis.

_____ The importance of listening is frequently brought up during class discussions.

_____ I share expectations for listening behaviors with caregivers and students.

EXHIBIT 8.6

Listening self-assessment checklist for teachers.

Are you aware of your listening behaviors? Circle yes or no.

1. I can hear just fine, so I am probably a good listener.	YES	NO
2. I often find myself interrupting a student or colleague when I am tired of listening.	YES	NO
3. I am a good listener, especially if I am interested in the topic.	YES	NO
4. I nod my head when listening during a conversation.	YES	NO
5. When listening during a presentation or faculty meeting, I often smile at the speaker.	YES	NO
6. My students and colleagues consider me to be a good listener.	YES	NO
7. I can listen well and do something else at the same time.	YES	NO
8. When I am busy in the classroom, it's difficult for me to really listen to my students.	YES	NO
9. At times I have to force myself to really listen to students and colleagues.	YES	NO

Adapted from Kline, J. A. (2003). *Listening effectively: Achieving high standards in communication.* Upper Saddle River, NJ: Prentice Hall.

Listening checklist

Assesses: Listening skills

Suggested grade level: Second grade and above

College and Career Readiness Standards	Common Core State Standard, grade example: Grade 5
Speaking and Listening: Comprehension and Collaboration	Speaking and Listening: Comprehension and Collaboration
SL.1 Prepare for and participate effectively in a range of conversations and collaborations with diverse partners, building on others' ideas and expressing their own clearly and persuasively.	**SL5.1** Engage effectively in a range of collaborative discussions (one-on-one, in groups, and teacher-led) with diverse partners on *grade 5 topics and texts,* building on others' ideas and expressing their own clearly.
SL.2 Integrate and evaluate information presented in diverse media and formats, including visually, quantitatively, and orally.	**SL5.2** Summarize a written text read aloud or information presented in diverse media and formats, including visually, quantitatively, and orally.
SL.3 Evaluate a speaker's point of view, reasoning, and use of evidence and rhetoric.	**SL5.3** Summarize the points a speaker makes and explain how each claim is supported by reasons and evidence.

EXHIBIT 8.7

Listening checklist.

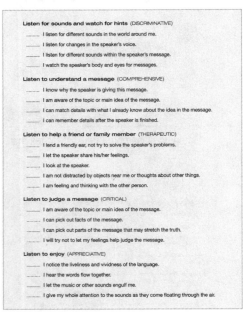

Listen for sounds and watch for hints (DISCRIMINATIVE)
_____ I listen for different sounds in the world around me.
_____ I listen for changes in the speaker's voice.
_____ I listen for different sounds within the speaker's message.
_____ I watch the speaker's body and eyes for messages.

Listen to understand a message (COMPREHENSIVE)
_____ I know why the speaker is giving this message.
_____ I am aware of the topic or main idea of the message.
_____ I can match details with what I already know about the idea in the message.
_____ I can remember details after the speaker is finished.

Listen to help a friend or family member (THERAPEUTIC)
_____ I lend a friendly ear, not try to solve the speaker's problems.
_____ I let the speaker share his/her feelings.
_____ I look at the speaker.
_____ I am not distracted by objects near me or thoughts about other things.
_____ I am feeling and thinking with the other person.

Listen to judge a message (CRITICAL)
_____ I am aware of the topic or main idea of the message.
_____ I can pick out facts of the message.
_____ I can pick out parts of the message that may stretch the truth.
_____ I will try not to let my feelings help judge the message.

Listen to enjoy (APPRECIATIVE)
_____ I notice the liveliness and vividness of the language.
_____ I hear the words flow together.
_____ I let the music or other sounds engulf me.
_____ I give my whole attention to the sounds as they come floating through the air.

Description: The ultimate goal is for students to monitor their own listening processes and make sure they are listening effectively. In order to do this, they need to know what makes for an effective listener. The listening checklist utilizes the five purposes for listening as described in Chapter 7 to encourage students to check their listening behaviors. Exhibit 8.7 displays the listening checklist, as created for fourth, fifth, and sixth graders. The checklist can also be used with younger students, but the statements and length of the list would likely need to be adapted. You could choose one of the purposes to focus on at a time, especially with younger students. Before a formal listening situation, give the checklist to the students to clarify the expected listening behaviors, then have them assess themselves after the event. Next, have the students conference with a partner or small group and discuss which aspects of listening they found the most challenging. In this way, a simple assessment tool can be powerful in changing listening behaviors.

8.3

OBSERVING

Kidwatching entails more than just watching students in the classroom. A skilled teacher with a trained eye becomes attuned to the subtle nuances of student learning in the same way a miner knows that it takes careful looking to spot gold dust camouflaged by dirt, rocks, and water. The key to turning your observations into valuable assessment data is to systematically record them in a way that lets you analyze the data to understand what a student knows and can do. Observing alone is not enough. You must know what to watch for, what observations to collect, how to collect them, how to analyze this data, and above all else, what to do next. The assessments included in this section present a variety of systematic ways to observe the reading, listening, and viewing modes.

Concepts about print

Assesses: Word, sentence, and book knowledge

Suggested grade level: Pre-K–first grade

College and Career Readiness Standards	Common Core State Standard, grade example: Kindergarten
Reading: Key Ideas and Details	**Reading: Foundational Skills**
R.1 Read closely to determine what the text says explicitly and to make logical inferences from it; cite specific textual evidence when writing or speaking to support conclusions drawn from the text.	**RF.K.1** Demonstrate understanding of the organization and basic features of print.

Description: Concepts about print assessments tell you how young readers might approach books and other texts. Children who know how to hold a book, where to begin reading, or how to move from one line of text to another can move forward with other reading skills. In a concepts of print assessment, you hand a book to the student and ask a few questions while she responds by pointing to specific features of the text. The term *concepts about print* was coined by Marie Clay (2000); several versions of concept about print assessments are available on the Internet.

On Patti's Electronic Classroom page (7:00, http://teams.lacoe.edu/documentation/classrooms/patti/k-1/teacher/assessment/print/conceptsqt.html) watch Patti give a concepts about print assessment and explain what she is observing about the student. A ten-item version of the assessment is available.

EXHIBIT 8.8

Example items from a concepts about print assessment.

	SEPTEMBER	JANUARY
Show me the front of this book.		
Show me with your finger how to read the words.		

Some teachers create a checklist with columns for two or three evaluations at different times of the school year (see Exhibit 8.8 for an example of how the first item might look). The teacher simply checks off the box for each correct response, and counts correct responses while noting areas where the student needs extra attention.

Fluency rubric

Assesses: Oral reading fluency

Suggested grade level: First grade and above

College and Career Readiness Standards	Common Core State Standard, grade example: Grade 1
Reading: Key Ideas and Details	**Reading: Foundational Skills**
R.1 Read closely to determine what the text says explicitly and to make logical inferences from it; cite specific textual evidence when writing or speaking to support conclusions drawn from the text.	**RF.1.4** Read with sufficient accuracy and fluency to support comprehension.

Description: One way to assess a reader's fluency is to listen to him read orally and to match what is heard and observed to a set of expectations described in a rubric. You can use an existing fluency rubric or design your own. The goal is to have a set of common descriptors for fluency that are understood and used among the teacher, students, and caregivers. Throughout the course of the school year, a fluency rubric can also be collected in a literacy portfolio and used to record student progress, possibly with accompanying audio recordings of oral readings as evidence of fluency growth. A fluency rubric typically includes the categories of expression, phrasing, fluency, pace, or similar elements as specified in the CCSS. A high-quality rubric has clear statements delineating the differences between the levels of quality, beyond simply using the words *all, some,* and *none* to describe behaviors. When creating your own fluency rubric, try it out with students before finalizing the content. What you envision during the tool creation process may be quite different from the ways students perform in real situations. Because a fluency rubric is an informal assessment tool, it can easily be adapted for different learning situations; rather than starting from scratch, consider locating a fluency rubric, such as the one at the link, and making adaptations from that point.

> See a sample fluency rubric: www.timrasinski.com/presentations/multi dimensional_fluency_rubric_4_factors.pdf

Purposeful listening rubric

Assesses: Listening skills

Suggested grade level: Second grade and above

College and Career Readiness Standards	Common Core State Standard, grade example: Grade 1
Speaking and Listening: Comprehension and Collaboration	Speaking and Listening: Comprehension and Collaboration
SL.1 Prepare for and participate effectively in a range of conversations and collaborations with diverse partners, building on others' ideas and expressing their own clearly and persuasively.	**SL1.1** Participate in collaborative conversations with diverse partners about *grade 1 topics and texts* with peers and adults in small and larger groups.
Integrate and evaluate information presented in diverse media and formats, including visually, quantitatively, and orally.	
SL.3 Evaluate a speaker's point of view, reasoning, and use of evidence and rhetoric.	

Description: The Common Core State Standards use the verbs *review, respond,* and *summarize* to describe listening expectations for students. While these concepts help listeners know what to do once information has been received through listening, we as teachers must also consider ways to promote listening behaviors among students that will facilitate active listening. The Purposeful Listening Rubric (www.hhpcommunities.com/teaching languagearts/IL-08-03.pdf) acts as an assessment tool as well as a tool for teaching positive listening behaviors. The rubric focuses on specific listening behaviors, including eye contact, body language, and attentiveness. It also relates directly to CCSS categories that identify what a listener does to confirm the message. Older students can be given a copy of the rubric prior to a listening event to clarify your expectations.

Show Me Framework

Assesses: Viewing skills

Suggested grade level: Kindergarten and above

College and Career Readiness Standards	Common Core State Standard, grade example: Grade 4
Speaking and Listening: Comprehension and Collaboration	**Speaking and Listening: Comprehension and Collaboration**
SL.2 Integrate and evaluate information presented in diverse media and formats, including visually, quantitatively, and orally.	**SL.4.1** Engage effectively in a range of collaborative discussions (one-on-one, in groups, and teacher-led) with diverse partners on *grade 4 topics and texts,* building on others' ideas and expressing their own clearly.
SL.3 Evaluate a speaker's point of view, reasoning, and use of evidence and rhetoric.	

Description: The Show Me Framework is an informal assessment of the viewing process used with multimedia, including picture books, digital images, and video. Because multimedia elements can vary so widely, the viewing process assessment will likely need to be adapted for the specific viewing situation. The Show Me Framework provides a comprehensive starting point by addressing the affective, compositional, and critical dimensions of viewing. Use the framework as an observation guide, recording notes about specific observations that match the visual features (e.g., "looks at images while reading," "comments on pictures") and performance indicators (e.g., "discusses favorite character, using pictures to assist," "gives reasons for disliking particular images or pictures").

 Read more about the Show Me Framework in the article "Show Me: Principles for Assessing Visual Literacy" (*The Reading Teacher,* 61(8), 616–626).

8.4

ANALYZING

Analyzing entails taking a closer, more detailed look at what students know and can do by closely examining the elements of their learning. For the miner, analyzing is like digging for the vein of gold deep below the earth's surface. Striking it rich takes specialized equipment, hard work, time, and patience. For the teacher, analyzing requires an assessment tool that focuses on breaking down the process of reading, listening, and viewing into elements or components and looking at these in greater detail, then sifting out what students know and what they need to learn next. This section discusses analyzing tools that test for phonemic awareness, decoding and comprehension, and listening.

Yopp Singer Test of Phonemic Segmentation

Assesses: Phonemic awareness

Suggested grade level: Pre-K–first grade

College and Career Readiness Standards	Common Core State Standard, grade example: Grade 1
Reading: Key Ideas and Details	**Reading: Foundational Skills**
R.1 Read closely to determine what the text says explicitly and to make logical inferences from it; cite specific textual evidence when writing or speaking to support conclusions drawn from the text.	**RF.1.2** Segment spoken single-syllable words into their complete sequence of individual sounds (phonemes).

Description: Knowledge of phonemes, or the individual sounds within a word, appears to be one of two powerful early predictors of reading difficulties; the other being a test of letter names (Torgesen, 1998). Together these simple assessments give teachers critical information about which students are at risk of not succeeding as readers. Armed with this information, you can provide the right instruction to the right student at the right time. The goal of targeted, intense, early literacy instruction is preventing reading failure by diagnosing reading difficulties and giving students a boost through instruction. The Yopp Singer Test of Phonemic Segmentation (Yopp, 1995) is a widely used assessment for phonemic awareness. Students are orally given a word and asked to say the word one sound at a time. For example, you might say, "Say the sounds in *cat*." To which the student would correctly respond "/c/ /a/ /t/." An incorrect response could be "/c/ /at/." You pronounce 22 specific items for the assessment, each having two to three phonemes, and you write the students' responses and mark them as either correct or incorrect—no partial credit is given. You may also consider making an audio recording of the session for future reference. No norms are available for analyzing the results, but a skilled teacher can gain a sense of a student's phonemic awareness skills, and coupled with other early literacy assessment data, the teacher can use this information to identify students who are at risk of failure. You can also use the information to plan for reading instruction in a kindergarten or first-grade classroom. This test is free and can be used for educational purposes without permission. You will obtain the most accurate results by giving the test in the second half of kindergarten or the first half of first grade.

For a copy of the Yopp Singer Test and for information on the research supporting the test, see the article "A Test for Assessing Phonemic Awareness in Young Children" (10 pp.): www.glassboroschools.us/cms/lib/NJ01000249/Centricity/Domain/14/OrigYoppSinger.pdf. To read more about preventing reading difficulties, read the article "Catch Them Before They Fail: Identification and Assessment to Prevent Reading Failure in Young Children": www.readingrockets.org/article/225.

Names Test: A test of phonics skills

Assesses: Phonics skills

Suggested grade level: Second–fourth grades

College and Career Readiness Standards	Common Core State Standard, grade example: Grade 2
Reading: Key Ideas and Details	Reading: Foundational Skills
R.1 Read closely to determine what the text says explicitly and to make logical inferences from it; cite specific textual evidence when writing or speaking to support conclusions drawn from the text.	RF.2.3 Know and apply grade-level phonics and word analysis skills in decoding words.

Description: The Names Test provides a test of phonics skills. Its simple format is in stark contrast to the wealth of valuable phonics information it provides about individual students. The Names Test was originally created in 1990 by Patricia Cunningham and F. A. Dufflemeyer. In 1994, Dufflemeyer and colleagues created an enhanced version that includes a longer list of names and additional scoring information. To give the test, a teacher needs the list of names for the student, the teacher's protocol sheet for recording responses, and a scoring matrix. These materials can be found here: www.hhpcommunities.com/teachinglanguagearts/IL-08-09.pdf. A detailed description of the research supporting the Names Test can be found in the article "Further Validation and Enhancement of the Names Test" (Duffelmeyer, Kruse, Merkley, & Fyfe, 1994). This one-on-one assessment entails the student reading the names (e.g., "Jay Conway," "Kimberly Blake") and the teacher recording errors in the student's pronunciation (p. 124). Directions are provided for assisting in analyzing the student's responses to determine the types of phonics errors. This information can then be used to guide phonics instruction. Although originally designed for older students, the Names Test has been adapted for young students and can be seen in the article "Adaptations of the Names Test: Easy-to-use Phonics Assessments" (Mather, Sammons, & Schwartz, 2006).

Giving the Names Test can be time-consuming and may only be necessary for those students struggling with decoding. The names on the list are chosen to represent a variety of phonics elements, and the simplicity of the assessment makes it a practical and useful choice.

Cloze test: A test of comprehension

Assesses: Comprehension

Suggested grade level: Second grade and above

College and Career Readiness Standards	Common Core State Standard, grade example: Grade 3
Reading	Reading: Literature
Key Ideas and Details	*Range of Reading and Level of Text Complexity*
R.10 Read and comprehend complex literary and informational texts independently and proficiently.	**RL.3.10** By the end of the year, read and comprehend literature, including stories, dramas, and poetry, at the high end of the grades 2–3 text complexity band independently and proficiently.

Description: A cloze test gives a broad picture of a reader's comprehension of a certain piece of text. The test is typically created by the teacher with a grade level passage students have not previously read, although commercially prepared cloze tests are available.

To prepare and administer the cloze test, use the following procedures:

- Select a passage of 275 to 300 words in length.
- Type out the passage, keeping the first and last sentence intact and deleting every *nth* word, inserting a blank. The fifth word is the typical number deleted, but the test will be easier if this number is higher, and more challenging if lower.
- Make the test less challenging by providing students with a word bank, or a collection of possible words, or by supplying the first and/or last letter of each correct response.
- Have students read the passage and fill in the blanks with the missing word.
- When scoring, make no deductions for spelling, but the exact word should be included, rather than a synonym.
- Upon completion, the calculate the percentage of correct responses and uses that score to determine a child's reading level:

- Independent: 58–100% correct
- Instructional: 44–57%
- Frustrational: 0–43%

You can use this information in conjunction with a reading level determined by a running record or informal reading inventory to form small groups for instruction or to identify students at risk for reading difficulties. The cloze test is also sometimes used as an instructional activity, and it requires an understanding of vocabulary and context. The reader makes inferences, using her understanding of words and their collective meaning to fill in the blanks. Because a teacher-created cloze test has no norms, it can only be used to draw general conclusions about a reader's comprehension and should be accompanied by further comprehension assessments to be of maximum value.

See an example of a cloze test, "Counting on Frank": https://svsudifferen tiatedinstruction.wikispaces.com/file/view/cloze_test.pdf/230897224/cloze_test.pdf

Running record

Assesses: Fluency, phonics, phonemic awareness, comprehension

Suggested grade level: K–fifth grade

College and Career Readiness Standards	Common Core State Standard, grade example: Grade 1
Reading: Literature	**Reading: Foundational Skills Phonological Awareness**
Key Ideas and Details	**RF.1.2** Demonstrate understanding of spoken words, syllables, and sounds (phonemes)
R.1 Read closely to determine what the text says explicitly and to make logical inferences from it; cite specific textual evidence when writing or speaking to support conclusions drawn from the text.	**RF.1.3** Know and apply grade-level phonics and word analysis skills in decoding words
	RF.1.4 Read with sufficient accuracy and fluency to support comprehension
	Reading: Literature
	Key Ideas and Details
	RL.1.2 Retell stories, including key details, and demonstrate understanding of their central message or lesson.
	Reading: Information Text
	Key Ideas and Details
	RI.1.2 Identify the main topic and retell key details of a text.

Description: Running records, developed by Marie Clay (1993), capture students' text processing strategies through oral reading and can be used on an ongoing basis throughout the year to inform instructional decisions. Running records can be taken during small group and one-on-one conferences with the text the student is currently reading. The teacher sits beside the student and, using a running record form (see Exhibit 8.9) or a blank sheet of paper and the coding system (refer back to Exhibit 5.7), records the student's reading of approximately 100 words from any point in the text. The oral reading can be followed up with a few comprehension questions or a retelling in which the reader tells the story in his or her own words. The running record can be analyzed for accuracy to determine the kinds of information the student is using to process the text (see Exhibit 8.9). Even very good readers make errors when reading. The difference is when the errors, or miscues, lead to lack of comprehension of the text.

Miscue analysis is based on the idea that the errors students make when they read are not random, but rather reflect their attempt to make sense of the text using the skills and strategies they possess. By paying careful attention to the miscues students make while reading, you can diagnose their areas of need as well as their strengths. By utilizing the running record and miscue analysis as a type of formative assessment, you can plan specific interventions and differentiate lesson plans based on the unique needs of each student.

Informal reading inventory

Assesses: Fluency, phonics, comprehension

Suggested grade level: First grade and above

College and Career Readiness Standards

Reading: Literature

Key Ideas and Details

R.1 Read closely to determine what the text says explicitly and to make logical inferences from it; cite specific textual evidence when writing or speaking to support conclusions drawn from the text.

Common Core State Standard, grade example: Grade 5

Reading: Literature

Key Ideas and Details

RL.5.1 Quote accurately from a text when explaining what the text says explicitly and when drawing inferences from the text.

Reading: Foundational Skills

Phonics and Word Recognition

RF.5.3 Know and apply grade-level phonics and word analysis skills in decoding words.

Fluency

RF.5.4 Read with sufficient accuracy and fluency to support comprehension.

Description: The informal reading inventory (IRI) is the Cadillac of reading assessments. This individually administered assessment, although time-consuming, provides a teacher with information about phonics, fluency, and comprehension in one shot. Some teachers reserve an informal reading inventory for struggling students, while some administer an informal reading inventory to all students at the beginning and end of the school year. A teacher or reading specialist may give an informal reading inventory to a student who is being evaluated for special reading or educational services.

Several different types of published informal reading inventories are available. This description will focus on the Qualitative Reading Inventory (QRI), version 5, but other high quality IRIs are available and should be considered if you have a choice.

The article "A Critical Analysis of Eight Informal Reading Inventories" (www.readingrockets.org/article/23373) provides more detailed information about these inventories and compares eight of those most commonly used.

EXHIBIT 8.9

An example running record shows an analysis of errors using the cueing systems; this text sample is from *Just Juice*, by Karen Hesse.

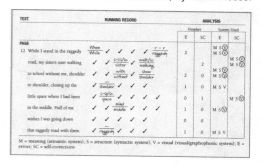

(Print a blank running record: www.hhpcommunities.com/teachinglanguagearts/IL-08-03.pdf)

One goal of an IRI is to determine a student's reading level (e.g., independent, instructional, frustrational). The first step in administering the QRI is to use a graded word or sentence list to help estimate the student's reading level and point you toward the proper beginning level for the oral reading portion of the assessment. The QRI also provides a brief assessment of the student's prior knowledge before beginning to read passages, in order to assist with describing her comprehension abilities. Next, a series of passages are read orally, each one containing more difficult words and concepts. The student reads while you record miscues, much like with a running record. After each passage, you calculate the student's rate of correct words and then analyze the miscues, looking for patterns that can lead to possible concepts for instruction. When this rate dips below a certain point, the student is considered to be reading at the frustration level, and the oral reading portion of the test is discontinued. Also, after reading each passage, you ask the student a series of comprehension questions and record the answers.

The QRI and other published IRIs are normed assessments, and you must follow the procedures correctly in order for these norms to be valid. Further study of IRI administration is encouraged, as this comprehensive assessment can contribute much valuable information about a student's reading ability.

Elementary discussion rubric

Assesses: Listening skills

Suggested grade level: Third grade and above

College and Career Readiness Standards	Common Core State Standard, grade example: Grade 4
Speaking and Listening: Comprehension and Collaboration	Speaking and Listening: Comprehension and Collaboration
SL.1 Prepare for and participate effectively in a range of conversations and collaborations with diverse partners, building on others' ideas and expressing their own clearly and persuasively.	**SL.4.1** Engage effectively in a range of collaborative discussions (one-on-one, in groups, and teacher-led) with diverse partners on *grade 4 topics and texts*, building on others' ideas and expressing their own clearly.

Description: The title of the elementary discussion rubric is misleading because the rubric's focus is on listening rather than discussing (see Exhibit 8.10). This rubric identifies elements of listening as engagement, interaction, collaboration, and reflection. Designed as a self-assessment tool, the rubric focuses on the thinking a listener does during a class discussion, which makes it a useful assessment for digging deeper into the listening process. Possible listening events for using this rubric include a literature circle, a collaborative project, or a class meeting. Prior to the listening event, you could give the student a copy of the rubric and discuss effective listening strategies and behaviors. After the listening event, you could have the student complete the listening rubric for his own listening habits. Just the act of sharing the rubric will raise the student's awareness of effective and appropriate listening behaviors and will also provide both of you with information about how students view themselves as listeners. Because students are asked to evaluate themselves, giving points or a grade for this rubric may cause students to rate them-

---

EXHIBIT 8.10

Elementary discussion rubric.

Elementary Discussion Rubric

	4	3	2	1
Engagement	While listening to a discussion, I think about how other students' comments relate to my knowledge and experiences. I always expect to learn something from a discussion. I like to hear what my classmates have to say about a topic. As I listen to a discussion, I analyze and evaluate other people's comments on a subject before I make up my mind. When I am not talking, I show I am interested in the discussion through appropriate body language, such as eye contact, smiling, and nodding.	During a discussion, I think about what everyone is saying. I usually like to hear what my classmates have to say about a topic. During a discussion, I think about whether I agree or disagree with people's comments and why. I show that I am interested in the discussion.	During a discussion, my mind sometimes wanders and thinks about other things. I sometimes think I will enjoy a discussion. I sometimes like to hear what my classmates have to say about a topic. Sometimes I think about whether I agree or disagree with people's comments. Sometimes I show that I am interested in a discussion, but sometimes I look like I'm not paying attention.	During class discussions, I usually am thinking of something else. I usually think discussions will be boring and a waste of time. I do not usually like to hear what my classmates have to say about a topic. I rarely think about whether I agree or disagree with my classmates' comments. My body language usually shows that I am not interested in the discussion.
Interaction	I look for opportunities in the discussion to appropriately share my personal experiences, beliefs, and opinions and think about what I am going to say before I speak. I use good reasons to support my opinions and explain where my information comes from. My comments during a discussion build on what others have said. I summarize and add to others' ideas. When appropriate, I ask my classmates to explain more about what they have said.	I often share my personal experiences, beliefs and opinions in a discussion. My comments during a discussion connect to what others have said. I often comment on what others have said. I often ask questions of my classmates.	Sometimes, if I am encouraged to, I share my personal experiences, beliefs, and opinions in a discussion. My comments usually connect to what others are saying, but sometimes I make comments that are kind of off the topic. Sometimes I comment on what others have said. Sometimes I ask questions of my classmates.	I rarely speak during a discussion. Sometimes when I speak, my comments are clearly not on the topic. I seldom make comments on what others have said, unless it is to say that they are wrong. I rarely ask questions of my classmates.
Collaboration	I speak when I have something significant to add, but I am careful not to monopolize the discussion. I encourage all members of my class to participate asking questions. I disagree respectfully by looking for areas of agreement, if possible. I actively and enthusiastically show my appreciation for the good comments made by my classmates. I carefully follow the rules for a discussion established by my class. I carefully consider respectful, intelligent criticism of my ideas and change my mind if I need to.	I speak when I think I have something important to say, but I try not to speak too much. I often encourage my classmates to participate by asking them questions. I disagree respectfully. I show my appreciation for good comments made by my classmates. I follow the discussion rules established by my class. I accept respectful, intelligent criticism of my ideas.	Sometimes I do not speak at all, and sometimes I talk too much during a discussion. I seldom encourage my classmates to participate. I usually disagree respectfully, but sometimes I get angry and act disrespectfully. I usually follow the discussion rules established by my class, but sometimes I forget. I usually accept criticism of my ideas, but sometimes I get mad when people disagree with me.	I do not speak at all during discussions OR I talk all the time and do not give others a chance to contribute. I do not encourage my classmates to participate. I often get angry when I disagree with my classmates and say and do disrespectful things. I have a lot of trouble following the discussion rules established by the class. I get mad when people criticize my ideas.
Reflection	I take time to think about what I have learned about a topic from a discussion and apply it to my learning in the future. I look back and evaluate my participation in a discussion and set goals for improving my skills during the next discussion.	I think about what I have learned from a discussion. I think about how well I did in a discussion and try to do better in the next one.	If I am reminded, I think about what I have learned from a discussion. Sometimes I try to improve my discussion skills.	Once a discussion is over, I usually do not think about what I have learned from it. I hardly ever think about my discussion skills and how to improve them.

selves higher than they might otherwise. Encourage students to be honest with themselves instead.

Read fourth grader Erin's comments about her own listening habits after using the elementary discussion rubric.

Wow, okay, I didn't know that listening takes so much thinking! I don't usually think about what I am hearing—I just hear it! I guess it would make sense to think more and maybe I will do it now that I know. I am a good listener though. At least my friends say so. I do look at them when they are talking, although we don't talk nearly as much as we text. But when we talk, I do try to look interested—even if I am not. I also nod my head and do the other things on the rubric. At least I think I do, which is why I circled mostly the 3 and 4 boxes.

8.5

CHAPTER SUMMARY

A gold miner searches for evidence of a big vein of gold, one that will lead to striking it rich. A teacher strikes it rich by using various assessment techniques to collect evidence of student progress toward standards. Examples of learning collected from monitoring, observing, and analyzing student work provide the key for a teacher to determine what an individual student knows and what she is ready to learn next. The assessment tools presented in this chapter and in Chapter 12 serve as possible ways of gathering information as each teacher seeks to understand the capabilities of students and also to evaluate the effectiveness of her own teaching.

APPLICATION ACTIVITIES

think like a teacher

Try It Out

Think a cloze test for comprehension sounds easy? After all, the student merely fills in the blanks of a selected text. How difficult can it be? Give it a try to find out. Visit the link for the Cloze Test for Reading Comprehension: www.useit.com/alertbox/cloze-test.html. Scroll down to the cloze passage taken from the Facebook Privacy Policy. Fill in the blanks with the missing words. Keep in mind, about 60 percent accuracy means reasonable comprehension. Synonyms are accepted and no deductions are made for spelling. If this seems difficult, know that this passage is written at a fourteenth grade level, or a college level, so it should be right at the reading level for a typical college student. After completing the Facebook cloze passage, scroll down the page, check your answers, and calculate your score as a percentage of correct responses. The purpose of this activity is to give you the experience of a cloze test, not to compare scores, so keep your score private. Once everyone has completed the passage, discuss your experiences. Did the test seem difficult? What factors may have contributed to a person's sense of difficulty? What might have made the test easier? How do you think students would respond to this type of test?

REFERENCES

Clay, M. M. (1993). An Observation Survey of Early Literacy Achievement. Portsmouth, NH: Heinemann.

Clay, M. M. (2000). *Concepts about print: What have children learned about printed language?* Portsmouth, NH: Heinemann.

Cunningham, P. (1990). The Names Test: An assessment of decoding ability. *The Reading Teacher, 44,* 124–129.

Dale, E. (1965). Vocabulary measurement: Techniques and major findings. *Elementary English, 42,* 895–901, 948.

Dufflemeyer, F. A., Kruse, A., Merkley, D. S., & Fyfe, S. A. (1994). Further validation and enhancement of the Names Test. *Reading Teacher, 48*(2), 118–128.

Kline, J. A. (2003). *Listening effectively: Achieving high standards in communication.* Upper Saddle River, NJ: Prentice Hall.

Mather, N., Sammons, J., & Schwartz, J. (2006). Adaptations of the Names Test: Easy-to-use phonics assessments. *The Reading Teacher, 60*(2), 114–122.

Torgesen, J. K. (1998). Catch them before they fail: Identification and assessment to prevent reading failure in young children. *American Educator.* Available: http://www.readingrockets.org/article/225/

Wesche, M., & Paribakht, T. S. (1996). Assessing second language vocabulary knowledge: Depth versus breadth. *Canadian Modern Language Review, 53*(1), 13–40.

Yopp, H. (1995). A test for assessing phonemic awareness in young children. *Reading Teacher, 49*(1), 20–29.

CHILDREN'S LITERATURE CITED

L'Engle, M. (1962). *A wrinkle in time.* New York: Crosswicks.

Writing as a Process

Access the book's Glossary, which defines the key terms boldfaced in this chapter, at www.hhpcommunities.com/teachinglanguagearts/glossary.pdf

KEY IDEAS

- Writing is one of the expressive modes of language arts, like speaking and visually representing.

- Writers develop their skills with time and practice, and this development follows a continuum of growth.

- The writing process is common to all writers, although the process is fluid and not always sequential.

- Digital writing workshop provides opportunities for students to develop independent writing skills while also using technology at all steps of the writing process.

- Technology can provide assistance for students who struggle with writing.

9.1

WRITING IS COMMUNICATING IDEAS

School days, school days

Dear old golden rule days

Readin' and 'ritin' and 'rithmetic

Taught to the tune of the hickory stick.

The lyrics from the song "School Days," published in 1908, harken back to the time of the one-room schoolhouse (Exhibit 9.1), when lessons focused on the basics. Reading, writing, and ciphering (mathematics) were seen as necessary for people to accomplish such daily tasks as reading the Bible, writing letters to family members, and keeping track of money. Writing, the focus of this chapter, involved practicing alphabet letters on a slate or honing handwriting skills using a quill pen and ink. Being able to sign your name in cursive was thought to be a sign of a well-educated person. Times have certainly changed! Today our students are not only putting pencil or pen to paper, they are creating text through digital stories, blog entries, and tweets. Although traditional forms of writing, such as poetry, letters, reports,

"Writing is an art; it can speak to people."

TAWN HAYES,
kindergarten teacher

EXHIBIT 9.1

School days.

and descriptions, continue, they are often shared with others through a class website, an email message, a collaborative wiki, or a personal blog. **Writing** has become *multimodal* in the sense that writing centers around arranging words to express ideas, but those words are often shared with others through a variety of modes involving not only written text, but also pictures, audio recordings, and videos (Labbo & Ryan, 2010; Lemke, 1998), just like the format of this ebook. With technology, the writer has the opportunity to enhance the message or add layers of meaning; but the heart of writing lies in expressing a message through written text. This has not changed. The slate, quill pen, and computer are only tools to **compose** a message.

Writing and the ways we encourage young people to write in schools are quite different from the act of practicing printed or cursive letters on a whiteboard or piece of paper. Keep in mind that writing is not handwriting, although many educators believe handwriting continues to have a place in the elementary school classroom (handwriting is discussed in Chapter 10, beginning with Section 10.10). Handwriting is practicing the formation of the letters on paper. Writing means expressing your ideas in written form, and although this process can involve handwriting, the focus is on communicating ideas.

This chapter begins with a focus on what it takes to become a writer. Then it identifies the stages of development students follow as they learn to write, describes the writing process, describes instructional practices that promote writing, and discusses how to work with writers who struggle.

9.2

BECOMING A WRITER

So where do writers get their ideas? For every writer, from professional published writers to kindergartners, ideas come from within ourselves by looking at the ordinary in a unique way. The world around us can provide inspiration; however, when writing, we must sift out all of the unneeded details to find the kernel of an idea that conveys our meaning. Latching on to an idea and nurturing it to a full-fledged piece of writing occurs through a process of listening, thinking, and writing.

In order to write, one must listen

First, the writer must have something to say, and that begins with listening. A writer is driven; that is, in order to create a written message, a writer must be compelled to set aside other activities in order to write. A person must mentally sift through knowledge and experiences and determine what is important enough to put into written words (Hillocks, 1988), which makes writing a cognitive, or thinking, process (Kress, 1999). Searching for what to write begins with finding a quiet place in our mind and listening to our own thoughts. Considering what is interesting and important requires a person to pay attention to his thinking and notice an idea that stands out or itches to be written down. This process is not always easy, and the challenge may cause some to shy away from it. Writer Jayne Anne Phillips describes writing as "being led by a whisper. If I listen closely enough the writing will tell me what to say and how to say it" (Newkirk & Miller, 2009, p. 81). Donald Murray, known for his skill both as a writer and a teacher of writing, describes writing as an ability to "chase a wisp of thinking until it grows into a completed thought" (Newkirk & Miller, 2009, p. 89).

What does it mean to be a writer?

Writing is about expressing an idea or message, and those ideas come from within ourselves, but what does it mean to *be* a writer? Some might say a writer is a person who has published a piece of work, such as a book, magazine, or newspaper column. Others might describe a writer as a person who writes extensively, possibly for several hours every day over the course of many years. Still others might say a writer is a person who has made a career of writing or who is getting paid to write. As Nick Leshi, writer and actor, states, "My definition is simple: A writer is someone who writes. Period" (Leshi, 2010). In *Forward Thinking*, the definition of a writer follows this same broad interpretation. A **writer** is anyone who chooses to use writing to collect and convey his or her ideas. A writer seeks to get a message across through the page, screen, or other writing tool (see Exhibit 9.2). The goal of a writer is to make people see what she is saying, and a writer does this by creating lists, jotting down notes, writing poetry, composing emails, drafting research reports, publishing stories, authoring a newsletter, or penning a birthday card. In other words, there are many ways to be a writer.

EXHIBIT 9.2

Writing for all kinds of reasons.

Why is it important for a teacher to be a writer?

Never underestimate the powerful influence you, as a teacher, have over the literacy development of your students. Students watch your actions and listen to your words. Through these, students determine what is important to you, and often embrace these same values and make them their own. When a teacher is a writer, talks positively about writing, and models the ways he uses writing, students sense this value. Seeking to emulate and please the teacher, they will often value writing as their teacher does. The opposite is also true, when a teacher does not believe himself to be a writer, when he speaks negatively about writing or not at all, students will sense this and may take their cues from him, making writing a low priority both in and out of school.

Furthermore, when a teacher is a writer, he also has credibility with his students. Would you want to take tennis lessons from a person who never plays tennis? The same is true for writing. When you talk like a writer, using terms such as ideas, draft, and revise, you are sharing your knowledge with students and providing a role model for learning a skill that will be important to them for the rest of their lives. Always remember the power to influence you hold in your pen, pencil, or keyboard and through your words and actions.

> **What if I do not feel I am a writer, how can I become one?** Read more: www.hhpcommunities.com/teachinglanguagearts/IL-09-01.pdf
>
> **Can I be a writer if I am not good at spelling, grammar, and punctuation?** Read more: www.hhpcommunities.com/teachinglanguagearts/IL-09-02.pdf
>
> **Books and websites about grammar and punctuation.** Read more: www.hhpcommunities.com/teachinglanguagearts/IL-09-03.pdf

points2ponder

QUICK REVIEW 1 How does being a writer help you become a better teacher of writing?

(Access the answer in the digital version of this book.)

9.3

UNDERSTANDING HOW CHILDREN LEARN TO WRITE: DEVELOPMENTAL STAGES

Writing is a process in which the writer grows and develops at her own pace, reflecting her own language development, experiences, and abilities. Writing leaves traces of a person's thoughts visible, and these traces can provide you with clues about what a student knows and can do when it comes to writing. Although each writer is unique in his development, educators have identified typical stages that all young people tend to pass through as they become writers (see Graves, 1985; Henderson & Beers, 1980; Juel, 1991). These stages seem to be stable even among different dialects, languages, and methods of instruction (Henderson & Beers, 1980). Graves (1994) points out that there is no certain point when a child is not, then is, a writer; just as there is no certain point when a child passes from one stage of writing to another. The process of becoming a writer is an accumulation of knowledge and experiences that builds over time. Young people accumulate knowledge at different rates, some quickly and some more slowly, depending on their oral language development and early language experiences at home (Shanahan, 2009), and their own abilities and motivation to learn.

In order for a writer to get a message across to others, her brain must coordinate several mental processes (Flower & Hayes, 1980), or all of the pistons must be firing at the same time, so to speak. A poem, a story, and a newspaper article represent the culmination of many mental processes coming together in unison, much like the various musicians performing a symphony. Obviously, writers do not begin at this level. They begin with a drawing, a word or two, or a brief sentence. As their knowledge of written language grows, so does their ability to convey their ideas. Children gradually move from *knowledge-telling* to *knowledge-transformation* (Bereiter & Scardamalia, 1987, pp. 5–6), from repeating facts and details to shedding new light on information through their own ideas.

Think of developmental stages as "overlapping and parallel waves rather than in discrete, sequential stages" (Berninger, 2000, p. 66). Some students may move quickly through one stage and more slowly through the next. Even within a stage, students sometimes appear to move two steps forward and one step back. In many cases, such stop-and-start development is normal; such is the nature of developmental stages. Imprecise guides, writing stages are general descriptors of what a student is learning and what he may be ready to learn next, although an age range usually accompanies the description of what the student learns at a given stage.

For the students in our classrooms, learning opportunities differ due to family income or education, ethnicity, or language background. These differences can dramatically affect the pace of learning for many students and may slow down the pace of so-called normal development. In addition, some students' learning may significantly lag behind or jump forward from what has been identified as typical, due to their own learning abilities. To be an effective teacher you must, first and foremost, know the students in your class and their abilities and interests. With this knowledge you can account for the varying differences in their learning. Then, for each student you can hold high expectations, set challenging yet achievable goals, and provide just the right level of scaffolding necessary to ensure success (National Association for the Education of Young Children, 2009). For those students who have had limited learning opportunities, you can design a classroom environment and learning activities that provide more intensive and enriched language experiences to enhance their written language development.

Knowing the stages of development provides you with professional knowledge about the level of performance you can expect from your students. Use this knowledge to design effective instruction and useful assessment. A knowledgeable teacher knows the skills students are expected to learn and watches for signals from students that they have learned these skills and are ready to move on to the next step. The next sections of this chapter describe the ten stages of development for written language, which take students from the preschool years through early adolescence. They include the following categories:

- Preconventional, ages 3–5
- Emerging, ages 4–6
- Developing, ages 5–7
- Beginning, ages 6–8
- Expanding, ages 7–9
- Bridging, ages 8–10
- Fluent, ages 9–11
- Proficient, ages 10–13
- Connecting, ages 11–14
- Independent

Notice the overlap of the age levels. These categories are rough estimates, rather than precise descriptors. A writer may fluctuate between two categories until new skills are firmly in place.

The Writing Continuum (www.hhpcommunities.com/teachinglanguagearts/IL-02-B.pdf) introduced in Chapter 2 provides an overview of specific elements of each stage. In Chapters 5 and 11, similar stages are used to describe the development of reading skills and oral language skills.

EXHIBIT 9.3

Scribble writing.

EXHIBIT 9.4

Letter strings.

Preconventional

Children in the **preconventional** stage of writing development are typically between three to five years old. These children are just discovering the ways writing is used to convey a message, but mostly focus on drawing a picture to get their idea across. Although in the early part of this stage their writing often looks like scribbles or random marks (see Exhibit 9.3), they are beginning to understand the usefulness of a shopping list, a reminder message, or a thank-you note. Pictures often accompany these early attempts at writing. As children move into the later part of this stage, a reader can recognize individual letters or a string of random letters or letter strings in their writing (see Exhibit 9.4). The growth from scribbles to readable simple words is fascinating to observe, as children put together the complex aspects of the written word.

Emerging

Emerging writers are beginning to combine both written letters and pictures to convey ideas. Some understanding of the connection between letters and sounds appears with the use of beginning and ending consonants, but con-

EXHIBIT 9.5

Simple sentence.

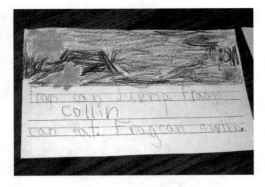

EXHIBIT 9.6

Complete sentences.

EXHIBIT 9.7

Inventive spelling.

ventional spelling is still a few stages down the road. These young children see themselves as budding writers as they become more skilled at communicating their ideas through words and pictures. Toward the end of the stage, some students will begin to write simple sentences, in preparation for becoming developing writers, the next stage. (See Exhibit 9.5.)

Watching the progress of emerging writers is fascinating because so much is learned over a relatively short time. View the video of kindergartner Collin (5:43). *(Access this video in the digital version of this book.)* Using the Writing Continuum (www.hhpcommunities.com/teachinglanguagearts/IL-02-B.pdf), see if you can identify at least three characteristics that place him at or close to the emerging level of writing.

Developing

Students between the ages of five and seven are usually at the **developing** stage of writing growth. Leaps and bounds beyond where they started at the preconventional stage, they can now write two to three sentences about a topic and enjoy the self-assurance that comes from knowing others can understand what they have written. They can spell names and **high frequency words** and make a close attempt at spelling less common words (see Exhibit 9.6). Written texts are often first attempted orally or in pictures, then in writing with more details added as they progress through the stage. Inventive or temporary spelling is used and reflects the young writer's early understanding of letters and sounds, focusing mostly on the sounds one hears when saying a word orally (see Exhibit 9.7). Consonants are used more accurately than vowels, and some sounds run together because this is how the student hears them. Students at this stage are developing a desire to have their written message be seen and understood by others and recognizing that what they do as a writer can facilitate this understanding.

Beginning

Simple informational pieces, such as a report on tree frogs, begin to appear. A single draft of a beginning writer's work is usually good enough to get the point across, but toward the end of the stage, these writers begin to make small edits and revisions, demonstrating their ability to convey ideas in a way others can read. Conventional letter formation and use of basic punctuation go a long way toward helping to communicate their ideas. Students generate their own writing ideas, and they may write stories involving a character or two and a familiar setting (see Exhibit 9.8).

View the video of Maddie (6:42), a second grader and beginning writer. Mentally list four writing skills Maddie displays that you did not see in the writing of Collin from the previous video. *(Access this video in the digital version of this book.)*

Expanding

Expanding writers are between seven and nine years old. These writers appear to be all grown up compared to their developing and beginning counterparts, although attempts at more sophisticated aspects of writing are still developing. Their writing is longer, often a full page to two or three, depending on the depth of their descriptions (see Exhibit 9.9) and includes short narrative, poetry, and informational texts created with guidance. They make attempts at a catchy beginning or an ending that wraps up ideas, although a reader may still find these attempts to be minimal at best. Spelling is more accurate with many high frequency words and other **content words** often spelled correctly or very close. Editing for punctuation and capitalization is done with guidance, although quotation marks, commas, and apostrophes are still a challenge.

Bridging

At the **bridging** stage, the purpose for writing goes beyond conveying ideas to include sharing feelings and expressing opinions. Paragraphs are sometimes used to organize ideas, although a text is often one long paragraph. Ideas for writing usually come from students' own experiences, but also books, movies, or television shows. Bridging writers often value the opinions and assistance of classroom peers in developing ideas for writing, spelling unknown words, or deciding where to place a detail. Sharing writing with others is an important motivator for bridging writers.

View the video of third-grade bridging writers, Mayra and Marisela (5:16) as they describe their motivation to write. Notice the way these students understand themselves as writers and their use of an inner motivation to write beyond the school day. *(Access this video in the digital version of this book.)*

Fluent

In the stages of development for elementary students, **fluent** writers are typically found in fourth and fifth grades, between the ages of nine and eleven. Teachers will likely find a wide range of abilities at this level. A few of these writers possess the skills approaching the level of some adult writers, while others may struggle to get thoughts in a clear and understandable format (see Exhibit 9.10). For the most part, writers at this stage understand the writing process and are able to edit and revise their writing. They recognize the importance of creating a final draft that is presentable to others, although some may not willingly put forth the effort to do so.

View Ethan (4:17), a fluent writer, as he shares about where he finds ideas for writing. Consider how Ethan's skill level compares to that of Collin, Maddie, Mayra, and Marisela. Identify and list five specific phonemic elements that Ethan appears to have mastered at this stage of his writing. *(Access this video in the digital version of this book.)*

Proficient

For some students, writing at the **proficient** level is a private act used to release emotions, possibly through a diary or journal (see Exhibit 9.11), or to describe situations that are difficult to discuss with others. This shift in

EXHIBIT 9.8

Simple story with characters.

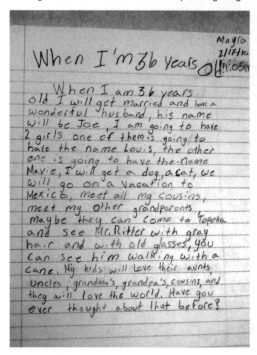

EXHIBIT 9.9

Longer text from a writer at the expanding stage.

Fluent writing.

> *Sixth grader Eric is at the proficient level and uses complex sentences, varied vocabulary, paragraphs, and an introduction and conclusion that show an awareness of the reader.*
>
> ### Family Portrait
>
> It's my mom, she's the one who gets up in the morning just to wake my sister and I up. She waits for the day when my sister and I are nice to each other, she waits until something funny happens, then embraces it. When my sister and I start to have fun, the kind of smile and laughter that can only be from a child comes out. But she still knows when enough is enough, and when to get down to work. Down to work she does, she goes into a fortress of a computer room, with cords everywhere, and papers sprawled on the ground. And when it comes to lunch and dinner, there's nothing better than her taco meat. When dinner is over, she does the dishes, my step dad says not to, but my mom likes washing dishes, it helps her relax. When cleaning up is done, she rests and washes T.V., some days she gets called by her sisters. My aunt Amy is in the hospital, and sometimes she gets worried, and times, cries. But she then forgets about everything, and lays down to sleep, just to do it all over again.
>
> It's Emily, she's the one who gets up to do her hair and get dressed for high school. She enjoys the day when we get along and look for videos on Youtube, to watch funny animals. Some days she tries to go driving but my mom won't let her. Feelings can be hurt, but everything ends up alright. She enjoys having a messy room and car, but still can find everything. She likes dressing up in nice clothes to go on dates with her boyfriend. She loves music and sometimes asks me for good bands. Times when it's time to eat, she decides not to eat what we're having. And when she gets busy, she forgets things, just to go to sleep early and wake up and do it all over again.
>
> It's my dad, he's the one who tries to sleep in, but ends up waking up early and feed the dogs. He wakes up and makes coffee for my step mom. He, some days, can get depressed, but can suck it up and not show anything. When you look in his office it looks like a tornado went through it. When he walks through the house he likes wearing jeans and a sweatshirt. Even going out, he likes to wear relaxing clothes. He doesn't really have a favorite food or dislikes a food. He's the kind of person who can go out to eat and will always like something. He likes it when he is busy, when he works he's happy. He doesn't like doing nothing. He has a fix for everything. When I procrastinate on my chores, he gives me a lecture. And when I talk back I get in trouble. When the day is through he retires early and sleeps, just to get up and do it all over again.
>
> It's me, I'm the one who plays sports but aren't too good at any sport. I can cry when I miss my family sometimes. I like an organized mess, when I leave something somewhere I like it ti stay there. I like to use the computer a lot. If I catch people in my room or touching my stuff I get mad at them. I'm the one who can reveal myself to a stranger easier than some. I only dislike a few foods, and love the rest. I usually don't care what I look like so I wear comfortable clothes around and outside. I like being busy, but not too busy, or else I get stressed. I like to stay up late, just to talk to friends, just to sleep and do it all over again.
>
> Its my family, they're the ones who loves to be with each other and laugh, and always share love.

Writing can be used to release emotions.

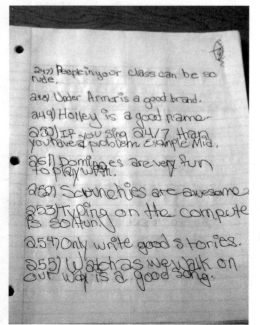

their thinking is a normal part of development, as they are moving into a time when the opinion of friends becomes as much, or more important than, the opinion of their families. At the same time, other students hold the opposite view and are eager to share drafts with classmates and seek their advice for writing. Proficient writers are capable of seeking tools to assist with writing and editing, including using a dictionary or electronic spell checker, but they do not necessarily use these tools when needed. Students at this stage often set personal goals for themselves as a writer, whether to write a longer text or to try a new genre.

Connecting

At the **connecting** stage, the structure of writing is more sophisticated, incorporating organized thoughts into several indented paragraphs with each focusing on a single idea and one idea leading into the next. Stories and informational writing usually have a catchy beginning, an organized middle, and a satisfying conclusion. Poems incorporate rhyme or other structures. Word choice is varied and may incorporate technical vocabulary or descriptive adverbs and adjectives. These writers have gained much control over grammar, punctuation, capitalization, and spelling, although new learning focuses on patterns and exceptions.

Independent

An **independent** writer is able to put all of the pieces together, easily moving from writing an email, to a report for school, to a personal narrative blog entry. Skillful application of spelling, grammar, and punctuation gives the independent writer's work a polished feel, and taking a piece of writing from an idea, to rough draft, to published piece gives the writer a strong sense of accomplishment. The level of confidence varies and can be strongly influenced by past experiences with writing or a perceived weakness in one aspect, such as spelling or punctuation. Independent writers continually work on being able to take suggestions about their writing with a thick skin and to also recognize their own strengths and weaknesses as writers.

One might think that the independent stage represents the pinnacle of writing development. However, writing skills continue to develop well into adulthood through the refinement of many skills described at the independent level. Words, organizational structures, appropriate use of grammar all become more complex for the adult writer, but these ten stages of development lay the foundation for adult writers to be successful.

9.4

THE ACT OF WRITING: STAGES IN THE WRITING PROCESS

Before delving in to what it takes to teach students to write, let's explore what the act of writing entails. Our example at the beginning of this chapter of the good ol' school days reminds us there was a time when writing was viewed as a finished product, a piece of work to be turned in as an assignment, kept for later reading, or published in a book or newspaper. The emphasis was on *what* the writer wrote, while little was known or shared about *how* the writer created the work. Currently, educators have a better understanding of the process writers use to create a piece of writing and of effective ways you can plan instruction to facilitate this process for your students (Atwell, 1988; Calkins, 1986; Graves, 1983; Murray, 1985; Routman, 2005). Based on this research, two general conclusions can be made about the writing process:

- Each writer and piece of writing is unique. No two pieces of writing follow the same exact process of development, because this process is influenced by the writer's background, experiences, knowledge, skill, motivation, and the purpose of the writing.
- Most writers use some similar elements, in varying orders and to varying degrees, in the process of writing.

In other words, the writing process is both similar and different for each writer.

Researchers during the 1980s and 1990s studied the writing process by closely observing students as they wrote freely about topics of their choice. Through these observations, reflections, and analyses, educators developed a description of common elements or stages in the writing process. These stages include prewriting, drafting, revising, editing, and publishing. The stages of the writing process are often described as discrete steps that happen in a certain order. This is misleading. The attention given to each stage varies with each writer and each piece of writing, depending on the purpose, audience, and context (Dyson & Freedman, 2003). In other words, there is no exact writing process; however, even with all of the variance among writers, they use a collection of common practices that lead to a finished product.

The process of bringing ideas to life on paper or screen is more like a cycle and less like a series of discrete steps. The stages become intertwined as a writer weaves the complex threads of his ideas (we can imagine these interwoven ideas like the circles in the illustration we see in Exhibit 9.12). Once one set of ideas moves through the stages of the writing process, a new set of ideas is often waiting in the wings to be brought out for others to see. Younger writers or those who struggle with writing may follow an abbreviated form of the writing process, appropriate to their age, background experiences, and ability levels (see Exhibit 9.13). For English language learners, writing is challenging because so many aspects of spelling, grammar, and punctuation must be put together to communicate effectively. For these students and others who may struggle, the writing process may include drawing, dictation, or a combination of English and the native language until the English skills become stronger. Your role is to help young writers find the process that works best for them on a given day with a given piece of writing by creating loosely structured routines that can be adapted to fit each student's writing situation.

EXHIBIT 9.12

The elements of the writing process are intertwined.

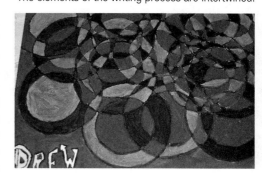

EXHIBIT 9.13

Adaptations to the writing process for younger, inexperienced, or struggling writers.

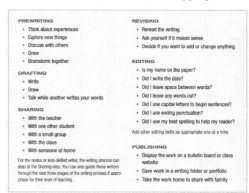

PREWRITING
- Think about experiences
- Explore new things
- Discuss with others
- Draw
- Brainstorm together

DRAFTING
- Write
- Draw
- Talk while another writes your words

SHARING
- With the teacher
- With one other student
- With a small group
- With the class
- With someone at home

For the novice or less-skilled writer, the writing process can stop at the Sharing step. You can also guide these writers through the next three stages of the writing process if appropriate for their level of learning.

REVISING
- Reread the writing
- Ask yourself if it makes sense
- Decide if you want to add or change anything

EDITING
- Is my name on the paper?
- Did I write the date?
- Did I leave space between words?
- Did I leave any words out?
- Did I use capital letters to begin sentences?
- Did I use ending punctuation?
- Did I use my best spelling to help my reader?

Add other editing skills as appropriate one at a time

PUBLISHING
- Display the work on a bulletin board or class website
- Save work in a writing folder or portfolio
- Take the work home to share with family

Adapted from Northwest Regional Educational Laboratory (1999). *Seeing with new eyes: A guidebook on teaching and assessing beginning writers.* Portland, OR.

spotlight ON A LITERACY LEADER

LUCY CALKINS

Lucy Calkins inspires and challenges both teachers and students to use writing to change the world and especially the world of your classroom by truly listening to your own writing and the writing of others. Calkins, through her work at the Reading and Writing Project at Columbia University in New York, is credited with the concept of the writing workshop (explored later in this chapter), which is an instructional framework for supporting the writing process in classrooms. Her book, *The Art of Teaching Writing* (1994), has inspired many teachers to make writing a key part of their instructional practices.

In the video Being a Good Writer: Writing Tips and Strategies (www.youtube. com/watch?v=WO29k1-RvsA), Calkins entreats writers to "read your writing as if it were gold." Her heartfelt enthusiasm and deep love of writing is contagious.

Prewriting

Before putting pencil to paper or fingers to keyboard, a writer works through the topic idea by thinking, talking, reading, drawing, making notes, and otherwise trying out concepts. Compare **prewriting** to a runner warming up before a race. Donald Graves suggests writers devote 85 percent of their writing time to the prewriting step in order to increase the flow of ideas later in the writing process (Graves, 1994). Sometimes called brainstorming or rehearsing, prewriting entails all of the plans a writer makes for writing. Although prewriting typically occurs before writing, it can also take place as a draft is being created when, for example, a writer takes a break from writing to consider what will be written next.

Encourage students to make plans for writing by providing opportunities for them to collect ideas in a writer's notebook, to talk with classmates about writing ideas, and to read and collect background information for writing.

Read Writer's Notebook (www.hhpcommunities.com/teachinglanguagearts/IL-09-04) to learn about the who, what, where, when, why, and how of using a writer's notebook. Consider how you might use such a notebook for your own writing assignments and how it might benefit your students. Read one of the suggested children's books that promote the writer's notebook to see how two young writers used them.

Concept maps, or graphic organizers, whether on paper or screen, can provide writers with a visual outline of their ideas before more involved writing begins. In a research study involving young people with learning disabilities, writing that began with a concept map was longer and of higher quality (Sturm & Rankin-Erickson, 2002). A graphic organizer provides students with a format for making notes before writing and can be a useful tool when a writer is unsure of what to write next when drafting.

In addition to generating ideas, prewriting is a time when the writer is making numerous decisions about the piece of writing by answering these questions:

- What is the intent or purpose of this piece of writing? (to inform, entertain, persuade, describe)
- Who is the audience, or who will read this piece of writing?
- How can I get my ideas across most effectively? Which form of writing is best for this piece? (letter, poem, story, report, poster, podcast, email, text, etc.)

Between generating ideas and making decisions, a writer has much to do in the prewriting stage.

A main idea graphic organizer (www.writingfix.com/PDFs/Process/main_idea_organizer.pdf) provides an example of the ways writers can organize their ideas before writing. See if this structure helps you to organize your own writing by using this or another graphic organizer the next time you need to write a paper for a college class.

Drafting

The process of **drafting** involves a writer putting her thoughts on paper or screen. Writers at this stage should focus on getting ideas down rather than on spelling, grammar, and punctuation, although pausing to correct a misspelling or add a period is fine. There is some debate among teachers about whether it is better to draft with paper and pencil or on the computer. Research shows pros and cons to each approach. Writers tend to make more minor changes while writing a draft on the computer. For some, the ease of making these changes is a distraction to getting their ideas in written form. For others, this ease facilitates the writing process (MacArthur, 2009).

Consider a draft as written in clay, rather than stone, because many aspects of a draft will change as the writing becomes more firmly defined during the later stages of the process. Creating a draft that is considered to be temporary or fluid can be challenging for students who often believe that their writing needs no further changes or improvements. For a personal journal or a grocery list this may be the case, but writing that will be seen by others often requires some polishing to make ideas clear to readers. What happens during drafting, as with each stage of the writing process, depends on the writer's intent or purpose. Also, drafting does not necessarily mean the end of prewriting. Students can benefit from taking brief pauses in drafting to talk with a writing partner or teacher about their draft or to read and collect more information.

Revising

Notice the similarity between the two words *revising* and *revisit*. **Revising** means taking another look at a draft to see if it makes sense and then clarifying the message. Throughout the writing process, a writer should be focused on clearly explaining ideas. Sometimes, when engrossed with getting ideas down, a writer may lose this focus. Revising allows the writer to pause and revisit the work to consider what the reader needs to know. A fresh perspective may arise if time has passed between creation of the original draft and the revision, whether this time ranges from a few minutes, to a few hours, or to a few days. Revising usually involves three basic steps:

EXHIBIT 9.14

Peers offer feedback to writers.

1. Reread the writing.
2. Pause at a portion of the writing that expresses a point. Ask yourself, does this point make sense?
3. Decide which option would help the writing make sense:
   a. Moving the text to another place in the writing.
   b. Deleting text that seems unnecessary or distracting.
   c. Adding text that seems to be missing or to provide more explanation, an example, or additional details.

A peer or teacher may provide a useful sounding board for determining if a piece of writing makes sense (see Exhibit 9.14). Young writers seem to revise more effectively when working with another person (Boscolo & Ascorti, 2004). Revising may happen after a sentence has been written, or it may not occur until the entire first draft is completed. Sometimes writers revise while they are drafting. Consider your own writing process. Do you wait until the entire piece is complete before checking yourself for clarity? Again, each writer and piece of writing is unique.

Chapter 12 will discuss the Six + 1 Trait writing model, a framework for writing instruction and assessment that also provides writers with a

framework for revising by encouraging a focus on seven (6 + 1) aspects of writing: ideas, organization, voice, word choice, sentence fluency, conventions, and presentation. Using this model, writers are able to give attention to the various aspects of a piece of writing.

Editing

When writing is to be shared with others, editing is a must. **Editing** involves analyzing the details of spelling, punctuation, and grammar. However, if the writing is not intended to be read by others, editing is not necessary. To undergo such a process with every piece of writing would be extremely time-consuming and frustrating for young or inexperienced writers. At the same time, lack of editing can cause the reader much difficulty in understanding a writer's message; thus a balance must be struck. Editing is an element of writing etiquette and shows an awareness of the reader's needs. The amount of editing a piece needs depends on the developmental level of the writer and the purpose of the writing. For first graders, simply checking for a capital letter at the beginning of the sentence and a period at the end may be the extent of editing. As students become more experienced writers and their knowledge of structure, meaning, and usage increases, the expectations for editing increase.

A primary goal of writing instruction is for students to become independent editors. Thus, you should not actually do the editing for your students. When you edit your students' writing, the learning stops. Many adults have experienced an instructor's red pen marking numerous corrections on their writing. These bold red marks may have caused dismay and contributed to their dislike of writing. Students should be taught to edit their own writing, which takes much modeling from the teacher and practice time for the students. Exhibit 9.15 displays a list of editing marks that students can use to guide the editing process. You can customize a list of revising and editing marks based on the elements emphasized during writing time.

Publishing

The culminating point in the writing process occurs during the **publishing** stage, when a writer prepares the piece to share with others. Some young people (and adults) write solely for the purpose of having their words seen by an audience. Through this sharing, a writer is putting his work out for others to see, enjoy, and possibly critique. Doing this requires writers to be confident, but it also makes them vulnerable. On a simplistic level, publishing might mean adding an illustration and displaying the work on a hallway bulletin board or recopying a story into a small stapled paper booklet with a construction paper cover. Publishing may entail writing on a blog or wiki or reading a work for a podcast. A more involved publishing project may be creating a hardback book through a children's publishing website, such as Student Treasures (www.studenttreasures.com). Each student can contribute a page of writing and an illustration or would write and illustrate their own complete book; the manuscript is then professionally published at no cost, and the teacher receives a free classroom copy. Students' families are invited to purchase their own copy of the book. One teacher, Sarah Lucero, holds a special author party and sharing session when the class receives their book (see Exhibit 9.16).

EXHIBIT 9.15

Revising and editing marks for writers.

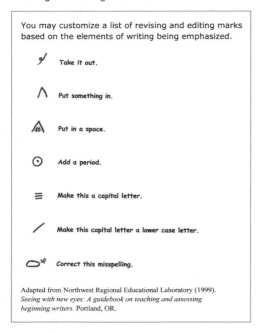

You may customize a list of revising and editing marks based on the elements of writing being emphasized.

Take it out.

Put something in.

Put in a space.

Add a period.

Make this a capital letter.

Make this capital letter a lower case letter.

Correct this misspelling.

Adapted from Northwest Regional Educational Laboratory (1999). *Seeing with new eyes: A guidebook on teaching and assessing beginning writers.* Portland, OR.

EXHIBIT 9.16

The published book produced by Sarah Lucero's second graders.

Animals

Written and Illustrated by Mrs. Lucero's Class
Whitson Elementary School 2009-1

English language learners face challenges to develop writing skills while also mastering the speaking of English. The article "Children's Writing in ESL" by Sarah Hudelson (www.readingrockets.org/article/287/) shares strategies for encouraging growth in writing for English learners.

points2ponder

QUICK REVIEW 2 Create a simple graphic organizer showing the stages of the writing process and how these stages are connected.

(Access the answer in the digital version of this book.)

9.5

CREATING A CLASSROOM WHERE WRITING FLOURISHES

How do you create a classroom where writing flourishes? Imparting the value of writing and showing enthusiasm for students' writing are both important first steps in this process. Students and their families take their cue about priorities in the classroom from the teacher. When teachers show enthusiasm, plan engaging writing activities, talk about their own writing, and share students' writing with others outside of the classroom, they demonstrate the value of writing. Students, families, and administrators sense this commitment to writing instruction and begin to value writing in similar ways.

Standards

At the same time you are setting your priorities for writing in the classroom, you are also making instructional decisions. These decisions are guided by standards at the district, state, or national level. The Common Core State Standards provide specific expectations for instruction in the area of writing, based on four categories:

1. Text types and purposes
2. Production and distribution of writing
3. Research to build and present knowledge
4. Range of writing

These four categories are addressed by the standards at all grade levels, and within these categories are specific indicators for each grade level. Indicators for younger students call for guidance and support from adults and peers until students can be expected to meet the indicator independently. This **scope and sequence** for writing displays the range of knowledge students need and the order in which that knowledge should develop.

Referring to the CCSS (www.corestandards.org/ELA-Literacy/W/introduction), notice the progression of learning described through the writing standards. Click on Writing to view grade levels; then examine across the grade levels, for example, the third standard under the category Text Types and Purposes. Notice that students are writing narrative texts at the various levels; yet as the grade level increases, so does the expectation for the depth of the narrative texts. A similar sequence is found among each of the standards. Presently, the CCSS are a guide for teachers and for state and district curriculum planning.

Along with the CCSS, states and local school districts have standards to guide writing instruction and assessments. Each set of standards provides teachers with a guide for what students should know and be able to do. Many school districts have aligned their standards with state and national standards so teachers can easily pinpoint the instructional expectations for each grade level.

Philosophy

In addition to standards, instructional decisions are also guided by your own philosophy of teaching, as described in Chapter 3. Your philosophy may or may not attend specifically to writing, but it will set the tone for the classroom. As discussed in Chapter 3, a philosophy is a reflection of your personal style and beliefs, which are often based on the research and theoretical work of others.

The next sections focus on the National Council of Teachers of English's (NCTE) principles for guiding effective writing instruction and the elements that make up the writing instructional philosophy for Donald Graves, a noted researcher and teacher in the field of writing. While reading the sections, consider which elements will help guide your philosophy about writing.

Key principles for guiding effective writing instruction

As discussed in Chapter 2, the NCTE is a professional association for teachers that focuses on literacy. It has identified key principles for guiding effective teaching practice in the area of writing (NCTE, 2004). These principles provide a foundation to help teachers develop a philosophy of teaching and in planning for writing instruction and assessment. The following are the 11 principles. Visit the NCTE website for a discussion of them (www.ncte.org/positions/statements/writingbeliefs).

1. Everyone has the capacity to write, writing can be taught, and teachers can help students become better writers.
2. People learn to write by writing.
3. Writing is a process.
4. Writing is a tool for thinking.
5. Writing grows out of many different purposes.
6. Conventions of finished and edited texts are important to readers and therefore to writers.
7. Writing and reading are related.
8. Writing has a complex relationship to talk.
9. Literate practices are embedded in complicated social relationships.
10. Composing occurs in different modalities and technologies.
11. Assessment of writing involves complex, informed, human judgment. (unpaged)

A common thread weaves through these 11 principles: Writing does not stand alone. It is inextricably linked to the other five modalities of language arts. Reading, listening, and viewing prepare the writer to understand the patterns of language; speaking serves as a springboard for writing or a tool for providing feedback to the writer; and visually representing often stems from a written idea. In this chapter, although the focus is on writing, keep the other five modalities in mind.

Seven conditions for effective writing

Some writers choose a special hat or favorite chair that inspires their writing. Other writers want a certain view out the window or are inspired when their cat curls up on their lap. For Donald Graves, seven conditions for learning promote effective writing. According to Graves, quality student writing does not result from a specific writing program or a method of instruction. It is not magic or elusive. Good writing develops when a teacher makes instructional decisions that foster the conditions of (1) time, (2) choice, (3) response, (4) demonstration, (5) expectation, (6) room structure, and (7) evaluation.

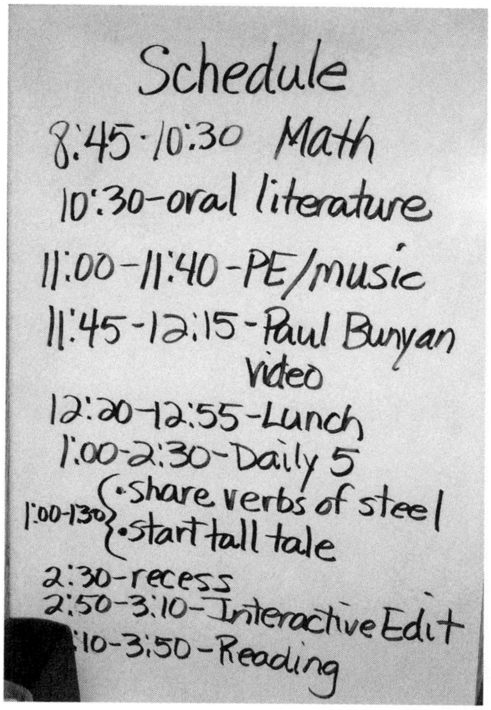

Here is a detailed description of how you can implement the seven conditions for effective writing in your classroom: www.hhpcommunities.com/teachinglanguagearts/IL-09-05

In order for your students to develop as writers, you must make time for writing. Regie Routman, in her book *Writing Essentials* (2005), expresses the belief teachers make time for the things they value. When writing time is a standard part of the classroom schedule (see Exhibit 9.17), students begin to think about writing even when they are not engaged in the process (Graves, 1994). Students should also have the opportunity to choose their own topics. Writers at all levels are more engaged when writing on a topic they care about or have chosen on their own (see Exhibit 9.18). Response or feedback lets writers know how well their message is getting across to others. Compliments and suggestions are the food of the writer, especially one who wants to share his words with others.

Demonstration or modeling is at the heart of teaching (see the discussion of gradual release of responsibility, Chapter 4). The mental part of the writing process is best modeled through thinking aloud while writing, sharing the struggles and the elations with selecting just the right word or completing an important thought. The role of the teacher is "to find out what your students know, show them how to put what they know into words, then *expect* [emphasis added] them to do it" (Graves, 1994, p. 110). By setting high but realistic expectations for all students in the class, we let them know that writing is not optional. Writing routines begin with the expectation that students write often and on a regular basis and might also include a quiet daily minute of brainstorming beforehand. Knowing this routine will occur each day of writing time lets students focus on their ideas rather than trying to figure out what will happen next. The word *evaluation* stems from the root word *value*. Evaluation is about placing value or making judgment about quality. When it comes to writing, two aspects of evaluation are important to consider: the teacher's evaluation of the students' writing, and the students' evaluation of their own writing.

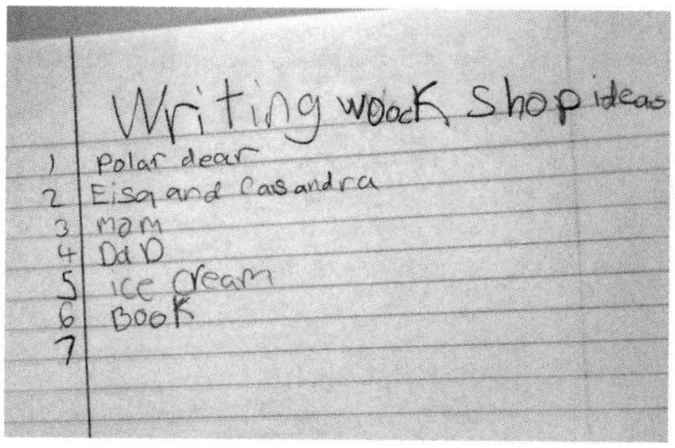

The NCTE principles of writing provide a foundation for creating a teaching philosophy that reflects the value of writing. The seven conditions

EXHIBIT 9.17

Daily schedule includes writing time.

EXHIBIT 9.18

Casandra's list of writing topics.

for effective writing are the building blocks of a classroom writing program. Together these beliefs and conditions support a teacher's decision to make writing an integral part of the school day, so students can blossom as writers and teachers can guide students in their writing growth.

points2ponder

QUICK REVIEW 3 Donald Graves identified seven conditions for learning that promote effective writing. Identify four of the seven and describe three ways you can create these conditions in your classroom.

(Access the answer in the digital version of this book.)

9.6

TEACHING STUDENTS TO WRITE

With a strong philosophy and a clear set of values about the importance of writing, you are ready to begin constructing a plan for teaching writing. When it comes to making the day-to-day instructional decisions that form the framework for writing instruction, keep two additional key ideas in mind:

- Children are active constructors of their own language and literacy (Clay, 1991).
- As children gain more control over their abilities to construct meaning from print, their competence and confidence grows (Vygotsky, 1962).

Again, this cannot be said enough: Students learn to write by writing. Decisions about instructional activities, room arrangement, feedback, assessment, all provide encouragement and opportunities for students to write. Only through extensive opportunities to write will students develop the skills needed to successfully communicate their ideas. How do these skills develop? They grow from a gradual release of responsibility (Pearson & Gallagher, 1983), as we described in Chapter 4, as applied to the writing process:

- First the teacher explains and models.
- Next the teacher and students practice writing together.
- Then the students write independently.

This gradual release may occur within one lesson, over the course of a week or two, or span the entire school year, depending on the students' developmental needs. Such a gradual release toward independence prepares students to use their language skills in new ways. The goal is to keep students working in their zone of proximal development (Vygotsky, 1988), where they feel challenged but not frustrated. By gradually turning over more of the responsibility for writing as students are ready to accept this responsibility, a skilled teacher guides them toward effectively communicating with others through writing. When discussing the gradual release of responsibility with students, teachers often use the motto, *I do, we do, you do* to help them understand the teacher's role in conjunction to theirs.

When teaching students to write, use various approaches to instruction, depending on the degree to which you are releasing responsibility to your students for their writing (see Exhibit 9.19). The decision about which writing instruction approach to use in your classroom will also be influenced by the developmental needs of the students and the skills to be taught. Each of the approaches described in the next section can be used with students of various ages, but all reflect the importance of teacher demonstration. "Modeling is the most powerful portion of any lesson. Try to do it as often as possible" (Oczkus, 2008, p. 84). Even as students become more independent in their writing, teacher modeling of new or challenging skills remains a key component of successful writing instruction.

EXHIBIT 9.19

Gradual release of responsibility and writing approaches.

I DO	WE DO	YOU DO
TEACHER WRITES	TEACHER AND CHILDREN WRITE TOGETHER	CHILDREN WRITE
Modeled writing	Shared writing *Language experience approach* *Morning message* *Digital shared writing*	Independent writing *Journaling* *Writing workshop*
	Interactive writing *"Share the pen or keyboard"*	
	Guided writing	
Whole class Small group	Whole class Small group	Partners Individuals

9.7

MODELED WRITING

Believe it or not, the human brain is not naturally hard-wired for written language. Speaking and listening, yes, but writing and reading are not natural processes for us. As evolutionary psychologist Stephen Pinker says, "Young people are wired for sound, but print is an optional accessory that must be painstakingly bolted on" (1998, p. ix). This "bolting on," so to speak, involves the development and strengthening of neural pathways in the brain. These pathways are developed through experience and are used to carry important information from one part of the brain to another. With each experience, neurons fire in the brain. One brain development theory suggests that neurons that fire concurrently strengthen the pathway and are more likely to fire together in the future (Fisher, Frey, & Lapp, 2009). Each time a first grader writes the word *horse,* the pathway becomes stronger and it becomes easier for her to remember how to write the word. Because of this complex system, our brain may actually be more active when we are first learning a new skill than when we have mastered that skill and can perform it without much conscious thought. By then, the neural pathways have become streamlined and efficient. In order to help our students develop their neural pathways, one of our jobs is to continually provide the experiences so our students can build and strengthen these pathways (Fisher, Frey, & Lapp, 2009). Besides the actual hands-on experience of writing, which will be described in the upcoming sections, modeling or demonstrating how to write is one of the most effective ways to teach someone a new skill that is not a natural process for the brain.

Modeled writing is the first step of the writing sequence, which moves from the teacher demonstrating to the student writing independently (see Exhibit 9.20). In order to arrive at that final destination of independence, the writer must begin with an understanding of what it means to write, and this understanding begins with watching and listening to a more experienced writer. Modeled writing begins with telling your class *what* you are going to write about and *why* you chose the topic. Write slowly, saying the words ahead of writing them, whether on an interactive whiteboard, an overhead projector, a chart paper, or a computer. During modeling, you may often dramatize or overly exaggerate the writing process, thinking aloud about how to spell a tricky word or contemplating the best way to describe a character. Though you are adept at these and many other writing skills, dramatizing them illustrates how a less experienced writer, like the students in your class, will approach them.

You may think aloud about any aspect of writing, but the following are common topics during a writing think-aloud.

EXHIBIT 9.20

Amanda Arndt models writing for her first graders using an interactive whiteboard.

- *Choosing and developing a topic.* Model the process of choosing a topic by contemplating the several sources students might consider for finding an interesting topic, explaining why they might discard a topic or two, referring to their own topic list, and keeping a writing folder as a source for possible ideas.
- *Gathering ideas for writing.* Guide students in gathering and organizing their ideas for writing by modeling the use of graphic organizers, writer's notebook, sticky notes, diagrams, illustrations, and even talking with a buddy.
- *Making decisions about writing forms.* Influence students to explore different forms of writing by modeling these different forms yourself. Suggest writing a poem, a descriptive blog entry, or a personal narrative. Through your interest and enthusiasm during a think-aloud, students will be motivated to try different formats.
- *Infusing the writer's voice.* **Voice** is the writer's style, personality, or individual touch. This quality is challenging to teach because each writer's voice is unique; however, modeling and thinking aloud is an effective way to make students aware of the tone conveyed in their writing.

During modeled writing, students are actively watching and listening while you are actively writing. Although you may engage the students in a brief discussion, most of the time you are doing the talking, writing, and thinking aloud. The students will become more active during other activities that may occur during the same lesson or during another lesson.

Use this list of additional *do's* and *don'ts* (www.hhpcommunities.com/teaching languagearts/IL-09-06.pdf) to guide your modeling of writing.

Encourage students to be active listeners (see Chapter 7 for more information about active listening) through simple activities such as the following (Oczkus, 2008):

- Pause to ask students to give thumbs up or thumbs down about a specific detail you add to the writing.
- Give students a few minutes to turn to a partner and discuss what they noticed about your writing. Invite a few students to share with the class.
- Invite a small number of students to dramatize an excerpt from the text to help the teacher/author decide if the text has enough details.
- Ask the students to use individual whiteboards and to write one thing they saw you do when you were stuck or unsure of what to do next.

For some teachers, the prospect of writing in front of students is daunting. What can you do about this? First, know that you are not alone; others, even experienced teachers, share this same concern. Next, consider composing your text ahead of time and later pretend you are writing it for the first time. This practice text lets you think through your teaching points ahead of time, thus heading off the uncertainty of on-the-spot composing. If you use this approach, you will likely become more comfortable writing in front of students after only a few times. Build the following prompts into your think-aloud to keep yourself on track, whether during practice or the real session:

- I am going to write this because . . .
- What should I write next? Let me think a minute . . .

- I am having trouble remembering how to spell this word. I think I will try . . .
- This part does not sound right. I think I will change it.
- It seem like I have left something out here. I will add . . .

When responding to these prompts, you are not asking a student what he should do, but instead you are describing the thoughts he should use to make these decisions on his own. You are modeling, not explaining.

Explaining is *not* modeling

Modeling Scenario 1: Modeling

On the interactive whiteboard, Mr. Baldwin writes an informational text about animal habitats. He thinks aloud while composing.

Writers, I want to use headings to help organize my ideas, but I am not sure what my headings should be. I am going to look back on the graphic organizer we prepared in science to remind me.

Mr. Baldwin continues thinking aloud about how he solves the problems he encounters when writing.

I want to use the word habitat, *but I am not sure how to spell it. I could choose an easier word, like* home, *but it doesn't seem to me like* home *really fits for animals that move around a lot. So let me think about how I could spell* habitat. *I could give it a guess, circle it, then go on and return with a dictionary later to check my spelling. I like this choice because it doesn't slow down my writing.*

Mr. Baldwin finishes his piece of writing and asks students to turn to each other and discuss one thing they noticed about what he did while writing his paragraph. Add these observations to a class chart.

Modeling Scenario 2: Explaining

Mr. Baldwin holds up a blank piece of paper and refers to a copy of an informational picture book propped on the ledge in the front of the room.

I am going to show you how I want you to write an informational book about animal habitats. First, I want you to think about what is in this picture book, such as headings and a table of contents. Also I want you to remember that informational texts are true and full of facts and details. You should put these in your writing. I am also going to add headings at the beginning of different sections. You can think about the graphic organizer we made to get ideas for your headings. Next you will write the text.

Mr. Baldwin passes out blank paper to each student and gives them time to write on their own.

Notice: In modeling, the teacher thinks aloud. In explaining, the teacher tells students what to do. Both have a place in teaching, but for modeled writing, the thinking aloud about what you do as a writer is key to creating understanding.

Some students need the rich, detailed description characteristic of modeling in order to fully understand just what they are expected to do themselves. Remember, there are no right or wrong answers in a think-aloud. There is only vivid description and not so vivid description. Students need vivid description in order to know exactly the type of thinking they should be using for their own writing. A teacher has the responsibility to demonstrate this thinking and action before expecting students to try a task, especially one as complex as writing, on their own.

COMPREHENSION *coach*

Active reading Are you able to process what you are reading in this chapter, cement it in your memory, and make it your own? Listen to this podcast by Elizabeth Dobler for comprehension coaching. *(Access this podcast in the digital version of this book.)*

9.8

SHARED WRITING

Shared writing is a *We do* type of writing instruction. Although you and the students are sharing the words of the text, you are actually doing the writing. A natural bridge between spoken and written language, conversations between the teacher and the students provide a fountain of words and ideas, which the teacher then models through his writing. Roach Van Allen (1986) described shared writing in this way:

> What I think about, I can talk about.
>
> What I say, I can write (or someone can write for me).
>
> What I can write, I can read (and others can read for me, too).
>
> I can read what I have written and I can also read what other people have written for me to read. (pp. 51–52)

During shared writing, the teacher and students work together to plan the text based on books previously read or experiences shared, both in and outside of the classroom. Then the students' thoughts are recorded on chart paper or an interactive whiteboard and displayed for students and visitors to read. The writing may follow a specific structure, such as an invitation to Doughnuts for Dads Day or the retelling of a favorite story, such as "Goldilocks and the Three Bears." Throughout a shared writing activity, the teacher receives and records the students' words, but also uses each word or phrase as an opportunity to teach an element of writing, such as beginning a name with a capital letter or putting a period at the end of a sentence (see Exhibit 9.21).

McKenzie (1985) says about shared writing:

> [The teacher] takes on a teaching role in which she enables children to develop and organize ideas. The emphasis is on the message or story they are creating. She receives their ideas, and through her comments and questions she sustains their interest and production of ideas. She encourages them to think about appropriate language as she helps them to elaborate, or to focus, their text. Throughout the process her guidance and the children's discussion contribute to a growing awareness and understanding of what writing is about and what readers can make of their writing. Children begin to "get in on" the craft of writing. (p. 8)

The teacher and students become partners in the text creation, although not necessarily equal partners. You play the key role of providing pinpointed

---

EXHIBIT 9.21

Example written language skills taught during shared writing.

- recognition and names of lower and uppercase letters
- proper letter formation
- letter and sound correspondence
- left-to-right progression of text
- concept of a letter, a word, and a sentence
- spacing within and between words
- common sight words
- ending punctuation
- patterns within words or word families

instruction based on what the students need, while at the same time drawing students into the conversation by using their own authentic words.

Because shared writing focuses on teaching the connection between the spoken and written word, this approach is typically used with students at the emergent stage of development, which may include English language learners and students with special learning needs, because instruction can easily be tailored to their needs. While composing together, shared writing gives a teacher the opportunity to think aloud in front of the students and grapple with the common challenges faced by writers of any age and ability. A shared writing text may be read and reread several times, with each visit to the text focusing on a new skill or providing opportunities for extended practice. Fun gadgets (see Exhibit 9.22) can be used to keep students interested and motivated to reread.

Language experience approach and morning message are two specific shared writing activities in which teachers facilitate students' gradual acquisition of writing skills through modeling and creating texts from the students' own words.

Language experience approach

The **language experience approach,** a type of shared writing activity, focuses on the students and teacher creating a text based on a shared experience. The students dictate a text and you serve as a scribe, with the goal of providing practice to prepare students to write independently (Ashton-Warner, 1965; Stauffer, 1980). A distinct characteristic of the language experience approach is that the teacher records the students' *own* words about the shared experience, making few changes to grammar or wording, thus facilitating the students' ability to reread their own words later (see Exhibit 9.23). In addition, the teacher thinks aloud about such skills as where to begin the sentence and how much space to put between words (see Exhibit 9.24).

Language experience topics usually stem from everyday sights and events (autumn, a field trip to the zoo), special occasions (Thanksgiving), common tasks (caring for a class pet), and new lyrics to familiar songs (*The Wheels on the Bus*). At times a language experience activity emerges spontaneously from an unexpected event, such as the first snowfall or the escape of the class pet, and becomes a learning opportunity that capitalizes on the natural enthusiasm of the students. The collaboratively written text serves as a record of their learning, thinking, and a free, useful, and authentic teaching tool. Students are encouraged to bring their varied experiences and backgrounds into the classroom to be shared during a language experience activity. For example, a language experience activity can be planned around a Cinco de Mayo celebration (see Exhibit 9.25). This authentic learning tool reflects the lives and words of the students, thus supporting students' diverse cultural and linguistic backgrounds. Exhibit 9.26 presents the steps to creating a language experience text.

Morning message

Morning message is another activity that encourages shared writing and is typically used by teachers with students at the emergent stage of writing (Kawakami-Arakaki, Oshiro, & Farran, 1989). Morning message is similar to the language experience approach in the sense that the teacher records the students' own words regarding their own experiences. Teacher

EXHIBIT 9.22

Gadgets to encourage rereading of shared writing.

EXHIBIT 9.23

Shared writing from Lucy Burdiek's first-grade class.

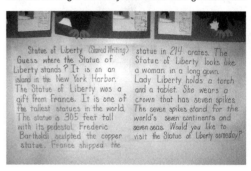

EXHIBIT 9.24

Thinking aloud during shared writing.

Emergent writers often confuse letters and words, running both together into one long string. One way to help is to teach "spaghetti and meatball" spacing through a teacher modeling and thinking aloud during shared writing, such as the following:

Derrick, you suggested the sentence "We went to the zoo." First, let's count how many words are in this sentence. Let's say the words slowly and put up a finger for each word. We ... went ... to ... the ... zoo. Five fingers. That's five words. When we finish writing our sentence, we will need to check and see if we have five words. Now, for the first word "We," I am going to write a capital W because it's the first word of the sentence. There is another letter in we, "e." Since these letters are in the same word, I am going to make a small space or a spaghetti space between the letters, a space the size of a piece of spaghetti.

The teacher uses his finger as a space marker between the letters while writing and then continues.

The next word is "went." Since this is a new word, I am going to use a meatball space to show whoever reads our story that "went" is a different word than "we." The teacher makes a fist to use as a space marker between the words.

This process continues until the sentence is complete and the teacher concludes by saying,

Now let's go back and count our words. Do we have five words like we said we would? Yes. Our spaghetti and meatballs are a little bit bigger than the ones we eat for dinner, but they helped us to use our spaces when we are writing on the board or chart paper.

Special occasions stimulate language experience texts.

Steps for creating a language experience text.

1. **Provide an activity or item that sparks interest.** Consider authentic events and objects such as field trips, guest speakers, children's literature, animals, items from nature or other real objects, and photographs. Use a language experience activity to meet grade level objectives or standards, especially in science and social studies.

2. **Stimulate ideas through discussion** between you and your students as well as between students. Weave new vocabulary into the discussion and provide examples to help define new words. Possibly create a web of ideas during the discussion or a list of "gist words" or important words to include.

3. **Model writing by serving as the scribe.** One at a time, have students dictate their thoughts. While you are writing, model spacing between words, capitalization, spelling, and handwriting, keeping the text as close to the student's words as possible. All students may not be able to share each time. Consider including the student's name to encourage interest and rereading at a later time. Use questions to guide the discussion. Questions might include:
   - What should we write next?
   - What sound do we hear at the beginning of that word?
   - What mark do I make at the end of the sentence?

4. **Read and reread what has been written.** This step occurs throughout the writing process, at the end of a sentence, and at the end of the whole text. When students are familiar with the text, invite them to read along as a group and use a pointer to help them.

5. **Honor the students by sharing the text** in various ways (display in the classroom, periodically reread, refer back to ideas from the text, look for familiar words in the text, illustrate the text).

Adapted from Van Allen, R. (1999). *Language experiences in communication.* New York: Houghton Mifflin.

modeling of the various aspects of writing remains an important feature of morning message, since the two approaches differ in the content of the writing, rather than the process. A morning message usually has three or four sentences, each one contributed by a different student, with a focus on their personal experiences or special events occurring at the school, such as pajama day, a visit by a firefighter, or treats for a classmate's birthday. Often, teachers begin morning message with a sentence pattern, such as "Today is (insert day of the week) the (insert month, date, year)," thus making it also an opportunity for practicing numbers, days of the week, and months of the year. Follow-up activities are similar to the language experience approach and focus on reinforcing emergent and beginning writing concepts, such as those listed in Exhibit 9.26.

stories FROM THE CLASSROOM

Morning message

Kimberly Nelson, a kindergarten teacher in Sarasota County, Florida, describes the importance of providing students with a "daily and predictable shared writing experience" and has created an extensive collection of web resources for morning message. Visit Kimberly's website (www.mrsnelsonsclass.com/teacherresources/teachingwriting/morningmessage.aspx) and scroll down the page to the sample morning messages. Be sure to read the example teacher/student dialogue boxes to see the type of interaction Kimberly uses with her students during the shared writing process. Also, click *About Mrs. Nelson* to read Kimberly's philosophy of teaching. Notice the ways the value of writing shines through in her philosophy.

Digital shared writing

The digital language experience approach and digital morning message can involve the use of technology to record and share students' words (Labbo, 2005; Labbo, Eakle, & Montero, 2002; Sampson, Allen, & Sampson, 1991). Similar steps are followed for the creation of a digital shared writing text as for a printed one. For example, students and teacher discuss an experience, then the students' words are recorded, possibly on a computer or a digital whiteboard. Digital photographs are often used to record experiences, which then inspire discussion and writing. The photos serve as a memory link for students as well as a prompt for the descriptive language needed to create a rich language experience text. Photographs can also be a source of vocabulary development for English language learners by providing clear images of the concepts at the center of the discussion and writing.

Text is created on the computer and may be projected onto an interactive whiteboard, through PowerPoint slides, or through the creation of an online booklet using free software available online, for example, RealeWriter (www.realewriter.com). Such software can be used to create simple online books with photos. Students, along with a more experienced helper, follow the writing process approach, first by authoring their text and taking digital photographs. Next, the text and photos are placed into the template. A review of the final draft emphasizes the importance of preparing a writer's work for publishing. Then copies are printed, bound, and shared with friends and families.

Using word processing software allows the teacher to model drafting, revising, and editing. Voice synthesizers can be used to read on-screen text and make stories accessible to those students who cannot read the text themselves. Printed copies of the language experience or morning message text can be given to students to take home and share with families, or bound into a booklet and shared in the classroom library, or posted on the class website. Collected over time, these texts form a digital or paper record of the students' activities and the literacy concepts taught throughout the school year.

Print directions for creating a digital language experience approach: www.hhp communities.com/teachinglanguagearts/IL-09-07.pdf

---

A digital recording can be made of you and students reading the text together, as seen in an example from special education teacher Andrea Keller in the upcoming Stories from the Classroom and accompanying video *The Plant Grows*.

When describing digital shared writing, Labbo, Eakle, and Montero (2002) adapted the words of Roach Van Allen (1986) presented earlier in this chapter.

What I think about, I can talk about.

What I can see in a digital photograph, I can talk about and remember.

What I can say, I can write down. What I can write down, I can revise on screen.

What I can write I can read or have read to me by the computer. I can read what others write for me to read. (pp. 51–52)

Digitally collecting and publishing students' words can enhance the traditional language experience and morning message approaches, although both the digital and printed texts are useful and authentic teaching tools. The key for both types of text is to capitalize on the students' interest and enthusiasm and to use their language to teach about the writing process.

stories FROM THE CLASSROOM

Digital shared writing

The six students in Andrea's K–2 classroom have autism to varying degrees along the autism spectrum. The students have limited or no verbal skills, yet Andrea plans language experience activities that encourage them to participate to the best of their abilities. For students with autism, ideas may be more easily communicated through pictures than written words. Andrea recognizes the value of the students first experiencing an activity, then communicating about this activity, whether orally, in writing, or through pictures. The video The Plant Grows (http://kellerbusybees.blogspot.com/search?q=the+plant+grows) shares the experience Andrea and her students had planting seeds and displays their shared writing about growing plants. Although the students require much support, they are able to participate in the planting and see how this experience can be turned into words and images.

The digital language experience approach can be used to meet the learning needs of individual students. The article "Digital Language Experience Approach: Using Digital Photos and Software as a Language Experience Approach Innovation" (www.readingonline.org/electronic/labbo2) describes the ways a kindergarten teacher encourages children to express their ideas in writing. Focus specifically on the description of India, the first of three students described in the article. Notice the way the process causes India to re-envision herself as a literate person.

All forms of shared writing capitalize on students' oral language skills, which are typically at a higher level than the written language skills of these emergent and beginning writers, as well as for English language learners and those students who struggle with writing. Through shared writing, students learn that their spoken words can be shared as written or typed words, and they, along with others, can return to these words over and over, thus giving them a sense of accomplishment.

9.9

INTERACTIVE WRITING

Interactive writing moves writing instruction further into the *We do* phase, with the students and teacher physically writing together to create a common text. Also known as *sharing the pen,* interactive writing involves the teacher's continued modeling of the writing process, with the students writing words with some support in the form of phonics or spelling prompts. Moving from shared writing to interactive writing allows for a gradual release of responsibility from the students sharing words orally, to them beginning to write. Exhibit 9.27 displays an interactive writing text written by the teacher and Eric, a five-year-old child. Much of the writing has been done by the teacher, but Eric has also joined in for some of it.

The roots of interactive writing stem from teachers and researchers experimenting with the language experience approach, searching for ways to promote the literacy skills of emergent and beginning readers and writers while increasing their active participation (McKenzie, 1985; Pinnell & McCarrier, 1994). Although interactive writing began as an approach to use with young students, teachers have adopted this approach for students with special needs (Mariage, 2001) and English language learners (Wall, 2008). "Interactive writing provides opportunities for teachers to engage in instruction precisely at the point of student need" (Button, Johnson, & Furgerson, 1996, p. 448). Interactive writing activities for older students focus on more challenging writing skills and more sophisticated topics. In classrooms where students have limited vocabulary, interactive writing activities can focus on developing key vocabulary words needed for understanding science or social studies concepts or grade-level English skills. The distinguishing characteristic is students' involvement not only in the discussion but also in the actual writing by sharing the pen or the keyboard. The lively pace and the students' active involvement keep them engaged.

During an interactive writing activity, each word is a literacy lesson that gives students the opportunity to practice skills to be used later in independent writing. The writing begins with a shared experience and discussion to stimulate ideas, then the text is collaboratively constructed. You think aloud while writing by pointing out specific skills, such as spacing or letter/sound combinations. When a student contributes to the writing by adding a sight word or a period, you supply prompts or clues, but only

EXHIBIT 9.27

Interactive writing.

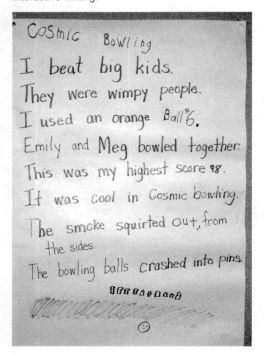

Cosmic Bowling
I beat big kids.
They were wimpy people.
I used an orange Ball #6.
Emily and Meg bowled together.
This was my highest score 98.
It was cool in Cosmic bowling.
The smoke squirted out, from the sides.
The bowling balls crashed into pins.

if needed. The goal should be for the student to do as much independent thinking and writing as possible. Clay reminds teachers that the purpose of scaffolding is to supply only the minimal amount of support needed for the student to be successful, and not to do for the student "anything that she can teach him to do for himself" (1989, p. 4). Throughout the interactive writing process the students and teacher reread and revise the text, applying growing knowledge of spelling skills, punctuation, or handwriting. Then, the text is displayed so the students and teacher can revisit the text again and again for brief literacy lessons or as a reminder of previous learning. Being surrounded by the classes' interactive writing may inspire students in their own independent writing.

BOOK REVIEW

Interactive Writing: How Language and Literacy Come Together

BY ANDREA MCCARRIER, GAY SU PINNELL, & IRENE C. FOUNTAS

Although published in 2000, this book remains a great resource for interactive writing. Few teacher resources focus specifically on this writing approach, so this book fills a gap along with providing high-quality information and numerous classroom examples. Pinnell and Fountas are both widely known for their work in the area of guided reading.

Locate a copy: www.worldcat.org/title/interactive-writing-how-language-and-literacy-come-together-k-2/oclc/42290734

Effective interactive writing activities can occur in the moment, when you capitalize on a spontaneous idea, such as the first snowfall of the year. At other times, you will give careful planning to create an interactive writing lesson. View this lesson on the Read, Write, Think website to see an example of an interactive writing lesson plan: www.readwritethink.org/classroom-resources/lesson-plans/teaching-audience-through-interactive-242.html. Notice the way this series of 13 short sessions leads students through reading, writing, reflecting, and sharing by tying together several modes of language arts.

9.10

GUIDED WRITING

Guided writing moves students another step closer toward independent writing, although this approach is still at the *We do* level. Shared and interactive writing help students see their spoken words transformed into written words, then guided writing provides the bridge to independently communicating their ideas through writing, taking on more responsibility by doing their own writing based on a topic or framework you provide. (See Exhibit 9.28.) Guided writing encourages students to

- learn a new skill, such as inserting quotation marks or creating an inviting lead.
- experiment with a purpose, such as persuasion.
- explore a new genre, such as mystery or informational writing.

EXHIBIT 9.28

Guided writing at the fourth-grade level.

- develop revising and editing skills.
- refine sentence structure or word choice.

The teacher plans structured writing activities and provides scaffolding for writers through writing projects such as jointly writing a poem about the class pet or having each student include information in his or her report about an animal habitat. Guided writing gives students the opportunity to practice with others before trying it themselves. As Regie Routman describes it: "The student is now in charge, holding the pen and attempting to apply what has been previously demonstrated and practiced with the direct support of the teacher and/or group. The students' guided practice is likely to be only as good as our demonstrations" (2005, pp. 81–82).

In the upcoming Stories from the Classroom, first-grade teacher Lucy Burdiek explains how she uses a science unit on penguins and the website Wallwisher for a guided writing activity that teaches science concepts using informational writing.

stories FROM THE CLASSROOM

Guided writing with first graders

In her own words, first-grade teacher Lucy describes the process she used to guide her students to write informational texts about penguins using Wallwisher.

We spent around seven days learning about penguins. First, we created a schema chart on a large penguin that I made. The sections were labeled as the following: Our Schema, New Learning, and Misconceptions. I asked students what they knew about penguins and wrote all of the students' responses on the same colored sticky note and placed them under the heading Our Schema. As we read books about penguins we charted Our New Learning on a different colored note. If we found out that some of our schema about penguins were misconceptions, we talked about why they weren't accurate and added them to the Misconceptions box.

The students wrote "All About Penguins" books, which included a table of contents and a diagram of a penguin. They also wrote five or six different facts about penguins. We continued to do many other penguin activities that week relating to math, language arts, poetry, and social studies.

Finally, on the last day I had students each write a fact about penguins that they wanted to share. These were edited. Then they posted them to Wallwisher in the computer lab as shown in the photo (see Exhibit 9.29).

Lucy Burdiek uses Wallwisher during guided writing with beginning writers.

Guided writing is often used immediately following modeled or shared writing as a way to give students more practice before writing independently. Whether used with the whole class or a small group, guided writing may also be a wise instructional choice when teaching a new writing concept or asking students to write in a mode of writing that is new.

Read more information about various modes of writing, their purposes, and related genres: www.hhpcommunities.com/teachinglanguagearts/IL-09-08.pdf

You may let students write independently first to informally assess which aspects of writing they need to work on, then plan a guided writing lesson matched to the group's learning needs. If the students are adept at the writing skill to be taught, a guided writing lesson may be skipped altogether and students can move right into independent practice. The flexible nature of guided writing lets you meet the goal of providing students with guided practice before they are expected to write on their own. Third-grade teacher Cherise Smith uses a class wiki and a study of spiders to design a guided writing activity, which has teacher modeling and students working in pairs to write informational text. After reading Cherise's story, view the project wiki and notice the similar structures, but unique perspectives of, her students' writing.

stories FROM THE CLASSROOM

Guided writing

After introducing the spider wiki project, third-grade teacher Cherise Smith guided her students through the writing project by creating the black widow spider page together (see Exhibit 9.30). As a group, they wrote a description of the spider and its eating habits, listed cool facts about it, and included a bibliography of websites used in their research. This guided writing clarified expectations as they set off to work with a partner to create their own spider page, using the same categories modeled by Cherise. After completing the wiki pages, Cherise evaluated the students' work using the evaluation tool she created (see Exhibit 9.31).

After her class completed the project, Cherise shared these thoughts:

I asked the children to tell what they liked about the project and what was difficult about this project.

Things they liked:

—the use of computers

—the idea that others can see their work by accessing the wiki, and their project will stay accessible

—finding so much new information (They unanimously agreed they learned a lot of new information about spiders.)

—the professional look of the projects

—reading each others' wikis to answer spider questions

Things they said were difficult:

—finding some of the information

—putting information from their research notes into their own words in paragraph form

—typing took a really long time

—typing the webliography with no typos

—being patient with their partner

They want to make more wikis again soon!

EXHIBIT 9.30

The black widow spider page created by Cherise's class.

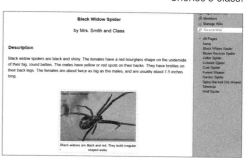

EXHIBIT 9.31

Spider wiki evaluation tool.

EVALUATION OF SPIDER WIKI PAGE	STUDENTS		TEACHER
The wiki includes a proper title, names of authors, and required headings. (Description, Habitat, Eating Habits)	YES	NO	1 2 3 4 5
A clear description of the spider is included. Details describe the color, shape, and size of the spider.	YES	NO	1 2 3 4 5
The habitat is clearly described. The description tells where the spider is found and tells about its web or place of shelter.	YES	NO	1 2 3 4 5
The eating habits of the spider are described. This includes what the spider eats and how it catches its food.	YES	NO	1 2 3 4 5
A webliography listing the websites used for research is included. At least 3 websites are used. The website names and URLs are written correctly.	YES	NO	1 2 3 4 5
A picture or pictures are included. The pictures are appropriate and help the reader to learn more about this spider.	YES	NO	1 2 3 4 5
Writing is clear and easy to understand. Complete sentences are used, and the writing includes correct capitalization, punctuation, and spelling.	YES	NO	1 2 3 4 5 (× 2)
Both team members worked cooperatively throughout the project. The team members stayed on task and treated each other with respect.	YES	NO	1 2 3 4 5 (× 2)
			TOTAL ____/50

In the video Engaging Boys: Engagement Through Choice: Guided Writing Session (5:06, www.youtube.com/watch?v=liOpNE-qFvQ), teacher Erika Chin uses guided writing with a group of older students to respond to a film. A graphic organizer provides a framework for discussion about the film, which leads to structured writing. View the video and make a list of the probing questions Erika asks to lead students into writing.

9.11

INDEPENDENT WRITING

Independent writing is the opportunity for students to try out their new learning with written language on their own. Independent writing may occur within an individual lesson, after you have modeled and you and the students have practiced together, or it may occur during a special writing time each day, when students are encouraged to practice the skills learned during modeled, shared, interactive, or guided writing. The key characteristics that set independent writing apart from the other writing approaches are that students choose their own topic and move at their own pace through the writing process. One effective way to facilitate independent writing is through journaling.

Journals

Journals give students the chance to reflect not only on their personal experiences and ideas, but also to make connections to their new learning. New thinking is given permanence through a journal, and thus can be revisited and prompt continued reflection. "Writing is how students connect the dots of their learning" (National Commission on Writing, 2003, p. 18). As a learning tool, journals are versatile, inexpensive, and readily available, which makes them an optimal tool for promoting thinking, writing, and reading. Whether in paper or electronic form, a journal is a place for students to summarize, illustrate, describe, evaluate, and connect ideas from various subjects, including math, science, and social studies all the while practicing language arts skills. They are a tool for practicing independent writing skills at each individual's level of development and to receive feedback from the teacher. For the teacher, journals have the power to enrich the relationship with each student through genuine and purposeful written responses, as well as providing an informal assessment of new learning.

By promoting choice and original thoughts in a journal, you confirm the value of the students' ideas and experiences (Calkins, 1994). For English language learners, a journal provides a chance for sharing stories from home, but also an opportunity for language skills to grow in the context of the classroom. "It is crucial for the teacher to provide opportunities for the language learner to gain access to the learning communities that are present in the classroom" (Salcedo, 2009, p. 440) while also maintaining the learner's unique cultural identity. Because literacy skills in their native language and English may develop at different paces, students who have strong writing skills in their native language may have more confidence in experimenting with English in the safe space of a journal (de la Luz Reyes, 1991). You can use these approximations as individualized teaching and learning opportunities.

The article "Raising Children's Cultural Voices" (www.rethinkingschools.org/special_reports/bilingual/bil144.shtml) describes how a third-grade teacher uses journals and other types of writing to teach English and Spanish in a bilingual classroom. Read the article and look for additional benefits of using journals with English language learners.

When implementing journals in the classroom, begin by making decisions about the purpose of the journal, how often students will write, and what is expected in each entry.

Purpose

Journals may be used to share daily happenings, record science observations, draw a model, or explain a math problem-solving activity. Identify the reason for using the journal or what knowledge and experiences students should gain from it. Once the purpose has been met, then take a break from using a journal and try a different type of writing activity.

The decision about which type of journal to use depends on its intent or purpose. Identify what should be accomplished through using the journal, then decide on the specific type of journal that meets the instructional focus. View a list of journal types and the type of purpose they can serve: www.hhpcommunities.com/teaching languagearts/IL-09-09.pdf

Frequency

In addition to deciding about purpose, you must decide how often journal entries will be written: every day, a couple of times a week, once a week, or a few times a month. Again, consider the purpose. A literature response journal may be used every day during the reading of a novel, and a science journal may be used once a week to record the changes in the growth of a plant. Keep in mind that if journals are used too often, students can become bored with them. Vary the purpose and frequency of journal use to hold student interest and attention.

Expectations

Also determine your expectations for handwriting, spelling, language usage, and length of entries. These decisions often also depend on the purpose for the journal. Some teachers think of a journal as a private writing space, to be only seen by the teacher and the student, in which case mechanics are not emphasized. Other teachers grade each journal entry and expect attention to editing. Some teachers, especially those at the intermediate grades, involve the students in establishing expectations for spelling and language usage. Together they decide if certain words are inappropriate or if abbreviations, such as LOL (laughing out loud), can be used to convey ideas.

One of the most common types of journals is the **dialogue journal,** which involves the student and the teacher embarking on a written conversation, as shared in Exhibit 9.32. The teacher can facilitate the dialogue about expectations by following these practices:

- **Support the message of the writer.** In your response, acknowledge the writer's ideas. Confirm, agree, or share similar thoughts. Keep your response to a similar or a bit shorter length than the writer's response.
- **Clarify ideas or provide information.** If you notice misperceptions or incorrect information, offer the correct information in a matter-of-fact, nonjudgmental way. If an idea is unclear, ask for clarification. Use the response as a chance to challenge the writer to rethink or to think more deeply.

Ethan's journal entry with the teacher's response.

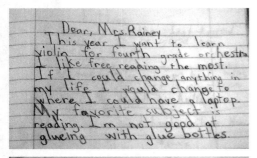

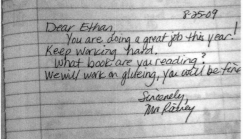

During independent writing, a teacher becomes a coach and a mentor.

- **Model correct grammar and spelling.** Rather than correcting errors in a journal, provide a correct model when you notice incorrect usage by the writer. One strategy suggested for English language learners, but appropriate for all writers, is to ask the writer, while writing, to underline a word for which he is unsure of the spelling or usage. When responding, you should correctly use the word in your response or spell the word and underline it.
- **Ask questions.** Make your questions genuine and open-ended, as a way to encourage more writing in the next response, as in Exhibit 9.32.

A **traveling journal** is another journal type frequently used in classrooms. The journal travels back and forth between home and school, sparking written conversation between the teacher and the family. Some teachers of young students give the journal a special purpose by including it in a backpack with a stuffed animal, a picture book, and a list of literacy activities that can be completed at home. Families are asked to use the journal to record the adventures of the stuffed animal on his visit to the student's home and write about their experiences reading the book and participating in the activities. A home–school connection can be forged through a traveling journal project. Journals are not only used to build writing skills but also to develop friendship and trust between the caregivers, students, and teacher (Peyton & Reed, 1990).

Writing workshop

Writing workshop promotes independent writing by providing intensive, targeted instruction and time for budding writers to practice their newfound skills, whether with pencil and paper or a keyboard. Students work through the writing process, including prewriting, drafting, revising, editing, and publishing. Although the goal is to have students writing independently, much structure and planning on the teacher's part must be in place for students to do so. Independent writing does not mean the teacher is not involved; instead the teacher becomes a coach or mentor rather than a director (see Exhibit 9.33). The day-to-day format of the writing workshop may vary slightly from classroom to classroom and age level to age level, but the key characteristics of the workshop are to give students the opportunity to

- be an active member of a writing community in their classroom.
- interact with adults who write, in this case teachers who share their writing with the students.
- write frequently and on a regular basis in school.
- choose their own topics for writing based on their experiences, background, and interests.
- receive explicit teaching about writing skills from the teacher through mini-lessons and writing conferences.
- use their spelling, grammar, and punctuation skills on real pieces of writing.
- use technology to produce and share ideas.
- receive responses about their writing from peers and the teacher.
- monitor their own progress on written texts collected over the course of the school year, possibly through an electronic portfolio.
- share their writing with classmates and the teacher on a regular basis.

Writing workshop had its beginnings in the early 1980s and was refined through the work of Nancie Atwell (1988/1998), Lucy Calkins (1986/1994), and Donald Graves (1983/2003) who all focused on the importance of teachers understanding the writing process and providing students with classroom opportunities to write about what is important to them while using the skills at their own developmental level.

Since its inception, several other educators have further defined writing workshop. Use this Writing Workshop Instructional Resource list (www.hhpcommunities. com/teachinglanguagearts/IL-09-10.pdf) of articles written by educators working in this field for more information about conducting a workshop in your class. Choose a resource that looks interesting to you and create a list of the authors' suggestions for these workshops.

These and other educators have identified the following elements that are common to writing workshops:

1. writing center
2. mini-lessons for explicit teaching of skills and strategies needed to be a writer
3. writing time for composing texts with minimal support
4. conferences to meet the individual needs of students and reinforce teaching points from mini-lessons
5. sharing time for celebrating finished work or seeking feedback from peers on work in progress
6. technology

Writing center

In order for students to develop the habits and routines of writing, writing workshop must be a regular, predictable part of the school day. Establishing a writing center promotes independence in writing by making supplies directly available to the students. Bookshelves, a small table, and computers are ideal, but at a minimum, students need access to supplies and materials that may include the following:

- paper (various sizes, shapes, and colors)
- writing utensils (pens, pencils, markers, various types and colors)
- letter ink stamps
- unused greeting cards, stationery, envelopes
- clear tape for fixing small tears or book binding
- stapler for making small paper books or creating a collection of work
- hole puncher for creating paper books
- plastic crates/tubs for storing writing folders
- anchor charts (writing workshop schedule, editing marks, the writing process)

Writing centers are as unique as the teachers and students who create them. View this link to see a collection of possible materials to include in a writing center: http://bdobler.edu.glogster.com/elements-of-a-writing-center. What materials could be added to the list above?

A small group work area, such as a table or carpeted area, is needed for holding conferences or guided writing lessons. A special chair provides a spot for the writer and signifies to the other students that attention should be given to this writer during sharing time. Teachers play an important role in helping students understand how, when, and why to use technology in the writing workshop. Internet access may be helpful for gathering facts for informational writing. Word processing and publishing programs are especially helpful in the revising, editing, and publishing phases of the writing process. Computers during writing workshop may be accessed at a classroom computer station, through individual laptops, or through a school computer lab.

Mini-lesson

Usually occurring at the beginning of writing workshop and lasting for five to ten minutes, the mini-lesson is a time to check in and tune up. Mini-lessons are short and focused, an arrow of writing instruction aimed at the needs of the writers. You provide direct instruction of the skills writers need to successfully convey their message. You may use a copy of your own writing or a sample of students' writing as a tool for instruction, thus modeling the use of writing skills in an authentic way.

How do you know what to teach in a mini-lesson? One place to begin is with the district curriculum or state standards for the grade level. Another source for mini-lesson topics is observing students while they are writing. During previous writing workshop sessions, perhaps you notice aspects of writing that the group as a whole struggles with. Rather than thinking of these topics as skills the students do not have, consider them mini-lesson opportunities. In this way, you are constantly informally assessing the students and providing instruction based on this information.

Whatever the source of the content, mini-lessons often fall into the following categories:

- Procedural: routines of writing workshop
- Writer's craft: effective ways of getting an idea across to others
- Skills: spelling, grammar, punctuation

Exhibit 9.34 shares specific examples of topics from these three categories. A mini-lesson is a time to introduce a single important skill and provide brief teacher modeling and guided practice. A whole class guided writing activity may be used to give students scaffolded practice of a specific skill before they are expected to use the skill during independent writing time.

EXHIBIT 9.34

Mini-lesson topics.

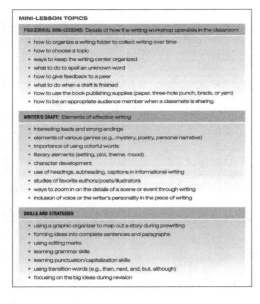

In the video Writer's Workshop 1st Grade Mini-lesson on Writing Booklets (8:29, www.youtube.com/watch?v=Dciu2f3fW3M), a first-grade teacher demonstrates a mini-lesson. View the first three to four minutes of this video to see the teacher's explicit instruction and modeling. Notice that the next element of writing workshop, writing time, is the chance for students to return to their individual writing projects, where they will apply skills taught in various mini-lessons. Visit this website (www.jmeacham.com/writing.mini.lessons.htm) for mini-lesson ideas and resources for the primary classroom created by Jessica Meacham, a first-grade teacher in Door County, Wisconsin.

Writing time

The biggest portion of time during writing workshop is devoted to actual writing. Independence is built through practice and an extended time to write allows students to develop their budding communication skills (see Exhibit 9.35). Because students are working on individual projects, each student may be at a different stage of the writing process. Some may be creating a graphic organizer to plan ideas or may be explaining an idea to a writing partner, while others may be absorbed in writing a first draft. Still others may be rereading their work to check for needed revisions, and some are editing for spelling or punctuation. The flexibility promotes differentiation so that students who need a bit more time, those learning English as a second language, and those who are prolific writers can all be challenged at their own level.

Writing time should be alive with the hum of productivity. At the beginning of the school year, giving structure to writing time helps students to adjust to the routines and expectations of writing for an extended period. As students become more familiar with the routines and have built up writing endurance by writing for longer periods of time, you may loosen up some of the structure, letting students sit in various comfortable places around the room (see Exhibit 9.36) or work collaboratively on a wiki or document sharing site for easy access. Students may also extend their collaboration beyond the school day, if home access to the Internet is available.

stories FROM THE CLASSROOM

Writing time meets individual needs

Within every classroom, each student has an individual set of learning needs that can be met through the flexibility of a writing workshop approach. Meet three second graders in Sarah Lucero's class—Jose, Maddie, and Andrew—and read about how writing workshop meets their individual needs. While learning about these students, keep the sociocultural theory in mind. Consider how their families and culture may influence their attitude and abilities as writers.

José (Exhibit 9.37)   Born in Mexico and now living in the United States with his family, José participates in a program for English language learners. During writing workshop, he is encouraged to write in English, although his teacher may conference with him in Spanish if she feels he will more easily understand the concept in his native language. José's writing skills are enhanced when he can hear his words aloud, which he does by reading his story into a whisper phone. José is eager to learn English and to share stories of his family and favorite activities with the other students in the class.

Maddie (Exhibit 9.38)   Maddie's reading and writing skills are a little more than a year above the second-grade level. Maddie wants to be a writer when she grows up, and her stories are rich with details, interesting characters, and unusual settings, with some stories spanning two or three pages in length. Maddie is an independent writer, only seeking a writing conference with the teacher to share finished work rather than to seek help. Maddie's generous spirit shows when she willingly helps classmates who need a writing idea, an interesting word, or the location of a quotation mark.

Andrew (Exhibit 9.39)   Andrew is friendly and eager to talk about his favorite topic, Bob the Builder, to anyone who will listen. Andrew's writing skills are about two years below the second-grade level. Typically, the paraprofessional

EXHIBIT 9.35

Ta'Janea and Jareea write independently during writing workshop.

EXHIBIT 9.36

A writer enjoys a comfortable writing spot.

EXHIBIT 9.37

José using a whisper phone to hear his written words as he reads them aloud.

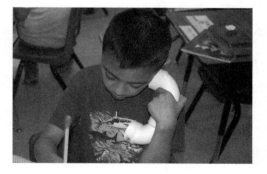

EXHIBIT 9.38

Maddie working independently to write a story.

EXHIBIT 9.39

Andrew receiving support as he participates in writer's workshop.

EXHIBIT 9.40

Spelling strategies that encourage spelling independence.

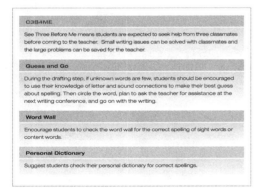

C3B4ME

See Three Before Me means students are expected to seek help from three classmates before coming to the teacher. Small writing issues can be solved with classmates and the large problems can be saved for the teacher.

Guess and Go

During the drafting step, if unknown words are few, students should be encouraged to use their knowledge of letter and sound connections to make their best guess about spelling. Then circle the word, plan to ask the teacher for assistance at the next writing conference, and go on with the writing.

Word Wall

Encourage students to check the word wall for the correct spelling of sight words or content words.

Personal Dictionary

Suggest students check their personal dictionary for correct spellings.

who works with Andrew most of the day because of his learning needs will write down Andrew's words for him. Then Andrew copies these words into his writing workshop notebook and adds an illustration. Gentle reminders are necessary to help Andrew stay on task. With support from his classmates, the teacher, and other adults, Andrew participates in writer's workshop, working at his own level.

These are just three of the 22 students in Sarah Lucero's second-grade class. The other 19 students each have unique learning needs of their own. The format of writing workshop provides just the right mixture of flexibility and structure to meet students where they are in their writing skills and to move them forward in their learning.

In addition to creating independent writers, the goal of writing time is to let students practice the writing skills needed to move to the next level of development. For the first five minutes or so of writing time, you also write with the students. As a model, you demonstrate how experienced writers work through the writing process. Students see you writing, thinking, rereading, revising, and writing again. Later in the writing workshop, during sharing time, you can periodically share a piece of writing and elaborate on the challenges, tentativeness, and successes experienced in creating a draft.

One question that new teachers often ask is how much help to give students with spelling when working on a first draft. Because the goal of writing workshop is to create independent writers, this independence definitely needs to stretch into spelling. First and foremost, spelling a word for a student should be a strategy of last resort. If you are constantly spelling for students, little time will be left for instruction on other aspects of writing, not to mention that students will never learn to spell for themselves. Instead, emphasize the strategies shown in Exhibit 9.40 to encourage spelling independence.

Some students may have difficulty moving forward with their draft unless their spelling is correct. Assure students that spelling is important to getting their message across to others and close attention will be given to spelling during the editing step of the writing process. A first draft is an opportunity to get words down on paper, and expecting everything to be spelled perfectly the first time often causes a writer to lose his train of thought.

Conferencing

While the students are writing, you are holding writing conferences with students (see Exhibit 9.41). Fletcher and Portalupi (2001) describe a writing conference as having "a marvelous kind of tai chi in which you work off the student's energy, affirming the writer yet slightly redirecting the flow" (p. 48). A writing conference is a time for you to learn as much about the student as a writer as for the student to learn from you. For you, this learning involves reading, listening, then providing feedback specific to that writer. For the student, a conference is a chance for a one-on-one audience to share and discuss her writing. Conferences are particularly valuable for English language learners who benefit from the oral language interactions in which pronunciation and translation issues can be given closer attention.

The conference begins with the student presenting the piece of writing to you. Try to hold the conference at a table or desk with both participants sitting side-by-side, and the piece of writing lying on the desk. This simple act of sharing the writing gives a sense of teamwork or collaboration and facilitates conversation because both can see the writing easily. Then initiate the conference with open-ended statements or questions such as:

EXHIBIT 9.41

A writing conference.

- Tell me about this piece of writing.
- Is there something specific you would like me to see?
- What is your favorite part of this piece of writing? Why?
- Is there something I can help you with?
- What do you intend to do next?
- What do you think of your beginning? Your ending?

The agenda for the conference is set by the student's response to one or more of these questions or statements. An observant teacher listens carefully and takes cues from the student about what is the most important lesson to be taught/learned from the conference. A writing conference is also an appropriate time for a brief guided writing lesson if you determine this type of scaffold practice would be beneficial to a specific writer.

View the first 5:45 minutes of the video Precision Teaching: Writing Conferences Student and Teacher (9:26, www.youtube.com/watch?v=njLGV3drzRo) to get an inside view of a writing conference. Notice the teacher's use of modeling to develop the writer's skills. Watch for the ways the teacher puts the learning back in the hands of the student.

Online feedback. Many students are highly motivated to write and have an authentic reason to pay attention to the details of editing and revising when they know others will see their work. Online tools can be an effective way to give feedback when a face-to-face conference is not an option. When working directly with the teacher, a student can submit a piece of writing electronically or in paper format. Once the teacher has read the work, feedback can be shared electronically. Real-time feedback may take the form of an instant message chat or a video conference. Here are some examples to include in your recorded feedback:

- an email message
- written comments shared on a secure social learning network, such as Edmodo (www.edmodo.com)
- an audio recording created as a podcast and uploaded as an attachment to an email
- a video recording shared through a free lecture capturing website, such as Panopto (www.panopto.com)

By recording feedback, you can give careful thought to comments and revise if needed. At the same time, the student has a chance to revisit the feedback several times as she grapples with communicating her ideas clearly. In addition, feedback recorded orally or in writing gives English language learners the chance to receive feedback in a format that best matches their English skill level, whether by listening, reading, or viewing.

Sensitive feedback. Writers of all ages can be highly sensitive to feedback about their writing, but this is especially true of inexperienced writers. On the topic of writers and feedback, Nancie Atwell says that "young writers want to be listened to. They also want honest, adult responses. They need teachers who will guide them to the meanings they don't know yet by showing them how to build on what they do know and can do" (1998, p. 218). Early in the conference, provide concrete positive feedback to boost the student's confidence and reinforce the notion that a writing conference is for learning, not criticizing. Also provide a specific suggestion or two about ways to make the writing stronger. Some teachers use the Oreo cookie model of giving feedback: Give two positive comments with a suggestion sandwiched in between.

Because a writing conference should be kept to about five minutes in length, the focus of the conference is *not* to identify all of the errors in the piece. The goal is to teach a concept or two that will help the writer move toward independence. This might mean teaching the student to identify unknown spellings and giving suggestions for where he can find the correct spelling. Above all else, the student should be doing more work during the conference than you, such as actually writing revisions on the paper, or making corrections on the computer screen. Some teachers write suggestions on a sticky note for the student to keep after the conference, rather than writing these suggestions directly onto the student's writing. The boldness of writing directly on a student's work removes the focus of the conference from the writer learning to the teacher fixing.

Peer feedback. Peer-to-peer writing conferences can also be an effective way of providing specific feedback to a writer, but only if you explain and model effective ways to give and receive feedback throughout the school year. When trained, students are better able to give constructive feedback leading to revisions and edits beyond the surface level. Although peer conferences can be effective with lots of teacher direction, keep in mind that the value of peer comments will vary. Some will consider peer comments more closely than comments from the teacher. Other students, possibly because of their cultural background, may perceive you, not their peers, as the authority in the classroom; these students may see little value in peer feedback. Being aware of these differences is important so you can guide peer conference frequency and duration.

When teaching the routines of peer conferences, first discuss with students specific expectations. Model for students the appropriate way to give feedback, the kind way to give a suggestion, or the thoughtful way to ask a question. Teach students to give the writer their full attention when a piece of writing is being shared and to look the writer in the eye when giving feedback. See Chapters 7 and 11 for additional suggestions for listening and speaking with a peer. A peer review checklist can be an effective tool for helping students to keep their peer conference on track (see Exhibits 9.42 and 9.43).

The National Writing Project incorporates three types of feedback into its peer review for its E-Anthology project, which features writing by teachers. These types of comments may be appropriate for students, too. During a conference, the teacher is asked to choose the type of feedback he would like to receive:

- Blessed: Only tell me the positive things about my writing.
- Addressed: Give me feedback on the specific questions I have about my writing, such as What would be a good title? or How can I describe this character more clearly?
- Pressed: I am willing to accept any critique that helps my writing to become stronger (NWP, 2009).

EXHIBIT 9.42

Peer review checklist for younger writers.

(Print a blank copy of this form: www.hhpcommunities.com/teachinglanguagearts/IL-09-11.pdf)

EXHIBIT 9.43

Self and peer review checklist for older writers.

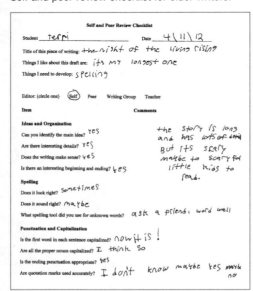

(Print a blank copy of this form: www.hhpcommunities.com/teachinglanguagearts/IL-09-12.pdf)

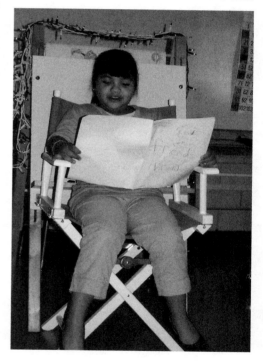

Fourth-grade teacher Tim Bedley incorporates peer review conferences into his writing instruction, which makes the students responsible for making the conferences effective learning tools. View the video Peer Review TOP 10 Mistakes (www.youtube.com/watch?v=iBuq4qgRhCc&feature=related), which shows Tim's students demonstrating the ways attitude can undermine the success of a peer conference. Join characters Pushy Paula, Loud Larry, and Off-Task Oliver to see the common problems that occur during peer conferences in the classroom. Consider the times you have given feedback to a peer about writing and see if any of these mistakes look familiar to you.

Sharing time

Sharing time gives the author a chance to share a piece of writing with the whole class (Exhibit 9.44). The author is in the spotlight but is also vulnerable, because after reading her piece, the audience provides feedback. For some students sharing time is a great writing motivation, creating a sense of accomplishment and pride. This convinces many teachers that sharing time should be an integral, not optional, part of writing workshop. In a digital writing workshop, sharing may entail posting one's work to an online source and seeking feedback either from a limited audience or from anyone on the Internet. Whether face-to-face or digital, feedback may be aimed at a work in progress or be a celebration of a finished piece of writing. In order for sharing time to be successful, you must give specific instruction to the audience about attentive listening and polite ways to ask questions and give feedback to a peer. Questions might include the following:

- What do you like best about your writing?
- Where did you get your idea?
- How does the introduction grab our attention?
- What is a place in your writing that needs more details?
- What was the problem? How was it solved?
- How does your ending tie the ideas together?
- What will you write next?

The Oreo cookie model works well here, and you can teach students to use it. Also, in preparation for sharing, teach students about eye contact, voice volume, and openness to suggestions. You may want to delay the addition of the sharing time element of writing workshop until students are adept in using these skills. Modeling and role playing with your students are effective ways to prepare them for their important roles in sharing time. Some students may be reluctant to share because they are shy or lack confidence. Time and patience will often bring these students around rather than requiring them to speak in front of the class if they are uncomfortable. You will probably want to develop a system for making sure students who want to share get a turn, either by instituting a checklist or a sign-up sheet.

One way to fine-tune sharing time to meet the needs of the students in your class is to form smaller response groups or set up partners for sharing. As students get older they write longer texts, so sharing time with the whole class may take more time than you have. When peers share with each other, students still gain a sense of audience and receive feedback. You can circulate among the groups to add to their feedback. Modeling and discussion about

EXHIBIT 9.44

Casandra in the author's chair.

appropriate ways to share and give feedback are equally important when using small response groups for sharing time.

📹 Seeing the elements of writing workshop in action may help clarify the concept. View A Day in the Life of Our Writing Workshop (3:56, www.youtube.com/watch?v=zPRM2ZXyrS0) to see how one teacher integrates writing workshop into the classroom routine. Notice the storage and variety of materials available to students for writing. Look for small group spaces and an author's chair. Think about the ways these elements might be incorporated into your future classroom.

Writing workshop, whether using paper and pencil or a digital tool, provides students with opportunities to learn about writing through authentic literacy experiences. Students are learning to write by writing, and this writing is about topics of importance to their lives.

Technology

When the writing process is infused with technology, as in a digital writing workshop, students have the opportunity to not only *write* a text, but to *create* a text that conveys their ideas in a variety of ways while also developing adeptness with technology (see Exhibit 9.45). Through multimodal composition (texts, images, sound, graphics) and sharing with a wide audience, students become aware of how ideas are represented and how these ideas are received by others. When you are deciding between print or digital for a writing project, consider the guiding question, "What is the purpose of this text?" If a key purpose is to inform or entertain others, and you or the writer wants those others to extend beyond the classroom or school, then a digital text would meet this purpose. For example, student writing can be posted on a class blog, which can be viewed by the public or restricted to an audience you choose. Feedback can be posted on the blog entry, so the writer and anyone else who views the blog can respond, creating a reciprocal cycle of writing and responding, thus promoting synthesis, analysis, and interaction (Richardson, 2006). On the other hand, a wiki is useful for collaborative writing and creating, but it does not provide a streamlined format for promoting feedback and discussion, as with a blog.

Collaborative writing may include *serial writing* (each person adds a part), *compiled writing* (each person adds their own element), and *coauthored writing* (several writers collaborate on one document) (Haring-Smith, 1994). A document sharing site offers invited participants the chance to write together, even allowing them to collaborate on one document at the same time from different computers. The key to making decisions about how to infuse technology into the writing workshop hinges on the purpose of the writing and the access to technology.

📹 Effective teachers strive for a balance between pencil and paper and the keyboard, so their students are adept at a variety of writing formats. View Mrs. Abernethy's wiki (http://jabernethy.wikispaces.com) and blog (http://ponderouspandas hungergames.blogspot.com) for her fifth-grade class in Greenville, Pennsylvania. She uses a wiki and a blog to share digital projects created by the students, including writing, videos, and podcasts.

EXHIBIT 9.45

Technology skills for writing workshop.

Two of the standards for the International Society for Technology in Education (ISTE) call for students to do the following:

- Apply digital tools to gather, evaluate, and use information.
- Demonstrate a sound understanding of technology concepts, systems, and operations.

Students can meet these goals during digital writing workshop through practice with the following skills:

- copying and pasting their own words
- editing features such as track changes, inserting comments, accepting changes
- highlighting text
- deleting, moving, or inserting text
- downloading or uploading an image or a document
- searching for and recognizing reliable Internet resources
- giving credit to a website for information or images created by others

Source: ISTE Standards at www.iste.org/standards/nets-for-students/nets-student-standards-2007.aspx.

The Digital Writing Workshop
BY TROY HICKS

This was a WOW book for me the first time I read it. Troy Hicks helped me make the transition in my thinking from written words on paper published with technology to technology as a way to gather ideas, create works, and share our message with a few people or a wide audience. He took ideas I am familiar with, such as writing workshop, conferencing, and publishing, and vividly explained how these same concepts can be expanded with technology. His inclusion of numerous web links within the text served as a model for *Forward Thinking*.

Locate a copy: www.worldcat.org/title/digital-writing-workshop/oclc/324776969

points2ponder

QUICK REVIEW 4 Identify the five approaches to teaching writing and list them in order from least student responsibility to most. Indicate the teacher's and students' roles for each.

(Access the answer in the digital version of this book.)

9.12

WORKING WITH WRITERS WHO STRUGGLE

Even with an effective array of writing approaches, some students may struggle to record their thoughts on paper or screen. Writers of varying degrees of skill and experience may have difficulty with numerous aspects of writing (Graham, Harris, & Larsen, 2001) such as:

- choosing a topic
- planning what to write and having a flow of ideas
- anticipating the needs of the audience
- word choice
- organizing ideas sequentially
- mechanics (capitalization, punctuation, and spelling)

Even experienced writers may struggle in these areas from time to time. But struggling writers are "much more likely than their peers to require writing instruction that is *frequent, intensive, explicit,* and *individualized*" (Dudley-Marling & Paugh, 2009, p. 3) to make progress. When it comes to writing instruction, they benefit most from more of the high-quality instruction provided to all students rather than interventions that tend to overemphasize the mechanics of writing at the expense of developing ideas (Dyson & Freedman, 2003). Studies also show that students with learning difficulties who are taught to set and monitor their own writing goals can increase the amount and quality of their writing (Graham, 1990).

The key to meeting the needs of all writers, especially those who struggle, is for you to provide as much individualized support as possible. Meet this challenge by organizing the classroom and promoting conferences, small group collaborations, and students' access to the tools they need to be successful. Specific instructional approaches, discussed previously in this chapter, provide teachers and students the opportunity for *frequent, intensive, explicit,* and *individualized* writing instruction.

Despite what you do, keep in mind that many writers who struggle are not motivated to write. Most people who are not good at something do not enjoy doing it. Writers are no different. Often a struggling writer has a negative view of himself as a writer and feels powerless to change this image. Nevertheless, do not underestimate your influence over students' attitudes about writing through your positive attitude toward, your explicit teaching of strategies, and your monitoring of students' writing behaviors (Troia, 2009).

An important characteristic of any writing instruction is for you to scaffold toward independence. The challenge is knowing just how much scaffolding each student needs. Make this determination through ongoing assessment of students' writing through observations, conferences, and reading their work. Chapter 10 further explores writing assessment, but for now consider assessment as the tool for revealing the specific areas students need to work on to be successful writers. Once these areas are revealed, a skilled teacher moves in to provide explicit instruction, modeling, and guided practice as needed. At times, you may need to back up a few steps if the instruction seems too difficult or the student needs a stronger foundation. Strive to have the student do as much for herself as possible. For example, if a student struggles to spell a word, suggest a tool like a word wall or an electronic spell checker. You could also provide a prompt by emphasizing a sound in the word or pointing the student toward letter/sound cards in the writing center. Spelling the word for the student should be done only after several other tools have been recommended and tried. Remember, the goal is independence at whatever level that might be for each individual student.

Even with high-quality, targeted instruction, some students need further assistance. These students may struggle with the mental or physical aspects of writing. Various technologies are available to facilitate the writing process. These tools are motivating and give support for drafting, revising, and editing written work. Students with learning and other disabilities, English language learners, and struggling writers seem to need the most help in these areas (MacArthur, 2009).

Word processing software

Drafting, revising, editing, or publishing through the use of word processing works smoothly for some writers, especially those who have difficulties with physically writing the text.

Speech recognition software

This software recognizes a person's voice and types what the person is saying, with some degree of accuracy. Dragon Dictation (www.nuance.com/for-individuals/by-industry/education-solutions/index.htm), a speech-to-text program, is available for computers and mobile devices. Speech recognition software lets the speaker create word documents, emails, instant messages, blog entries, and even web searches all by speaking clearly into the microphone. For writers who struggle with handwriting, typing, or spelling, but can clearly enunciate words, speech recognition software provides a way to collect their thoughts in writing.

Text-to-speech software

Speech synthesis is the electronic production of speech based on words on the computer screen, whether a document or website. For the writer, hearing his words read back to him may assist with drafting, revising, or editing. The quality of synthetic speech continues to improve, making this tool a more realistic option for elementary students. Software programs such as Natural Reader (www.naturalreaders.com) can convert any text to speech that sounds natural.

Electronic spell checkers

Electronic spell checkers can help writers of all levels who struggle with spelling. Whether embedded within a word processing program or as a handheld device, such as the Franklin Talking Dictionary and Spell Corrector (www.franklin.com/for-children/children-s-talking-dictionary-spell-corrector), these powerful spelling aids require the writer to supply at least some of the letters to spell the word. The spell checker then provides possible spellings, or determines whether a spelling attempt is correct or not. Spell checkers do have limitations. The writer must be able to recognize the correct spelling provided by the electronic device. Words with double meanings, those spelled similarly to another word, or those that do not fit the syntax of a sentence may not be noticed by the spell checker.

Electronic translator

Useful for English language learners, an electronic translator provides assistance with translating a word in the native language to English or vice versa. As a writing tool, an electronic translator assists with fluency of writing, so a student does not become stuck on a single word and can quickly move back into the flow of writing. Google Translator (http://translate.google.com) can translate written text into 64 possible languages, and other free translation tools are available online.

Although technology cannot form the writer's idea, many tools help her get this idea across to others. The novelty of technology may motivate even the most reluctant of writers, while also providing a conduit for meeting the individual writer's learning needs.

points2ponder

QUICK REVIEW 5 List three tools that can be used with writers who struggle. Explain how each helps writers.

(Access the answer in the digital version of this book.)

9.13

CHAPTER SUMMARY

Although those good ol' school days are long gone, writing continues to play an important role in teaching and learning. The basic process of writing—finding ideas, getting your thoughts down, and making your writing easy for others to read—is still at the heart of quality writing instruction, whether it be with paper and pencil or a keyboard. Today, though, the term *writing* describes a process of creating a text that can be shared in a plethora of technology tools that enhance the process. The writing process—prewriting, drafting, revising, editing, and publishing—provides a framework for guiding a writer toward the goal of communicating thoughts and ideas with others. Students are taught the skills of effectively communicating their ideas through a gradual release of responsibility, which may occur in an individual writing lesson or over a time period through modeled writing, shared writing, interactive writing, guided writing, and independent writing. Students who struggle with the writing process may need assistive technology, and a skilled teacher recognizes these needs and provides appropriate tools. In Chapter 10, we explore the fundamentals of writing, including spelling, grammar, and handwriting, along with a variety of effective ways to assess students' progress with writing.

APPLICATION ACTIVITIES
think like a teacher

Exploring Your Experiences, Beliefs, Attitudes About Writing

Your views of writing and the role it plays in your life are shaped by your family, culture, and community. Being aware of this can help you understand how you came to be where you are today. These views will influence you as a teacher. Getting in touch with your past and present can impact what you do in the future, especially when it comes to providing a role model for students. Take the time to explore how these forces have shaped your views about writing and feelings about yourself as a writer. Consider the childhood, school, and adult experiences that have helped you form your current values and attitudes about writing. Think about important people in your life (parents, teachers, friends) and how they have influenced your current preferences toward writing, handwriting, spelling, grammar, and word processing.

Steps of the Project

1. Create a graphic organizer using the categories of childhood/family, school, and adult experiences. Brainstorm ideas that come to mind in these areas and add them to your graphic organizer.
2. If there are gaps in your memory, contact a family member or friend and talk about your past experiences with writing. Sometimes talk can jog a person's memory.
3. Write a narrative description about your experiences, beliefs, and attitudes toward writing. Possible topics to include:
    types of writing you enjoyed as a young person
    family attitudes that influenced you as a writer
    participation in a spelling bee
    frustrations you felt about writing
    a teacher who influenced you positively or negatively
    how you learned to write
    family activities that involved writing

Remember, there is no right answer here. The purpose of the activity is to explore your own feelings so that you can understand how you arrived at your current beliefs and attitudes. Why is this important? As teachers, we each bring part of ourselves into our classroom. Our past influences what we do today, and this includes teaching writing. If you understand yourself, you will be more likely to understand your instructional decisions and make the best instructional decisions for your students.

Change

"Technology does not drive change, it enables change."

UNKNOWN

A theme of this chapter is change, especially the ways writing has changed, as described in this quote. These changes have come about because our communication tools have changed. Explore the rationale behind these changes through this reading, thinking, writing, and speaking jigsaw activity. The premise of a jigsaw activity is that the collective knowledge of a small group is greater than the knowledge of a single member. Plus, dividing the work makes for an easier task.

1. Form groups of six, with each member having access to the Internet.
2. Visit the site Why Teach Digital Writing: www.technorhetoric.net/10.1/coverweb/wide/introduction.html
3. Have each group member choose one of the topics listed on the left side of the webpage:
   - introduction
   - how technology changes writing practices
   - changed context for writing
   - rhetorical view of writing
   - how we should teach digital writing
   - some conclusions
4. Each group member reads his or her topic individually and creates a bulleted list or a graphic organizer of the six to eight most important points. Be sure to click on the stars, which lead to more in-depth information.
5. The group meets together and each member shares a summary of their reading using the list or graphic organizer.
6. Merge your individual summaries into one list of the top dozen key points from the website. This list can be created on a shared document or a piece of chart paper.
7. As a class, compare lists of key ideas. Note ideas that are common to all groups and ideas that are unique. Discuss how these ideas could be applied to writing instruction in an elementary classroom.

Solve a Problem, Create a Plan

"Big problems are rarely solved with commensurately big solutions. Instead, they are most often solved by a sequence of small solutions, sometimes over weeks, sometimes over decades."

DAN AND CHIP HEATH, *Switch: How to Change Things When Change Is Hard*

Finding time to teach writing in today's busy classrooms is a big challenge. Each day is filled with many expectations, and writing instruction can easily be pushed to the side. Creating a plan for teaching writing is one way to get moving in the right direction. Create a plan for the writing program in your future classroom that you could share with your students' families when they come for open house or back-to-school night at the beginning of the year. Consider what families will want to know about the writing program. Address issues such as time, materials, skills, meeting the needs of all students, and assessment. Put your plan into a presentable format using technology, and include the following components:

1. Identify the goal(s) of your writing program.
2. Identify the national and/or state standards that your writing program meets.
3. Describe the classroom setting. Include specific room arrangement, furniture, and supplies to promote writing.
4. Describe how the writing time will fit into the weekly and daily schedule.
5. Describe what will typically occur during writing time. Identify the daily routines of writing and their purpose.
6. Share your project using some type of technology (paper brochure, PowerPoint, Prezi, blog, wiki, video, podcast, etc.).
7. Carefully edit the final version of your project. Consider the needs of parents when selecting words; avoid educational jargon. Scour your project for spelling, grammar, and punctuation errors, because parents and others will judge your teaching abilities if your project has more than one or two small errors.
8. Use the project rubric, which your instructor may use for grading, to assess your work to determine your level of quality before submitting your project.

Print a blank Scoring Rubric for Writing and Instructional Plan: www.hhp communities.com/teachinglanguagearts/IL-09-13.pdf

Catch Phrase

Writing workshop has been described as a way to support students as they transition into independent writers. This activity is designed for you to explore the issues surrounding writing workshop and to think more deeply about how writing workshop can be used as an approach to meet the learning needs of students in your future classroom. Issues to consider for this discussion include the following:

- Finding time to teach writing
- Integrating content areas (math, science, social studies) into writing instruction
- Your level of comfort with teaching writing
- Students who are unmotivated to write
- Students with special needs
- Meeting the needs of English language learners
- Supporting students who are enthusiastic and prolific writers

  1. Explore the list of issues. Have a general, brief discussion about each issue.
  2. Break up into groups of three or four.
  3. Each group selects an issue to discuss further.
  4. After conversing for 15 minutes or so, summarize your discussion.

5. Create a slogan reflecting a key idea that surfaced during your discussion. The slogan should be a phrase or sentence and may include a simple graphic. Display this for others to see and share a brief synopsis of the discussion leading to your slogan.

REFERENCES

Allen, R. V. (1986). *Language experiences in communication.* New York: Houghton Mifflin.

Ashton-Warner, S. (1965). *Teacher.* New York: Simon & Schuster.

Atwell, N. (1988). *In the middle: Writing, reading, and learning with adolescents.* Portsmouth, NH: Heinemann.

Atwell, N. (1998). *In the middle: New understandings about writing, reading, and learning* (2nd ed.). Portsmouth, NH: Boynton/Cook.

Bereiter, C., & Scardamalia, M. (1987). *The psychology of written composition.* Hillsdale, NJ: Lawrence Erlbaum.

Berninger, V. W. (2000). Development of language by hand and its connections with language by ear, mouth, and eye. *Topics in Language Disorders, 20*(4), 65–84.

Boscolo, P., & Ascorti, K. (2004). Effects of collaborative revision on children's ability to write understandable narrative texts. In L. Allal, L. Chanquoy, & P. Largy (Eds.), *Studies in writing: Vol. 13. Revision: Cognitive and instructional processes* (pp. 158–182). Norwell, MA: Kluwer.

Button, K., Johnson, M. J., & Furgerson, P. (1996). Interactive writing in a primary classroom. *Reading Teacher, 49*(6) 446–454.

Calkins, L. M. (1986/1994). *The art of teaching writing.* Portsmouth, NH: Heinemann.

Clay, M. M. (1989). *The early detection of reading difficulties: A diagnostic survey with recovery procedures.* Portsmouth, NH: Heinemann.

Clay, M. M. (1991). *Becoming literate: The construction of inner control.* Portsmouth, NH: Heinemann.

de la Luz Reyes, M. (1991). A process approach to literacy using dialogue journals and literature logs with second language learners. *Research in the Teaching of English, 25,* 219–313.

Dudley-Marling, C., & Paugh, P. (2009). *A classroom teacher's guide to struggling writers: How to provide differentiated support & ongoing assessment.* Portsmouth, NH: Heinemann.

Dyson, A. H., & Freedman, S. W. (2003). Writing. In J. Flood, D. Lapp, J. R. Squire, and J. Jensen, (Eds.), *Handbook of research on the teaching of English language arts* (pp. 968–992). Mahwah, NJ: Lawrence Erlbaum.

Fisher, D., Frey, N., & Lapp, D. (2009). *In a reading state of mind: Brain research, teacher modeling, and comprehension instruction.* Newark, DE: International Reading Association.

Fletcher, R., & Portalupi, J. (2001). *Writing workshop: The essential guide.* Portsmouth, NH: Heinemann.

Flower, L. S., & Hayes, J. R. (1980). The dynamics of composing: Making plans and juggling constraints. In L. W. Gregg & E. R. Steinberg (Eds.), *Cognitive processes in writing* (pp. 31–50). Hillsdale, NJ: Lawrence Erlbaum.

Graham, S. (1990). The role of production factors in learning disabled students' compositions. *Journal of Educational Psychology, 82,* 881–891.

Graham, S., Harris, K. R., & Larsen, L. (2001). Prevention and interventions of writing difficulties for students with learning disabilities. *University of Maryland Learning Disabilities Research and Practice, 16*(2), 74–84.

Graham, S., & Perin, D. (2008). *Writing next: Effective strategies to improve writing of adolescents in middle and high schools— A report to Carnegie Corporation of New York.* Washington, DC: Alliance for Excellent Education.

Graves, D. H. (1983/2003). *Writing: Teachers & children at work.* Portsmouth, NH: Heinemann.

Graves, D. H. (1985). An examination of the writing processes of seven-year-old children. *Research in the Teaching of English, 9,* 228–241.

Graves, D. H. (1994). *A fresh look at writing.* Portsmouth, NH: Heinemann.

Haring-Smith, T. (1994). *Writing together: Collaborative learning in the writing classroom.* New York: HarperCollins College.

Henderson, E. H., & Beers, J. W. (Eds.). (1980). *Developmental and cognitive aspects of learning to spell: A reflection of word knowledge.* Newark, DE: International Reading Association.

Hicks, T. (2009). *The digital writing workshop.* Portsmouth, NH: Heinemann.

Hillocks, G. (1988). Synthesis of research on teaching writing. *Educational Leadership, 44,* 81–82.

Juel, C. (1991). Beginning reading. In R. Barr, M. L. Kamile, P. Mosenthal, & P. D. Pearson (Eds.), *Handbook of reading research, Vol. 2* (pp. 859–888). New York: Longman.

Kawakami-Arakai, A., Oshiro, M., & Farran, D. (1989). Research to practice: Integrating reading and writing in a kindergarten curriculum. In J. Mason (Ed.), *Reading and writing connections* (pp. 199–218). Boston: Allyn & Bacon.

Kress, G. (1999). Genre and the changing contexts for English language arts. *Language Arts, 86,* 461–469.

Labbo, L. D. (2005). From morning message to digital morning message: Moving from the tried and true to the new. *Reading Teacher, 58*(8), 882–885.

Labbo, L. D., Eakle, A. J., & Montero, M. K. (2002). Digital Language Experience Approach: Using digital photographs and software as a Language Experience Approach innovation. *Reading Online, 5*(8). Available: http://www.readingonline.org/electronic/labbo2/

Labbo, L. D., & Ryan, T. (2010). Traversing the "literacies" landscape: A semiotic perspective on early literacy acquisition and digital literacies instruction. In E. A. Baker (Ed.), *The new literacies: Multiple perspectives on research and practice* (pp. 88–105). New York: Guilford.

Lemke, J. L. (1998). Metamedia literacy: Transforming meanings and media. In D. Reinking, M. McKenna, L. D. Labbo, & R. D. Kieffer (Eds.), *Handbook of literacy and technology* (pp. 283–302). Mahwah, NJ: Lawrence Erlbaum.

Leshi, N. (2010, January 26). What does it mean to be a writer? *Salon.com.* http://open.salon.com/blog/kikstad/2010/01/26/what_does_it_mean_to_be_a_writer

MacArthur, C. A. (2009). Effect of new technologies on writing. In C. A. MacArthur, S. Graham, & J. Fitzgerald (Eds.), *Handbook of writing research* (pp. 248–262). New York: Guilford.

Mariage, T. V. (2001). Features of an interactive writing discourse: Conversational involvement, conventional knowledge, and internalization in "morning message." *Journal of Learning Disabilities, 34*(2), 182–196.

McCarrier, A., Pinnell, G. S., & Fountas, I. C. (2000). *Interactive writing: How language and literacy come together, K–2.* Portsmouth, NH: Heinemann.

McKenzie, M. G. (1985). Shared writing: Apprenticeship in writing. *Language Matters,* 1–2, 1–5.

Murray, D. (1985). *A writer teaches writing* (2nd ed.). Boston: Houghton Mifflin.

National Association for the Education of Young Children (2009). *Developmentally appropriate practice in early childhood programs serving children from birth through age 8.* Available: http://www.naeyc.org/files/naeyc/file/positions/PSDAP.pdf

National Commission on Writing. (2003). *The neglected "R": The need for a writing revolution.* http://www.collegeboard.com/prod_downloads/writingcom/neglectedr.pdf

NCTE (2004). *Beliefs about the teaching of writing.* http://www.ncte.org/positions/statements/writingbeliefs

National Writing Project (2009). *2009 E-Anthology* http://www.nwp.org/cs/public/download/nwp_file/12476/2009%20E Anthology%20PDF.pdf?x-r=pcfile_d

Newkirk, T., & Miller, L. C. (Eds.). (2009). *The essential Don Murray: Lessons from America's greatest writing teacher.* Portsmouth, NH: Heinemann.

Northwest Regional Educational Laboratory (1999). *Seeing with new eyes: A guidebook on teaching and assessing beginning writers.* Portland, OR.

Oczkus, L. D. (2008). *Guided writing: Practical lessons, powerful results.* Portsmouth, NH: Heinemann.

Pearson, P. D., & Gallagher, G. (1983). The gradual release of responsibility model of instruction. *Contemporary Educational Psychology, 8*(3), 112–123.

Peyton, J. K., & Reed, L. (1990). *Dialogue journal writing with nonnative English speakers: A handbook for teachers.* Alexandria, VA: Teachers of English to Speakers of Other Languages.

Pinker, S. (1998). Foreword. In D. McGuinness, *Why our children can't read—and what we can do about it: A scientific revolution in reading.* New York: Simon & Schuster.

Pinnell, G. S., & McCarrier, A. (1994). Interactive writing: A transition tool for assisting children in learning to read and write. In E. Hiebert & B. Taylor (Eds.), *Getting reading right from the start: Effective early literacy interventions* (pp. 149–180). Needham, MA: Allyn & Bacon.

Richardson, W. (2006). *Blogs, wikis, podcasts, and other powerful web tools for classrooms.* Thousand Oaks, CA: Corwin.

Routman, R. (2005). *Writing essentials: Raising expectations and results while simplifying teaching.* Portsmouth, NH: Heinemann.

Salcedo, J. B. (2009). Inviting students and teachers to connect. *Language Arts, 86*(6), 440–448.

Sampson, M., Allen, R. V., & Sampson, M. (1991). *Pathways to literacy: A meaning-centered approach.* Fort Worth, TX: Holt, Rinehart & Winston.

Shanahan, T. (2009). *Relations among oral language, reading, and writing development.* In C. A. MacArthur, S. Graham, & J. Fitzgerald (Eds.), *Handbook of writing research* (pp. 181–183). New York: Guilford.

Sloan, M. S. (2009). *Into writing.* Portsmouth, NH: Heinemann.

Stauffer, R. G. (1980). *The language experience approach to the teaching of reading.* New York: Harper & Row.

Sturm, J. M., & Rankin-Erickson, J. L. (2002). Effects of hand-drawn and computer-generated concept mapping on the expository writing of students with learning disabilities. *Learning Disabilities Research and Practice, 18,* 124–139.

Troia, G. A. (2009). Writing instruction for students with learning disabilities. In C. MacArthur, S. Graham, & J. Fitzgerald (Eds.), *Handbook of writing research* (pp. 324–336), New York: Guilford.

Vopat, J. (2009). *Writing circles.* Portsmouth, NH: Heinemann.

Vygotsky, L. S. (1962). *Thought and language.* Cambridge, MA: MIT Press.

Vygotsky, L. S. (1988). *Mind in society: Development of higher psychological processes.* Cambridge, MA: Harvard University Press.

Wall, H. (2008). Interactive writing beyond the primary grades. *Reading Teacher, 62*(2), 149–152.

CHILDREN'S LITERATURE CITED

Moss, M. (2006). *Amelia's notebook.* New York: Simon & Schuster.

Moss, M. (2003). *Max's logbook.* New York: Scholastic.

Writing Tools for Enhancing Meaning

Access the book's Glossary, which defines the key terms boldfaced in this chapter, at www.hhpcommunities.com/teachinglanguagearts/glossary.pdf

10.1

WRITING TOOLS

Just as a hammer, a tape measure, and a level are the tools of a carpenter, spelling, grammar, and handwriting are the tools of a writer. A carpenter takes wood and crafts a bowl or a rocking chair with his tools; he creates an item of functionality and beauty. In much the same way, a writer takes words and crafts a poem or a letter with her tools; she too creates an item of functionality and beauty. The tools themselves are useless alone. A hammer without wood creates nothing. Knowing the parts of speech is meaningless without a piece of writing in which to use them effectively. This chapter presents spelling, grammar, and handwriting as tools for creating a message. Taught within the context of writing, these tools are often the objective of a mini-lesson or explained in conjunction with the conventions or presentation traits in the six-trait writing model. Whether assessed through an informal checklist or more formally, spelling, grammar, and handwriting can reveal helpful information to an observant teacher about what students know, are able to do, and are ready to learn next. As with the creation of an object of functionality and beauty, the focus should be

> *"Instead of asking What skills should I be teaching? we need to ask . . . How can I engage my students' hearts and minds so they want to write and do their best writing?"*
>
> **REGIE ROUTMAN** (2005, p. 141)

on the end product—the way our words create an effective message that is understood by others.

A misspelling is a window into the mind of a speller.

10.2

SPELLING OVERVIEW

A misspelling or a mistake is like a window into the mind of the student (see Exhibit 10.1). Now, this idea may seem a bit odd at first, considering the purpose of this section is how to teach spelling, so it seems contradictory to consider misspelling as valuable. When learning anything new, a mistake reveals a learner's knowledge and what he or she is ready to learn next. When learning how to play tennis, for example, a ball hit into a certain part of the net reveals information about the player's hand grip, body position, and stroke, and signals the instructor which skill should be taught next. According to the seminal research of Charles Read (1971), spelling errors follow regular and predictable patterns, which, when studied as a whole, reveal a clear developmental continuum. Thus, words are not just right or wrong; rather, misspellings are clues to understanding the student's stage of spelling development. This knowledge helps a teacher know what the student is ready to learn next, which is the key to effective instruction and the creation of independent and confident writers.

In order to put effective spelling instruction into action in the classroom, a teacher must understand several concepts. You must comprehend the process of spelling, the connection between spelling and reading, and how spelling skills develop (discussed in Section 10.3).

The process of spelling

An independent and confident writer.

Understanding the value of spelling errors represents one small but significant part of your knowledge about spelling instruction. To further develop this knowledge let's look deeper at exactly how spelling works in the mind, and the strong connections between elements of spelling and elements of reading. Sophisticated thinking skills and processes are at work during the act of spelling. First, a person must be able to break up a word into the approximate sounds or **phonemes,** which entails **phonemic awareness** and the ability to distinguish the unique quality of one sound compared to another. Next, **phonics** skills are applied as the phonemes must be converted into **graphemes** or the written letters, which entails knowledge of what the letters look and sound like and how to form them. A speller encounters several challenges along the way, because many sounds can be written in various ways (e.g. /f/ as *f* or *ph*; *ee, ea, ey* for long *e*), so a visual memory of how words are spelled gives the speller an extra boost. In addition to this already challenging process, the speller needs to include graphemes that are not heard (e.g., silent *e* in bike). Conventional, or correct, spelling requires all of this knowledge to be firmly in place. Some spellings occur frequently enough that the student memorizes it, thus bypassing the conscious attention needed to move through the spelling process.

The ability to hold a mental impression, or to remember the spelling for individual words, varies from one person to the next, and a person may struggle with spelling for reasons related to memory, visual perception, or auditory discrimination. Research in the field of spelling suggests the brain processes letters into recognizable patterns almost instantaneously (Adams,

1990). Also, researchers are seeking to understand the possibility of a visual coding mechanism in the brain for storing spellings of words (Frith, 1985), and the neurological, environmental, social, cultural, and education factors that influence the development of the brain's ability to spell. Gaps in one or more of these areas may cause a delay or even a disorder in the development of spelling ability.

To find out where the spelling area is located in the brain, view Richard Gentry's video Teaching Spelling in the 21st Century (1:01): www.youtube.com/watch?v=hcd0 xgGetKk&feature=related. How does Gentry think that teaching spelling should change now that researchers have found the brain's spelling region?

Connection between reading and spelling

Although spelling is often taught as a separate subject in elementary schools, literacy research does support the connection between reading and spelling, especially for young students. Both learning to read and learning to spell follow a similar process of moving through stages of development along a continuum (Ehri, 1997). When encountering an unfamiliar word in reading, for example, a reader uses **decoding** skills to break the code of the word in order to pronounce and understand it. For spelling, the writer is **encoding,** or creating the code or sounds mapped to letters. Both spelling and reading, especially at the early stages of literacy learning, lead to a similar goal: fully grasping the **alphabetic system** with all of its complexities. Along the path to this goal, learners progress from one level to the next, each stage bringing new knowledge and new ways of using the alphabetic system, both as a reader and a speller. A developmental stage is the "tangible evidence in children's productions of shifts in their thinking" (Gentry, 2004, p. 5). What teachers observe students doing, saying, and creating serves as evidence of students' thinking at a particular developmental stage. A student's misspellings provide a knowledgeable teacher with clues of how he thinks the alphabetic system works and guides a teacher to know what he is ready to learn in order to proceed from one stage to the next.

points2ponder

QUICK REVIEW 1 Explain why a misspelling may be helpful to a teacher.

(Access the answer in the digital version of this book.)

10.3

DEVELOPMENTAL STAGES OF SPELLING

As with other aspects of language arts, spelling skills follow predictable developmental stages, which most students pass through as they become proficient spellers. You must know these stages in order to make competent instructional decisions. In addition, you must understand your students as developing spellers. This understanding is refined through observing students, collecting and analyzing their writing samples, and talking with them about spelling in order to gain a clear sense of what they know.

Development stages are spelling guideposts.

Differences between a skilled and less-skilled speller.

SKILLED SPELLER	LESS-SKILLED SPELLER
Forms a mental picture of a word	Is unable to form a mental picture of a word
Chooses useful strategies to spell a new word	Uses a hodgepodge of spelling strategies, unaware of which works best
Is aware of spelling patterns and uses them to spell new words	Is oblivious of spelling patterns and does not see patterns when they are misused in spelling.
Knows where to turn when stumped with spelling	Stops writing and waits for help when stumped with spelling
Understands that spelling an unknown word is mental work	Expects the spelling of an unknown word to magically appear
Develops confidence in herself as a speller when able to figure out how to spell an unknown word	Does not develop confidence as a speller because she is often unable to figure out the spelling of an unknown word
Is pleased and positive when successes with spelling outweigh the mistakes	Becomes frustrated when mistakes outweigh the successes with spelling
Has spelling consciousness, or an awareness of words and spellings, a sense of caring about expert spelling	Is unaware of correct and incorrect spellings and appears to have no concern for expert spelling

Researchers who have worked to identify the stages of spelling development since the early 1970s include Charles Read, Edmund Henderson, Shane Templeton, Richard Gentry, Linnea Ehri, Marcia Invernizzi, Darrell Morris, Robert Schlagal, and Carol Chomsky. Although the names and descriptions of the stages vary slightly, these researchers agree on the basic developmental continuum of spelling. Two main models have emerged and are based on the same premise: knowing the student's stage of development can guide instruction. *Words Their Way,* developed by Bear, Invernizzi, Templeton, and Johnston (1996, 2012), pinpoints the spelling skills students use but confuse as a signal of their growing knowledge. The Developmental Stages of Spelling, Gentry's broader model (1982), describes linguistic elements of words and seeks to understand the thinking behind the spelling and for a teacher to use this thinking to guide instruction. While both models are widely used by teachers, *Forward Thinking* presents more in-depth information on Gentry's Developmental Stages of Spelling model. However, you may explore further with Words Their Way: Word Study in Action (4 pp.): www.mypearsontraining.com/pdfs/TG_WTW_WordStudy.pdf. Formal study of spelling begins in second grade, and most students will need to study these patterns for the next five to seven years in order to spell as well as adults (Gentry, 1997). Prior to formal spelling instruction, students pass through several developmental stages. As discussed previously for reading and for writing, stages of development are simply guideposts or accomplishments expected at certain age levels, which point the way toward what should be taught next (see Exhibit 10.3). For spelling, developmental stages signal the use of specific spelling strategies over half the time, which means a writer is thinking basically the same way most of the time he or she is spelling a word (Beers & Henderson, 1977; Gentry, 1982; Read, 1971). A student who has difficulty with spelling, on the other hand, may demonstrate his difficulties by randomly trying various spelling strategies, revealing little or no consistency. Exhibit 10.4 shares the differences between a skilled and less-skilled speller. Once a student reaches a certain spelling stage, she may occasionally revert to a previous stage when tired, frustrated, or unmotivated. An occasional spelling from a previous stage is not cause for alarm. Just like a child who is learning to walk may revert to crawling for a bit, he generally returns to the upright position when he is ready and has the energy and motivation.

Review the overview of Stages of Spelling Development: www.hhpcommunities.com/teachinglanguagearts/IL-10-01.pdf

Precommunicative stage

Children at this stage are between three and five years old and are just beginning to grasp the concept of the written word. Throughout their short life, they have observed adults writing in various situations, and they often mimic or pretend to write as an adult would. In addition, their knowledge of the alphabet is just emerging, and they have not yet made the connection between letters, sounds, and the written word. Their thought processes are focused on creating marks on a paper to give a message to another person, which is the basis for all their written communication. Occasionally, a few random alphabetic letters may appear in the writing, or even several random letters may be strung together to form a letter string. The child is thinking about putting letters together to make a word, but does not recognize the need to link these letters to sounds. So a seemingly disjointed collection of letters may mean a word, a sentence, or a whole story (see Exhibit 10.5). The young child is the only one who can read her scribbles or letter strings. She may share a long, elaborate story based on the markings one day, whereas on another day, when asked the meaning of the writing, she may share a very different explanation. At the precommunicative stage, the writing's meaning lies with the writer.

Even though understanding the written work of children at this stage is challenging, families, caregivers, and teachers are thrilled with these early attempts because they are evidence of a child's budding ability to communicate in a new and exciting way. Of course, the thrill may vanish when children move beyond the confines of a piece of paper and onto walls and floors, where their gross muscles can be more fully engaged. Preschool teachers let children practice these movements with sidewalk chalk, painting outdoor walls with water, or stirring in sand.

Semiphonetic stage

Early literacy experiences at home and school have helped children between ages four and six develop enough alphabetic knowledge to understand that letters have sounds and can be put together to represent words. This understanding is an important milestone as students inch toward using writing to effectively communicate their ideas to others. Since alphabetic knowledge is not fully in place, students are thinking about using sounds and letters, but can only partially map the letters to the sounds or create an abbreviated spelling of a word. Students grasp the initial sound first, then add the final sound, and eventually they add the medial sound(s). So the word *night* may be spelled *n* or *nt*, and *Christmas* as *kms* as seen in Exhibit 10.6. At this stage, others can just begin to grasp meaning of the writing, especially if a drawing accompanies the writing and provides clues to the meaning. An ability to segment sounds is crucial to the success of spelling at this stage, and this skill develops through oral phonemic awareness activities, thus building that connection between reading and spelling.

Phonetic stage

Five- to seven-year-olds are commonly at the phonetic stage and are thinking about the connections between letters and sounds. Students use their alphabetic knowledge to map out the sounds within a word by matching a letter to each sound. This mapping ability hinges on a student having a full phonemic awareness or the ability to segment sounds within a word, often called "bubble gum words" or "turtle talk" because of their slow sound-by-sound pronunciation. At the phonetic stage, all or most of the sounds are represented within a word rather than the limited letters used for a semiphonetic spelling. So the word *hope* might be spelled *hop* or *merry* as *mere*, or *year* as *yer* as in Exhibit 10.7. Students at this stage have also begun to memorize spellings of common or simple words, so phonetic spellings may be intermixed among these sight words.

The link between what a student hears and what a student spells is very strong at this stage. Silent letters are left out as are consonant and vowel sounds that are difficult to hear, such as the /m/ in *stomp*.

Precommunicative stage with letters.

Five-year-old Eric uses strings of random letters to label illustrations and represent ideas. His letters have no connection to sounds.

Semiphonetic spelling.

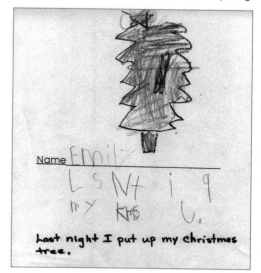

EXHIBIT 10.7

Phonetic spelling.

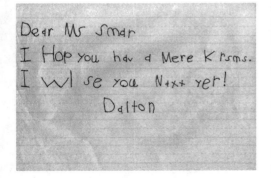

EXHIBIT 10.8

Common phonetic errors.

LETTER COMBINATION	SAMPLE WORD	PHONETIC SPELLING
Short vowel sound	mat	mut
	met	mat
	sit	set
	hot	hut
	tub	tob
Long vowel combination	weight	wat
	seat	set
	nice	nis
	soak	sok
	you	u
N or M before a consonant	bump	bup
	bank	bak
Ed endings	hopped	hopt
	trimmed	trimd
	waited	watad
R-controlled vowels	hurt	hrt
	stir	str
Consonant combinations (dr, ch)	drip	jrip
	chop	trop
Strong consonants (l, m, n)	token	tokn
	bottom	botm

Directions: Say the correct word slowly and become aware of the movement and placement of your tongue, lips, and mouth. Do this several times so that you can feel the word. Next, say the phonetic spelling of the word in the same slow way. Notice similarities and differences in the ways your mouth, lips, and tongue are working. In most cases, one can easily understand why these unusual phonetic spellings might be tricky.

Adapted from Gentry, J. R. (1978). Early spelling strategies. *Elementary School Journal, 79*, 88–92.

Research reveals the elements missing in phonetic spellings follow systematic omission. Exhibit 10.8 explains these systematic errors made by phonetic spellers. A close look at these error patterns reveals detailed thinking behind the student's phonetic spellings, based on how the lips, tongue, and mouth form each sound. For example, return to the word *stomp* and say it slowly to yourself. Notice the way the parts of your mouth work to make each sound. Notice how the /m/ sound is not distinct during a slow pronunciation of the word. Now say the word *stop* slowly to yourself. Again, notice the work of the lips, tongue, and mouth, and the similarity in physical formation to *stomp*. With such similar ways of forming these two words, it is no wonder young spellers can confuse the spelling of *stomp* and *stop*! Understanding common spelling errors at the phonetic stage lets a skilled teacher design both spelling and phonics instruction appropriate to this stage of spelling development. (Section 10.6 includes word study activities.)

Phonetic spelling may also be referred to as **invented,** or temporary, **spelling.** What appear to be merely misspellings to the untrained eye may represent the cognitive movement of the student from one spelling stage to the next. Sometimes children will linger in the phonetic stage, spelling phonetically words that are practiced and used frequently in the classroom. You may need to give some students a nudge toward conventional or correct spelling for common words, while accepting phonetic spelling for challenging, unknown, or longer words.

Before reading further about the stages of spelling development, view the video Invented Spelling (4:00): www.readingrockets.org/firstyear/fyt.php?CAT=34. The video will activate what you already know about the phonetic stage and provide additional mental hooks for hanging new information about the next two stages, transitional and conventional.

Transitional stage

Transitional spellers, ages six to eight, have progressed beyond the letter-sound correspondence of phonetic spelling to think about not only what is heard in a word, but also what is seen, or the visual patterns of spelling. These spellers think of spelling in chunks of phonics and use letter combinations that contain silent letters, double letters, **digraphs,** and **diphthongs,** and even some of the tricky letter combinations identified in Exhibit 10.8. One of the most distinguishing characteristics of this stage is the inclusion of a vowel in every syllable, an important feature of correctly spelled words. A misspelling of *attack* as *utack* displays the inclusion of a vowel in each syllable and the use of the *ck* combination, a visual pattern (see Exhibit 10.9). This misspelling exhibits rich knowledge and is just one small step away from correct spelling, the final stage of the developmental spelling model.

Another characteristic of the transitional stage involves the student spelling a long vowel sound with an incorrect but logical pattern, for example, spelling *pray* as *prae* (as we saw in Exhibit 10.9). A perceptive teacher will notice the attempt to apply the silent *e* to make a long vowel sound and place the speller at the transitional stage. A transitional speller experiments with alternative ways to spell a sound, based on her sophisticated collection of both visual and auditory clues. For example, the long *a* may be spelled in the following ways by a transitional speller: *dae* [day], *naybor* [neighbor], *traid* [trade]. No longer should a misspelled word be merely considered wrong. Instead, ask yourself, "What smart thing has a student done to create this spelling?"

Conventional stage

The conventional, or correct, stage of spelling development simultaneously represents the end and the beginning of spelling growth and development. The student is applying a vast array of orthographic knowledge collected in about ten years of experience with listening, slightly fewer years with speaking, and even fewer with reading and writing. Spellers at this stage can usually generate one or more alternative spellings, and their knowledge and experience helps them choose the correct form, drawing from knowledge of word structure, including root words, prefixes, suffixes, contractions, and compound words.

Being at the conventional stage of spelling does not, however, mean all words will be spelled correctly. It means most words will be spelled correctly, especially those words that have been identified as appropriate for students at that grade level. For example, fourth-grade conventional spellers should spell words correctly that are appropriate for fourth graders. As students advance in the elementary and middle grades, so does the expectation for better spelling. As new and specialized vocabulary is introduced, students will constantly be challenged with new words to spell, which explains the need for continual growth even at the conventional level. In this sense, conventional spelling is a beginning for students as they are able to independently apply their orthographic knowledge more successfully, gaining confidence as their message is understood more easily by others.

Your role with spelling is similar to a parent's role in helping his child transition from crawling to walking. You create a supportive environment for spelling growth, provide lots of models of spelling strategies and correct spellings, and set the expectation that each student is moving forward at her own pace.

Transitional spelling.

Stages of spelling and native Spanish speakers

Students from another alphabetic system of spelling, such as Spanish, tend to follow similar stages of spelling development, with a few slight differences (Rubin & Carlan, 2005). At the precommunicative stage, both Spanish- and English-speaking students create letter strings and random letters to represent words. Spanish-speaking students will even use the same letters for both the Spanish and English words, even though they know the spoken words are different. At the semiphonetic stage, Spanish-speaking students, like native English speakers, represent a whole word with a single letter. The Spanish language has an emphasis on vowels, which may explain the frequent use of a single vowel to represent a word, rather than the consonant typically used by English speakers. Because Spanish is strongly phonetically based, students at the phonetic stage are often very close to spelling Spanish words correctly, matching a letter to a sound. Elements of the transitional stage usually entail doubling the *r* or *l* and adding an accent, before students move into the conventional stage. Keep in mind a student may be at one stage of spelling development in English and a different, likely more sophisticated, stage in their native language, especially if the student developed some literacy skills before learning English. Rubin and Carlan (2005) advocate giving students the opportunity to write in both English and their native language so literacy skills can be developed in both languages (see Exhibit 10.10).

Students in a dual language classroom study their Spanish spelling list.

Using knowledge of spelling development to assess spelling progress

Knowing the stages of spelling development gives a teacher valuable insights into the ways students express their ideas through writing. A spelling inventory allows the teacher to monitor growth. By analyzing students' misspellings over time, you will have visual evidence of the spelling patterns a student knows and those he is still learning. This evidence can then guide instruction, provide focus for a writing conference, lead the development of a leveled spelling list, and be shared with caregivers to show progress. The Words Their Way, Assessment: Placement and Grouping as well as the Developmental Spelling Test are examples of spelling inventories, and more information about these spelling assessments is provided in Chapter 12.

points2ponder

QUICK REVIEW 2 Name the stages of development for spelling and give two characteristics for each stage.

(Access the answer in the digital version of this book.)

10.4

CREATING A CLASSROOM SPELLING PROGRAM

Traditional spelling programs focus on giving students a word list, providing time and activities to memorize these words, and having a spelling test, usually on Friday. This pattern is repeated week after week. With the current knowledge we have available to us as educators, and our goal to meet the varying learning needs of all students, this method seems inadequate at best, and unconscionable at worst. A quality spelling program is multifaceted and focuses on three key components: assessment, attitudes, and instruction. The previous section discussed the developmental stages of spelling and how to assess a student's spelling level. More information about spelling assessment and observing students' spelling progress over time is presented in Chapter 12. The next section in this chapter discusses the teacher's and students' attitudes toward spelling, and Section 10.6 describes spelling instruction.

Analyzing spelling errors is like putting together an intriguing puzzle. As a teacher, you will look for the predictable and logical ways students misspell words to identify their stages of spelling development. Then you can select or design instructional activities to promote interactions with sounds, letters, and words. A perceptive teacher recognizes the role attitude plays in motivating students and provides opportunities for students to set their spelling goals, keep track of their progress, and share their feelings and experiences with spelling. In the upcoming Stories from the Classroom, Sarah Lucero uses writing workshop to keep the focus of spelling on communicating your ideas to others. Her students are highly motivated to share their writing, and Sarah capitalizes on this motivation to impress upon them the importance of spelling.

stories FROM THE CLASSROOM

Keep spelling in perspective

Although the students in Sarah Lucero's second-grade classroom have a weekly spelling list and test on Friday, both Sarah and her students know that the goal of learning to spell is to become a better writer. During writing workshop, Sarah's students have the opportunity to apply their spelling knowledge.

View the video Writing Workshop Part 1 (6:48) to see how writing workshop functions in Sarah's classroom. Watch for the ways spelling is naturally integrated into the workshop. *(Access this video in the digital version of this book.)*

10.5

ATTITUDES ABOUT SPELLING

Spelling is a polarizing topic; people tend to like it or hate it. Consider your own feelings toward spelling. Does it come easily for you? Or do you have negative memories of studying spelling words and taking spelling tests in elementary school? Did you win the school spelling bee? Or did you receive lots of red marks for spelling errors on your writing? Whatever your experiences, you will carry them with you into your teaching career (Ladson-Billings, 2001).

View a Wallwisher page (http://wallwisher.com/wall/XpTYzxzvwB) showing the viewpoints of a group of preservice teachers. Do you relate to these sentiments? It can be quite challenging to overcome negative attitudes enough to convince students that their experiences with spelling will be better than yours, but your own attitude can affect your students' attitudes.

Our society also has strong opinions about spelling. Often undeservedly, those who are poor spellers—just like those with poor handwriting—may be seen as less intelligent, uneducated, or lazy. Misspellings can have serious consequences. A job application with a misspelled word may end up in the trash. A misspelling on a food package could cost a company thousands of dollars to correct. A public official who makes a spelling blunder may be ridiculed in the media. Misspellings can be more than an embarrassing nuisance; they may create a lasting impression with far-reaching consequences, including financial, professional, and personal.

Poor spelling often leads to frustration, low motivation, and a lack of confidence. This may cause a person to shy away from spelling by writing as little as possible, choosing only words he knows how to spell or over-relying on aids like spell checkers. All of these tactics can keep a person from developing stronger spelling strategies and becoming a better speller. Consequently, less skilled-spellers are often unmotivated to practice and thus become even less-skilled spellers (Stanovich, 1986) (see Exhibit 10.11). Over time this gap widens until it becomes very difficult for less-skilled spellers to catch up to the level of their skilled peers. A knowledgeable teacher seeks to break this cycle by understanding the learning and emotional needs of each student and designing spelling instructional activities to meet these

EXHIBIT 10.11

A less-skilled speller can become unmotivated and want to give up.

needs. A one-size-fits-all spelling list given to the whole class each week may not be the best choice.

Students' attitudes

When it comes to developing positive attitudes toward spelling, try a two-pronged approach. First, become aware of the students' attitudes toward spelling by asking them to share their views through writing and discussion. Getting to know students' views on spelling can be as simple as asking a few basic questions through an inventory—collection of questions about spelling habits and patterns—that can be adapted to any age level based on which questions are important in your classroom. Ask questions that will provide a glimpse into each student's thinking and allow you to create a unique profile of each student as a speller, which can be used to guide instructional decisions. Chapter 12 describes a spelling attitude inventory that can be used as an informal assessment tool. A spelling log, similar to a journal, provides students the opportunity to record spelling words, learning goals, new understandings, or reflections about spelling. You can provide prompts (see Exhibit 10.12) or the journal could be used for free writing about spelling experiences. A spelling log also provides a record of the student's development as a speller, writer, and literate person. You may want to periodically respond to spelling log entries with words of encouragement, thoughtful questions, or personal connections, although this may not be necessary for each entry. This written conversation can provide insights and strengthen connections between the teacher and student.

Teacher's attitude

Students will often mirror your enthusiasm, which is the second part of the two-pronged spelling approach. Sharing new or interesting words with students sets the stage for developing an awareness of words. Collect unusual or tricky words seen in the newspaper, magazines, signs in the community, or online, and enthusiastically explore these with students. As a class, develop a plan to become spelling sleuths, searching for misspellings and bringing them to the classroom to share. If you are not a confident speller, make it your personal goal to become a better speller by implementing some of the strategies described later in this chapter. Also, share your own feelings about spelling with students, and if these feelings are less than positive, use this as a teaching moment. Consider saying something like the following:

- "When I was in elementary school, spelling was difficult for me. One thing I did to improve my spelling was _____." (e.g., *to write in a journal at home. It seemed like the more I wrote, the more my spelling improved*).
- "I still struggle with spelling, which is why I always _____." (e.g., *keep an electronic spell checker close by, so I always have spelling help at my fingertips*).
- "Sometimes I am unsure of my spelling, so I _____." (e.g., *ask a buddy, or in this case all of you students, to look over my writing and help me find misspellings*).

When you make a spelling mistake in front of the students, which most teachers eventually do, use it as a teachable moment. Own up to misspellings by taking responsibility, then modeling how to make the necessary correction. Think aloud throughout the process of deciding on a strategy

---

EXHIBIT 10.12

Prompts for a spelling log.

- Explain what you learned today about contractions (*or another topic*).
- Describe your feelings about spelling.
- Write about a time when you felt frustrated with spelling.
- How would you feel if your teacher asked you to be in a spelling bee?
- I used to think _____, but now I know _____. (e.g., I used to think spelling was easy, but now I know it takes lots of thinking.)
- I didn't realize _____. This makes sense because _____. (e.g., I didn't realize there are three ways to spell to and too and two. This makes sense because they mean different things.)
- What is the most important thing to remember about what you learned about spelling today?
- What is your goal for yourself as a speller?
- Did you reach your spelling goal? Why or why not?

(Print the prompts: www.hhpcommunities.com/teaching-languagearts/IL-10-02.pdf)

for correction, whether it is mentally picturing the word, using a dictionary, or asking a friend. Students can learn much about developing their own spelling habits from our actions and our words.

One way to help shape a positive attitude toward spelling is to give students choices, as described in Chapter 3. "Allowing students to participate in decision making related to spelling words and tasks helps them to develop their own personal sense of success and to see their own literacy strengths" (Alderman & Green, 2011, p. 604). Involve students in choosing spelling words, analyzing their own writing for misspellings, developing a list of useful spelling strategies, and keeping records of their growth in spelling.

points2ponder

QUICK REVIEW 3 How can teachers determine their students' attitudes toward spelling? How does a teacher's attitude about spelling influence the attitudes of students?

(Access the answers in the digital version of this book.)

10.6

SPELLING INSTRUCTION

The goals for spelling instruction are for students to learn how to spell with accuracy and ease and to understand why spelling matters. Experienced teachers would agree that mastering the art of teaching spelling by moving beyond spelling worksheets and a Friday spelling test takes time, effort, and persistence.

According to Sandra Wilde, author of "A Speller's Bill of Rights" (1996) (www.asdk12.org/MiddleLink/LA/spelling/Spelling_BillofRights.pdf), students are entitled to high-quality spelling instruction that meets their learning needs. Yet, even some experienced teachers wonder what high-quality spelling instruction actually looks like because their experiences have always centered around memorization and tests. Some students can learn to be successful spellers using these methods. Others struggle with this limited approach and could benefit from new tactics that use sight, sound, touch, and action. Whatever the approach, your responsibility is to teach students how to spell.

Teaching spelling is anything but easy. As author Cindy Marten puts it, "teaching a child to compose through thoughtful, clear, well-written work is a complicated process" (2003, p. 9). Quality spelling instruction means students are learning and practicing spelling patterns and words that match their stage of development (Newlands, 2011). Vygotsky (1986) uses the term *zone of proximal development,* meaning the mental space where the learner has the greatest potential for learning. Quality spelling instruction relies on you knowing just how much support to give students by not making spelling instruction too easy or too hard. A skilled teacher pays attention to what the budding speller is able to do with ease, what causes frustration, and what spelling knowledge is just within her grasp.

Leaders in the field have yet to determine the *best* way to teach spelling, but current thinking supports differentiating spelling instruction based on each student's needs by using knowledge about developmental stages, homogeneous grouping, and leveled spelling lists (e.g., Bear, Invernizzi, Templeton, & Johnston, 2012; Gentry, 2000; Graham, Harris, Fink, &

EXHIBIT 10.13

Elements of effective spelling instruction.

- Teach spelling strategies.
- Teach memorization of high frequency words.
- Teach spelling patterns.
- Integrate a word-study approach into classroom spelling routines.
- Promote the development of spelling consciousness.
- Involve families with spelling development.

EXHIBIT 10.14

Map of spelling skills for third grade.

2011-2012 Scope and Sequence
Ashlay Parker's Third Grade
Lanwood Elementary, Ft. Pierce, FL

NEW GENERATION SUNSHINE STATE STANDARDS (NGSSS)	CONCEPTS	OBJECTIVES
1st quarter The student will: Spell grade level core words	Short and long vowel spelling patterns (long a: stay, train, space) Spelling by analogy (est: best, guest, quest)	The student can: Correctly spell and use root words and other word parts to define words.
2nd quarter The student will: Know and apply rules of spelling compounds, blends, and homophones.	Compounds Blends (_r: try, group, throne) Homophones	The student can: Use appropriate blends and recite and spell the differences between homophones. Correctly spell compound, blended, and homophone words.
3rd quarter The student will: Learn and use the spelling rules of double constant, vcv, vccv, and -ed and -ing endings.	Double consonant VCV, VCCV -ed , ing endings	The student can: Use appropriate -ed and -ing endings. Correctly spell vcv, vccv and double constant words in my daily writing.
4th quarter The student will: Spell, define, and use prefixes and suffixes. Learn and use the spelling rules of changing y to i and -tion, -sion endings.	Prefixes Suffixes Changing y to i -tion, sion endings	The student can: Use appropriate -tion and -sion endings. Correctly use a y or i ending word. Understand the difference between prefixes and suffixes and use them in writing.

MacArthur, 2003). Spelling instruction that addresses what educators *do* know about spelling and meets the learning needs of students includes the teaching of spelling strategies, effective memorization techniques, spelling patterns, word study practice activities, and spelling consciousness (Marten, 2003). (Exhibit 10.13 lists elements of effective spelling instruction.) Involving families with spelling development can also be a positive influence. Also necessary are ongoing assessments, daily opportunities to write, and recognizing students' attitudes and interests toward spelling.

This video (5:08, www.youtube.com/watch?v=5mKQcjxzr0I) shows how several teachers use tablet computers to differentiate spelling and reading practice for their students.

You can create a study sequence by mapping out the expected spelling skills for your grade level, based on district, state, and national standards (see Exhibit 10.14). This map should identify the underlying linguistic sequence that will guide the classroom spelling program. Use spelling assessments to determine where to begin and how fast to move through the curriculum map, providing students with guidance and practice time as needed.

Teach students spelling strategies

Spelling strategies are the mental and physical tools used to determine how to spell a word. Pause for a moment to consider which two strategies are recommended most often to students. Keep in mind that spelling strategies are about teaching students *how* to spell, not *what* to spell. Because no single strategy works for every word, a speller needs a collection of strategies from which to choose.

The two most common strategies are *look it up in the dictionary* and *sound it out*. Both of these strategies may are useful in certain situations, but a speller should consider the following additional strategies:

- Use visual memory by creating a mental picture of the word or writing the word several ways to see which one looks right.
- Recall experiences with other words that have a similar pattern of letters or phonics elements, words that look or sound similar.
- Break words into parts (e.g., root word, prefix, suffix) and consider what is known about each part.
- Use a mnemonic device (e.g., for *arithmetic*: a rat in the house might eat the ice cream).
- Look around the room or in a book.
- Consider the word's history (morphology).
- Ask another person.

Teach students the importance of equipping their mental toolbox with various tools. Introduce one strategy at a time, and encourage them to try it out with several different words. When students have a small collection of strategies, discuss how to choose the best strategy for each type of word.

Teach memorization of high frequency words

Memorization plays a strong role in spelling. Writing would be a slow and laborious process if we had to carefully consider how to spell every single word. At the same time, most people cannot memorize every word they may need to spell. In a traditional model of spelling instruction, memorization is the main route to successful spelling (Chapter 12 will discuss Weekly Spelling Tests). When you give students a spelling list on Monday and a test on Friday, with little or no instruction in between, spelling is assigned and assessed rather than taught. You must find balance between memorization and other aspects of instruction.

Teach students a study or memorization strategy (www.readingrockets. org/article/269/) that incorporates the use of various senses to increase the likelihood students will mentally move the words into their long-term memory. Avoid having students write words over and over again; Henderson (1990) likens this to the aspirin theory: "One helps a lot; two are almost twice as helpful, a third adds very little more, and four are bad for the stomach" (p. 90). Instead, encourage caregivers to support the study of spelling words using a multisensory approach.

When considering which words to have students memorize, one possible source are grade-level word lists: www.spelling-words-well.com/spelling-word-lists.html. A school district may develop lists of words determined to be appropriate at a certain grade level. Additionally, grade-level word lists can be found on the Internet or as a part of commercially developed spelling materials. Although word lists may vary, no exact set of grade-level words has been established, so teachers need to choose the list that seems most appropriate for their students. One online source for grade-level word lists is Spelling-Words-Well (www.spelling-words-well.com/spelling-word-lists. html), although many other sources exist.

Other word lists include lists of frequently misspelled words: http://academic.cuesta.edu/acasupp/as/819.htm. These lists may also vary, depending on the intended age level. Teachers may also create word clusters, or a small group of words centering around a content topic or a linguistic element to be used for memorization (see Exhibit 10.15).

EXHIBIT 10.15

Word clusters for spelling.

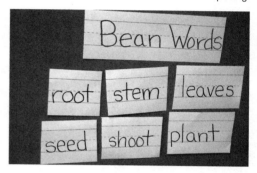

First-grade teacher Glynis Kickhaefer selects this week's spelling words based on the class's science unit on plants and their experiment of growing bean seeds. She chooses science words that match the vowel and consonant combinations in the first-grade curriculum.

Teach spelling patterns

Our brain naturally searches for patterns as a way to understand the world around us. Patterns serve as signals that support a prediction of what will occur or be found next. Just as a pattern of noises from under the hood may signal a problem with the car, words with similar spelling patterns may signal a speller about how to spell a new, but similar, word. Patterns give the speller a starting point or a clue of how a word might be spelled. **Word families** represent a pattern or a group of words that vary in beginning letter but have the same ending chunk (e.g., *bike, like, strike*), similar to the concepts of **onset** and **rime** described in Chapter 5. A skilled teacher creates opportunities for students to recognize and describe patterns among words, which helps them strengthen the link between known words and new words.

View the spelling patterns students should be learning at certain grade levels: www.hhpcommunities.com/teachinglanguagearts/IL-10-03.pdf. To understand how to teach spelling by emphasizing patterns, watch the video Word Study in Action: Spelling Patterns (8:44, www.youtube.com/watch?v=rpoMk-Ncv8o) featuring a teacher who guides students toward uncovering the pattern for adding the -ed ending to short vowel words. Notice the way the teacher presents the opportunity, but the students discover and explain the pattern.

A hands-on approach facilitates identifying and understanding the patterns in spelling. *Words Their Way* is an example of a research-based, systematic approach to spelling that focuses on the study of words and an understanding of spelling patterns (Bear, Invernizzi, Templeton, & Johnston, 2012). Recognizing patterns within and between words is taught through word sorts and other hands-on activities, several of which will be shared in this next section.

Integrate a word study approach into classroom spelling routines

Word study is an instructional approach that allows students to manipulate and examine word features through hands-on activities. Gaining notoriety through the *Words Their Way* model (Bear, Invernizzi, Templeton, & Johnston, 1996, 2012), word study teaches spellers to look more closely at how words are constructed based on sounds, visuals, and meaning (see Exhibit 10.16) and apply their ever-increasing spelling knowledge and experiences with word features. *Words Their Way* offers one specific approach, although other variations and similar approaches can be found in classrooms. Word study activities promote the following advantages when learning about spelling:

1. Hands-on activities are motivating and keep students engaged.
2. The search for similarities and differences among words promotes identification of spelling patterns.
3. The act of sorting words promotes a different way of thinking than memorization, giving more students an opportunity for success with spelling.
4. Word study activities can be easily differentiated for students with different abilities by adjusting the type of the spelling patterns.
5. Flexible grouping of students is based on each student's stage of spelling development and instructional needs.
6. Literacy center activities may include experiences with sorting words and letters and the use of word study games to review spelling knowledge.

The featured element of a word study program is the sorting activity. You can focus the activity on sound (rhyme, syllable), pattern (word families, onset/rime, consonant and vowel sounds), or word meaning (homophone, root words, prefixes, suffixes), which are the three layers of English **orthography.**

Students receive picture, letter, or word cards and may record their sort on paper, a whiteboard, or a computer (see Exhibit 10.17). During a closed sort, you identify the sorting categories and give instructions for the sort, thus providing a high level of teacher support. An example of a closed sort would be a group of ten pictures to be sorted into words that rhyme and words that do not. For an open sort, students receive the same set of ten pictures, but without any guidance. An open sort presents students with a puzzle to solve and sets a high expectation for independent thinking and effort. Word sorts can be used during spelling practice time as a way to have students synthesize their reading and spelling knowledge.

Bailey and Martin share their long e word sorts.

Jasymn records her word sort on a whiteboard.

study program and Beth's rationale for incorporating each. Afterward, see if you can identify at least one spelling activity that occurred each day of the week. (In the video, Beth mentions the *Words Their Way* Spelling Inventory, www.mypearsontraining.com/products/wordstheirway/tutorials.asp).

Electronic word sorts, or eSorts, integrate the use of patterns to teach spelling with the use of technology (Zucker & Invernizzi, 2008). The first step for this activity is creating a digital language experience story (described in Chapter 9) representing a personal literacy event, which creates a group of meaningful words for the students to sort. The teacher and students select words from the story, and may also select words from other literacy activities and texts. The selected words are put into a digital graphic organizer created through software such as Inspiration. The user can manipulate and move the words electronically. Students can customize their eSort by using different shapes for the word boxes, various background colors, or by adding photographs, music, or voice recordings.

To read more about eSorts: Digital eSorts and Digital Experience Stories for Word Study and Creative Literacy (20 pp.): http://tilesig.wikispaces.com/file/view/Digital_eSorts_DigitalExperienceStories_Zucker.pdf

Promote the development of spelling consciousness

Ever notice that when you are considering buying a certain car, suddenly you notice that model everywhere you turn? When spelling is in the front of your mind, you notice unique spellings, misspellings, and your own spelling; this is **spelling consciousness.** Accurate spelling does not happen by magic, nor does it happen unconsciously. Students will often rise to the expectations we set, so set high expectations for spelling. Create a *no excuses* word wall for words students are expected to spell correctly in their daily writing (see Exhibit 10.18), then hold students accountable for it. *No excuse* words are those that are appropriate for the grade level or high frequency words that students have had many opportunities to practice. Talk to students about when to give closer attention and care to correct spelling. When writing for ourselves in a journal or on a grocery list, correct spelling may not be required, but an entry on the class blog, which will be seen by classmates, parents, and anyone on the Internet, needs more careful attention. "When we care about what we are writing and about who is going to read it, our spelling improves considerably" (Marten, 2003, p. 17).

All teachers occasionally have trouble with spelling. When that happens, they let the students know, ask for help with proofreading, and model the correction of misspellings. In order to improve as a speller, students *and* adults must take responsibility for their own spelling. Teaching self-sufficiency does not mean leaving students to seek out the English orthographic system on their own, but it does mean that you lay the foundation, create the opportunities, and model these behaviors by monitoring your own spelling (Graham & Harris, 1994). You can promote self-regulated spelling development by encouraging students to set goals for spelling, work toward reaching these goals, and evaluate and record their progress. For younger students, much teacher guidance may be needed to help them take on this responsibility, but the rewards will be invaluable. Students can

EXHIBIT 10.18

No excuse words.

In this first-grade classroom, children are expected to spell the word wall words correctly in their independent writing.

Developing spelling consciousness among students.

A writing conference is the perfect time to provide individualized spelling instruction, based on a student's needs. In order to raise spelling consciousness, try using these questions:

- Does this word look right?
- What part of this word is giving you trouble?
- What other way could you spell this word?
- There is a silent letter missing in this word. Where might it go?
- What other letter(s) could you use to make the same sound?
- What strategy(ies) have you used already to spell this word?
- What is the next strategy you could try?

select spelling words for a weekly spelling test, identify spelling patterns to be practiced in word study, and record words they know how to spell in a spelling log or on a word wall. This creates a sense of ownership, even for a reluctant speller, when students are accepted at their individual stage of development and encouraged to move forward (see Exhibit 10.19).

Involve families in spelling

Many caregivers grew up when the Friday spelling test was the norm, and memorization was the predominant teaching method. Teach the family, along with the student, effective spelling strategies or hands-on word study activities for building word knowledge and spelling skills. A brief presentation at back-to-school night or a series of newsletters with spelling information can be useful tools for helping parents understand the developmental stages of spelling or the value of authentic writing in spelling development. In the upcoming Stories from the Classroom, Melissa Hill describes a spelling activity and how she shares it with families.

Caregivers want to feel included in what the student is learning and experiencing. You may share word study activities, favorite spelling websites or apps, for example. Here are resources for sharing:

Additional examples of materials teachers have created to share spelling information with families: www.hhpcommunities.com/teachinglanguagearts/IL-10-11.pdf

Spelling games that can be played at home: www.hhpcommunities.com/teaching languagearts/IL-10-12.pdf

stories FROM THE CLASSROOM

A spelling game for home

Melissa Hill, a second-grade teacher, understands the importance of working with caregivers to impact students' spelling progress. Throughout the school year, Melissa shares spelling activities for students to do outside of school and under the guidance of a caregiver. This perceptive teacher recognizes that forging a spelling partnership between school and home requires communication. Melissa created the Spelling Tic-Tac-Toe activity based on the thinking that follows. Notice how Melissa wants to help caregivers understand the value of these games and activities as ways to encourage both practice and fun with words.

I chose to make Tic-Tac-Toe cards to use with my second graders as a different way for them to study the week's spelling words. I send homework packets with the students every Monday and they are due on Friday. The packets contain math, reading, and spelling assignments. The spelling assignments are either to put the words in alphabetical order or to use the words in a complete sentence. I knew that this was probably going to get boring for the students, but wasn't sure what else to do. Through listening and reading about differentiated instruction and getting a clearer picture of what it was, I decided that completing Tic-Tac-Toe cards would not only give the students a chance to pick the activities they were interested in, but keep them from getting bored at the same time. I chose to make up four different cards so that I could send one home each week of the month. This helps to keep the activities new because most of them are unique to each card. There are a few that are repeated, but not many.

I explain these activities to the students before the cards are sent home and I also send home a note to accompany each card the first time it is given out. The note explains that the student may choose any three activities to complete as long as they are in a row, like tic-tac-toe. If the activity requires that something be written or made, the actual product needs to be returned with the homework packet. If the activity doesn't require that something be returned to school, the activity is followed by an asterisk (*), and the parent must sign the box so that I know it was completed. There are also some directions for the activities that need further explanation.

It is my hope that with eight options each week the students will find this homework more fun and therefore put forth more effort when completing it. This in turn will help them to gain more knowledge from the activity.

Exhibit 10.20 shares a description of Spelling Tic-Tac-Toe.

EXHIBIT 10.20

A spelling game for home.

SPELLING TIC-TAC-TOE

Choose any 3 activities in a row to get tic-tac-toe. You can choose up and down, left to right, or corner to corner. Use this week's spelling words.

Create a picture for each word.	Look up each word in the dictionary and write the guide words for each.	Spell words while bouncing a ball—once for each letter.*
Spell each word aloud, jumping as you say each letter.*	Write a poem, rap, or story using all of the words. It must make sense.	Write the word in the shape of the first letter.
Write the words using one color for vowels and another color for consonants.	Spell each word using toothpicks for each letters.*	Write each word and how many syllables there are in each word.

*Parent signature required in the box (activities that do not require actual products to be returned with the homework packet).

Remind caregivers to be enthusiastic about the student's growing awareness of words and knowledge of letters and sounds and promote this enthusiasm by sharing reports of progress the students are making in their spelling growth. Suggest caregivers create a spelling tool kit to promote spelling practice at home. Here are some items to include in the tool kit:

- Small whiteboard
- Magnetic letters and cookie sheet
- Alphabet stamps and ink pad
- Paper of different sizes, shapes, colors
- Various writing tools (gel pens, markers, colored pencils, etc.)

Emphasize the value of spelling in your communication with families. Through your words and actions, model the importance of spelling as a tool for effective communication, not just as something to memorize for a weekly test.

points2ponder

QUICK REVIEW 4 Teaching students strategies takes spelling instruction beyond memorization into more active involvement. Name at least five strategies you can teach your students. Also, identify the two strategies you use the most and why you think those strategies are helpful to you.

Describe spelling consciousness and why it is important to spellers.

(Access the answers in the digital version of this book.)

Spelling FAQs

Even with a solid background in teaching spelling, questions may still arise. Here are questions teachers often ask about spelling. Visit the URLs listed for the answers.

Does texting impact spelling? Answer: www.hhpcommunities.com/teachinglanguagearts/IL-10-04.pdf

Do spell checkers make spelling consciousness obsolete? Answer: www.hhpcommunities.com/teachinglanguagearts/IL-10-05.pdf

What if students take home some of their work that has spelling errors? Answer: www.hhpcommunities.com/teachinglanguagearts/IL-10-06.pdf

What role does vocabulary play in spelling instruction? Answer: www.hhpcommunities.com/teachinglanguagearts/IL-10-07.pdf

10.7

GRAMMAR OVERVIEW

Spelling knowledge helps the writer put letters together to form words; grammar knowledge helps the writer join words together to form coherent sentences. Together spelling and grammar are foundational tools for communicating your message to others.

What, how, and why should we teach grammar?

The goal of grammar instruction is for students to use grammar to create a clear and eloquent message, whether through writing or speaking. Grammar is powerful, because when others can understand your message, you can inform, persuade, entertain, and build connections. Grammar facilitates communication, but just knowing about proper grammar is not enough. To get a message across effectively, a person must determine which aspects of grammar are important in which situation. For example, the use of the word *yeah* for *yes* may be perfectly acceptable in a conversation with a close friend, but may not be eloquent in a job interview. The term **linguistic etiquette** (Hartwell, 1985) refers to an awareness of language usage and the social consequences of misuse, which may include being considered uneducated, poor, or even lazy. Grammar knowledge allows a person to make effective choices about speaking and writing in any situation (Wheeler & Swords, 2006). According to the NCTE, "grammar is important because it is the language that makes it possible for us to talk about language" (2002). In this sense, knowing about grammar helps us to use it more effectively.

Although few would disagree about the importance of grammar in getting our message across to others, there seems to be some question among literacy leaders about the effectiveness of grammar instruction. In 1986 writing researcher George Hillocks stated that "traditional school grammar has no effect on raising the quality of student writing. Taught in a certain way, grammar and mechanics instruction has a deleterious effect on student writing" (p. 248). Actually, this issue was raised as early as 1936 by the NCTE (Weeks) and expressed again in the 1963 work of Braddock, Lloyd-Jones, and Schoer. Not teaching grammar in the traditional way may seem like a welcome respite to many teachers. Grammar is complicated and full of rules; rules many teachers were expected to memorize as students but cannot recall as adults. Traditional grammar instruction focused on memorizing definitions for parts of speech, diagramming sentences, and filling in missing punctuation or capitalization.

Because students need to know grammar in order to communicate and to be taken seriously as productive citizens, you should not ask, *Should we teach grammar?* Rather, you should ask, *How do we teach grammar in a way that is engaging and raises the quality of student writing without detracting from the classroom time devoted to writing?* Sometimes this occurs during a teachable moment (see Exhibit 10.21).

EXHIBIT 10.21

Effective grammar instruction can occur through a formal lesson or a teachable moment.

Third-grade teacher Diane Kimsey conferences with Ashley about her use of ending punctuation in her story.

stories FROM THE CLASSROOM

From grammar to journals

Pam Albin, a first- and second-grade teacher, has focused much of her writing instruction on the rules of grammar, teaching her students about periods, commas, and capital letters. Pam decides to integrate journal writing into the daily writing routine to give her students the opportunity to apply what they have been learning about grammar.

View the video *A Teacher New to Journals* (1:53) to learn about Pam's and her students' experiences and enthusiasm for journal writing. *(Access this video in the digital version of this book.)*

EXHIBIT 10.22

Grammar words.

Clarifying the terms used to describe grammar seems like a good place to begin, because these words can be a bit confusing (see Exhibit 10.22). People may interchangeably use the terms *mechanics, conventions, punctuation, usage,* or *grammar* when referring to writing skills, such as whether to use a period or an explanation mark at the end of a sentence. In the broad sense, **grammar** is about being a courteous writer and considering the intricacies of language that will help the reader gain meaning. More specifically, grammar refers to the patterns of language we internalize through listening and speaking and also through reading and writing. For our purposes, grammar includes the following:

- **Mechanics:** using correct punctuation, capitalization, spelling, paragraphing.

  Example: *As the red ball rolled down the hill, Jose chased it as fast as his legs would carry him.*

  Mechanical elements for this sentence include the capital letter for the beginning of the sentence and for a proper noun, a comma after an introductory clause, and a period at the end of the sentence.

- **Sentence Completeness:** using proper parts of speech to construct a complete sentence.

  Example: *As the ball rolled down the hill.*

  This phrase lacks sentence completeness. It is a dependent clause and cannot stand alone as a sentence because it does not contain a complete thought with a subject and verb.

- **Syntax:** placing words in the spot that makes sense and sounds correct, according to the guiding principles of the language; the flow of a sentence.

  Example: *As the red ball rolled down the hill, Jose chased it as fast as his legs would carry him.*

  Knowledge of English syntax guides us to place the adjective *red* before the noun *ball.*

- **Usage:** using the right word in the right situation.

  As the red ball rolled down the hill, Jose chased it as fast as his legs would carry him. His brother shouted, "You ain't never gonna catch that ball!"

Decisions such as using informal words instead of formal words (e.g., *ain't* for *isn't*), or choosing the right word (e.g., *affect* or *effect*) are influenced by a person's intended meaning and audience.

When students begin school, they have already internalized many of the guiding principles of grammar, and likely without a single formal lesson.

Much of what we know about grammar is learned intuitively and resides on a subconscious level, and we may notice incorrect grammar if something does not sound or look right. This knowledge alone will carry many students a long way toward communicating effectively; however, in some situations, the expectations for grammar are different from what we use in our daily interactions. For these times, students need the knowledge and skills to communicate in a way that meets these expectations, such as when giving an oral presentation to be posted on the Internet or publishing a piece of writing to be displayed at the school's annual Writers Open House. Having a strong working knowledge of **Standard English** gives students an academic boost during their school years and a professional boost during their work years. As teachers, we are responsible for preparing students for these situations. In fact, people often judge our effectiveness as educators by how well students use grammar outside of school. This may not be fair, but it happens.

Along with this responsibility comes two specific challenges for teachers. First, Standard English varies, in subtle and not so subtle ways, between spoken and written language (Krauthamer, 1999), between print and digital texts, and between informal and formal situations. In other words, standard English falls within a range, and this range varies from situation to situation; standard English is not a precise set of rules. Some people see these variations as a positive and valuable reflection of the diversity of our society, while others see these variations as an erosion of traditional English. You must determine which elements of grammar you should teach your students. At the same time, students bring a wealth of experiences, ideas, and vocabulary from language learned at home—whether English, Spanish, Vietnamese, or another language—to the classroom. You face the challenge of teaching the grammar of standard English, while also acknowledging and valuing the home language, because wise teachers know that to value the home language is to value the student.

Zeroing on the target: Which aspects of grammar to teach

Grammar instruction needs to be focused on useful, important knowledge that can be applied immediately to writing; it must be engaging and purposeful. Instead of memorizing a complicated definition of a preposition, students need a working knowledge of prepositional phrases and how words such as *since, above, toward,* and *with* orient the reader to time, space, and relationships.

Teachers should focus on aspects of grammar that help students write more effectively. In other words, do not focus on obscure grammar rules for aspects of writing that occur infrequently. Focus on the skills students at your grade level need to know. First graders need practice writing complete sentences (i.e., subject, verb, capital letter, ending punctuation). They do not need to know about dashes, semicolons, or colons. How do you know what skills students at your grade level need? Look to the students' writing, the school district curriculum, the state standards, and the CCSS.

10.8

A GRAMMAR CURRICULUM

One place to begin identifying aspects of grammar to teach is the CCSS, first introduced in Chapter 2. These standards clarify the instructional expectations at various grade levels. The Common Core English Language Arts Standards center around four grammar elements: (1) concept of a sentence and parts of speech, (2) syntax, (3) punctuation, and (4) usage.

The Common Core English Language Arts Standards, Language Progressive Skills by Grade (www.corestandards.org/ELA-Literacy/L/language-progressive-skills) shows the breakdown of grammar skills to be taught at each grade level, beginning with third grade. Review the chart and note specific grade levels where formal instruction begins for certain skills. Consider how to use these key elements to form a curriculum, keeping in mind "a minimum of grammar for maximum benefits" (Weaver, 1996, p. 142). Focus on what students need to know, which includes a basic understanding of what makes a sentence, patterns of punctuation, and usage of words.

Concept of a sentence and parts of speech

You may recall from elementary school that a noun is a person, place, thing, or idea and a verb is an action word. These simple descriptions may be the key to understanding a complete sentence, a basic element of grammar instruction. Knowing the definitions for the parts of speech does not make one a good writer, but knowing how to use words to do different jobs within the sentence does. Students need to know that certain words name things and other words explain what those things do and how they do it (see Exhibit 10.23). They also need to know the difference between a complete sentence with a subject and verb, a run-on sentence, and a sentence fragment. With this working knowledge, students can construct grammatically sound sentences.

The basic terms, such as *pronouns, adjectives,* or *fragments,* give teachers and students a shared vocabulary for talking about language. Deborah Dean, in her book *Bringing Grammar to Life* (2008), advocates having students work with the teacher to develop the definitions of parts of speech by investigating texts together to determine what an adverb is and how it works in a sentence, then creating a generalization and testing this out on other texts. A discussion could then center on the ways adverbs can be helpful to writers. Another resource is the Grammar House collection of videos, published as part of the *Schoolhouse Rock* television series, which first aired in the 1970s. Snappy music and catchy lyrics spell out each part of speech by emphasizing what the words do through colorful graphics. Some adults may even remember the parts of speech and elements of a sentence specifically from these videos, and many teachers incorporate these videos into their instruction today. (A few of the videos are available on YouTube.)

Patterns of punctuation

The visual aspects of grammar come in to play when considering punctuation within sentences. Punctuation signals the reader how to read that portion of the text. Each mark is a clue to the text's meaning by indicating places to raise your voice, pause, or stop. Consider the following three statements and their different meanings based on the placement of punctuation.

A woman without her man is nothing.

A woman, without her man, is nothing.

A woman: without her, man is nothing.

Parts of speech help us name things and describe what they do.

Using punctuation is like walking a tightrope, keeping the balance between flexibility and rules, which can be both a blessing and a curse for writers. Many punctuation rules remain consistent, such as using a period at the end of a sentence. But some elements of punctuation vary depending on the style of the writer and the writing. For instance, English experts differ on whether a comma should be used before the last item in a consecutive list. Both are acceptable uses of the comma, but a grammarian stresses the importance of being consistent in using commas throughout a piece of writing.

Punctuation has room for flexibility, which can cause confusion when teaching students. Emporia Public Schools in Kansas, like many school districts, created its own style handbook, giving teachers at all grade levels consistent writing and grammar guidelines. The skills included in the handbook, coupled with the state standards and the CCSS, form the Emporia School District's grammar curriculum. While providing consistent expectation is helpful, teachers must also prepare students for the experiences with college and work where expectations for writing style may vary.

In Emporia Public School's Writing Style Handbook (56 pp., www.usd253.org/home/documents-and-publications/curriculum-resources/writing-style-handbook/view) note the specific information available to teachers.

Another resource may be an electronic grammar-checking tool, which works much like a spell checker, although use with caution. Grammar is a complex system full of subtle nuances, which an electronic tool may or may not be able to apply accurately to a piece of writing. Needless to say, a grammar checker has the potential to miss errors or mark a correct sentence as incorrect. Free grammar-checking sites exist, and commercial grammar-checking tools, such as Grammarly (www.grammarly.com), claim to fix all grammar errors and improve writing, but charge a fee after a free trial period.

Word usage

From birth, children hear their language constantly during waking hours. Through modeling, individuals usually develop an intuitive sense about word usage and recognize when a sentence or word does not sound right. Syntax refers to the order or pattern of words in a sentence and how this flow of words creates a message. Students who are native English speakers bring to school a basic understanding of how a sentence is put together, knowing that an adverb is usually placed before or after the verb, and that an adjective is almost always before the noun. Teachers work to expand this knowledge. Noam Chomsky, a linguist and leader in the field of grammar, believes the way a person speaks and writes represents a vast amount of intuitive syntactic knowledge about his or her native language (Chomsky, 1965). A person's linguistic knowledge and cognitive abilities create the conditions for developing an expertise with her native language. Non-native English speakers acquire their knowledge of word usage in similar ways as native speakers, first by listening and viewing nonverbal cues, then knowledge of English is extended to reading, writing, and speaking.

Variations in language

The term **dialect** describes variations in the way a language is spoken. Within a single language, such as English, one encounters variations that reflect social, cultural, economic, and geographic differences. On a simple level, dialect is sometimes used to refer to differences in pronunciation, but these are more accurately referred to as *accent* (for example, a Southern drawl or a Midwest twang). Do you say "wash" or "warsh"? These small differences often cause friends or relatives from different regions of the United States to laugh or tease us about pronunciation and usage. At a slightly more complex level, dialect may account for differences in vocabulary, pronunciation, and grammar.

American English comprises a wide range of dialects. Variety should not be mistaken for value; no dialect is of lesser value or considered to be ungrammatical. In truth, each dialect is acceptable in a given situation. Choosing which dialect to use in which situation is known as **code-switching,** a term gaining more prominence during the past decade or so, as the United States becomes increasingly diverse in ethnicity and language.

Some might think students are too young to understand the nuances of switching dialects in different situations. Actually, some students begin to learn this skill long before coming to school. Your role in grammar instruction is to give students alternative ways of using words, depending on each student's purpose and audience (Wheeler & Swords, 2006). Having this knowledge allows students to choose how to get their ideas across to others, deciding which words to use and how to use them (see Exhibit 10.24). Without this knowledge, students have no choice to make.

Some educators distinguish between what language users *actually* do with language and what language users *should* do with language. This distinction may cause tension among teachers as they try to pin down the grammar concepts that should be taught in their classroom. An initial step might be to collaborate with the students by noticing and discussing discrepancies between a usage rule and the way a word is actually used. Together the class could make a list of these words, create a questionnaire, and survey their friends and families about how they use the word. This type of "grammar detective" activity brings to light the usage variations among those speaking the same language, from the same geographic area, and even the same family.

For some students, grammar instruction will be about minuscule shifts in the ways they already use language. For others, the shifts will be immense and will require much patience and practice.

Language changes

English changes constantly. One of the tricky aspects of teaching grammar, and especially word usage, is becoming accustomed to the adaptability of language. "It changes constantly; it grows with an almost exponential joy. It evolves eternally; its words alter their senses and their meanings subtly, slowly, or speedily according to fashion and need" (Winchester, 2003, p. 29). For instance, consider the word *blog*, which started out as a noun, but through widespread use in a certain way is now also a verb. When explaining this idea of the changing nature of language to students, the book *Frindle* by Andrew Clements (1996) provides an entertaining story describing one boy's creation of the new word—*frindle* for *pen*—and the subsequent chain of events triggered by this new word.

EXHIBIT 10.24

Blake, a second grader, edits his own writing with an eye to grammar.

Blake prepares his writing to be published and read during sharing time. He knows his second-grade classmates will listen closely and point out any grammar errors he makes, so Blake tries to catch these mistakes before he shares.

Students can and should be taught about the changing nature of English. Grammar rules are not set in stone nor are they black and white. You can use recent publications, such as advertisements, editorials, magazines, blogs, newspapers, and websites to provide examples of our current use of words and expectations for grammar. To emphasize this point, use the Internet to locate a copy of writing from over 50 years ago, such as the Declaration of Independence or an excerpt from a person's diary or journal, and compare their word usage to the word usage of today. To take this idea a step further, have students interview adult family members and make a list of words that used to be in style but are not anymore. Two of our favorites are the words *groovy* and *bell-bottom*. Students can share their list to create a class list of outdated words. Discuss the ways words change and remind students today's popular words will likely not be so common or popular when they are adults.

points2ponder

QUICK REVIEW 5 The four aspects of grammar identified in this section include mechanics, sentence completeness, syntax, and usage. Explain each aspect and give a one-sentence example.

(Access the answer in the digital version of this book.)

10.9

TECHNIQUES FOR TEACHING GRAMMAR

Most teachers tend to teach the way they were taught. Many adults were taught to memorize grammar rules, to diagram sentences, and to edit sentences from a workbook. For today's teachers to make grammar interesting and meaningful, we must move beyond our own experiences toward teaching methods that engage students and build an appreciation of the value and usefulness of grammar. Teaching grammar skills through explicit instruction in the form of guidelines, mini-lessons, and mentor texts provides students with a strong foundation. Some of these teaching techniques are described in the following sections.

Teach guiding principles of grammar through mini-lessons

Teaching grammar requires clear, explicit instruction and abundant modeling. It must go beyond merely mentioning the difference between *there* and *their* or correcting quotation mark errors. Teachers must teach grammar, not merely mention or correct errors. The mini-lesson during writing workshop provides a prime instructional opportunity within an established writing time, thus encouraging students to put newly acquired grammar knowledge into practice. The Guiding Principles for Grammar Usage provides a starting point for mini-lesson content (see Exhibit 10.25). This list can also be extended to include elements from the CCSS for English Language Arts and state and district writing standards. A mini-lesson may include the following:

- An explanation of the grammar element.
- A teacher or student modeling correct usage.

EXHIBIT 10.25

Guiding principles for grammar usage.

- Use fragments (incomplete sentence) rarely, only purposefully and for effect.
- Avoid run-on sentences.
- Use precise pronoun referents.
- Strive for subject-verb agreement.
- Include a comma in a compound sentence.
- Add commas in a series.
- Use apostrophes for possession or contraction.
- Choose the correct form: e.g., *there*, *their*, and *they're*.
- Use quotation marks accurately.
- Avoid overuse of the exclamation point.

Based on the most common grammar errors among children as identified by Conners & Lunsford (1988). Because spelling errors occur three times more frequently than the next most common error, Conners & Lunsford did not include spelling in their collection of the most common grammar errors. Our list reflects this.

■ A summarization of the grammar element and encouragement and opportunity for students to use this element in their own writing.

Students need wall charts as visual reminders of the mini-lesson. These charts, created by you and the students, display patterns in writing, organize information, and remind students of important grammar guidelines. Wall charts become a living, growing part of the classroom and provide students with an instructional resource when you are busy with other students. In the following Story from the Classroom, fourth-grade teacher Ashley Williams uses anchor charts for grammar instruction and other aspects of language arts.

stories FROM THE CLASSROOM

Anchor charts

Ashley Williams believes that effective wall charts grow throughout the year as she and her students add examples and explanations to clarify ideas. When creating a wall chart, she writes big; uses bright colors; and adds arrows, stars, or other symbols to organize and feature ideas. In her fourth-grade classroom, anchor charts hang in an area designated for writing resources. Charts about a similar topic are grouped together and are organized so all can see and easily add information (see Exhibit 10.26). During a lesson, Ashley stands by the chart and points to specific examples. She also invites students to add new or interesting examples to the chart, and she returns to them often, both during writing time and at other times of the day. Ashley reminds students to use the wall charts when they are writing, and encourages them to imprint the information from the wall charts into their minds, so they can take this knowledge anywhere.

EXHIBIT 10.26

Anchor charts serve as visual reminders of learning.

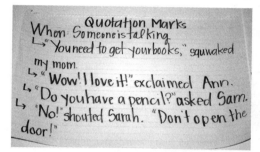

In this fourth-grade classroom, anchor charts for writing and reading are grouped in the reading/writing center. When wall space runs short, charts are layered for easy access.

To prepare for mini-lessons, you may want to brush up on your grammar skills. Online resources can provide grammar guidelines and become a home-based grammar resource for students who have Internet access. Web grammar (www.webgrammar.com/index.html) and Grammar Tips (www.grammartips.net/) are both quality websites for learning more about grammar, whether a person is a native English speaker or an English language learner. Teachers and students will both enjoy electronic grammar games and apps (www.hhpcommunities.com/teachinglanguagearts/IL-10-13.pdf) as a fun and instructional way to practice grammar skills so these skills can be accurately and easily incorporated into writing and teaching.

Use mentor texts as models for grammar instruction

A **mentor text** can be any text used to shed light on a specific aspect of grammar. The term *mentor* refers to the idea of guiding, supporting, or coaching, in this case, a writer. Using mentor texts emphasizes a piece's positive aspects, whether it was written by a class member, you, or a published author. For young people, "the goal is not to point out what is wrong with their writing, but to encourage students by showing them what they are ready for now" (Anderson, 2005, p. 23). A mentor text, be it a phrase, a sentence, or a paragraph excerpted from a complete piece of writing, provides an opportunity to move forward. It lets you zoom in on a specific grammar element, rather than focusing on an entire piece of writing and overwhelming the students with too many words. Teachers should be "sen-

Using the teacher's writing as a mentor text for grammar instruction.

Sixth-grade teacher Robin Dixon uses a piece of her own writing during a class writing lesson. The text is a letter for families about the upcoming field day, and the students help Robin make changes to the draft she prepared for the lesson.

Children's literature as mentor texts.

Dear Fish by Chris Gall
Rich language forms vivid descriptions of the many sea creatures that come to visit Peter Alan after he puts an invitation in a bottle and throws it in the sea. Rhyming nouns and verbs are used for effect. Before reading, encourage students to listen for the verbs and nouns. After reading, discuss how these words add to the story.

Flossie and the Fox by Patricia McKissack, illustrated by Rachel Isadora
This tale of a young girl outfoxing a sly fox was told to the author as a child by her grandfather. The story moves between the standard English of the narrator and the vernacular English of the girl and her grandmother. When read aloud, the story provides a model of blending both dialects.

Seedfolks by Paul Fleischman
This story of an urban garden is told by 13 different characters, from different cultures and with different language experiences. During a read-aloud, dramatize the tone and dialect of each character, bringing their words to life. Students enjoy hearing models of dialect because when they encounter unusual forms of English in their reading, they often are unsure of pronunciations and may even stop reading because of it.

Heads or Tails: Stories from the Sixth Grade by Jack Gantos
Jack is a lively sixth grader who seems to find good-natured trouble at every turn. A collection of eight short stories, this book describes his adventures and is full of humorous dialogue, which can be used as mentor texts for mini-lessons on grammar and punctuation.

Bedhead by Margie Palatini, illustrated by Jack E. Davis
It is school picture day, and Oliver cannot get his hair to behave. Palatini uses words like shuffle-shlump to describe the beginning of Oliver's bad hair day. During read-aloud time, demonstrate how punctuation drives the way we read a story through the author's vivid use of descriptive and unusual words.

When I Was Little: A Four-Year-Old's Memoir of Her Youth by Jamie Lee Curtis, illustrated by Laura Cornell
A young child feels grown up when she tells what she used to do as a baby. Using sing-song language, the text is enhanced by introductory phrases and conjunctions, which promote the use of commas.

Recognize approximations as baby steps toward accuracy.

tence stalkers" (Anderson, 2005), constantly looking out for well-crafted mentor texts to use in grammar mini-lessons. You could record them in a writer's notebook or keep them in an electronic file. Students' own pieces of writing, your writing, and age-appropriate literature provide fertile sources of relevant examples that can be incorporated into brief grammar lessons (see Exhibit 10.27).

In order to use students' writing as a source for grammar instruction, students must be writing. Constance Weaver, in her book *Teaching Grammar in Context* (1996), believes an important first step toward improving grammar is to have students write, write, and write some more. Choose examples by periodically perusing students' writing, looking for successful sentences and also for patterns of errors. The goal is to gain a sense of which elements of grammar students need the most help with.

In addition, literature can be an abundant source of mentor texts (see Exhibit 10.28). Reading and listening to age-appropriate literature fills students with models of flowing, elegant, and correct grammar. Choose books that are more difficult than students would typically read on their own, opting for literature full of rich and vivid syntax that easily demonstrates the point you are trying to make. When using a mentor text, consider the following steps as an instructional framework:

1. Read the entire text without stopping to emphasize or teach. Focus on the enjoyment of listening to the flow of the language.

2. Point out a specific aspect of grammar students should listen for during the reading, and then share the text again.

3. Discuss the grammar element that is the focus of the lesson.

4. Model this grammar element in your own writing.

5. Encourage students to apply their new learning in their own writing. Set an expectation, saying something like, "I am hoping to see you create a new paragraph when beginning a new idea in your writing, in the same way I modeled for you."

Using a mentor text during a mini-lesson or a full writing lesson can be an effective way to provide students with a daily dose of both high-quality writing and targeted grammar instruction.

Recognize approximations

As students become more independent in using grammar, keep in mind that "we must make mistakes while moving toward correctness" (Anderson, 2005, p. 4). This idea of **approximation**, moving closer to getting it right, is true when learning just about anything new. Part of this process may involve the learner gaining a short burst of confidence with a newfound skill and over-applying the skill in similar situations (Vygotsky, 1986). For example, often young students will put a period at the end of every line rather than just at the end of a sentence. An approximation often seen with older students is combining sentences to add interest, which often turns into a collection of run-on sentences. Both of these examples are normal.

Recognize these early attempts as important and necessary steps toward growth—not merely as mistakes (see Exhibit 10.29). Eric, a four-year-old, created two new words that turned into family favorites: *whobody* (means anyone or who; Whobody ate the last cookie?) and *tagapus* (means octopus; A tagapus has eight legs). Eric's early attempts at spoken language reflect his knowledge about words and syntax while also being precious examples of his growth as an English language user. With the help of a supportive teacher (or in Eric's case, family), students can quickly move beyond their pseudo-concepts toward correctness.

stories FROM THE CLASSROOM

Approximations in writing workshop

Writing workshop provides an environment ripe for promoting approximations. Sarah Lucero values the structure of writing workshop for giving students at all levels of writing proficiency to flourish. Through writing conferences and the self-paced nature of the workshop approach, Sarah can work to meet the individual needs of each student.

View Writing Workshop Part 2 (5:30), a continuation of Sarah's previous video, to see more about writing workshop in action. *(Access this podcast in the digital version of this book.)* By the end of the video, see if you can answer the question, *What are the features of writing workshop that facilitate differentiated instruction?*

Look to yourself

If your students do not seem to be grasping grammar concepts or transferring this knowledge to their own writing, your first step of action is to look at yourself and your instruction. Jeff Anderson, a middle school English teacher and author of the book *Mechanically Inclined*, suggests teachers ask themselves the following questions when grammar instruction does not appear to be successful (2005, p. 11):

- What have I done to teach this grammar or mechanics pattern?
- Have I immersed students in correct models? Visually and orally?
- Have I demonstrated how to use the mechanics pattern in a piece of my own writing?
- Have I modeled correcting this type of error in focused edits?
- Have I given students ample practice in editing this particular type of error?
- Have I directed the students to edit their own writing for this type of error on multiple occasions?

Just like a garden requires tending to thrive, quality grammar instruction requires purposeful, intentional, and repetitive teaching, rather than just a single mention or modeling. Making grammar part of a daily routine, such as drawing out a treasure (grammar tip) from the Grammar Treasure Box, provides students with a consistent, yet interesting, structure for learning about grammar. Keep in mind, some students will need more repetition than others. A less-skilled reader may need to see a word 40 times before making it a permanent part of her vocabulary (Beers, 2001). Struggling writers or English language learners may need at least this many opportunities to see and hear grammar elements before making the transfer to their own writing. Your attitude and willingness to continually learn about grammar sets the tone for how grammar is valued in your classroom. Instead of viewing it as a chore, help students to see the integral role grammar plays in communicating their message to others.

EXHIBIT 10.30

Grammar requires constant practice and awareness, much like tending a garden.

10.10

HANDWRITING OVERVIEW

Handwriting may be one of the most controversial topics encountered in *Forward Thinking* or in a new teacher's career. Educators, families, and the general public ask, "Will handwriting continue to be necessary in the computer age?" This is not a new question, nor one with an easy answer. Beatrice Furner, in her work with computer-assisted instruction, posed this very question in a paper presented at the 1985 NCTE conference. Over the years, the question about handwriting instruction has moved from the education field to the mainstream. In 2009 *USA Today* journalist Megan Downs asked, "Is Cursive Writing Worth Teaching?" in an article that looked at both sides of the handwriting question.

Read the brief article "Schools Debate: Is Cursive Writing Worth Teaching?": www.usatoday.com/news/education/2009-01-23-cursive-handwriting_N.htm. Then scroll down and review the posted comments to read what others are saying about handwriting. People, and especially teachers, remain unsure of the role handwriting will play in our digital world. As you read the article, think about whether time would be better spent teaching keyboarding than handwriting, thus enabling students to focus on the skills they will be using most frequently in their future.

For some teachers, the decision about handwriting instruction is out of their hands, made by school district administrators in an effort to provide a structured handwriting curriculum. For other teachers, the school district provides little or no direction so she can make those decisions herself. Whether or not handwriting is a priority in the school district, a new teacher must have a strong rationale for all instructional decisions within the classroom, and handwriting is no exception. The next section of this chapter will answer the why, what, when, and how questions about handwriting instruction.

Why should we teach handwriting?

One might think with the prolific use of texting, email, and instant messaging, handwriting is out of date or old-fashioned. After all, how much do we really use handwriting as adults? Very little handwriting went into creating *Forward Thinking*. Consider how much you use handwriting in the average day. Think about the last time you received a handwritten letter in your mailbox. As educators, we must ask ourselves if handwriting should remain an important part of our curriculum.

Although it might be tempting to conclude that handwriting is obsolete, don't render this opinion until you explore the benefits of handwriting. First, handwriting is portable. Handwriting can occur at any time, any place, and with any writing utensil (see Exhibit 10.31); no power cord, battery, or wi-fi needed. Handwriting is convenient, and this makes it valuable. Whether used for writing directions on the back of a napkin, creating a shopping list, taking notes at an impromptu meeting, or writing a dying person's last will and testament, handwriting's usefulness has not become antiquated. In fact, a more likely scenario is the continued co-

EXHIBIT 10.31

Handwriting can occur just about anywhere.

existence of handwriting and keyboarding, depending on the needs of the person creating the message. In addition, handwriting allows the writer to add a creative flair or an expression of one's personality. Handwritten words can set a writer's style apart from others and can add voice to a written message. In schools, many students at all grade levels still complete assignments using handwriting, even with the influx of technology into classrooms. Various standardized assessments at elementary, middle, high school, and college continue to require students to produce handwritten responses and essays. Handwriting continues to be ingrained in our society and the ways we communicate with each other. Wise teachers recognize the continued role of handwriting and seek to balance both handwriting and keyboarding instruction. These teachers also understand that teaching handwriting is a responsibility; being skilled at handwriting can impact other aspects of school learning and may be one of the keys to academic success for many students.

Regie Routman expresses her opinion about the handwriting question in this way: "Handwriting matters. Not being able to form the letters easily constrains writing. That's common sense. If your energy is taken up forming letters, you're not able to concentrate on your message" (2005, p. 66). In fact, Routman feels so strongly about the importance of handwriting instruction that she advocates more, rather than less, handwriting instruction in schools. Teachers must raise their expectations for quality handwriting from the students, but not before explicitly teaching, modeling, and valuing it. Although questions have been raised regarding the need for handwriting instruction, the truth is, many people in the general public expect students to learn it in school. In fact, some express a sense of dismay when seeing students use poor handwriting, even making judgments about the state of education and the quality of teachers based on it.

Teacher attitude

The key to successful handwriting instruction is your attitude. If you are enthusiastic, knowledgeable, value handwriting, and are willing to be flexible about handwriting expectations, you will inspire in students these same values and attitudes. Also important is recognizing the genuine struggle some students face when it comes to handwriting, finding it difficult to focus on neat handwriting *and* quality content at the same time. Do not assume these difficulties are due to laziness, a poor attitude, or defiance. The struggling student needs your understanding, patience, and belief in her. Handwriting should not be used as a punishment for misbehavior, nor as an assignment to be done only when other work is completed. Focus on the positive by helping students understand nice handwriting makes the reader feel valued, like putting on your best clothes for a special event (see Exhibit 10.32). The goal is to have your message read easily.

Phases of handwriting development

To better understand how young people learn the complexities of handwriting, let's explore what is known about the ways children develop in this area. Researcher and writing expert Donald Graves has identified the stages of development for handwriting (1995). Graves believes these phases may overlap and that some children move through the phases more rapidly than others, which is the nature of development of any new skill. Most of the phases seem to occur before second grade.

EXHIBIT 10.32

Praise students for their handwriting efforts.

Pam Albin, a first- and second-grade teacher, uses a bird puppet to help her evaluate students' handwriting during practice time. When Pam sees a student making a letter correctly, the bird's soft beak gives him or her a gentle little peck as a sign of praise.

1. *Get-it-down phase:* Young children have a natural desire to write, often using whatever writing utensil or surface they can find. Many children bring this enthusiasm to school and are eager to make their marks on paper, without being concerned with letter formation, spacing, or size.

2. *First aesthetics:* In this phase, children show an initial awareness of what the writing looks like on the page. Cleanliness of the page is highly valued. Mistakes cause anxiety, and much time may be spent erasing. Underdeveloped fine motor skills make controlling an eraser a challenge, and the student often tears or smudges the paper, thus increasing anxiety.

3. *Growing age of conventions:* Around the age of six, children move into the phase of wanting their writing to look like that of adults, with correct size, spacing, and margins. These children are beginning to look at their work with a critical eye, and some will hesitate to write or spell if they cannot do so correctly. Correctness of handwriting becomes more important than the content of the writing; thus written pieces often become shorter.

4. *Breaking conventions:* Handwriting concerns strongly affect the amount of writing at this phase. Students at this phase hesitate to make changes, whether correcting, adding, or deleting, that will make the paper look messy; they opt for neatness over content. Modeling editing marks and maintaining an attitude of acceptance of changes can help students understand that a first draft may not be their last (see Exhibit 10.33).

5. *Later aesthetics:* Students begin to see a progression from rough draft to polished final copy and may cross out a mistake and go on rather than stopping to eradicate the mistake with an eraser. Creating an aesthetically pleasing final draft is a priority, and students at this phase enjoy using special paper, pens, markers, stickers, and such to embellish their final draft. They may also develop a favorite pencil, pen, type of paper, or a favorite writing spot.

The amount of time set aside for writing, the topic of writing, and the audience can also influence students' commitment to quality handwriting at any age. Again, modeling a positive attitude toward handwriting goes a long way toward encouraging your students to make handwriting a priority in their own work.

EXHIBIT 10.33

A first draft may not be the last draft.

spotlight ON A LITERACY LEADER:

DONALD H. GRAVES

Dr. Donald Graves left an indelible mark on the field of teaching and writing. In the 1970s, he pioneered the study of the ways children learn to write, and up to the end of his career he remained passionate about the importance of teachers writing with their students and seeing themselves as writers. Graves was a prolific writer himself, publishing 26 books in 25 years, mostly on the topics of writing and teaching writing. Starting his education career as a classroom teacher, Graves became a school principal and eventually a professor of English at the University of New Hampshire, where he inspired many new and experienced teachers to bring the joys of writing into their classrooms. Read more about Donald Graves at Remembering Donald H. Graves: www.nwp.org/cs/public/print/resource/3284.

points2ponder

QUICK REVIEW 6 Give two reasons why cursive handwriting should still be taught in elementary school and two reasons why it should no longer be taught.

(Access the answer in the digital version of this book.)

10.11

HANDWRITING CURRICULUM

Whether in the world of school, home, or work, "handwriting is the vehicle carrying information on its way to a destination. If it is illegible, the journey may not be completed. Handwriting, like skin, shows the outside of the person. But beneath the skin beats the living organism, the life's blood, the ideas, the information" (Graves, 1983, p. 17). Graves's view of handwriting illustrates the important connection between handwriting and creating a message easily read by others. The goal is for the writer to produce a message with efficiency, speed, and neatness by forming the letters through an automatic process. Automaticity comes with practice and skill. Pride in handwriting develops when the teacher values and expects quality handwriting and expresses this to the students on a regular basis. The elements of shape, size, spacing, and slant provide a structure for teaching the mechanics of handwriting. The physical ability of the student can impact the amount of time it takes to develop the handwriting elements.

Physical skills

Formal instruction in handwriting begins when children are physically able to control a pencil and paper. Various parts of the body work together to bring a person's ideas to the page (see Exhibit 10.34):

EXHIBIT 10.34

Parts of the body work in unison to make handwriting possible.

- A strong and steady trunk (upper body and abdomen) provides physical support for arms and shoulders.
- Supportive shoulders lend stability to the arms and hands.
- The hand, thumb, and fingers work in tandem to control the pencil, while the other hand steadies the paper (bilateral coordination).
- Visual perception skills aid in recognizing letters, recalling what letters look like, and knowing the difference between similar letters (e.g., *b, d*).
- Visual motor skills facilitate the ability to copy shapes, numbers, and letters.

If a student's skills are not fully developed in one of these areas, handwriting may not come easily. You can help build up these skills by providing students with activities that build small muscles, such as tracing, stringing beads, working puzzles, or moving manipulatives like pattern blocks or color tiles. Gross motor arm skills can be developed through coloring with crayons, finger painting, and stirring water or sand. A strong trunk and stable shoulders can be developed by throwing a beach ball, shooting a Nerf ball into a ring, or moving with a song, rhyme, or chant. Exploring letter tiles or magnetic letters gives students an opportunity to play with letters and become more familiar with their shapes. These activities are typically a part of an early childhood program, a time when students are both physically and mentally preparing for handwriting instruction.

Proper pencil grip.

Correct handwriting position.

Alleya uses the left hand for an anchor and moves the right hand across the paper as she forms the words.

Once these physical and mental skills are developed at a certain level, a student is ready to begin formal handwriting instruction, usually starting with **manuscript,** which is also called printing. Pressure and control are key to the legible formation of letters. To apply the proper pressure to the pencil—not too heavy and not too light—and to control the strokes used to form the letters, several elements must work in unison:

- Furniture: must be the correct size for the writer.
- Paper: placed slightly to the right of mid-body range and tilted to the right at a forty-five degree angle. This helps the writer maintain control at the top and bottom of the page.
- Pencil grip: coordinate the action of the thumb, index, and middle fingers to hold the pencil at an angle with the right amount of pressure (see Exhibit 10.35).
- Posture: upright, both feet flat on the floor.
- Arm and wrist placement: rest on the table so large muscles provide stability for the small muscles of the fingers and hand (see Exhibit 10.36).
- Eye and hand coordination: work in unison to create the basic shapes of handwriting, the circle and line. The circle requires fine motor control, while the line requires stability in the trunk, shoulder, and arm in order to maintain consistent pressure and not become wobbly, too light, or too heavy.

Most adults can perform the physical aspects of handwriting without thought, but for children, orchestrating these elements together to produce legible handwriting requires instruction, modeling, and practice. Give students opportunities to trace letters in the air, on the desk, or on their hand. Instructive apps for electronic notebooks provide handwriting models, opportunities for tracing the letters with a finger or stylus, and even feedback about letter formation accuracy. Fun handwriting practice apps (www.hhpcommunities.com/teachinglanguagearts/IL-10-14.pdf) give students a chance to write letters using creative techniques such as glitter, glow, steam, or fire. Over time young writers gain more control and they form their letters with more clarity and steadiness (see Exhibit 10.37).

Growth in clarity and steadiness of handwriting.

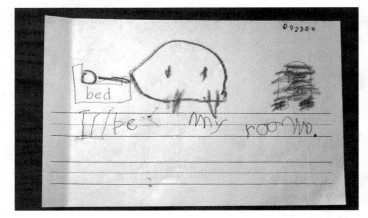
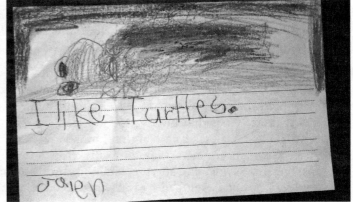

Jalen's handwriting during the first month of kindergarten (first sample) reflects his underdeveloped fine motor skills. His letters are a bit wobbly and several are flying, rather than sitting on the line. For the letter *k*, Jalen has difficulty making the two small lines meet at a point in the middle, a skill requiring much precision. By the last month of kindergarten (second sample), Jalen has made much progress with his handwriting. The letters are written with a smooth line and almost all letters are sitting on the line correctly. He has mastered the precision needed to form the letter *k* correctly, although Jalen appears to still struggle a bit with the letter *s*.

Shape/letter formation

Shape, or letter formation, refers to the way a letter is formed. There are two basic forms of letter formation: manuscript and cursive. Manuscript, also known as print or block handwriting, consists of individual letters separated by a space. Manuscript is usually taught before cursive, with instruction often beginning in preschool or kindergarten. Most manuscript letters are created with one continuous stroke using a vertical style, which makes them physically easier to form than the connected letters of cursive. Stemming from the Latin word *curro*, **cursive** means to run or hasten, which is fitting for this handwriting form designed to be written quickly by connecting each letter of a word through one continuous stroke, which saves time and effort. Cursive is typically introduced in first, second, or third grade. Instruction usually begins with individual lowercase letters, then connecting lowercase letters together, then adding capital letter formation. It can take one to two school years to teach cursive handwriting. Handwriting programs from various publishers represent a certain style of manuscript and cursive and are often named after the company or creator of the style. Each style has its own guidelines regarding the precise formation of individual letters, which makes handwriting a bit of a challenge for novice teachers who should be at least familiar with the various styles. When teaching a specific style, further study of specific letter formation is necessary; Exhibit 10.38 provides a comparison of three different handwriting styles.

Good handwriting should be consistent, with letters formed the same way each time they are written. Teachers need to model the correct letter formation in order for students to learn this skill. For some, this means changing your own handwriting style and habits and may require practice.

In the video Handwriting Lesson: Letter Formation (3:28, www.youtube.com/watch?v=Jukn9cEeXek) the teacher models letter formation, offers guided practice, and invites the student to make the letter on her own, thus completing the sequence of gradual release of responsibility. Watch for the teacher's clear modeling, guidance, and feedback to the young writer.

Accuracy with letter formation improves when students always begin the letter at the same place; visual cues and oral directions can aid novice handwriters in formation. A visual cue reminds the student where to begin forming the letter, such as the placement of a star on the top line to indicate where to begin the letter *h*. Oral directions provide a brief description or catchy chant for how to make the letter. For example, in the program Handwriting Without Tears, the oral directions for making a capital E are: "Start at the top. Big line down. Then a frog jump (pick up the pencil). Then a little line across, another little line, and another little line." The advantage of oral directions, such as this simple chant from the previous video with Ella writing her name, is that she can carry those directions with her always, serving as a simple yet helpful reminder.

Watch Hannah Makes an N (1:27): www.youtube.com/watch?v=hqysiXGHEN8. In the video, young Hannah practices a chant to help her remember where to begin writing the lowercase manuscript letter *n*. As Hannah is writing, notice what the adult does when Hannah switches and begins the letter *n* at the bottom line. When practicing your own handwriting, make up a chant as a reminder of letter formation.

EXHIBIT 10.38

A comparison of print styles.

HANDWRITING STYLE	PUBLISHING COMPANY	DESCRIPTION	
D'Nealian Print: slant Cursive: slant Named for Donald Neal Thurber, the style's creator. Introduced in 1978.	Pearson www.pearson school.com Reading/Language Products, D'Nealian Handwriting *D'Nealian Handwriting* is copyrighted by Pearson Education, Inc. or its affiliates. Used by permission. All rights reserved. D'Nealian is a registered trademark of Donald Neal Thurber.	The D'Nealian style, used worldwide, was designed to ease the transition from print to cursive. Print letters have slant and monkey tails, which can easily lead into the connecting stroke used for linking cursive letters. In fact, 87% of D'Nealian lower case letters are the same as their cursive partner. Go to http://www.dnealian.com/lessons.html to see the transition strokes.	
Continuous Stroke Style Print: vertical Cursive: slant Developed by educators and used nationwide for over 75 years. Zaner-Bloser explains that the current program is "informed by best practices in handwriting instruction and recent brain research in handwriting."	Zaner-Bloser www.zaner-bloser.com Educator, Language Arts and Reading Products, Hand-writing *From Zaner-Bloser Handwriting © Zaner-Bloser, Inc. Used with permission from Zaner-Bloser, Inc. All rights reserved.*	In the continuous stroke style, all of the print letters can be formed by four basic strokes: vertical, horizontal, circle, and slant forming all letters with one continuous stroke, when possible. These strokes mimic the same strokes and hand movements made by children in their early attempts at drawing and writing, beginning around the age of three; thus making the continuous stroke style an easy transition for six and seven year olds. Additionally, the ease of reading this vertical letter style makes it the one most commonly used for highway signs, contracts, newspapers, textbooks, computers, and novels. When students are ready to move on to cursive, they learn to join their letters.	
Vertical Style Print: vertical Cursive: vertical Created by Jan Olsen, an occupational therapist. Current program has been developed over the past 30 years.	Handwriting Without Tears www.hwtears.com Used with permission from Handwriting Without Tears. All rights reserved.	This vertical style, simple and clear, is taught through a multisensory approach, with unique materials (CDs, wood pieces, slate, workbooks, etc.) that make handwriting easy to learn and easy to teach. Lessons are sequenced developmentally from capital and lowercase printing to a simplified cursive. The materials and instruction are inclusive, with the goal of being equally effective for left-handed children, English learners, and children who struggle with handwriting. The curriculum ties to Common Core State Standards and cross-curriculum learning. Visit the site to see samples and videos and to learn about teacher training.	

Explore the online resources to learn more about each style, including the cursive forms.

Other tips for teaching letter formation:

- Provide a visual cue for where to begin the letter (star, dot, arrow).
- Teach similarly formed letters together, such as *b, h, n, m, r*.
- Teach reversible letters separately (e.g., *b* and *d*, or *g, p,* and *q*).
- Use a song for helping students remember the direction for *b* and *d*.
- For cursive, teach the connections between letters once the formation of single letters is mastered.

Spacing

Spacing refers to the amount of space between individual letters within a word, between separate words, and the space on the page as a whole. Because so many physical and mental skills come into play with handwriting, at times the writer may pay too little attention to the amount of space needed to make handwriting legible. In addition, young writers may not fully grasp the concept of a letter, word, or sentence, making spacing quite a challenge. A sentence should begin on the left side or margin and move right across the page, stopping at the right margin or side, then proceeding down to the next line. These seem like simple concepts, and by the time students are in second and third grade, little instruction is given to spacing. But before then, students need a lot of modeling and instruction to understand where letters and words should sit on the page. Encourage students to use small items as space holders between words, such as a finger, a Popsicle stick, a piece of yarn, or a pencil eraser (see Exhibit 10.39). Model where to start a new line, leaving space between words, writing from left to right across the paper, and beginning a new sentence after the preceding sentence's punctuation. With the gradual release of responsibility, students will need less and less modeling of spacing as they grasp the concepts of words and sentences.

Size

For the most part, formal handwriting instruction and practice take place on lined paper, although early practice activities may include tracing letters in the air, sand, water, or shaving cream. When using paper, the focus is on the size of a letter within the paper's lines. Tall letters, such as *t* and *f*, should touch the top and bottom line. The short letters *c* and *m* should touch the bottom line and come halfway between the top and bottom line. The dangling letters, like *j, g,* and *p* should begin at the middle of the lines and hang down below the bottom line. The amount of space between the lines varies with different styles of paper. A wider space between the lines is typically used for younger writers whose fine motor skills are still developing. The space between lines narrows as students progress in their development. College-ruled notebook paper is not usually used with students until third grade or later. Once students have mastered letter formation or even before, their handwriting frequently begins to drift to their own style. By about fourth or fifth grade, students have adapted cursive or manuscript to fit their personality and ability. (See Exhibit 10.40.)

Slant

Slant in handwriting occurs when letters lean in one direction, usually to the right, and most often in cursive. Some styles emphasize slant and some do not. The D'Nealian style uses slant in both printing and cursive. Accord-

EXHIBIT 10.39

A finger space between words.

EXHIBIT 10.40

Handwriting's unique flair.

Notice the extra touches Emily has added to her handwriting. The dot above the *i* is an open circle. The *y* and *g* have extra long tails. The *k* has a fat and curved lower piece. The middle of the *m* does not touch the line on the page. The *s* has an extra curve at the top. Emily, a fifth grader, has taken the basic handwriting formation learned in school and added her unique flair to make a style all her own. Once students learn the basics, their handwriting becomes an expression of themselves.

ing to this program, slant used in printing makes the transition to cursive easier. On the other hand, the Handwriting Without Tears style uses no slant in either print or cursive, claiming a clean, vertical style is easier for the young writer. Both programs have evidence to support their view.

When slanting letters, the writer should aim the letter for the one or two position on the face of an imaginary clock, while vertical style letters with no slant point straight up to the 12 on a clock. When writing on paper, a stronger tilt of the paper will enhance the slant. When teachers are writing on a board, they achieve the slant by turning the wrist, which can feel a bit awkward at first. Novice teachers are strongly encouraged to practice the handwriting style to be used for instruction, which may be quite different from their own personal style.

stories FROM THE CLASSROOM

Handwriting

Pam Albin teaches in a first- and second-grade combination classroom. Familiarity with the curriculum for both grade levels is crucial for Pam, because it lets her make adjustments for individual needs as students move beyond grade level expectations for handwriting.

Pam knows that the principal and her students' parents expect quality handwriting from the students, and look to Pam to model, explain, and integrate handwriting practice into the classroom routines. Listen to the podcast from Pam (2:56), in which she discusses the role handwriting plays in her classroom and her high expectations for students' handwriting. (Access this podcast in the digital version of this book.)

points2ponder

QUICK REVIEW 7 Identify and explain at least five physical skills and environmental elements that can effect handwriting development.

(Access the answers in the digital version of this book.)

Assessment of handwriting

In order to effectively assess students' handwriting, you must be knowledgeable about quality handwriting, which means knowing if letters are made correctly, if correct spacing is used, or if the amount of slant is appropriate. You can set these expectations by creating informal assessment tools, such as a rubric or checklist. The tool helps to define what is expected, and they should be shared with students on a regular basis. Students should be encouraged to self-assess by giving them time and directions to look critically at their own handwriting (Troia & Graham, 2003). For example, when working on a handwriting practice page, ask students to pause once or twice to look over their work and select their handwritten letters that most closely match the models presented in class or the description provided in a rubric (see Exhibit 10.41). The checklist in Exhibit 10.42, another informal assessment, presents handwriting guidelines. A more formal handwriting assessment, the Screener of Handwriting Proficiency, is discussed in Chapter 12.

EXHIBIT 10.41

Handwriting rubric.

	PROFICIENT	IMPROVING	STRUGGLING
Size	Nearly all letters are the appropriate size and touch the lines as needed.	Some letters are the appropriate size and touch the lines as needed.	Only a few letters are the appropriate size and touch the lines as needed.
Shape	Nearly all letters follow the style or are formed correctly.	Some letters follow the style or are formed correctly.	Only a few letters follow the style or are formed correctly.
Slant	Nearly all letters follow the appropriate slant.	Some letters follow the appropriate slant.	Only a few letters follow the appropriate slant.
Spacing	Nearly all spacing between letters and words is appropriate.	Some spacing between letters and words is appropriate.	Only a little of the spacing between letters and words is appropriate.

(Print this rubric: www.hhpcommunities.com/teaching languagearts/IL-10-08.pdf)

EXHIBIT 10.42

Handwriting suggestions.

Remember to use these suggestions for creating your best handwriting.

_____ Start each letter at the top

_____ Make tall letters touch both the top and bottom lines

_____ Make half-way letters touch the dotted line

_____ Make round parts of letters round like a ball (a, b, c, d, e, g, o, p, q)

_____ Make straights parts of letters straight like a stick (a, b, d, f, h, i, k, l, m, n, p, q, r, t, u)

(Print this checklist: www.hhpcommunities.com/teaching languagearts/IL-10-09.pdf)

10.12

SPECIAL CONSIDERATIONS WITH HANDWRITING

So far, our explanation of handwriting instruction has been fairly simple: explain, model, and practice. This is the basic recipe for effective handwriting instruction. Yet, as most experienced cooks know, preparing a favorite recipe often requires a little extra know-how that goes beyond the basic instruction. This section on special considerations in handwriting addresses the challenges posed by a classroom full of unique handwriters.

Left-handedness (left-hand dominance)

Estimates show the number of people with left-hand dominance is between 10 and 15 percent of the population. Recognize the special attention these students require in order to learn handwriting. This attention may begin as students first enter school, especially if hand dominance has not yet been determined. In the past, students who favored their left hand were often forced to switch to right-hand dominance through such tactics as tying their left hand behind their back or punishing them for writing with their left hand. Current practice emphasizes patience and understanding with hand dominance; however, if a child has not identified a dominant hand upon entering school, you can assist with this identification. Over the course of a few days, carefully observe the student in a variety of fine and gross motor activities (without her knowledge). This may include cutting with scissors, throwing a ball, pointing out the window, painting with a brush, or screwing a lid on a jar. Record the dominant hand during these observations and look for a pattern. A student may be ambidextrous, or may be able to switch between hands for various tasks, but one hand is usually preferred for writing.

If you identify the left hand as dominant, give the student special attention when teaching paper position and pencil grip. Encourage the use of a plastic pencil grip (www.thepencilgrip.com) or physically help the student place the pencil between the thumb and first two fingers, about an inch above the point. The top of the pencil should point in the direction of the left elbow, not toward the shoulder as when writing with the right hand. Teach the student to gradually shift the paper to the left as writing progresses across the page. Next, position the paper with the lower right corner pointing to the midsection of the body. A similar position with slightly less slant is used for cursive.

Some cultures consider a person who is left-handed to possess magical or healing powers or to be creative, while other cultures consider left-handedness to be unlucky or sinister. Whatever the qualities this student possesses, recognize that adaptations in instruction and modeling will help him participate fully in handwriting instruction.

Letter reversals

Writing involves orchestrating several different thinking paths simultaneously. Sometimes the pathway needed by each of the processes becomes a bit overloaded or may be missing some key information. When children reverse letters, such as *b* and *d* or *p* and *q*, it may represent a little glitch in their thinking pathway. The glitch may be due to insufficient experiences with letters, a weak visual perception of the letters, difficulty with visual motor skills, or getting the hand to create what is in the mind. For the most part, this glitch works itself out through repeated experiences and practice with letters and writing.

EXHIBIT 10.43

Handwriting on a tablet computer exaggerates the motion of making the letters.

📹 Sometimes an oral cue can remind young learners about correct direction. View the brief video B and D Song (:40, www.youtube.com/watch?v=cGTFB54WodQ) and join in with the hand motions. Commit the verse to memory so you can teach it to students who struggle with the reversal of these two letters.

Letter reversals are very common among children ages four through seven, and are no cause for alarm at this age. Early research in this area showed that letter reversals in writing among young children are not an indicator of poor reading ability or dyslexia (Liberman, Shankweiler, Orlando, Harris, & Bell-Berti, 1971), as some people still believe. Students can move beyond reversals through awareness, formally teaching left to right progressions, and the use of oral directions. For example, the directions for *b* are "start at the top, down, back up to the middle, circle around," while the directions for *d* are "start at the middle, circle around, up to the top and back down." Also, practicing the motions in a bigger space, such as a wall whiteboard or an electronic tablet computer, which can help to create a feel for the correct way to form the letter (see Exhibit 10.43). Knowing where to start and which motions to make can help reduce reversals.

If a student has reached third grade or the age of seven or eight and reversals are still occurring frequently, consider consulting with a specialist such as the special education teacher or the occupational therapist. Both can help to create individualized handwriting activities to assist with straightening out reversals, and they may help determine if the student should be considered for more specialized services.

COMPREHENSION *coach*

Synthesizing to get the gist Can you describe the focus of this chapter in a sentence or two? If so, you will be more likely to remember the information. If not, listen to this podcast by Elizabeth Dobler for comprehension coaching. *(Access this podcast in the digital version of this book.)*

10.13

HANDWRITING AND ENGLISH LANGUAGE LEARNERS

Students who are learning English as a second language are simultaneously learning how to understand, speak, read, and write in English. Handwriting reinforces the letter and word knowledge being learned through reading, writing, and spelling, thus providing an additional layer of practice. For English language learners with a primary language based in alphabetic principles, English handwriting practice may be an extension of handwriting practice done while working in the student's native language. Although the words and meanings may be different in Spanish, French, or Italian, the formation of the letters is similar. When the student's first language utilizes a non-alphabetic script, such as Chinese or Arabic, or for beginning non-English speaking writers, you need to provide clear and simple verbal directions, specific modeling of letter formation, and verbal cues and gestures. For making the letter *t*, you might say and do the following: "We make the letter *t* by starting at the top of the line." Pat the top of your head. "Now make a line going straight down." Model this on the board. "Then we make a small line going across." Make a *t* with your fingers or a hand movement across your stomach. Here are some other suggestions for handwriting instruction that will benefit all students, but are essential for non-native speakers:

- Say the stroke sequence aloud while modeling.
- Make sure you are facing the students.
- Model the movement for forming the letter with broad hand and arm gestures and invite students to join in.
- Have students apply the new handwriting skill in their own practice and daily writing as soon after instruction as possible.
- Teach students to self-evaluate their own handwriting, noticing strengths and weaknesses with shape, size, spacing, and slant.

Giving students of all language backgrounds ample time to write their own thoughts and ideas and to share these with others creates a purpose for learning handwriting.

10.14

ADAPTATIONS FOR STUDENTS WHO STRUGGLE WITH HANDWRITING

Even with quality handwriting instruction full of modeling and clear explanations, some students may struggle with forming the letters on a page. Their difficulties may stem from slower development of the muscles needed to control the pencil or from a scrambling of the message from the brain to the hand. Occupational therapists typically work with students who have severe difficulties with handwriting, often designing an individualized education plan for each student, specifying certain skills to be developed through various activities chosen to address individual concerns. Students with less severe difficulties may not qualify for an individualized plan, but may need more support from you. Regina Richards, author of *Eli, the Boy Who Hated to Write: Understanding Dysgraphia* (2008), suggests the following ways you can make adjustments in handwriting expectations for students who struggle.

Break into smaller chunks. Break up handwriting tasks into smaller steps, so greater concentration can be given to each step. Have students write a letter, or two, or three, then take a short break, rest the hand, look around, and return to finish the word.

Decrease the quantity. Expect fewer practice items to be completed, especially if the student demonstrates proficiency with the handwriting skill early in the activity. For example, on a handwriting worksheet, the student may complete two of the four practice lines.

Increase the time. Give more time for the student to complete the practice activity. This time could be stretched into another time during the school day or practice time at home.

Reduce or eliminate copying demands. Finding the words on the board or screen and reproducing them on paper can be a challenging task even for students who are adept at handwriting. Determine if copying activities genuinely help students reach the handwriting goals set for the class. Practicing on a pre-made handwriting worksheet may allow students to focus on the handwriting rather than transferring words to the paper.

Recognize hand fatigue. Talk about why the hand becomes tired and teach students simple stretching activities to relieve sore and stressed muscles. Avoid hand fatigue by teaching students a standard way to hold the pencil each time they write. Use special pencil or pen grips, such as Penagain (www.penagain. com) or a writing frame (http://shop.zaner-bloser.com/p-24-writing-frame. aspx) to help reduce hand fatigue and create a steady, smooth stroke.

Give students a choice. Give students who have the foundational skills in manuscript, cursive, and keyboarding the opportunity to choose their mode for classroom writing projects. Choice motivates students and lets them capitalize on their strengths and writing preferences.

Develop efficient keyboarding skills. Teach keyboarding skills as part of the school curriculum, along with manuscript and cursive, especially for students who struggle with handwriting. Keyboarding provides students with an alternative way to express their ideas, but for keyboarding to be an effective and efficient tool, instruction and practice must be a priority.

Utilize adaptive software. Train students with a genuine need how to use text-to-speech software, such as Dragon NaturallySpeaking (www.nuance.com/for-individuals/by-solution/speech-recognition/index.htm), which types the words spoken by the writer, thus eliminating the need for keyboarding or handwriting skills. Word prediction software, such as Co:Writer (www. donjohnston.com/products/cowriter/index.html), can also assist with writing by predicting what the next word will be based on the first few letters typed by the student, thus cutting back on the words needed to be typed. A talking word processor, such as Write:OutLoud (www.donjohnston.com/products/write_outloud/index.html?gclid=CLyXv4ru4KkCFZFY7AodcTh8Vg), reads aloud letters, words, and sentences as the student types, giving the student auditory feedback to promote their writing.

Find shortcuts. Assist slow, laborious handwriters with tools for cutting back on the amount of writing they need to perform. Use a template or prewriting graphic organizer with some information already filled in and spaces for the student to add some information. Livescribe (www.livescribe.com/en-us/?gclid=CNCy1L7r4KkCFcYE2god0Cf5Yg) is a portable note-taking device that includes a special pen and paper to record both the written words and the spoken words simultaneously. Both the writing and the speaking can be uploaded into one file for later use.

10.15

CHAPTER SUMMARY

Return to the carpenter analogy from the beginning of the chapter. A carpenter may learn to use the tools of his trade by working as an apprentice, side by side with a more experienced craftsman. He observes, he tries, he often fails, but again he returns for more lessons in measurement, sanding, and staining. The students in our classroom are apprentices to us as writers, and throughout the school day, they observe, listen, try, and sometimes fail, sometimes succeed, and return again for more learning. Their goal, and our goal for them, is to effectively get their ideas across to others. As teacher Sarah Lucero said in the video *Writing Workshop Part 2*, "Children love to express themselves!" Spelling, grammar, and handwriting are the tools that facilitate this expression. Teachers use formal and informal assessments of these tools to determine what students know. National and state standards and knowledge of the stages of development help to guide teachers in determining what students are ready to learn next. Focusing instruction on the skills students need to be effective communicators helps them, caregivers, and teachers to see how spelling, grammar, and handwriting fit into the expressive modes of language arts.

APPLICATION ACTIVITIES
think like a teacher

Identify the Stage of Spelling Development

This activity gives you the chance to put your new knowledge about the stages of spelling development into practice.

1. Examine the chart Stages of Spelling Development (www.hhp communities.com/teachinglanguagearts/IL-10-01.pdf) and formulate a mental picture of what students can do at the various stages.

2. Watch the video of Richard Gentry (www2.scholastic.com/browse/media.jsp?id=422) (Sample 2) as he works with a young student during a writing activity.

3. Make a list of six things you observed Gentry do to recognize the student's learning while also giving her encouragement. On your list, give the time of your observation and the specific thing Gentry did or said. (For example: 0:26, Gentry says. . . .)

4. Identify the student's stage of spelling development.

5. List the characteristics that support your stage identification.

6. Discuss your discoveries with a partner, then share with the whole group.

Code-Switching

1. As an introduction to the activity, brainstorm as a class a list of words that are pronounced or used differently by people with various backgrounds or from various geographic regions (for example, "wash" or "warsh" and "pop" or "soda"). This part of the activity raises people's awareness of the many variations within English.

2. Read the article "Code-switching" by Heather Coffey: www.learnnc.org/lp/pages/4558?ref=search

3. Working in small groups, discuss personal experiences related to both the correctionist and contrastivist approach. Recall experiences from elementary, middle, high school, and college, along with experiences outside of formal education.

4. Make a chart of home language phrases and how they are adapted for more formal settings, such as school, work, or a performance.

Be the Researcher

For this activity, consider yourself a researcher of handwriting practices. Your task is to collect data regarding the physical handwriting habits of three people with the purpose of identifying and describing the various physical elements of the handwriting. To be a qualitative researcher, you must be an observer, putting your sense of sight into high alert and following these steps:

1. Identify your participants: Ideally you would choose three students of any age from four years old and up. If access to students is not possible, then choose three people from outside of this class, so they are not likely to be aware of the specific elements you are observing.

2. Seek permission from the participants to observe them while they are writing. A formal research study would require written permission, but this is an informal study so verbal agreement is fine.

3. Be sure **not** to let the participants know exactly what you are looking for when they are writing. This may cause them to do something different than usual.

4. Be prepared with your researcher materials: Observation recording sheet (www.hhpcommunities.com/teachinglanguagearts/IL-10-10.pdf), writing utensil, hard surface (clipboard). Watch each participant for five to ten minutes. Make notes about what you see in relation to the physical elements described in this chapter (furniture, placement of paper, pencil grip, posture, arm/wrist placement, eye-hand coordination).

5. Make informal notes about your observation for each category.

6. After completing the three observations, use your notes to write a paragraph or two about each participant. The case study format should give you a description of the physical handwriting habits of the three participants. Knowing about the habits of these three people may help you better understand the habits of an entire class of students.

REFERENCES

Adams, M. J. (1990). *Beginning to read: Think and learning about print.* Cambridge, MA: MIT Press.

Alderman, G. L., & Green, S. K. (2011). Fostering lifelong spellers through meaningful experiences. *Reading Teacher, 64*(8), 599–605.

Anderson, J. (2005). *Mechanically inclined: Building grammar, usage, and style into writer's workshop.* Portland, ME: Stenhouse.

Bear, D. R., Invernizzi, M., Templeton, S., & Johnston, F. (1996/2012). *Words their way.* New York: Pearson.

Beers, J. W., & Henderson, E. H. (1977). A study of developing orthographic concepts among first grade children. *Research in the Teaching of English, 11,* 133–148.

Beers, K. (2001). Contextualizing grammar. *Voices from the Middle, 8*(3), 4.

Braddock, R., Lloyd-Jones, R., & Schoer, L. (1963). *Research in written composition.* Urbana, IL: NCTE.

Chomsky, N. (1965). *Aspects of the theory of syntax.* Cambridge, MA: MIT Press.

Conners, R. J., & Lunsford, A. (1988). Frequency of formal errors in current college writing, or Ma and Pa Kettle do research. *College Composition and Communication, 39,* 395–409.

Dean, D. (2008). *Bringing grammar to life.* Newark, DE: International Reading Association.

Downs, M. (January, 2009). Schools debate: Is cursive writing worth teaching? *USA Today.* http://www.usatoday.com/news/education/2009-01-23-cursive-handwriting_N.htm

Ehri, L. C. (1997). Learning to read and learning to spell are one and the same, almost. In C. A. Perfetti, L. Rieben, & M. Fayol (Eds.), *Learning to spell* (pp. 237–269). Mahwah, NJ: Erlbaum.

Frith, U. (1985). Beneath the surface of developmental dyslexia. In K. Patterson, J. Marshall, & M. Coltheart (Eds.), *Surface dyslexia, neuropsychological and cognitive studies of phonological reading* (pp. 301–330). Mahwah, NJ: Erlbaum.

Furner, B. (1985). Handwriting instruction for a high-tech society: Will handwriting be necessary? NCTE. http://eric.ed.gov/PDFS/ED257119.pdf

Gentry, J. R. (1978). Early spelling strategies. *Elementary School Journal, 79,* 88–92.

Gentry, J. R. (1982). An analysis of developmental spelling in GNYS AT WRK. *Reading Teacher, 36,* 192–200.

Gentry, J. R. (1997). *My kid can't spell!* Portsmouth, NH: Heinemann.

Gentry, J. R. (2000). A retrospective on invented spelling and a look forward. *Reading Teacher, 54*(3), 318–332.

Gentry, J. R. (2004). *The science of spelling.* Portsmouth, NH: Heinemann.

Graham, S., & Harris, K. R. (1994). The role and development of self-regulation in the writing process. In D. Schunk and B. Zimmerman (Eds.), *Self-regulation of learning and performance: Issues and educational applications* (pp. 203–228). Mahwah, NJ: Erlbaum.

Graham, S., Harris, K. R., Fink, B., & MacArthur, C. A. (2003). Primary grade teachers' instructional adaptations for struggling writers: A national survey. *Journal of Educational Psychology, 95,* 279–292.

Graves, D. (1983). *Writing: Teachers and children at work.* Portsmouth, NH: Heinemann.

Graves, D. (1995). *A fresh look at writing.* Portsmouth, NH: Heinemann.

Hartwell, P. (1985). Grammar, grammars, and the teaching of grammar. *College English, 47,* 105–127.

Henderson, E. H. (1990). *Teaching spelling* (2nd ed.). Boston: Houghton Mifflin.

Hillocks, G., Jr. (1986). *Research on written composition: New directions for teaching.* Urbana, IL: NCTE.

Krauthamer, H. S. (1999). *Spoken language interference patterns in written language.* New York: Peter Lang.

Ladson-Billings, G. (2001). *Crossing over to Canaan: The journey of new teachers in diverse classrooms.* San Francisco: Jossey-Bass.

Liberman, I. Y., Shankweiler, D. P., Orlando, C., Harris, K., & Bell-Berti, F. (1971). Letter confusions and reversals of sequence in the beginning reader: Implications for Orton's theory of developmental dyslexia. *Cortex, 7,* 127–142.

Marten, C. (2003). *Word crafting: Teaching spelling, grades K–6.* Portsmouth, NH: Heinemann.

NCTE (2002). Guideline on some questions and answers about teaching grammar. http://www.ncte.org/positions/statements/qandaaboutgrammar

NCTE (2006). Teacher to teacher: What is your most compelling reason for teaching grammar? *English Journal, 95*(5), 18–21.

Newlands, M. (2011). Intentional spelling: Seven steps to eliminate guessing. *Reading Teacher, 64*(7), 531–534.

Read, C. (1971). Preschool children's knowledge of English phonology. *Harvard Educational Review, 41,* 1–34.

Richards, R. G. (2008). *Eli, the boy who hated to write* (2nd ed.). Riverside, CA: RET Center Press.

Routman, R. (2005). *Writing essentials: Raising expectations and results while simplifying teaching.* Portsmouth, NH: Heinemann.

Rubin, R., & Carlan, V. G. (2005). Using writing to understand children's bilingual language development. *Reading Teacher, 58*(8), 728–739.

Stanovich, K. E. (1986). Matthew effects in reading: Some consequences of individual differences in the acquisition of literacy. *Reading Research Quarterly, 21*(4), 360–407.

Troia, G. A., & Graham, S. (2003). Effective writing instruction across the grades: What every educational consultant should know. *Journal of Educational and Psychological Consultation, 14,* 75–89.

Vygotsky, L. S. (1986). The genetic roots of thought and speech. In A. Kozulin (Trans. & Ed.), *Thought and language.* Cambridge, MA: MIT Press.

Weaver, C. (1996). *Teaching grammar in context.* Portsmouth, NH: Boynton/Cook.

Weeks, R. M. (1936). *A correlated curriculum.* NCTE Educational Monograph No. 5. New York: Appleton.

Wheeler, R., & Swords, R. (2006). Code-switching: Tools of language and culture transform the dialectally diverse classroom. *Language Arts, 81,* 470–480.

Wilde, S. (1996). A speller's bill of rights. *Primary Voices K–6, 4*(4), 7–10.

Winchester, S. (2003). *The meaning of everything: The story of the Oxford English Dictionary.* New York: Oxford University Press.

Zucker, T. A., & Invernizzi, M. (2008). My eSorts and digital extensions of word study. *Reading Teacher, 62*(8), 654–658.

CHILDREN'S LITERATURE CITED

Clements, A. (1996). *Frindle.* New York: Atheneum.

Curtis, J. L. (1990). *When I was little: A four-year-old's memoir of her youth.* New York: HarperCollins.

Fleischman, P. (1997). *Seedfolks.* New York: HarperCollins.

Gall, C. (2006). *Dear fish.* New York: Little, Brown Young Readers.

Gantos, J. (1995). *Heads or tails: Stories from the sixth grade.* New York: Farrar, Straus & Giroux.

McKissack, P. (1986). *Flossie and the fox.* New York: Dial.

Palatini, M. (2003). *Bedhead.* New York: Simon & Schuster.

Speaking and Visually Representing

Access the book's Glossary, which defines the key terms boldfaced in this chapter, at www.hhpcommunities.com/teachinglanguagearts/glossary.pdf

KEY IDEAS

- Oral language is an integral component of human nature, and the skills of oral language can be taught.

- Successful oral work, like written work, addresses context and audience.

- Images, including photographs, drawings, and video, are a useful form of expression in their own right; however, when paired with written or oral language, their power grows exponentially.

- Words and images together appeal to the human desire to tell an intriguing story.

11.1

SPEAKING AND VISUALLY REPRESENTING AS EXPRESSIVE MODES

In Chapter 2 we explored the idea that writing, speaking, and visually representing are expressive modes of the language arts and reflect the ways humans get their ideas across to one another. The word *express* means state, reveal, show, signify, communicate, convey, symbolize, and put into words. Words, whether spoken, written, or symbolized through images, hold power. Words can entertain a listener, convince a doubter, and teach a learner. Words are used to tell the stories of our lives and maintain our heritage. The ability to use language sets humans apart from the other creatures of our planet. Writing and visual creation are accomplished with tools such as paint brushes, computers, pens, and paper. Spoken words are created with the tools of the mind and enhanced by gestures, facial expression, and tone of voice. This chapter explores the expressive modes of the language arts not explored previously in *Forward Thinking*, speaking and visually representing. Effective teachers understand that the expressive modes can inform their own use of oral language and images in the classroom as they scaffold and improve their students' ability to use language

"Our lives with stories start early and go on ceaselessly; no wonder we know how to deal with them."

J. BRUNER,
Making Stories

fluently and express their ideas visually in a variety of contexts. As Bruner (2002) notes, much of the world of humans is contained in stories. Those stories are often told aloud and recounted in pictures.

Sharing ideas through speaking and visually representing is a process, similar to the writing process. We gather ideas, put them into a cohesive format, check to make sure they make sense, and then share them with others. When it comes to speaking, this process often occurs in a split second; an exception is a formal speech, which may take much thought and planning. Bereiter and Scardamalia wrote that "what distinguishes the more studied abilities is that they involve deliberate, strategic control over parts of the process that are unattended to in the more naturally developed ability" (1987, p. 6). When writers create texts that transform their thinking into words, they compose the words and sentences and choose how to represent their ideas. This same principle applies in other **media** as well. The three expressive modes, visual creation, oral expression, and writing, all follow a similar process for developing ideas in many important respects. A painter may transform the subject of a painting through the process of composition. In creating a podcast, a student might transform understanding of the topic or a theme.

The expressive and receptive modes are often paired together (e.g., reading and writing, speaking and listening, viewing and visually representing); however, educators recognize that the cognitive process of each mode, although connected, is unique. For example, writing and reading are sometimes presented as mirrored processes; however, we agree with Berninger and Richards (2002) that the cognitive processes involved in writing are substantively different than those of reading. One involves encoding and the other involves decoding. A similar comparison could be made about speaking and listening, and viewing and creating a visual text, such as a drawing. The sensory modes are related in that one listens to what others speak, or one views what others have painted or drawn, but these cognitive processes are not exactly mirrors. Anyone who appreciates art but cannot complete a paint-by-numbers kit successfully will know exactly what we mean. The focus in this chapter is on how one composes an oral text, such as a podcast, or a visual text, such as a political cartoon, thus emphasizing the process of expressing an idea rather than receiving or comprehending that idea by reading, listening, or viewing the work.

Throughout *Forward Thinking*, we use the term **text** to mean any form of expressing an idea. This is not to be confused with **textbook**, a type of text written specifically for instructional purposes. In its most literal interpretation, text is written; but a broader interpretation of text recognizes the many ways people communicate an idea. Cultural codes influence the ways texts, or words and symbols, convey ideas and interpret meaning (Barthes, 1967), as we learned from our study of semiotics in Chapter 3. Thus, a text is a way to construct and convey meaning, and any symbol or sign system that a culture might use in this endeavor can be considered a text. Speaking, visually representing, and writing are the ways people convey meaning, and the reading, listening, and viewing processes, explored in Chapters 5 through 7, are used to construct meaning.

Teachers can use this broad definition to develop their students' abilities to use language to make meaning. When explaining the concept of a text to them, you may say that a text can be a book that uses letters to make words, and words are combined to make sentences, and so on. A text can be a poster about Dr. Seuss, or a podcast explaining global warming, or a cartoon describing cellular mitosis. In short, texts are all around us, and they are not limited to books or webpages. Moreover, students can learn to create texts as an act of composing their own thoughts about some aspect of the world. In creating texts—oral or visual—learners also create meaning, not just for those who read or view the text, but also for themselves.

11.2

SPEAKING OVERVIEW

Speaking entails sharing an idea or creating a message through spoken words. Excuse the pun, but sometimes this is easier said than done. Eloquent and meaningful speech does not come easily to all of our students, or even to all adults. Effective oral communication hinges on a well-developed vocabulary, clear organization of one's thoughts, and a balance of enthusiasm and conviction. The knowledge and skills for speaking clearly do not develop overnight, however. Just as writing develops in stages, as described in Chapter 9, so too does oral language.

Oral language acquisition

Although oral language develops in predictable stages, many variables affect young speakers' capacities for using language as a tool. Language is the ultimate tool of the human being, and oral language is our species' first mode of communication see (Exhibit 11.1). Language conveys values (Hughes, 2004), as well, and for teachers this concept is paramount. Language is an important part of every class and all content areas, including physical education, music, and art. While teachers and students may not think of these subjects as depending on language, consider what the coach says during half-time to the players, what the piano teacher says during the lesson, and what the teacher tells students about operating the digital camera. Language and communication are indelibly intertwined.

EXHIBIT 11.1

Language is the ultimate tool of the human being.

Oral language develops in a fairly regular order. Lessow-Hurley (2009) synthesized the research on early stages of language development between birth and the age of 4 years. After crying (which is a form of communication), infants begin cooing and then start babbling. Later in this stage, babbling becomes **echolaic,** which means that the baby is starting to replicate speech sounds in the environment. At some point in the latter part of the first year and into the second (9 to 18 months), the baby begins uttering single words. Around 2 years of age, two-word utterances debut and expand to three-word utterances. These often take a telegraphic form that demonstrates that the child is associating concepts but has not yet acquired more sophisticated language structures. For example, a child might express ownership by saying, "Ball mine." Syntax, or word order used to convey meaning, begins to develop. Between the ages of 2.5 and 4, the child begins using recognizable syntax and expanding vocabulary.

While it is commonly accepted that language (all forms, including oral language) is intended to convey information, Gee (2004) disagrees. He views the functions of language in two ways, both as scaffolding interactions. Language scaffolds (1) "the performance of action in the world, including social activities and interactions," and (2) "human affiliation in cultures and social groups and institutions through creating and enticing others to take certain perspectives on experiences" (p. 117). For him, language use is primarily about the context in which it occurs, and it is more

Speaking as a way of establishing identity within the classroom.

than just a means of getting across a point. Rather, language is a means of interacting in the world, within and between cultures, and establishing one's identity within those constructs (cf. Erikson, 1968) (see Exhibit 11.2). For teachers, the idea of language as a tool by which children construct their identities and interact with the world of the classroom and the world at large forms the foundation of language arts instruction. Language is the tool by which children learn who they are and what their role in the world will be. This concept should be firmly planted in your mind as a teacher and guide your instructional decisions. The next section explains how language manifests itself in the classroom, and we assert that in no other form of the language arts is this more evident than in oral language.

Halliday's functions of language

Over the years, researchers and theorists have derived a number of theories of language and its purposes. One of the most useful is Halliday's (1969) functions of language model that postulates seven functions of children's language. You may recall our introduction to the work of Michael Halliday in Chapter 3, which describes the semiotic theory, as well as those functions of language that center around the communication of ideas through social interactions and texts. The functions of language described in Chapter 3 focus on the end result, or the ways adults use language. Prior to reaching this point, children use language in seven basic ways, and these seven ways begin to merge as children gain more experiences with language and mature. Here are the seven functions:

1. Instrumental: relating basic needs
2. Regulatory: influencing the behavior and responses of others
3. Interactional: relating how the language user relates to others with language as a mediating factor
4. Personal: relating self-expression
5. Heuristic: related to exploration of the environment
6. Imaginative: relating the capacity of the mind, and especially of the child, to pretend and imagine a world that is not physically present
7. Informative or representational: informing others.

As the language user matures, these purposes merge into three more generalized functions of language. Pinnell and Jaggar (2003) describe these as:

> The pragmatic, or interpersonal function that has to do with maintaining social relationships; the mathematic, or ideational, function that has to do with reflecting on personal experience and exploring the environment, and the textual function that involves the use of language resources to construct oral texts (e.g., stories, conversation), that are coherent within themselves and within the context of the situation. In adult language, all three of these functions are used simultaneously. (pp. 896–897)

For teachers, these models of language inform what we know about our students' use of language, and particularly how we scaffold their oral language. For example, Holliway (2004) noted that young children may use language in very egocentric ways: "Perspective-taking in oral referential communication is a developmental achievement, moving from egocentric language use to a more decentered language use that includes listener-useful descriptions" (p. 337). Put another way, children experience and express their understanding in terms of their own lives. As they grow older, they begin thinking about how the messages they wish to convey relate to other people. Instruction can help children understand how their own experiences and understandings can be conveyed in terms others might also understand. A young child who has not decentered may expound, during a discussion, about his favorite toy, ignoring questions and listener confusion. You can help young students learn to decenter their language from the strictly personal toward more imaginative and informative constructs that take into account the expectations of those who are listening to or reading the students' work (Lapp, Shea, & Wolsey, 2011).

The astounding ability of the human brain to acquire language is often evident to teachers as they observe the complex cognitive work of their young learners. Sometimes, the most remarkable evidence of the brain as a pattern-finder can be witnessed by listening to children as they acquire and try out new language structures. Honig (2007) provides the example of a toddler who characterizes a baby pig as a "piggy" or "baby pig" because the child does not know the term *piglet*. Thus, the toddler generalizes from language structures he does know, such as adding the long *e* sound to the end of a word or to apply a descriptor, such as *baby* to convey the meaning intended.

The Junior Oral Language Screening Tool (JOLST) (www.minedu.govt.nz/NZ Education/EducationPolicies/SpecialEducation/PublicationsAndResources/Resources ForEducators/JuniorOralLanguageScreeningTool11908.aspx) is a useful tool for understanding and assessing the oral language of children approximately five years of age and is available from the Ministry of Education, New Zealand (2009). The JOLST focuses on vocabulary, language use, and grammar for English, and assessment data help a teacher make decisions about grouping children for differentiated instruction and identifying those possibly needing further testing for speech-language therapy. The categories on the screening tool are also effective indicators of oral language proficiencies that might be expected of primary-grade students. Additional examples of difficulties with speech that a teacher might encounter are available on the Ministry of Education website, along with suggested approaches for working with students who exhibit these difficulties. Examples include children with autism spectrum disorders, which impair communication and understanding of social roles and routines.

Recognizing cultural differences and influences on communication

Achievement gaps are differences in performances between different demographic groups. Data gathered by the National Assessment of Educational Progress (NAEP, 2011) indicate gaps between the achievement of students who are Hispanic and white or between African American and white students, for example. Many studies have found correlations between socioeconomic factors, such as family income, and student achievement in school (e.g., Hart & Risley, 2003; National Reading Panel, 2000). However, the cause of the gaps is not fully understood. Some suggest students from low-income homes or communities have fewer experiences with language and fewer life experiences on which to draw (e.g., Dahlin & Cronin, 2010; Neuman & Celano, 2001). For example, in some lower-income homes, parents have fewer financial resources for travel to places such as a zoo, a museum, or a vacation spot. With fewer language experiences, children recognize and understand fewer words, a key component of teaching and learning.

Some researchers have also argued that schools do not routinely tap the knowledge students do have, nor do schools build on that knowledge (e.g., Moll, 2010). Thus, teachers can and should consider what students do know, even when that knowledge is unfamiliar to or outside the context of the teacher's own culture. In our discussion of the role of oral language, these factors are especially relevant because students' spoken language is what teachers notice first. Cummins (2005) described conversational fluency for English language learners as a proficiency that students might acquire within one to two years if they experience "intensive exposure" (p. 7) in school or in the environment outside of school. **Conversational fluency** for English language learners is often characterized by the use of high frequency words and sentences that are relatively simple. For teachers and other educational professionals, this notion is significant because students who sound as if they are fully fluent in English may actually struggle with tasks that require academic English. Academic English, in contrast to conversational language, requires familiarity with complex sentence constructions, terms that are not common outside of school, and abstractions that often lack environmental cues to provide context.

You can promote proficiency in conversational and academic English in a variety of ways. A first step is to honor the language students use, including their **registers,** or the variation of language used in different situations and for different purposes; even ones not considered standard in school. Understand that the language students bring with them is nonetheless complex and meets specific purposes in their lives. Sometimes, these registers are considered not proper in school. Diane Lapp (Townsend & Lapp, 2010) describes how she scaffolded students' use of academic register by having her students identify the registers they use and then teaching her to use those registers. Through role play activities, her students learned to determine which settings are appropriate for conversational registers and which are appropriate for more formal or academic registers.

In this book, we use the term *standard*, rather than *proper*, when describing English. The language students use is a reflection of the language their parents, brothers and sisters, and friends use at home and elsewhere. When teachers tell students to use proper English, the message students glean is that the language of their families and friends is, in some way, defective. Commenting on the nature of African American Vernacular English (AAVE), sometimes known as "Black English," bell hooks (who does not capitalize her name) wrote,

> For in the incorrect placement of words, in the incorrect placement of words, was a spirit of rebellion that claimed language as a site of resistance. Using English in a way that ruptured standard usage and meaning, so that white folks could often not understand black speech, make English into more than the oppressor's language. (1994, p. 170)

As with AAVE, other forms of language deserve your respect and that of the community even as students learn to use other registers, dialects, or languages. Language is central to humanness. "Language is . . . the universal and biologically specific activity of human beings. We engage in it communally, compulsively, and automatically. We cannot be human without it," wrote Lewis Thomas (1974, p. 89). Because language is so integral to our personalities, our identities, and our humanity, we find it problematic to tell children that the language they use is not *proper*. Teachers can respectfully work with students to expand the ways they can use language without thinking of one form as more useful or more sophisticated than others. Perhaps the most significant contribution any teacher can make in terms of language learning is to provide contexts in which students can speak and try out different registers, including dialects, slang, and colloquial as well as academic registers. When you honor the variety and richness of language, students will quickly mirror the practice in their own language use.

Bongolan and Moir (2005) at the New Teacher Center, University of California, Santa Cruz, developed the following six effective practices teachers can use to assist students to develop language proficiency in academic contexts:

1. Introducing vocabulary through discussion of target concepts (often expressed as lesson objectives).
2. Providing guided interaction in which students work with one another through language as they grapple with academic concepts.
3. Modeling and explicitly teaching the thinking skills necessary to work through complex ideas. Teachers use authentic assessments to determine students' progress and, when appropriate, avoid tasks that rely solely on advanced language skills.
4. Directly teaching concepts, academic language, and comprehension skills.
5. Connecting instruction to students' lives through meaning-based contexts and universal themes that students recognize regardless of English proficiency.
6. Modeling products, processes, and behaviors. They can employ graphic organizers that help students see the relationships between ideas. Teachers can use visuals, paired with language, to clarify both target concepts and academic language.

EXHIBIT 11.3

Give English language learners opportunities to interact.

Teachers may wonder what types of speaking tasks are appropriate for English language learners whose proficiencies with English can vary widely. We recommend the matrix of strategies and applications from the English-Language Development Standards for California Public Schools (91 pp.): www.cde.ca.gov/be/st/ss/documents/englangdevstnd.pdf (California Department of Education, 2002). Starting on page 17, a helpful matrix lays out example oral language tasks for students at each level of proficiency (e.g., beginning, early intermediate, intermediate, early advanced, and advanced) and for each grade level band (kindergarten through second grade, third through fifth grade, sixth through eighth grade, and ninth through twelfth grade).

All students benefit from classroom opportunities to develop expressive language skills. Resourceful teachers look for authentic ways to encourage expression. The article "Tech How To: Podcasts" ((http://stage30.scholastic.com/browse/article.jsp?id=3752278)) talks about giving your students a voice.

points2ponder

QUICK REVIEW 1 How might teachers help students increase their proficiency with language while honoring the language they already use?

(Access the answers in the digital version of this book.)

Oral language and reading

One of the most common oral language activities in schools is reading. Though we don't always recognize it as such, reading is an oral language activity when reading aloud. In some instructional situations, we benefit from having a student read aloud as students attend closely to the material with opportunities for explanations and inquiry regarding what is going on in the text. Other beneficial examples of oral reading are explained below, along with some of its drawbacks. Reading aloud is not a replacement for other reading formats, but it does play a role if we keep its limitations in mind.

Benefits to oral reading

Effective silent reading is the desirable end result of most reading tasks; however, silent reading does have one drawback: the processes of reading are largely hidden from the teacher's view. When students read aloud, many of the reading processes they employ become apparent to the teacher, who can offer encouragement, correction, and other feedback. When students read orally and respond orally to what was read, we can assess comprehension, enunciation, miscues, and so forth (Dechant, 1991). When we need to assess aspects of decoding, word recognition, and fluency, oral reading is an indispensable tool. We gain valuable information from hearing our students read out loud and can use this information to tailor our teaching to give individual students what they need to progress as readers.

Oral reading can be beneficial in other ways. Students learn from oral reading that in many ways the written word is a record or reflection of the oral tradition. Oral reading activities can also provide effective scaffolds for students who need models of effective readers. For example, students may read aloud with a partner to compare interpretations or as a read-along peer who can model intonation or pose interesting questions (Tompkins, 2003). From read-alouds conducted by a fluent reader (such as the teacher) students can acquire knowledge of text structures, learn content from texts that are beyond their current reading abilities, hear fluent oral reading on which they can model their own reading, and witness the great pleasure that reading gives the skilled reader. Oral language, via reading aloud, has a multiplicity effect; that is, many purposes are served when teacher and students read aloud.

Unhelpful oral reading practices

Though oral reading is useful in many ways, a subset of oral reading practices is quite popular but not useful. Strategies that require students to read by turn-taking (round-robin) or by the popular "combat" approaches are worth noting here. In round-robin, a student simply reads a short passage, perhaps a paragraph or to the end of a page. Then another student continues where the first student ended. The combat approaches include the "popcorn" method, wherein students try to catch their peers who are not reading the exact word from the text. Studies show that neither approach is effective for improving content learning or reading proficiency (Ash, Kuhn, & Walpole, 2009; Rasinski, 2006; Wolsey, Lapp, & Dow, 2010). The round-robin and combat approaches persist, largely because they have classroom management implications; that is, everyone is doing the same thing at the same time, and the activity looks like reading on the surface. However, both approaches actually reduce opportunities for students to read widely, fluently, and well, and they may actually inhibit students' reading proficiency by promoting word-by-word reading. Such approaches also discourage students from using appropriate study strategies such as skimming or scanning already-known information in order to read more closely those sections of a text that present new learning (Wolsey, Lapp, & Dow, 2010).

COMPREHENSION *coach*

Making connections How can we make a connection between what we read in a difficult text and what we already know to help us to cement the new information into memory? Listen to this podcast from Thomas DeVere Wolsey for tips on making connections. *(Access this podcast in the digital version of this book.)*

11.3

ORAL WORK IN THE CLASSROOM: TEACHERS AND STUDENTS SPEAK

The following sections explore some of the many ways that students can use spoken words and images to convey meaning and express emotions. It is not as easy as it sounds, and students at all levels benefit from thoughtful instruction. Though the tradition of public speaking is as old as the first town meeting, it is also a tradition that places the speaker in a vulnerable position, subjecting the speaker to public scrutiny.

People routinely indicate in surveys (Bruskin Associates, 1973; Stein, Walker, & Forde, 1994) that they are uncomfortable in, and even fear, public speaking situations. However, as long ago as 1923 (Winans), educators noted that speaking is routinely pushed aside in the curriculum in favor of reading and writing tasks that are more easily measured. He wrote: "I confess that I know no better way to improve speaking of all kinds than to encourage and help pupils to acquire something to say worth saying, to think straight, and practice saying it to their fellows" (1923, p. 228). Ninety years later, schools and the public at large still value the talents of those who can compose their thoughts verbally and have something worth saying. However, in the past these skills have received little attention in the elementary and middle school curricula. Neglect of this important mode of language arts may be changing, as the CCSS include standards specifically for speaking and listening (www.corestandards.org/ELA-Literacy/SL/introduction), which will place speaking in the instructional spotlight (CCSS Initiative, 2012). As with the standards for reading and writing the CCSS provide specific expectations for instruction in the area of speaking and listening in categories, in this case, "Comprehension and Collaboration" and "Presentation of Knowledge and Ideas." Notice the progression of learning described through the standards related to speaking. Closely examine, for example, the progression related to participation in collaborative discussion from kindergarten to grade six.

As students work to understand key ideas and practice important literacy processes, they often construct meaning through the composing processes, such as those explored in Chapters 9 and 10 regarding written communication. However, students also use oral processes to compose their thoughts and construct meaning. Students who have the opportunity to speak as they learn are much more likely to be engaged and to construct meaningful understandings of processes and content. Be assured that what you say and do is an important factor in the quality of students' speech.

spotlight ON A LITERACY LEADER

SPENCER KAGAN

Dr. Spencer Kagan has devoted his career to helping teachers help their students work together for more powerful learning. His cooperative learning structures are known all over the world as a way to help students engage with learning tasks through thoughtfully constructed interactions with peers. Speaking and listening, hallmarks of effective cooperative learning, are a key focus of the Kagan strategies, which give students opportunities for authentic classroom application of these skills. Dr. Kagan spent much of his career at the University of California at Riverside before becoming the director of Kagan Publishing and Professional Development.

View this video to learn more about cooperative learning and Kagan structures (6:04): www.youtube.com/watch?v=S0s_qxJDuas&feature=youtu.be. Notice how Kagan structures differ from traditional notions of how classrooms are structured. The emphasis is on working together rather than competing for the attention and approval of your teacher. How might cooperative learning, including Kagan structures, help you improve you teaching of speaking as well as the other language arts?

Teachers speaking

Teachers' words have critical instructional implications for students. They can encourage or stymie thinking. Just as important, sometimes words intended to be supportive actually have the reverse effect. Johnston, Ivey, and Faulkner (2012) write, "When a first-grade teacher says, 'How did you do that?' instead of 'Good boy!' is a consequential instructional decision" (p. 233). The first question promotes deeper thinking, while the second statement tends to unintentionally shut students down. A large body of research shows that generalized statements of praise that are not specific to the task or criteria tend to encourage students to please the teacher rather than understand what is good about the performance or process (Kohn, 1993).

You can promote students' oral language learning in a variety of ways simply by choosing your own words carefully. As explained above, words of praise (e.g., "great work!") that are not tied to a specific criterion tend to encourage students to simply reproduce knowledge they think you want. What words or phrases might you say to encourage learning? Johnston et al. (2012) suggest that teachers notice and comment on features of students' work. When teachers notice specific aspects of a student's work, they point out exactly what the student has done that is noteworthy (see Exhibit 11.4). This helps students know specifically what they are doing that should continue. Consider this exchange about the book *The Young Man and the Sea* (Philbrick, 2004) during small group work:

> **Teacher:** I noticed that you are all reading different passages in the book. It seems you are trying to understand something and needed to consult the book. What is it that is puzzling you?
>
> **Student 1:** We're stuck because we realized that Skiffy's dad was pleased that the boat was repaired, but he was sad, too. We wanted to find out why he was sad.
>
> **Student 2:** Yeah, on page 19, Skiffy is talking to a neighbor about his dad's boat that sank. Mr. Woodwell asked what his father said, and Skiffy replied, "Nothin' much."

EXHIBIT 11.4

Positive interactions by third-grade teacher Scott Ritter.

Teacher: So you are thinking that . . .

Student 3: Skiffy's dad loves him, but there is something about that boat that caused his dad's heart to sink when the boat sank, too.

In the sequence above, the teacher noticed the students' behavior in trying to understand *The Young Man and the Sea.* She did not evaluate what they were doing; rather, she noticed and pointed out the process students were using to make sense of the book. Her words helped the students explain their thinking. Students also learned that their approach was an effective one in trying to understand complex works of literature. In so doing, she exemplified two other principles that Johnston et al. (2012) suggest are important. First, she listened to their explanations, and second, she kept their attention on the process they were using to make sense of the literature with the simple statement "So you are thinking that . . ." and let the students finish the sentence.

Your words can also help students expand their thinking in a way that helps build their identities as competent people with knowledge to share. Holyoak and Thagard (1995) worked with graduate students at a university and found that they often struggled to generalize a solution to a problem from one domain to another. When teachers ask, "How else might you apply this?" they are asking students to identify important attributes of the solution in a way that helps them apply the solution to various contexts. In these exchanges, the students own the problem and they own the solution to it. Moreover, the teacher prompts them to use oral language to make sense of the problem and notice its key attributes.

Oral presentations

Conversational oral language is an important aspect of helping students learn; however, formal oral **presentations** are an important part of schooling, as well. Some time-honored traditions give students a chance to stand in front of their classmates to have their say. Incorporating digital technologies in oral presentations can enhance the effective use of oral language for learning, expressing, and demonstrating what has been learned.

Show and tell: Is it worth the time?

Show and tell is a ubiquitous practice in primary grades throughout the United States and other English-speaking countries. Though it sometimes goes by different names, the idea is that students bring a mediating artifact or prop from home (see Exhibit 11.5). Whatever the student brings becomes the basis for a brief presentation to the rest of the class providing the student with a chance to develop public speaking skills. Show and tell also helps develop a sense of community as classmates come to know each other through the practice. Later in this chapter, we will further explore the role of mediating artifacts in oral language activities. For now, discussion of some effective practices for show and tell will suffice.

To plan an authentic and purposeful show and tell event, begin by identifying the standards and objectives to be met. Show and tell should not be just a time-filler. The CCSS (2012), for example, ask kindergarten students to "describe familiar people, places, things, and events and, with prompting and support, provide additional detail." By contrast, first graders are asked to "describe people, places, things, and events with relevant details, expressing ideas and feelings clearly." Both of these standards can inform show and tell activities.

EXHIBIT 11.5

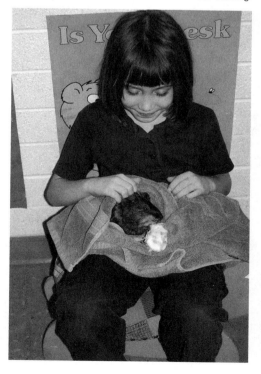

Joy shares her guinea pig during show and tell. Using a physical prompt may encourage students to keep on track with their show and tell sharing.

EXHIBIT 11. 6

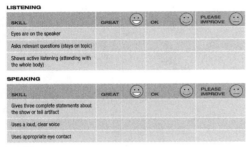

EXHIBIT 11. 6

Rubric for show and tell in kindergarten.

Contributed by Cheryl Isaacson.

(Print this rubric: www.hhpcommunities.com/teaching languagearts/IL-11-01.pdf)

Themes for show and tell may also give the presentations more focus and purpose. Students might be asked to continue a theme from other instructional areas, like bringing an item made from plants during a science unit. Students may be asked to think of their families as members of a community by bringing an item that shows their family as part of a neighborhood, possibly through a favorite family photo. Some evidence indicates that show and tell in the form of a report is more effective when related to students directly; that is, when students are retelling something that happened to them rather than retelling events of which they were not a part (Murachver & Pipe, 1996).

An important purpose of show and tell is that students learn to share with their classmates in a supportive environment. Rubrics or other scoring criteria can help direct students', teachers', and parents' expectations for show and tell. The person showing and telling can learn how to present information orally, and those in the audience can learn to be reflective listeners. Exhibit 11.6 presents a rubric that clarifies expectations for speakers and listeners. Because show and tell often involves the cooperation and involvement of caregivers, speak with them and share a copy of the rubric at an open house, parent/teacher conference, or through a classroom newsletter. This communication may lead to support of speaking skills development at home. Practicing the show and tell presentation at home may contribute to more interesting and meaningful show and tell presentations at school.

Formal oral presentations

Public speaking is a skill that can be learned, and if it can be learned, it can be taught. Learning to speak in public serves students' interests in later life when they enter college, the workforce, and civic life. More immediately, composing one's thoughts to speak in public is a form of composition that develops thinking skills and depth of understanding about content.

The well-known Toastmasters International offers ten tips for public speaking (www.toastmasters.org/MainMenuCategories/FreeResources/NeedHelpGivingaSpeech/TipsTechniques/10TipsforPublicSpeaking.aspx) (Toastmasters International, 2011). For students and teachers, the first three items on the Toastmasters' list seem most relevant. While the Toastmasters' tips are intended for adult speakers, the principles can be learned in a scaffolded manner by elementary school children, as well.

Toastmasters (2011) suggests that:

1. Speakers know their content. For teachers, this means that students need adequate time to prepare for the presentation and access to appropriate resources.

2. Speakers should practice. In fact, Toastmasters is emphatic: "Practice, practice, practice." Practice integrates principle number one. The principle also means that students should be able to rehearse with any equipment or props they might use (e.g., microphones, webcams, artifacts as those used in show and tell).

3. Speakers should know the audience. Toastmasters suggests greeting participants at the door, bantering before the presentation, and so on. For students, we add that knowing the audience means making reasonable assumptions about what the audience already knows and what they might like to learn. For students who share a classroom, this means that they must actively consider what new contributions they can make, rather than repeating ideas previously shared by others.

As with show and tell, more formal oral presentations should address relevant standards, such as the CCSS, and advance students' skills as learners of relevant content and as knowledgeable contributors to the classroom community. Rubrics and checklists can help here, as well.

Typically, formal oral presentations are given in front of the entire class, and there are times when whole-class presentations are the best choice for sharing work. Digital technologies provide additional opportunities for oral presentations, such as creating digital audio recordings, or podcasts, to post on a class website or in Voice Threads and make available for others to hear. Creating visuals, such as a digital poster on Glogster, or a digital slide show, can enhance an oral presentation to both large and small groups.

Small group oral presentations

While students need the practice of making formal presentations, they have many more opportunities to use language informally as they explore ideas, construct meaning, and expand on ideas they have encountered in class. When they make a presentation to small groups of peers, the power of the presentation is multiplied. Imagine students in a classroom with five computer stations. Two students at each station present information as a team about a topic of interest, for example, the periods of geologic time. Four or five other students rotate between the stations to learn about the different periods of geologic time. Each student is armed with a checklist that includes several of the features of oral language presentations found in Exhibit 11.7. Additionally, the audience members are responsible for writing a two-sentence summary of each geologic time period as they move through the stations during three or four days. Over the course of the presentations, students learn about all the time periods, develop their listening skills (see Chapter 7), and hone their oral presentation skills and receive checklist feedback from their peers.

EXHIBIT 11.7

Attributes of oral presentations for inclusion on a checklist.

Pitch	Pauses	Comprehension	Enthusiasm	Attire	Preparedness
Speaks clearly	Props	Vocabulary	Uses complete sentences	Stays on topic	Posture and eye contact
Evaluates peers	Listens to other presentations	Time limit	Content	Collaborates with peers	Volume

Categories derived from Rubistar.

Informal speaking opportunities

Spontaneous or informal speaking opportunities abound in school. Recess and the lunchroom may be popular places for speaking, and non-native speakers definitely build conversational skills in both places. In the classroom, however, informal speaking experiences are opportunities for you to provide scaffolds to help students develop effective speaking skills. Lapp, Grant, and Johnson (2012) used photographs as artifacts to help students grapple with essential questions in science. According to Wiggins (2007), an essential question is one that:

1. causes genuine and relevant inquiry into the big ideas and core content;
2. provokes deep thought, lively discussion, sustained inquiry, and new understanding as well as more questions;
3. requires students to consider alternatives, weigh evidence, support their ideas, and justify their answers;
4. stimulates vital, on-going rethinking of big ideas, assumptions, and prior lessons;
5. sparks meaningful connections with prior learning and personal experiences;
6. naturally recurs, creating opportunities for transfer to other situations and subjects. (unpaged)

In the science project mentioned earlier, the teacher provided students with a photograph of the phenomenon they were studying (in this case, places where man-made structures had failed) and a language frame. Language frames (www.reading.org/general/Publications/blog/engage/engage-single-post/engage/2012/01/10/teaching-tips-language-frames-support-literacy-in-science) give students a way to begin discussing their understanding. Next to each photograph of structural failure, a frame prompted students to respond to key attributes of the photograph. For example, students might examine the photograph, then comment to a peer: "I noticed in this photo . . ." or "This collapsed structure looks different from the others because . . . ."

In the example above, key attributes of the photographs prompted students to notice things that led them to greater understanding of the science concepts and standards for their state. Scaffolds, like the ones used in this study, can jump-start students on the right thinking and speaking path. In classrooms every day, students have many opportunities to learn through speaking and listening. Visualize the classroom where the teacher has to say to students, "It is way too quiet in here. Don't you think you'll learn more if you have to explain/summarize/wonder about this material? Let me hear a little talking, please." Following are informal ways to foster learning through classroom talking.

Think–pair–share

Cooperative learning structures are powerful ways to encourage students to construct and share knowledge (see Exhibit 11.8). Think–pair–share (Kagan, 1994) encourages oral language use to enhance thinking about learning by working with a partner (the *pair* in think–pair–share). This relatively simple structure is powerful in terms of the learning it can engender. The process has four steps:

1. Pose a problem yourself or have another member of the class pose one.
2. Encourage students to think about the problem and consider related evidence or how the problem might be solved. This can be done individually, and you can also ask students to jot down some notes about their thinking.
3. Then, have students turn to their assigned partners to discuss the available evidence and possible solutions. In this phase, they compare their thinking and generate new ideas that come from the discussion.
4. In the final step, students share their ideas with the class or small group.

Common terms associated with this approach are *shoulder partners* or *knee buddies* (see Exhibit 11.9). If the problem is particularly complex, an additional step (Kagan, 1994) can be introduced between pair work and sharing with the class. In this modification, pairs share their thinking with another pair sitting near them before sharing with the class.

Talking chip

Sometimes in small groups, one or two students tend to dominate the discussion. One of our favorite structures for fostering participation in small groups is the *talking chip* (Kagan, 1994). Talking chip helps students establish the norm that everyone participates (Cohen, 1994) in group discussions. Students receive either a game chip used in checkers, a large plastic button, or any small plastic or wooden disk. Even a pencil that recognizably belongs to the owner will work. The rule is simple: As each person talks, the speaker

EXHIBIT 11.8

Cooperative learning encourages students to construct and share knowledge together.

EXHIBIT 11.9

Shoulder partners.

places the chip in the center of the group. No one can talk again until every member of the group has contributed to the discussion and placed a chip in the center of the group. Then, each person can reclaim the chip and the cycle starts again. Students tend to contribute in a circle; that is, with each student contributing in a clockwise (or counterclockwise) direction, so it is may be helpful to tell students that they do not need to participate in order.

Class discussion plus

Students become increasingly capable of conveying ideas orally when conversational exchanges that support practice and self-reflection are regular features of the classroom routines (see Exhibit 11.10). Conversational participation is therefore important for students throughout the grades (Pinnell & Jaggar, 2003), and these conversations are more effective when building from the home languages that students bring to school (Au, 1993; Ball & Farr, 2003).

Speaking is an important part of learning together.

Twenty-first-century classrooms are typically composed of students who have had a wide array of language experiences (Ball, 2002), including native English speakers whose home registers often differ from their teachers or classmates (Baugh, 2000) and English language learners who speak languages other than English (Allen, 1991; Gonzales, Moll, & Amanti, 2005). Sociocultural theory guides teachers to make instructional decisions that support language expansion through classroom experiences and that acknowledge the students' home language and add to rather than erase from it. Tharp and Gallimore (1989) noted that a common approach to discussion includes the teacher posing questions to which the teacher already knows the answer. Even after reading and engaging in other activities, students may still be unable to determine what it is the teacher is trying to ascertain, since there may be only one right answer—the one in the teacher's mind (Green, 1983; Mehan, 1979). The purpose of such exchanges, often characterized as *discussion*, is to quiz or assess students rather than foster new information and engage them in conversation. Tharp and Gallimore (1989) pointed out that this model has been around schools since the beginning of the twentieth century and continues to this day.

In contrast, skilled teachers are willing to accept various student responses to open-ended questions and use these responses to further guide discussion. The challenge teachers face is to ask genuine and thought-provoking questions. Through the questions they ask, teachers also model the type of thinking they value. Based on this modeling, teachers demonstrate that they expect their students to ask high-level questions of themselves and others. In a study of teacher questioning patterns, Daines (1986) defined **interpretive questions** as those that ask students to consider information from many sources, including their own experiences. Interpretative questions include those that require students to make inferences, compare or contrast, determine cause and effect relationships, and make predictions based on trends. Daines's research, however, showed that 93 percent of the 5,289 questions teachers asked in her study were at the literal level. Just less than 7 percent were interpretive questions that asked students to think deeply about the content they were learning in class.

In Chapter 4 we discussed the importance of instructional planning. When it comes to discussion, planning is equally important, which may seem counterintuitive. Plan a discussion? But aren't discussions spontaneous and organic? An effective discussion does have certain spontaneous qualities and arises organically in many ways; however, a quality discussion is more likely to occur if foundational elements are in place. Questions should lead students to think critically and deeply. Questions usually require planning, because they are reflections of thought processes that require time to develop on the part of the questioner. Questions that are created on the fly tend to be literal; questions that are planned in advance can be far more effective in seeding students' discussions.

Effective discussion is a way of wondering and a way of inquiring into the things that puzzle students and their teachers. In preparing for effective discussions with students, we suggest using the following framework:

1. What background knowledge do students have about the topic? How should the instruction be tiered to support these differences?

2. What knowledge might students need to be exposed to before they can engage in meaningful discussion about the topic?

3. What discussion skills might students need to develop in order to participate in an effective discussion?

4. Will discussion help promote learning and inquiry about this topic? Are multiple constructions of knowledge possible? (Wolsey & Lapp, 2009, p. 373)

Working with this framework, you can design questions to help students look beyond the surface and come to a deeper understanding of concepts and processes outlined by the standards and objectives of the lesson.

🔊 Listen as third-grade teacher Scott Ritter talks about his expectations for students (3:54) when they are participating in whole class discussions. *(Access this podcast in the digital version of this book.)*

Following are activities that promote effective discussion that results in achievement of learning outcomes.

Socratic seminar

One time-honored practice for discussion is the Socratic seminar. In this activity, students who have interesting questions to explore are encouraged to treat discussion as an inquiry rather than as a quiz. In Socratic seminars, the teacher's role is different from standing in the front of the classroom posing questions that students must answer correctly. In the Socratic format, the teacher has three tasks:

1. Prepare the questions that define the discussion.

2. Probe the responses of the students to elicit reasons, support, or implications of the claims they make.

3. Engage the students with one another, especially if their ideas seem to be in conflict (Adler, 1984).

In addition to this list, keep in mind that students who help define the guiding questions are far more likely to be engaged in the discussion (e.g., Wiggins & McTighe, 2005). When classes are large, a kind of fishbowl approach in which students sit in two concentric circles (Cornett, 1997) can be effective. The inner circle is responsible for the discussion, and the students sitting in the outer circle provide feedback on the quality of the discussion. After a predetermined time has elapsed, students switch places.

Online discussions

Discussions in real time with students who are sitting face-to-face are effective ways to promote learning through interaction. However, online discussions, often in the form of **threaded discussion groups** or live online chats, are another way students can learn from one another. Some of these digital tools promote student thinking because they are asynchronous; that is, they do not require an immediate response from the participants (Boling, Castek, Zawilinski, Barton, & Nierlich, 2008; English, 2007; Grisham & Wolsey, 2006). Students may hear or read their peers' posts, think about what they have heard or read, then respond at a later time. This delayed response time is an important strength of the online discussion. Other online chats occur during real time (i.e., they are synchronized), where students use their first name and a profile picture or avatar representing themselves (see Exhibit 11.11). Online discussions teach students to negotiate meaning with others as in a face-to-face discussion; however, the sense of community that develops and the engagement with the content (e.g., Bowers-Campbell, 2011) are benefits that are sometimes magnified.

Voicethread (http://voicethread.com) is one tool used by students from primary grades to graduate school where users can post an image and record their ideas. Voicethread includes features of threaded discussions; in addition, it can include oral commentary by teachers and students, images, and drawing tools. Hayes and Desler (2009) reported that students spontaneously used the tool to start discussions of their own on political topics or works of poetry they had created and wanted to share. The students wanted to hear from others about their written creations, and Voicethread was just the tool for the task because of its appeal to students and teachers alike. Users can integrate visual and text-based content, hear what others have to say, and add their own comments to the dialog without fear of someone else speaking over them.

EXHIBIT 11.11

Live online chat.

stories FROM THE CLASSROOM

Preeti's story

Fourth-grade teacher Preeti Singh recognizes the importance of not only teaching speaking skills to her students, but also providing opportunities for students to practice these skills in authentic settings. Preeti uses Voicethreads to connect her students with children's authors and to explore various content. She and her students can post, view, and listen to audiorecorded responses. Although a Voicethread can be kept private, when it is made available to others, the quality of students' work begins to reflect the seriousness of having a worldwide online audience. Humans need and want to discuss their ideas and find out what others are thinking. While discussion has been a facet of learning since humans uttered their first words, new technologies increase the opportunities for humans to interact beyond geographical boundaries. As Preeti's students experienced, technology can help students to learn through their interactions with others with web-based and other digital tools.

As you view Mrs. Singh's Voicethread (14:00) notice how students interact with each other and how they use oral language, drawings they created, and responses to each other to teach and learn new ideas. *(Access this resource in the digital version of this book.)*

Discussion invites interaction by its very nature. The Flat Stanley project is one example of the power of discussion. Flat Stanley is a character from the children's book *Flat Stanley* by Jeff Brown, who travels and records his adventures.

The Flat Stanley project (www.flatstanley.com/about) invites participants from around the world to create a Flat Stanley and share his traveling adventure through written descriptions and photographs. The popularity of the mail-based and digital versions of the Flat Stanley project attests to the desire of students to connect with those outside their classroom walls.

EXHIBIT 11.12

Face-to-face dialog with other educators is a form of professional development.

For teachers, regular participation in online and face-to-face dialog with other educators can be an effective means of professional development that promotes both learning and professional friendships (Exhibit 11.12).

Consider adding an online discussion tool to your personal learning network. Edge (http://ascdedge.ascd.org) from the Association of Supervision and Curriculum Development is one example of an educational discussion tool. Edmodo (www.edmodo.com) an additional site for educators, supports discussions about various content areas (e.g., language arts, special education, technology).

Video conferencing tools are another effective way to merge discussions in the classroom with those outside of the classroom. With a tool such as Skype, you can figuratively flatten the walls of the classroom and extend its reach throughout the community, the state, the country, and the world. In the upcoming Story from the Classroom, read how fifth-grade teachers Jill Simons and Brian Thompson used Skype between their classes in Rhode Island and Arizona to have a literature discussion. Both teachers found the students' enthusiasm to be a powerful motivator for developing speaking skills.

stories FROM THE CLASSROOM

Online literature discussion with Skype

Dead End in Norvelt, by Jack Gantos, the 2012 Newbery Award winner, is the topic of a literature discussion between students in two classrooms literally across the country. Teachers Jill Simons of Rhode Island and Brian Thompson of Arizona met virtually in a Twitter discussion group called the Nerdy Book Club (@ nerdybookclub). Both had already made plans for a novel study using the same book, so their logical next step was to connect their students for a discussion. To give structure to the discussion, they divided their students into groups of four and assigned each group a set of chapters to prepare for discussion, although all students read the entire book. The discussions were held on Tuesdays and Thursdays for 40 minutes, and throughout the discussion the teacher's computer was projected on the screen, so all students could see the other students. The group of four sat closer to the computer microphone and presented their ideas, while a group of four at the other site responded. Between the discussion group meetings, each class was studying the home state of their partner class, learning about the other state's location, climate, geography, and unique features. A virtual friendship formed between the two classes, and they finished the school year by making spring May Day cards for each other.

Preeti Singh also uses technology to connect her students with those of her colleague, Lisa Wilson, in Michigan. The classes read and discussed books together using Skype (2:26). This digital book club gives students the opportunity to use their budding speaking skills to communicate with peers, often miles apart. *(Access this podcast in the digital version of this book.)*

Assessing speaking skills

To assess speaking skills, teachers most often rely on listening and observing. A strong understanding of the development stages of speaking will provide you with the foundation needed to make knowledgeable observations. A rubric can also guide you to make insightful observations and collect useful information. You can prepare speaking rubrics yourself or find some already prepared in a teaching resource. The Rubistar (http://rubistar.4teachers.org) website, for example, makes it possible for teachers to create rubrics online and save them for future use, download them, and customize them (for more on rubrics, see Chapter 4). For oral presentations, Rubistar includes several generic categories that teachers can customize to meet the instructional needs of the students at a particular grade level and studying specific content. A word of caution about rubrics: limit rubric categories to a small number, perhaps three to five, that emphasize the important traits students should work on to achieve literacy standards. A rubric assessing speaking attributes may not focus solely on speaking, but also may assess the content of the speech, as it relates to science, social studies, or other content topic. A specific example of a speaking rubric is available in Chapter 12.

For some students, more detailed information about speaking skills might be needed to determine if the student is progressing as expected. A standardized assessment, such as the JOLST mentioned earlier in this chapter and the Teacher Rating of Oral Language and Literacy (refer to Chapter 12) analyzes a student's speaking skills through observations in the natural classroom setting and compares these skills to established norms. Both types of speaking assessments provide useful information to the classroom teacher. An evaluation by a speech therapist may be necessary for a small number of students with a need for more specialized assistance.

points2ponder

QUICK REVIEW 2 How might praise be used effectively? How is it used ineffectively? In what ways might teachers make good use of show-and-tell time?

(Access the answers in the digital version of this book.)

11.4

VISUALLY REPRESENTING OVERVIEW

The term *literacy* has traditionally meant the ability to read and write, but in today's world of instant information, bombardment from visual images, and a need to translate images and information quickly and effortlessly, this definition of literacy seems woefully inadequate. As stated in Chapter 2, to-

EXHIBIT 11.13

Visual images convey ideas.

day's definition of literacy must be multidimensional, representing the varied ways we express and receive messages. Visual literacy is a key component to this definition. As described in Chapter 7, **visual literacy** is the ability to skillfully evaluate, apply, or create a conceptual image (Riddle, 2009). When a person creates a graph of the most popular flavors of ice cream, or when a person views such a graph and uses the information to decide which type of ice cream to serve at the school picnic, visual literacy plays a role. Simply put, "visual literacy means to read and create images" (Stafford, 2011, p. 1).

The term *visual literacy* may seem new, but actually it was coined in 1969 by John Debes, who focused on the importance of people understanding the actions, objects, and symbols of their environment (Debes, 1969). In 1973, Dondis described visual literacy as "vital to our teaching of the modern media as reading and writing was to print" (1973, p. 18). People have been using visual literacy skills since the prehistoric times of petroglyphs by creating simple stone drawings to convey messages to others (see Chapter 2). Today, visual literacy is an essential component of the skills needed to be successful in a world where information is increasingly being delivered through visual media. The image is a fundamental part of the way people express ideas, whether through an illustration in a book, an icon on a website, a symbol on a street sign, or a photo attached to an email message.

Knowing how to create and interpret images does not occur naturally, but requires the accumulation of a certain set of skills. Since school is the place where students are taught how to read books, it only makes sense that it should be the place where students are taught how to read images. A curriculum for teaching visual literacy would include the following skills (Kiefer, 1995):

- observing details.
- inferring and perceiving.
- identifying and interpreting symbols, shapes, and colors.
- generalizing information.

The most effective form of visual literacy instruction would embed these skills in real world experiences, because that is where visual literacy skills will be actively applied. Amidst this real world application, knowledgeable teachers would capitalize on the natural interest and motivation students have to use visually representing and viewing to create meaning (Callow, 2008).

Visually representing is a mode of language arts dating back to the petroglyphs. When an idea is conveyed or a message created through an image, then visual representation has occurred. In modern times, ideas represented through symbols and images are often created with technology and presented through photographs, videos, billboards, posters, charts, graphs, maps, and many other media.

11.5

VISUAL WORK IN THE CLASSROOM

Visual expression, or expressing an idea through images, is an important complement to traditional learning in linguistic or mathematical modes (e.g., Unsworth, 1996) and it is a worthy means of learning and expression in its own right. Visually representing in the classroom focuses on how best to teach students to think through the media of language and images. The creator of a visual message must first consider his intention or purpose as the author/creator, along with making decisions about the tone and mood of the message. The creator must then determine the best way to convey his message, whether through a sketch, a video, a photograph, or some other type of visual display. If images or words are borrowed from the work of others, the creator must do this in a fair and ethical manner. As one can see, visually representing one's ideas has as rich and complex background as both speaking and writing.

View the video Teacher Case Study Video Elementary (5:49, http://media educationlab.com/teacher-case-study-video-elementary) as an introduction to visually representing in the classroom. Watch for the teacher's emphasis on the use of critical thinking skills when creating a visual project. Jot down at least two examples of the teacher's expectation for students using critical thinking in the video.

---

author's story   THOMAS DEVERE WOLSEY

Statistics was a tough class for me and many of my college classmates. One day in class, as we were struggling with a particularly difficult concept, our professor reminded us to draw the statistics or to put the data into a graphic form. The visual display helped us make sure the meaning of the statistic was clear. We were reminded that drawing leads to greater understanding, and who knows, maybe this one hint is what tipped the scales for me passing statistics that semester.

Although not specifically listed as a standard, visually representing is a skill of importance in the CCSS Initiative (2012). For example, under Speaking and Listening, Presentation of Knowledge and Ideas, the CCSS (www. corestandards.org/ELA-Literacy/SL/introduction) asks for kindergarten students to "Add drawings or other visual displays to [oral] descriptions as desired to provide additional detail" (p. 23). By contrast, second graders are asked to "Create audio recordings of stories or poems; add drawings or other visual displays to stories or recounts of experiences when appropriate to clarify ideas, thoughts, and feelings." In fifth grade, students are asked to "include multimedia components (e.g., graphics, sound) and visual displays in presentations when appropriate to enhance the development of main ideas or themes."

In the following sections, we explore how students might represent ideas they encounter in the world with images, often coupled with written text and how those images inform their ability to use language in its traditional sense. An emphasis is placed on the ways students create images in the digital age that empower them to think critically about their learning. Creation of visual art is an act of understanding, just as writing is. It is an act of expression, just as speech is. It is an act that complements written expression and speech, as well.

Expressing ideas through photography

Photographs give a realistic interpretation of our world and can be visual tools for representing ideas (see Exhibit 11.14). In the classroom, photographs can help communicate and support an idea that a student is also conveying through words. Students can either create their own photographs

EXHIBIT 11.14

A photograph conveys the idea of being alone.

EXHIBIT 11.15

The focal point of a photo should be at the point where two lines on a grid of thirds intersect.

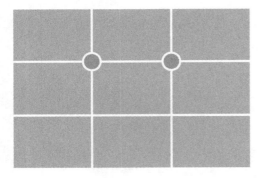

EXHIBIT 11.16

Anna and Franco's photograph of the school fountain.

or use photos from safe and appropriate websites. Before putting a digital camera in the hands of students, teach basic photography guidelines, such as the following, to increase the likelihood of students creating images that clearly and effectively portray their ideas.

- Get in close: zoom in on the subject to show the details.
- Try a different point of view: look above or below the subject for a unique perspective.
- Use the rule of thirds: image a grid, breaking up the lens into nine squares and put the focal point of the photo at the point where two lines on the grid intersect (see Exhibit 11.15).
- Notice the background: before taking the picture, notice what is in the background and consider how it may add or detract from the photograph.
- Take multiple shots.

A few years ago, Wolsey and some colleagues wanted to understand more about how the physical attributes of school buildings affected student learning. Students were given cameras and asked to take ten photographs that portrayed aspects of the school building and grounds that either helped them learn or inhibited their learning (Uline, Tschannen-Moran, & Wolsey, 2009; Uline & Wolsey, 2011). Often, students knew what they wanted to say about their school buildings, but they struggled with the unfamiliar vocabulary of architecture. The photographs provided a point of reference for when their understanding outstripped their vocabulary. The photographic art that students made became an important way for them to understand their schools as learning places. Two students described a decorative fountain. They imported their photograph into presentation software and explained the fountain as a peaceful place when they were on campus (see Exhibit 11.16). In this study, the students used images to enhance their abilities to explain what they experienced and knew. Digital and cell phone cameras are relatively inexpensive tools that, when put in the hands of students, can be used to create powerful messages.

For additional information, see the article "Exploring Learning Spaces and Places: The Photo Interview" (4 pp.): http://media.cefpi.org/efp/EFP45-1and2Uline-Wolsey.pdf

EXHIBIT 11.17

Art created with paper, ink, and paint.

Make thoughtful choices when selecting photograph websites for students to use for school projects. Two of our favorites are Edupics (www.edupic.net/index.html) and Pics 4 Learning (www.pics4learning.com) because these sites include free, copyright-friendly images for teacher and classroom use.

Expressing ideas through illustration

Art composed with paper, ink, paint, or on the computer can mediate students' understanding of the world and enhance the linguistic expressions they need to understand content. These media may appeal to students for a variety of reasons, including the use of large and fine motor skills that creation of such art requires (see Exhibit 11.17). Each work of student-created art helps students explain, summarize visually and orally, or synthesize from many sources their understanding (see Exhibit 11.18). Marzano (2009) described how a teacher might incorporate student-created visuals to help students better learn vocabulary. In his model, the teacher provided an example, an anecdote, a definition, or a description of the target term. Students then restated the teacher's example and drew or constructed an image illustrating their understanding of the new term. In this way, student-created images and language learning intersect to create rich knowledge of the vocabulary terms and the concepts those terms represent. Putman and Kingsley (2009) used teacher-created podcasts to help students learn science-related vocabulary, and in the process modeled audio presentation skills and innovative approaches to content (i.e., science) learning their students could later emulate. Building on this idea, podcasts can be combined with images and video. Images are also useful forms of communication for students who are just learning to work with written texts. In Exhibit 11.19, students use teacher-created images to create sentences explaining what they know about seeds.

EXHIBIT 11.18

Using art to express new learning.

Link to a collection of online drawing and graphics tools (http://previous.delicious.com/tdwolsey/graphics) that can be used in the classroom for encouraging students to express their ideas through images.

Expressing ideas through digital multimedia

When more than one medium is used to represent an idea, we use the term **multimedia**. A sculpture may be created with wire and paint, a sketch with colored pencils and charcoal, and a digital poster with a podcast and animation. **Multimedia literacy** refers to the skills needed to express and understand ideas presented through various media and interpreted through various modes, which leads to the term **multimodal** (Hobbs, 2011). One may interpret a video through listening, viewing, and possibly some reading, which would make the ways the person perceives the video multimodal. At times the terms *multimedia* and *multimodal* are used interchangeably, which is understandable but technically incorrect.

Creating digital multimedia is an act of composing involving multiple modalities. Visually representing in multimedia format means attending to what the viewer will see, but may also consider what the viewer will hear and read. In the case of video, for example, creators must consider: Where will actors or commentators stand? What will they wear? What other information is conveyed by the camera angle and what is or is not included in the frame? Will a musical soundtrack help convey evocative content that enhances the video? How will the title be conveyed?

Earlier, we described written and oral language tasks as a composing process, and the same is true for creating digital multimedia work. However, additional layers of complexity are added as students design video compositions that include oral language, written text, still images, and video (see Exhibit 11.20). Students can easily become more absorbed in using the composing tools than in their learning; it is up to you to ensure that students are focused on what they are learning, not just the tools that are used to create the product.

Digital multimedia projects are often thought of as the culmination of what students have learned, and they can range from a simple PowerPoint presentation to a complex movie project. The success of multimedia projects in the classroom hinges on the following key concepts:

EXHIBIT 11.19

Teacher-created images to scaffold student language learning.

EXHIBIT 11.20

Public speaking and video merge when students become commentators.

Camera, computers, and visual composition.

Checklist for creating videos.

Checklist for Creating Videos

1. What resources are available?
   ☐ microphones ☐ cameras ☐ software ☐ computers ☐ props
   ☐ other ___

2. How much time might this project take?

3. What enhancements might it include?
   ☐ animation ☐ text ☐ music
   ☐ other ___

4. Will we need to go to different locations in school or outside of school to create the video?
   ☐ No ☐ Yes If yes, where?

5. How will we plan and compose the spoken portions of the video?

6. How will we compose written portions, including credits for any works cited and those who assisted?

7. How might we compose the visual portions of the video? Will we need a storyboard?

8. Once we have captured the video and audio elements, will we need to process them using software to add effects, transitions, and titles, or to reorganize the elements of the show?
   ☐ No ☐ Yes If yes, what software will we use?

9. Who are the class experts with video processing software?

10. How might those class experts share their knowledge with other members of the group?

11. How will we host the final video? (Will it be uploaded to YouTube, Vimeo, TeacherTube, Edmodo, or another site?)

12. Will it be linked to the class webpage so that parents may view it?

13. Will we permit comments from the class, parents, or from anyone on the Internet?

(Print this checklist: www.hhpcommunities.com/ teachinglanguagearts/IL-11-02.pdf)

- Establish clear goals for learning, content, and technology.
- Link the goals of the project to the district or state standards.
- Focus on the content and not the glitz of technology.
- Utilize a checklist or project rubric to clarify expectations and give this rubric to students at the onset of the project.
- Evaluate the quality of the content, the project, and the presentation using a project rubrics or checklist. (Chapter 12 discusses the assessment tools Project Checklist and Digital Video Project, for example.)

Video

Video cameras are no longer a luxury reserved for Hollywood, and the other equipment and software needed to create videos are increasingly common in schools (see Exhibit 11.21). Inexpensive, high-quality video cameras can be purchased for less than $100, and many still image cameras are also capable of making videos. Cell phones often include video cameras that can produce good quality video images.

The checklist below for students who are creating videos is fairly straightforward; however, it is important that each item is attended to if students are to create videos that help them learn *and* share what they have learned (see Exhibit 11.22). The items in the list do not need to be followed in order, but all need to be addressed.

As mentioned in Exhibit 11.22, students may need to prepare a storyboard before shooting their videos. A **storyboard** is a graphic organizer type of tool for planning their digital work and can aid in keeping students focused on the task at hand. Although the exact format of a storyboard can vary, typical elements include a sequential box for each scene, which contains a sketch of the scene, dialogue, and a written description of what will occur. These detailed plans, much like the outline some writers make before embarking on a writing project, will set students on a course for efficient and effective multimedia production. Typing *storyboard template* in an image search engine (for example, Google images[http://images.google.com/] will return a number of storyboard templates. Tables created in word processing and spreadsheet programs also make excellent storyboards for planning videos. Freeware is also available with additional features, for example, Storyboard Pro from Atomic Learning: www.atomiclearning.com/ storyboardpro.

For teachers interested in learning more about video production, Michael Snowdon (2011) created a blog for video novices, Making Better Video, that elaborates on what good video creation entails: http://makingbettervideo.com/2011/08/10/8-steps-to-making-a-video

For an example of a student video, view My Snow Pit (www.youtube.com/ watch?v=hj_xO8KFfrY) created by fifth grader Keyghan Reed. The video records his learning during a science experiment with snow. On a day when school was canceled because of snow, the teacher shared possible snow activities with students via Skype. Keyghan's use of music, images, and written words tells the story of his learning. To assess the content and visually representing knowledge a student demonstrates in a video like Keyghan's, you could use a tool such as the Digital Video Project Rubric discussed in Chapter 12.

stories FROM THE CLASSROOM

Video creation

Cherise Smith, a third-grade teacher, embarked on a learning adventure with her students when they merged a science unit on the solar system with a project for creating a digital video, which enticed earthlings to visit their planet. Cherise provided an itinerary or map of the unit and each day's activities, although students could work ahead if time permitted. Students created a plan for their project, which required factual information about the planet and persuasive arguments for visiting it. Next, students researched the planet and used this information to write a script for their video. Cherise noted the script step required the students to make their wording creative, more like a television commercial than a research report. Students also created a backdrop and cue cards to use during filming and spent class time recording their video. The videos were then edited, with titles and effects added, and posted to a video sharing site. Throughout this project, Cherise continually reminded students to be aware of what their audience will see and hear and of the need to express their ideas clearly.

🔊 The podcast Sharing Impacts Quality (17:40 min) provides an excerpt from an interview with Cherise about her iMovie project. The podcast Students' Perspective (11:47 min) shares an interview with a group of third graders involved in the project (see Exhibit 11.23). Together these podcasts bring to life the myriad of issues surrounding a digital video production project. (*Access these podcasts in the digital version of this book.*)

Third-grade students share their thoughts about preparing a digital media project.

Multimedia presentations

Multimedia presentation tools can bring a student's project to life by facilitating the use of the student's own images, voice, animation, and presentation and sharing their digital creation with an audience outside of the classroom. For a class project, students might learn about the Civil War, choose a Civil War-era person of interest, and then create a poster, a PowerPoint, a Prezi, or a Voki, sharing what they have learned. Choice is an effective tool for engaging students in their work, but it is important for students to know why the media they choose is the most effective for their purposes. This section shares a brief description and some examples of multimedia presentation tools. You do not need to be an expert about each tool, but you should be willing to learn along with your students. When encountering an issue with a presentation tool, we have found the best source for help is the Internet. Multimedia presentation tool users are a friendly group, and many have helpfully created tutorial videos and posted these on the Internet. A quick Google search can often turn up many useful problem-solving resources.

Based on the work of Garr Reynolds (2012), we recommend a process for creating a multimedia presentation that includes the following considerations, in order:

- First design, don't decorate (that is, consider the message and the elements needed to convey that message first).
- Who is the audience?
- To what should the audience attend?
- What are the strengths and limitations of the presentation tools (for example, what does PowerPoint offer that Prezi does not, or vice versa)?

■ Decorate (add clip art, backgrounds, and fonts that add to the appeal of the presentation medium).

When choosing the multimedia presentation tool, base your decision on what it can do for the presentation and for your intended audience, which may mean trying multimedia tools that are new and unfamiliar. In our experience, teachers and students should try creating a project with a new or different tool occasionally. Doing so can give the creator a feeling of pride and sense of accomplishment. So next time you are creating a project, consider trying one of the tools described in this section. If you always use PowerPoint, why not try Prezi? If you like posters on paper, consider giving Glogster a try.

Glogs. Lapp (2011) asserts that Glogs (http://edu.glogster.com) are a useful way for students to engage in literary analysis, author study, and literature discussion in real time and online. A Glog is a digital poster resembling the collage format of a scrapbook. With predesigned backgrounds, graphics, and picture frames, students can create a dynamic multimedia poster presentation. Students can add images, video, audio podcasts, and other media layered into the Glog post. Viewers are encouraged to browse the Glog's links, images, and text.

To learn more about using Glogs in her classroom, read the article "Teaching Tips: Going Graphic with Glogs" by Diane Lapp: www.reading.org/general/Publications /blog/engage/engage-single-post/engage/2011/05/04/teaching-tips-diane-lapp-glogs. Glogs invite viewers to browse the eposter exploring the links, images, and text presented there. Also visit Glogster: http://edu.glogster.com.

Prezi. Another online presentation tool, Prezi (http://prezi.com), leads viewers on a presentation journey developed by the Prezi user. Each idea slides, rotates, or turns into the next, making still images and text into an active flow of ideas. Video elements created by the student or found online can be integrated into Prezis, and links to audio files can also be added. Prezi works well as a visual complement for oral presentations for a whole class or small groups, as well.

Though technology has increased the opportunities for students to construct meaning through multimedia tools, one useful tool for learning is as old as time, and it is as relevant in the age of the cell phone as it was when Socrates used it as a pedagogical tool about 2,500 years ago. Learners still use oral language and they still use images to create and explain their understandings of the world.

View the presentation of Hispanic Culture Children's Literature (http://prezi. com/s5hrg8ngtekb/hispanic-culture) to see how this tool can be used.

Voki. Using Voki (www.voki.com) students and teachers can design an avatar, or animated character, to say their words for them. Their Voki can be shared with others when posted to a blog, wiki, website, or profile. Teachers may use a Voki to give project instructions or make class announcements, and when used judiciously, the novelty of the Voki captures students' attention. For students, the Voki provides a variety of uses including preparing oral presentations such as those in the second-grade Voki examples in the link below. In addition, Voki gives students a text-to-speech tool helpful in the writing process, as students can write a story, type it into the Voki program, listen to their words being read back to them by their avatar, and return to their writing to make revisions.

📹 View examples of second-grade Voki avatars (http://obeelibrary.wikispaces. com/Vokis) and the video Conferring with an Avatar: Using Voki for Proofreading (3:26, www.youtube.com/watch?v=Y9gHpIH9RTA), showing students using an avatar to assist with the revising and editing process.

Digital storytelling. Multimedia presentation tools can also be used to create digital stories. Oral language and visual representation is integral to the art of telling a story. A story transforms significant moments by making them memorable to the storyteller and to the listener, as well. For millennia, stories have been an oral tradition, often accompanied by images and gestures. From petroglyphs to picture books, images and spoken words go together. Many readers remember having a parent or another important person read a picture book aloud. In the twenty-first century, **digital storytelling** continues to build on the synergy of the oral and visual traditions. As students work in digital environments, their capacity to illustrate and narrate the stories they want to tell increases. Not only is it possible for them to find images that help them tell their stories, but software makes it possible for even the youngest students to record narration and create or match appropriate images to the story. Online, with guidance from their teachers, students can share their stories with each other, with other classrooms, and with their parents and others.

stories FROM THE CLASSROOM

Digital storytelling

Oral storytelling traditions have been used to bring people together for thousands of years and can be found in many cultures. Teacher Preeti Singh capitalizes on this tradition to encourage her students to visually represent their stories. Preeti begins by creating a lesson plan (www.hhpcommunities.com/teaching languagearts/IL-11-03.pdf), which identifies the purpose of the digital storytelling lesson and guides her instructional decisions. As the lesson plan indicates, she has the students begin by writing a story. Preeti then has the students block their story into sections (www.hhpcommunities.com/teachinglanguagearts/IL-11-04. pdf). Next, she asks them to create a storyboard to map out their stories (www. hhpcommunities.com/teachinglanguagearts/IL-11-05.pdf), with one box for each of the story's sections. Preeti then has students create full-size illustrations for each storyboard box. Finally, the students use Photo Story 3 (www.microsoft. com/en-us/download/details.aspx?id=11132#overview) to create a digital story.

📹 View the digital story (2:05 min) of one of Preeti's fourth graders. Notice the many language arts modes that are involved in creating and "reading" a digital story like this one. *(Access this resource in the digital version of this book.)*

Multimedia presentation tools abound, and we've presented only a handful of them. The key for you and your students is to create a clear message and then choose a tool that best conveys your message, whether that includes voice only, voice with images, digital video, or a combination. A list of possible presentation tools would be ever-changing, because designers are continually creating new ones. To access an easily updated list of presentation tools created for readers of this book, visit http://previous.delicious.com/tdwolsey/presentation on the bookmarking site Delicious.

Adapting work from one format to another

Creativity may entail developing an idea from scratch or taking an existing idea and crafting it into a new form. For instance, adding mango to a traditional salsa recipe can cause tomatoes, jalapenos, and onions to take on a unique taste. One way to help students adapt work into their own creative format is to critically examine the attributes of various media (e.g., video, image, oral presentation). A study of various cultural versions of the Cinderella story can help students identify the elements of the traditional tale **genre.** Just as D. DeCristofaro (2001) asked her students to notice the style of the authors they were reading, adapting a work from one form of media to another (i.e., print book to digital book trailer) is an effective way to help young thinkers determine the important attributes and concepts of a given work. Stafford (2011) suggests that "examining how and why artistic material is altered and remoulded into new forms provides children with a unique opportunity to develop their critical understanding of narrative elements across a range of media and reinforce what they have learned about each individual medium" (p. 140).

A novel, for example, might be recast as a comic strip, a stage drama, a readers' theater, a podcast, a video dramatization, a news commentary using video or podcasts, and so on. When creating an adaptation, focus on the features of the media or genre that are appropriate for conveying the key ideas and attributes of the original source. The term *remix* is used to describe the process of altering or recombining a previous work, typically music, film, or literature. Through remixing, artist/creator borrows from the work of another to create a new work.

Never before has it been so easy or tempting to find someone else's work and use or reuse it; however, teach your students to credit the sources they use and adhere to principles of **fair use.** Creative Commons is a nonprofit organization seeking to promote the legal, free sharing of creativity and knowledge by establishing various levels of license for original work. Creators seeking a Creative Commons license identify the degree to which they want to share their work, then license it to let others remix, share, or tweak it as long as attribution is given to the original creator. The Creative Commons site (http://creativecommons.org) explains other types of licenses and the rationale behind the structured sharing of work.

⌨️ View the video Code of Best Practices in Fair Use for Media Literacy Education (6:27, http://mediaeducationlab.com/intro-video-code-best-practices-fair-use-media-literacy-education) to learn more about the expectations for teachers and students when it comes to reusing and adapting others' work, especially from the Internet. Whenever you create presentations or models for students, address the principle of fair use by crediting sources and making sure students know how to do the same.

The Code of Best Practices in Fair Use for Media Literacy Education is a set of expectations and opportunities for educational use of media.

Assessing visual representation skills

Determining your students' visual representation skills depends first on how clearly you have communicated your expectations. Vague criteria will likely yield projects that focus on the media rather than the content. Be sure to share your criteria with students *before* beginning the project. As mentioned earlier in this chapter, Chapter 12 includes two helpful assessment tools, Project Checklist and the Digital Video Project Rubric, that can be adapted for various grade levels and types of projects.

At times, the students get lost in creating projects, focusing on the tool and forgetting about the purpose. Use questions and carefully placed checkpoints to ensure that students are focused on learning, not on a flashy end product. Throughout the process, encourage students to think critically about how the words and images they select can best convey their intended message. Doing so requires a constant awareness of one's audience, a sense of what the audience needs to know, and knowledge of the most effective way to convey these ideas.

points2ponder

QUICK REVIEW 3 What processes are involved in creating a visual representation? What are some items that students should consider when creating videos that help them learn and share what they have learned? How can you help students choose appropriate technologies (such as Prezi, PowerPoint, or Glogster) that fit their presentation purposes?

(Access the answers in the digital version of this book.)

11.6

CHAPTER SUMMARY

Literacy is a function of a person's ability to read and write; however, it is also a function of one's ability to listen and to speak, make sense of the world, and communicate with others through all the signs and systems that are intended to convey meaning (Lankshear & Knobel, 2003). Students who create visual and oral representations tend to understand the content and processes they encounter in school more effectively.

- What was your definition of literacy before reading this chapter?
- How has reading this chapter expanded your thinking about what literacy is and what it means to your students?
- How might you work with students to build on their understandings of the content and processes in your curriculum using oral language and visual expression?
- How do the practices you identified stand on their own? How do they intersect with traditional literacies?

Literacy is a multifaceted concept that captures many aspects of human communication. In this chapter, we explored two expressive communication modes, speaking about ideas and representing them visually. Each is a powerful expressive tool on its own; however, in the twenty-first century, many educators and their students are finding that when visual and spoken media are combined, students' learning increases.

think like a teacher

Picture Walk

To better understand the impact of photographs for conveying ideas, take a picture walk. This mini-field trip can occur inside or outside. Keep in mind the photography tips presented previously in this chapter. Take 20 photos, return to the classroom, and upload them to a photo-sharing website, such as Flickr. To facilitate the process, consider creating the online photo group before class time. After photos have been shared, all participants can view them and leave comments. Give feedback to three or four of your classmates, commenting on the quality of the photo, based on the photography suggestions previously mentioned. After this activity, discuss ways teachers can promote these same photography tips with their students.

Language Development

Consider a lesson you have designed, observed, or found on the Internet. In what ways does it incorporate students' oral language or visual expression skills? Don't worry if the lesson does not incorporate both. Rather, consider how the lesson might be adapted for the times when both modes are appropriate.

- What could you do differently?
- How could you incorporate visual expression or oral language activities to help students to better use these processes and achieve other learning targets, as well?

REFERENCES

Adler, M. (1984). *The Paideia Program: An educational syllabus.* New York: Macmillan.

Allen, V. G. (1991). Teaching bilingual and ESL children. In J. Flood, J. M. Jensen, D. Lapp, & J. R. Squire (Eds.), *Handbook of research on teaching the English language arts* (pp. 356–364). New York: Macmillan.

Ash, G. W., Kuhn, M. R., & Walpole, S. (2009). Analyzing "inconsistencies" in practice: Teachers continued use of round robin reading. *Reading and Writing Quarterly, 25,* 87–103, 2009. DOI: 10.1080/10573560802491257.

Au, K. H. (1993). *Literacy instruction in multicultural settings.* Orlando: Harcourt Brace Jovanovich.

Ball, A. (2002). Three decades of research on classroom life: Illuminating the classroom communicative lives of America's at-risk students. In W. Secada (Ed.), *Review of Research in Education* (Vol. 26, pp. 71–112). Washington, DC: American Educational Research Association.

Ball, A., & Farr, M. (2003). Language variations, culture and teaching the English language arts. In J. Flood, D. Lapp, J.

Squire, & J. Jensen (Eds.), *Handbook of research on teaching the English language arts* (2nd ed., pp. 435–445). Mahwah, NJ: Erlbaum.

Barthes, R. (1967). *Writing degree zero.* (A. Lavers & C. Smith, Trans.) New York: Hill and Wang. (Original work published 1953).

Baugh, J. (2000). *Beyond Ebonics: Linguistic pride and racial prejudice.* New York: Oxford University Press.

Bereiter, C., & Scardamalia, M. (1987). *The psychology of written composition.* Hillsdale, NJ: Erlbaum.

Berninger, V. W., & Richards, T. L. (2002). *Brain literacy for educators and psychologists.* Boston: Academic Press.

Boling, E., Castek, J., Zawilinski, L., Barton, K., & Nierlich, T. (2008). Collaborative literacy: Blogs and Internet projects. *Reading Teacher, 61*(6), 504–506. DOI: 10.1598/RT.61.6.10.

Bongolan, R., & Moir, E. (2005). Six key strategies for teachers of English-language learners. Alliance for Excellent Education. Available: http://www.all4ed.org/files/archive/publications/SixKeyStrategies.pdf

Bowers-Campbell, J. (2011). Take it out of class: Exploring virtual literature circles. *Journal of Adolescent and Adult Literacy, 54*(8), 557–567. DOI: 10.1598/JAAL.54.8.1.

Bruner, J. (2002). *Making stories: Law, literature, life*. New York: Farrar, Straus & Giroux.

Bruskin Associates. (1973). What are Americans afraid of? *The Bruskin Report, 53*. Edison, NJ: Author.

California Department of Education. (2002). *English-Language Development Standards for California Public Schools, Kindergarten Through Grade Twelve*. Sacramento, CA: Author. Available: http://www.cde.ca.gov/be/st/ss/documents/englang devstnd.pdf

Callow, J. (2008). Show me: Principles for assessing students' visual literacy. *The Reading Teacher, 61*(8), 616–626.

Cohen, E. G. (1994). *Designing groupwork: Strategies for the heterogeneous classroom* (2nd ed.). New York: Teachers College Press.

Common Core State Standards Initiative. (2012). The Standards: English Language Arts Standards. Retrieved from http://www.corestandards.org/ELA-Literacy.

Cornett, C. E. (1997). Beyond retelling the plot: Student-led discussions. *Reading Teacher, 50*(6), 527–528.

Cummins, J. (2005). Teaching the language of academic success: A framework for school-based language policies. In C. F. Leyba (Ed.), *Schooling and language minority students: A theoretico-practical framework* (3rd ed., pp. 3–32). Los Angeles, CA: LBD Publishers.

Dahlin, M., & Cronin, J. (2010). Achievement gaps and the proficiency trap. *Northwest Evaluation Association*. Available: http://www.eric.ed.gov/PDFS/ED521963.pdf

Daines, D. (1986). Are teachers asking higher level questions? *Education, 106*, 368–374.

Debes, J. L. (1969). The loom of visual literacy. *Audiovisual Instruction, 14*(8), 25–27.

Dechant, E. (1991). *Understanding and teaching reading: An interactive model*. Hillsdale, NJ: Erlbaum.

DeCristofaro, D. S. (2001). Author to author: How text influences young writers. *The Quarterly, 23*(2), 8–12. Available: http://www.nwp.org/cs/public/print/resource/146

Dondis, D. (1973). *A primer of visual literacy*. Cambridge, MA: MIT Press.

English, C. (2007). Finding a voice in a threaded discussion group: Talking about literature online. *English Journal, 97*(1), 56–61.

Erikson, E. (1968). *Identity: Youth and crisis*. New York: W. W. Norton.

Gee, J. P. (2004). Reading as situated language: A sociocognitive perspective. In R. B. Ruddell & N. J. Unrau (Eds.), *Theoretical models and processes of reading* (5th ed., pp. 116–132). Newark, DE: International Reading Association.

Gonzales, N., Moll, L. C., & Amanti, C. (Eds.). (2005). *Funds of knowledge: Theorizing practice in households, communities, and classrooms*. Mahwah, NJ: Erlbaum.

Green, J. L. (1983). Research on teaching as a linguistic process: A state of the art. *Review of Research in Education, 10*, 151–252.

Grisham, D. L., & Wolsey, T. D. (2006). Recentering the middle school classroom as a vibrant learning community: Students, literacy and technology intersect. *Journal of Adolescent & Adult Literacy, 49*, 648–660.

Halliday, M. A. K. (1969). Relevant models of language. *Educational Review, 22*, 26–37.

Hart, B., & Risley, T. (2003, Spring). The early catastrophe: The 30 million word gap by age 3. *American Educator*. Available: http://www.aft.org/newspubs/periodicals/ae/spring2003/hart.cfm

Hayes, S., & Desler, G. (2009). Changing writers: Bridging gaps and divides. *Voices from the Middle, 17*(2), 49–51.

Hobbs, R. (2011). *Digital and media literacy: Connecting culture to classroom*. Thousand Oaks, CA: Corwin.

Holliway, D. (2004). Through the eyes of my reader: A strategy for improving audience perspective in children's descriptive writing. *Journal of Research in Childhood Education, 18*(4), 334–349.

Holyoak, K. J., & Thagard, P. (1995). *Mental leaps: Analogy in creative thought*. Cambridge, MA: MIT Press.

Honig, A. (2007). Oral language development. *Early Child Development & Care, 177*(6/7), 581–613. DOI:10.1080/030044 30701377482.

hooks, b. (1994). *Teaching to transgress: Education as the practice of freedom*. New York: Routledge.

Hughes, T. P. (2004). *Human-built world: How to think about technology and culture*. Chicago: University of Chicago Press.

Johnston, P. H., Ivey, G., & Faulkner, A. (2012). Talking in class: Remembering what is important about classroom talk. *Reading Teacher, 65*(4), 232–237. DOI: 10.1002/TRTR.01033.

Kagan, S. (1994). *Cooperative learning*. San Juan Capistrano, CA: Kagan Cooperative Learning.

Kiefer, B. Z. (1995). *The potential of picturebooks: From visual literacy to aesthetic understanding*. Englewood Cliffs, NJ: Merrill.

Kohn, A. (1993). *Punished by rewards: The trouble with gold stars, incentive plans, A's, praise and other bribes*. Boston: Houghton Mifflin.

Lankshear, C., & Knobel, M. (2003). *New literacies: Changing knowledge and classroom learning*. Berkshire, UK: Open University Press.

Lapp, D. (2011, May 4). *Teaching tip: Go graphic with glogs*. Engage: Teacher to teacher. Newark, DE: International Reading Association. Available: http://engage.reading.org/READING/READING/Go.aspx?c=BlogViewer&BlogKey=2f8717ff-9921-4274-83e9-5fb90282762d

Lapp, D., Fisher, D., Wolsey, T. D., & Frey, N. (2011/2012). Graphic novels: What teachers think of their instructional value. *Journal of Education, 192*(1), 23–35.

Lapp, D., Grant, M., & Johnson, K. (2012, Jan. 10). *Teaching tips: Language frames support literacy in science*. International Reading Association. Available: http://www.reading.org/general/Publications/blog/engage/engage-single-post/engage/2012/01/10/teaching-tips-language-frames-support-literacy-in-science

Lapp, D., Shea, A., & Wolsey, T. D. (2011). Blogging and audience awareness. *Journal of Education, 191*(1), 33–44.

Lessow-Hurley, J. (2009). *The foundations of dual language instruction* (5th ed.). Boston: Pearson.

Marzano, R. (2009, September). Six steps to better vocabulary instruction. *Educational Leadership, 67*(1), 83–84. Available: http://www.ascd.org/publications/educational-leadership/

sept09/vol67/num01/Six-Steps-to-Better-Vocabulary-Instruction.aspx

Mehan, H. (1979). *Learning lessons: Social organization in the classroom.* Cambridge MA: Harvard University Press.

Ministry of Education New Zealand. (2009). *Junior Oral Language Screening Tool (J.O.S.T).* Available: http://www.minedu.govt.nz/NZEducation/EducationPolicies/SpecialEducation/PublicationsAndResources/JuniorOralLanguageScreeningTool11908.aspx

Moll, L. C. (2010). Mobilizing culture, language, and educational practices: Fulfilling the promises of *Mendez* and *Brown. Educational Researcher, 39*(6), 451–460. DOI: 10.3102/0013189X10380654.

Murachver, T., & Pipe, M. (1996). Do, show, and tell: Children's event memories acquired through direct experience, observation, and stories. *Child Development, 67*(6), 3029–3044. DOI:10.1111/1467-8624.ep9706244846.

National Assessment of Educational Progress (NAEP). (2011). Achievement gaps. Available: http://nces.ed.gov/nations reportcard/studies/gaps/

National Reading Panel. (2000). *Teaching children to read: An evidence based assessment of the scientific research literature on reading and its implications for reading instruction.* Washington, DC: National Institute of Child Health and Human Development.

Neuman, S. B., & Celano, D. (2001). Access to print in low-income and middle-income communities: An ecological study of our neighborhoods. *Reading Research Quarterly, 36,* 8–26.

Pinnell, G. S., & Jaggar, A. M. (2003). Oral language: Speaking and listening in elementary classrooms. In J. Flood, D. Lapp, J. R. Squire, & J. M. Jensen (Eds.), *Handbook of research on the teaching the English-language arts* (2nd ed., pp. 881–913). Mahwah, NJ: Erlbaum.

Putman, M., & Kingsley, T. (2009). The Atoms Family: Using podcasts to enhance the development of science vocabulary. *Reading Teacher, 63*(2), 100–108.

Rasinski, T. V. (2006). A brief history of reading fluency. In S. J. Samuels & A. E. Farstrup (Eds.), *What research has to say about fluency instruction* (pp. 4–23). Newark, DE: International Reading Association.

Reynolds, G. (2012). Presentation Zen. Available: http://www.presentationzen.com/

Riddle, J. (2009). *Engaging the eye generation: Visual literacy strategies for the K–5 classroom.* Portland, ME: Stenhouse.

Snowdon, M. (2011). 8 steps to making a video. *Making a better video.* Available: http://makingbettervideo.com/2011/08/10/8-steps-to-making-a-video/

Stafford, T. (2011). *Teaching visual literacy in the primary classroom: Comic books, film, television, and picture narratives.* New York: Routledge.

Stein, M. B., Walker, J. R., & Forde, D. R. (1994). Setting diagnostic thresholds for social phobia: Considerations from a community survey of social anxiety. *American Journal of Psychiatry, 151,* 408–412.

Tharp, R. G., & Gallimore, R. (1989). Rousing schools to life. *American Educator, 13*(2), 20–25, 46–52.

Thomas, L. (1974). *The lives of a cell: Notes of a biology watcher.* New York: Penguin.

Toastmasters International. (2011). Ten tips for public speaking. Available: http://www.toastmasters.org/MainMenuCategories/FreeResources/NeedHelpGivingaSpeech/TipsTechniques/10TipsforPublicSpeaking.aspx

Tompkins, G. (2003). *Literacy for the 21st century (3rd ed., p. 42). New York: Merrill Prentice Hall.*

Townsend, D. R., & Lapp, D. (2010). Academic language, discourse communities, and technology: Building students' linguistic resources. Teacher Education Quarterly, Special Online Edition. Available: http://teqjournal.org/townsend_lapp.html

Uline, C. L., Tschannen-Moran, M., & Wolsey, T. D. (2009). The walls still speak: A qualitative inquiry into the effects of the built environment on student achievement. *Journal of Educational Administration, 47,* 395–420. DOI: 10.1108/09578230910955818.

Uline, C. L., & Wolsey, T. D. (2011). Exploring learning spaces and places: The photo interview. *Educational Facilities Planner, 45*(1/2), 24–27. http://media.cefpi.org/efp/EFP45-1and2Uline-Wolsey.pdf

Unsworth, J. (1996). Dare to think new. *Arts & Activities, 119*(3), 26.

Wiggins, G. (2007, November 15). What is an essential question? http://www.authenticeducation.org/bigideas/article.lasso?artId=53

Wiggins, G., & McTighe, J. (2005). *Understanding by design* (2nd ed.). Alexandria, VA: Association for Supervision and Curriculum Development.

Winans, J. A. (1923). Aims and standards in public speaking work. *English Journal, 12,* 223–234.

Wolsey, T. D., & Grisham, D. L. (2012). *Transforming writing instruction in the digital age: Techniques for grades 5–12.* New York: Guilford.

Wolsey, T. D., & Lapp, D. (2009). Discussion-based approaches for the secondary classroom. In K. Woods & B. Blanton (Eds.), *Promoting literacy with adolescent learners: Research-based instruction* (pp. 368–391). New York: Guilford Press.

Wolsey, T. D., Lapp, D., & Dow, B. (2010). Reading practices in elementary schools: Format of tasks teachers assign. *Journal of Research in Innovative Teaching, 3,* 101–112. http://www.nu.edu/assets/resources/pageResources/journal-of-research-in-innovative-teaching-volume-3.pdf

CHILDREN'S LITERATURE CITED

Brown, J. (1964). *Flat Stanley.* New York: Harper &Row.

Gantos, J. (2011). *Dead end in Norvelt.* New York: Farrar, Straus & Giroux.

Philbrick, R. (2004). *The young man and the sea.* New York: Scholastic.

Assessing the Expressive Modes

Access the book's Glossary, which defines the key terms boldfaced in this chapter, at www.hhpcommunities.com/teachinglanguagearts/glossary.pdf

KEY IDEAS

- Assessing the expressive modes of writing, speaking, and visually representing involves looking at both the process of expressing an idea and the final product of that expression. Progress can be monitored with formal and informal assessment tools.

- Teacher observations look for signs of student learning.

- Analyzing expressive skills entails digging deeply into the various components to look at distinct elements of learning.

12.1

ASSESSING THE PROCESS AND PRODUCT

Assessing the expressive modes entails determining how well a student expresses an idea through writing, speaking, and visually representing. On the surface, this may seem fairly easy to do; however, experienced teachers know there is nothing simple about assessing how students share thoughts with each other. The process of getting your idea across to another means exposing a little bit of yourself, and this can be risky (see Exhibit 12.1). Consider the myriad factors that can enhance or detract from the expression of an idea (e.g., gestures; facial expressions; subtle nuances of word meaning; and the use of color, light, or music). Asking the question, "Is the message clear?" is too simple, just as a single score on a spelling test may be too simplistic an indicator of a student's spelling ability. An effective way to determine what students know and can do when it comes to the expressive modes is to gather information about the *process* of expressing an idea and the final *product* that is created. Assessing the process might include observing a small group discussion and making anecdotal notes about individual contributions. Assessing the product might include determining the quality of a podcast or

"Assessing children's writing is a soulful job."

ANONYMOUS TEACHER

Assessment should recognize the heart and soul a student puts into sharing an idea.

video production using a rubric. Regardless of the form, a useful assessment provides both the teacher and the students with information about what the students know and can do, which can then be used to determine what students are ready to learn next. In this way, assessment guides instruction.

Although this chapter is about assessment rather than instruction, the two are closely related. Remember that assessment is gathering evidence about what students know and can do. Evaluation is making a judgment about their progress based on this evidence. As in Chapter 8, which focused on assessing the receptive modes of language arts, we follow a similar flow of ideas in Chapter 12, beginning with the ways a teacher monitors, observes, and then analyzes to determine student learning. Information for each assessment begins with the purpose of the assessment and a suggested grade level range. Next, a chart provides one or more relevant College and Career Readiness Standards and a grade level example from the Common Core State Standards. The standards we've included for an assessment are not an exhaustive list, but are presented as sample links between the assessment and the standards. Finally, we provide a description of the assessment tool. This chapter will guide you in choosing tools to assess the expressive modes given the age level and learning needs of your students.

12.2

MONITORING

We use the term *monitor* as an assessment term, but let's first consider how it is used in another context. When baking a chocolate cake, a baker monitors the cake. She sets a timer with the expected time needed for baking, but she also checks along the way to make sure the cake is rising. When the timer goes off, she opens the oven door, gingerly pulls out the pan to test if the cake is done, looks at the height of the cake, and determines whether it pulls away from the edges of the pan. All are ways the baker monitors the cake—a process similar to how a teacher monitors the progress of her students by checking and collecting evidence periodically. The writer's profile and the Writing Attitude Survey are two assessments a teacher can use to monitor students' writing progress.

Writer's profile

Assesses: Preferences about aspects writing

Suggested grade levels: All (with adaptations)

College and Career Readiness Standards	Common Core State Standard, grade example: Grade 3
Writing	Writing
Production and Distribution of Writing	*Production and Distribution of Writing*
W.4 Produce clear and coherent writing in which the development, organization, and style are appropriate to task, purpose, and audience.	**W.3.4** With guidance and support from adults, produce writing in which the development and organization are appropriate to task and purpose.
W.5 Develop and strengthen writing as needed by planning, revising, editing, rewriting, or trying a new approach.	**W.3.5** With guidance and support from peers and adults, develop and strengthen writing as needed by planning, revising, and editing.

Description

Learning your students' preferences toward various aspects of writing gives you valuable information about how to structure lessons and identify possible writing topics. This information helps you get to know your students, which then facilitates teaching that addresses their needs. A writer's profile is an informal way to collect useful information. Typically given at the beginning of the school year, a profile lets students present themselves as the unique individuals they are, while also asking them preferences they may not have thought of before. You can use the information gathered from this informal assessment to form an impression of writers as individuals and of the class as a whole. During writing conferences or mini-lessons, encourage students to try a genre that may not be their favorite but that may be important for future writing, such as an informational report or a science project. Students complete the writer's profile on paper or electronically, and it can be stored in an assessment notebook, a word document file, or in students' individual portfolios. You can adapt the items on the profile to best fit the age level of your students.

Exhibit 12.2 is a writer's profile from Julia, a fourth grader. Her positive attitude about writing comes through clearly, as well as her preferences for writing in a journal over a poem and for typing or using lined paper and a sharp pencil.

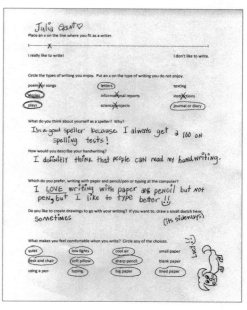

EXHIBIT 12.2

Sample completed writer's profile.

(Print a blank form: www.hhpcommunities.com/ teachinglanguagearts/IL-12-01.pdf)

Writing Attitude Survey

Assesses: Attitudes about writing and motivation to write

Suggested grade levels: First through 12th

College and Career Readiness Standards	Common Core State Standard, grade example: Grade 5
Writing	Writing
Production and Distribution of Writing	*Production and Distribution of Writing*
W.4 Produce clear and coherent writing in which the development, organization, and style are appropriate to task, purpose, and audience.	**W.5.4** Produce clear and coherent writing in which the development and organization are appropriate to task, purpose, and audience.
W.5 Develop and strengthen writing as needed by planning, revising, editing, rewriting, or trying a new approach.	**W.5.5** With guidance and support from peers and adults, develop and strengthen writing as needed by planning, revising, editing, rewriting, or trying a new approach.

Description

The emotional, or affective, aspects of writing play an important role in a writer's interest and enthusiasm toward writing. Collecting information about students' attitudes and interests can occur through informal conversations or questionnaires and also through a valid and reliable norm-referenced instrument such as the Writing Attitude Survey (www.professorgarfield.org/ parents_teachers/printables/reading.html) (Kear, Coffman, McKenna, & Ambrosio, 2000). The purpose of this questionnaire, designed for students in grades one through twelve, is to provide information about a writer's feelings toward various types of writing. The assessment has 28 items; students respond by indicating which animated character best represents their feelings about each item. The choices range from very happy to very unhappy. First-

and second-grade teachers can read the survey aloud to the class while students respond on their individual handouts. Older students can complete the survey independently. Results can be compared to national norms and a percentile determined. In addition to the score provided by the questionnaire, you may also add a narrative description, like the one below written by teacher Ruth Slappy, to accompany the score in a student's literacy portfolio collection:

> Chelsea's raw score was a 79 that places her in the 63rd percentile. Half of her responses were twos, which is an indifferent attitude toward writing. I was surprised with her answers since she indicated at the beginning of the session that she likes to write. Her scores indicate that she would be more likely to write if the topic was not school related.
>
> I would recommend that Chelsea partner with a higher level writer to create a silly story together to be shared with the class later. I will closely monitor her writing assignments to make sure she does not fall behind because of lack of interest. I believe with some continued interventions that Chelsea's writing skills will improve. I would also encourage her to write expressively every chance she gets.

 For additional informal interest inventories, writing profiles, and attitude surveys, visit this site: www.region15.org/file/3465/download

Spelling attitude inventory

Assesses: Attitudes about spelling and toward oneself as a speller

Suggested grade levels: First and above

College and Career Readiness Standards

Conventions of Standard English

L.2 Demonstrate command of the conventions of standard English capitalization, punctuation, and spelling when writing.

Common Core State Standard, grade example: Grade 4

Language

Conventions of Standard English

L.4.2 Demonstrate command of the conventions of standard English capitalization, punctuation, and spelling when writing.

Description

While knowledge of phonics, onset and rime, and high frequency words is helpful to becoming a successful speller, attitude also plays a key role. A spelling attitude inventory informally assesses a student's feelings toward spelling and herself as a speller. (See the example in Exhibit 12.3.) This type of assessment tool can be given at the beginning and end of the school year to record changes in attitudes and stored in a writing portfolio, becoming another data tool that adds insight about the student as a literate person. Items on the assessment can be adapted for the students' age level. You may wish to take the assessment to the next step and conference with the student about specific items, especially if strongly negative attitudes persist.

Completed spelling attitude inventory.

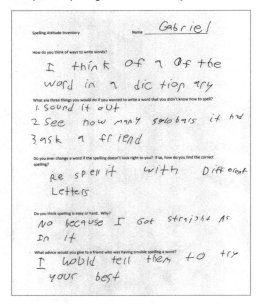

(Print a blank form: www.hhpcommunities.com/teachinglanguagearts/IL-12-02.pdf)

12.3

OBSERVING

A meteorologist must be a keen observer, watching for subtle shifts in weather data and using this information to draw conclusions about what is happening and what is to come. A teacher must also be a keen observer, watching for subtle shifts in a student's progress from one stage of learning to the next and drawing conclusions about what the student has learned and what he is ready to learn. As a classroom assessment technique, observing means an alert teacher notices the signs of learning—or not learning—and makes adjustments to meet the students' needs. What is a sign of learning? A sign is evidence that a student has met the expectation or standard. For example, third graders are typically learning how to write a complete paragraph, beginning with an indentation. A sign of learning could be consistently indented paragraphs. A sign does not guarantee learning, just as clouds do not guarantee rain. Both meteorologists and teachers must continue to collect data and make more observations to determine if clouds lead to rain and if indentations lead to complete paragraphs. Four tools for collecting assessment data through observation include a project checklist, a writing skills checklist, the Teacher Rating of Oral Language and Literacy, and a speaking rubric.

Project checklist

Assesses: Criteria met for various projects

Suggested grade levels: Second through fourth grades

College and Career Readiness Standards

Writing

Text Types and Purposes

W.2 Write informative/explanatory texts to examine and convey complex ideas and information clearly and accurately through the effective selection, organization, and analysis of content.

Production and Distribution of Writing

W.4 Use technology, including the Internet, to produce and publish writing and to interact and collaborate with others.

Common Core State Standard, grade example: Grade 2

Writing

Text Types and Purposes

W.2.2 Write informative/explanatory texts in which they introduce a topic, use facts and definitions to develop points, and provide a concluding statement or section.

Production and Distribution of Writing

W.2.6 With guidance and support from adults, use a variety of digital tools to produce and publish writing, including in collaboration with peers.

EXHIBIT 12.4

A completed project checklist and the fourth-grade student project to which it applies.

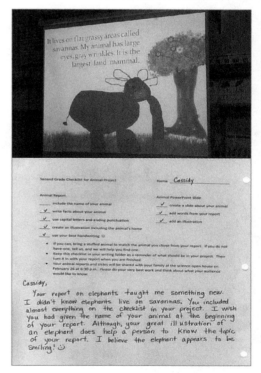

(Print a blank form: www.hhpcommunities.com/ teachinglanguagearts/IL-12-03.pdf)

Description

A checklist is unique to each project and consists of the key elements needed for students to demonstrate their proficiency in the areas that apply to their grade level. Standards and classroom objectives guide the creation of a project checklist, which will give you a quick, simple way to tick off those elements and provide specific feedback. Elements not present could be addressed in narrative comments (see Exhibit 12.4). Prepare and share the checklist with students prior to beginning the project so they know the criteria expected for success. (A checklist, by its nature, does not provide a way to evaluate the *quality* of each individual element; a rubric is a tool better suited for evaluating quality, as will be discussed below.)

Writing skills checklist

Assesses: Writing skills

Suggested grade levels: Fourth-grade example, but a checklist can be adapted for any grade

Writing skills checklist.

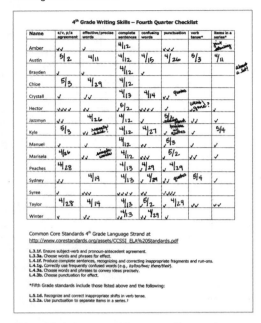

4ᵗʰ Grade Writing Skills – Fourth Quarter Checklist

Name	s/v, p/a agreement	effective/precise words	complete sentences	confusing words	punctuation	verb tense*	items in a series*
Amber	✓✓	✓	4/12		✓✓✓		
Austin	5/2	4/11	4/12	4/15	4/26	5/3	4/11
Brayden	✓	✓	4/12	✓			
Chloe	5/3	4/29	4/12				
Crystall	✓	✓✓	4/13	4/14	✓✓		
Hector	✓✓✓	✓✓	5/2	✓✓✓	✓		
Jazzmyn	✓✓	4/26	4/12	✓	5/2	✓✓	✓
Kyle	5/3	✓✓	4/12	4/27	✓	✓	5/4
Manuel	✓	✓	4/12	✓✓	5/3	✓	✓
Marisela	4/26	✓✓	4/12	✓✓✓	5/2	✓✓	✓
Peaches	4/28		4/13	4/29	4/29		
Sydney	✓✓	4/19	4/13	4/29	✓	5/4	✓
Syree		✓✓✓	✓✓✓✓	✓✓	✓✓✓✓		
Taylor	4/28	4/14	4/13	5/2	4/29	✓✓	✓✓
Winter	✓	✓✓	4/13	✓✓ 4/29	✓		

Common Core Standards 4ᵗʰ Grade Language Strand at
http://www.corestandards.org/assets/CCSSI_ELA%20Standards.pdf

L.3.1f. Ensure subject-verb and pronoun-antecedent agreement.
L.3.3a. Choose words and phrases for effect.
L.4.1f. Produce complete sentences, recognizing and correcting inappropriate fragments and run-ons.
L.4.1g. Correctly use frequently confused words (e.g., to/too/two; there/their).
L.4.3a. Choose words and phrases to convey ideas precisely.
L.4.3b. Choose punctuation for effect.

*Fifth Grade standards include those listed above and the following:

L.5.1d. Recognize and correct inappropriate shifts in verb tense.
L.5.2a. Use punctuation to separate items in a series.†

(Print a blank form: www.hhpcommunities.com/
teachinglanguagearts/IL-12-04.pdf)

College and Career Readiness Standards

Language

Conventions of Standard English

L.1 Demonstrate command of the conventions of standard English grammar and usage when writing or speaking.

L.2 Demonstrate command of the conventions of standard English capitalization, punctuation, and spelling when writing.

Common Core State Standard, grade example: Grade 4

Language

Conventions of Standard English

L.4.1f Produce complete sentences, recognizing and correcting inappropriate fragments and run-ons.

L.4.2b Use commas and quotation marks to mark direct speech and quotations from a text.

Description

This teacher-created checklist focuses on fourth- and fifth-grade skills identified in the CCSS. When the student exhibits each writing skill, the teacher adds a checkmark next to the item and notes the date. The teacher may add brief comments to serve as reminders. This checklist provides a snapshot of which skills students have learned and which are still developing (see Exhibit 12.5).

A third-grade teacher came across a checklist similar to the one in Exhibit 12.5 while perusing materials for her new classroom. Although the format of the checklist was appealing, the specific items did not match the curriculum at her school. She adapted the checklist by adding two columns ("confusing words" and "verb tense") as shown in Exhibit 12.5. She explained her reasons for the changes:

I found a writing skills checklist on the Internet, but I wanted an assessment tool that matched what I am expected to teach fourth graders. These are the things I must mark on end-of-quarter report cards. So when I observe children and check their work, I can transfer what I see directly to what I share with parents. After I found the checklist, I began adapting the headings to what I think are important. I added the heading about confusing words, because I want my students to limit their use of words they don't understand. Sometimes they will just find words in the thesaurus, even if they don't know what the words mean. I want to monitor this. I also added verb tense because this is an item from our district's fourth-grade curriculum. Then I took this list and compared it to our state writing standards, which have just been approved to follow the Common Core State Standards. Items five and nine were added based on this comparison. Of course I could include many more items, but I was worried the list would get too long, plus I was trying to focus on what we are learning about writing in the fourth quarter of the school year. I share the checklist and the child's writing folder with parents at the end of the school year.

Teacher Rating of Oral Language and Literacy (TROLL)

Assesses: Oral and written language usage and understanding

Suggested grade levels: Preschool to first grade

College and Career Readiness Standards

Speaking and Listening

Comprehension and Collaboration

SL.1 Prepare for and participate effectively in a range of conversations and collaborations with diverse partners, building on others' ideas and expressing their own clearly and persuasively.

Common Core State Standard, grade example: Grade K

Speaking and Listening

Comprehension and Collaboration

SL.1.1 Participate in collaborative conversations with diverse partners about *kindergarten topics and texts* with peers and adults in small and larger groups.

Description

The TROLL is a standardized assessment that provides teachers with information about a young student's oral and written language understanding and usage. It requires a teacher to observe a student in various speaking, writing, and reading situations in the classroom. The teacher then chooses a statement that best describes the students based on a collection of observations. For example, one question asks: "How often does the student use a varied vocabulary or try out new words (e.g., heard in stories or from teacher?)"; the choices are never, rarely, sometimes, and often. Each choice is accompanied by a score between 1 and 4 (in this example, never = 1 and often = 4); then a total score is calculated for writing, reading, and oral language.

Find further information about the TROLL, including the assessment form, a chart for interpreting assessment data, and the research behind the TROLL: www.ciera.org/library/reports/inquiry-3/3-016/3-016.pdf

Speaking rubric

Assesses: Skills needed to convey ideas effectively in a formal speaking situation

Suggested grade levels: Third through fifth

College and Career Readiness Standards

Speaking and Listening

Comprehension and Collaboration

SL.1 Prepare for and participate effectively in a range of conversations and collaborations with diverse partners, building on others' ideas and expressing their own clearly and persuasively.

Presentation of Knowledge and Ideas

SL.5 Present information, findings, and supporting evidence such that listeners can follow the line of reasoning and the organization, development, and style are appropriate to task, purpose, and audience.

Common Core State Standard, grade example: Grade 5

Speaking and Listening

Comprehension and Collaboration

SL.5.1 Engage effectively in a range of collaborative discussions (one-on-one, in groups, and teacher-led) with diverse partners on *grade 5 topics and texts,* building on others' ideas and expressing their own clearly.

Presentation of Knowledge and Ideas

SL.5.4 Report on a topic or text or present an opinion, sequencing ideas logically and using appropriate facts and relevant, descriptive details to support main ideas or themes; speak clearly at an understandable pace.

Description

This speaking rubric focuses on the skills students need to effectively convey their ideas in a formal speaking situation, such as giving a presentation to a small group or the whole class (see Exhibit 12.6). Developed by the Topeka Public Schools, this rubric defines the speaking criteria and relies on the teacher's observations during an oral presentation to determine how closely the student's performance matches the criteria listed in the advanced column on the rubric. Teachers and students focus on the categories of ideas and content, language, organization, delivery, and visual aids. This rubric should be shared with students before they begin preparing for their oral presentation. It can also be shared with caregivers, especially when the teacher encourages students to prepare for their presentation at home.

EXHIBIT 12.6

Speaking rubric.

(Print a blank form: www.nhpcommunities.com/teachinglanguagearts/IL-12-05.pdf)

12.4

ANALYZING

Not only is a teacher like a baker and a meteorologist, she is also like a mechanic who checks out a car to determine the source of that unusual noise. Based on knowledge and experience, a mechanic knows a rattling sound may mean a rock in the hubcap, a clicking sound could mean a nail in the tire, and a high-pitched squeal could mean a loose belt. A teacher uses knowledge and experience to identify the essential features of writing, speaking, and visually representing and then make a judgment about student progress in these areas by digging deeper to find evidence of learning. This digging may mean analyzing misspellings for phonics patterns or looking closely at the individual components of a multimedia project. Suggested tools for gathering this data include the digital video project rubric, spelling inventories, weekly spelling tests, Screener of Handwriting Proficiency, and the 6 + 1 Trait Writing Assessment.

Digital video project rubric

Assesses: Quality of the planning, time management, and communication skills in creating a digital video

Suggested grade levels: Third and above

College and Career Readiness Standards

Writing

Production and Distribution of Writing

W.6 Use technology, including the Internet, to produce and publish writing and to interact and collaborate with others.

Research to Build and Present Knowledge

W.8 Gather relevant information from multiple print and digital sources, assess the credibility and accuracy of each source, and integrate the information while avoiding plagiarism.

Common Core State Standard, grade example: Grade 3

Writing

Production and Distribution of Writing

W.3.6 With guidance and support from adults, use technology to produce and publish writing (using keyboarding skills) as well as to interact and collaborate with others.

Research to Build and Present Knowledge

W.3.8 Recall information from experiences or gather information from print and digital sources; take brief notes on sources and sort evidence into provided categories.

Description

Creating a digital video project takes planning, time management, and communication skills. A rubric provides an assessment tool that lets a teacher evaluate the quality of a student's performance in each of these areas. Focusing on the content of the project encourages both the teacher and the students to avoid becoming enamored by the glitz and glamour of the video production. In one example of a Digital Video Project Rubric (http://www.dartmouth.edu/~videoprojects/files/digital-video-project-rubric.pdf) students are expected to create a storyboard to plan the various elements of their video, write a script, and keep a work log. Along with assessing the technical elements of the video, a teacher also analyzes the cooperative group work and students' attention to copyright expectations. Sharing this rubric at the start of the project and including such a broad spectrum of elements clarifies the teacher's expectations and reinforces the *process* of visually representing, rather than just the creation of an end product. To use this tool as an assessment, you would evaluate the storyboard, work log, script, and video, while also observing the cooperative group work throughout the project. This rubric calls for the teacher to assign points to certain elements, calculate a total, and identify where this total falls on a scale. A letter grade could also be assigned to the point total, if required.

Spelling inventory

Assesses: Stage of spelling development and overall word knowledge

Suggested grade level: Second grade and above

College and Career Readiness Standards	Common Core State Standard, grade example: Grade 3
Language	Language
Conventions of Standard English	*Conventions of Standard English*
L.2 Demonstrate command of the conventions of standard English capitalization, punctuation, and spelling when writing.	**L3.2f** Use spelling patterns and generalizations (e.g., *word families, position-based spellings, syllable patterns, ending rules, meaningful word parts*) in writing words.

Description

A spelling inventory can provide pinpointed information for determining the stage of spelling development, monitoring spelling growth over time, or forming leveled spelling groups. Given to the whole class, a small group, or an individual student, a spelling inventory may look like a traditional spelling test with a teacher pronouncing a list of words, but it has three key differences. (1) The words are selected to represent specific phonics elements; (2) the same words are used over time; and (3) the words are not given to the students ahead of time for practice. Like a running record, a spelling inventory is an informal assessment meant to be completed in a short amount of time, although rather than assessing miscues made during decoding, a spelling inventory is assessing miscues made during encoding.

A spelling inventory seeks to answer the following questions:

1. Which phonetic elements is the student using correctly?
2. Which phonetic elements is the student attempting but using incorrectly?
3. What knowledge is the student trying to apply when a phonetic element is used incorrectly?

An analysis of a student's spelling inventory can estimate his stage of spelling development based on the patterns in his correct and incorrect spellings. Although useful in determining a student's overall sense of word knowledge, a spelling inventory does not indicate which specific spelling patterns he has mastered. Because a spelling inventory includes between ten and twenty words, it is only a snapshot of what the he knows about spelling. For example, if the student misspells a word with an *ea* long vowel combination such as spelling "treat" as "treet," one should not assume he needs practice specifically with that combination. The student who misspells the long *e* word likely needs more practice with various long vowel combinations because this is a characteristic of the transitional stage of spelling development. This limited sample of words, and the spelling inventory itself, are not meant to target specific skills, but to determine at what stage spelling breaks down and to gain an overall sense of word knowledge.

Beyond identifying the stage of spelling development, a spelling inventory can also be used to document growth over time. Inventory words should not be specifically practiced, and the inventory is only useful if students do not spell all the words correctly. Comparing a student's spelling of specific words at the beginning, middle, and end of the school year can serve as powerful evidence of what she has learned through spelling, reading, and vocabulary activities. The Developmental Spelling Test (www.gse.uci.edu/docs/DEVELOPMENTAL_SPELLING.pdf) developed by Richard Gentry, consists of ten words that represent various spelling patterns. When administered and compared over time, as displayed in the chart on page 5 of the test, you can see a student's spelling move through the stages as described in Chapter 10.

Analyzing spelling inventory data for all your students can be time consuming, but with practice you can gauge students' orthographic knowledge with a quick glance at their everyday writing. Thus, reserve a formal spelling inventory for two to three times a year. For a skilled teacher, answering these questions about spelling progress becomes a fluid part of spelling assessment, and the answers lead to more pinpointed instruction for each student based on your solid knowledge of spelling stage features. The more you know about each student, the better you can teach, and a spelling inventory is an important tool for obtaining this knowledge.

A spelling inventory can also be a useful tool for determining leveled groups for spelling instruction and practice. Students at similar stages of development can be grouped together and benefit from word work with the specific spelling patterns appropriate for their stage of development.

View the document Words Their Way, Assessment: Placement and Grouping (www.mypearsontraining.com/products/wordstheirway/tutorials.asp) for a description of how to use the Primary Spelling Inventory and the Upper Elementary Spelling Inventory to gather spelling data and use it to make instructional decisions.

Weekly spelling test

Assesses: Spelling a certain set of words and spelling knowledge

Suggested grade levels: First and above

College and Career Readiness Standards	Common Core State Standard, grade example: Grade 4
Language	Language
Conventions of Standard English	*Conventions of Standard English*
L.2 Demonstrate command of the conventions of standard English capitalization, punctuation, and spelling when writing.	**L.4.2d** Spell grade-appropriate words correctly, consulting references as needed.

Description

A weekly spelling test, consisting of a different list of words each week and usually given on a Friday, has been a long-standing part of traditional spelling instruction and is often expected by parents and administrators. High scores typically are rewarded with good grades or positives such as stickers or candy. A spelling test is a snapshot of how well a student can spell a certain set of words in a given week, another set of words the next week, and so on. When the words are organized by similar phonetic elements, you can glean valuable information about the class as a whole and each individual's spelling knowledge. This knowledge can then be used to make adjustments to the weekly word list or to plan lessons in order to better meet the students' learning needs.

Two simple adjustments to the traditional weekly spelling test can increase its effectiveness. Giving a pretest to determine which words on a given list are already known or need more attention can provide both the teacher and the students with information to guide study practices. Also, it provides students with immediate feedback when misspellings are corrected, which helps cement the correct spellings into a student's memory. An effective practice is to have students correct their own spelling test immediately after taking it. Prior to correcting the tests, however, have students color over their answers with a yellow crayon or highlighter to prevent students from changing their spelling before you have a chance to analyze the incorrect spelling. Students can then write the correct spellings in the margins of their own test.

In the article "Promote Smart Spelling with Partner Quizzes" (http://teacher. scholastic.com/lessonrepro/lessonplans/instructor/spell198a.htm), Gentry describes how to structure spelling tests so students work with partners to give and check the test, which is especially effective if students do not all have the same spelling list. An additional resource, Spelling City (www.spellingcity.com) is a comprehensive spelling website that provides online tools for creating an individualized spelling list, taking a practice test, and playing spelling games for practice.

A word of caution: words learned for a weekly spelling test do not necessarily transfer into students' writing as one might hope (Beckham-Hungler & Williams, 2003). A transfer of knowledge may be more likely if students have some interest or choice in the selection of words for the spelling list. You and your students could collaboratively create the week's spelling list, selecting words together from the district spelling curriculum, topics currently being studied in the classroom, a grade-level list, or other sources.

The Screener of Handwriting Proficiency

Assesses: Various aspects of handwriting

Suggested grade levels: Kindergarten and up

College and Career Readiness Standards	Common Core State Standard, grade example: Grade 3
Writing	Writing
Production and Distribution of Writing	*Production and Distribution of Writing*
W.4 Produce clear and coherent writing in which the development, organization, and style are appropriate to task, purpose, and audience.	**W.3.4** With guidance and support from adults, produce writing in which the development and organization are appropriate to task and purpose.

Description

The Screener of Handwriting Proficiency is a formal handwriting tool that is free to teachers and can be given to the whole class at the same time to assess:

- memory of letters and numbers through dictation
- orientation or directionality
- placement of letters in relation to the lines
- sentence writing

Because this screener does not focus on letter formation, it can be used with any style of manuscript or print handwriting. You can use the online scoring and reporting tool to keep track of data through the generation of class, individual, and specific skill reports. Students' handwriting performance is compared to a set of benchmarks. When the screener is administered two to three times per school year, the results mark both individual and class progress. Specific suggestions for handwriting remediation are generated based on the scores in each category.

The Screener of Handwriting Proficiency is published by the company Handwriting Without Tears, and one might wonder if it promotes their program. But because the screener can be used with any style of manuscript writing and is available to all teachers for no charge, it has gained credibility and popularity among teachers as a valuable handwriting tool.

View the Screener of Handwriting Proficiency (3:52, www.hwtears.com/hwt/online-tools/screener) and the video clips describing the screener.

6 + 1 Trait Writing Assessment

Assesses: 6 + 1 writing traits

Suggested grade levels: Kindergarten through second; third through 12th

College and Career Readiness Standards	Common Core State Standard, grade example: Grade 5
Writing	**Writing**
Production and Distribution of Writing	*Production and Distribution of Writing*
W.4 Produce clear and coherent writing in which the development, organization, and style are appropriate to task, purpose, and audience.	**W.5.5** With guidance and support from peers and adults, develop and strengthen writing as needed by planning, revising, editing, rewriting, or trying a new approach.
Language	**Language**
Vocabulary Acquisition and Use	*Vocabulary Acquisition and Use*
L.4 Determine or clarify the meaning of unknown and multiple-meaning words and phrases by using context clues, analyzing meaningful word parts, and consulting general and specialized reference materials, as appropriate.	**L.5.4** Determine or clarify the meaning of unknown and multiple-meaning words and phrases based on grade 5 reading and content, choosing flexibly from a range of strategies.

Description

The 6 + 1 Trait model identifies and describes the key traits, or elements, of effective writing, Although it began as an assessment tool, the 6 + 1 Trait model directly links to writing instruction. Assessment teaches us what good writing looks like and how close students are to meeting these expectations. The gap between performance and expectations is the space where quality instruction can make a difference. As Vicki Spandel, one of the teachers who developed the model, says, "You cannot repair a car until you know specifically what is not working. You cannot rework writing unless you can hear the problems within the text" (p. 5). The 6 + 1 Trait model lets teachers and students see the goal of writing by making the target visible through the analytic rubric (http://educationnorthwest. org/resource/464), which identifies the traits of ideas, organization, voice, word choice, sentence fluency, conventions, and presentation. See Exhibit 12.7 for a description of the 6 + 1 traits.

Naming, describing, and assessing the traits using the analytic rubric helps both teachers and students understand the multifaceted aspects of writing. Once these traits were identified in 1984 (Spandel, 2009) and teachers started using this model in their classrooms, the 6-trait model began to spread across the United States. The extra trait of presentation was added, and the 6 + 1 Trait model now forms the foundation of writing assessment and instruction in at least one school district in every state, and also in many other countries, including Australia, Great Britain, Turkey, Bahrain, China, and Venezuela (Education Northwest, 2011). Some educators have adapted the model to use four traits, seven traits, or other variations. The common thread is the emphasis on individual characteristics of what makes writing work and the various uses of the trait model:

- teaching about writing.
- giving written or oral feedback to a student about a piece of writing.
- assessing a piece of writing for one, a few, or all of the traits.
- talking with students and families about the expectations for writing.
- assessing writing for a large-scale writing assessment, such as a state assessment.

In addition, the traits provide a lens that allows students to evaluate their own writing, which strengthens reflection on their own learning (Bransford, Brown, & Cocking, 2000). As soon as students are able to read the rubric, they should keep a copy in their writing folder to aid them in checking their own progress.

Learning to rate a piece of writing with the 6 + 1 Trait rubric

Reliably and consistently rating student writing takes training and practice. Skilled raters have usually attended several days of professional development training and have rated dozens of writing samples. As an introduction, Exhibit 12.8 shares a brief step-by-step explanation for how to rate a piece of writing, using Education Northwest's 5-Point Rubrics: http://education northwest.org/resource/464.

Teachers use their best professional judgment to rate writing, which grows as they gain more classroom experiences with the 6 + 1 Trait model (http://educationnorthwest.org/traits) and with this judgment comes consistency.

Additional information, practice activities, and scored samples papers to be used for comparison are available at the Education Northwest website: http://education northwest.org[end box]

Issues to consider when rating students' writing

Even with practice and knowledge, you will still encounter some issues when using the 6 + 1 Trait rubric. The word *value* is at the heart of the

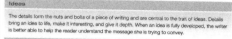
EXHIBIT 12.7

Description of the 6 + 1 traits.

Ideas

The details form the nuts and bolts of a piece of writing and are central to the trait of ideas. Details bring an idea to life, make it interesting, and give it depth. When an idea is fully developed, the writer is better able to help the reader understand the message she is trying to convey.

Organization

Organized ideas seem to flow naturally from one to the next. The opening or lead provides the initial structure for organization and should capture the reader's attention while also drawing the reader into the writing. The beginning should ignite a spark of interest, which increases as the reader continues. The ending or conclusion should tie the key ideas together in informational writing and provide a solution to any problems arising in most stories.

Voice

Third-grade teacher Diane Kimsey encourages students to "write with your heart and not the pencil." A writer's heart, personality and style, is his voice. One of the hallmark descriptors for voice is that the writing sounds like the person who wrote it. Voice may also be seen in the illustrations that accompany a piece of writing, or for young writers, in the illustrations they create first, which serve as an inspiration for a piece of writing. Effective voice for informational or persuasive writing stems from knowledge rather than emotion.

Word choice

The trait of word choice involves carefully selecting just the right words to effectively convey an idea—words that create a mental image, clarify an idea, or evoke an emotion. Often these words are lively, colorful, or descriptive, but for informational writing these words may be informative, specific, or technical. The best word choice sounds natural, reflects the writer's voice, and is not full of words from an overused thesaurus.

Sentence fluency

When read aloud, a piece of writing should have a rhythm, or cadence, that stems from a variety of sentence lengths and styles. Short, simple sentences intermixed with longer, complex sentences provide a variety that translates into interest. Run-on sentences and sentence fragments, addressed in the trait of sentence fluency, are a problem for the reader. They cause readers to expend much effort to insert pauses where punctuation is missing, or figuring out the relation between ideas in clauses, or adding ideas when words are not present.

Conventions

Although perfection may be the goal, it is not the expectation for the trait of conventions. A strong piece of writing shows editing has been given careful consideration, although a small number of minor errors may have been missed. Conventions include the elements of spelling, grammar, and punctuation. The goal of conventions is to make the paper readable to others by giving attention to spelling, punctuation, and grammar.

Presentation

Presentation is about paying attention to the visual and textual elements, or the way the writing is presented on the page or screen, which includes such elements as handwriting, font selection, layout, and neatness. The trait of presentation is meant to be an integral part of the writing process, especially publication, rather than an afterthought.

EXHIBIT 12.8

How to rate a piece of writing.

STEP 1. Gather a piece of writing and a copy of the **6 + 1 Trait** rubric linked in the previous paragraph for either younger or older students. At no point would you be expected to memorize the rubric, although after you use it extensively, the words will come to you without thinking. Novice raters also may want to have other information about the traits close by, maybe a website, a book, or a set of handouts to serve as reminders if needed.

STEP 2. Read the writing aloud to yourself. This may feel a little awkward at first, and you do not have to read loudly. By reading aloud you can better hear the flow of the language, an important consideration for sentence fluency, word choice, and voice.

STEP 3. Identify a specific trait and read the writing again, focusing on this trait.

STEP 4. Decide if the writing is closer to weak or to strong for this certain trait.

STEP 5. Go to the rubric. Begin at the level that matches your general impression. If the writing is closer to strong, start in the 5 category and move to the 3 category if needed. If closer to beginning, start in the 1 category and move to the 3 category if needed. If your general impression is somewhere in the middle, begin with the 3 category and move to the 5 or 1 categories as needed.

STEP 6. Read the descriptors for the category you selected. Decide which descriptors seem to match the piece of writing. If you find at least two descriptors that are a close match, then give the writing this rating. If not, move to a category above or below to find at least two descriptors that are a close match. If you find descriptors in two adjacent categories that are a close match, then assign the rating in between. For example, descriptors from the 5 category and the 3 category would lead to a rating of 4.

STEP 7. Follow this sequence for each of the 6 + 1 Traits.

Note: If working with a partner or small group, pause after step 6 and discuss your rating and rationale. Through such discussions, educators come to understand the perspectives of other raters, and all involved will be better prepared to interpret and apply the rubric.

(Print this information sheet: www.hhpcommunities. com/teachinglanguagearts/IL-12-06.pdf)

word *evaluation,* and rating a piece of writing is a form of evaluation. The goal of the 6 + 1 Trait model is for a trained teacher to set aside biases in order to make a judgment based on professional knowledge and evidence.

Be aware that a rating is not a score. The 6 + 1 Trait rubric ratings work along a continuum from beginning, emerging, developing, maturing, to strong. A one rating is equivalent to beginning, a three rating to developing, and a five rating to strong. The 6 + 1 Trait rubric ratings are not meant to be converted into percentages, letter grades, or added together to determine a total. Each trait is rated individually so that a writer can receive feedback about his strengths and weaknesses. This is the beauty of the 6 + 1 Trait model; it allows each writer to be analyzed in an individualized, structured, and consistent way.

Beware of your own biases. In order to minimize your subjectivity, you must be aware of your own biases, or basing a score on some factor other than actual writing performance as described in the rubric. Your bias may include the length or topic of the paper, or your attitude toward writing. The challenge for you as a teacher is to set aside these biases when using the 6 + 1 Trait rubric to rate a piece of writing. In order to do this, you must first become aware of your biases, neatly tuck them into a box, and then close the lid during assessment. You will have a chance to assess your possible biases in the Application Activities at the end of this chapter.

Rating the writing of young students

The 6 + 1 Trait model was originally created with more experienced writers in mind, specifically third through twelfth graders. These older writers generally have more length, depth, and sophistication in their writing than younger students, which facilitates the application of the 6 + 1 Trait model. The rating system of the 6 + 1 Trait model, a key to the short-hand feedback given to writers, is not as appropriate for younger writers who often are not able to grasp the meaning of a rating or how it applies to their writing. Yet, each of the traits can be adapted to the writing of students in kindergarten through second grade. Instead of giving a younger students' writing ratings, teachers often use an adapted form of the 6-trait rubric to guide verbal feedback to both parents and students. Resources are available to help teachers of young students understand the unique ways the traits can be adapted for early writers.

To learn more about using the 6-trait model with young writers, listen to the podcast *Teaching Traits to Young Children* (7:00, www.allynbaconmerrill.com/podcasts/episode.aspx?e=1e588e41-da11-44cf-8610-fd9d7b10e639) from Vicki Spandel, or view the video *Empowering Young Writers* (2:41, www2.scholastic.com/browse/media.jsp?id=723) by Ruth Culham as she describes the role the traits have in creating an "I can" attitude among young writers. *Also, be sure to review these examples by young writers, with teacher feedback:* www.hhpcommunities.com/teachinglanguagearts/IL-12-07.pdf

Portfolios

Assesses: Student progress and achievement

Suggested grade levels: All grades

College and Career Readiness Standards	Common Core State Standard, grade example: Grade 4
Writing	Writing

Text Types and Purposes

W.1 Write arguments to support claims in an analysis of substantive topics or texts using valid reasoning and relevant and sufficient evidence.

W.2 Write informative/explanatory texts to examine and convey complex ideas and information clearly and accurately through the effective selection, organization, and analysis of content.

W.3 Write narratives to develop real or imagined experiences or events using effective technique, well-chosen details, and well-structured event sequences.

Text Types and Purposes

W.1.1 Write opinion pieces in which they introduce the topic or name the book they are writing about, state an opinion, supply a reason for the opinion, and provide some sense of closure.

W.1.2 Write informative/explanatory texts in which they name a topic, supply some facts about the topic, and provide some sense of closure.

W.1.3 Write narratives in which they recount two or more appropriately sequenced events, include some details regarding what happened, use temporal words to signal event order, and provide some sense of closure.

Description

Portfolios are a collection of work designed to highlight student progress and achievement. Though there are many types of portfolios and purposes for using this approach, they tend to share common attributes. First, the items included in the portfolio are purposefully selected to represent progress, achievement, or both. The criteria for what can be placed in the portfolio are determined in advance (see Exhibit 12.9 for an example of portfolio criteria). Well-designed portfolios often include a reflective component intended to give students the opportunity to reinforce what they know about the qualities of the work contained in it. Though sometimes teachers specify exact items (called artifacts) that must be placed in the portfolio (e.g., last Friday's spelling test), in our experience, portfolios are usually very powerful learning tools when students choose the items that demonstrate high-quality work. When students have some choices about what they believe are good examples of their progress and achievement, they recognize key attributes of quality work and take pride in what they have accomplished. For students who may have specific learning goals, such as English language learners, portfolios are easily customized as a demonstration of student achievement relative to specific goals, such as oral language fluency or English spelling accuracy.

Portfolios are frequently a collection of work on paper, and many portfolios are intended for display or further assessment, often both. On the other hand, electronic portfolios offer great opportunities. Many commercial websites allow teachers and students to create a portfolio. However, shared document sites (such as Google Docs) and blog sites can often serve as excellent hosts for electronic portfolios. An English language learner who struggles with oral presentations might create a podcast that meets grade-level standards and upload it to an electronic portfolio. Parents like to be involved in education, and portfolios offer them an opportunity to see their child's work collected over time. Exhibit 12.10 shares a parent portfolio response focusing on the positive aspects of a student's work.

Read the article "Using Technology: Electronic Portfolios in the K–12 Classroom" (www.educationworld.com/a_tech/tech/tech111.shtml) for more about electronic portfolios and links to additional online resources.

EXHIBIT 12.9

Portfolio contents and score sheet.

An introduction (10 points)
The introduction is an overview of your portfolio. It describes how the work in your portfolio demonstrates:
* Your accomplishments in writing this year
* How you use the writing process and several writing strategies learned in class
* How you have grown as a writer, use writing for various reasons, and use writing to understand parts of your world

Evaluated work (10 points)
The evaluated work is one you have chosen as your best writing this year. The teacher will evaluate it using these criteria:
* The piece is focused and coherent
* The piece is based on a suitable design worked out mainly during prewriting
* The piece varies sentence structures to suit the purposes for writing
* The piece demonstrates an awareness of the audience
* The piece uses humor, metaphor, imagery, and demonstrates a clear written voice
* The piece has no errors described on the mechanics and usage checklist

Process work (10 points)
This piece should demonstrate how well you use a writing process and includes all drafts, notes, and prewriting. This artifact shows that you:
* Use prewriting strategies effectively
* Draft work in paragraph form
* Use drafts to further discover and shape ideas
* Use response groups and other readers to refine your writing
* Edit your work thoroughly
* Produce a polished piece of published writing

The entire portfolio (25 points)
In addition to the written work described above, the portfolio should include:
* Your best creative piece (either fiction or poetry)
* One piece you feel challenged you the most this year
* Your best informative piece
* A reflection for each of these that describes why each is your best example.

About the author (5 points)

Parent response (extra credit: 5 points)

(Print this form: www.hhpcommunities.com/teachinglanguagearts/IL-12-08.pdf)

EXHIBIT 12.10

Parent/caregiver portfolio response sheet.

Parent/Caregiver Portfolio Response Sheet

The portfolio is a place where students display and evaluate their best work. It is a place to show you who they are as readers, writers, and learners.

Please read through your student's portfolio and write a short response to five or six of the questions below. Please attach your responses or write them on the back of this page. Then sign it and send it back with the portfolio.

What do you notice that he or she is able to do well?

What impressed you about your student's portfolio?

What is your favorite sentence in the portfolio?

Did you find any surprises?

Did the portfolio help you to understand your student's progress? How?

What would you like to know more about concerning your student's progress?

Do you have any questions for your student?

Do you have any writing goals for your student you would like to share?

Thank you!

[Your name]

Parent Signature   Date

Student Signature

(Print this form: www.hhpcommunities.com/teachinglanguagearts/IL-12-09.pdf)

12.5

CHAPTER SUMMARY

A baker, a meteorologist, a mechanic—one might wonder when a teacher has a chance to just be a teacher. This question can best be answered with another question, which is, when are words just words? Words are never just words; there is always a meaning behind the message in the form of subtle nuances, facial expressions, juxtaposed images, and the many other ways we express an idea. Making sense of words, whether written, spoken, or visually represented, is a complex process, as is the process of evaluating the progress students make in their ability to create these messages. A teacher is often described as a jack-of-all-trades because she must know how to recognize learning in so many forms. Recognizing learning is at the heart of assessment, and the various assessment tools presented in this chapter create a multifaceted picture of what students know and can do.

APPLICATION ACTIVITIES

think like a teacher

Rating a Piece of Writing Using the 6 + 1 Traits

In the section we described the process for determining a rating in this chapter, which involves finding descriptors from the rubric to match evidence in the writing. As discussed, when rating piece of writing, teachers usually focus on rating one trait at a time. The links below connect to student writing samples, which you can use to practice rating the six traits of ideas, organization, voice, word choice, sentence fluency, and conventions.

Ideas: Kids and Parents, www.hhpcommunities.com/teaching languagearts/IL-12-10.pdf

Organization: Soccer, www.hhpcommunities.com/teaching languagearts/IL-12-11.pdf

Voice: Father of the Year, www.hhpcommunities.com/teaching languagearts/IL-12-12.pdf

Word Choice: Little Cats, www.hhpcommunities.com/teaching languagearts/IL-12-13.pdf

Sentence Fluency: If My Bed Had a Built in Alarm Clock, www.hhp communities.com/teachinglanguagearts/IL-12-14.pdf

Conventions: Dangeresqe U.S. Mark, www.hhpcommunities.com/ teachinglanguagearts/IL-12-15.pdf

Once you have determined your rating for the trait using a copy of the 6 + 1 Trait rubric (http://educationnorthwest.org/resource/464) for either younger or older students, discuss your rating with a partner or small group of classmates. This discussion is a particularly important step for novice raters. See if everyone in the group can agree on a rating, or at least be within one point of each other. Throughout the discussion, return to the rubric and the paper to provide evidence to support your rating.

After your discussion, review the scored examples (www.hhpcommunities. com/teachinglanguagearts/IL-12-16.pdf) to see the authors' suggested scoring and consider how their score is similar to or different from your score. Also, read the authors' comments and see how closely these align with your thoughts and your group's discussion. Follow this process for each of the traits, keeping each score separate and recording your scores on a scoring chart (www.hhpcommunities.com/teachinglanguagearts/IL-12-17.pdf).

What Are Your Biases When It Comes to Writing?

All teachers favor an aspect of writing assessment, which seems a little more important than the others. Are you impressed with neat handwriting? Are spelling errors your pet peeve? These opinions are often engrained in us over many years of experiences; however, when it comes to assessing writing using the 6 + 1 Trait rubric, these biases need to be put on the shelf. Awareness is the first step in containing these opinions.

1. Work with a partner using the Chapter 9 writing sample, Exhibit 9.10. Each person should read over the sample and make an individual brainstormed list of general impressions. Try not to think of scoring the paper or of specific traits, just think of your overall perceptions.

2. Come together to discuss your lists. Listen to your partner, but also listen to yourself. What stands out to you about your comments? Try to identify your own biases toward writing.

3. As partners, make a top 10 list of biases to avoid. Put your personal biases at the top of the list.

Pros and Cons of Rubrics

Not everyone agrees with using rubrics to rate writing. Regie Routman, the author of *Writing Essentials* (2005), cautions teachers about focusing on the rubric instead of the student and questions whether ratings are an accurate representation of a writer's abilities. While Routman is not alone, few alternative assessment tools have been proposed. To prepare for a discussion of pros and cons of rubrics, read the following article and watch the video clip. Then divide into two groups, one that supports using rubrics to rate writing and one that questions or has issues about using rubrics to rate writing. The purpose of this activity is to consider the issues so that when rubrics are used, they can be used in a professional way. Afterward, as a group prepare a list of ten recommendations for the professional use of rubrics.

Read the article "Things That Make Us Smart Can Also Make Us Dumb" by Suzanne L. Porath (4 pp.): http://wisc.academia.edu/SuzannePorath/Papers/332572/6-Traits_Writing_Rubric_Things_That_Make_Us_Smart_Can_Also_Make_Us_Dumb)

View the video of Maja Wilson (2:52, www.youtube.com/watch?v=kH3PSjh2G20), author of *Video Rethinking Rubrics* at Adapting Rubrics.

A rubric can be a useful tool for evaluating student performance if the criteria is specific and appropriate. Because a rubric is an informal assessment, you can easily adapt this tool to meet different assessment situations, and the Adapting Rubrics activity gives you a chance to develop the skills to do this. For this activity you will need a copy of the writing developmental continuum first discussed in Chapter 2 (www.hhpcommunities.com/teaching

languagearts/IL-02-B.pdf). Also, you will need either the third through fifth grade Speaking Rubric (www.hhpcommunities.com/teachinglanguagearts/IL-12-05.pdf) or the Digital Video Project rubric (http://www.dartmouth.edu/~videoprojects/files/digital-video-project-rubric.pdf), both discussed in this chapter.

Your task is to take one of the rubrics and adapt it for younger students. Work with a partner and use the developmental continuum as a reminder of what students are able to do at certain stages of development and the CCSS as a reminder of what students are expected to do. Decide if your adapted rubric will have the same categories and the same levels of quality as the original rubric. Will you delete anything? Add anything? Adjust anything? As you are making changes, keep in mind that you will have to justify your changes to others. To create your rubric, use the website Rubistar. Sign up for a free account, then select a topic and begin creating your rubric. Print a copy, and meet with a set of partners who created a different kind of rubric. Each set of partners should explain their rubric and justify their changes. Base your rationale on what you know about the ways students develop and the expectations for student performance. After the discussion, each individual writes an explanation of his or her rubric and the changes and submits it to the instructor with the final copy of your adapted rubric.

REFERENCES

Beckham-Hungler, D., & Williams, C. (2003). Teaching words that students misspell: Spelling instruction and young children's writing. *Language Arts, 80*(4), 299–309.

Bransford, J., Brown, A., & Cocking, R. (2000). *How people learn: Brain, mind, experience and school.* Washington, DC: National Academy Press.

Education Northwest. (2011). About 6+1 trait writing. http://educationnorthwest.org/resource/949

Kear, D. J., Coffman, G. A., McKenna, M. C., & Ambrosio, A. L. (2000). Measuring attitude toward writing: A new tool for teachers. *Reading Teacher, 54*(1), 10–23.

Routman, R. (2005). *Writing essentials.* Portsmouth, NH: Heinemann.

Spandel, V. (2009). Creating writers through 6-trait writing assessment and instruction (4th ed.). New York: Pearson.

Author Index

Subject Index

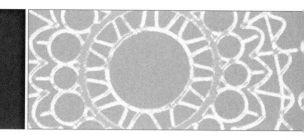